RENE
DA
DEC 0 8 2009

D0764317

WITHDRAWN
UTSA Libraries

Government by Contract

Government by Contract

OUTSOURCING AND AMERICAN DEMOCRACY

Edited by

JODY FREEMAN

MARTHA MINOW

HARVARD UNIVERSITY PRESS

Cambridge, Massachusetts, and London, England   2009

Copyright © 2009 by the President and Fellows of Harvard College
All rights reserved
Printed in the United States of America

Library of Congress Cataloging-in-Publication Data

Government by contract : outsourcing and American democracy / edited by Jody Freeman
and Martha Minow.
    p. cm.
  Includes bibliographical references and index.
  ISBN 978-0-674-03208-8 (alk. paper)
    1. Contracting out—United States. 2. Privatization—United States. I. Freeman,
Jody. II. Minow, Martha, 1954–
  HD3861.U6.G678 2009
  352.5'30973—dc22   2008027501

Library
University of Texas
at San Antonio

Contents

Acknowledgments

We have had the good fortune to share conversations for nearly two decades about the nature of governance in a large democracy that formally divides public and private spheres yet depends so heavily on their interconnections. Our work has been enriched over the years by many conversations with many colleagues who approach governance questions imaginatively from within their own fields and disciplines. We are deeply grateful for those conversations and for the support of Dean Elena Kagan for the Harvard Law School conference we convened in March 2005 to explore the subject. Entitled "Governance by Design: Cost, Effectiveness, and Democratic Norms," the conference brought together a diverse group of participants with different perspectives on the legal, political, and economic implications of outsourcing government work, including experts in administrative law and practice, experts in democratic theory and institutions, and people with special knowledge of the markets and industries on which the government relies so heavily to accomplish public goals. A distinctive agenda emerged from that conference, one that moves beyond the increasingly calcified debates over privatization that simply divide outsourcing's cheerleaders from its critics and that embarks on a broader inquiry into the challenges posed by contractual governance. This book, which collects essays emerging from the conference, is a first step in that broader inquiry. We are especially thankful to the authors for their willingness to engage across the usual lines that divide disciplines and separate academic work from practice. In addition, we thank the other conference participants, all of whom made lively contributions to the day's discussions: David Barron, Archon Fung, Steve Goldsmith, Dan Gordon, Brian Gran, Dan Guttmann, Jacob Hacker, Nan Hunter, Alexandra Lahav, Orly Lobel, John Manning, Jon Michaels, Kal Raustiala, Nancy Rosenblum, Steve Schooner, David Sklansky, Susan Sturm, Rebecca Weiner, and Alexandra O'Rourke. For her help organizing and managing the conference we are grateful to Miriam Seifter.

The quality of each chapter in this volume reflects the superb assistance of a devoted team of student research and editorial assistants, orchestrated by the extraordinary Lena Konanova. Melinda Atkinson, Elizabeth Bell, Thomas Davies, Sushma Gandhi, Miriam Glaser, David Kellis, Michael Kolber, Sydney Leavens, Anthony Oliva, Naomi Reed, Summer Smith, Brendan St. Amant, Emily Ullman, and Janelle Weinstock each brought dedication, precision, and clarity to the task, and Lena Konanova deserves more thanks than we can express for her tireless and imaginative work as an editor, coordinator, and interlocutor. Our staff assistants Kathy Curley and Kristin Flower performed impressive governance of this project, and Kristin Flower in addition supplied constant help in tracking down authors and sources and in producing the manuscript for publication. Michael Aronson at Harvard University Press early recognized the value of the project, found anonymous outside reviewers who supplied insightful comments, and stayed with it through each phase. Over the course of our work, the issues posed by governmental contracting moved into the headlines, reflecting the legitimate questions about ballooning government expenditures in Afghanistan, Iraq, and New Orleans, making us all the more appreciative of the foresight and engagement of everyone contributing to this volume.

Finally, as always, we thank our partners and families for their support, enthusiasm, and love.

Government by Contract

Reframing the Outsourcing Debates

Jody Freeman

Martha Minow

This book is about a simple but striking development: we live in an era of pervasive government outsourcing—what we call government by contract.[1] Over the last few decades, the United States government has outsourced to private actors a significant portion of its work, including both a broad range of service provision and important aspects of regulation and policymaking. Moreover, these contracts increasingly encompass what many consider to be core government functions. Although outsourcing is not new to the American scene—all levels of government in the United States depend on private contractors to some extent—our claim in this book is that its current scope and scale are unprecedented.[2] Recent developments raise new questions about the government's ability to manage its outsourcing relationships, and, more broadly, about the compatibility of the American outsourcing regime with the country's professed commitment to the democratic values of public participation, accountability, transparency, and rule of law. The purpose of this book is to shed light on what is now a pervasive, and in many contexts, a presumptive use of private contractors to perform work we might think of as governmental, and to spark a public discussion of the issues posed by this increasingly dominant form of governance.

The Current Context

It is a propitious moment to take stock. In the last seven years alone, since September 11, 2001, the federal government has exponentially increased its use of outsourcing, especially in the areas of national security, intelligence, warfare, development of governmental infrastructure, and disaster relief. These contracts go beyond traditional government procurement contracts for goods, services, and military weaponry.[3] Recent contracts extend to particularly sensitive functions, and involve private firms in activities once thought to be the exclusive responsibility of government, such as military target selection, interrogation of detainees, border control, security training, surveillance systems design, intelligence operations management, control over the collection and use of classified or confidential information, and significant military support in a combat zone.[4] In contexts where contractors once provided support, they now play a significant role in planning and operational decision making.[5]

The recent intensification and expansion of outsourcing related to intelligence and security functions is particularly noteworthy. It can be attributed in part to unprecedented circumstances—the wars in Afghanistan and Iraq, and Hurricane Katrina, a major natural disaster. Yet these seemingly exceptional circumstances sit within a broader trend. Government contracts for military, security, and disaster management build on the already extensive outsourcing that has developed in more mundane circumstances, and less visibly, over time. Quite apart from the exigencies presented by wars and hurricanes, contractors have come to provide what Dan Guttmann calls "the basic work of government"— writing regulations and budgets for government agencies, producing statutorily required reports, interpreting laws, delivering social services, administering foreign aid, and managing nuclear weapons sites, among other things.[6] The primary concern, voiced in recent years by critics in public policy circles and in academia, is that the ubiquity of governance-by-private-contractors strikingly outstrips our legal and political capacities of oversight meant to ensure that the contractors' execution of these governmental functions complies with democratic norms. This worry animates many chapters in this book.

Some, and perhaps even much, of private government contracting works well, as some of the chapters in this collection make clear. For example, contracts for run-of-the-mill supplies and routine commercial services may pose few problems while generating significant savings or quality improvements for taxpayers. From this perspective, examples of egregious contractor conduct seem few and far between, and should not be the rationale for unnecessary systemwide reform. Yet one of the points made in this volume is that it can be hard to tell whether such instances are exceptional or common. Too often, the nature and extent of government contracting is invisible or inaccessible to the public, despite procurement laws and policies and other rules that are ostensibly designed to ensure their disclosure. Some of the most controversial contracts are literally off the books;[7] others are awarded under suspicious circumstances, hurriedly and without competition.[8] Although contracts themselves can be a source of accountability in theory, many contracts are so underspecified as to afford contractors almost unlimited discretion. And even when contractual terms are clear, there can be a stunning failure of government oversight. At times, it seems as if no one in any branch of government—executive, legislative, judicial—has the knowledge and capacity, not to mention the political will, to enforce contractual terms.

The chapters in this volume explore how the three accountability regimes of law, markets, and politics can all break down in the face of extensive government contracting. First, despite elaborate rules and procedures, in some cases, legal regulations and sanctions simply do not apply to contractors. When legal rules do apply, government agencies often lack the capacity to enforce contractual terms or keep up with contractors who know how to exploit gaps in the legal framework.[9] Second, markets can fail to exert meaningful control over contractors. For many contracts, the government itself creates the market by generating demand, and then, through devices like no-bid and cost-plus contracts, fails to use market discipline. Third, political checks, which are inconsistent at best, can collapse entirely. This happened recently when one party controlled both Congress and the executive branch, and oversight investigations dropped off significantly.[10] Yet even when Congress does actively investigate wrongdoing, the hearings and follow-up measures tend to be reactive and superficial, offering relatively little by way of meaningful reform. Thus, although proponents of outsourcing often defend bypassing the rules traditionally enforced by administrative agencies and courts with assurances about the alternative accountability afforded by private market competition or electoral politics, these other accountability devices fail for a significant portion of contracts. Of course, none of the three main accountability mechanisms can function effectively if basic information about performance, costs, and effects is hard to obtain. The relative inaccessibility of the contracting process (to all but the competing contractors themselves and the most intrepid academics) only heightens the risk that serious problems will be identified too late, or never.

Critiques

For many if not most Americans, government contracting has been unknown or unimportant. Over the last few years, however, there have been a number of shocking revelations about the behavior of contractors in Iraq and Afghanistan, as well as reports of widespread fraud and abuse concerning contractors involved in the response to Hurricane Katrina. These events have put government contracting on the front page of major newspapers and fueled complaints about a host of problems with the contracting process, including misconduct in the selection of contractors, illegal or abusive action by private actors who elude public sanction, ineffective and inefficient performance by contractors, and end runs around the demands of transparent democratic accountability. Those voicing such concerns reject the argument that these problems are limited to a few unusual instances, and claim that they occur in patterns that suggest the problems are potentially widespread. The most prevalent and provocative objections to contracting are as follows:

· *Fraud and waste:* Recent government reports have identified serious problems with no-bid and noncompetitive contracts, as well as cost-based and monopoly contracts.[11] The sheer scope of federal contracting makes the possibility of fraud and waste acute.[12]

· *Insufficient oversight:* Recent reports also cite poor contract planning and inadequate oversight by government officials as a reason for poor performance.[13] Agency personnel are insufficiently resourced and badly trained for contract management.[14] As a result, in some cases oversight itself is contracted to private parties who face conflicts of interest because they seek, and at times hold, direct service contracts as well.[15] Neither the agencies supervising the contracts, nor Congress, which supervises the agencies, is able to ensure that contracting is done in a fair or effective manner, resulting in millions in wasted taxpayer money.[16] Courts play virtually no meaningful role in contracting oversight.[17]

· *Illegal and abusive conduct by private actors outside public sanction:* The notorious example of such conduct is the cruel and humiliating treatment of Abu Ghraib detainees, with the participation of private employees present under government contracts and outside the supervision, monitoring, and sanctioning applicable to military and other governmental personnel.[18] The other glaring example is the incident in Iraq in which Blackwater employees, who provide security services to U.S. diplomats and are answerable to no legal system, allegedly opened fire on civilians, killing several.[19] Especially when the private contractors perform outside the jurisdiction of an operating legal system—as in wartime Iraq or in New Orleans immediately after the Hurricane Katrina disaster—risks of illegal and abusive conduct, however exceptional, increase dramatically.[20]

· *Undermining democratic norms of transparency, rationality, and accountability:* Much contracting is immune from the traditional laws and procedures that would apply to public agencies doing the same work, simply because it is performed by private contractors. They operate free from the legal obligation to defend their discretionary decisions as rational. Moreover, to the extent that government contracting operates in a "no-man's-land" beyond the reach of traditional disclosure requirements, the public lacks access to relevant information.[21] Even the most serious kinds of abuses, such as violations of human rights, may go unnoticed, or, even if noticed, unpunished. Outsourcing itself impairs the visibility necessary to check for such abuses, because private companies control information about cost, performance, and other vital data that otherwise would be open to review by government agencies, Congress, the media, and the general public.[22] This diminished accountability can undermine the legitimacy of public action.

· *Diminished government capacity:* Many discrete instances of outsourcing may not be particularly troubling when viewed in isolation. Yet when one considers the cumulative impact of contracting on government capacity and character over the long term, there is reason for more concern. For example, if government performs less and less of its own basic work, will government employees retain sufficient expertise to oversee the work of private contractors effectively? Can government continue to attract competent employees under current civil service rules and pay structures, while opportunities to perform essentially the same work in the private sector for more money expand? Does this situation create a significant "revolving door" problem and worsen the potential for conflicts of interest? Will meaningful oversight become impossible without reliance on nongovernment entities?

Some of the chapters in this book voice objections like these, whereas others respond to and challenge them. The early chapters set the stage for this exchange by describing in detail how the contracting process works and by explaining its historical genesis. Importantly, the authors in this collection approach the phenomenon of contractual governance from different disciplines and perspectives, which helps to provide a rich treatment of the topic.

Historical Context

The historical context of government by contract is illuminated in this book by William Novak in Chapter 1 and John Donahue in Chapter 2. Reliance on private providers for many functions valued by the public has long been part of the American landscape.[23] Yet, as these authors show, the last decade has produced palpable changes both in the scope of outsourcing and in the kinds of mechanisms by which it is executed.

First, there is simply more outsourcing now, and the value of the contracts amounts to ever greater sums. During fiscal year 2006, federal agencies spent over $400 billion on procurement of goods and services from private firms, an increase of almost 90 percent since 2000. Contracts are the fastest-growing component of federal discretionary spending.[24] Second, the scope of functions and services for which the government now relies on private (and primarily for-profit) actors has grown to encompass activities that fall closer to the "core" of what the public in the twentieth century came to identify as the state's responsibility in a democratic society. As the chapters in this volume show, private contractors are now supporting American military operations in Afghanistan and Iraq, supplying security for American diplomats, reconstructing the Iraqi oil infrastructure, handling domestic and international security and training services, conceptualizing and operating an elaborate American border security project, running prisons and detention centers, and certifying that hazardous waste cleanups conform to statutory requirements. This is just a small subset of contracted activities, but it illustrates some of the dangers to democratic norms about which critics are concerned.

Third, for most of the nineteenth and twentieth centuries, public reliance on private actors proceeded largely through indirect means. Federal and state governments offered subsidies to private actors to encourage enterprises to enhance general welfare. Public charters and municipal corporations straddled the public-private divide in the eighteenth and nineteenth centuries, and even the private corporation held charters calling for public benefit, imbuing the private sphere with public-mindedness.[25] In contrast, the government now uses contracts with private providers to accomplish tasks specified by the government. Whereas government in the past pursued the public interest by organizing and subsidizing private initiatives, contemporary outsourcing adopts private provision, measured by private measures of performance and efficiency even when pursuing public ends, such as environmental protection, public safety, and military logistics. Rather than using public subsidies and public charters to stimulate private enterprises to advance economic growth and to take up public service ideas, the contemporary movement pays private actors to accomplish specified tasks and permeates the public sector with private-sector notions of competition and efficiency.

Government in the nineteenth and twentieth centuries did purchase goods—including armaments—from private companies. In areas like human services, local governments also regularly arranged contracts to provide counseling, foster care, and sanitation. But toward the end of the twentieth century and the start of the twenty-first, federal and state governments[26] have relied heavily on ongoing contracts with private providers for a much broader range of government functions, making contract the primary mechanism of government action, and arguably government's most important means of control over the provision of public services. This development makes the contracting process—from negotiation to oversight to remedies for breach—a key accountability mechanism in modern government. It also exposes the critical need for capacity *within* the government to develop and monitor such contracts. In this sense, outsourcing does not lessen government's burden; it changes it and may even increase it.[27]

Present-day outsourcing cannot be understood, however, without locating it as a reaction to an intervening period—beginning with the Progressive Era and lasting through the New Deal. After the Great Depression, widespread disillusionment with the private sector led to popular support for entrusting public institutions with greater responsibilities, and the government grew dramatically. By the late 1970s, however, the pendulum had swung in the other direction: there was newfound enthusiasm for private markets and competitive practices. Indeed, both the Ford and the Carter administrations, building on initiatives begun by President Nixon, took significant steps to deregulate industry[28] and introduce market competition. In the 1980 presidential campaign, Ronald Reagan ran on an explicit agenda of downsizing a wasteful and bloated public sector. Since then, outsourcing has been embraced with greater or lesser enthusiasm by both Democratic and Republican administrations. In the 1990s, the Clinton administration sought to "reinvent government" largely by shrinking the federal workforce and infusing it with private-sector methods and metrics. The goal of the administration's National Performance Review was to create a government that "works better and costs less."[29] It was President Clinton who declared, "The era of big government is over."[30]

The administration of President George W. Bush has pursued outsourcing even more aggressively.[31] The President's Management Agenda adopted a policy of cutting thousands of civil service jobs through "competitive sourcing."[32] Mitch Daniels, Director of the Office of Management and Budget (OMB) during President Bush's first term, announced the new orthodoxy when he said, "The general idea that the business of government is not to provide services but to see to it that [services] are provided seems self-evident to me."[33] Following the events of September 11, 2001, outsourcing accelerated considerably. This was of course made necessary by the demand on government created by the wars in Afghanistan and Iraq, and later, by the burden of responding to the devastation wrought by Hurricane Katrina, which taxed the resources of the federal government.

Notwithstanding the OMB's "competitive sourcing" process, which maintains a formal posture of neutrality between civil service and private service provision, the clear trend over the last few decades, at all levels of government, is toward outsourcing. In policy and academic circles, the shift is notable—the purported efficiencies of private service provision tend to be assumed, and the onus of argument falls on those who believe a particular function ought to remain exclusively in the government's hands. The impetus to outsource government work is driven to a significant extent by both pragmatism and ideology. Some supporters of outsourcing see it primarily as a way to reduce costs. They believe that private companies are simply more effective than government—more "nimble"—and therefore more capable of responding to rapidly changing events, partly because they are not constrained by civil service rules and other legal restrictions that could impede their flexibility. Others embrace outsourcing as a way to limit government.

This account suggests how far contemporary expectations of government have evolved since the Progressive Era and the New Deal. In the United States today, government is just one among alternative forms of organization. Private for-profit, private not-for-profit, and hybrid state-sponsored enterprises each deliver services to the public. The government is not indispensable—even for functions we might think of as "inherently governmental."[34] There is also a perceptible and relatively new understanding of the citizen as customer: someone who pays taxes and expects value in return, and who cares less about the identity of the provider than about the timely and affordable provision of the good or service. It is hard to know whether this shift in public attitudes helped fuel the demand for smaller government and more outsourcing, or vice versa. Likely it is both.

Critiques of the Current Outsourcing Regime

The benefits of outsourcing—access to talent, technology, and innovation—can be significant, as at least two chapters in this volume attest, and as many others concede. Stan Soloway and Alan Chvotkin argue in Chapter 8 that the government is driven to outsource higher-end functions such as military logistical support and military intelligence services because it can no longer keep up with the technological innovations developed in the private sector. Outsourcing is both inevitable, and largely desirable, argue Soloway and Chvotkin in their chapter and Steven Kelman in Chapter 7, and it would be a mistake to overreact to particular instances of abuse by burdening agencies and contractors with additional legal red tape.

Yet other contributors to this volume claim that the promised efficiency and effectiveness of outsourced work is often belied by faulty performance, which can be indulged or made worse by inadequate government supervision. The legal constraints that do exist, while arguably extensive, are clearly inadequate. More broadly, critics argue, the outsourcing trend of the last few decades jeopardizes important twentieth-century reforms aimed at enhancing the visibility and accountability of governance decisions, through public participation and clear legal limits on government discretion.

Since 1900, periodic statutory reforms have improved democratic participation and government responsiveness and required public agencies to solicit comments from the public on important policy decisions, to provide an explanation of those decisions, and to submit them to sometimes searching judicial review.[35] Government records have been made largely accessible to the public through statutes like the Freedom of Information Act (FOIA), subject to limited exceptions.[36] Interest group pressure behind the scenes has been brought into the light of day by recordkeeping and disclosure requirements. Yet much outsourced work evades these efforts at openness, as a number of chapters show.[37] For example, despite repeated public questions since 9/11, neither the Army nor the Pentagon directly answered how many private contract employees worked for the military; public officials report that they simply do not know the answer. It is thus not surprising that Congress and the wider public have a limited understanding of the actual extent of outsourced activity.[38] Moreover, until there is a big scandal, public ignorance about the scope of government contracting and its attendant problems reflects the historically shallow media coverage of contracting, which in turn "contributes to civic disengagement, including ignorance of public affairs, disenchantment with government, and political apathy."[39] The damage to democratic participation is exacerbated when the media cannot even gain access to relevant information about government activities and the associated private contract work.

Many of the contributors to this volume find this state of affairs deeply troubling. They are concerned that contractors, as private entities, are not governed by the same laws as public agencies. For example, as Fred Aman explains in Chapter 10, private actors are not bound by the Freedom of Information Act, the Administrative Procedure Act, or other "government in the sunshine" laws designed to ensure that agency decision making is transparent, participatory, and rational. Unlike government agencies, private actors do not face judicial review of their policy decisions, even though under government contracts they make discretionary decisions affecting the course of public action and allocation of public resources. As a result, courts play a very minor role in overseeing the contracting process, especially in contrast to their review of policy decisions by agencies. Proponents of outsourcing may see this absence of meaningful judicial review as a plus because it is exactly what makes the private sector more flexible, innovative, and willing to take risks than the government. But for critics, it is a source of dismay.

As Paul Verkuil explains in Chapter 12, the U.S. Constitution appears to prohibit delegations of significant discretionary governmental power beyond "Officers" of the United States, but in practice, such delegations are pervasive. Gillian Metzger shows in Chapter 11 how the Supreme Court's conception of the state action doctrine currently offers little constraint on executive delegation of governmental functions to private actors. At present, there is no recognized constitutional duty to supervise delegated power. Although members of Congress presumably could face political consequences for failing to oversee contractual governance, they have no affirmative legal duty to do so.

The extreme consequences of the problem are illustrated by the scope of military outsourcing. As Martha Minow describes in Chapter 5, the Department of Defense outsources much of its own outsourcing tasks, such as oversight and selection of providers , to military contractors, who fall outside the protocols for government contracting. Contractors are subject neither to the oversight of military authority nor to the accountability of competitive markets. In theory, procurement law sets controls on contracting, but in practice, military contractors potentially can evade any system of domestic accountability within the United States, and they typically fall outside the practical reach of foreign governments even when performing their work on foreign soil. In Iraq, military contractors have enjoyed explicit immunity even from criminal prosecution under Iraqi law, pursuant to an order of the U.S. Coalition Provisional Authority—a fact that prompted international controversy after the employees of Blackwater were accused of killing Iraqi civilians while accompanying diplomats in Baghdad.[10]

This picture of disorder may surprise experts who know well that government contracting is subject to the elaborate rules and procedures that constitute federal procurement law, described in this volume by Mathew Blum in Chapter 3 and examined further by Stan Soloway and Alan Chvotkin in Chapter 8 and Steven Kelman in Chapter 7. For example, Office of Management and Budget Circular A-76—the government directive for competitive sourcing—ostensibly forbids outsourcing of "inherently governmental" functions. Contracts must also comply with the extensive Federal Acquisition Regulations, which aim to ensure a fair and open competition process. This federal procurement process operates well in many instances. Detailed rules generally ensure that competitions operate in a fair and transparent way, and, as Blum explains, a significant percentage of the competed functions wind up remaining with the government, proving that the civil service still plays a robust role. Moreover, as we noted earlier, contracting for many of the goods and services the government procures—such as laundry services at Veterans Administration hospitals or office supplies at the Environmental Protection Agency[41]—might be relatively uncontroversial. Although such standard contracts may occasionally result in fraud or waste, they tend not to present the severe accountability deficits that concern many commentators.[42]

Yet the process does not always work as it should. In practice, agencies contract out a number of traditional governmental functions, notwithstanding the A-76 directive.[43] And many contracts—some for huge sums of money and involving highly sensitive functions—sidestep the procurement process entirely. Of course, at times, making exceptions to normal procedures seems necessary and appropriate because of special circumstances. In time of war, for example, the government needs to act quickly but often lacks the capacity itself promptly to muster or redeploy necessary goods and personnel. Such extraordinary circumstances can justify suspending the usual procedures. But when this occurs, contracts also tend to be less transparent: they are subject to less public deliberation and often bypass competitive bidding.[44]

There may be reasonable explanations for such contract awards, but they create an appearance of impropriety.[45] In addition, contracts initiated on a rushed timetable outside of the procurement rules imperil effective control by public officials over the course of the expected performance. Such contracts are likely to lack effective accountability mechanisms, such as a system enabling real-time auditing and guarding against excessive subcontracting, which raises overhead while reducing both efficiency and transparency.[46] Large-scale contracts executed under exigent circumstances may also well exceed the government's capacity to manage and monitor private company performance. Increased government reliance on private contractors carries with it increased need for capacity within the government to oversee the contracts, yet no one attended to the increased oversight needs when government contracting escalated surrounding the Katrina disaster and the Iraq war.[47]

These accountability deficits go beyond the simplest notion of "mismanagement," which connotes technical failures and bureaucratic inattention to detail, and conjures up images of cost overruns. The broader understanding of mismanagement pursued in this book points to the risk of a double failure: that contracts will both fail to conform to the accountability regime associated with "public governance" *and* that they will fail to use an adequate substitute to provide assurances of transparency and accountability—whether market based or not.

Perhaps the failures are inevitable. The very qualities of innovation and initiative associated with the private sector defy the "by the book" dimensions of conventional government bureaucracy, in which "everything not authorized is prohibited."[48] Indeed, it is this contrast that in many instances motivates the outsourcing decision. The private sector preoccupation with the financially profitable bottom line, along with proprietary prerogatives that foster secrecy, is at odds with the public-mindedness and disclosure expected of government action.[49] There may be irresolvable clashes between the improvisational, entrepreneurial, profit-driven motives of the private sector and the world of public governance that demands direct, explicit, and participatory terms of accountability.[50] But such tradeoffs between private entrepreneurship and public governance should be made mindfully and with public input rather than ad hoc and largely invisibly, as seems to be the case now. If there are reasons not to impose the full panoply of traditional administrative law constraints on private contractors, then at least functional substitutes must be pursued if the benefits of private enterprise are to be captured by the government outsourcing process without too great a cost.

Contributors to this volume express differing views about the reliability of governmental versus profit-making organizations, which no doubt affect their assessments of the relative virtues and vices of governance outsourcing. A significant overhaul and strengthening of the contracting process, paired with a greater measure of government oversight strikes some critics as a promising avenue for achieving sufficient transparency and accountability, while others question whether any increased governmental role would be worth potentially undermining the efficiencies of private enterprise. Still other contributors to this book question whether outsourcing can ever be appropriate for functions such as military combat, national security, or domestic law enforcement. For example, Sharon Dolovich, in Chapter 6, argues against contracts for private prison management on normative grounds because the conflicts of interest in these settings can be so serious, the evasion of meaningful accountability to the public so complete, and the nature of the tasks so ill-suited to the pursuit of profit. For functions such as these, which involve the use of force, or expose vulnerable populations to substantial risks to life and liberty in the name of the public interest, perhaps no amount of contract specification will suffice and they must be performed by the state itself.

Many critics are also concerned about the instability of the "inherently governmental" designation and its failure in practice to rule functions in or out of eligibility for contracting. If the government may contract with private companies to provide military, national security, and criminal justice functions, why not contract out criminal prosecutions and executions or the Federal Reserve Board's regulation and supervision of national monetary and financial systems? Why should the federal government not outsource the Quadrennial Defense Review—the statutorily mandated regular evaluation of national defense strategy, force structure, force modernization plans, infrastructure, budget plan, and other elements of the defense program and policies?[51] Such questions might once have been dismissed as rhetorical. Yet they are not, given the recent expansion of outsourcing and the instability of the "inherently governmental" designation in practice. We hope that the arguments in this book will stimulate a normative debate over just this question, Where and how do governments—and the people they serve—draw boundaries between what should and should not be subject to outsourcing? That should prompt the related question, What happens to democratic values and sheer effectiveness if we become unable to draw any distinctions, or if we fail systematically to manage the government contracts entered into in our name?

A Reform Agenda

Neither indifference nor panic will help address what we view as vital questions about the scope and quality of government by contract. As difficult as it may be to stimulate public debate on a subject that may seem technical or arcane, it is just as challenging to resist pressures to frame this conversation in ideological or absolutist terms. It is all too common to see the "private" sector as energetic, nimble, and efficient on the one hand, or greedy, unaccountable, and corrupt on the other, while the "public" sector is imagined as either virtuous and public spirited or alternatively lazy, wasteful, and stupid. Yet the breadth and variety of public and private-sector organizations that actually join in contemporary American governance defy such caricatures. Crude ideological frameworks will fail to generate solutions to the genuine weaknesses in our contractual governance system to the extent they pose false "either-or" alternatives. It is not sensible to suggest that we simply stop much of government contracting, but neither should we ignore evidence of its problems.

Despite their different perspectives and prescriptions, the authors contributing to this volume share a commitment to the nuanced and careful analysis of government outsourcing. A total rejection of the practice emerges as unrealistic and unhelpful. As Stan Soloway and Alan Chvotkin in Chapter 8 and Steve Kelman in Chapter 7 suggest, it is not possible and may not even be desirable to address the range of challenges tackled by government without engaging a host of private actors. In many instances, there are genuine advantages to relying on the private sector, including for-profit and non-profit organizations, for expertise, innovation, energy, and flexibility. Government provision can be slow, ineffective and costly. By using for-profit, non-profit, and governmental organizations, the government can enhance society's capacity to deliver more of the goods, information, services, and protections that we all need. And whenever we can reduce costs without losing quality performance, which some say is the primary aim of outsourcing, we should.

At the same time, one of the main themes of this book is that the effectiveness or quality of services and programs paid for by the government should be measured in light of democratic as well as economic values. Considerations beyond those that apply in the private sector matter when the government is the customer and when the functions implicate collective needs.

It may seem easiest to advance public values by keeping all government work within government. But a significant amount of outsourcing will persist in the United States for the simple reason that government cannot do everything its citizens want done without growing into a behemoth they refuse to support. Of course, the contracting regime we now have is not necessarily inevitable. What the public "wants" is not exogenous to government; public preferences reflect choices the government has already made and which it has the power to reverse. Still, we think it unlikely that the American public is prepared to abandon outsourcing in favor of a larger and more powerful state. It is also worth noting that the patterns of government contracting currently in place reflect foibles in the contemporary political process. For example, private contractors that gain so much from the federal contracting regime would not easily allow sharp reductions and currently spend considerable resources on lobbying and advocacy.

With contractual governance here to stay, the real question is not whether to outsource at all, but to what ends, using which strategies, and under what constraints. New energy must be devoted to determining which essential functions must remain not only formally directed by the government in theory, but actually performed by the government in fact. The "inherently governmental" designation used for this purpose for over half a century has proven woefully inadequate, both conceptually and in practice.[52]

The problem lies not just with the contractors, of course, but with Congress, which does not take the responsibility for ensuring government capacity for the programs that it authorizes and funds;[53] the executive branch, which has failed to retool and retrain for its new role in contract management and oversight; and even the courts, which assiduously adhere to a formal but increasingly unrealistic public-private distinction that protects contractors from significant legal and constitutional accountability. Many contractors themselves can and do call for significant reform so they can more reliably know the rules to which they should be trying to adhere. The problems of contractual governance should be viewed as shared by the public and private sector, with models of accountability from each sector supplying important elements of workable solutions.

We recognize that it is not enough to call for more government oversight when our current oversight system has not been effective. Nor is it adequate to demand more of the familiar legal and procedural checks if those checks will ossify the contracting system to the point of paralysis. This is why we propose an expansive approach to accountability and envision going well beyond the most familiar mechanisms available within the traditional paradigm of administrative law and process.

What do we mean by accountability? Here, Jerry Mashaw's definition supplies a useful guide: "in any accountability relationship, we should be able to specify at least six important things: *who* is liable or accountable to *whom; what* they are liable to be called to account for; *through what processes* accountability is to be assured; *by what standards* the putatively accountable behavior is to be judged; and, what the potential *effects* are of finding that those standards have been breached."[54] Public governance accountability historically has deployed a mix of political and legal mechanisms including electoral processes, hierarchical control between principals and agents within bureaucracies, and enforcement of legal rules in courts and adjudicative settings. This setup contrasts sharply with private market accountability, dominated by customer satisfaction, shareholder concerns with market performance, and greater return on investment.[55] As the lines between public and private functions have blurred, features of market competition have been brought into public functions, and elements of public oversight and rule compliance extended well into private enterprises.[56]

Minimal accountability for government contracting requires sufficient investment in human capital and deliberate selection of the mechanisms for gathering information, setting the requirements for effective performance, and managing and enforcing the contracting and oversight process. Planning before entering into any contract, determining procedures for large-scale contracting, and anticipating the impact of the use of contractors on the government's capacity to comply with law and public policies are crucial elements both for decisions about whether to contract and for the redesign and administration of the framework for government contracting.

As a first step in any serious discussion of reform, the accountability system for contractual governance must be honest. The costs of adequate supervision must be calculated as part of the outsourcing program, even if this means that outsourcing will not reduce costs as much as projections suggest. To be capable of performing oversight—and playing its role as a contracting party—the government must invest in the mechanisms of accountability, whether they take the form of legal regulation, measurable contract performance terms and government contract management capacity, or political review. Clarity about actual requirements, roles, and responsibilities is the central precondition so that each contracting arrangement specifies who is accountable to whom, for what, through what processes, by clear standards, and with specific consequences.[57]

Securing sufficient capacity within the government for the planning and oversight such clarity demands is difficult for several reasons. It runs counter to the rationale for cost savings often used to justify privatization. It is challenging to stem the significant "brain drain" from government to the private sector, since government agencies cannot compete with the salaries offered by private industry for individuals with relevant technical expertise. This diminishing government capacity further increases the government's reliance on the private sector. Dramatic and quick expansions of government contracting often emerge precisely because of the government's limited ability to respond to emergencies, as John Donahue documents in Chapter 2. The government typically lacks the internal capacity to ramp up services and logistics quickly or to deploy personnel and to collect and distribute goods and services suddenly needed due to an emergency or new challenge. In turn, this limitation also hampers the government's ability to draft and manage the outsourcing contracts used to substitute for the government's missing capacity. Especially in light of recent experience with this problem, the inspector general offices of government agencies should be drawn into the outsourcing process early during an emergency ramp-up. And, as James Jay Carafano and Alane Kochems have proposed, "government agencies should consider creating a corps of reserve contracting officers. Such an organization ideally would be identified, recruited, trained in advance, and regularly exercised to meet contracting needs in the aftermath of [a] crisis or conflict to assist in reconstruction."[58]

Of course, although they attract significant public attention and consume enormous resources, wars and natural disasters are not the typical contexts for government contracting. With this in mind, Kelman in his chapter, and Soloway and Chvotkin in theirs, warn against excessive focus on such outlier examples when proposing reforms. This is a concern that we take seriously. In particular, Kelman argues that adding more legal procedure to the outsourcing process will likely go too far in the direction of protecting against fraud and abuse while failing to design systems that will increase speed and improve quality of services. We agree that a satisfactory system must seek to provide all of these things: speed, quality, transparency, and compliance with democratic norms. At a minimum, where tradeoffs are inevitable, the risks should be made more explicit, and the decision to take them should be subject to public debate—certainly more than is currently the case.

Setting aside these emergency situations, though, even routine and uncontroversial contracting can be improved, perhaps with relatively minor reforms. In Chapter 9, Nina Mendelson describes a number of relatively modest changes to existing statutes or legal doctrines that could improve contract performance and accountability significantly across the board. In the same vein, Laura Dickinson in Chapter 13 explains how better structuring of contracts could improve accountability between government and private contractors in the international setting. This and other chapters consider strengthening civil liability under private law as another vehicle for tightening accountability of private contractors for defective work.

The effectiveness of even relatively modest reforms will depend to a significant extent on whether they are well matched for the contexts in which they are deployed. These contexts will vary with respect to a number of features, including the relative clarity with which performance measures can be stated; the distribution of relevant expertise between the private sector and the government; the competitiveness of supplier markets; and the extent to which the incentives of potential providers and monitors are aligned or misaligned. The case studies and examples pursued by Miriam Seifter in Chapter 4, Martha Minow in Chapter 5, Sharon Dolovich in Chapter 6, and Paul Verkuil in Chapter 12 open a window onto the contextual variability that will demand such a refined approach to accountability design. Institutional accountability mechanisms should be designed to produce the relevant information, address the most serious concerns, and report to appropriate people—meaning those in a position to take remedial action and answer to the public—for each specific context.

One size does not fit all accountability needs, and yet, in every setting, public accountability requires some degree of transparency, participation, and legality, with effective and independent review by actors responsible and responsive to the public.[59] In devising flexible yet rigorous accountability regimes across many contexts, policy makers in this country could learn from the emerging field of global administrative law, which focuses on the variety and interaction of accountability structures operating in the public and private realms, and in both national and international settings.[60]

Attention to context should not mean, however, a piecemeal reform agenda. Although it will be useful in some instances to separate out different species of contracting—because particular problems might be unique to one category and call for a tailored response—such subdivision can hide patterns that emerge only when outsourcing is considered cumulatively. For example, modest improvements to routine contracts for consumer goods, and even specialized reforms aimed at contracts for emergency situations like war or natural disaster, will help in some respects, but will not be sufficient to address the full set of issues raised by the shift to government by contract.

Recognizing the larger trend toward government by contract, which is possible only by aggregating contracts across a number of issue areas, raises a new and more challenging set of questions than any subset of contracts does alone. When substantial outsourcing is at stake, special problems of scale arise if government is to maintain its internal capacity to perform its essential supervisory and oversight role, and ensure responsiveness to the general public for decisions made in its name. A government engaged in such a high volume of outsourcing across many different areas must actively retool and obtain sufficient resources to keep on top of the increased reliance on private partners.

Although it is not yet clear what mix of measures would be adequate to address the large-scale shift to government by contract, clearly something systematic must be done. A wide variety of approaches must be considered beyond modest or targeted proposals, including significant civil service reform, new requirements for greater transparency both from agencies and contractors, creative use of third-party monitors, mandated self-regulation and disclosure, minimum requirements for public participation, robust conflict of interest rules, and meaningful, if selective, judicial review. Some functions should be brought back into the government, even if it costs more.[61] Some should remain outsourced, even if accountability is less than perfect. Taken as a whole, the collection of chapters calls for a robust and creative reform agenda: smaller-scale revisions of the contracts themselves to clarify standards and adjust incentives; medium-scale reform of the existing legal regime to build in greater transparency, public participation, and accountability; and farther-reaching proposals for revising the structures of oversight themselves, or even deeming certain functions ineligible for contracting.

Our current government contracting system does not work. It is largely invisible and unresponsive to the public in whose name it is undertaken. The existing rules and procedures fail to guard adequately against inefficiency, conflict of interest, and abuse. And much of the power being exercised through contracting is largely unaccountable to *any* regime of oversight—market, legal, or political. Yet government by contract has arrived, and it is here to stay. This fact should prompt serious and sustained public dialogue about the short- and long-term implications of outsourcing for American democracy. Offering contrasting and at times conflicting views, the contributors to this book aim to spark that dialogue in pursuit of better governance in this challenging age.

PART ONE

Recent Developments

CHAPTER ONE

Public-Private Governance

A Historical Introduction

WILLIAM J. NOVAK

Ius publicum privatorum pactis mutari non potest.
Public law cannot be changed by private pacts.

—DIGEST OF JUSTINIAN 38.2.14

Introduction

Much of the language and practice of current American policymaking, international as well as domestic, suggests that we are in something of a new age. The end of the cold war and the demise of the totalitarian states that dictated so much of the world history of the twentieth century has convinced many commentators that one great historical era has passed and that a new and comparatively unencumbered future is upon us. Speculations about the decisive end of one great historical epoch have produced a series of provocative neologisms for talking about the distinctive nature of the present, from rich theoretical literatures on postindustrialism and postmodernism to more policy oriented discussions of globalization and neoliberalism.[1]

The chapters in this volume are part of that broader conversation. They concern themselves with one particular trend in contemporary American policymaking: the turn to privatization—the tendency of policymakers to increasingly rely on the private sector, through outsourcing, contracting, disinvestment, and the selling and leasing of governmental properties and resources, to meet obligations formerly thought of as distinctly public. Part of a larger set of neoliberal policy shifts that includes deregulation and an increased reliance on market mechanisms, this preference for exploring private over public solutions has permeated current policy issues ranging from international security and prisons to welfare and public health to highways and public parks.[2]

The job of the historian in this conversation is to place this sudden and dramatic turn to the private in broader historical, socioeconomic, and theoretical context. Such historical contextualization provides several useful services. First, it challenges some of the linear and teleological thinking that has accompanied many normative theories about the beneficent inevitability or predictability or finality of this shift to the private. There is nothing natural, neutral, or necessary about privatization, deregulation, or neoliberalism.[3] Things could be, and have been (in other contexts, in other times and places), decidedly otherwise. Indeed, as recently as the early 1930s in the United States, all of the normative, political, and economic arrows were pointing in exactly the opposite direction. The private sector and market mechanisms were in a state of disrepute even among the most traditional of economists. Private economic actors could not be counted on to produce and distribute even the most basic of human commodities—for example, milk and coal.[4] In that critical period, it was the public sector—the government, the state—that was called on to provide distinctly public remedies to pervasive private sector ills through increased public regulation (e.g., the SEC), public welfare (e.g., Social Security), public works programs (e.g., the PWA, WPA, and the CCC), public ownership and management (e.g., TVA), and public planning (e.g., NRPB).[5] As historical times change, history reminds us that our current policy preferences are time-bound and contingent—a product of a particular politics and a politically-charged economics. The solutions of the present are no more privileged and perhaps no more enduring than some of those of the past.

Second, and relatedly, history calls attention to the particular socioeconomic context of public policy formulation—the changes in the distribution of wealth, power, and authority that affect collective policy preferences over time. For the historian, such extant distributions of power in economy and society are not exogenous to determining the best policy choices. Rather, they are understood as causal agents of change. The context, in other words, is crucial. History thus brings a critical perspective to bear on the models and formulae that offer up policy prescriptions on the basis of supposedly timeless and apolitical—anti- or transhistorical—principles like efficiency or utility.

Finally, and perhaps most importantly, history provides an alternative perspective—the different point of view offered by confronting the alterity and the otherness of the past. As L. P. Hartley opened *The Go-Between*, "The past is a foreign country; they do things differently there."[6] With respect to public and private, contemporary advocates of outsourcing, privatization, and deregulation might be surprised to discover that past American approaches to government, regulation, and the public interest do not conform to present priorities. Rather than interpret neoliberalism as but the latest turn in a consistent and continuous American liberal tradition favoring individual rights, economic interests, and the private sector, history suggests that present policies might mark a significant departure from historical precedent—a great transformation in American policymaking and a potential breach in what previous political and legal commentators understood as "the public trust."

The Great Dichotomy: Public and Private

As the Italian legal and political philosopher Norberto Bobbio has noted, the public-private distinction is one of the great dichotomies in Western jurisprudence and politics. Like war and peace or individual and collective, the public-private dichotomy serves as an influential intellectual template ordering much of our thinking (positive as well as normative) about the nature of society, polity, and economy. The public-private distinction has several characteristics that account for its peculiar power in shaping our views of the world. First, from a historical perspective, the public-private distinction is particularly foundational. Bobbio traces its roots through Justinian's original demarcation of public law and private law as the distinction upon which the entire edifice of Western legal rule was built. In jurisprudence, the public-private distinction is primary—all other legal distinctions are subsumed beneath this first-order division of legal life. Second, the public-private distinction is complete and comprehensive. No third sphere need be contemplated in order to account for and classify the vast range of human activities, relations, and institutions.[7] Third, the public-private distinction divides the world into two separate spheres that at least purport to be mutually exclusive—something designated as public cannot at the same time be deemed to be private, and vice versa.[8]

Such characteristics make public and private a powerful device for interpreting social life, past as well as present. Consequently, interpretations of American history and policymaking deploy the public-private dichotomy with great regularity. Indeed, one of the most dominant trends in historiography is the tendency to interpret the American past completely with primary reference to but one half of the great dichotomy.

According to one school, the key to American history is the supremacy of the private in American life—the predominance of private property, individual rights, private interests, civil society, and market forces. In this classical liberal model, the private sphere is the motor of American history, the reason for American prosperity, and the raison d'être of the American state. Americans turn to the public sphere only reluctantly in a self-interested Lockean bargain that aims only to further secure other private rights and interests. Private liberty against public government is the mantra of this school of historical and political thought.[9]

On the other hand, an equally powerful, alternative interpretation of American history emphasizes the opposite side of the great dichotomy. With an emphasis on popular democracy, collective action, and general welfare, this school endorses the formative role of the public in American life. Drawing attention to the great episodes of public governmental activism in United States history—e.g., Progressive Era reform, the New Deal, the Great Society, the civil rights movement—the dominant theme of American history from this perspective is the never-ending struggle to protect the public from powerful and resilient private interests.[10]

Such is the power of the interpretive tendency to put things wholly in one category or another—public or private. But one of the more interesting things about American history is the degree to which it frequently resists such simple, bifurcated categorization. Despite the pretensions of the public-private dichotomy to be a complete and seamless analytic, one of the dominant characteristics of American policymaking over time has been the curious blending of public and private initiatives, techniques, and institutions. Indeed, while many commentators have been drawn to thinking about public and private in the American past as a normatively charged *either/or* proposition—as *either* a matter of the overweening predominance of private individual right and market self-interest *or* a matter of the triumph of public good and governmental activism—the great mass of the best analyses of American legal-political life (e.g., work like that of John Commons, Harold Laski, Adolf Berle, V.O. Key, Grant McConnell, Joseph Schumpeter, John Kenneth Galbraith, Theodore Lowi, Morton Keller, Theda Skocpol) has frequently rejected the two extremes in favor of an emphasis on the close interrelationship and interpenetration of public and private in American history.[11] These scholars reject the idea of simply splitting the problem of power (political, social, or economic) along a single private/public binary: right or sovereignty, individual interest or social welfare, market or regulation. They argue instead that the problem of power in America is complex, and that one of its defining features over time is the intersection or convergence of public and private authority. The hallmark of American politics from this perspective is the distinctive way in which power has long been distributed along an exceedingly complex array of persons, associations, and institutions that are not easily categorized as fundamentally *either* public *or* private. Highlighting the everyday nexus of the legal-political and the socioeconomic, these scholars present the public-private interplay in actual social and economic life of forces often separated out in more polemical forms of inquiry: power and right, coercion and contract, solidarity and autonomy.

With this historical and social-scientific perspective in mind, it is worth asking exactly what is truly "new" in the recent policy turn to privatization, and what might be understood as part of a broader tradition or more structural trend in the history of American governance. For while the language of "outsourcing," "contracting," and "deregulation" is certainly contemporary, the history of U.S. government reliance on intersecting public-private partnerships runs much deeper. Indeed, the interrelationship of public and private in policymaking is at the center of a distinctive national style of American statecraft that stretches back to the founding and beyond.

Public-Private Partnerships in American History

The deepest roots of American public-private governance extend back to early traditions of English legal rule first identified by Frederic William Maitland.[12] When Maitland went looking for the historical foundations of English governance, he passed by some of the standard sources of national public law like Magna Carta and the Bill of Rights. He went instead to the actual practicing institutions of English local government—the shire, the hundred, the vill, the township, the borough, the trust, and the corporation. What Maitland found there in the charters, properties, membership, organization, rules, and bylaws of these group associations was not an absolute demarcation of institutions of public authority, but rather a strange mélange of private, public, and associative functions. In short, he uncovered the medieval origins of public-private governance. Where the manor and the corporation upon first glance seemed to be quintessentially "private" entities, Maitland detailed the extensive public responsibilities they carried out, from the keeping of public order to the construction and management of roads and public works. Meanwhile more classically "public" institutions like the hundred, the vill, and the township frequently operated autonomously as quasi-private entities with their own independent property and charter rights. Even courts had an ambiguous public-private nature. As Maitland noted about the hundred courts, "Many of these courts had fallen into private hands . . . , and the kings had freely given and sold the right of holding courts. To a great landowner this right was very profitable, it enabled him to keep his tenants in hand, and we must further remember that throughout the Middle Ages jurisdiction was a source of income—the lord of a court has a right to the numerous fines and forfeitures which arise out of the doing of justice."[13] The great modern public-private dichotomy is not much help in categorizing such early and basic institutions of English governance, for they frequently involved a strange mixture of seemingly private charters, rights, and properties granted by the king for the achievement of seemingly public purposes—local governance, public order, taxation, and the administration of justice.

This distinctive style of ancient English public-private governance through law was imported rather seamlessly into the American colonies. The most obvious symbol of the continuity of this governmental regime was the role of the charter in colonial rule. It is important to remember the true origins of American government in the series of twenty-eight major colonial territorial grants, patents, and charters from 1606 (Virginia) to 1681 (Pennsylvania) that established English jurisdiction over and directed colonial settlement of North America.[14] Like the institutions of old English governance, the diverse colonial charters displayed the same odd mix of public and private terms, conditions, and strategies. Charter conditions varied greatly over time and place, ranging from a vague royal licensing of unincorporated exploration and settlement, to a partnership between the Crown and a group of formally incorporated investors, to incorporation of the colony as joint-stock company, to more neofeudal forms of territorial proprietorship. The first charter of Virginia (1606) licensed "Sir Thorn as Gales, and Sir George Somers, Knights, Richard Hackluit, Clerk, Prebendary of Westminster, and Edward-Maria Wingfield, Thomas Hanharm and Ralegh Gilbert, Esqrs. William Parker, and George Popham, Gentlemen, and divers others of our loving Subjects . . . to make Habitation, Plantation, and to deduce a colony of sundry of our People into that part of America commonly called VIRGINIA." The license allowed the formation of two separate companies and included the all-important grant of land and property: "They shall have all the Lands, Woods, Soil, Grounds, Havens, Ports, Rivers, Mines, Minerals, Marshes, Waters, Fishings, Commodities, and Hereditaments, whatsoever, from the said first Seat of their Plantation." But in addition to such private-sounding provisions for property rights and company formation, the overarching public purposes of the colonization enterprise were never far from view: "Each of the said Colonies shall have a Council, which shall govern and order all Matters-and-Causes, which shall arise, grow, or happen, to or within the same several Colonies, according to such Laws, Ordinances, and Instructions, as shall be, in that behalf, given and signed with Our Hand or Sign Manual, and pass under the Privy Seal of our Realm of England."[15] Public governance *and* private organization and investment were mutual objectives and distinguishing characteristics of the entire American colonization project. Colonization was a powerful example of the potential force and effectiveness of techniques of public-private governance.[16]

Like the reception of English common law more generally, the public-private governing system reflected in the English colonial chartering system continued to influence American policymaking after the revolution, independence, and the establishment of new constitutional standards for American governance. Examples are legion, but one of the most complete analyses of this perseverance is Hendrik Hartog's examination of the legal status and powers of the Corporation of the City of New York. New York City, like the American colonies, legally originated in a royal charter—the Montgomerie Charter of 1730—as a formal and quintessentially mixed public-private corporation. The powers of the city were originally based on its relatively autonomous control of the municipality's own private estate, that is, its royally granted private property rights. The charter continued to exert influence after independence, when the original royal grant of property contributed to the emergence of a distinctive style of municipal governance wherein city property management became a useful tool of public planning and development. A classic example of early American public-private governance was the use of waterlot grants to develop New York City's waterfront. While many have seen only private interests and perhaps more than a bit of private speculation and public corruption in the distribution of the city's waterfront property to private entities, Hartog portrays the waterlot system as a creative mode of public-private development and regulation. The city marshaled private energies and equity for development through the granting of private property rights while at the same time maintaining public control and regulatory oversight. For Hartog, the waterlot grants exemplified a distinctive public-private technology and instrumentality of governmental action. The waterlot grants provided New York City with the streets, bridges, wharves, and port infrastructure necessary to a developing municipal entrepôt. The city's original charter property rights "allowed it to plan and initiate action. . . . The fact that the corporation held its property as a private landowner made it possible for the city to delegate to private individuals major responsibility for the construction of its commercial heart, without at the same time abandoning control over that process."[17]

But it was not just American municipal corporations that displayed this curious mixture of public-private forms and functions. Historians have now completed a couple of generations of work on the legal history of the development of the American business corporation.[18] And there is now a fairly strong consensus that the business corporation was devised in the early American republic as a peculiar instrument of statecraft—a quasi–public or public service corporation—to aid funds-strapped state governments in accomplishing public objectives like the construction of a national infrastructure in a capital-scarce economy. As Willard Hurst among others has noted, before the advent of general incorporation statutes, most corporations were created through the grant of a special charter from the state legislature. The pubic act signified the private corporation's official status as a creature and instrument of governance—as an artificial legal entity dependent upon sovereign authority for its existence. Corporations received special benefits and privileges through the legislative act of incorporation such as limited liability, powers of eminent domain, control over public rights of way, and so on. In return, legislatures extracted what Ernst Freund called "an enlarged police power" for supervising and controlling corporate activities.[19]

The special public nature of early American business corporations is even more evident in the kinds of activities pursued by the first corporations. The vast majority of early American corporate charters were granted to associations with a special public-utility or public-interest character. Of the 335 chartered corporations formed before 1800, 219 were turnpike, bridge, and canal companies; 67 were banks and insurance companies; and 36 concerned water, fire protection, or harbor facilities. Between 1790 and 1860, 88 percent of Pennsylvania's 2,333 special charters were granted to transport, infrastructure, utility, and financial corporations (only 8 per cent went to manufacturing or general business firms).[20] In short, like New York City's waterlot grants, the early American business corporation was aimed squarely at the development of the nation's public infrastructure. It was a legal tool of state action that empowered private investors and groups with special privileges so as to allow them to undertake costly but necessary public improvement projects. Such public-private partnerships allowed cash-starved state governments to promote, encourage, direct, and regulate infrastructural development without taking on the full financial and political risks of such an enormous enterprise. During the nineteenth century, the great mass of the U.S. national infrastructure—turnpikes, bridges, canals, railroads—was created through a nexus of such public-private partnerships.[21]

But public-private governance was not just a feature of American economic policy a useful tool of economic and infrastructural development. Historians of American social policy have detected a similar mixture of public and private means and ends in the administration of policies concerning such things as crime, health, education, and welfare. Arguably there is no more "public" area of social policymaking than the criminal law, wherein the state directly punishes with the most severe pains and penalties the most noxious offenses to the society as a whole. Yet within this most public of policy places, one also notes the curious presence of the private in American history. Allen Steinberg, among other historians, has documented the long hold of private prosecution as an instrument of criminal justice in the United States.[22] Allowing, indeed encouraging, private persons to prosecute violations of public law sprang from some of the same motivations seen in the economic arena. Private prosecution allowed for the wide distribution of the policing function—stretching capacity, spreading costs, and lessening the need for an expansive, professional bureaucracy. Private prosecution was particularly effective in the enforcement of local regulatory laws. New York ensured effective oversight of its fire regulations in the early nineteenth century by allowing any private person to prosecute violations of the city's prohibition on gunpowder, with the additional incentive that the illegal gunpowder would be forfeited to the private person bringing suit.[23] Through the early twentieth century, private groups like the YMCA and the WCTU as well as special citizen's committees on crime and vice continued to wield inordinate private power in the definition and enforcement of public criminality in the United States.[24]

This short survey suggests that public-private governance has deep roots in American history. But while most of the examples surveyed thus far are primarily products of the eighteenth and nineteenth centuries, it should be apparent that American public-private governance is not just a thing of the past. Despite the rise of a powerful public nation-state as well as the systematic development of a private corporate economy in the twentieth century, public-private partnerships and policies have remained mainstays of American governance. In social policy, the best new work on the nature of the modern American welfare state has especially emphasized the distinctive role and influence of the private sector in education, social insurance, and health care.[25] In economic policy, long after the huge public interventions of New Deal policymaking, quasi-public/quasi-private entities like the Federal Land Bank, Fannie Mae, port authorities, utility districts, sports and convention authorities, and other government created, government-sponsored enterprises continue to dominate whole sectors of the economy from land, housing, and urban infrastructure to entertainment, recreation, and tourism.[26] The current turn towards privatization needs to be understood in the context of this longer history of near-constant American governmental public-private cooperation in economic as well as social policy development.

Public Corruption and Private Coercion

There are several sets of interpretive, analytical, and normative implications for this long tradition of public-private collaboration in American history. The first revolves around the all-important question—"Why?" What explains this peculiar policy preference for public-private initiatives in the American past?

One answer to that question involves two great American historical preoccupations. The first concerns the political preoccupation with the problem of public corruption at the turn of the nineteenth century, and the second concerns the equally powerful political problem of private coercion at the turn of the twentieth century. In the context of these twin concerns about the potential for public corruption in state-directed projects and private coercion in the free market, it is not an accident that the United States developed a preference for balancing public direction with private initiative and regulating the private excesses and market failures of competition and monopoly with what John Kenneth Galbraith termed "countervailing" public power.[27] Public-private governance, in short, is a prime example of a dominant American constitutional tendency to attempt to separate, divide, balance, and most importantly *distribute* power. The primary constitutional principles that Americans learn in grade school—federalism, the separation of powers, checks and balances—are but classic examples of a prevailing constitutional preference for the distribution of power. Legal historian James Willard Hurst characterized this principle this way: "Any kind of organized power ought to be measured against criteria of ends and means which are not defined or enforced by the immediate power holders themselves. It is as simple as that: We don't want to trust any group of power holders to be their own judges upon the ends for which they use the power or the ways in which they use it." Separating legislative, executive, and judicial power; distinguishing local, state, and federal governments; establishing bicameral legislatures and a multilevel court system, and, most importantly, *balancing the public and the private spheres through law* were but alternative means of realizing this distributive constitutional ideal—of assuring that "any kind of organized power," public as well as private, should be held accountable by other forms of organized power. Counterbalancing public and private forms of initiative and regulation was a creative constitutional means of distributing authority, thus providing checks on the use and abuse of both public and private power.[28]

Public Corruption

The United States was born amid a pervasive original fear of public corruption—not a fear of government or public power per se (as mistakenly portrayed in so many ideological histories of the American founding)—but a fear of the misuse or the perversion of power. As Hannah Arendt so correctly noted in *On Revolution*, "[t]he true objective of the American Constitution was not to limit power but to create more power, actually to establish and duly constitute an entirely new power centre."[29] Public governmental power wielded in the public interest was lauded for its ability to create order and wealth, to promote economic development, and to expand social and cultural opportunity. What was to be feared (and guarded against politically) was the possibility that the enormously disproportionate power available to government in the public sphere could be put to corrupt uses and purposes—to ends that served selfish, private, or despotic interests rather than the general welfare and the common good.[30] In the eighteenth and early nineteenth centuries, the most powerful entities that could be most dangerously corrupted—that could be harnessed so as to do greatest damage to the interests of humankind—were the public, collective, and rulemaking bodies of secular and theocratic governance. Private powers were comparably less threatening (if no less susceptible to corruption)—smaller in scale, comparatively unorganized, fragmented, and widely distributed. It is no accident in this environment that the private sector was looked to as a safe counterbalance—a democratic countervailing power—to the possibility of public corruption. Many of the great policy debates of the early nineteenth century over general incorporation, banks, canals, railroads, and other public improvements were shaped by this overarching concern with the potential for public corruption and the possibility of employing the private sphere as an effective hedge against despotism. The private sector, in other words, was an attractive mechanism for distributing power.

Private Coercion

Twentieth-century policymaking is still frequently influenced by the founding fear of public corruption. But of course, with the advent of industrial corporate capitalism in the late nineteenth century, the political and institutional context had changed dramatically. Private power, private property, and the private sector could no longer be seen as simple and innocent antidotes to public corruption. On the contrary, the problem of private coercion—of the possibility of private despotism through the powerful actions of unprecedentedly large and influential corporations and property holders—for the time being displaced the overriding concern with the corruptibility of public power. Indeed, in the progressive and new liberal reform movements of the early twentieth century, activists and intellectuals explicitly endorsed an expansion of public state power to redress the rampant private abuses of a "gilded age." The idea that the private sphere was corrupting the public sphere (rather than the other way around) marked a lasting redirection of American political thought and action.[31] In a host of public legal, legislative, and administrative reforms that only climaxed with Franklin D. Roosevelt's New Deal, reformers created an expanded public sphere—a new liberal state—to regulate, police, and rein in private excess.[32]

This new concern with private coercion rather than the traditional American obsession with public corruption yielded an extraordinarily perceptive discourse about the relationship of public and private that remains highly relevant given resurgent neoliberal faith in the purities and efficiencies of the private sphere. Arguably some of the best work on the theme of public-private governance in America remains that of sociological jurists and legal realists like Roscoe Pound, Morris Cohen, and Robert Hale. As early as the 1910s and 1920s these scholars worked to deconstruct an overly stark public-private distinction in American law—a distinction they saw as a barrier to socioeconomic reform. In "Property and Sovereignty," Cohen brilliantly complicated the naturalistic distinction between civil private property (dominium) and political public sovereignty (imperium) by demonstrating their deep historical and legal interdependence. Like Brooks and Henry Adams and Roscoe Pound, Cohen feared that the United States was entering something like a new feudal age marked by the reemergence of private power as a despotic force in public life. Collapsing the traditional public-private distinction that seemed to align the public sphere with force and coercion and the private sphere with voluntarism and freedom, Cohen examined certain similarities in the coercive, real-world effects of private property and public sovereignty, suggesting in the end the fundamental "character of property as sovereign power compelling service and obedience." Similarly, in *Freedom through Law: Public Control of Private Governing Power*—a text that very much deserves to be resurrected given contemporary debates—Robert Lee Hale contended that the sharp theoretical separation of public and private obscured the actual proactive role of public power in structuring the so-called private bargains that had such an immense effect on the distribution of wealth and power in American society. Reversing the nineteenth-century solution to the problem of public corruption, Hale endorsed a more powerful role for the public state in regulating the "governing power" of the new private entities rapidly dominating American economic and social life.[33]

The lasting effect of this critical reappraisal of the public-private distinction in American law was a more realistic understanding of the public construction of private power, emphasizing the degree to which the private sphere is positively constructed by law and government and is consequently always suffused with (as opposed to immune from) sovereignty, force, violence, and coercion. In an era that witnessed the forceful emergence of new forms of private property sanctioned by positive law with rather severe consequences for American society and economy, the realist project cultivated a perspective that no longer naively viewed private right as the natural opposite of public power and a necessary counterweight to public corruption. They opened the door to a more critical perspective wherein private power could be seen as a threat to public right and to democratic self-government. The realists forever complicated thinking about public and private by insisting upon always seeing the sovereignty, seeing the power, and seeing the political and public consequences of the legal allocation of the designation "private" in human activities and interactions. In that spirit, our present neoliberal moment—our preoccupation with deregulation, privatization, and the expansion of "millennial" global capitalism[34]—should not fool us into thinking that the American state is again somehow retreating (after the New Deal and World War II, after the Great Society and Vietnam) to a more familiar, some might say "natural" pattern of statelessness, privatism, or laissez-faire. From a realist perspective, we must not lose sight of the fact that despite the rhetoric, from the perspective of history the powers of the U.S. government to regulate, punish, study, discipline, order, and affect its citizens (as well as others' citizens)—have never been greater. As we analyze current rhetoric about leaner central governmental organization and outsourcing, privatization, and deregulation, we should remember what Sheldon Wolin calls the "paradox of power" in late modernity—that "power is simultaneously concentrated and disaggregated."[35]

Public Trust and Publicity

The other important set of interpretive and normative issues that emerges from this historical look at public and private in the United States concerns the public good. The idea of public interest or common welfare was at the heart of the classical American conception of a commonwealth or a republic founded upon *res publica*—defined by Cicero as a "thing of the people," wherein "people" represents not a mere assemblage of discrete individuals, but a society bound together by common interest and advantage *(utilitatis communione)*. Though late eighteenth- and nineteenth-century Americans feared public corruption and distinctly used the private sphere (private property, private associations, and public-private partnerships) to mitigate the threat of public despotism, they never lost sight of the fact that, in the end, the public was prior to and superior to *any* private interest. The idea was as old as Justinian's original distinction. Public law was superior to private law, with private law frequently being treated as a residual category defined as "not public." Private contracts could not dictate, alter, abrogate, or enforce public law, and public law frequently controlled the terms and guaranteed the enforcement of private agreements.[36] In Anglo-American jurisprudence, this sentiment about the ultimate superiority of public over private was best captured in the ancient common-law maxim *salus populi supreme est lex*—the welfare of the people is the supreme law.

The *salus populi* maxim suggested that in the final balance, the collective public interest always trumped mere individual private advantage. As New York Chancellor James Kent put it in his influential commentary on property and police power, "[p]rivate interest must be made subservient to the general interest of the community."[37] This legal idea lay behind some of the most important doctrines and institutions in nineteenth-century governance—from general state police powers to pass regulations protecting public health, safety, morals, and welfare to the power of eminent domain to the more obscure emergency provisions of the common law of overruling necessity.[38] One of the more pertinent examples, given contemporary preoccupation with privatization, was the law of public trust. Public trust was in some ways the public antipode of eminent domain. Whereas eminent domain held that private property could be taken for public use with just compensation, public trust held that the opposite should not be true—that is, public property should not be taken for private use—period. Though twenty-first century privatization is replete with examples of the selling off and leasing of public resources to private entities with only modest controversy,[39] some nineteenth-century efforts at privatization encountered more legal and political resistance.

Given contemporary policies and powerful mythologies about the overriding role of private property and individual rights in American history, one might think that in the early republic the privatization of public property would have been routinely accepted. History suggests otherwise. In the 1840s and 1850s, many cash-strapped municipalities latched on to the idea of selling off portions of their public squares to replenish dwindling public coffers (motivations not dissimilar to some contemporary privatizations). The result was not a celebration of an ingenious merger of private and municipal interests, but a flurry of lawsuits defending overriding public rights in the public's property. And early American judges defended the public trust with vigor. When Allegheny, Pennsylvania, tried to privatize its public square in 1849 to pay for a recently constructed city waterworks, the Pennsylvania

Supreme Court ruled that the appropriation of the park to private interest was "an offense against the public, and indictable as a common nuisance." In a similar case, the Vermont Supreme Court held that the dedication of public property to public use was primary and irrevocable. The public rights could not be traded, sold, or bartered away to private interests no matter what the offsetting benefits to the city. As the court put it, "[t]he taking of property dedicated to the use of the public, and appropriating it to private use, thereby wholly excluding the public from enjoyment of it," was not tolerated by American law. Even existing public officers and duly elected councils had no right to separate public property from its true and lasting owner—the public.[40] Such was the power of the legal idea of the superiority of public rights in early America.

An important corollary to the supremacy of public law and public interest in early American legal and political thought was the ideal of publicity—the notion that truly public affairs should be conducted publicly (literally, "in public"), transparently, and with as much democratic public participation as possible. The structure (if not always the function) of early American political institutions demonstrated an intense regard for publicity and participation, again originally as a check on the potential for public corruption. Primary constitutional guarantees concerning speech, press, and assembly encouraged an active and engaged public sphere. The local nature of much day-to-day governance in early America only added to the substantively public and participatory nature seen in such institutions as the New England town meeting or the county court day. From the important role of the jury in legal governance to the recruitment of ordinary citizens for routine public service, nineteenth-century American government was visible, accessible, and almost tangible in everyday life. With the rise of a concern with private coercion and the threat of business corrupting American politics at the turn of the twentieth century, a new wave of reforms (including the direct election of senators, an expanded suffrage, and innumerable election laws) was enacted to try to ensure accountable government in the public interest. This overriding concern with publicity— with political power as essentially nonprivate and open to the public, as visible rather than hidden, and as subject to public scrutiny, checks, and remedies—has been at the center of the American governmental experiment from its founding. Current fascination with the increased privatization of the public should not overlook an essential publicity, visibility, and accountability at the heart of the historical struggle for popular government and the security of a democratic republic against despotisms, private as well as public.

Conclusion

From the perspective of American history, public-private governance is distinctly old rather than surprisingly new. Current fascination with public-private policymaking should acknowledge this longer history of public-private governance as a distinctive form of American policymaking with roots back to the earliest settlements and the constitutional foundations of the republic. That longer history offers up several important lessons and perspectives to contemporary advocates of increased public-private partnerships.

First, the power of public-private governance as a technology of public action flowed from its ability to counter the twin evils of *both* public corruption *and* private coercion. Public-private forms were developed in past American policymaking to guard against both the excessive publicization of private life as well as the privatization of public things, both of which were seen as corrupting crossroads to serfdom and despotism. American legal and political history draws equal attention to the formative struggles against age-old public corruption at the turn of the nineteenth century and to the progressive battle to rein in new forms of private coercion in the twentieth century. Contemporary policymakers should take heed of both of these twin dangers when rebalancing public and private strategies for the twenty-first century.

Second, the main historical strength of public-private governance comes from its usefulness as a pragmatic policy instrument for the distribution of power—offsetting public power with private distribution and checking private jurisdiction with public regulation. Embedded in this idea is the notion that the complicated American governmental regime of distributed sovereignty, separation of powers, federalism, multiple and competing jurisdictions, and the frequent downward delegation of rights and powers through charters, incorporations, associations, properties, and the rule of law creates a system of rule that penetrates civil society and acquires a public legitimacy frequently denied more direct and authoritarian mechanisms of governance. But this system of distributed public-private governance also raises some important questions for democratic politics in terms of the consequences of delegating and distributing the state's monopoly power over the legitimate use of force and violence (to use Max Weber's terminology).[41]

What are the political implications and requirements of distributing public power through private actors, groups, and institutions in a democratic republic? Although normative distributive claims have been notoriously difficult to make when investigating the allocation of "private" economic resources in the United States, when we are also talking about the distribution of public powers (as shown in the work of Pound, Cohen, and Hale) distributive concerns should be able to get more traction.

Finally, in all this discussion of the long history and positive and negative distributive effects of public-private governance, the ultimate supremacy of public law and the public interest should not forgotten. As the pendulum of American public life has once again swung toward a preoccupation with public corruption and toward rather uncritical assumptions about the comparative virtues and efficiencies of the private sphere, it is important to reaffirm the historic origins of the American republic in an unambiguous assertion of the superiority of public things, public rights, and public goods. Public-private governance should not be confused with private government. Private government has a longer and comparatively more ignominious history than the one covered in this chapter, from the power of the lord over serfs in the medieval manorial system, to the firm rule of the slaveholder over the Southern plantation, to the power of some corporations and private police forces over laborers in late nineteenth-century industrial capitalism. As we investigate and analyze new ways to distribute power and make policy through private mechanisms, we should remember past autocratic and theocratic regimes that capitalized on private power and an enervated public sphere. At the beginning of the previous century, progressive and new liberal thinkers worried about the power of private wealth versus commonwealth and the possibility of a new feudalism built upon new forms of unchecked private coercion in a modernizing world. In response, they reinvigorated older conceptions of republican government for the general welfare and crafted new instruments of public power to regulate and control private excess in the public interest. At the beginning of a new century of globalizing capital and a relentlessly aggrandizing private sphere, their warnings and their remedies might still hold the most important lessons that American legal and political history can provide.

CHAPTER TWO

The Transformation of Government Work

Causes, Consequences, and Distortions

JOHN D. DONAHUE

This is a transformative era for government—at least on paper, and by intent. Books and articles heralding a brave new public sector roll off the presses. Government has become, or is poised to become, or at the very least is assiduously *trying* to become leaner, more agile, performance-oriented, densely networked, ever more flexible and efficient. At the federal level the roll call of major transformation campaigns includes the Grace Commission during the Reagan administration, the National Performance Review under Clinton, and the President's Management Agenda of George W. Bush. Few states have gone without at least one high-level task force dedicated to root-and-branch restructuring.

It would be both churlish and inaccurate to claim that all this is a sham. Some real changes have taken place in how public organizations operate and in the allocation of public missions within and beyond governmental institutions, including some undeniably sound changes. Transforming government is an urgent, noble mission embraced by many people of good will and great talent. It would be surprising indeed had the quest proven fruitless. But many aspiring reformers, among whom I count myself, are plagued by a sense that progress has been meager relative to both the effort applied and the distance to be traveled. The transformation of America's public sector to date is both limited and, perhaps more importantly, distorted. Some eminently sensible changes remain stubbornly stalled. Some questionable revisions to government's structure and operations have outpaced fundamental reforms.

In part this is just the elemental inertia that torments all would-be reformers and comforts all true conservatives. But the results of the far-flung transformation campaign—both its torpid pace and its peculiar pattern—become easier to understand in light of the segregation between the public and private worlds of work. As America's middle-class economy has unraveled, less-skilled workers have seen their private-sector prospects shrivel so that government, by comparison, has become an attractive employer. Workers with high levels of education and training, conversely, have seen private-sector rewards soar beyond what government offers. Thus government employment has become a safe harbor for less fortunate workers, and a backwater in the eyes of the most ambitious, best educated, and luckiest. This development has motivated a generally expanded but frequently distorted use of the option of contracting for government services. Outsourcing can be a sensible managerial approach, but not if chosen for the wrong reasons. The best candidates for contractual outsourcing satisfy the three straightforward criteria of specificity, ease of evaluation, and competition. These criteria allow the separation of "commodity" tasks—appropriate for contracting out because they involve discrete, measurable functions—from custom tasks—the complex, sophisticated activities that are less suitable for outsourcing. We take up these considerations shortly, after an overview of what has been happening to government work, and why.

Lumping and Splitting

One illuminating way to understand major shifts within the private economy over recent decades is to focus on the integration or disintegration of economic activity—the degree to which the chain of value creation is lumped together into a unified entity, or split up across separate, specialized units. At the extreme of "lumping," imagine an automobile factory where raw materials pour in at one end (from company-owned mines, on company-owned ships) and finished cars roll out the other, as designers, accountants, and managers direct the whole productive symphony from offices overlooking the shop floor. (Ford's River Rouge plant actually came close to this image of ultimate integration.) At the extreme of "splitting," consider the way many movies reach the screen today, through fleeting interactions among numerous writers, agents, producers, actors, distributors, and other free agents.

Scholars have long been fascinated by the forces that account for lumping and splitting in a single industry or the economy as a whole. A vast literature can be traced to a brief 1937 article by Ronald Coase, "The Nature of the Firm."[1] Coase puzzled over why formally structured, long-lasting firms should exist when economic theory (by the current state of the art) stressed the irrelevance or perversity of managed production and the virtues of production by independent economic actors guided by the invisible hand of price signals. When theory so clearly prescribed disintegrated production coordinated by prices, why did integrated production coordinated by managers seem to be working out reasonably well in the real world?

The answer, Coase suggested, had a lot to do with flaws in the flow of information. For the price system to work perfectly, information about what is available on the market, the characteristics of each product, and the alternative ways to obtain them needs to be universally available and consistently accurate. In the mid-twentieth century this standard was often glaringly unrealistic. The less complete and reliable market information becomes, the stronger the case for lumping economic activities under the direction of managers. Lumping has its costs—not just the overhead of management and its administrative apparatus but, more seriously, having to forfeit the cost-paring power of market competition for any functions brought into the corporate tent—but under circumstances that are far from rare these costs are less than those of relying on a treacherous external market.

Integration was the dominant theme when Coase first wrote because the profusion of economically relevant information outpaced the price system's capacity to capture it. But radical improvements in information processing over recent decades have triggered a shift towards disaggregated productive capacity. As information becomes more widely shared, easier to access, and simpler to process, the theoretical ideal of fully informed market actors is at least roughly approximated in reality. The more closely we approach this ideal, the more we can harvest the benefits of splitting—flexibility, rich menus of options, rapid innovation, and cost reduction through both specialization and competition.[2]

Lumping and Splitting Government's Work

Disaggregating the value chain—parceling out each separable function to whoever can perform it best—promises even more of a payoff to government than to business. It is no slur against government to say that productive efficiency is not and should not be its strong suit. The public sector's cardinal virtue—precious when present, crippling when absent—is legitimacy in citizens' eyes. Public organizations are answerable to a broad range of constituencies whose interests, on a wide spectrum of dimensions, must be taken into account. Private organizations, conversely, are answerable to a narrower set of masters, but in a far more focused way.

Once the ends are established and it's down to a question of means, therefore, private organizations should have a considerable edge in pure operational efficiency. Shifting some function from one private firm to another may generate gains from specialization, optimal scale, and the spur of competition. Shifting some function from government to a private firm can do this too, but it also transfers the task from an institutional setting in which productive efficiency is a secondary concern into one in which productive efficiency is the prime directive.

A great deal has been written about the generic make-versus-buy decision in the private sector and the closely related, though not quite identical, choice between direct and indirect production for government.[3] Multiple terms refer to indirect governmental production, including outsourcing, competitive supply, contracting out, and privatization. A full account of the criteria that determine whether or not a task is suitable for privatization would include many layers of rationale, exceptions, nuance, and caveats. But most of it can be summarized as three characteristics whose presence makes a task appropriate for delegation and whose absence renders privatization hazardous: specificity, ease of evaluation, and competition.

SPECIFICITY

You can only delegate what you can define. Splitting off a function requires specifying it in sufficient detail to solicit bids, select a provider, and structure a meaningful contract. So tasks that are predictable, stable, and separable from the rest of the value chain are good candidates for contracting out. It is hard to write a sturdy contract for the performance of tasks that are entangled with other functions and subject to continual revision (in timing, scale, or purpose) as circumstances change. For such tasks the appropriate contractual form—you pay me to hang around and follow your instructions as you figure out what needs doing—is what we call "employment." It is technically possible, of course, to rely on outsiders for ill-defined and changeable tasks, but it is usually not very smart.

EASE OF EVALUATION

To outsource a function you not only need to be able to say what you want (specificity), but you also need to be in a position to know what you've gotten—clearly enough and early enough to take corrective action if what's delivered isn't what was promised. Otherwise, there can be no assurance that government is equipped to perform, as it must, as the agent of the people in ensuring that public value is produced in exchange for public resources. The easier it is to monitor performance and assess the quality of the work, the more safely can a task be delegated. For many functions, fortunately, it is not too hard to distinguish between a good job and a bad job, and for such functions a well-crafted contract can enforce accountability. But other tasks resist clear evaluation. Outcomes may be inherently ambiguous or opaque. Consequences may play out over a very long period of time. Results may have multiple causes, making it impossible to infer good or bad efforts from a good or bad outcome. No matter how producers are organized, it is inherently tricky to elicit good performance if you can't measure it. But the problem is worse for delegated functions, since producers' behavior is veiled behind organizational boundaries.

COMPETITION

Private providers tend to outscore government on productive efficiency not because there is something magic about the private sector, but because competition eliminates, or at least narrows, the opportunities to survive without being efficient. Competitive markets weed out the laggards and keep the winners in a state of healthy anxiety. The whole point of privatization is to harness for the government the salutary effects of competition. Contracting out can transplant into public undertakings some of the intensive accountability that characterizes the private sector. Without competition much of its rationale collapses. When external providers are comfortable, not spurred on by rivals, privatization offers far fewer benefits and far greater hazards.

Commodity Tasks and Custom Tasks

Determining the degree to which these three criteria—specificity, ease of evaluation, and competition—apply is a matter of careful, case-by-case analysis. The privatization decision is contingent on the details of the mission, the capabilities and deficits of the public organization, the number and nature of available private suppliers, and other considerations. Yet in general these conditions will be met more fully for relatively straightforward functions—what might be called "commodity tasks." For more complex and sophisticated functions, or "custom tasks," the odds are generally higher that one, two, or all three of these conditions will fail to hold.

The transition of many functions from custom to commodity status has done a great deal to enable the surge of economic splitting in the private sector. It is business orthodoxy that a company should cleave to its core competency, maintaining tight control over those functions on which its fate pivots. This does not preclude the outsourcing of some sophisticated functions, but custom tasks that are commonly split off from the rest of the value chain (such as advertising, specialized aspects of design, or market analysis) tend to display a reasonable degree of specificity, ease of evaluation, and competition. The splitting trend in the private economy is far more pronounced at the commodity end. Beyond paring costs, a major part of the rationale for splitting off routine functions is to tighten managers' focus on those custom tasks that define a company's core. The less managers are distracted by routine chores, the more they can concentrate on those key functions that cannot be delegated. This goes for government, too.

In an alternate universe, where the public and private worlds of work had evolved in the same ways, government would be undergoing a transformation that is not quite identical but closely parallel to that of the private sector. Specialized outside organizations would handle most of the routine commodity work. The transformation would have occasioned some turmoil and sparked some resistance, of the same sort that we see marking the private sector's reconfiguration. Nobody likes to have change forced upon them, and even amid proliferating alternatives it is usually preferable to retain the status quo as an option. But if sector switching imposed only modest burdens on government workers—that is, had no gulf developed between the conditions of employment in the two sectors—the turmoil would have been manageable and the resistance milder.

Direct governmental employees would confine their attention to functions that are so intimately entwined with subtle and shifting public missions that they cannot be specified with much precision, or so entangled with other factors that they resist clear evaluation, or that are available on the market, if at all, only from monopoly suppliers. Even in this alternate universe there would still be many such tasks, and government employment would not be limited to a handful of procurement officers. But the public workforce would be appreciably smaller than it had been twenty or thirty years ago and heavily tilted toward the more skill-intensive and sophisticated kinds of work. In our own universe, the picture is very different.

The Pace of Public-Sector Outsourcing

As unions point with alarm at the evaporation of public jobs, trade associations representing private contractors celebrate the long boom in profitable opportunities to provide services to the public sector. Yet assertions of a surge in outsourcing—whether gleeful or grim—turn out to lack anything that approaches a convincing empirical base. The record is replete with case studies of both successful and unsuccessful privatization. But the cases may be typical of what is going on in this big and diverse country, or they may be odd exceptions. Without systematic data we simply don't know, and there are no official data series explicitly focused on direct versus indirect public-service delivery. There have been a few efforts to survey governments on their outsourcing habits, but these have been spotty, episodic, or marred by low response rates. Some ambitious and generally sensible studies hinge on idiosyncratic definitions and handcrafted data that are hard to test or replicate.[4] So the debate over privatization rests, to a remarkable extent, on simple assemblages of anecdotes.[5]

The closest approximation to an authoritative statistical series is the "National Income and Product Account" data assembled by the Commerce Department's Bureau of Economic Analysis. These data permit us to track the share of public spending that goes to compensate employees and the share that goes to engage outside suppliers. The two categories are not exactly comparable—the costs of external services include equipment and overhead, for example—but they are close enough to make trends meaningful. For government as a whole, the external share of service spending ran just over 23 percent in the 1950s, growing to a little over 33 percent, on average, between 2000 and 2005. So outsourcing *does* seem to be on the rise in the public sector. But there are several complicating factors to keep in mind.

First, the story differs sharply across segments of the public sector. Figure 2.1 shows the trends for the three big categories—federal defense-related spending, other federal spending, and by far the largest category, state and local government. State and local outsourcing starts low and grows steadily but modestly. Federal outsourcing leaps sharply between the 1950s and the 1960s, but changes little thereafter. The

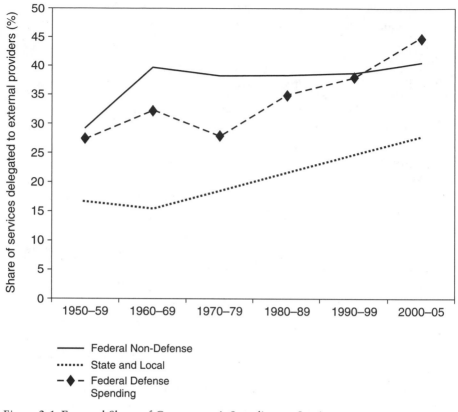

Figure 2.1 External Share of Government's Spending on Services.
Source: Bureau of Economic Analysis.

most dramatic action is with federal defense spending, where out-sourcing surges from the 1970s onward, and especially after the turn of the century. Such diversity across segments makes it hard to talk about a single trend.

Second, much of the apparent boost in outsourcing is an artifact of the soaring share of health-care spending within public-sector budgets. The Bureau of Economic Analysis implicitly treats Medicare and Medicaid as governmental operations, like maintaining a park or tracking a missile, which can be either performed by public workers or split off to private suppliers. But setting up a big public medical system (instead of having government pay for much of the private health services of the poor, the elderly, veterans, and other groups) has never been a serious option in the United States. The share of external services including

Medicare and Medicaid has grown not because we changed our minds about lumping and splitting medical services, but because the big health programs—always heavily private—account for so much more of the government's spending than they used to. An experimental reprocessing of the official data that pulls out Medicare and Medicaid suggests that growth in outsourcing has been only about one-fourth to one-third as great as the raw data suggest.[6]

Much of this modest bump, moreover, reflects the shift in America's center of gravity southward and westward, toward regions that have always been somewhat more inclined to choose private providers, rather than the shift of existing functions from public to private suppliers. It does happen, of course, that a task is wrenched away from public workers and handed to the private sector; the case studies are not based on hallucinations. It just does not happen all that often.

Whatever its scale, enthusiasts and skeptics alike should concur that privatization should go furthest and fastest in the areas where its advantages are greatest and its downsides smallest. Recall the three criteria that permit a function to be split off—specificity, ease of evaluation, and competition—and the distinction, derived from those criteria, between commodity tasks and custom tasks. These suggest a general taxonomy of governmental duties that are strong or weak candidates for delegation. Custom tasks, all else equal, should be done by government itself. Many commodity tasks should be outsourced. But this is not what we see. Pressures set in motion by the widening of the gaps between public and private work are warping the pattern of government's transformation.

The Retention of Commodity Tasks

Commodity jobs—tasks that are well defined, relatively easy to evaluate, and available from competitive private suppliers—remain plentiful in the public sector. Consider the twenty-five jobs most common in government, drawn from the Bureau of Labor Statistics' helpful Occupational Employment Survey and listed in Table 2.1. While job titles obscure a multitude of detail, it seems only slightly risky to suggest that many of these jobs, in principle, could be split off from the core public sector and delegated to private organizations. There are excellent reasons why this doesn't happen in some cases. It may be imprudent for the president to rely on even a top-of-the-line temp as his personal assistant, and it is probably advantageous to have duly vetted government

Table 2.1 Twenty-five most common jobs in government, 2005

Job title	Number	Median annual pay
Elementary teachers	1,315,650	$47,487
Teacher assistants	1,115,454	$20,090
Police and sheriff officers	609,960	$46,470
Correctional officers	394,320	$34,390
Mail carriers	347,180	$46,330
Office clerks	329,420	$26,730
Firefighters	273,540	$39,350
Business operations specialists	235,920	$59,520
Mail sorters and processors	208,600	$43,420
Secretaries	162,500	$31,900
Information and record clerks	151,530	$41,120
Executive secretaries	139,270	$35,780
Registered nurses	136,970	$56,470
Highway maintenance workers	134,600	$30,310
Maintenance and repair workers	125,270	$32,600
Office managers	114,680	$46,240
Managers, not otherwise specified	108,740	$77,770
Bookkeeping clerks	108,480	$31,370
Social workers	108,040	$38,130
Janitors	107,880	$23,730
Bus drivers	106,930	$35,170
Lawyers	105,180	$83,650
Recreation workers	102,710	$20,570
Accountants	102,110	$48,500
Court, municipal, and license clerks	99,060	$29,560

employees empty the National Security Council's wastebaskets. But it is doubtful that a persuasive argument against delegation, anchored on the three criteria outlined earlier, could be mounted for every job on the list. To advance the conversation, imagine that fourteen of government's top employment categories—those shaded in the table—turn out to contain enough commodity tasks that some large fraction of these jobs ought to be plausible candidates for outsourcing.

The frequency with which commodity tasks are retained in government is due in part to the circumscribed ardor for cost minimization inherent in public organizations, which (however much managers prefer low to high costs) lack the intense incentives to cost consciousness that characterize competitive private firms. But at least as important is the uniform awareness that splitting off such functions entails casting workers out into a far harsher world of private work. It is not in the least surprising that they resist. There are scores of struggles over service outsourcing every year in the federal, state, and municipal governments—some of them dramatic, high-profile confrontations, most of them small scale and obscure. Public workers doing commodity tasks demonstrably lose some of these struggles. But not many. To gain a better appreciation of public workers' determination to hold their ground, let us shift the focus from the multitude of commodity tasks marbled throughout government to a few particular functions.

The Postal Service

Even in the age of cheap electronic communications, the post remains a vital public function. The right of every individual and organization in America to send almost anything from anywhere to anyplace else, for a relative pittance, plays a major role in knitting together the country's economic and social fabric. This is surely true, but conceding that a task is extremely important does not make it ineligible for delegation. The question, again, is whether it can be specified, evaluated, and competitively obtained. The legal notion of "inherently governmental" tasks that has long served as the touchstone for federal decision rules on outsourcing (see Office of Management and Budget Circular A-76) is (aside from the extreme cases) too ambiguous to be very helpful.

The postal service has traditionally delegated mail delivery in many rural areas to independent contractors, and spends billions of dollars every year on air and land transportation contracts. Many—indeed, most of its processing and delivery functions are the kinds of commodity tasks that are routinely split off in the private sector. And while only the United States Postal Service can use official mailboxes, there are many private firms providing services closely equivalent to those of the post office. Retreating again to our alternate universe, where no gulf separates public from private work, it is not hard to imagine a highly disaggregated postal system in which a small number of public workers carry out a core set of custom tasks and orchestrate a network of private organizations charged with the commodity tasks that constitute the bulk of the work. Many other countries have sharply expanded the private sector's role in moving the mail (with Sweden, perhaps surprisingly, in the vanguard).[7] The technical feasibility of splitting up postal functions is manifest in the covert outsourcing achieved by offering "worksharing discounts" to mass mailers who process, sort, or transport their mail before it reaches the post office.[8] It would certainly be possible to bungle the shift to a disaggregated postal system, but there is nothing unsound in concept about a heavily delegated model for moving the mail.

No such shift has happened, and it is unlikely to happen soon. This is not for any want of pressure to change. Unlike most public organizations, the post office is supposed to be self-supporting, and costs have consequences. It is also atypical in facing serious competition. Private courier services such as Federal Express, DHL, and UPS skim away the more lucrative segments of the market, while the inexorable growth of electronic communications chips away at the mundane commercial mail—the torrent of bills sent to households each month and the torrent of checks sent back to businesses—that has kept the Postal Service solvent.

Despite the organization's precarious status, postal workers and their union leaders have steadfastly resisted calls for fundamental change in the structure, scale, or employment practices of the USPS. This opposition provokes charges of pigheadedness. Pay and benefits account for the bulk of postal costs;[9] postal personnel practices, from a business perspective, are relics from a vanished age; and the very survival of the enterprise is in question. How can labor refuse to consider fundamental change? Yet any different stance would have been surprising. The explicit goal of a turn-of-the-century presidential reform commission, for example, was to make the postal service more "businesslike."[10] The entire rationale of postal unionism is to prevent any such thing. The business world has become a barren realm for the kinds of people postal unions represent. The defining mission of the unions and their congressional allies is to defend a blue-collar redoubt where the old rules still apply. Critics who indict the recalcitrance of postal labor leaders as economically unrealistic and ultimately self-destructive, as the postal service enters what many see as a death spiral, are missing the point. From labor's perspective, a businesslike post office is not worth saving. The prophets of insolvency may be bluffing, after all, or Congress may step in to halt the slide. But if not, postal labor would prefer to go down fighting than to surrender its bastion without a struggle. Even those who do not share the postal unions' goals should be able to understand them, and to appreciate that they are unlikely to change.

Support Services in Schools

About 45 percent of all public jobs are related to education. This army of education workers includes many teachers, superintendents, principals, and other people dedicated directly to the core mission; Table 2.1 lists teachers as the most common public job, and teaching aides as the second most common. But the educational workforce also includes people doing support jobs that are important in enabling the actual teaching but distinct from it. In 2002 there were about 3.1 million state and local education employees doing noninstructional work—a corps of education support workers outnumbering the entire federal civilian workforce, including the postal service.[11]

A fraction of these noninstructional education workers certainly perform what I have termed custom tasks, as senior administrators, counselors, personnel managers and the like, but a great many are occupied with relatively straightforward commodity tasks. There were about half a million food-service workers in the education sector, another half-million cleaning and maintenance workers, and well over a million administrative support workers (clerks, secretaries, receptionists and so on). There were also over 300,000 transportation workers—mostly bus drivers, unsurprisingly—and about 200,000 construction and repair workers such as carpenters, painters, plumbers, and general handymen.[12]

In contrast to core teaching functions—where delegation implies both significant risk and considerable transactional complexity—educational support functions, in general, present a far simpler case. One can certainly conjure up calamities stemming from careless delegation—a catering company might serve nothing but junk food; a bus contractor might hire child molesters—but to observe that a policy option can be implemented stupidly should not settle the debate. Much of the work of these three million noninstructional workers in the education sector consists of the kinds of tasks that are routinely, and for the most part uneventfully, split off by private organizations. Retreating again to our alternate universe, there is no systematic technical reason why many or most of these support functions could not be delegated to private providers. Even in the fantasy world where public and private compensation is the same, this could yield cost savings from specialization, innovation, and economies of scale. The strongest argument for such an approach is not financial, however, but managerial. Principals have better things to worry about than the balky steam table in the cafeteria or the schedule for collating the parent handbooks. The best reason for handing off support functions is to free educators to focus on the schools' core mission. Indeed, an ideal model—while we are still in the realm of make-believe—might be an industry of educational logistics-management companies competing to handle nearly all of a school's functions except for direct instruction.

The pattern we actually see looks nothing like this. Support staff comprised a little over 30 percent of the workforce in public primary and secondary schools as of 2000—almost precisely the same share as in 1969.[13] A unit of the federal Department of Education maintains statistics on school operations that are wonderfully detailed but, unfortunately, not very current; the most recent available are from the 1999–2000 school year.[14] Spending to buy services from outsiders, for schools as a group, was about 11 percent as great as spending for employees' salaries and benefits. The data suggest some sharp departures from the decision rule—hold on to custom tasks, split off commodity tasks—outlined earlier. Outside providers' share of transportation, operations, and maintenance functions actually declined a bit in the second half of the 1990s. Food service (with contracts just 15 percent as large as payroll) was somewhat less likely to be delegated than "instructional staff services," a category that includes curriculum development, teacher training, and other functions closely tied to the core mission. The fastest growth in split-off school support tasks was in this instructional staff services category; the second-fastest growth was for student support functions such as guidance counselors, health services, and speech pathologists, mostly tasks that call for fairly advanced training. And outsourced teaching, while relatively rare, was growing faster than outsourced food services.

It seems highly improbable that these patterns indicate rational assessment of gains that outweigh the difficulties in specifying, assessing, and ensuring competition in the areas of curriculum development, teacher training, and instruction itself. Yet these curious patterns become easier to understand by reference to the different ways the public and private sectors treat the sorts of workers who carry out commodity tasks in the schools. Food-service workers in the education sector earn about 13 percent more than the same category of workers in the restaurant industry. The "accommodation" industry—covering hotels, motels, and the like—employs about the same number of cleaning and maintenance workers as the education sector, but schools pay these workers about 37 percent more. "Installation, maintenance, and repair" workers earn 24 percent more in education than in the accommodations industry. Clerical and support workers in school offices earn about 12 percent more than their counterparts in the "administrative and support services" industry.[15] Comparably detailed data on benefits are not available, but all the evidence suggests that disparities in job security and in health, retirement and other benefits are even greater than the pay difference between the two sectors.

Splitting off support functions would be very bad news for the workers doing commodity tasks in America's public schools. Their resistance is correspondingly ferocious. Attempts to outsource this kind of work, when it is currently carried out by public workers, tend to be thoroughly miserable political episodes—particularly when the support workers are sympathetic local residents with children in the same school system. Even in Houston during the 1990s—at that time America's undisputed mecca of freewheeling market approaches, in a state with notoriously weak public-employee unions—Superintendent Rod Paige, later the Secretary of Education in the Bush administration, was forced to backtrack on many of his plans to outsource school support services.[16]

The Delegation of Custom Tasks

The sorts of workers most battered by today's private sector find a kinder climate in government, creating a highly motivated constituency opposed to the delegation of government's commodity tasks. Workers with the skills required for high-end custom tasks, conversely, tend to find public employment dull and stingy relative to their private-sector options. This imposes a second, symmetrical twist in the public sector's transformation. Work that, without these distortions, would be done in-house—whether because it is too entangled with other functions to specify with precision, or hard to evaluate objectively, or sheltered from competitive pressure—is frequently delegated to private firms that are able to access talent pools largely barred to government. Sometimes this works out tolerably well; sometimes delegating custom tasks carries a heavy price.

An obscure agency called the Federal Procurement Data Center keeps detailed statistics on everything Washington buys from the private sector. For fiscal year 2002 the federal government was a party to some 8 million separate transactions summing to almost exactly a quarter-trillion dollars.[17] Many of these acquisitions reflect entirely logical make-versus-buy decisions. It is unremarkable and unobjectionable for the government to buy its aircraft ($15 billion), ships ($7 billion), guided missiles ($4 billion), computer equipment ($6 billion), and live animals (a mere $7 million) rather than setting up its own factories and farms. Even among services (as distinct from goods) there are categories rich with commodity tasks that are quite sensibly split off from direct public performance, such as construction ($10 billion), property maintenance and repair ($7 billion), or research and development for defense systems ($14 billion.) But there are also many custom tasks for which Washington spends heavily on outside services. The largest single category of federal procurement, at more than $25 billion, is "professional, administrative, and management support services."

The Lockheed Martin Corporation has long been a preeminent federal supplier, accounting on its own for over $20 billion in contracts in 2002. It is significant, if little noted, that this famous maker of airplanes, missiles, and cutting-edge defense systems has been furiously diversifying into high-end government services. Its $5 billion in research and development contracts, $1.4 billion in information-technology services, and nearly $5 billion in "other services"—for both defense and civilian agencies—together eclipsed Lockheed's $9 billion in hardware sales. By 2006 Lockheed was responsible for more federal money than either the Department of Justice or the Department of Energy.[18]

As the scarcity of internal talent forces government to outsource much of its thinking, markets expand for policy analysis, strategic planning, and other functions that a naïve observer might expect agencies to treat as core competencies. Leaving aside scores of smaller operations, three big consulting firms alone (Booz Allen & Hamilton, BearingPoint, and Accenture) billed the federal government for close to $2 billion in 2002. Some such arrangements seem decidedly questionable. One federal contractor, for example, was engaged to investigate charges of malfeasance against several other federal contractors[19] with no indication that this private firm was equipped or motivated to carry out, accountably and dispassionately, this delicate duty.

A thriving industry provides analysis and strategic advice to state and local government as well. For instance, in the wake of the 1996 legislation reshaping the welfare system, the private sector—for-profit as well as nonprofit—has become the mainstay of social services in many cities and states, in part because public-agency staff proved ill equipped for the shift from an income-maintenance to a work-based mission.[20]

As with the retention of commodity tasks, a bit of detail on a few particular areas in which custom tasks have been outsourced may provide more clarity on the delegation of tasks that fall short on specificity, clear evaluation, competition, or all three criteria.

Information Technology Services

"Automatic data processing and telecommunications services" accounted for about $16.7 billion in federal contracts in 2002—an IT service bill nearly three times as large as the cost of IT equipment.[21] There are no comparably complete data for procurement by the cities and states, but information technology is a large, growing, and strategically significant category of delegated services at every level of government.[22] It can be wholly rational to outsource some IT services, in both public and private organizations.[23] Certain tasks are so technically exacting and so infrequently performed that delegating them to specialized outsiders makes more sense than developing internal capacity. Other IT functions are so routine and so widely available that they meet every definition of a commodity task. Most well-run organizations maintain a network of IT contractors. But they also take care to retain a strong nucleus of their own highly qualified employees to orchestrate and monitor that network.[24]

The danger lies in crossing the line from commodity to custom tasks, and outsourcing IT functions that are integral to strategic management, resistant to evaluation, or vulnerable to monopoly power. In the private sector this would represent a simple management blunder—which does not mean it never occurs. In the public sector, however, the tilt of the economic terrain places government in continual danger of sliding across that line. Many IT services require the sort of high-end labor that is systematically scarce in government. If a public organization wants its IT services to be within shouting distance of the state of the art, it often has no choice but to outsource aggressively.

The trend in public-sector IT procurement is away from the healthy pattern of engaging specialized contractors for separate tasks, and toward comprehensive contracts with large "integrated system providers."[25] Such arrangements can be far from ideal in terms of all three criteria for delegation. It is virtually impossible to specify in advance every requirement for an IT system that weaves throughout an agency's operations. As new requirements emerge and old ones evolve in the course of a contract, the customer agency must either live with the original terms of the deal or renegotiate, at a decided disadvantage, with its contractor. Clear-cut contractor evaluation tends to be elusive, in part because the customer and the contractor are jointly involved in the system's performance, and in part because it is often the case that nobody in the customer agency really understands what the contractor is doing.

Competition for integrated IT service contracts is often vigorous at the start; there are many firms in the government information systems market and the rivalry is fierce. But once a contractor is selected and becomes indispensable to an agency's work, market discipline ebbs. Disentangling an organization from one integrated system provider and bringing in another is so traumatically disruptive a prospect that, short of truly egregious performance or blatant exploitation, it rarely happens.

I do not mean to fault public managers who cross the line from commodity to custom tasks when delegating IT services. Given the constraints within which they operate, this can be the least bad option at their command. The point, rather, is to highlight both the causes and the costs of those constraints. Information technology is an arena where the gap between the public and private working worlds is especially wide. Many agencies cope remarkably well with a degree of IT delegation that, in principle, is strategically unsound. But they would do even better—and produce a more efficient, accountable, and managerially coherent public sector—if the great divide in the labor market had not denied them the option of an internal corps of top information technology talent.[26]

Space Shuttle Operations

The space shuttle was meant to transform space travel into a commodity. The orbiter itself and its solid-rocket boosters—the costly parts of the system—could be reused for mission after mission. Only the massive but relatively inexpensive external fuel tank was jettisoned to burn up in the atmosphere. The National Aeronautics and Space Administration (NASA) expected orbital launches to become cheap and mundane once the shuttle system matured.

Predictions of routine space operations proved premature at best, however, and by the mid-1990s the shuttle program was in deep trouble. Cost overruns were straining the patience of Congress, and operational demands were draining resources and management attention from other NASA missions.[27] The Clinton administration seized upon a bold strategy of delegation to lower the cost, and the management burden, of running the shuttle. NASA's tangled skein of separate shuttle contracts, along with most NASA personnel involved with the shuttle, were folded into a single "Space Flight Operations Contract." A company called United Space Alliance won what turned out to be an eight-year, nearly $10 billion contract to handle virtually every aspect of a shuttle mission, from astronaut training and system assembly to the management of launch and reentry. NASA technicians and other workers with direct shuttle duties switched their badges to USA, a small remnant staying behind to oversee the contract.

The splitting off of shuttle flight operations occasioned remarkably little controversy for so radical a change. General acquiescence was partly due to worries that the status quo was unsustainable. It is surely significant, though, that most of the NASA workers affected were at the upper end of the skills spectrum—many of them above the point where public pay exceeds private, and some bumping up against binding constraints on governmental compensation. No precise reckoning is possible, since USA's compensation data are proprietary. But it is revealing to compare public-sector salaries for these kinds of jobs to salaries prevailing outside government. Private-sector pay for avionics technicians ranges from a little less than government to markedly more, depending on the specific industry, but even at the lower end the difference is small enough to be outweighed by profit sharing and other inducements USA can offer. Public and private salaries are comparable for aerospace engineers, and senior managers (eligible for stock options and bonuses) likely fare considerably better than they had on the public payroll.[28] In contrast to the outsourcing of most commodity tasks, the delegation of shuttle operations was far from devastating for government workers.

The delegation strategy seemed to pay off in its early years. Shuttle operations claimed less of senior managers' attention, while costs declined somewhat as USA deployed its advantages in streamlining procedures and driving hard bargains with subcontractors. Most people are aware, of course, that the subsequent history of the space shuttle has not been a happy one. It is impossible to know whether this aggressive delegation contributed to the 2003 loss of *Columbia* and its crew. One shuttle has been lost under both direct and delegated arrangements, after all, and NASA's contract with USA left key decisions, at least formally, in government's hands.

It is instructive, nonetheless, to consider how far the shuttle departs from the criteria defining a task's suitability for delegation. Despite heroic efforts to codify every element of shuttle operations, the contract was not and could not be fully specified. The shuttle system was simply too complex and volatile. Periodic upgrades, altered missions, process improvements, and continuous technological tinkering meant that literally every launch was different. Nor, even with a sophisticated set of incentives built into the contract, could NASA unambiguously evaluate

USA's performance. The operations model continued to evolve following the handoff, and the remnant of NASA personnel involved was too small—and, to an increasing degree, too unfamiliar with the details of the enterprise—to exercise full oversight. NASA eventually shifted its aspirations from oversight to what it called "insight"—a less intensive form of monitoring that left much to the contractor's discretion. Some shuttle managers became intensely concerned that the growing knowledge gap between NASA and USA imperiled flight safety and called for reuniting decision-making authority with flight operations, either by unwinding the delegation or by making shuttle operations more conventionally private.

The sharpest shortfall from the criteria for delegation, however, concerned competition. Very few private firms had the scale, experience, and technical know-how to be plausible contenders for the shuttle operations contract. The short list was limited to two companies: Lockheed Martin and Boeing. United Space Alliance was a joint venture formed by Lockheed and Boeing to bid for the contract, and USA's corporate bylaws specified that neither of its parents would compete against it.[29]

Multiple causes typically drive decisions to delegate functions that might be better handled internally. One factor, seemingly secondary but often influential, is public managers' urge to transform *something,* as enlisting private competence has been enthroned as managerial orthodoxy. Commodity tasks, where the substantive case for delegation is stronger, tend to be too hard politically, so reformers turn by default to custom tasks. Bids to make custom functions more businesslike, or to turn them over entirely to business, often inspire little or no "defense" from high-end public employees. For example, White House pressure for some kind of action led the Office of Personnel Management to outsource security screening for new federal workers in the second Clinton administration. Preemployment vetting is at best a borderline candidate for delegation. But worker resistance was limited and, as it happened, many of the former federal employees did a great deal better under private management.

Private firms may find it less rewarding to deliver true commodity services to the government than to perform custom tasks that involve more discretion. Tightly specified contracts for commodity tasks leave little wiggle room. Close evaluation means constant pressure to perform as promised. Even worse, from the firms' perspective, ongoing competition puts a ceiling on potential profits. From the perspective of the private company, custom tasks that are imperfectly specified, hard to monitor, or secure against competition tend to offer more attractive rewards in terms of revenues and discretion for the individual employee.

Distortion of Government Work: Why the Warping Matters

The divide in the working world imposes distortions at both ends of the labor market. It limits government's access to the human assets required for custom tasks. And it hobbles government's flexibility to alter commodity tasks. Public missions that demand highly qualified workers are frequently performed less adroitly than they ought to be (if carried out internally despite skills shortfalls) or less accountably than they ought to be (if delegated despite the downsides). Simpler public missions that require less specialized workers are performed less flexibly and more expensively than they ought to be. This happens both because the outsourcing option is often barred and because rules, institutions, and cultures by which public workers safeguard their status tend, alas, to straitjacket management and undermine efficiency. Both aspects of the segregation of government work—its attraction for less-skilled workers, its repulsion of the most fortunate—make government fall short of the performance it could attain had the great divide in the working world never happened.

The same syndrome also contributes to a twisted transformation of American business. As supplying firms shift their strategies to shore up government's deficits of high-end labor, their business models become dependent on the public sector's enduring disabilities. Just 5 percent of Lockheed-Martin's $32 billion in 2003 sales was to private-sector customers.[30] Companies such as Corrections Corporation of America (which runs prisons for state and federal customers), Maximus and America Works (welfare services), Electronic Data Systems (integrated IT services) and many more earn a substantial share of their revenue doing things for government that, by a plausible or even compelling substantive case, government ought to be able to do for itself. One need not credit every charge of cronyism or corruption to perceive the moral hazards inherent in such arrangements.

No less lamentable is the warping of America's labor movement. Labor is hunkering down in its public-sector stronghold as private-sector unionism continues to shrivel. At the tactical level, this focus on government employment is entirely understandable: public workers are easy to organize, intensely motivated to embrace labor's agenda, culturally congenial, and politically reliable. But on the strategic level, it threatens disaster for American unionism. The conscious and conspicuous defense of employment conditions that are superior to what the market offers most taxpayers for the delivery of tax-funded services promises to breed hostility both to government and to the labor movement.

One might object that my anxious overview of public-sector transformation efforts has focused too narrowly on reform ideas that force government to collide with the separate world of private work. The reformers' repertoire includes other options, such as performance measurement, classic reorganization, and electronic government initiatives, which can proceed in substantial isolation from the private economy. It is certainly true that the "lumping versus splitting" framework fails to exhaust all of the options, and many reformers are doing valuable things within the constraints I have sought to describe. But the deepening segregation of government work makes the menu of realistic options a meager one. It is possible to transform government without exposing less-skilled employees to the private world of work they rightly fear, and without expanding government's share of top talent. It is also possible to write a sonnet without using the letters "E" or "T". But the effort is far more arduous than it would be without the constraints, and the outcome, by long odds, will be less satisfying.

CHAPTER THREE

The Federal Framework for Competing Commercial Work between the Public and Private Sectors

MATHEW BLUM

Introduction

In 2001, the President's Management Agenda (PMA) called upon agency managers to make competitive sourcing (that is, public-private competition) a key management tool for creating a more efficient and effective government.[1] Competitive sourcing involves the use of competition to determine the best and most cost-effective public or private sector provider of commercial activities that agencies need to support their mission.[2]

Encouraging the use of public-private competition to bring cost control to the daily tasks that support government operations is not a new idea. However, the attention paid to competitive sourcing as a result of the PMA distinguishes this administration's efforts from most in the past.[3]

The administration's focus on competitive sourcing derives from a number of historical reports evaluating past experiences with public-private competition, mainly by the Department of Defense (DOD), as well as some states and municipalities. These reports conclude that the reasoned and responsible use of competition can bring cost control and better performance to the daily commercial tasks that support government operations, including savings of between 10 and 40 percent, irrespective of whether the competition is won by a private sector contractor or by the government.[4]

Competitive sourcing is often confused with the concepts of "outsourcing" and "privatization."[5] Both outsourcing and privatization presume that the taxpayer is always better served through private sector performance and, for this reason, seek to have work directed to private contractors without considering the cost or other benefits of continued performance by a federal agency. In the case of outsourcing, which is also referred to as "contracting out," the government continues to maintain responsibility for providing the service, but the work is always performed by the private sector under contracts administered by the agency. In the case of privatization, ownership of the agency's equipment and facilities is transferred to the private sector along with the workforce and management responsibility for the function. In essence, privatization results in an agency selling a business line.[6]

In contrast to outsourcing and privatization, the principles of competitive sourcing make *no presumption* as to which sector is the better provider of a commercial service.[7] Instead, the competitive sourcing model assumes that *both* the public and private sectors offer important efficiencies and accepts that many commercial activities will likely be accomplished for agencies by a blended workforce of federal employees and private sector contractors. Under competitive sourcing, an agency remains responsible for the provision of the service and associated management decisions. Public-private competition is used as a catalyst for better results, giving in-house sources the opportunity to restructure their operations into a most efficient organization and the private sector the chance to demonstrate how it can improve performance and lower costs. The competition process is intended to produce information that a federal manager can use to identify the more efficient sector—including the cost of public sector performance versus private sector performance and the manner in which work will be performed. Decisions on which sector will perform the work are expected to vary, even for similar activities, since agencies have different missions, and different operational strengths and weaknesses.

Statutes and executive branch policies require agencies to perform a series of analyses and follow certain procedural requirements when considering and undertaking a public-private competition. This chapter describes the framework governing competitive sourcing under the PMA. The chapter first discusses the various analyses that agencies are required to undertake to determine if an activity should be considered for public-private competition and the process for comparing government performance to private sector performance, if competition is pursued. The chapter then looks at the results of public-private competitions conducted under the PMA over the past four years and the potential effect of competitive sourcing on the workforce and its continued ability to manage agency programs.[8] Finally, the chapter considers the future of competitive sourcing and why its general principles are likely to remain relevant even if the focus or nature of its application changes.[9]

The Decision-Making Framework for Selecting Activities for Public-Private Competition

Before conducting a public-private competition, agencies are required to perform a series of analyses. These analyses are designed to ensure both that the activities selected for competition are potentially suitable for performance by the private sector and that a private-sector contractor may help to achieve cost savings and performance improvements.

The actions agencies must take prior to engaging in public-private competition are addressed in Office of Management and Budget (OMB) Circular A-76,[10] the Federal Activities Inventory Reform (FAIR) Act of 1998,[11] and a variety of supplemental OMB guidance documents issued in connection with the PMA.[12] The decision-making framework established by these documents consists of the following four steps:

Step 1: Create inventories that identify workforce activities, distinguish commercial activities from inherently governmental activities, and exclude inherently governmental activities from consideration for competition;

Step 2: Differentiate commercial activities that may be suitable for competition from those that should continue to be performed by federal employees;

Step 3: Develop plans for public-private competition that are tailored around the agency's mission and workforce mix; and

Step 4: Perform preliminary planning to ensure the agency is fully prepared to proceed with a competition.

Each of these steps is described below.[13]

Step One: Distinguishing Inherently Governmental Activities from Commercial Activities

The preparation of workforce inventories is the first step agencies undertake to determine where competition may be applied. Agencies are required to annually prepare two inventories of the activities performed by their employees: one inventory must identify commercial activities, the other must identify inherently governmental activities.[14] Only the activities on the commercial inventory may be considered for competition and potential performance by the private sector.

The FAIR Act defines an inherently governmental function as one that "is so intimately related to the public interest as to require performance by Federal Government employees." The term includes activities that require "either the exercise of discretion in applying Federal Government authority or the making of value judgments in making decisions for the Federal Government."[15] If the activity falls within this definition, it may not be performed by the private sector.

In 2006, agencies reported a civilian workforce of approximately 1.8 million full-time equivalent employees (FTEs). Agencies categorized approximately 720,000 (41 percent) of these FTEs as inherently governmental.[16] Examples of functions identified as inherently governmental on agency inventories included those that involve (1) the determination of agency policy (such as setting regulations) or priorities, (2) the award or termination of contracts, (3) the direction and control of federal employees (including hiring decisions), and (4) the direct conduct of criminal investigations or prosecutions.[17]

Determining whether a particular function is an inherently governmental function depends upon an analysis of the totality of the circumstances. The FAIR Act makes clear that not every activity involving the exercise of discretion is inherently governmental. It states that inherently governmental activities do not normally include activities that involve "gathering information for or providing advice, opinions, recommendations, or ideas to Federal Government officials." Similarly, the statute makes clear that inherently governmental functions do not encompass all activities involving the "interpretation and execution of the laws of the United States" but instead only those that, for example, have the effect of "[binding] the United States to take or not to take some action by contract, policy, regulation, authorization, order or otherwise," or "[exerting] ultimate control over the acquisition, use, or disposition of property"[18]—in other words, decisions that involve the exercise of discretion of a substantial nature.

OMB Circular A-76 further explains:

> While inherently governmental functions require the exercise of substantial discretion, not every exercise of discretion is evidence that an activity is inherently governmental. Rather, the use of discretion shall be deemed inherently governmental if it commits the government to a course of action where two or more alternative courses of action exist and decision

making is not already limited or guided by existing policies, procedures, directions, orders, and other guidance that (1) identify specified ranges of acceptable decisions or conduct and (2) subject the discretionary authority to final approval or regular oversight by agency officials.[19]

For example, the fact that an investigator must review confidential business records or exercise judgment does not mean the work is necessarily inherently governmental. But an investigator's responsibilities would be inherently governmental if the investigator exercises substantial discretion in applying the government's authority or in making decisions for the government (for example, whether to initiate enforcement proceedings).

The Federal Acquisition Regulation (FAR) provides an illustrative list of activities that are generally not considered to be inherently governmental functions, although they may approach being in that category "because of the nature of the function, the manner in which the contractor performs the contract, or the manner in which the Government administers contractor performance."[20] Examples of contractor services in this category include assistance (for example, analysis) that is used by federal employees to (1) plan activities, (2) develop statements of work, (3) evaluate contractor proposals, (4) develop regulations, or (5) interpret statutes and regulations.[21]

The Circular requires the agency's Competitive Sourcing Official (CSO) to justify, in writing, any designation of government personnel performing inherently governmental activities. (The CSO is an assistant secretary or equivalent-level official with responsibility for implementing the Circular.) The justification must be made available to the public on request.[22]

Pursuant to §2 of the FAIR Act, OMB reviews agency inventories prior to their publication. After review and consultation, OMB publishes a notice announcing the availability of the inventory. The agency provides its list to Congress and makes it available to the public.

Final determinations regarding the designation of an activity on an inventory as inherently governmental or commercial are made by the agency—not by OMB. An interested party[23] who disagrees with the agency's initial judgment may challenge an omission of a particular activity from, or an inclusion of a particular activity on, an agency's inventory. Under the FAIR Act, initial challenges must be made within thirty days after OMB publishes its notice of availability. The agency must decide the challenge within twenty-eight days after receipt of the challenge. An interested party may appeal an adverse decision to a higher -level agency official within ten days after receiving notification of the decision. The agency has an additional ten days to resolve the challenge.[24]

Step Two: Identifying Commercial Activities That May Be Suitable for Competition

After an agency has identified the inherently governmental activities performed by its employees and has excluded them from potential competition, the Circular requires the agency to subdivide the remaining activities—that is, the commercial activities—into two main groups: those suitable for competition with the private sector and those that are not.[25]

Agencies have considerable latitude in deciding if a commercial activity may be suitable for public-private competition.[26] Agencies take a number of factors into consideration in deciding whether an activity should be considered for private sector performance. For example, an agency could exclude an activity from consideration for competition in order to preserve a "core capability." OMB guidance provides that an activity may be considered core to an agency's operation to the extent that loss of in-house performance of the function would result in substantial risk to the agency's ability to accomplish its unique mission.[27] Other reasons agencies cite for excluding commercial activities from consideration for competition include the need for confidentiality in support of senior-level decision making and the need to permit rotation of personnel for career growth or to maintain maximum productivity.[28]

Agencies make the final determination as to whether an activity is identified on the inventory as suitable for competition, just as they make the final determination as to whether an activity is inherently governmental.[29] They have reached different results regarding the extent to which activities are potentially suitable for competition. In 2006, the majority of agencies identified somewhere between 5 and 45 percent of their total workforce inventory as available for competition. Two agencies (the Department of Education and the Department of Housing and Urban Development) reported more than 50 percent as available for competition. Three agencies (OMB, the Social Security Administration, and the Smithsonian) identified less than 5 percent as available for competition.[30] These differences are a reflection, in part, of the divergence in agency missions. In all, of the approximately 1 million FTEs identified as commercial in 2006 inventories, around 390,000 (37 percent) were identified as potentially suitable for competition.

Step Three: Developing Competition Plans

OMB requires agencies to develop plans that lay out a reasoned approach and timeline for considering and conducting competitions of the activities that have been identified in their inventories as suitable for potential performance by the private sector.[31] OMB's guidance calls for agencies to tailor plans around their individual priorities. There is no predetermined timeframe for the development of plans, which are a major consideration in how agencies are evaluated in scorecards issued in connection with the PMA. As explained in OMB's September 2003 report, "Timeframes will be based on an agency's analysis of its mission and workforce mix and other factors."[32] Other factors may include the complexity and diversity of the competitions planned, the agency's demonstrated ability to conduct competitive sourcing reviews and competitions, and other extenuating circumstances.[33] Significant management reforms, such as agency reorganizations, may also affect the suitability and timing of competition.

Most agencies build time into their plans to perform additional analysis, such as feasibility studies or business cases, to further validate the potential benefits of competition. The additional analyses are generally used to prioritize which activities are the best near-term candidates for competition and to determine how activities are best grouped for competition.

A number of factors are taken into account to validate an agency's initial assessment of an activity as suitable for competition.[34] These factors include

- private sector capability and availability of the function in the marketplace (for example, does market research indicate that there is interest in performing the function? Has the function been considered as a business unit, grouped with the same or similar activities at other locations?);

- efficiency of current operations (for example, can operations be improved through the types of changes facilitated by competition, such as process reengineering, workforce realignment, better leveraging of technology, consolidation of operations, clearer performance standards?);

- customer satisfaction with current operations (for example, is there a history of poor performance or budget increases?);

• long-term demand for the function (for example, is this a recurring need that will exist in the future? Will this need change based on pending realignments, reorganizations, consolidations, or restructurings?);[35] and

• a variety of human capital considerations (for example, does the activity face a high rate of attrition, retirements, recruitment/retention difficulties, or skill imbalances?).[36]

Agencies have developed a number of approaches for conducting these analyses. For example, at the Internal Revenue Service (IRS), employees who are subject matter experts and high-level managers develop business case analyses to evaluate if (1) competition can achieve sizable potential return on investment and significantly improved performance, (2) risks are manageable, and (3) results are likely to align with IRS's strategic business objectives.[37] Similarly, the National Institutes of Health (NIH) developed a software program to aid its competitive sourcing decision makers in considering the effectiveness of current operations, human capital impact, and demand for the function.[38] NIH used this software to select real property and grants support functions as suitable candidate for competition. The Department of Energy (DOE) conducts feasibility studies to determine whether a function may be competed as a business unit. Feasibility assessments are reviewed by a high-level executive steering committee, chaired by the deputy secretary, to ensure that the interests of affected agency stakeholders are taken into account.[39]

Step Four: Conducting Preliminary Planning

Once an agency decides to compete an activity, or multiple activities, the Circular identifies a number of steps to ensure the agency is fully prepared when it formally announces the competition. Preparatory actions include

• determining the incumbent provider's baseline costs (which will be used to assess the potential savings that could be achieved through the implementation of a most efficient organization (MEO) or use of a private sector contractor);[40]

• identifying competitions officials—for example, the "agency tender official" (ATO) who will develop, certify, and represent the agency tender; the contracting officer; the human resource advisor; and the source selection authority;[41] and

• ensuring access to available resources (for example, skilled manpower and funding).[42]

The Circular imposes no timeframes on preliminary planning leading up to the announcement of a competition. OMB explains that this flexibility helps to "ensure competitions are adequately and properly planned."[43]

Procedures for Conducting Public-Private Competitions

The Main Elements of a Public-Private Competition

After an agency has completed the steps described above and has made the decision to consider the conversion of work from public to private sector performance, the agency would proceed to announce and conduct a public-private competition. Circular A-76 establishes the procedures for conducting public-private competitions.[44]

The Circular provides for two types of competition: *standard competitions,* which may be used for any activity, and *streamlined competitions,* which is available for small activities involving up to 65 FTEs. Standard competitions are used for the majority of activities competed.[45] The main elements of a standard competition are as follows:

1. *Public announcement.* The competition begins with a formal announcement, both in FedBizOpps.gov (the officially designated Web site for publicizing federal business opportunities) and at the local level. The announcement identifies, among other things, the activity being competed, and the name of the competition officials—for example, the CSO, who has overall responsibility for competitive sourcing in the agency; the agency contracting officer, who will award the contract or performance agreement; and the ATO, who is responsible for the agency tender. The announcement must also identify the projected end date of the competition, which generally is to be no more than one year after public announcement.[46]

2. *Issuance of solicitation.* The agency develops and issues a solicitation inviting *both* interested private and public sector sources to submit offers. As a general matter, public-private competitions involve full and open competition, where all responsible sources are permitted to compete.[47] The solicitation must include a performance work statement describing the government's needs and desired outcomes, the factors and process to be used to evaluate sources (for example, sealed bid, negotiation of offers), the closing date for offers, the performance period, and a quality assurance surveillance plan describing how the selected source's performance will be measured.[48]

3. Development of offers and tenders. The incumbent federal provider and other interested public and private sector sources must develop offers. The incumbent federal provider's offer, referred to as a tender, must include a staffing plan that reflects the agency's "most efficient organization" (MEO) for performing the work with federal employees. This process effectively empowers federal employees to identify new and more cost-effective business practices. MEO plans typically involve reorganizations, and often propose better leveraging of technologies. MEO plans may also involve consolidation of facilities and restructuring of contracts that support the federal providers.[49] The Circular recognizes that federal employees, unlike contractors, do not generally have experience competing for work. For this reason, the Circular requires agencies to ensure that their in-house providers have access to available resources (for example, skilled manpower, funding) necessary to develop competitive agency tenders.[50] In most cases, the incumbent federal provider will contract with a private sector consultant to assist in the development of its tender. Public-private competitions have been won overwhelmingly by federal employees. OMB cites federal employee success as evidence that agencies are giving their employees meaningful opportunities to demonstrate their value to the taxpayer.[51]

4. Evaluation and award (source selection). The contracting officer must evaluate timely received offers and tenders against the factors set forth in the solicitation. As part of the evaluation process, the contracting officer must perform price analysis of all public and private proposals to ensure that prices are fair and reasonable.[52] The Circular requires agency tenders to identify the full cost of performance by the government.[53] An agency tender must identify personnel costs (calculated based on the amount of manpower that will be dedicated to perform the function), material and supply costs, overhead, and other costs.

Since different agencies account for costs in different ways and agency accounting systems generally do not track the full cost of performance, the Circular prescribes standard cost factors to estimate costs of government performance. These cost factors are designed to ensure that proposed costs reasonably reflect the actual cost of performing commercial activities with government personnel and are calculated in a standard and consistent manner.[54] For example, agencies are required to calculate fringe benefits (insurance and health benefits, retirement benefits, Medicare benefits, and miscellaneous fringe benefits) as a set percentage of personnel costs.[55] A similar approach is taken for the calculation of overhead costs.[56]

In addition, the Circular requires certain adjustments to the private-sector bids. For instance, the proposed private-sector prices are adjusted upward to reflect "one time conversion costs"—that is, costs that will be incurred because of the conversion from the public sector to the private sector, such as the cost of relocating or separating federal employees displaced as a result of a decision to contract out.[57] Similarly, the proposed cost of private sector performance is adjusted downward to reflect the tax revenue that is gained by contracting out the work.[58]

The results of the analysis must be provided on a standard form prescribed by the Circular.[59] The agency tender is certified by the ATO and costs of the private sector are certified by the contracting officer. The selection official will then select a provider and certify the decision. As a general matter, the work will continue to be performed by federal employees, under the reorganized MEO, unless the difference between the two adjusted costs exceeds a minimal conversion differential. That differential is 10 percent of the government's personnel costs or $10 million, whichever is less.[60] An agency must formally announce its performance decision (that is, award) locally and on FedBizOpps.com.[61]

5. *Challenges.* The Circular authorizes directly interested parties to file administrative challenges (known as contests) with the agency over actions taken in connection with standard competitions.[62] Directly interested parties include (1) the ATO, (2) a single individual who is a directly affected employee and is appointed by a majority of directly affected employees as their agent, (3) a private sector offeror, or (4) the official who certifies the public reimbursable tender.[63] The GAO is also statutorily authorized to hear bid protests arising from public-private competitions, including protests from "the official responsible for submitting the Federal agency tender"—that is, the ATO.[64] The ATO must file a protest if requested by a majority of the employees who are engaged in the performance of the activity subject to competition, unless the ATO determines that there is no reasonable basis for the protest. If the ATO makes such a determination, the official must notify Congress.[65]

6. *Postcompetition accountability.* The agency is required to hold the selected provider—public or private—accountable for achieving results.[66] If award is made to the private sector, a contract is issued. If

award is made to the incumbent federal provider (or another federal re-imbursable source), a performance agreement, known as a letter of obligation, is established between the MEO and the agency. OMB guidance describes the main elements of an accountability structure as follows:

- "If the . . . agency selects a private sector contractor, [it] must ad-minister the contract in accordance with the FAR. In particular, the [agency] must: (i) have a quality assurance surveillance plan (QASP) and a team in place to implement the plan and (ii) eval-uate the contractor's performance on an ongoing basis for con-sideration in future competitions for federal work."[67]

- If the agency selects its incumbent provider (or a federal provider from another agency), the agency and federal service provider will enter into a letter of obligation, identifying the workload, performance levels, the method of quality surveillance, and the cost for performance. The agency must have a QASP and a team in place to implement the QASP. The agency must also be pre-pared to evaluate the provider's performance on an ongoing basis for consideration in future competitions.[68]

- Contracts and agreements must include performance metrics so that performance can be periodically evaluated and adjustments made where necessary, including consideration of a new provider over the longer term if service is not satisfactory.

- Agencies must incorporate appropriate performance periods into their agreements with federal service providers and contracts with the private sector, considering the nature and risk associated with the service to be provided.[69]

Recent Changes to the Competitive Sourcing Process

In April 2002, the Commercial Activities Panel, chaired by the Govern-ment Accountability Office (then the General Accounting Office), is-sued a comprehensive report reviewing the policies and procedures gov-erning the use of competitive sourcing.[70] The panel found that public-private competitions can produce significant cost savings, re-gardless of whether a public or private entity is selected, and improve the quality of service delivery.[71] At the same time, the panel identified a number of shortcomings limiting the use and effectiveness of this tool. Among other things, it found that

- agencies lacked sufficient flexibility to factor quality into the performance decision;

- the competition process was complicated and not well understood (half of the bid protests taken to the GAO on public-private were sustained versus 21 percent of GAO protests overall);

- the process was time-consuming (the average competition took over two years);

- conflicts of interest were not being adequately addressed, resulting in instances where individuals with a stake in the outcome participated in the evaluation process; and

- accountability for results was limited.[72]

The GAO did not call for changes to the costing principles used to calculate the cost of in-house performance. It noted that the principles "reflect a reasoned, if only partially successful, effort to calculate (in the context of inadequate systems) the direct and indirect costs of performing the work in house."[73]

In May 2003, OMB substantially revised Circular A-76 to "improve the management of commercial activities."[74] To clarify the intent of competitive sourcing, OMB eliminated a long-standing policy principle that discouraged the government from competing with the private sector. OMB explained that the change was not meant to diminish the role played by the private sector. Rather, it was designed to reinforce the "Circular's main function of providing policies and procedures to determine the best service provider—irrespective of the sector the provider represents."[75] Along with this policy clarification, OMB eliminated authority provided in prior versions of the Circular for agencies to directly convert work to the private sector.[76]

These changes clearly distinguish competitive sourcing policies from outsourcing, which presumes private sector performance is always superior and seeks to convert work to private sector performance without considering the benefits of continued public sector performance. Likewise, the change distinguishes current OMB policies on government performance of commercial activities to those proffered by the executive branch for many years. The original policy addressing government performance of commercial activities, issued in January 1955 by the Bureau of the Budget (which later became OMB), stated that "the Federal Government will not start or carry on any commercial activity to provide a service or product for its own use if such product or service can be procured from private enterprise through ordinary business channels."[77] The value of public-private competition, as opposed to simply converting commercial work to private sector performance over time, emerged in earnest when OMB issued a detailed handbook for comparing the cost of government operations with private sector costs.[78] However, as explained above, it was not until 2003 that the policy of discouraging public sector performance of work offered by the private sector was eliminated.

To improve the overall effectiveness of competitive sourcing as a management tool, OMB's 2003 revisions to the Circular

- authorize trade-offs between cost and quality considerations in order to determine which public or private sector source is offering the "best value";[79]

- treat public and private sector offers in similar fashion to the maximum extent practicable;[80]

- impose time limits on the length of competitions;[81]

- create firewalls to avoid the appearance of conflicts of interest and build public confidence in the process;[82] and

- establish postcompetition accountability.[83]

The GAO stated that the revised Circular should result in better transparency, increased savings, improved performance, and greater accountability.[84] DOD, which has the most experience with competitive sourcing, testified that the new Circular offers "a fresh start with employees, industry, and managers of the competitive sourcing program."[85]

The Impact of Public-Private Competition

According to OMB, competitive sourcing is serving to accelerate the pace of management improvements and cost-savings measures, including operational consolidations, reengineering of processes, workforce realignments, leveraging of technologies, customer-focused performance standards, and reductions in contract support costs.[86] Improvements include better help desk services to support internal operations, more efficient vendor payment processing, state-of-the-art delivery of flight services to general aviation pilots, more cost-effective facilities maintenance, and better service to the public for tax-related forms and publications.[87] Table 3.1 provides a list of examples at various agencies.

Table 3.1 Examples of improvements facilitated by public-private competitions

Management objective	Cost-saving changes facilitated by competition	Estimated savings
FAA: Modernize Automated Flight Service Stations	• Consolidation of stations from 58 to 20. • Modernization of facilities and technologies.	$2.2 billion over 10 years
Army Corps of Engineers: Reengineer IT support	• Consolidate redundant IT activities. • Leverage enterprise-wide purchasing to enable greater compatibility in IT solutions.	$950 million over 6 years
IRS: Reengineer support operations	• Consolidation of distribution centers from 3 to 1. • Leveraging of technology. • Reduction of labor costs.	$207 million over 5 years
Forest Service: Improve IT support	• Consolidation of operations from 150 locations to 10 server farms. • Reduction of labor costs.	$147 million over 5 years
Navy: Make facilities management more cost-effective	• Leveraging of technology. • Restructuring of workflow to adopt customary commercial practices.	$73 million over 5+ years
NASA: Eliminate redundant investments in shared services	• Consolidation of HR, procurement, financial management & IT transactional activities from 10 centers into 1 center. • Leveraging of technology. • Process re-engineering.	$42 million over 10 years
SSA: Make IT support more efficient	• Consolidation and streamlining of help desk and administrative support activities. • Redeployment of labor to understaffed IT-related positions.	$36 million over 5 years

(continued)

Table 3.1 (continued)

Management objective	Cost-saving changes facilitated by competition	Estimated savings
Energy: Make the delivery of financial services support more efficient	• Consolidation of financial services operations from 15 to 2. • Restructuring of job mix. • Leveraging of telecommunications technology.	$31 million over 5 years
Centers for Disease Control (HHS): Reduce cost of editorial support services	• Process reengineering. • Realignment of workforce.	$21+ million over 5 years
Public Buildings Service (GSA): Obtain less costly custodial services	• Reliance on a more cost-effective mix of federal and contractor support (identified through a series of regionalized competitions).	$14 million over 5 years
Justice: Reduce the cost of vehicle maintenance	• New performance standards. • Consolidation of operations. • Reduction of labor costs. • More efficient use of resources.	$11.5 million over 5 years
OPM: Reengineer test administration services	• Leveraging of technology to automate test scheduling and materials ordering. • Reduction of labor costs. • Restructured customer-focused processes.	$10 million over 5 years
Employment & Training Admin (DOL): Improve delivery of financial support	• Consolidation of accounts payable operations. • Reduction of labor dedicated to payment processing/restructuring of job mix.	$5 million over 5 years
Coast Guard: Make public works support for the Academy more effective & efficient.	• Streamlined work order process & reporting. • Fewer FTEs dedicated to administration. • Clear, customer-focused performance standards.	$6 million over 5 years

Source: Office of Management and Budget.

Competitive sourcing has been an especially useful tool for closing performance gaps in routine—but nonetheless essential—services. Between fiscal years 2004 and 2006, 65 percent of the positions competed were for maintenance and property management, information technology, or logistics. Human resources/education, finance and accounting, and administrative support represented 20 percent of the remaining activities.[88] Because these services are common among agencies, federal managers planning competitions have been able to leverage the knowledge of both their colleagues at other agencies and industry consultants who have successfully used the Circular's processes to close similar performance gaps in other organizations.

Agencies project that improvements put in motion by competitions completed in fiscal years 2003–2006 will help taxpayers save approximately $7 billion over the next five to ten years[89] for redirection to higher priorities or deficit reduction. See Table 3.2. Annualized expected savings are about $1.1 billion, which translates to an average savings rate of approximately 28 percent or about $25,000 for every FTE studied.[90] See Table 3.3. One-time out-of-pocket expenses for conducting competitions were $226 million—meaning taxpayers stand to receive about $31 for every dollar spent on competition.[91] Additional data are provided in Tables 3.4 and 3.5.

In October 2006, OMB estimated that if half of the activities identified as suitable for competition in agencies' fiscal year (FY) 2005 FAIR Act inventories were competed over time, and agencies continued to achieve the savings per FTE estimated for competitions completed

Table 3.2 Estimated savings from completed competitions

Savings	FY 2003	FY 2004	FY 2005	FY 2006	Four-year total
Gross	$1.2 B	$1.5 B	$3.1 B	$1.3 B	$7.1 B
Net[a]	$1.1 B	$1.4 B	$3.1 B	$1.3 B	$6.9 B
Annualized gross	$237 M	$285 M	$375 M	$220 M	$1.12 B

Source: Office of Management and Budget's May 2007 report, 17 tbl. 4.
a. Net savings = gross savings less incremental costs (i.e., out-of-pocket expenses). Incremental costs attributable to completed competitions were $88 million in FY 2003, $74 million in FY 2004, $50 million in FY 2005, and $15 million in FY 2006. Net savings reflect adjustments for fixed costs in FYs 2006, 2005 and 2004, the first year OMB started to collect such costs. Adjustments have not been made for transition costs.

Table 3.3 Savings per FTE

Factor	FY 2003[a]	FY 2004	FY 2005[b]	FY 2006
Annualized net savings per FTE	$12,000	$22,000	$25,000	$34,000
Savings rate[c]	14%	25%	27%	36%

Source: Office of Management and Budget's May 2007 report, Appendix G; April 2006 report, Appendix G; May 2005 report, Appendix G; and May 2004 report, Appendix E.

Note: These figures have not been adjusted to reflect fixed costs (which were not reported by agencies in FY 2003). They also do not reflect transition costs.

a. FY 2003 figures reflect savings achieved by 5 standard competitions completed in the first quarter of FY 2004 by the Departments of Commerce, Energy, Health and Human Services, Justice, and the Office of Personnel Management but reported by OMB as part of its FY 2003 report. If the savings from these 5 competitions were removed from the FY 2003 data and added to the FY 2004 data, annualized net savings per FTE for FY 2004 would be $23,000 and the savings rate for FY 2004 would climb to 28 percent.

b. This figure does not reflect additional savings achieved by the Federal Aviation Administration's standard competition of Automated Flight Service Stations, covering 2,300 FTE. If these savings are included the FY 2005 annualized net savings per FTE increases to $45,000 and the savings rate for FY 2005 climbs to 56 percent.

c. These percentages assume the government paid roughly $83,000, $89,000, $93,000, and $97,000 per civilian FTE annually in salary and benefits in FYs 2003, 2004, 2005, and 2006, respectively. The salary and benefit cost figures are based on average actual costs, as reported in the *Analytical Perspectives* volume of the President's Budget for FYs 2005, 2006, 2007, and 2008.

between FYs 2003–2005, the government could save more than $4 billion annually.[92]

OMB's projections notwithstanding, a number of concerns have been voiced regarding the viability of competitive sourcing as a management model.[93] Some fear that competitive sourcing will dismantle the workforce—that is, that the government will be left without adequate personnel to manage its affairs. Others question whether anticipated improvements and cost savings will materialize.

OMB's reports on competitive sourcing include a number of data elements that respond to these concerns. These data points and other relevant OMB management initiatives that address these concerns are discussed below.

Competitive Sourcing and the Workforce

OMB's reports on competitive sourcing include a number of data points to suggest that public-private competition and Circular A-76 are neither dismantling the workforce nor impairing agencies' ability to oversee their activities.

Table 3.4 Competitive sourcing activity in FYs 2003–2006:
Competitions completed

Element	FY 2003	FY 2004	FY 2005	FY 2006	Average
Total competitions completed	662	217	181	183	311
Streamlined	570	116	124	120	233
Standard	92	101[a]	57	63	78
Total FTEs competed	17,595[b]	12,573[b]	9,979[b]	6,678	11,706
Streamlined	5,474	1,201	1,296	2,158	2,532
Standard	12,121	11,372[a]	8,683	4,520	9,174
Percentage of competitions where agency determined best result provided in-house (based on FTE studied)	89%	91%	61%	87%	83%

Source: Office of Management and Budget.

a. Excludes 5 competitions completed by the Departments of Energy (DOE), Health and Human Services (HHS), Justice (DOJ), and Commerce (DOC), and the Office of Personnel Management (OPM), respectively, that were assessed in the FY 2003 report (involving a cumulative total of 1,240 FTEs); also excludes DOD "direct conversions" (despite the name, DOD does not convert activities to private sector performance until after having considered the cost of in-house performance, as required by 10 U.S.C. 2462).

b. According to the 2003 FAIR Act inventories of agencies tracked by the PMA, there were approximately 380,000 FTEs identified as suitable for competition. Thus, approximately 4.6% the FTEs potentially eligible for competition were competed in 2003, 3.3% were competed in 2004, 2.6% were competed in 2005, and 1.7% were competed in 2006.

First, competitive sourcing is being applied to a relatively small segment of the government's overall activities in any given year. Agencies have considerable discretion to determine the best timing for a competition and typically coordinate competitions with other management initiatives, such as achieving human capital goals and agency reorganizations. Competitions completed between FYs 2003–2006 involved approximately 47,000 FTEs, representing about 12 percent of the commercial activities identified as suitable for competition and about 3 percent of all government activities.[94] DOD, which historically has had the most extensive competitive sourcing program, estimates that public-private competition represents only a small fraction of its total service contracting.[95]

Second, federal employees have enjoyed considerable success in competitions conducted under the PMA. Federal employees were selected to

Table 3.5 Competitive sourcing activity in FYs 2003–2006: Costs

Element	FY 2003	FY 2004	FY 2005	FY 2006	Average
Incremental (out-of-pocket) costs[a]					
Cost directly attributable to conducting *completed* competitions	$88 million	$74 million	$58 million	$15 million	$59 million
Average incremental cost per FTE studied	$4,900	$5,800[b]	$5,100	$2,800	$4,700
Fixed costs for central direction & oversight					
Total fixed costs	Data not collected	$36 million	$31 million	$37 million	$35 million

Source: Office of Management and Budget.
a. These are one-time expenses.
b. The increase from FY 2003 to FY 2004 likely reflects the increased use of standard competitions (versus streamlined competitions).

perform over 80 percent of the work competed between FY 2003 and FY 2006.[96] In other words, the talents and skills of federal employees continue to be relied on for the performance of many of the government's commercial needs—and all of its inherently governmental needs. In many cases, employees will work under MEOs that offer new and better ways of delivering services. For example, the Army Corps of Engineers is one of several agencies that have undertaken to significantly transform how information management and information technology is provided. The employees' team developed the blueprint for an MEO that was selected by the Army's senior management following a public-private competition. Implementation of the MEO is expected to save taxpayers $950 million over six years through leveraged enterprise-wide purchasing and "virtual teams that allow local commands to draw upon a greater breadth of knowledge and capabilities than could be done under the old command-by-command approach."[97]

Although the implementation of MEOs typically involves a reduction in the amount of labor devoted to the activity, many (if not most) employees who wish to stay in the workforce are generally retained in the workforce, through retraining or reassignment, to fill skills gaps in other program areas.[98] Studies show that the rate of involuntary separation is low—historically around 5 percent.[99] The Army Corps anticipates a minimal number of involuntary separations, if any, as a result of its commandwide competition, involving over 1,400 government positions. Many of the labor-related reductions have been achieved through attrition.[100]

Third, as explained above, competitive sourcing principles require that federal employees perform *all inherently governmental work* and maintain a sufficient presence in the performance of *core commercial activities* to provide effective stewardship. As noted above, agencies have identified just over 40 percent of the workforce as inherently governmental. In addition, they have identified about 60 percent of the commercial positions as unsuitable for competition, in many cases because these positions involve core activities. OMB considers a function to be core to an agency's operation if loss of in-house performance of the function would result in substantial risk to the agency's ability to accomplish its unique mission. Core commercial activities could include, for example, strategic planning, capital or resource planning, asset management, architecture and infrastructure planning, and technology assessment. Agencies are expected to exempt these activities from competition to the extent necessary to provide and preserve an internal core competency.[101]

Fourth, efforts are being taken to ensure that work performed by federal contractors is managed effectively. OMB's Office of Federal Procurement Policy (OFPP) is working to strengthen the contract workforce.[102] Recognizing that each agency's acquisition workforce differs in terms of size, capability, and skill mix, OFPP partnered in the spring of 2007 with the Federal Acquisition Institute (FAI), a federal entity dedicated to training and professional development of the acquisition workforce, on a survey tool to help civilian agencies assess their proficiency in core contracting competencies.[103] DOD is also working to evaluate the competencies of its existing workforce.[104] Agencies have used these analyses to develop plans to tailor recruiting, training, and deployment efforts to their individual capability gaps. Equally important, OFPP has established an acquisition certification program to train program and project managers in acquisition planning and contract management. These officials have critical knowledge about the government's requirements. A better understanding of the acquisition process will allow them to partner more effectively with contracting personnel in the creation of clear contract work statements and the oversight of resulting contracts.[105]

The General Services Administration Modernization Act[106] allows federal agencies to hire retired annuitants to fill critical vacancies in the acquisition field.[107] In anticipation of a significant loss of experience and corporate knowledge as the baby boomer generation retires, OFPP has instructed agency chief acquisition officers, senior procurement executives, chief human capital officers, and acquisition career managers to work together in drafting implementation plans.[108] The guidance explains that reemployed annuitants may supplement and strengthen acquisition operations in a variety of ways, such as by (1) acting as mentors and providing on-the-job training and coaching, (2) helping agencies meet surges arising from emergencies and other situations, and (3) providing support to program managers.[109]

The Department of Homeland Security, which has been criticized for relying too heavily on contractors to address immediate staffing shortfalls,[110] is taking steps to improve the management of its contractors. DHS stated its intention to "develop a mature acquisition workforce that will enable [the department] to build [its] own 'pipeline' of people, create a career-path from within the Department, and reduce [its] inefficiencies in areas of oversight and project management."[111] The GAO issued recommendations for additional steps DHS should take to improve its ability to manage risk and ensure government control of decisions associated with professional and management support services currently provided by contractors.[112]

FAR 37.114 reminds agencies that "contracts for services which require the contractor to provide advice, opinions, recommendations, ideas, reports, analyses, or other work products have the potential for influencing the authority, accountability, and responsibilities of Government officials."[113] As a result, agencies are required to ensure that

- a sufficient number of qualified government employees are assigned to oversee contractor activities;
- functions performed are not changed or augmented to become inherently governmental;
- a greater scrutiny and an appropriately enhanced degree of management oversight is exercised when contracting for functions that closely support the performance of inherently governmental functions (for example, services to support the development of policies, reorganization and planning, or the drafting of statements of work); and

· contractor personnel attending meetings, answering telephones, and working in other situations where their contractor status is not obvious to third parties identify themselves as such, to avoid creating an impression that they are government officials unless, in the judgment of the agency, no harm can come for failing to identify themselves.[114]

Implementation: From Projections to Results

Skepticism regarding the long-term benefits of competitive sourcing is likely to remain until actual savings are achieved.[115] A number of steps have been taken to increase transparency and demonstrate results.

First, Circular A-76 requires agencies to track the implementation of their competitions.[116] This requirement is further reinforced by §647(b) of the Departments of Transportation and Treasury, and Independent Agencies Appropriations Act, 2004, which requires agencies to report annually on their competitive sourcing efforts, beginning with FY 2003 efforts.[117] OMB has developed a standard reporting format and provided guidance to help standardize the calculation of (1) baseline costs of operation,[118] (2) fixed costs associated with overseeing competitive sourcing efforts in the agency, and (3) the incremental cost of competition.[119]

OMB cautions that savings will not accrue evenly over the entire implementation period, with actual savings likely to be small during the initial implementation:

[A]ctual savings are likely to be *smaller* in the near term and *greater* in the out years of implementation. In particular, near term savings are likely to be offset by investment costs, such as transition costs and capital expenditures. In addition, some letters of obligation with MEOs or contracts may not call for full performance until the second or third year of implementation, so the opportunity to achieve the full benefit of new efficiencies may not be realized in the early stages of implementation.[120]

OMB requires agencies to identify cost projections for each performance period throughout the duration of the contract or letter of obligation. OMB explains that by "identifying estimated costs of the selected service provider by performance period (rather than assuming costs are incurred evenly over each year of performance) agencies will be able to see more easily if the provider is meeting its requirements" after appropriate adjustments are made to reflect changes in scope, inflation, and wage rates.[121]

Second, OMB has deployed a government-wide database to document the results of public-private competitions. According to OMB, the database facilitates comprehensive and consistent reporting of data.[122] Information is being collected both on contracts awarded to the private sector and letters of obligation established with MEOs to ensure work is being performed at the agreed-upon level irrespective of the provider.[123]

Third, OMB has issued guidance to help agencies substantiate savings and performance improvements.[124] The guidance requires agencies to have plans in place to ensure the independent validation of a reasonable sampling of competitions. In selecting competitions for validation, agencies are advised to consider factors such as the impact of the activity on the agency's operation, the projected savings for the agency, and the results of prior agency reviews.

Agencies have entered into agreements with a variety of independent sources to assist with the evaluation of results. At the Office of Personnel Management, for example, the Office of Inspector General has reviewed MEO implementations to determine whether actual costs were within the agency cost estimate and whether the letter of obligation was being adequately administered. The Department of the Treasury assigns implementation responsibilities to a number of offices; the Deputy Chief Financial Officer validates that the MEO is a properly established organization while its budget office compares projected costs to actual costs.[125]

The Future

Agencies have always relied on a mix of federal employees and contractors to carry out their missions and they will need to continue relying on a blended workforce to address the increasingly complex challenges posed by the defining events of this decade, including 9/11, Iraq reconstruction, and Hurricane Katrina. As has been the case for the past fifty years, there will be an ongoing need for a standard evaluation process to help agencies that wish to consider the conversion of commercial work from one sector to the other, in circumstances where either sector could appropriately perform the work. The executive branch and Congress must work together to preserve agencies' ability to conduct public-private competitions—involving work currently performed by federal employees, work performed by the private sector, or new work—in situations when such competitions make sense.

Agency use of public-private competition for potential conversion of work to the private sector will likely be modest. Even with the attention placed on competitive sourcing by the PMA, agencies competed less than three percent of the workforce between FYs 2003 and 2006. This level of activity is not surprising. The preponderance of activities performed by federal employees is either inherently governmental or unsuitable for competition (for example, the activity is core to the agency's mission, or private sector interest, capability, or capacity is lacking). In addition, most agencies have generally proceeded with caution before announcing public-private competitions. As explained above, agencies often perform multiple analyses. It is not uncommon for agencies to forego competition based on these analyses.[126] Moreover, agencies already rely heavily on the private sector to bring expertise and innovation to government programs and supplement the skills and competencies of the workforce.[127]

Congressional support for competitive sourcing will probably be tenuous, creating uncertainties regarding the availability of funding and limitations that might be imposed on a competition. Since FY 2003, Congress has imposed a variety of statutory restrictions on public-private competition. Some provisions restrict the process used to evaluate competitors (for example, restrictions on the use of trade-offs between cost and quality when choosing between in-house federal providers and the private sector).[128] Others limit the activities that may be competed (for example, competitive sourcing is precluded for immigration information activities at the Department of Homeland Security[129] and for rural development and farm loan programs at the Department of Agriculture[130]). At least one caps resources available for competition (a cap is imposed on the funding available to conduct competitions at the Department of Interior[131]). Some restrictions go so far as to prohibit any public-private competitions by the organization (no funds appropriated in fiscal year 2008 may be used to conduct competitive sourcing at the Forest Service[132] or the Army Corps of Engineers;[133] the Department of Labor may not conduct public-private competitions until sixty days after GAO completes a report on the Department's use of competitive sourcing—no deadline is provided for the GAO to complete its review;[134] the House-passed Defense Authorization Bill for FY 2009 proposes a moratorium on the use of competitive sourcing at the Defense Department through the end of fiscal year 2011[135]), while others declare *all* activities performed by the organization to be inherently governmental.[136]

Congressional actions to restrict competitive sourcing appear to be driven by concerns that public-private competition will dismantle the workforce, projected savings will not materialize, and contracts will not be properly managed.[137] Some of these concerns should be addressed by the efforts described above to increase attention on contract management, strengthen the skills of the workforce, and validate the results of public-private competitions completed in recent years.

Congress has shown increased interest in "insourcing," where work is converted from contract to government performance, as well as increased consideration of agency performance for new work.[138] Competitive sourcing is one means for evaluating the comparative cost, capacity, and capabilities that exist within each sector, including the cost of developing an infrastructure within an agency where one does not currently exist. However, recent statutory changes restrict use of public-private competition prior to federal performance of commercial work in certain circumstances.[139]

Where work is being performed by federal employees and public-private competition is not suitable, recognition should be given to alternative processes that rely on principles similar to those in the Circular to achieve performance improvements and cost savings.[140] For example, many of the steps required to internally reengineer activities not suited for competition may be the same as those required to develop an MEO through competition, namely, (1) workload measurement, (2) establishment of clearly defined performance expectations and standards to measure results, (3) cost analysis to determine the full cost of government performance, (4) meaningful involvement in the restructuring process by interested stakeholders and technical experts (for example, affected employees, experts in human resource management, industrial engineering, and cost analysis), and (5) documentation of performance agreements and the results of implementation. Giving appropriate recognition to an agency that creates a "high-performing organization" through disciplined internal reengineering will provide an additional incentive for federal managers to increase government effectiveness in areas where use of public-private competition is not likely to bring about this result.[141]

Conclusion

As stewards of taxpayer resources, federal managers have a fiduciary responsibility to close performance gaps using appropriate management processes. For those commercial activities that may be successfully performed by either the public or private sector without substantial risk to the agency's ability to accomplish its mission, competitive sourcing can be a suitable process for addressing performance gaps. However, competitive sourcing, like any other management tool, must be used reasonably and responsibly. If competitive sourcing is approached in a fair, transparent, and accountable manner, experience suggests that federal managers can leave their operations better than they found them.

PART TWO

Cases and Critiques

CHAPTER FOUR

Rent-a-Regulator

Design and Innovation in Environmental Decision Making

MIRIAM SEIFTER

Introduction

Debates over the reach, effects, and desirability of privatization[1] are imprecise without attention to the particular tools, strategies, and personnel a particular program deploys.[2] Although others have noted the variety of component parts in privatization efforts,[3] particular variations seldom receive in-depth evaluation.

This chapter seeks to examine one such under-the-radar model, both to put another variation of privatization on the table for discussion and to show that the design of a privatization initiative may bear heavily on the initiative's success or failure. The model, which I nickname "rent-a-regulator," transfers regulatory decision making to licensed professionals who directly serve regulated "clients." Rather than contracting out regulatory functions or privatizing them entirely, the government licenses professionals, just as it would doctors or plumbers, to make compliance decisions pertaining to regulated parties—their paying "clients." By examining this model, the chapter seeks to refocus overbroad denouncements or praise of privatization itself.[4] The model's pathologies provide a base from which to investigate the connection between the structure and performance of a regulatory program.

Recent efforts in the governance of hazardous waste remediation provide a revealing case study of the rent-a-regulator model. Hazardous waste law, and more prolifically, brownfields law,[5] has increasingly embraced privatization as part of a shift away from what some saw as heavy-handed command-and-control regulation. New elements of privatization are part of the innovative regulatory patchwork of voluntary cleanup programs, financial incentives, and liability relief states have woven to address the hundreds of thousands of contaminated properties across the country.[6]

The rigid, lengthy process of state-administered hazardous waste cleanups—in which a regulated party must obtain state permits and approval through multiple phases of remediation—is among the vestiges of traditional regulation that is giving way. Resonant with privatization in other contexts[7] and with the philosophy that an entrepreneurial state government "understands that sometimes the most helpful thing to do is to get out of the way,"[8] at least six states have aimed to increase the expediency, predictability, and flexibility of environmental cleanups by entrusting private professionals with oversight and approval of remediation efforts.[9]

Although agencies have long enlisted private actors to carry out environmental protection functions,[10] the recent initiatives step boldly beyond the familiar service delivery model. The privatization initiative in Massachusetts was the first and remains the prototype: state law requires regulated entities to hire private consultants—licensed site professionals (LSPs)[11]—and receive their approval before mandatory remediation can be considered complete. There is no option for state oversight. Except at the minority of sites the state audits, the LSPs make the final decision whether the investigation and remedy comport with the best practices embraced by the regulations' broad standards. Unlike typical regulators, however, LSPs often design and carry out a cleanup in addition to approving it. And unlike most private delegates, LSPs are not government contractors; once licensed they are selected and hired by regulated parties. Free of a government contract and seeking to edge out competitors, the LSPs strive to represent the best interests of their regulated clients and minimize the cost of cleanups.

Ascertaining the impact of the program's design on its performance requires a metric by which to measure performance. To focus on inherent tendencies without passing judgment on policy ends, this chapter evaluates privatization initiatives on their own terms. Have private actors done what the government has asked?[12] In the LSP program, the key question is whether the LSPs have properly executed the regulatory compliance decisions entrusted to them. Performance requires "regulatory adherence," faithful upholding of both the letter of the regulations and the government's understanding of them.[13] This means that, despite economic incentives and client demands to cut corners, LSPs must only design, perform, and approve cleanups that fully comply with the regulations. The adherence criterion is substance neutral; it would mandate enforcing regulations requiring the LSP to pollute as much as to remediate.

The state agency's audits of the LSPs' work[14] reveal widespread "regulatory slippage"—a failure to take regulatory action or a decision to take action less rigorous than promulgated requirements mandate.[15] The audits indicate that LSPs routinely permit—or execute—deviations from state regulations governing hazardous waste site cleanups, sometimes creating serious risks to human health and the environment.[16]

Examination of the LSP program's structure reveals that design flaws likely contribute in great part to the regulatory slippage. First, conflicts of interest—both within workplaces and with respect to clients—may prompt the private regulators to cut corners. Second, a dearth of management procedures and avenues for discipline may prevent detection and remedy of malpractice—and in turn fail to incentivize good behavior. These factors together invite slippage; LSPs have motivation to underenforce the regulations and little fear of getting caught. But this chapter argues that the design flaws in the LSP program and rent-a-regulator model are not irreparable, and some—like conflict-of-interest prohibitions—could be implemented at low cost.

More broadly, the LSP experience indicates that attention to design issues can illuminate causes of failing privatized programs and solutions for rehabilitation. In particular, the LSP experience underscores the importance of aligning interests between government principals and their private agents—creating relationships and incentives that establish "a shared understanding of common values and goals"[17]—and instating management mechanisms to monitor performance. To the extent that these reforms entail costs that would jeopardize the benefits sought from privatization in the first place, political officials must make judgment calls. A key point of this chapter is that those judgment calls need not involve a stark choice between public and private; rather, decision makers can select from a variety of design alternatives.

Here it is worth emphasizing what this chapter does *not* attempt. First, it does not seek to weigh the LSP program's overall costs and benefits. Thus, it does not take up the question of whether the program's comparative expedience, flexibility, and productivity—the program is widely praised for enabling the cleanup of thousands more sites per year—sufficiently offset the decreases in regulatory adherence. This chapter also does not address the potential immeasurable effects of the privatized program, such as the potential for government's withdrawal from hazardous waste decision making to express diminishment of environmental protection as a public value,[18] or the political implications of privatizing functions that may be "inherently governmental."[19] For purposes of this analysis, such results are merely interesting second-order effects worthy of further study.

Similarly, this chapter does not suggest that regulatory slippage necessarily warrants a return to publicly administered decision making. That suggestion would be unfounded in the LSP context, where data limitations preclude comparative analysis; there are no records of how well Massachusetts's predecessor public program adhered to the regulations, and thus no empirical basis for concluding that a state-run program would do better. Moreover, a reflexive call for public control would run counter to what the chapter *does* argue—that a program's design and organization, rather than merely its public or private status, go a long way toward determining its performance.

Instead, the chapter situates itself in the existing landscape of pervasive privatization,[20] in which the scarcity of state funds[21] would prevent many states from providing all of the functions associated with environmental regulation.[22] From this vantage point, it identifies shortcomings in and possible solutions for the rent-a-regulator model, noting the connection between design and performance. The next part of this chapter explains how privatized hazardous waste decision making works in Massachusetts and provides data on its performance; the following part describes the rent-a-regulator model of privatization, building upon existing models of service provision versus regulation and of relationships between private regulators, the government, and regulated entities. The final part of the chapter draws upon the LSP experience to examine the factors that affect the behavior of private decision makers. I suggest that if regulatory adherence is the goal, regulatory provisions to limit conflicts of interest, to institute procedures for screening and monitoring, and to create opportunities for discipline should be focal points of future design.

Case Study

Imagine that an entity, public or private, is building a school on an abandoned lot that contains PCBs and other toxic pollutants in the soil. Numerous decisions must be made, and the stakes are high. How much investigation must be done to ascertain the scope of the pollution? What models should the engineers use to extrapolate the level of risk presented? Do the pollutants need to be removed altogether, or can they safely be left in the ground? How much should factors like the cost of remediation or the expected usage of the property affect the decision? If the pollutants are left in the ground, what kind of precautions— "institutional controls," in the brownfields jargon[23]—need to be taken at the site to prevent human exposure to the chemicals? In making these compliance determinations, the decision maker acts as a gatekeeper of public health.

The potential for substantial public health threats has historically justified the cumbersome, involved nature of hazardous waste remediation regulation. In a traditional command-and-control cleanup regime like that in New York state, the school in the above hypothetical would need state approval for every phase of the cleanup process and would need to solicit public input at several times along the way.[24] The state-administered process, however, can be extremely time-consuming[25]— and delay may have significant consequences, harming real estate transactions while leaving vulnerable communities exposed to pollution. The Massachusetts LSP program, resonant with privatization in other contexts, was instituted as an attempt to improve the expediency, predictability, and flexibility of a program that had become backlogged and ineffective.[26]

In the LSP program, the state does not oversee hazardous waste cleanups. Instead, the relevant chapter of the state regulations, codified as the Massachusetts Contingency Plan (MCP),[27] requires landowners to hire an LSP and receive his or her approval before mandatory remediation can be considered complete. Other than auditing 20 percent of completed cleanups as required by statute,[28] the state Department of Environmental Protection (DEP) does not get involved. The state licensing board possesses authority to discipline LSPs for unprofessional conduct.[29] The structure of the LSP program is illustrated in Figure 4.1.

Once hired, the LSP's official service to the client is providing a series of "waste site cleanup activity opinions"—also known as "professional opinions" or "LSP opinions"—that designate a cleanup as compliant with state regulations.[30] The professional opinions must bear the LSP's signature and state-issued seal and are due at each of the remediation phases set out in the regulations.[31]

The approval process allows LSPs substantial discretion. Although the regulations are lengthy, they leave ample room for interpretation;

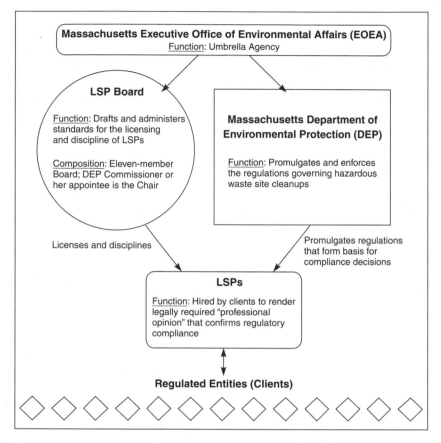

Figure 4.1 Organization of LSP Program.

they dictate procedure more than substance and require the decision maker to choose between multiple alternatives at each stage. For example, guidelines provide for several permissible risk assessment techniques, which can produce vastly different conclusions regarding the type and scope of remedy necessary. Similarly, the LSP must wrestle with ambiguous determinations of whether recommended solutions are "feasible."

Although LSPs only act in their official capacity when they approve and seal a document, their range of services may be far broader; LSPs often perform the very work they are approving. They frequently design site investigations, crunch the numbers of a risk assessment, and draft work plans. They or their firms may also carry out the physical remediation, and some LSPs also provide legal or regulatory advice, acting as a point person for the entire project. At the other end of the spectrum, subject to minimum requirements for LSP involvement, LSPs may have little to do with a project until providing their opinion at the end.[32]

Audits prepared by DEP suggest that LSPs routinely fail to comply with the regulations governing hazardous waste site cleanups, sometimes creating serious risks to human health and the environment.[33] Table 4.1 shows that a minority of sites—as low as 13 percent in fiscal year 2003—receive "passing" outcomes. Most sites—approximately 70 percent for the past three years—receive "follow-up required" outcomes. At these sites, LSP errors are significant enough to warrant further remedial work, but not enough to flatly invalidate the LSPs' decisions; usually DEP asks for more evidence to fully support a conclusion. Finally, between 5 percent and 21 percent of sites audited have violations severe enough to invalidate the final approval of the cleanup.

Even when cleanups are technically compliant, LSPs may exercise their discretion in ways inconsistent with DEP's perception of the public interest by taking shortcuts where DEP would have been more thorough.[34] This may occur when an LSP finds a response action infeasible, though guidance documents suggest infeasibility findings should be rare.[35] It may also occur when an LSP settles on a temporary solution instead of a permanent one by opting for containment and monitoring rather than actual remediation.[36] As shown in Table 4.2, whereas fewer than 1 percent of sites in the first year of the privatized program received approval for temporary solutions (classified in the regulations as Class C outcomes), over 10 percent of sites received approval for temporary solutions in 2004.

LSPs may also exercise discretion in a way that DEP disfavors by failing to reach background pollution levels in their cleanups.[37] The regulations identify three classes of cleanup outcomes: a Class A outcome

Table 4.1 Audit results

	FY94–00	FY01	FY02	FY03	FY04	FY05
Passing	29%	18%	14%	13%	19%	25%
No follow-up required	28%	31%	21%	15%	11%	4%
Follow-up required	43%	50%	65%	71%	70%	71%
Invalidation/retraction	5%	6%	12%	15%	21%	9%

Table 4.2 Temporary solutions

Year	Class C	Total	% Class C of total
1994	2	554	0.36
1995	9	1,829	0.49
1996	17	1,540	1.10
1997	27	1,901	1.42
1998	24	1,780	1.35
1999	33	1,721	1.92
2000	42	1,752	2.40
2001	52	1,816	2.86
2002	85	2,250	3.78
2003	107	2,060	5.19
2004	295	2,807	10.51

means that a "permanent solution" was implemented; a Class B outcome means that the LSP certified that no remedial action was required; and a Class C outcome, as discussed above, means that a temporary solution was reached. Despite DEP guidance that background conditions *must* be achieved unless infeasible,[38] only 6.5 percent of sites reached background conditions, or an A1 outcome, between 1994 and 2006.[39] As shown in Figure 4.2, the more common permanent solution—at 46.9 percent of sites—was an A2 outcome, a risk-based solution in which contamination remains. And over 9 percent of sites that reached permanent solutions reached only an A3 or A4 outcome, meaning that less aggressive remediation was permitted in exchange for an activity and use limitation (AUL)—a restriction on how the site can be used in the future given that contamination will remain.[40] Another 26.4 percent of sites reached a B1 outcome, a decision not to take any remedial action because the contamination does not pose a "significant risk," and 4.6 percent received a B2 outcome, in which remediation is avoided altogether through an AUL. Finally, 3 percent of sites reached only a temporary solution.

Lessons Learned: Designing Privatized Decision Making

Despite its important role in Massachusetts and the interest other states have expressed in adopting a similar program, the rent-a-regulator model does not appear in the privatization literature. While the enlistment of LSPs is generally consistent with the rise of third-party governance,[41] it differs from delineated models of privatization on at least

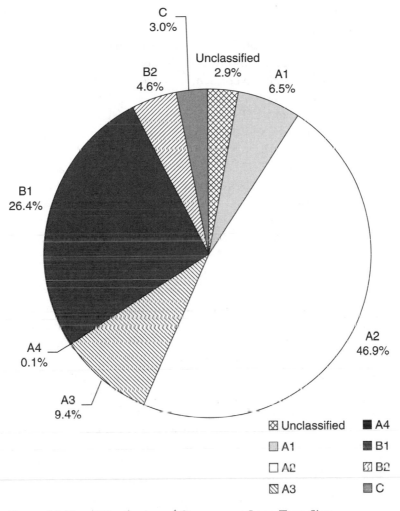

Figure 4.2 Total Distribution of Outcomes at Long-Term Sites.

three scores. First, LSP duties resemble regulation more than service delivery; to the extent that one expects privatization to involve pure "rowing"—execution of discrete and limited tasks like garbage collection[42] and highway maintenance[43]—LSPs' coercive responsibilities seem to reach into government's domain.[44] A second variable that sets LSPs apart is that their relationship with the regulated landowners is not adversarial. LSPs are a form of openly "captured" regulators; their decisions are dominated by the interests of the entities they regulate.[45] A third distinguishing characteristic of the rent-a-regulator model is that while LSPs are licensed, and while they base their opinions on agency-promulgated regulations, they do not contract with the government. The result is that government's control over the private decision makers is indirect and often limited.

Indeed, though many LSPs would cringe at the comparison, the relationship between LSPs and their regulated-party clients bears a significant similarity to that between attorneys and clients. The LSP signs a contract with the client and agrees to render professional advice on the client's behalf. Correspondence between the LSP and client beyond the documentation of the official opinion may be protected by a work-product privilege.[46] The LSP becomes an advocate for the client, defending the client's wishes to concerned third parties (such as abutters). LSPs, like lawyers, are bound by codes of professional conduct; they must ensure that "the actions undertaken are within the permissible limits" of the regulations.[47] Within those limits, however, the LSP—again like an attorney—is bound by the client's wishes and financial resources.[48] The LSP is not an "environmental crusader," and the professional opinion the LSP delivers is not the environmental equivalent of a "Good Housekeeping Seal of Approval."[49]

Zeroing in on the components of the LSP program's rent-a-regulator model permits analysis of the potential connection between design and performance. This connection is best viewed as an inquiry into the forces affecting how private regulators will exercise their discretion. Hence, I explore here the incentives that influence how the LSPs pursue their primary responsibility and the first-order goal of the LSP program, which is enforcement of the MCP regulations. As an alternative to abandoning the model altogether, I then explore whether the incentives can be adjusted or improved through structural changes.

Two main structural pitfalls of the LSP program impede adherence to the MCP regulations. First, conflicts of interest—both within LSPs' workplaces and with respect to clients—encourage LSPs to cut corners. Second, management procedures and disciplinary opportunities are too sparse to detect and remedy LSP malpractice, and in turn fail to incentivize good behavior. Alone, neither of the factors is likely to make or break the effectiveness of a privatization initiative; together, they become a reason to worry that privatization will lead to regulatory slippage.

Conflicts of Interest

IN-HOUSE BIAS

What determines how will LSPs exercise their discretion? The first issue is the simplest. The LSP program involves internal conflicts of interest; the LSP rendering the professional opinion is often approving her own work (frequently with input from other members of her firm, or subcontractors she hires). Donald Kettl has stated the problem succinctly: "Contractors who check their own work are clearly vulnerable to conflicts of interest."[50] These conflicts may lead to biases that influence the way that the decision makers exercise their discretion;[51] what is the likelihood that the decision maker will find that her own work is insufficient? The effect is to push the true moment of decision making earlier in the process, when the investigation and remediation plans are designed—and to eliminate the check on those decisions.

In a redesigned system, the decision maker could be separated from the consultants preparing the work plans. This could happen, as discussed below, if relationships were altered so that the decision maker contracted directly with the government; the regulated party could hire its own consultants to design and perform the cleanup, and the government could deploy an LSP to sign off on the work at each stage. As a more modest suggestion, a redesigned system might require the input of an impartial referee before a cleanup could be certified.

RENT-A-REGULATOR, REDUX: CLIENT DEMANDS
AND EXTERNAL CONFLICTS OF INTEREST

In addition to in-house conflicts of interest, the LSP program illustrates several ways in which objectivity can be overtaken by clients' wishes. First, the contractual relationship between the decision makers and regulated parties affords the regulated parties substantial power. Given the competitive market for LSP services,[52] LSPs must carry out their jobs fearing that they will be fired or not rehired if they consider the public interest in their decision, at least where doing so leads to more costly or risk-averse cleanups.[53] This arrangement threatens to punish any LSP who might otherwise be inclined to do an A+ rather than a D+ job.[54] The power of regulated entities is even greater when they employ LSPs as part of their full-time staff.[55] Second, the regulated party's power as the "hirer" can produce informational asymmetry; regulated parties may withhold key information that would have compelled the LSP to insist on a more aggressive cleanup.[56] Third, the contract structure itself may incentivize underperformance; the commonly used fixed-price remediation agreements may increase corner cutting so that LSPs can finish the job under budget (and if they get paid early on, they may have stronger incentives to shirk at the end of the job).[57]

Taken together, the power dynamics and contract structure between LSPs and clients create a degree of influence of the regulated over the regulators that many would regard as governmental failure.[58] Reform should entail greater separation between client and decision maker by prohibiting, through regulation addressing conflicts of interest, any contractual relationship between the regulated entity and the private decision maker. If LSPs were agents of DEP rather than of their regulated "clients," LSPs would be less likely to deviate from agency interests. If a contractual relationship must exist, its terms should be regulated[59] to encourage performance rather than mere outputs. Commentators have suggested that pay-for-performance contracts, for example, would improve the quality and reliability of services rendered in the brownfields context and elsewhere.[60]

Management and Discipline

The conflicts of interest plaguing LSPs are more problematic in light of the lack of adequate management practices. Specifically, the program fails to provide adequate screening, monitoring, and discipline. I take each of these structural flaws in turn. In restructuring the management of the LSP program, the agency should acknowledge that market forces alone cannot police third-party regulators.[61] Active steering, not cruise control, is necessary; agencies must attentively manage the incentives and relationships of authority that govern private decision makers to keep them on course.[62]

EX ANTE SCREENING

The advisory committee that helped design the LSP program envisioned that DEP would stay involved ex ante by screening sites, requiring both permits and agency involvement at complex or risky (Tier IA) sites.[63] However, severe budget cuts in 2003—as of September 2005, the agency only had 165 FTEs[64]—forced DEP to pare down its ex ante involvement. Although the agency has done its best, striving to focus available oversight resources on imminent hazards,[65] the lack of ex ante management creates the risk that DEP might become incompetent to exercise "step-in power"[66] when LSPs run amok or fail to deliver.[67] In addition, the lack of screening is a missed opportunity to limit LSPs' discretion. In a redesigned system, the agency might screen projects before cleanup begins and set limiting criteria for the sites eligible for the privatized program, an approach that has been successful in New Jersey.[68]

ONGOING MONITORING

The LSP program fails to provide ongoing monitoring. Although the advisory committee envisioned that DEP would conduct "vigorous" audits to ensure "compliance with all aspects of the program,"[69] and that audit rates would increase if the agency detected "significant levels of noncompliance,"[70] the audit process has been far less robust. Only 20 percent of sites are audited to begin with, meaning that the work at most properties goes unchecked. At the 20 percent of sites that do receive an audit, the agency must triage. As Table 4.3 shows, the vast majority of sites are checked by merely reviewing the file to see if the paperwork appears complete—a Level I audit.[71] In fiscal year 2004, after the 2003 budget cuts, only 5.7 percent of all audits and 1.9 percent of all sites received a Level III audit—a full-fledged "comprehensive evaluation" involving actions like sample collection and site visits to ensure compliance with the MCP.[72]

Perhaps more importantly, DEP does not provide long-term monitoring. While Massachusetts law requires an audit of all AUL sites and allows unlimited monitoring in light of their long-term threat,[73] DEP does not have the resources to audit sites more than once.[74] The agency is currently considering changes to its audit procedures.[75]

The lack of meaningful monitoring means that the agency is not provided with the necessary information to allow a true evaluation of

Table 4.3 Breakdown of audits

	FY01	FY02	FY03	FY04
Level III audits	332	208	196	131
Total audits	1,616	1,369	2,095	2,281
Total sites paying annual compliance fee	4,804	5,008	5,143	6,723
Percentage of audits with Level III	20.5	15.2	9.4	5.7
Percentage of all sites with Level III	6.9	4.2	3.8	1.9

LSPs' performance, either individually or collectively. Indeed, without more data, DEP may not even be able to ask the right questions—and the agency cannot "know what it [does] not think to ask."[76] Perhaps more importantly, without a management plan that provides for long-term monitoring to ensure that property owners adhere to use limitations, institutional controls like AULs do not solve the problem they were implemented to address. Under the current system, violations are likely to be detected by chance rather than design. For example, in one case, an AUL was used to prohibit excavation on school grounds, but the school planned an expansion only months later.[77] Excavation was only stopped because a local public health official aware of the AUL happened to drive by the site and notice the work being done.[78]

More attentive monitoring and evaluation of LSPs' performance would serve a dual purpose. First, knowledge that such management is operative may inspire fear of getting caught, making private decision makers more faithful to government interests. Second, in the event that private decision makers nonetheless deviate from governmental interests, proper oversight can allow government to detect and remedy poor performance.[79] The old adage bears repeating: you manage what you measure.[80] Absent attentive monitoring, the agency cannot know the extent and source of, and thus cannot address, regulatory slippage.

DISCIPLINE

In addition to the lack of monitoring of LSPs' work, there are few avenues for meaningful discipline of LSPs who underenforce or actually violate the MCP. In theory, three groups possess some form of disciplinary authority over LSPs: DEP, the LSP Board, and the public. However, the design of the relationships between these groups, and the limitations on the power wielded by each one, makes meaningful discipline unlikely. In turn, the disciplinary architecture fails to deter regulatory slippage.

First, DEP has no direct authority over LSPs. Although its actions against noncompliant *parties* alter LSPs' incentives at least somewhat—clients expect LSPs to avoid attracting enforcement actions, and may hold them responsible for fines[81]—enforcement actions continue to be limited by DEP's own knowledge. Absent tips from outsiders, it primarily has information about the sites that it audits—only 20 percent. Moreover, when DEP wants to penalize LSPs, it must rely on the LSP Board as an intermediary.[82] The agency may have little practical power over the board in any given case, because after the agency refers a matter to the board for discipline, the board may choose not to punish the LSP.[83] DEP's limited influence over LSPs, combined with the LSP Board's frequently deferential posture, thus fails to align the interests of LSPs and the agency.

DEP's limited provisions for public involvement further reduce the checks on private decision makers, as the public could otherwise exert pressure to comport with the public values expressed by agency regulations.[84] Currently, the only public participation occurs if a group of ten or more citizens petitions for special public involvement provisions,[85] but unlike in other states, there are no requirements that potentially interested groups be identified and notified of remediation activities. Copies of certain documents need to be filed with the Department of Public Health and published in the legal notices section of a local newspaper, and submittals become part of the public record that interested parties can request to view,[86] but citizens may remain unaware of response actions if they do not see the backhoe across the street or search DEP records.[87]

To increase the discipline imposed on LSPs without imposing such burdensome constraints that the benefits of private sector flexibility and innovation are lost, the agency could exact agreements to incentivize respect for its authority.[88] If DEP switched to a contracting rather than licensing scheme, it could negotiate penalties for noncompliance directly into the contract. Even in the extant licensing system, DEP could easily, by regulation, include provisions for sanctions and incentives as conditions of licensing. For example, the agency could provide bonuses to LSPs who achieve background pollution levels at a certain percentage of the sites they oversee; the bonus could take the shape of a monetary payment or a marketable endorsement from the agency. Similar benefits could accrue to LSPs who voluntarily participate in a program to increase transparency and recordkeeping at sites with AULs.

SUMMARY OF LESSONS LEARNED

Despite its success in other areas—namely volume and speed of cleanups completed—the LSP program exhibits several structural flaws if regulatory adherence is a goal. As the above discussion suggests, future initiatives could be altered in several ways to increase interest alignment.

First, the agency should recognize and address conflicts of interest. To limit in-house bias, DEP could promulgate a rule requiring that an LSP cannot render a professional opinion on a site for which she herself drafted the plans. To restrict external conflicts of interest—pressure from clients—DEP should consider switching to a contracting-out arrangement such that clients do not pay LSPs directly. If this change seems too drastic, the agency might also consider increasing its regulation of the contractual relationship between parties and LSPs, perhaps to proscribe fixed-price remediation.

With respect to management, the agency should consider reinstituting its ex ante screening process to retain state capacity and cabin LSP discretion, as well as expanding its monitoring to increase knowledge of slippage and incentives for good behavior. Finally, the agency should seek to expand the disciplinary channels through which DEP, the LSP Board, and the public can address LSPs' underperformance. Among other possibilities, increasing disciplinary opportunities might involve including incentives for achieving background conditions in the licensing agreement.

Conclusion

The Massachusetts LSP program is instructive on two levels. The program itself is a significant and potentially problematic development in state environmental governance. Even accepting the ideological palatability of delegating regulatory decision making to private actors—a premise this chapter does not assess—the program raises concerns. Audits reveal that it has contributed to pervasive departures from promulgated environmental regulations, and many of the regulatory decisions involve high stakes for public health and the environment. As more and more states consider privatizing all or part of their oversight of contaminated property cleanups and admire the expediency and flexibility of the LSP program, they must also consider the program's shortcomings.

On this score, the lesson from Massachusetts seems intuitive: if you give private decision makers broad discretion, pit their interests against those of the government, and offer little chance of getting caught for misconduct, they are likely to deviate from regulatory standards and the public values the regulations represent. Agencies could minimize such slippage through a number of reforms: ex ante screening that places the most sensitive projects under public control, regulations that restrict internal and external conflicts of interest, and mechanisms for monitoring and discipline.

More broadly, the LSP program's difficulties should cause agencies considering privatization—or those facing underperforming private initiatives—to contemplate the wide variety of arrangements through which the private sector might aid in environmental protection. And if regulatory slippage becomes systematic, designers of privatization should return to the drafting table to modify the incentives and relationships that make their program tick.

These interest alignment strategies may be costly. While improving compliance, they may jeopardize the gains of expediency, flexibility, and predictability that privatized decision making offers by reconstructing aspects of hierarchical bureaucratic control—and states may thus face political decisions that require weighing tradeoffs. But attention to design should aid these political decisions by refocusing all-or-nothing, public-versus-private debates and highlighting incremental and hybrid reform possibilities. Because the structure of relationships and authority in a governance system—not merely its public or private packaging—affects performance, careful attention to program redesign may provide a viable middle ground between inaction and complete abandonment of underperforming private initiatives.

CHAPTER FIVE

Outsourcing Power

Privatizing Military Efforts and the Risks to Accountability, Professionalism, and Democracy

MARTHA MINOW

A student asked President George W. Bush what law governs the action of private military contractors in Iraq. President Bush laughed awkwardly and said he would ask Secretary of Defense Donald Rumsfeld.[1] The student expressed disappointment with Secretary Rumsfeld's previous response that contractors employed by the United States would be regulated by domestic Iraqi law, given the low probability of enforcement amid civil disarray. In fact, neither the traditional accountability techniques of public oversight under U.S. law nor private markets adequately govern private contractors working for the U.S. military.

This is not a minor problem. After 9/11 and Katrina, President George W. Bush and the Congress increased overall federal spending from $1.8 trillion to $2.5 trillion between 2000 and 2005.[2] During that period, the fastest-growing part of the discretionary budget involved federal contracts for private-sector goods and services, which grew 86 percent, twice as much as the rest of discretionary spending.[3] By far the largest contributor to this growth in spending was the Department of Defense (DOD), whose contracting budget grew 102.3 percent between 2000 and 2005.[4] In a letter to the House Armed Services Committee on May 4, 2004, Secretary Rumsfeld estimated that the department employed 20,000 private security workers in Iraq, which would make these private workers easily the largest group—larger than the British deployment—working alongside the United States military there.[5] One estimate indicates that 130,000 civilians are working alongside 160,000 personnel from the U.S. military.[6]

This chapter identifies failures of contract enforcement and oversight of the contracting process, and gaps in domestic and international law concerning the conduct of private military contractors. Given escalating military reliance on private contracts, these failures risk undermining the integrity and effectiveness of the military and the interests of society in minimizing financial waste, maximizing military effectiveness, guarding against atrocities, and ensuring a functioning democracy. The most basic elements of public accountability are in jeopardy when actors paid by the government are not governed by anyone but themselves.[7]

Increasing Reliance on Military Contractors

Presidents Bill Clinton and George W. Bush both embraced outsourcing to help downsize the military.[8] Congress adopted caps on the number of civil servants employed by the government—but did not limit the number of persons who could be employed through contracts with private companies.[9] This has allowed policymakers to shield the true size of the government from public view.[10] Government functions subject to outsourcing include not only commercial activities such as transportation, laundry, and food services, but also planning, policy development, managing weapons systems, and managing the military workforce. President Clinton used private contract employees to administer the nuclear nonproliferation agreement with Russia.[11] As armed conflict and war have erupted, these functions have come to include target selection, interrogation, and strategic planning.

The first president with a master's degree in business, George W. Bush turned to private business to downsize government before 9/11 and then to ramp up both the war on terror and, later, disaster relief. When first elected, President Bush identified outsourcing as one of his five top government-wide priorities.[12] Although privatization in the abstract could mean ending government involvement altogether either by selling off public assets or by terminating government funding and involvement in a particular activity, for most federal governmental privatization—and most DOD initiatives—the term simply means reliance on both for-profit and nonprofit nongovernmental actors, paid under publicly funded contracts or vouchers. The U.S. military has pursued this form of outsourcing. The day before 9/11, Secretary Rumsfeld announced an "all out campaign to shift DOD resources from the bureaucracy to the battlefield."[13] He challenged the Pentagon to eliminate any but the core activities of defense and committed to take advantage of the private sector's expertise in management, technology, and business practices.[14]

Thus, well in advance of 9/11, the U.S. military contracted with private corporations—often employing former military personnel[15]—for weapons and technology development, logistical services and planning, and weapons management and servicing.[16] The Pentagon delivered $300 billion worth of contracts to private military industries between 1992 and 2002.[17] The government turned to private individuals to perform core military tasks and to private companies to orchestrate operations.[18] It outsourced security even at Army bases.[19] When national defense demands dramatically increased after 9/11, the Pentagon escalated the use of private military companies, compensating for the downsized military.[20] Private contractors played key roles in the U.S. war in Afghanistan. They served in paramilitary units with the CIA, maintained combat equipment, provided logistical support, and worked on surveillance and targeting; they worked to locate Osama bin Ladin.[21] After 9/11, the military increasingly turned to contractors to pull together information for the military and homeland security.[22]

In advance of the war in Iraq, the Army announced that it would permit contractors to compete for 154,910 civilian jobs—more than half of its civilian workforce—as well as 58,727 military positions.[23] Privatization at the DOD meant buying the time of people who work alongside both Pentagon officials and ground troops. These people do, as Dan Guttmann puts it, "what citizens consider the stuff of government: planning, policy writing, budgeting, intelligence gathering, nation building,"[24] but essentially as temp workers. After research and development and aircraft, the third-largest category for military expenditures on contracted work recently has been for "professional administrative and management support services."[25]

These developments depart from the past because never before have private companies been so intimately and extensively involved in the planning and conduct of day-to-day U.S. military and security activities.[26] Private military companies, as well as mercenaries,[27] have a long lineage,[28] but they have not played such direct or extensive roles in operations, strategy, weapons management, and communications.[29]

Medieval-era private military companies diminished with the rise of the idea that sovereign nation-states alone may legitimately use force.[30] States replaced their multinational armies, composed of soldiers recruited from many places, with the citizen army.[31] By the twentieth century, only those places with legacies of imperialism or temporary shortages of manpower deployed soldiers for hire.[32] These exceptions (such as Saudi Arabia, Libya, Angola, and Nigeria) are global trouble spots.

Private military companies resurged in the 1990s, generating about $100 billion in annual revenues globally.[33] One U.S. company trained the Croat leadership, which then defeated Serb forces in 1995.[34] Companies from the United States, South Africa, and elsewhere now routinely select targets, operate communication systems, gather and interpret intelligence, and provide armed security in combat zones for client countries.[35] The downsizing of major national military efforts after the cold war and apartheid left a supply of individuals with military training who could market their services.[36] Private military companies seemed to offer both former Communist countries and long-standing democracies improved efficiency, reduced costs, and specialized communication and transportation technologies—the roots of privatization. For the potential labor force, private security companies can offer much higher salaries than the national military can.[37]

Potential benefits to society from privatizing the delivery of any government services include innovation and efficiency. Outside the context of military and security operations, nonprofit and religious groups participate alongside for-profit companies in local, state, and federal initiatives, providing social and educational services. Privatization enhances pluralism, produces savings through the in-kind contributions of non–market-oriented players, and, in global operations, generates savings through the use of local workforces.[38] With any private actor doing government work, though, there are risks of fraud, mismanagement, cost overruns—and lack of transparency to the public.[39]

With privatized military services, the scale of the money involved, the sensitivity of the services provided, and the potential interference with military discipline and public review of military action each present benefits and risks distinguishing this from many other fields of government contracting. As a chief benefit, the private companies provide an unusual degree of flexibility. A private company can handpick the team for a given project, and disassemble the team when the job is done or changes. A company can hire and send twenty former colonels, while the U.S. Army would have to "strip more than an entire combat division to muster that many," observed Colonel Bruce Grant of the Institute of National Strategic Studies.[40] This nimbleness is especially difficult for the DOD when it deploys its own civilian employees, who increasingly perform key roles in defense policy, intelligence, acquisitions, and weapons system maintenance.[41] By outsourcing, the military

can obtain the newest technology and the staff trained to maintain it—
and avoid costs of retraining simply by shifting to new teams. With experienced, trained personnel willing to take extraordinary risks, private
security companies may be able to perform work that is crucial to a military initiative.[42]

Yet the enormous scale of private military contracts since 9/11 presents more than the usual problems of supervising contractors and ensuring their effectiveness and efficiency. Federally financed contracts
through the DOD grew from $132.10 billion in 2000 to $268.43 billion in 2005, and contracts through the State Department grew from
$1.23 billion in 2000 to $5.49 billion in 2005.[43] Bypassing accountability that otherwise operates in the military command structure and
military law poses risks to the success of military missions, to the
morale of the military, and to the long-term capacity of the armed
forces. Further risks arise due to the failures of the contracting process
and of oversight, the absence of competitive market checks, and the
gaps in substantive law, law enforcement, and congressional oversight.

Impairments of Contracts, Markets, Military Discipline, and Public Oversight

Bringing private contractors within the rules of engagement governing
military action would be one crucial step in advancing effectiveness and
coordination of action, and proposals to that effect are pending in Congress.[44] Private contractors may commit crimes and frauds; they may
charge too much money and fail to perform tasks they agreed to perform; and they may elude oversight and meanwhile wield large influence
on where public resources are spent and even on foreign policy. For these
risks, there are four potential sources of accountability for outsourced
government action in the United States: the government contracting process and enforcement; a genuinely competitive market; military discipline, including military law, international law, and if these are unavailable, domestic criminal and civil liability; and democratic oversight
through congressional hearings and ultimately elections. These four potential sources of accountability are either absent or impaired in the context of federal contracting with private military companies.

Breakdowns in Granting and Enforcing Contracts
Outsourcing governing tasks and spending public dollars, the government has to guard against hiring people who cannot or will not do the

jobs—and also make sure that the jobs are ones that private actors should do. Because of the urgent situations in Afghanistan, Iraq, and Guantánamo Bay, as the United States quickly launched invasions and captured enemies, Congress permitted departures for defense and homeland security from established procurement procedures.[45] But the government lacked the capacity or commitment to oversee and manage the contracts and perhaps even to set the benchmarks for the government work.[46] Financial and conduct abuses followed.[47]

The Halliburton Company, a Houston-based oil services firm previously headed by Vice President Dick Cheney, received the two largest contracts in Iraq. Halliburton received the contract to manage the logistical planning for the Iraq war, without competitive bidding.[48] One participant reported that "[i]n my 12 years doing government proposals, I had never seen anything as arrogant, as egregious as the ways in which Pentagon officials, in particular Corps of Engineers contracting staff at the Fort Worth district, treated the bidders, how they ignored our federal laws and regulations and the procedures that I still believe normally ensure fair play."[49]

Under one $6.5 billion contract, Halliburton was to provide the troops with housing, food, laundry, and other services; it promptly reported a 62 percent jump in revenues.[50] Its additional contract governed reconstruction plans with $2.5 billion to restore the oil infrastructure.[51] The contracts guaranteed the company a profit while passing on all expenses to the government.[52] Exposing cost overruns or fraud,[53] congressional and media sources reported that Halliburton overcharged $61 million worth of gasoline and $186 million for meals not actually served.[54] Halliburton could not later account for an estimated 43 percent of its billing.[55] In 2006, the Army decided not to renew a major exclusive contract with Halliburton to provide logistical support to the U.S. military.[56] The Inspector General at the DOD found that contracting officials failed to develop adequate surveillance plans on 87 percent of the contracts under review and did not document the performance of the contractors in 43 percent of the reviewed contracts.[57] The Policy Administrator of the Office of Federal Procurement observed as she left office in September 2003, "There is still not a lot of oversight in some areas of our contracting system, and I think it will haunt us."[58]

Even more than financial mismanagement, what will haunt Americans for decades to come are the shocking digital photographs of cruel and abusive practices used at the U.S.–run prison at Abu Ghraib in

Iraq.[59] Investigative reports into the abuses at the Abu Ghraib prison identify poorly supervised private contractors as one cause.[60] Civilian interpreters and interrogators working for CACI International, Inc., and Titan Corporation in conjunction with military officers were either directly or indirectly responsible for the abuses at Abu Ghraib.[61] The lack of clear command structures and the absence of contracting authorities in charge each contributed to the disastrous conduct by the contract employees.

The contracts involved in the Abu Ghraib abuses bypassed standard contracting procedures.[62] Agencies can now streamline the usual purchasing processes by paying a fee to a program manager in another agency, which then can select a favored contractor without competitive bids.[63] This shortcut is still supposed to protect against conflicting interests between procurement and management, but a new conflicting interest arises with fee seeking by external agencies. The Inspector General for the Department of the Interior concluded that chasing fees distorted the judgment of procurement officials of the Department of the Interior and the General Services Administration, who neglected to maintain actual records of the contracts, devise content for them, or monitor them.[64]

Many DOD contracts lack on-site monitors and neglect to work out lines of authority.[65] At the Abu Ghraib prison, military personnel did not receive guidance about how to use contracted personnel and knew neither the terms of the contracts nor their procedures.[66] This lack of clarity about contract workers and military is not anomalous.[67] The Government Accountability Office (then the Government Accounting Office) (GAO) found the same problem in the Balkans in 2000. Military officers were confused about whether they could control the actions of contractors, and the government proved unable to control contract costs.[68]

The contract enforcement failures at the DOD are pervasive and basic.[69] Its financial management and related business operations, when reviewed by the GAO, show persistent fundamental failures that produce waste, provide inadequate accountability, and threaten its mission.[70] The GAO found that contractors received inadequate oversight because the military lacked sufficient staff.[71] In 2004, the GAO concluded that fundamental flaws in the DOD's business systems damaged the agency's effectiveness, and contributed to fraud, waste, and abuse.[72] Yet the government rarely suspends contractors, even for misconduct, overcharging, and other violations.[73] The GAO documented year-long

... $_{j}$ security clearances for contractor employees (indi-
... mi... services failed to respect the security clearances granted
... other ...e),[74] poor assessment of the use of small businesses in
... pr...cess,[75] and millions of dollars to adjust mistaken
...   ...neglected best management practices, like ana-
...   ...s to enable savings,[77] and repeatedly failed to
... actors accountable for failures under their Iraq con-
...   ...ector General for Iraq Reconstruction reported ... ... National (a business unit of Bechtel Corporation)
met fewer than half of the objectives in its $1.8 billion reconstruction
contract—and assigned blame to the government for failing to oversee
the contract.[79] The Office of the Inspector General issued a 2004 report
on the Coalition Provisional Authority contracts in Iraq, and found not
only missing and incomplete records, but an ineffective system for contract review, tracking, and monitoring.[80]

The pervasive incapacity of any government agency to monitor and
enforce agreements with private contractors in the context of security,
reconstruction, and other activities in Afghanistan and Iraq is well established. An Army investigatory commission discovered an increase in
workload of over 600 percent for contracting personnel with an apparently declining number of in-house contracting staff—but also reported
that it could not obtain consistent data on military and civilian contracting personnel.[81]

Perhaps recognizing its own limited capacity,[82] the DOD regularly
outsources the task of monitoring other private contracts.[83] In the Iraq
war, the DOD has turned the process of contracting out over to private
companies—resulting in multiple layers of contracting and subcontracting. At a congressional hearing about Halliburton cost overruns
and inefficiencies, Halliburton employee Marie DeYoung (a former
Army captain) testified that with several layers of subcontractors,
"[w]e, essentially, lost control of the project and paid between four and
nine times what we needed to in order to fund that project."[84] Maintaining sufficient control over outsourcing should be an inherently governmental function that, by law, should not be outsourced.[85] The
House of Representatives passed legislation to reform government contracting in March 2007 that would limit the length of noncompetitive
contracts, require justifications of no-bid contracts, and disclosure of
overcharges,[86] and the Senate passed a related bill.[87] But how this law
will emerge, and whether it will produce any more enforcement than
prior efforts, remains to be seen.

Market Failure

Privatization supposedly brings market discipline to government. This makes sense for laundry services and meals, where competitive private markets already exist. Competition is difficult or impossible, however, for products and activities—like weapons systems and target selection—that have no private market analogue.[88] When the government is the sole purchaser, a handful of contractors dominating the field often enjoys power that undermines market efficiency and contractual accountability. The government finds it difficult to bar or suspend a major contractor or even to get contractors to perform and document their costs.[89] With neither competitive market discipline nor effective government oversight, government contracts with private military corporations evade accountability.[90] With oversight itself outsourced during the Afghanistan and Iraq conflicts and reconstructions, costs and expenses grew out of control. Suitcases of cash full of the public's money disappeared. Any market-based checks on prices and performance that might be relevant to outsourcing in other contexts have no relevance here.

Interference with Military Discipline and Legal Confusion

Military training, unit discipline, the Uniform Code of Military Justice,[91] and international legal standards governing war and armed conflicts ensure accountability for the military, but not for private corporations and their employees engaged in military work. Serious questions have been raised about whether Congress can use its oversight of the military on private contractors.[92] And difficult issues about what source of law even applies to private contractors have rendered ambiguous the relevant standards of conduct and relevant enforcement mechanisms, potentially jeopardizing the success of military missions as well as domestic, military, and international norms.

Potential legal frameworks for private security forces working abroad alongside the U.S. military include: (1) domestic civilian criminal law—if it applies extraterritorially; (2) the law of the nation, such as Iraq, where the contractors do their work; and (3) the Uniform Code of Military Justice, which governs the conduct of soldiers including their clothing and respect toward commanding officers.[93] In the first category, Congress enacted the Military Extraterritorial Jurisdiction Act to authorize domestic prosecutions of contractors under domestic criminal law for offenses occurring while they are deployed abroad, but its scope is confined to conduct that would be considered a felony in the

United States.[94] The law emerged after U.S. military and Bosnian law enforcers discovered that they lacked authority to prosecute employees of a private military company for sex trafficking while working in Bosnia.[95] That company was DynCorp International, currently under contract with the U.S. military to train the Iraqi police.[96] Through the prostitution ring, employees of DynCorp "purchased" young women and children to serve as their sexual slaves.[97] Once the practice was exposed, the company fired the individuals involved—but there were no prosecutions for statutory rape, human trafficking, or anything under military, Bosnian, or U.S. law.[98] While members of the military can face swift courts-martial,[99] civilian contractors fall outside that authority and elude any domestic legal system.

The Military Extraterritorial Jurisdiction Act was meant to close these gaps, yet its procedures and scope have been unclear from the start.[100] Some concluded that it did not apply to civilians who do not work directly for the government.[101] As exposed by investigation into a shooting by Blackwater personnel who apparently killed eleven Iraqis while the company's employees traveled with an American diplomatic convoy in Baghdad, the Act seemed not to cover private security contractors supporting State Department officials rather than working for the DOD.[102] The House of Representatives introduced specific legislation in 2007 to extend the Act to apply to contractors "supporting the mission" of the DOD,[103] though some observers believe that this interpretation was already available given earlier reforms.[104] Even if fully applicable, actual enforcement of the law remains a problem; who precisely will pursue the prosecutions, with what incentives, and at what cost? And its effect in strengthening the authority of military commanders over the conduct of contractors is at best unclear, and potentially nonexistent. The law provides for after-the-fact criminal sanctions for acts that would be felonies if committed in the United States; it requires decisions by prosecutors, judges, or juries, and operates as a sanction remote from and after the fact of felonious conduct. Hence, the law offers military commanders and civilian supervisors only indirect and limited control. Misdemeanors, poor performance, or failure to coordinate with military authority remain beyond its scope.

The law of Iraq, or another nation where the contractors do their work, could conceivably apply to contractor conduct that breaches criminal or civil norms, but the legal systems of a region in conflict usually lack the capacity to proceed with ordinary business, much less reach noncitizens who work for the United States. Moreover, U.S. officials often create special immunities for private contractors working for them. In 2004, L. Paul Bremer, acting as the administrator for the U.S. Coalition Provisional Authority in Iraq, issued "Order 17," which exempts security companies and their employees from accountability under Iraqi law for deaths and injuries caused while performing their duties.[105] This in effect immunized civilian contractors from responsibility under both U.S. law and Iraqi law. Several years passed without alteration in this order, even though in 2005 Congress directed the military to bring contractors accompanying an armed force even without a declared war within the scope of the Uniform Code of Military Justice,[106] and thus to subject them to military discipline. Even with congressional action, security contractors may remain immune from sanction under the military's own code;[107] it was this immunity from accountability under domestic civilian law and military law that became the target of international scrutiny after Blackwater was accused of killing Iraqi civilians.[108] Ironically, the outrage over the incident seemed to unite the otherwise divided factions within Iraq's political sphere in efforts to curtail the immunity and reassert legal authority.[109]

Congress took steps to bring contractors working in the Iraq war zone within the jurisdiction of American criminal law,[110] and in 2007 it finally explicitly extended the Code of Military Justice to encompass civilian contractors accompanying the military even in a contingency operation rather than a declared war.[111] As an alternative to extending U.S. law extraterritorially or relying on the law of the host country, this extension of military justice to civilian contractors appeals to many observers, but it raises its own issues.[112] First, it is not clear that Congress has the authority to subject civilians to military discipline.[113] Even if constitutional, the overlap with U.S. criminal law raises questions of double jeopardy and coordination between the two systems. Third, application of the Uniform Code of Military Justice to civilian contractors awaits answers to basic questions about the scope and responsibility for implementation: who would be responsible to carry out the prosecution of civilian contractors, and will capacity to prosecute ever really be used? Would offenses pertaining to military honor and command structure apply to contractors as well?[114] And many note that even preexisting U.S. laws would be sufficient to hold contractors accountable—but the country lacks the political and expert will necessary to pursue prosecutions within either the military system or the civilian justice system.[115]

Military lawyers have worried for a decade about what law applies to contractors working in military settings.[116] Even with the recent legal changes, contract employees are not governed by unit discipline; unlike government actors, they are not regulated by civilian statutes such as the Freedom of Information Act (FOIA).[117] Ambiguities remain over what law applies if contract employees are captured or injured by the enemy,[118] and whether they have the legal authority or actual competence to defend themselves with force.[119] Nor is it clear whether they are liable under American tort law for conduct occurring abroad.[120]

If they operate outside of military command, contractors may work at cross-purposes from military strategy. Retired Army officer and analyst Ralph Peters stated in an e-mail to contracting expert Peter Singer: "Armed contracts *do* harm [counterinsurgency] efforts. Just ask the troops."[121] When private security contractors have the protection of State Department officials as their priority, they may engage in behavior that conflicts with military operations, including efforts to build better relations with local residents. Proceeding with their own agendas, under their own leaders, contractors may literally collide with military initiatives, and no coherent coordination of information and personnel yet exists to bridge the contractor-military divide.

The GAO reported confusion by Army officers over whether they could control the actions of contractors in the Balkans in 2000.[122] Ground commanders often lack basic information about the number of contractors located nearby, or their movements and engagements. Commanders may not even be authorized to examine the contracts to determine the intended tasks. Individual employees typically are responsible to their employers, not to the military command structure. A key Abu Ghraib report concluded that a properly trained contracting officer's representative must be on site to prevent a recurrence of that situation.[123] Even if the lines of authority clearly locate the civilian contractor employees under military command, these civilians do not face the same rewards and sanctions as do the members of the military, including military culture and command structure.[124]

As one former soldier working in private security in Iraq wrote in a note to a reporter, "Being motivated, and also somehow restrained, by the trappings of history, and by being part of something large, collective, and, one hopes, right" characterizes the military experience, but "being a security contractor strips much of this sociological and political upholstery away, and replaces it with cash."[125]

International law might seem to offer norms even where U.S. law is inadequate. For example, the Third Geneva Convention would seem to cover combatants who are civilians if they are under the command of a superior, wear distinctive fixed signs recognizable at a distance, carry arms openly, and conduct themselves in accord with the laws of armed conflict, although each of these elements may be ambiguous in the case of particular contract employees.[126] Civilian contract workers may, however, be viewed as unlawful combatants.[127] Protocol I to the Geneva Convention deprives mercenaries of lawful combatant status and prisoner-of-war immunity upon capture.[128] Civilian contractors thus may elude military discipline, U.S. law, and the law of the host nation, and may fall outside the categories used in international law. And even with patches to these gaps in the law, the political will and institutional capacity to discipline civilian contractors in war zones have yet to be well developed.

Democratic Oversight

Political will is perhaps even more severely lacking when it comes to congressional oversight of the contracting process and the conduct of civilian contractors in the context of military action. Even if the issue rises to the top of the agenda for some members of Congress, Congress has only partial authority; it lacks the power to review all actions and practices of private military contractors. Media, ordinary citizens, and competitors are hampered without disclosure and public oversight. Private firms disclose some activities in promoting their services, but they can resist media and congressional inquiries by claiming protection for proprietary information.[129] Private companies are free from the disclosure obligations placed on the government by FOIA, meant to ensure public access to all government information compatible with security.[130] Private companies can even stop the government from disclosing information they have shared with the government in the course of doing business together.[131]

Courts have construed FOIA to exempt private contractor records compiled for law enforcement purposes from disclosure.[132] Combining the Trade Secrets Act and FOIA exemptions for trade secrets and confidential commercial or financial information, the judiciary has rejected the release of prices paid by the government for servicing planes to be flown by military personnel on dangerous missions.[133]

Although private contractors are doing the military's work, they often evade legal and political oversight.[134] This puts abusive or incompetent behavior beyond democratic review. Moreover, "the use of private contractors also hides the true costs of war. Their dead aren't added to official body counts."[135] An estimated thirty to forty private contractor employees were killed fighting in Iraq in 2004, and many more were killed in accidents, notably increasing the total casualties and injuries over those estimated in public reports.[136]

Use of contractors contributes to lack of transparency about the total numbers of people deployed and the total scale of the government-sponsored effort.[137] The scale is outside of public awareness and democratic choice.[138] Even information about procurement decisions and practices has been privatized, rendering them further out of public reach.[139] Bypassing public debate may make it easier for the government to plan and launch either an aggressive war or a humanitarian intervention—or to purchase and veil abusive interrogation techniques.

Jeopardy to Society's Interests

Due to impairments of legal and political oversight and defective private markets, the escalating use of private military contractors by the U.S. government poses serious jeopardy to the integrity and effectiveness of the military and to the interests of society. These interests include minimizing financial waste, maximizing military effectiveness, guarding against atrocities, and ensuring a functioning democracy.

Sheer Cost, Inefficiency, and Corruption

Waste and fraud accompany contracts awarded without competition.[140] The form of some government contracts makes cost management difficult. Cost plus contracts, common with private military companies, ensure that the government absorbs all costs incurred, exposing the government to potentially limitless payments.[141] Questionable accounting practices appear even with government contracts intended to produce savings.[142] Waste, mismanagement, and fraud in government contracts extend to Department of Homeland Security and Hurricane Katrina responses, and indicate pervasive incompetence or indifference about protecting taxpayer dollars.[143]

But the problems with military contractors are unique. Private contractors can exploit the chaos and fear of wartime. War profiteering, a concern even of the nation's founders,[144] diverts the money raised by taxes to private hands through overcharging and fraud.[145] It also jeopardizes peacemaking and broader confidence in government. Private contractors get away with cronyism and corruption.[146]

Risks to Integrity and Effectiveness of the Military

The military can be harmed if the option of retiring to a new career with a better-paying private contractor appeals to talented officers. An officer who retires continues to receive 50 percent of his or her salary in retirement benefits. If rehired by a private contractor and paid any more than 50 percent of that salary, the officer essentially gets a bonus for performing the same job.[147] Reenlistment bonuses cannot rival the cash offered by the private companies.[148] As one account reported, "Army Gen. David H. Petraeus, the top U.S. commander in Baghdad overseeing more than 160,000 U.S. troops, makes roughly $180,000 a year, or about $493 a day. That comes out to less than half the fee charged by Blackwater for its senior manager of a 34-man security team."[149]

Reliance on private sources for advanced technological weapons and logistics relieves the military from developing those capacities internally—to the long-term detriment of military strength.[150] Depending upon contracts for leasing trucks and equipment without ensuring appropriate maintenance plans can leave the military vulnerable to failures beyond its control.[151] If the contractor in turn does not pay subcontractors—as was the case apparently with Halliburton—vendors may grow resentful, collapse under bankruptcy, or halt performance, putting troops in jeopardy.[152]

The military also may compromise its strength by subcontracting with people it would never use directly, or who are paid little and shift loyalties on the basis of who pays them[153]—the mercenary problem.[154] During the Gulf War, illustrating Machiavelli's warning[155] that soldiers working for pay would not take crucial risks, some contractors fled from a possible chemical weapons attack.[156] Perhaps if the contractors build a team of retired military officers, the ethos of loyalty to the country and the military can be sustained even among these civilian employees.[157] Yet Machiavelli's warnings become relevant, especially when low-paid employees are brought in from third countries under subcontracts.[158]

Risks of Atrocity

Falling outside of military culture and discipline and having unclear status under international law, private contractors may commit abuses. Abuses are a predictable risk during any armed conflict, but the training and command structure of the military are more aligned to reducing that risk than is the set of economic incentives guiding private-contractor employees and companies. Some of the people drawn to private security may aspire to a kind of daredevil behavior that mimics violent movies more than military discipline.[159] Moreover, individuals offering security and combat services for pay may not have the proper training, sound incentives, or psychological profile to guard against wartime atrocity.[160] One contract employee turned out to be a fugitive charged with embezzlement and previously convicted of assault in the United States.[161] One American general personally tracked at least a dozen shootings of civilians by private security employees in Iraq over a three-month period in 2005.[162] In *Fiasco: The American Military Adventure in Iraq*, Thomas E. Ricks describes an incident in which Marine Colonel T.X. Hammes found himself staring down the barrel of a private contractor's weapon—just four pounds of trigger pressure away from eternity—after the contractor's group forced Hammes off the road because they thought he looked suspicious.[163] Ricks provides Hammes's account of the incident: " 'Fundamentally, the bodyguards' mission differed from that of the U.S. military,' noted Hammes. 'The contractor was hired to protect the principal. He had no stake in pacifying the country. Therefore, they often ran Iraqis off the roads, reconned by fire, and generally treated locals as expendable.' Yet Iraqis saw them as acting under American authority. 'You have loosed an unaccountable, deadly force into their society, and they have no recourse.' "[164] Without the discipline and internal monitoring of professional military or civilian oversight, contractors lack crucial restraints against abuses.[165]

As noted above, investigation of Abu Ghraib abuses revealed that private contractor employees "wandered about with too much under supervised free access in the detainee area."[166] The situation in Abu Ghraib, we can hope, was anomalous in many respects. But it exposed the threat to the command structure and security present when personnel working together include both military and private contract employees. In Iraq, the government has lost control under layers of contracting and subcontracting,[167] and confused lines of authority and accountability. It remains to be seen whether the extension of the Military Code of Justice to contractors will alter the widespread perception that private contractors operate under different rules, and evade military law, discipline, and the peer solidarity, culture, and sense of patriotic duty that have been key to military effectiveness.[168] Working side by side or in neighboring deployments, private security forces and military personnel can be rivals and mutual critics rather than a coordinated force.[169]

Risks to the Civilian Employees

When the military employs civilians to attack enemy computer networks with viruses or to operate and maintain remote-controlled unmanned aircraft, it blurs the line between civilians and military. This potentially makes the contractors fair military targets, jeopardizing other civilians, especially if the contractors are positioned far from combat.[170] The Iraqis do not distinguish between civilian contractors and the military in judging the conduct of the U.S. occupation.[171]

The Department of Defense reports that 3,672 members of the U.S. military died in Iraq between March 2003 and August 2007, but it does not keep data on the injuries and deaths of private contractors. Although data on mortally wounded civilian contract employees in Iraq are not publicly available, estimates indicate 1,000 fatalities among civilian contractors.[172] Private employers must require medical insurance for workers in a war zone, but many lack treatment, especially for mental health issues particularly once they return from the war zone.[173] The contract employees face health problems without the supports accorded to military veterans.

Risks to Democracy

The lack of transparency and public oversight accompanying private military contracts offers some potential benefits to government officials that are simultaneous harms to democracy. Precisely because their services are bought, private military contractors allow public officials to avoid instituting a draft. Officials may also take advantage of the private status of the companies and their employees to avoid disclosing and reporting details, such as troop and casualty numbers.[174] The uses of authority over those in a position to blow the whistle on misconduct and abuse in the military contract domain also jeopardize even this avenue for disclosure and political responsiveness.[175]

Democracy can be hampered in another way as the private military companies influence the political process. Revenues from government contracts feed into lobbying. Iraq contractors DynCorp, Bechtel, and Halliburton donated more than $2.2 million to political causes—mainly Republican—between 1999 and 2002, according to the Center for Responsive Politics.[176] Lobbying efforts by private contractors demonstrably affect weapons policies. Political scientists have documented the correlation between defense spending and domestic political goals.[177]

By using private contractors, the government can avoid the democratic system's checks and balances[178] on foreign policy.[179] The government can pursue end runs around legal duties; apparently, the United States used private contractors to transport terrorism suspects to countries where torture is a known practice.[180] The government can even license a private military company to assist another government—while the United States itself can deny involvement.[181]

Conclusion

Massive outsourcing has drawn civilian contractors into military work without cost controls or assurance of contractual compliance. Investigation of military abuses has exposed poor coordination between private contractors and military personnel. Private contractors can jeopardize civilian safety and democratic accountability. These risks could be inevitable effects when military tasks are outsourced, but they could instead result from incompetence and poor implementation. Which explanation fits the waste, mistakes, and abuses arising with the Department of Defense and the State Department's massive reliance on private contractors in Iraq? An initial test of the alternative explanations could come with the adoption of reform proposals to require private security firms to disclose costs, training, insurance, compensation, and casualties.[182] As noted by Congressman David Price, who introduced the bill, requiring accountability by private contractors is not anti contracting.[183] The extraordinary scale of recent military outsourcing, far outstripping government oversight and planning capacities, makes many dangers entirely foreseeable. Unless measures of accountability commensurate with the risks are implemented, the massive outsourcing of military tasks puts citizens, the military, and the democracy at unacceptable risk.[184]

CHAPTER SIX

How Privatization Thinks

The Case of Prisons

SHARON DOLOVICH

> Institutions create shadowed places in which nothing
> can be seen and no questions asked. They make other
> areas show finely discriminated detail, which is closely
> scrutinized and ordered.
>
> —MARY DOUGLAS, *HOW INSTITUTIONS THINK*

Debates over contracting out government functions to private, for-profit entities often play out within a deliberative framework that can be thought of as "comparative efficiency."[1] From this perspective, the decision whether to privatize any given government function turns on which sector, public or private, would perform the relevant function more efficiently. Comparative efficiency thus has two defining features. First, it views the motivating question as a choice between public and private. Second, it assumes efficiency to be the sole value guiding the analysis.

That comparative efficiency is the appropriate way to approach the issue of privatization tends to be taken for granted. Comparative efficiency, after all, takes no position as to the functions the state ought to perform. It simply holds that whatever tasks the state undertakes should be performed as efficiently as possible. And if fulfilling a chosen aim is good, how could fulfilling it more efficiently not be better?

By remaining agnostic as to which needs society ought to seek to satisfy, comparative efficiency seems to have the virtue of value neutrality. As I show below with the example of private prisons, however, comparative efficiency is not value neutral, nor does the existence of the privatization option make the adoption of this framework inevitable. Why, then, does the perspective of comparative efficiency continue to dominate the privatization debate? The answer, I suggest, is that comparative efficiency operates as a rhetorical device that keeps the debate within particular bounds, excluding some concerns altogether and reframing others in ways consistent with its own priorities.[2]

This process is clearly discernable in the debate over private prisons.[3] In this debate, the persistent focus is on comparing the performance of private prisons with their public counterparts in terms of their relative efficiency. This comparative focus, however, obscures troubling features common to public and private facilities alike, including the imposition of gratuitous inhumane punishment, indifference to the risk of imposing unjustifiably long sentences, and the distorting effects of financial interests on prison policy. Moreover, the exclusive concern with the value of efficiency shapes the inquiry to crowd consideration of all other normative implications of incarcerating convicted offenders out of the picture.

In this chapter, I explore the mechanisms through which the "thought style"[4] of comparative efficiency achieves these effects in the private prisons context. Doing so helps explain why critics concerned with the normative implications of privatization have had so little success in influencing, much less defining, the terms of the private prisons debate. I do not attempt to make the empirical case for this lack of success; the minimal traction broader normative concerns have had in this context will be familiar to anyone who has tried—whether in print or in conversation—to introduce issues of justice or legitimacy or any other considerations bearing on the state's obligations to the incarcerated into discussion about private prisons. True, debate over broad-based penal reform itself may be carried out in overtly normative terms. But the more focused debate over private prisons has somehow remained impervious to such considerations, as has the more general discourse regarding prison administration, such that the priorities of comparative efficiency have come to exert a sort of gravitational pull over the thinking of those whose job it is to run the prisons.[5] In this deliberative climate, virtually all policy challenges prison administrators face are likely to be framed in comparative efficiency terms—even those challenges that arguably call out for more explicitly normative analysis.

Readers already steeped in the privatization literature may wonder at yet another treatment of private prisons.[6] Isn't everything to be said on that topic already in print?[7] And given the many as-yet-unanswered questions posed by the nature and extent of privatization in the twenty-first century, wouldn't we be better served spending less time on the special case of private prisons and focusing instead on issues relevant to the main run of privatized governmental functions?

In fact, the topic of this chapter—why the debate over private prisons takes the particular shape it does—is as yet unexplored in the literature.

But my main purpose is to use this example to illustrate a phenomenon with applicability to privatization in general, namely how ways of thinking about matters of policy can shape the collective understanding of what is at stake and limit our capacity to question or transcend that collective understanding, and can even have tangible effects on the world quite independent of what the individuals employing these ways of thinking might intend or prefer or even realize.

In what follows, I offer an account of the rhetorical effects of comparative efficiency with the aim of explaining its dominance over, and effects on, the private prisons debate. I then consider the interests and values served by the ways comparative efficiency structures this debate, and argue that it is the project of privatization itself that is the beneficiary.

The Insistence on Comparison

From the perspective of comparative efficiency, the sole issue in the private prisons debate is whether responsibility for incarceration should remain in public hands or be privatized. Comparative efficiency, in other words, wants only to know which is better, public or private. But framing the issue this way can lead us to miss altogether the more likely possibility that neither alternative is satisfactory or even adequate. Instead, what is most urgently needed may not be a change in the existing management structure, but meaningful reform of the prison system in general.

The problem arises as follows. Comparative efficiency frames the issue solely as a choice between public and private. What matters most are thus the *differences* between these two management forms. Similarities, in contrast, tell us nothing about the relative merits of one over the other, and thus offer no grounds for choosing between them. Similarities therefore fade or recede into the background on a comparative efficiency analysis, even when their content ought to be of great moral concern. It can thus be hard to see that the most troubling features of our penal institutions may be those that public and private have in common.

Consider, for example, levels of violence. Prisons and jails across America, public and private alike, are violent places.[8] That this is so ought arguably to prompt policymakers to conduct a systemwide examination of the causes of violence in order to combat them. Yet, for comparative efficiency, prison violence is relevant only if there are appreciable differences between the levels of violence in private as opposed to public prisons. Should no such differences exist, levels of violence will offer no basis for choosing between public and private, and would therefore be viewed as irrelevant.

Absurd as it sounds, this process of dismissing as irrelevant even the most disturbing features of public and private prisons is standard fare in the private prisons debate. Horror stories about violence or serious deprivation and neglect in private prisons, evidence that there are aspects of this carceral form that ought to give us pause, are matched by equally horrific stories of violence, deprivation, or neglect in *public* prisons. This response, however, is not offered to confirm that there are serious problems with prisons across the board, but as a way to neutralize the concern, to demonstrate its ultimate irrelevance to the discussion. If the relevance of prison violence is acknowledged at all, it is only to the extent that one system can be shown to be worse than the other. Discussions of private prisons can thus devolve into contests over which system can be charged with a worse litany of suffering and abuse, in order that one alternative may emerge as the marginally more palatable.

Other disturbing features common to both penal forms are likewise sidelined in the private prisons debate. For example, some commentators have expressed concern over the fact that private prison providers have a financial interest in increased incarceration and that industry members might therefore be tempted to use their political influence (which is often considerable)[9] to press for harsher sentencing policies regardless of whether increased punishments are warranted.[10] This concern is generally met with the response that the formulation of criminal justice policy is *already* subject to influence by a number of interest groups with a financial interest in increased incarceration regardless of what legitimate punishment requires[11]—groups that include correctional officers' unions,[12] purveyors of goods and services to prisons and prisoners,[13] and even voters in rural communities for whom prisons are a source of community economic development.[14] The point of this response is not that the worry is unfounded as regards private prisons, nor that it is not of serious concern that sentencing policy may be driven by the economic interests of the politically influential. It is simply that, if this danger is in fact created by the state's use of private prisons, it is not *unique* to private prisons, and is thus irrelevant to the privatization discussion.

Or, to take one final example, consider the possibly worrisome effects of the profit motive in the prison context. Private prison contractors receive a set payment per inmate per day, and profit only when they spend less than this amount to run the facility. At the same time, if the state is to cut costs through privatization—the promise of private prisons—the contract price must *already* be less than the total cost the state would otherwise incur in operating the facility. If they are to make any profit, therefore, private prisons must be run for considerably less than the state would otherwise spend. Some observers have consequently expressed the concern that contractors will be tempted to cut corners in ways that cause harm to inmates. What tends to follow expression of this concern, however, is not investigation into whether this combination of factors does in fact generate abusive practices, but rather the observation that public prison officials too are under pressure to cut costs, and at times may also do so at the expense of inmates' health, safety, and well-being.[15] Again, the response does not deny the force of the concern, but waves it away as besides the point.

There is, of course, a different conclusion one could draw from exchanges of this sort. Perhaps the value in focusing on private prisons is not the promise of greater efficiency, but rather that they help us see in a fresh light troubling aspects of the penal system in general that are currently taken for granted. Thus, highlighting the violence in private prisons[16] might prompt us to acknowledge the extent of the violence in the penal system in general. Or recognizing the worrying possibility that private prison providers might be tempted to lobby for stiffer sentences in order to expand their business possibilities may lead us to notice that the development of sentencing policy is *already* prone to be shaped by parties who benefit financially from increased incarceration. Or exposing the incentives private contractors face to cut costs even at the expense of basic inmate needs might suggest the dangers that arise *whenever* prison administrators are pressured to prioritize their bottom lines. Comparative efficiency, however, is premised on a view of public and private as fundamentally distinct. There is thus no room in a debate framed on its terms for the possibility that public prisons and private prisons might create the same dangers.

As it is, comparative efficiency uncritically accepts the current state of incarceration in the public system as the baseline against which private prisons should be measured. That present conditions in public prisons and jails are wholly inconsistent with the realization of important public values and thus represent an inadequate standard against which to judge policy alternatives is never considered.

That comparative efficiency structures the analysis in this way calls into question a claim that is sometimes made in the context of private prisons:[17] that privatization offers the possibility for broad innovation, for radically rethinking how we approach the practice of incarceration.[18] In fact, the motivating question for comparative efficiency is not what approach to incarceration offers the healthiest, most promising, or most normatively defensible approach to imprisoning convicted offenders—a question that might drive an approach focused on meaningful innovation. It is instead whether, given how we as a society already incarcerate, private prison providers could save states money by doing essentially the same thing for less.[19]

Whether the same is true in the other contexts in which privatization is contemplated is an open question. But it is certainly true in the case of prisons. When policymakers discussing the privatization option ask the hallmark question of comparative efficiency—whether private providers "can do it cheaper than the state"[20]—they have a very particular "it" in mind: what the state is already doing in this area. The presumption is that we already know what we want to do. The only question is whether it can be done more efficiently if it is done by private actors.

Adopting the perspective of comparative efficiency is thus at odds with the possibility of true reform. Comparative efficiency is solely about increasing government efficiency by challenging public institutions to conduct themselves more like private actors or risk being replaced by private actors. By introducing state bureaucracies to competition, comparative efficiency aims to bring the logic of the market to the public sphere. And where the privatization question is framed in comparative efficiency terms, it can make it hard even to recognize the need for reform of existing penal practices, much less to move the debate over how to run the prisons onto a more explicitly normative plane.

Recognizing these effects suggests that, however natural and obvious comparative efficiency may seem as an approach to privatization, it is in fact bound up with a particular normative vision, one on which the public sphere is viewed primarily as a site of exchange where citizens qua taxpayers seek to maximize the return on their investment. The broad acceptance of this market-driven vision is integral to the possibility of privatization. As the next section demonstrates, its hold is only further reinforced by the nature of comparative efficiency's exclusive focus on the value of efficiency.

The Exclusive Focus on Efficiency

EFFICIENCY AS COST-BENEFIT CALCULUS

Comparative efficiency is exclusively concerned with maximizing efficiency. It assumes that, if the private sector can perform a task more efficiently than the public sector, there is no reason not to privatize. Arguably, in many contexts where privatization is contemplated, there are other values at stake that merit more focused attention than efficiency. Yet where the perspective of comparative efficiency dominates the debate, it can be hard to recognize these other values, much less take adequate account of them in any policy deliberation.

The prison example effectively illustrates this effect. Certainly, efficiency is a necessary and appropriate consideration for those officials running the prisons. Incarceration is expensive, and the more efficiently it can be achieved, the more taxpayer money may be freed up for satisfying other public needs. But ensuring efficient prisons is hardly the only or even the most urgent consideration raised by the incarceration of convicted offenders. Incarceration is among the most severe and intrusive manifestations of power the state exercises against its own citizens. When the state incarcerates, it strips offenders of their liberty and dignity and consigns them for extended periods to conditions of severe regimentation and physical vulnerability. Such an act implicates any number of values—legitimacy, humanity, dignity, respect, justice, and fairness among them—that are distinct from and arguably more pressing than a prison system's relative efficiency. When viewing the penal system from the perspective of comparative efficiency, however, these other concerns necessarily become subordinated, if they are considered at all.

The deeply normative implications of the act of imprisonment suggest that penal policy, if it is to be consistent with the state's obligations to those it incarcerates, must be designed with those obligations in mind. Elsewhere, I have argued that two principles in particular capture these obligations in the penal context: the *humanity principle,* which obliges the state to avoid imposing punishments that are gratuitously inhumane, and the *parsimony principle,* which obliges the states to avoid imposing punishments of incarceration that are gratuitously long.[21] In each case, gratuitous punishment is that which cannot be justified to all members of society under fair deliberative conditions.[22] Although this conception of legitimate punishment may not be universally shared, it does represent an understanding of the moral obligations, grounded in the foundational values of liberal democratic society, that bind such a society when it decides to incarcerate convicted offenders.[23] And if penal policy is to be consistent with these values, it is the requirements of these values, and not those of efficiency maximization, that ought to drive the policymaking process.

To some, the opposition just suggested between a commitment to honoring moral values and the goal of maximizing efficiency may seem to misunderstand the concept of efficiency. In any system of limited resources, it might be argued, no policy alternatives will fully satisfy all relevant values or yield a perfect result.[24] The best possible outcome is therefore that which most increases social welfare or overall well-being.[25] And understood in these terms, efficiency is not *opposed* to the realization of society's moral obligations. To the contrary, to the extent that honoring these obligations is properly understood as a component of society's welfare, an analysis geared toward the most efficient outcome will necessarily *include* them in any ultimate weighing of the costs and benefits of a given policy alternative.

This, of course, is the basic idea behind cost-benefit analysis.[26] This is not the place to engage the vast economics, public policy, and legal literatures analyzing the idea of cost-benefit analysis or the many features associated with it.[27] For present purposes, it is enough to recognize this approach as a tool through which policymakers attempt to determine how best to meet society's needs.[28] And the suggestion to be considered is simply that, through its use, policymakers are able adequately to account for all relevant normative concerns.

There are, however, grounds for thinking that a cost-benefit approach to the private prisons question would not ensure adequate consideration of normative concerns. For one thing, the suggestion that the value of satisfying a given moral obligation or the disvalue of its violation may be weighed against other implications of a given policy assumes that such values may be meaningfully captured in quantitative terms suitable for comparison with other costs and benefits. This possibility, however, is by no means a given. Certainly, where the arguably negative effects of the state's use of private prisons include, for example, a compromise in the extent to which citizens will trust in the integrity of the state's criminal justice institutions or an increase in the extent to which prisoners are regarded by state officials as financial burdens rather than humans, it is not obvious that the various harms at stake may be adequately expressed in terms that allow for such comparison. This problem of the "incommensurability" or "incomparability" of goods in a choice situation has received extended treatment by moral philosophers.[29] Here, it is enough to note that this problem exists for any efforts to incorporate normative concerns into a cost-benefit analysis, and represents a serious obstacle to any fully adequate consideration of such concerns.

Another key reason to doubt the potential of cost-benefit analysis to adequately consider incarceration's normative implications stems from the inability of cost-benefit analysis to fully grasp the import of moral obligations. Assume that privatizing a prison would have only two identifiable effects: a reduced cost to taxpayers and an increase in the extent to which the humanity principle would be violated.[30] As is true of consequentialism more generally,[31] a cost-benefit calculation that the money-saving benefits of privatization would outweigh the costs in terms of moral obligations left unfulfilled would yield the conclusion that privatizing would be the right thing to do.[32] But this conclusion reflects a fundamental misunderstanding as to the force of a moral obligation. It assumes that we ought to honor our moral obligations only when—and because—the balance of utilities will thereby be maximized. What this perspective thereby fails to recognize is that an extant moral obligation binds us regardless of the results of any welfare calculus.

It is not that such obligations always necessarily trump; in the real world, policymakers must balance many competing demands and partial compliance is inevitable. But a perspective that made space for meaningful debate over the normative implications of a given policy alternative would recognize that in such a case, a decision to privatize would represent only partial compliance with our collective obligations. Moreover, such a perspective would allow—indeed, it would *require*—further debate as to how, notwithstanding our limited resources and capacities, we could still attempt to do better. There would be, in other words, a collective recognition that we had fallen short, and that we are still bound to satisfy the full reach of our obligations as soon as we are able.[33] In contrast, a cost-benefit approach is generally unable to contemplate the possibility that under some circumstances, even actions consistent with maximizing efficiency may violate our collective moral obligations.[34]

A still further obstacle this approach creates to ensuring adequate consideration of incarceration's moral implications stems not from a problem with cost-benefit analysis per se, but from the likely rhetorical effects of its use. Even granting that in some contexts, analysts using sophisticated valuation techniques might be able meaningfully to capture explicitly normative concerns in quantitative terms, if such is even to be possible, there must first be a concerted effort to *identify* all such concerns and determine how best to quantify even those effects that are hard to capture in easily measurable terms. Otherwise, the analysis is sure to include only the most easily quantifiable "practical" considerations at the expense of the less easily quantifiable. Such an analysis is thus likely to be underinclusive. And in the prison context, what are most likely to be excluded under such conditions are the hard-to-measure benefits of ensuring a punishment regime consistent with society's moral obligations to the incarcerated.

Take, for example, the humanity principle introduced above.[35] To some extent, a prison's humanity may be understood in terms of the quality of conditions of confinement and the extent of inmate safety.[36] And plainly, there are any number of quantifiable measures readily available to capture these concerns: What is the ratio of correctional officers to prisoners? How many assaults on prisoners occur? Is the facility overcrowded? If so, by how much? How large are the cells? How much light do they get? Are they clean? Does the plumbing work? How many calories and nutrients do prisoners receive a day? How much programming is available? How many GEDs or GED equivalents do prisoners earn? Etc., etc.

But these questions do not capture the whole of it. If a penal institution is to qualify as humane, it is not enough that it satisfy a checklist of items. It must also foster a particular culture, one of mutual respect between staff and prisoners, in which brutality and the humiliation of prisoners are at a minimum and prisoners are able to feel and function like full human beings as much as possible.[37] A crucial component of a humane institution is thus the attitude with which prison officials approach the inmates in their charge. Do they view prisoners as fellow human beings, deserving of respect as such? Or do they instead see them as "garbage," rightly "written off" by society?[38]

It may be that a nuanced cost-benefit approach could incorporate into its calculations an awareness of the cultural and psychological dimensions that shape prison life—the fears, anxieties, hatred, and even disgust with which prisoners and custodial staff often approach one another. Perhaps, that is, given the highly developed methods available for characterizing the value of even intangible effects of various policy alternatives,[39] it would be possible to develop measurable standards to determine the extent to which prisoners are accorded dignity and respect in a given institution. I take no position on this possibility here. Instead, I mean simply to point out that even assuming this possibility, absent an explicit commitment to identifying the full range of concerns, approaching the problem through the lens of efficiency would direct the inquiry in a way that focuses on the most easily and obviously quantifiable aspects of a given facility and thus makes us less likely even to *recognize* the more intangible dimensions of a humane environment.

This problem will be even more pronounced with concerns less obviously open to empirical investigation than that of a prison's humanity. Consider, for example, the implications for the integrity of the criminal justice system of introducing an overt concern with profit into the carceral context. Will the use of private prisons compromise the legitimacy of sentences officially imposed or actually served? Will it undermine the public trust in the system? And what will it mean for the communities that most feel the weight of the criminal justice system?[40] Perhaps these questions could be answered empirically at least to some extent. But absent explicit attention to the particular dangers private prisons create for the legitimacy of punishment and the integrity of the system, we will be unlikely even to recognize this set of concerns, much less to address them in any meaningful way.

This concern suggests that if policy deliberation is to take account of the full range of moral issues incarceration raises, we need a genuine commitment to supplementing the language of efficiency with the language of moral obligation. Honoring this commitment would require inviting moral philosophers and political theorists to join a conversation presently dominated by economists and policy analysts.

Admittedly, to openly acknowledge and debate explicitly normative concerns can be difficult and even contentious—difficult because there may appear to be no obvious anchors to shape the inquiry,[41] and contentious because by definition attention to such issues places one immediately and explicitly in the realm of value, about which disagreements are inevitable. Not to do so, however, brings its own risks, most notably that we will lose sight of prisoners as fellow human beings and fellow citizens to whom we owe obligations, and come to see them instead as consumers of services who owe us for the privilege. Indeed, the recent history of the professionalization of prison administration,[42] with its focus on standard setting, statistical analysis, and efficiency maximization, illustrates this very process.[43] The language of comparative efficiency simply reinforces the tendency. As Sarah Armstrong nicely puts it, "an enthusiasm for economic techniques to manage public services and values ignores the way that the techniques of management can re-shape values and . . . compromise them."[44]

Efficiency as Cost Minimization

Whether or not a cost-benefit approach could adequately consider the full set of normative issues incarceration implicates, the fact is that policymakers contemplating the use of private prisons are little concerned with addressing this set of issues, whether through cost-benefit analysis or otherwise. Instead, the efficiency standard actually driving the debate is what can be thought of as cost *minimization*—that is, how to run the prisons at the lowest possible price. This approach is akin to what is known in the public policy literature as "cost-*effectiveness* analysis." An alternative to cost-benefit analysis, cost effectiveness simply asks which of the available policy options *can produce a given output at the lowest cost.*[45] The difference between cost-effectiveness analysis and what I am calling "cost minimization" is that, unlike more sophisticated versions of cost-effectiveness analysis, which consider a range of costs including those that are hard to measure, in the private prisons debate the only cost that tends to command much attention is the financial cost to taxpayers. This means that even if theoretically an efficiency analysis could take adequate account of broader normative concerns, in the case of private prisons there is no meaningful effort on the part of policymakers to do so.[46] The possibility that some concerns are more urgent than cost savings, even if not ruled out in theory, is rarely if ever taken seriously in practice.

True, the private prisons debate does not completely ignore considerations other than cost. In fact, one finds therein a general acceptance of the view that private prisons must be *at least as good as* public prisons on measures of quality and safety, which are important factors in any humanity determination. But this concession is wholly consistent with—and even demanded by—an approach that aims to identify the cheapest way to perform a specified task. The reason is this: such an approach takes as given the nature and scope of the job to be done. For cost minimization to remain the operative efficiency standard in the private prison debate, therefore, privatization must be thought not to alter the character of the service in question fundamentally. Otherwise, it could not be argued that private contractors would perform the specified task for less money, since they would not be performing the specified task at all but rather some other, fundamentally different task. This is why advocates of privatization insist that privatization would effect no meaningful change to the character of the governmental function to be privatized—so, for example, private prisons would be no more violent, and at least as safe, secure, humane, and so on as public prisons. It is also why debate over privatization is so often a contest between competing characterizations of the government function at issue and the likely effects of privatization, with advocates arguing strenuously that the nature of the function would be unchanged by privatization, and opponents arguing just as strenuously that it would be thereby transformed.[47]

That comparative efficiency's crude version of cost effectiveness—what I am calling "cost minimization"—makes it difficult to find space in the debate for the full range of incarceration's normative implications is itself unsurprising. If cost minimization is the only thing that matters, those adopting this approach will have no call to look beyond considerations of cost to society's moral obligations to the incarcerated. But the problem with comparative efficiency's cost-minimization approach is not merely that it does not consider other implications of incarceration. It is that, with its implicit adoption of this approach, comparative efficiency affirmatively *obscures* a set of broader normative concerns. What's more, by keeping the focus on relative cost, comparative efficiency subtly reinforces the prevailing approach to criminal punishment in ways that belie comparative efficiency's apparent value neutrality.

To understand how comparative efficiency achieves these effects, it is necessary to say a little more about cost-effectiveness analysis, with which cost minimization shares a basic structure. Cost-effectiveness analysis developed as a response to a particular criticism of cost-*benefit* analysis touched on above, that is, that it reduces all effects of a given policy to pecuniary (or at least quantitative) values, whether or not a numerical value is fully able to capture the concern at issue.[48] In contrast, cost *effectiveness* allows at least one value-laden policy consideration to be quantified not in monetary terms but in "physical units," thus avoiding the need to assign a putatively objective number to a consideration the moral significance of which cannot adequately be captured in numerical terms.[49]

The health policy context makes clear the benefits of this difference. The difficulty faced by health policy analysts is in assigning a dollar amount to the value of saving a human life. Cost-effectiveness analysis avoids this problem by simply quantifying the number of quality-adjusted human life years (or "QALYs") saved by a given medical technology, and then comparing the ratio of the years saved to the cost of that technology.[50] This move allows analysts to determine which approach provides for the most QALYs saved at the lowest cost, without having to confront the difficult question of how much a year of human life is worth.[51]

A cost-effectiveness approach thus necessarily takes for granted the desirability of the specified goal. And by framing the policy analysis in terms of how best to achieve that goal, it reinforces the likelihood that it is this goal, rather than any other, that society will ultimately realize. In the health policy context, this effect is relatively unproblematic. If the aim of medicine is to allow people to live longer healthy lives, any health policy seeking to maximize the number of QALYs will be arguably consistent with society's best interests.[52] But the same cannot be said of the prison context. What comparative efficiency's cost-minimization approach seeks in the prison context is not the lowest cost per healthful human life year saved—an incontrovertibly positive social end—but *the lowest cost per human life year incarcerated*. And since this approach takes as given the specified goal and seeks only to achieve it at the lowest possible cost, and since, as we have seen, it frames the goal of incarceration in terms that take existing conditions for granted, we must also assume for purposes of comparative efficiency that this is a human life year incarcerated *under existing conditions of confinement*.

But—and here is the key point—unlike a healthful human life year saved, a human life year incarcerated under existing conditions is only an obvious social good if one assumes that both (1) the prison sentences imposed and (2) the conditions under which those sentences will be served are justified and appropriate.

These twin assumptions are therefore necessary premises of cost minimization in the private prisons context. That is, cost minimization will remain a plausible approach to corrections policy only if we assume that prison sentences currently imposed and existing prison conditions are justified and appropriate.[53] In taking these assumptions for granted, comparative efficiency focuses the inquiry in a way that effectively forecloses reexamination of the very aspects of state punishment a more normatively capacious standard would want to question.

This aspect of comparative efficiency further confirms its normative bias: in adopting a cost-minimization approach, comparative efficiency favors the criminal punishment status quo. Some might think this stance wholly appropriate. It is, after all, the democratic process that defines social goals, and any objections to current sentencing policy or existing conditions in prisons and jails ought therefore to be addressed through the political process. On this view, comparative efficiency is simply a tool for deciding how to house most cheaply those prisoners society has deemed it appropriate to incarcerate, and is rightly agnostic on the more difficult normative questions of who should be imprisoned, for what and for how long, and under what conditions.

But this account fails to appreciate the way that taking comparative efficiency for granted as the appropriate tool for addressing the challenges of prison administration has a direct and palpable limiting effect on any political debate over the nature and scope of state punishment. In framing whether privatization will reduce the cost of corrections as the key issue for prison administration, comparative efficiency prompts the very people who ought to be most focused on the hard normative questions raised by mass incarceration—state legislators, prison officials, and other policymakers and analysts—to gloss over these difficult questions. Moreover, in redirecting attention away from these hard questions, comparative efficiency makes it less likely that those in a position to shape penal policy will even register the existence of more urgent issues in this arena.[54]

Again, we see that comparative efficiency is not value neutral, but instead plays a key role in shoring up the existing penal system. Once this role is appreciated, the relentless focus on comparative efficiency no longer seems obviously appropriate, but instead seems a way to distract from the more difficult and contentious questions of the appropriate limits on what the state may legitimately do to fellow citizens in the name of criminal punishment and whether existing practices adequately conform to these limits. Notice that when these latter questions come to the fore, privatization no longer appears the appropriate centerpiece of prison reform efforts. Widespread acceptance of the claim that the animating question of comparative efficiency is value neutral is thus arguably integral to the continued appeal of private prisons.

The success of private prisons did not always rest on painting the relevant issues in wholly nonnormative terms. In fact, when the modern private prison emerged,[55] privatization appealed partly because it promised to relieve the considerable overcrowding that marked prisons and jails across the country. Private prisons were thus seen as the means through which states could continue to imprison convicted offenders at prevailing levels while reversing the deterioration in prison conditions that is overcrowding's inevitable result.[56] Private prisons could thus be promoted and defended in terms of quality and safety, which have obvious normative implications.

But this particular justification soon dissolved as private prisons quickly became as overcrowded as the public facilities they were intended to relieve.[57] What remained was solely their potential for greater efficiency. For privatization to maintain pride of place on the corrections agenda, therefore, any concern with the problem of overcrowding, along with the most obvious solution to that problem—rethinking prevailing sentencing policies—had to be downplayed. Hence the appeal of cost minimization, which in taking for granted the legitimacy of prevailing incarceration levels and existing conditions of confinement steers us away from critical assessment of either the character of prison conditions or the extent of imprisonment. For those committed to ensuring the legitimacy of state punishment, however, this effect is problematic, since these aspects of the penal system are arguably the very ones most urgently demanding justification.

Comparative Efficiency: How Privatization Thinks

The foregoing account sketches the rhetorical mechanisms through which comparative efficiency structures the debate over private prisons. The puzzle that remains is how this particular perspective came to dominate the debate in the first place. Because the forces that shape individual and collective deliberation are multifaceted and complex, one can only speculate. Still, some explanations will fit a given phenomenon better than others. In this spirit, I suggest that, far from a free-floating set of premises that stands or falls on the strength of its justifying arguments, comparative efficiency is best understood as a key cognitive component of the entrenched political/structural institution of privatization. There is, moreover, a discernibly symbiotic relationship between the cognitive framework of comparative efficiency and the political/structural framework of privatization; each simultaneously produces and is reinforced by the other.

The path from privatization to comparative efficiency is a straightforward one. Comparative efficiency is not just coincidentally consonant with the interests and values of privatization but is presupposed by the very idea of privatization itself, that government functions may be appropriately delegated to private contractors. The operative assumption when privatization appears an appropriate move is that society has a need for *x* task to be performed or *x* service to be provided in the most efficient way possible. Either the state can do it, or it can contract with the private sector to do it. Once the issue is understood in these terms, the only remaining question is which method is more efficient, which is the motivating question of comparative efficiency.

Somewhat more excavation is required to understand the process by which the structuring assumptions of comparative efficiency reinforce the perceptions and values on which the possibility of privatization depends. But careful examination suggests that comparative efficiency does indeed perform this role. For privatization to be regarded as an acceptable policy option, it must be thought to make no meaningful difference whether a public official or a private actor fulfills the state's assigned role. Government must be perceived simply as an agent of service provision. A robust program of privatization in any given context thus depends on widespread rejection of a rich normative understanding of the moral obligations of the state and its citizens, in favor of this "depoliticized" view.[58] And although comparative efficiency did not create this stripped-down view of the public sphere, it nonetheless sustains and fortifies it. As we have seen, for example, the adoption of this deliberative framework in the context of prison administration obscures the normative concerns posed by current penal practices, thus reinforcing the notion that the exercise of state power in the prison context raises no meaningful normative issues. In this way, notwithstanding its implicit claim to value neutrality, comparative efficiency shores up the normative picture on which the possibility of privatization depends.

Comparative efficiency also channels debate in other ways conducive to the privatization project. For example, the comparative component of comparative efficiency divides state actors into two kinds, public and private. This move validates the basic assumption, noted above, on which the possibility of privatization depends: by taking for granted that the sole issue is which state actor is more efficient, it casts the private sector as a wholly appropriate candidate for carrying out the government's work, thereby steering the focus of the debate well past the point at which this role might be questioned. Moreover, by defining the terms of the debate in this way, comparative efficiency reshapes the very concepts of "public" and "private" to make any notion of public actors as the morally appropriate agent of state purposes seem quaint, outdated, and even naïve. From this seemingly more sophisticated perspective, the difference between public and private is no longer understood in terms of their respective purposes, with the public sector doing the state's business on behalf of society as a whole, and the private sector working on behalf of private interests to accumulate private wealth. Instead, consistent with its presupposition that public and private are just two different kinds of actors available to perform the state's business, comparative efficiency recasts the public-private distinction as simply one between different organizational forms. On this redefinition, "public" means only that the task in question is done directly by state employees, and "private" means that the task has been contracted out. To successfully frame the issue in this way prepares the ground for the legitimacy and thus the possibility of privatization—and is thus a victory for the institution of privatization regardless of whether a given privatization effort succeeds or fails.

Comparative efficiency thus recasts the public-private distinction. But it nonetheless continues to posit a fundamental and inherent difference between the two spheres.[59] We have already seen the way this foundational assumption of inherent difference between public and private can obscure the similarities that exist between the two.[60] It is, moreover, this assumed difference that grounds the necessary choice comparative efficiency constructs: because, on this view, public and private are essentially different and there are two and only two alternatives, we must choose one or the other. In fact, there is arguably a wide variety of options for realizing any governmental purpose, some "public" in the sense of being run by state employees in state agencies, others "private" in the sense of being run by nonstate actors working by contract. But to recognize the range of choices that exist within this array of options—say, between state corrections agencies as currently organized and such agencies operating with significant independent state oversight, or between private, for-profit companies seeking a financial return and nonprofits with a stated commitment to reducing recidivism—would require acknowledging that there is more to the success of a public policy than whether state agents are public employees or private contractors. It even introduces the notion that the public prison system may be improved and its problems resolved without contracting out to private parties. These possibilities, however, are at odds with the essential logic of privatization. By excluding them from the debate, comparative efficiency reinforces the perceptions on which the possibility of privatization depends.

This account of the symbiotic relationship between privatization and comparative efficiency helps to explain why critiques of privatization on grounds other than efficiency have had so little success at influencing the debate. Once privatization has come to be affirmed as an appropriate alternative to the public provision of a given government function, a broad-based commitment to the view that society has particular obligations which demand the collective engagement of citizens qua citizens must have already been displaced by a view of state officials as managers, who are obliged only to carry out their assigned responsibilities as efficiently as possible (and who can thus be replaced by other, private actors should these others prove the more efficient alternative). And once this displacement has occurred, it becomes difficult to generate debate as to whether privatization is the best way to satisfy our collective normative obligations to those we punish, or even what those obligations might involve. At that point, it is as if the words necessary to frame these questions are no longer widely understood.

It might be argued that even assuming the power of comparative efficiency to shape debate over privatization in the ways I have described, nothing prevents those concerned with the state of American prisons from directly criticizing prison conditions or sentencing policy in other terms. But although this claim has intuitive appeal, it fails to appreciate the extent to which the privatization option, with its "thought style" of comparative efficiency,[61] has come to occupy the deliberative field of prison administration. Comparative efficiency's success in this regard is partly because of the way the very possibility of privatization has channeled the energy of interested parties. Those individuals and institutions most inclined toward expanding the conversation beyond the normative vision of comparative efficiency are also most likely to be privatization's biggest opponents, and the widespread acceptance of privatization as a viable policy option has meant that much of the energy of this group has been directed toward fighting privatization and away from considering other issues. Private prisons, moreover, are the single biggest innovation in American corrections in the past three decades (save perhaps supermax prisons). As such, they have also commanded the attention of those policymakers, academics, journalists, and other interested parties who are not predisposed either way regarding the possibility of privatization but have still found themselves engaging the issue, and who, in its absence, might have focused on other aspects of the prison system.

But even more central to comparative efficiency's success at occupying the deliberative field is the success of the privatization movement itself in placing the possibility of privatization—not only of whole penal facilities but also of discrete prison services like health care, dental and psychiatric care, laundry, food service, transportation, and so on—at the center of the corrections agenda. Privatization has become a lens through which to view virtually all problems of prison administration. It defines available options even when the problem at issue does not obviously call for choosing between public and private management for maximum cost effectiveness. And appropriate or not, once privatization appears as a possible solution, comparative efficiency immediately arises to sct the deliberative terms, with predictable effect: other ways of understanding the problem, along with the solutions suggested by alternative constructions, are crowded out of the picture.

PART THREE

Responses and Reforms

A. Don't Increase Regulation

CHAPTER SEVEN

Achieving Contracting Goals and Recognizing Public Law Concerns

A Contracting Management Perspective

STEVEN J. KELMAN

The interest of many public law scholars in government contracting—demonstrated by the chapters in this volume—creates a new set of issues for scholars and practitioners involved in government procurement. The government contracting community has traditionally been concerned with two broad sets of issues. One is how well the procurement system performs in achieving its goal—supporting the missions of the agencies on whose behalf it buys by providing them with products and services of good quality at good prices from responsive contractors. The second is administrative law issues involving the fair and impartial operation of the procurement system in terms of how government officials treat those seeking to sell to the government, particularly regarding the government's selection of which contractor to do business with for any particular contract. Thus, administrative law has by no means been absent from the procurement system, but the focus has been on issues in the treatment of those wishing to sell to the government, not on those involving third parties (members of the public who might deal with contractors directly, or others concerned about democratic governance, the exercise of state power, and respect for individual rights).

Authors of the chapters in this volume partly raise questions similar to those traditionally raised by those interested in the substantive mission performance of the system, particularly questions of how and whether the government can successfully manage contracts so that contractors deliver what they are supposed to. But the public law questions of treatment of citizens and of democratic governance are largely new.[1]

This chapter has two purposes. The first is to introduce a public law–oriented reader to important mainstream policy and management issues in the world of government contracting. The second is to react, from a mainstream contracting perspective, to some public law concerns expressed in this volume.

I have several reasons to devote the bulk of this chapter to mainstream contracting issues. Most importantly, I seek to remind people from the public law world that contracting has substantive goals and aims—to help government agencies meet their missions to serve the public—that should not be lost while attending to public law issues. Additionally, as just noted, in the area of administering contracts after they have been awarded, there is overlap in concerns of the mainstream contracting and public law worlds. Finally, by understanding issues in the mainstream contracting community, people in the public law world will be better positioned to understand why many from that community are inclined to worry about some of the proposals public law scholars make for addressing problems they have identified.

Thinking Theoretically about the Make-Buy Decision Where Public Law Considerations Are Not at Stake

Casual inspection reveals that contracting out the production of products or services is by no means limited to contracting between government and private businesses, but includes contracting between one private business and another. Toyota contracts for many of the parts that make up its automobiles and for the steel used in its manufacturing plants. Most corporate advertising is developed by advertising agencies, not in-house, most companies have outside counsel as well as in-house lawyers, and consulting is a multibillion-dollar business. At the same time, firms don't contract for everything, even in a world where issues of concern to public law scholars do not arise.

There is a moderate amount of economic theory—the tradition of so-called transaction cost economics (TCE)—addressing when it makes economic sense for an organization to produce a product or service internally and when it makes sense to contract for it. This question is referred to in business as the "make-buy decision." In TCE, it is often referred to as the choice between "market," that is, contracting, and "hierarchy," that is, in-house production inside the bounds of an organization. It is helpful to consider this question because it sheds light on how decisions to contract or produce in-house might be made absent public law concerns.

The starting point for the economic theory of the make-buy decision is somewhat the opposite of the starting point for public law scholars worried about government contracting. In the seminal paper that established the field, Coase started by asking why firms exist at all, why *all* production does not occur through contracts among individuals or teams to produce the various components of a product or service.[2] After all, economists believe that the competitive market is normally superior to central direction as a way to reduce costs, improve quality, and encourage innovation. Yet firms, while they participate in the competitive market to sell their production, are not *internally* organized as markets, but rather as hierarchies.

Coase's basic argument was that firms come into existence to economize on transaction costs, which Arrow succinctly defined as the "costs of running the economic system."[3] The costs of negotiating and enforcing the multifarious contracts that would be needed to organize production can outweigh the benefits of contracting and hence explain the existence of firms.

This basic insight has been developed much further by the founder of modern TCE, Oliver Williamson.[4] Contracting, compared with hierarchy, brings the well-known advantages of the marketplace: if one looked only at *production* costs, contracting would be universal. Competition lowers costs and prices. Specialization (e.g., steel being produced by a modest number of steel companies rather than by each steel user) creates economies of scale and room for greater investment in learning about improved production methods. These have more recently been referred to as advantages growing out of an organization specializing in its "core competencies."[5] A good example is Halliburton's work for the government under the LOGCAP contract, under which the firm has provided various support services—running cafeterias, delivering mail, constructing facilities—for the Army. The basic idea is that these activities are not part of the core competency of the Army, which is war fighting, and that it makes little sense to employ soldiers, expensively trained to fight wars, at jobs requiring less, and different, training. By contrast, these support activities *are* the core competency of the Halliburton unit performing the LOGCAP contract.

Finally, even in the private sector—and more so in government—issues of internal morale and equity make it more difficult for organizations immediately to dismiss underperformers or to adopt a highly incentivized compensation system for rank-and-file employees, while such techniques are more acceptable to use toward outside firms with whom one contracts.

However, under certain circumstances contracting creates transaction costs outweighing its production-cost benefits. The two sources of transaction costs Williamson emphasizes are uncertainty and asset-specific investment. First, the more unknowable relevant conditions in the world are at the time a contract is signed or the more the world changes during the period of contract performance, the harder it is to develop a contract that covers important contingencies ex ante; under these circumstances, bounded rationality produces incomplete contracts. Second, the more ongoing competition is available to provide the product or service, the more attractive contracting is. Lack of competition occasionally occurs because the product or service itself is highly unusual, or because the customer's location is very isolated. More often, it occurs after a first contracting competition, when the winning vendor makes asset-specific investments in the relationship with its customer that are valuable for the customer but make it more difficult for competitors to wrest business from the incumbent when there is a contract recompetition. Examples range from physical investments tied to the customer (such as a train line spur to deliver material right to a customer's plant) to learning by experience with the customer that tends to make the vendor's employees more valuable to the customer than another firm's. The greater the asset specificity, the lower the level of competition after the first award. Williamson refers to this move from initial high competition to subsequent low competition as "the fatal transformation." A third source of transaction costs, discussed but not emphasized by Williamson, is the cost of measuring whether the contractor has delivered the appropriate-quality product or service.[6] Particularly for services production when there are no readily available quantitative or other easily observable performance measures—situations where one can only ask the contractor to produce "best efforts"—measurement can be costly.

Either of the first two problems alone does not create big difficulties for contracting.[7] But together they dramatically increase contracting's transaction costs, because each side fears the other will take advantage of changes in the world to renegotiate the contract to one-sided advantage in a situation where recompeting the contract is difficult. The parties must therefore invest in dispute resolution, auditing, and other governance structures. If they contract, the buyer, in making new contract awards, will want to reward good past performance or punish bad past performance, as a way to discourage ex post exploitation of reduced competition arising from asset-specific investments.

If the transaction costs of these investments outweigh production-cost benefits of contracting,[8] it makes sense to keep the function in-house. In such circumstances, one replaces a contracting with an employment relationship, whereby the employee agrees to take general direction from a boss, without the need to specify the expected output in advance or negotiate about changes. Uncertainty is dealt with by fiat, using hierarchy.[9]

Typically, it makes more sense to keep an operation in-house:

- the more it represents an organization's core competency (the production-cost advantage of contracting is likely to be less);

- the greater the combination of future uncertainty and asset specificity;

- the harder it is to measure whether contracted-for quality has been delivered.

There is evidence that organizations' make-buy decisions generally track TCE predictions. A recent meta-analysis of empirical research concluded that both uncertainty and asset specificity predicted hierarchy or interfirm alliance, although there was no significant interaction effect between the two variables, suggesting they were not jointly required to produce nonmarket transactions. The meta-analysis also concluded that organizational performance was worse when transactions were *not* organized in a TCE-appropriate way.[10] Brown and Potoski found that municipal services with high asset specificity and low measurability were somewhat less likely to be contracted out to private firms than those low on these variables, although effect sizes were not large.[11]

Often, both the production cost advantages of contracted production *and* its transaction costs are high. Many large-scale information technology or other infrastructure projects fit into this category.[12] In such cases, contracting makes sense, but it must become "relational"—long term and with significant investment in a governance structure.[13] Without a large investment in contract administration (governance structures), contracting under these conditions runs a great risk of failure.

Improving the Performance of the Procurement System

During the "reinventing government" program of the Clinton administration, the focus of procurement system efforts was on improving the ability of the procurement system to meet its goals. Even as we worry about other problems, real or alleged, involving government contracting, we must never lose sight of the basic goal of the procurement system in the first place—as stated in the "core guiding principles" of the Federal Acquisition Regulation[14] adopted as part of 1990s procurement reform—"to deliver on a timely basis the best value product or service to the customer."

Philosophically, this effort was informed by an analysis of why government underperforms in the first place. Government underperformance is overdetermined. One explanation, which economists favor, is that agencies are protected monopolies and thus lead an easy life, without performance pressures;[15] monopoly, writes Savas, produces a situation where citizens are "subject to endless exploitation and victimization," where "so-called public servants have a captive market and little incentive to heed their putative customers."[16] The very universality of popular obloquy regarding government performance across time and place suggests the monopoly criticism is not entirely groundless, since the most obvious common feature of agencies is monopoly status. However, it is inaccurate to state that agencies generally lead an easy life without outside pressures. Pressures come from the political system and the media, not the marketplace, but that doesn't make them innocuous: if one asked people whether they would rather be attacked on the front page of the *Washington Post* or subjected to the punishment firms typically mete out for poor performance, it is not obvious most would choose the former. Another explanation is that few of the best people choosing government careers do so because of an interest in managing an organization's performance, but rather to influence formulation of policies addressing such issues as AIDS or terrorism. A third explanation is that, while firms can use the profit metric, agencies often have a hard time developing good metrics. Even when metrics for performance improvement are available, agencies may be embroiled in controversy about goals.[17]

"Reinventing government" argued that government underperforms because, compared with firms, it pays less *attention* to performance in the first place. Every organization has both goals and constraints under which it operates.[18] Goals are *results* an organization seeks—for firms, profit, market share, or customer satisfaction; for the Environmental Protection Agency, improved air quality; for the National Cancer Institute, a better understanding of cancer. Constraints are *limits* on the acceptable behavior of organizations or their members, even to meet goals.[19] Respecting constraints leads to avoiding evils or abuses. For firms, constraints include respecting accounting rules, not dumping toxic waste, and not kidnapping competitors. For agencies, constraints include those familiar to public law, for example that officials not take bribes or lie to the public, that citizens be treated fairly, that due process be respected, and that there be accountability to the public for agency actions. One may also note, broadly, that the world of constraints is a world of *law* (laws set limits on behavior and, in a classical view, establish fences *within which* individuals may pursue goals as they see fit), while the world of goals, at least as far as organizations are concerned, is a world of *management*. Perhaps not surprisingly, then, lawyers worry more about constraints, managers more about goals.

Because they often embody important ethical values such as accountability, rationality in decision making, respect for persons, honesty, and integrity, constraints are not unimportant. This is particularly so in government, where behaviors often communicate signals about social values: while equal treatment of citizens signals the social importance of equality, dishonesty lowers the moral tone in society.[20] Furthermore, an important line of research suggests that procedural fairness encourages people to accept decisions that go against their personal interest.[21]

At the same time, organizations (or individuals) about which it can only be said they have respected constraints would typically not be judged successful.[22] Imagine a journalist who during a long career never revealed a source or fabricated evidence—but who had never uncovered a good story. Or imagine a company that never cooked its books, but also never succeeded in making a sale. Nor are organizations (or individuals) normally successful if they need to focus significant energy on assuring that constraints are respected, because that energy is unavailable for goal attainment. Instead, a healthy organization (or individual) is one that takes constraints for granted. An individual who needs to spend hours each day worrying about how s/he will avoid murdering others is unlikely to be successful at achieving substantive goals. We seldom think that "don't kidnap your competitors" is a constraint for firms, because we take the constraint for granted. Russia in the early 1990s was in bad shape, in part, because operation of this constraint could not be taken for granted.

Traditionally in government in general and the procurement system in particular, however, the tail wagged the dog—constraints have loomed larger than goals, inhibiting good performance.[23] This is so for several reasons. First, in government goals are often controversial (Should affirmative action be required? Should free trade be pursued?), but "everybody can agree" it's wrong to lie or show favoritism. This makes constraint violation an easier story for media or (opposition) politicians to tell. Second, goal achievement is not fully under agency control and occurs over time, while constraint violation is immediate. Third, pursuing goals is about "maximizing good government," respecting constraints is about "minimizing misgovernment";[24] many people have such limited aspirations for government that reducing misgovernment is all they ask, a standard for success firms would find incomprehensible.[25] Fourth, democratic accountability of agencies is a central value in democracy. This focus is a constraint since it says nothing about results, only process.

"Reinventing government" in general, and the procurement reform efforts of the 1990s in particular, were designed to raise the importance of goal attainment in government, including contracting. Again, the "core guiding principles" of the Federal Acquisition Regulation expressed the new philosophy: after stating the goal of the system as being to provide best-value products and services for agency missions, the regulation added that achieving the goal needed to occur "*while* maintaining the public's trust and fulfilling public policy objectives."[26] This expresses the right relationship between goals and constraints—achieve goals while respecting constraints.

"Reinventing government" was strongly associated with reducing the importance of rules in guiding the behavior of people in the procurement system—"empowering" procurement officials to develop buying approaches that promised to provide the government the best ways to achieve the procurement system's goals (to use the phrase the reformers themselves also used), or to provide procurement officials with greater discretion (to use the phrase lawyers would be more inclined to use, with its less positive associations, at least for lawyers).

The dominance of bureaucratic organizational forms—that is, the important role of rules and hierarchy[27]—in government relates to the importance of constraints over goals, since rules and hierarchy are important control tools.[28] As Kaufman famously noted, "[o]ne person's 'red tape' may be another's treasured procedural safeguard."[29] If one cares about minimizing misgovernment rather than maximizing good government, one will be disinclined to grant officials discretion; as Theodore Roosevelt stated a century ago, "[y]ou cannot give an official power to do right without at the same time giving him power to do wrong."[30] The main argument for the bureaucratic organization of the procurement system was to inhibit abuse, both by government officials and by contractors. Officials free to make decisions unconstrained by rules might give contracts to relatives or take bribes.[31] They might "take the easy way out" and lazily refrain from doing the work necessary to protect the government's interests (together, to use the term of art employed, referred to as "administrative convenience").[32] Or they might ask for products or services that were too fancy, and hence too expensive,[33] or pay excessive prices for what they were buying, unconcerned because they weren't "spending their own money." Finally, unconstrained by rules, some contractors would cheat the government. Applied by honest and conscientious people, the various rules might typically produce bad results. But the system was more moved by respecting constraints than by achieving goals.

Many source selection rules were associated with the policy of "full and open competition," a standard established in law under that name in the Competition in Contracting Act of 1984 but connected with the growing ruleboundedness of the procurement system well before that. Many common practices—such as buying from the low bidder or giving no consideration to a supplier's past performance in awarding new contracts—did not form part of any regulation. Rather, they were practices reflecting the spirit of a system that tried to render rulebound as much behavior as possible.

In the bid solicitation document,[34] the government was required by the 1984 Act to specify what it wanted (so that bidders bid on the same thing, reducing the danger of favoritism). Specifications could not ask for more than the agency's "minimum needs," to prevent the government from buying products and services of "excessive" quality. The bid solicitation also had to express criteria (such as price or technical performance) for evaluating bids; at a minimum, the relative weights of the various criteria were required to be presented (such as "price is the most important factor, followed by technical approach and management plan, which are of approximately equal weight").[35] Bids could be evaluated only based on the criteria, and using the evaluation weights, laid out in advance in the solicitation. In response to government solicitations, interested bidders prepared written proposals, explaining in detail how they would meet the requirements of the procurement. Written proposals would often be hundreds or even thousands (occasionally tens of thousands!) of pages long; sometimes, proposals were delivered using forklift trucks, and frequently the proposals from all the bidders might fill an entire room. This situation arose because government could use only the material in the written proposals to evaluate bidders. Proposals were often written by professional proposal writers, as often as not the same people who would actually be working on the contract once it was awarded. Proposals were widely seen as "essay writing contests."

Unless an award was being made on price alone, the government frequently entered into "discussions" (to use the term of art) with those bidders deemed, after evaluation of the proposals, to have the greatest chance of being awarded the contract. Typically, the government was hesitant to eliminate bidders at this phase of the competition (because this might show favoritism) and included most bidders in discussions. Despite the phrase, "discussions" were conducted only in writing and did not include what would normally be thought of as negotiations. During "discussions," bidders were invited to lower their prices. Bidders were also informed of weaknesses in their proposals and given an opportunity to improve. However, bidders were not allowed to improve elements of their proposal that met the minimum requirements of the solicitation; for example, if the bidder offered a one-year warranty, which was the minimum the government required, the government could not ask it during discussions to increase the warranty to two years. Refusal to allow the government to negotiate about elements of a proposal other than the price reflected a fear that the government might provide a favored bidder with hints about how to improve its bid.

One feature of the traditional system especially perplexing to outsiders was the inability to use the past performance of contractors on previous contracts as an evaluation factor in making new contract awards. This prohibition appeared neither in statute nor regulation, but grew out of worries about favoritism, excessive discretion, and using material beyond what appeared in a bidder's proposal. Bidders were chosen based on statements about the future appearing in their proposals, not about actual accomplishments.[36]

Additionally, more and more rules were promulgated over the years to limit the ability of contractors to speak one-on-one with government officials in the run-up to the award of the contract, often taking effect as soon as the government began to think about a procurement. Government-industry communication occurred in meetings open to all potential bidders and in written communications, which were public information.

Most of the rules regulating contractors were designed to protect the government against being overcharged or otherwise cheated. Many government contracts are "cost based." This may mean, as for many contracts for services (such as consulting services or research) that the contract reimburses contractors for costs incurred, plus a profit. Or it may mean that the contract is a fixed-price contract but has been negotiated sole-source with only one supplier (such as a production contract for fighter jets that a defense contractor has earlier developed). In both cases, rules governed what costs were allowable (that is, could legitimately be charged to a cost-reimbursement contract or be included for negotiating a fixed-price sole-source contract). A simple example is a prohibition against charging corporate entertainment costs to the government. There were also complex rules about accounting for indirect costs (for example, the cost of corporate headquarters or of non–contract-specific corporate research), designed to prevent a contractor from charging too many indirect costs to cost-based contracts rather than other government contracts or to nongovernment work.

The Truth in Negotiations Act of 1962[37] established rules for the information contractors must provide the government prior to (and as a basis for) the award of a contract. The regulatory exceptions for the requirement to provide such data were so narrow, and became interpreted even more narrowly, that gradually the government began to demand cost data for all but the most straightforward products. Contractors typically needed to develop special accounting systems to remain in compliance with these rules.

Frequently, the *only* ground for justifying rules was to reduce abuse. Rules preventing government officials from having one-on-one meetings with potential bidders once a procurement process was under way deprived government of valuable information and feedback on whether the requirements the government was considering made sense, since in these group settings competitors didn't want to say anything of interest lest they reveal information about their bidding strategy. The rule was contrary to commercial purchasing practice, which regarded vendors as invaluable sources of information in early stages of a procurement. Furthermore, the government's insufficient or incorrect information could be exploited by bidders who realized that doing what the government asked for would not produce results the government intended and then counted on lucrative contract modifications (providing additional work) when what the government had requested did not solve the underlying problem.[38] Again, the only justification for the rule was to prevent abuses—government officials giving information to one potential bidder that had not been given to others or plotting to "cook" a solicitation to favor a bidder. The same applies to the rule enjoining use of past performance information. The result was chronic overpromising prior to contract award, poorer contractor performance once a contract was signed, and less customer satisfaction, compared to comparable contracts in the private sector.[39] This counterproductive practice could only be justified on grounds that it would prevent the use of this evaluation factor corruptly to favor one supplier over another.

Rules the traditional system imposed also frequently created unintended consequences that made the government worse off. One example was the so-called price reduction clause in General Services Administration (GSA) contracts for government-wide use. In negotiating these contracts, GSA required vendors to offer the government a price at least equal to the lowest price offered any commercial customer under similar terms and conditions. The price reduction clause, placed in these contracts pursuant to regulation, was a rule requiring vendors to lower their price for all government customers whenever they provided a lower price to any government customer. The purpose was to avoid contractor abuse. The result, however, was that vendors were unwilling to provide temporary discounts, sale prices, or quantity discounts, because doing so would trigger the price reduction for all other customers and all times. The rule thus kept GSA prices higher than they otherwise would have been.

A second example was the notorious system of Department of Defense (DOD) specifications for everyday items, ranging from ketchup to troop underwear to chocolate chip cookie mix.[40] These emerged from the "buy low bid" practice. To buy low bid, the government needed to specify what it was buying, so it could choose among comparable offers. Whenever it was discovered that a previous low bidder had cut a corner in such a way as to make the product unacceptable, a new element was added to the specification to "tighten" it. Over time, some element of the growingly complicated spec emerged that commercial vendors of the product could not meet. Unwilling to adapt their products for the government, which was a tiny part of their business, these vendors exited from bidding. The unintended negative consequence was that eventually the only firms bidding on these items were those with no commercial marketplace presence, which had come into existence solely to bid on these government spec items, and which generally had high costs and poor customer satisfaction.

In a related vein, rules imposing detailed cost reporting requirements on contractors under the Truth in Negotiations Act frequently caused commercial companies to stay out of government business, whether because they lacked accounting systems to comply with the rules, were unwilling to reveal sensitive internal cost information, or refused to accept profit margins this cost-plus-fixed fee environment imposed. For example, as of 1992 five of the country's ten largest semiconductor firms refused to accept DOD contracts requiring the provision of such cost data.[41] The unintended negative consequence was to limit participation in significant parts of defense contracting to firms that bid only on government business and that were often more expensive and less innovative.[42]

A final example involves the unintended consequences of the rules establishing "bid protests," the ability of disappointed bidders to challenge government source selection decisions. This was an example of a rule that was justified as providing oversight of government officials and thus preventing abuse. However, the fear of being subjected to a traumatic lawsuit (not to speak of the fear of losing such a suit) inhibited government officials from using procurement practices not specifically sanctioned by other procurement rules, even if the rules did not forbid the practices, because such a course of action was perceived to increase one's risk of being sued. Furthermore, bid protests had the unintended consequence of establishing an adversarial relationship between government and suppliers—at the extreme, resulting in a situation in which a court ordered the government to do business with an unwanted supplier. This harmed government's ability to establish trusting relationships with suppliers, as commercial buyers increasingly have done.[43] Trusting relationships promote valuable sharing of information and investments in the relationship, as well as easier cooperation by individuals and organizations, factors that create greater value in mutual endeavors; trust is therefore typically seen as an important source of organizational social capital.[44]

More generally, rule proliferation produced the unintended consequence of slowing down decision making—marring the system with red tape. The sum of all the rules in the traditional procurement system slowed the system down enormously, so that buying products or services took far longer than in the private sector and following the rules took up much of the time of contracting officials. Simply evaluating proposals could take months. Indeed, one can easily imagine a situation where the benefit of each individual rule in the system outweighs its costs, but where the agglomeration of rules creates so much delay that the *system* unintentionally has greater costs than benefits.[45]

The most important changes in the procurement system in the context of "reinventing government" may be divided into the following broad categories: (1) streamlining, (2) "best value," (3) using commercial items, and (4) government-industry partnership.

1. Streamlining: No single change has had more of an impact on the average government employee than granting users a government-issued credit card for making small purchases of ordinary-use items (desktop PCs, software, office supplies, or simple services such as vehicle repair for a forest ranger or an FBI agent in the field). Before the introduction of the credit card, every purchase, even a $25 buy, had to go through an agency's contracting organization. This meant that a user would need to fill out a requisition form explaining what s/he wanted, send it to the contracting office, wait until it got on top of the pile, perhaps answer questions about the item from a semiclerical purchasing agent, and wait until the item arrived. Miscommunications frequently led to the need to return the original product and start the process anew. Users often waited weeks or months to receive even minor items. To allow users to buy directly necessitated eliminating the statutory applicability of seven contract clauses (such as Buy America restrictions) and the requirement to buy from small business for purchases under $2500. A second rule that needed to be eliminated was that only contracting officials could authorize the government to spend money, not program officials. After passage of the Federal Acquisition Streamlining Act ("FASA"),[46] a major expansion of a previously experimental government credit card program began. The card meant that transactions previously requiring a lengthy detour through an agency's procurement organization could now be undertaken immediately and directly. Administrative costs for these transactions, often greater than the actual cost of the item being bought, also were slashed.

The other most important streamlining change was the dramatic expansion of simplified vehicles for larger purchases through an expansion of GSA contracts and the development of so-called government-wide acquisition contracts (GWACs). The elimination of two rules produced a dramatic expansion of the popularity of the GSA schedules. In 1996 GSA eliminated the price reduction clause (one of the examples mentioned earlier of a procurement rule with unintended negative consequences), to allow vendors to offer some customers price reductions not offered to every customer. Elimination of the clause had an electrifying effect. Contracting officials at the Internal Revenue Service came up with a new idea—inviting a number of computer hardware/software GSA contract holders to bid for "blanket purchase agreements" with their agencies, specifying discounts off GSA prices they would offer on their whole range of items; the IRS would choose a smaller number of these bidders to be agency providers of choice. IRS's innovation spread quickly throughout the government.

For buying services, there had grown up before procurement reform the practice of awarding so-called task order contracts, where agencies competitively chose a contractor who would then be permitted to undertake individual smaller jobs, called "task orders," without further competition. These lived a shadowy existence, without recognition in the rules (lawyers in the Office of the Secretary of Defense stated they were illegal, though Defense continued to award them). FASA included a provision establishing an authority to award "multiple award task order contracts," whereby a stable of contractors could be selected upfront, with simplified competitive procedures limited to the selected contractors for choosing a contractor for individual orders. In 1995 the Department of Transportation took the initiative to establish a multiple award information technology services contract that would be open to orders (for a small fee) from the entire government. Thus was born, out of an authority granted in FASA but not imagined for a contract open to the whole government, the "government-wide acquisition contract." In 1996 a competitor to these new contracts arose when GSA established its first government-wide contracts for information technology services, which basically consisted of prenegotiated labor rates for various labor categories, along with a set of standard terms and conditions. The many new contracts that resulted quickly became the preferred way to buy information technology and some other professional services.

2. *"Best value"*: At the time procurement reform was beginning, the idea that contracts should not necessarily be awarded to the low bidder had emerged and was fighting to survive against many critics, especially in Congress. By the end of the reform decade, "best value," which involved considerably greater room for judgment by government decision makers, was the rule rather than low-bid source selection decisions. Furthermore, refusal to use a supplier's past performance in source selection vanished, and past performance emerged

as a major factor in choosing suppliers. The procedure for evaluating past performance was relatively bureaucratic, with due process protections for contractors allowing them to challenge a negative past performance rating at a higher level within the organization;[47] this discouraged agencies from being fully honest in filling out their reports. Introduction of use of past performance in source selection was a major change—recalling again its special importance in the context of relational contracting—in the procurement system. Thanks to "due process" restrictions for contractors, it was not as effective as it could have been, but it was definitely better than nothing. In particular, it worked well in conjunction with the new streamlined GWAC/GSA vehicles. Since streamlined procedures made it easier to get *on* contract, it also became less traumatic to get *off* contract,[48] so agencies began giving out work in smaller chunks, and simply did not renew or continue work when a contractor performed poorly. Also, agencies could pick and choose from among a larger number of contract holders in deciding who to allow to bid on a contract, meaning that only the best performers got asked to bid in the first place.

Furthermore, in recent years, partly successful efforts, have been made to express the government's requirements in performance terms in contracts for services as well as for products, without contractual design, personnel requirements or postaward technical direction. Such contracts leave it to the contractor to decide how to meet the metrics.[49] In such contracts, performance standards replace specific technical direction.[50] Here, too, a strong case can be made that government can easily end up exerting more control over contractors than over its own employees, because use of performance standards is more accepted as uncontroversial by contractors than by civil servants.

Finally, in the reform environment, experiments with new ways of structuring contractual relationships with suppliers flourished to improve the value government obtained from contracting.[51] For example, consider changes like the introduction to government of commercial practices such as Internet-based reverse auctions for buying products. Commenting on experiments with reverse auctions, *Federal Computer Week* noted that Internet auctions had "been around for only about a year" in the private sector and that "[i]n the past, government would have taken much longer to follow the private sector's lead."[52] Interest also grew in new forms of incentive contracting to increase the probability that the contractor would perform well. These included "share in savings" contracts, whereby the contractor was paid exclusively as a percentage of the savings its efforts generated, and "award term" contracts, according to which a contractor could be rewarded for outstanding performance by extending the contract's duration. Few of these new business practices required rule changes, but in the new environment, as the initiators of reform had hoped, less focus on rules opened psychological space for more focus on ways to accomplish the job better.

3. Commercial items: DOD undertook a number of steps to change practices that restricted the military's access to commercial suppliers and commercial products. The first major reform initiative the new team at DOD undertook was a 1994 directive creating a presumption *against* using milspecs to buy products. The department also sponsored provisions, adopted in FASA, to scale back dramatically the applicability of rules requiring submission of cost data when commercial items were being purchased.

4. Government-industry cooperation: The traditional system, with the many bid protests, emphasis on the danger of abuse, and extensive use of rules expressing lack of trust of contractors, was not an environment promoting government-industry cooperation. With procurement reform, two rule changes were made to promote such cooperation. One was elimination of the rule prohibiting one-on-one meetings between the government and potential bidders during early stages of the procurement process; such meetings were now permitted, provided that a contracting official was present.[53] The second rule change involved bid protests. In the Federal Acquisition Reform Act Congress eliminated a bid protest body whose standard of review made it especially easy for protesters to win. This left only bid protest bodies whose rules gave greater deference to the government, thus discouraging protests. In addition, an important purpose of reductions in contractor oversight, both rule changes involving fewer demands for cost data and management changes involving greater targeting of oversight based on past performance, was to reduce adversarial relations between government and industry.

Under procurement reform, it has become normal for government to have extensive early contact with prospective bidders to get their suggestions about what requirements the government should ask for. Some suggest that the government limit itself in a solicitation to a "statement of objectives," asking bidders to promote performance metrics and target values for such metrics.[54]

Many changes associated with procurement reform arose neither from statutory change nor from reinventing government initiatives emanating from the White House, but from innovations in the field. This includes GWACs, changes in GSA contracts, award-term contracting, reverse auctions, and others not discussed here for reasons of space. This underlines the point that just as important as the changed rules was the message that following the rules was not *enough*. If one looks at the genuine failures of post–Hurricane Katrina contracting in 2005, they mostly involved—in addition to not nearly enough people available to manage contracting—failure of the FEMA procurement organization to make use of new tools that spread in the context of procurement reform, particularly prenegotiated streamlined contract vehicles (which would have allowed quick ordering off contracts that had already been negotiated in a competitive environment before the crisis) and Internet reverse auctions (which allow contracting in real time that is both competitive and fast).

Finally, the system emerging from reform was not without rules. There are good reasons for many rules in the traditional system, and these remained in force. Most fundamentally, rules frequently serve as aids to producing good decisions. It is absurd to ask an aircraft maintenance worker to decide personally which parts should be checked or replaced after a plane had flown various numbers of miles, or figure out each time the best way to replace part of a complex wing assembly. Furthermore, rules incorporate organizational learning: if an organization has learned over time that certain approaches to dealing with recurring situations work, while others do not, it can use rules to codify and transmit that information.[55] Reform did not even eliminate all the rules designed mostly as constraints. In source selection, for example, the rule remained that proposals need to be evaluated based only on criteria established in the original solicitation; transparency requirements for explaining the grounds for decision were also retained. Nor was oversight of contractors by any means eliminated.

Nonetheless, it is fair to say that the architects of procurement reform thought the existing system was overly rulebound and overlegalized, as applied to how the government organizes the buying process itself. This predisposes reformers—and indeed all those in the system (which probably includes most government employees dealing with contracting issues, with the exception of agency lawyers) who believe too much "law" surrounds government contracting—to react with instinctive skepticism to proposals by administrative law scholars to add yet another corpus of law into government contracting.

Contract Management and the Performance of the Procurement System

By "contract management" is meant efforts undertaken after awarding a contract to obtain successful contractor performance. Unsuccessful contract management increases the chance both that the contractor will not perform well in achieving the goals of the contract and that the contractor will violate constraints on its behavior, including constraints of interest to public law scholars. A number of the chapters in this volume therefore display concern with the ability of the government to manage (a process often referred to in the chapters as "supervising" or "monitoring") contracts.

Any reasonably impartial person with experience in government contracting would draw the conclusion—unsurprising from a range of human affairs—that the quality of contract management varies widely, from contracts that are actively and successfully managed to ones where management is perfunctory or nearly nonexistent.

There is an image of contract administration, shared to some extent in many of the chapters in this collection, suggesting an environment where government is "asleep at the switch" or where nobody is "minding the store" (phrases often used by critics)—and, therefore, where contractors run roughshod over the public and hapless agencies. This is a world of cost overruns and performance failures. Academic concerns about a "hollow state" where government contracts rather than produces, sometimes citing similar accounts of contracting problems, have sounded a parallel alarm.[56]

We should take such images with a grain of salt. Surely, to take the best known exhibits for the prosecution, there are "cost overruns" in many weapons and technology projects. But these should not be seen simply, or even mostly, as due to sloth or fraud. Much cost growth results from unrealistically low initial cost estimates, reflecting positive illusions people tend to have that they are "above average" and therefore will be able to manage costs better than most, or, often, used to garner political support for a project that will be harder to sell the more expensive it is said to be.[57] To be sure, such gaming is problematic for other reasons, but it suggests skepticism about any assumption that the original cost estimate is what the project "should" have cost and that any final figure over that estimate means government is paying "too much." Cost growth also results from changes in project specifications, so what government ends up buying includes performance features not in the original contract.[58] And, of course, many of these projects involve very complex, first-time tasks going beyond the current state of the art. In fact, studies comparing "megaprojects" in DOD and the private sector found that a universe of forty-seven nondefense projects such as construction of refineries, process plants, and nuclear plants[59] showed greater average cost growth than did DOD major weapons projects in the 1960s, although technological uncertainties in the weapons systems development were surely greater on average than for these projects.[60] A study of private sector major information-technology systems development projects found that most came in considerably over budget and delivered less performance than expected; many were abandoned entirely.[61]

Nor is the evidence consistent with the suggestion that wily contractors are able to rip off a government asleep at the switch. Although the return on equity of the aerospace/defense industry was higher than that of the S&P Industrials index during the defense boom years of the 1980s, since 1988 that industry's return has typically been lower, often dramatically lower, than the S&P Industrials.[62] To take one example of a publicly traded information technology corporation that reports separate results for its commercial and U.S. federal government divisions, Computer Sciences Corporation reported a return on sales of 7.8 percent for commercial work and 6.3 percent for federal work for 2000, numbers in line with the observations of other large information technology firms selling into both markets.[63]

Although one might not guess as much from "asleep at the switch" accounts, the government maintains a significant infrastructure dealing with contract administration, including contract and program officials and an entire organization in DOD, the Defense Contract Management Agency. On the financial side, DOD has an entire organization of contract auditors, the Defense Contract Audit Agency, that also works for civilian agency customers, along with contracting officers who manage day-to-day financial issues in real time. Brown and Potoski found that municipalities contracting out garbage collection supplemented their own in-house contract management efforts (spot checks of quality, tracking missed streets and citizen complaints, and customer satisfaction surveys) with activities of these types that they required the contractor to perform, leading to a situation where the total level of monitoring was higher for contracted than in-house services.[64] Brown and Potoski also found that monitoring activities increased as competition for the original contract decreased; contracts for which fewer than three bids were received monitored the contractor more than in situations where three or more bids had come in.

Furthermore, it would be misleading to draw generalizations about the overall quality of contract management from experiences in Iraq. The ability to deploy contract management personnel on the ground there is limited by rules prohibiting DOD from ordering civilian employees outside the United States, largely limiting contracting personnel there to volunteers. Additionally, although dedicated funds were appropriated for inspector general positions to look for contracting mistakes after the fact, no additional funds were authorized for hiring more contracting personnel (to reduce the incidence of mistakes in the first place.[65] The security situation outside the Green Zone in Baghdad makes it difficult for contract monitoring to occur on-site. And contracting is occurring in a local culture where corruption is endemic.

Having noted all this, however, the fact remains that contract administration has traditionally not been given sufficient attention in most parts of government. In the early 1990s, before procurement reform, the Office of Federal Procurement Policy sent "SWAT teams" to a number of agencies to suggest improvements in contract administration. Much of contract administration is not amenable to rules; hence in the traditional system it suffered from the lack of attention accorded everything not treated at length in the rules. It would, finally, be fair to note that contract administration was largely a stepchild of procurement reform, which focused on encouraging innovative acquisition strategy ideas and on improving source selection, partly in order to free up time that, it was hoped, could then be devoted to contract administration.

To make the problem worse, government also currently suffers from a shortage of trained bodies to manage contracts. During the 1990s, the overall size of the procurement workforce shrank from about 39,000 to about 29,000,[66] pursuant to a mandate of the Clinton administration's "reinventing government" initiative to shrink the size of the federal workforce in general, and of "overhead" (sometimes called "micromanagement") functions such as procurement in particular. Some commentators, such as Schooner, have been critical of 1990s downsizing.[67] It might be noted, however, that downsizing was accompanied by reforms significantly reducing workload, which alleviated the need for additional personnel; the most dramatic reduction was achieved by the use of credit cards.[68] Moreover, procurement spending remained stable during the 1990s, and with the end of the cold war new weapons programs declined dramatically. Nonetheless, downsizing did deprive the government of a decade of new recruits, meaning that when hiring began again in recent years, there was a lack of people in the midcareer age range (35–44) to act as mentors and first-line supervisors, while the number of people 55 years or older had risen.[69] Further, downsizing did not allow workload freed up by reforms to be redirected into contract management, already underresourced. A generous reading of the 1990s experience is that government emerged with a workforce that was "lean and mean," but without much wiggle room.

The potential problem at the end of the 1990s has become indisputable during this decade as procurement spending, in the wake of 9/11, has doubled, while the size of the contracting workforce has increased only to a minor degree. The situation is now difficult, but it is not easy to solve, since few elected officials are eager to support hiring more "bureaucrats." Public law scholars worried about inadequate contract management need to add their voices to the meager, albeit growing, ranks of those making such a request.

What needs to be done well if contract management is to be successful? The vast majority of what good program and contract managers[70] need to be good at are the same things *any* good manager needs to be good at. In fact, the most important responsibilities are analogous to those of a senior executive, not a first-line supervisor or middle manager. It is the job of the *contractor's* management to supervise its employees directly on a day-to-day basis. What a *government* program or contract manager needs to be good at is executive-type functions such as (1) strategy and goal-setting, (2) inspiring those doing the work, including contractors, with commitment, enthusiasm and public purpose, (3) performance management, including traditional "monitoring" (financial and nonfinancial) where appropriate given the type of contract, (4) managing horizontal interfaces between the contractor and end users of the contractor's services, and (5) managing interfaces with higher organization levels and the external environment.

The most fundamental problem with the current system is that it insufficiently recognizes contract management as in the first instance a management function; correspondingly, too many contract managers selected from the ranks of program or technical officials are "wannabe doers" dealt the short straw by being given contract administration duties.[71] Technicians and other scientifically trained managers thus have had strong motivation to escape from the task—what one official whom Kettl interviewed called the "administrative stigma"—as quickly as possible.[72]

One observation that critics of contracting frequently raise is that if government does not retain significant work in-house, it will lack the substantive expertise required to administer its contracts.[73] According to this argument, if government has no "doers" who have written software code, it cannot successfully manage contractors writing code. In this view, contracting must be self-limiting, or else government will do a poor job getting good performance of the work it contracts for.

I disagree with the critics' argument. Before exploring this further, three remarks are in order. The first is that, typically, government has *subject matter expertise* on the goals of the contract—government people are still running business processes being reengineered by contractors or are the customers for new products and services and can express what results they seek. Government loses subject matter expertise only if a function both is completely outsourced and if there are no government customers of the service (such as when garbage collection is outsourced). Second, procurement reform has reduced government's need for *functional expertise* on the technology (the term is being used broadly here) the contractor is using to achieve the contract's goals. The more government evaluates bidders on past performance, the smaller the role of a bidder's technical approach in source selection on the new job being bid. In a performance-based contract, requirements for functional skills on the government's end, particularly after contract award, decline dramatically. Third, one should not overestimate the number of situations where government needs access to its own functional expertise. It is easier to recognize a good idea than to come up with one. It is easier to judge whether performance metrics have been met than to know how to meet them oneself.

But there still remain significant situations where the government needs functional skills. How can it have these skills available without its own "doers"?

1. Perhaps the most important requirement is for government to recruit people with several years of "doer" experience in the private sector into midlevel contracting management positions, rather than assuming such midlevel hires must move up from entry-level positions

within the government. Such jobs may appeal to young people who are generally job-mobile, who wish to do a few years of public service, who have young children and might prefer less travel or a more family-friendly environment, or who might be attracted to positions with fairly significant responsibility. This requires changing the reliance in government on a model according to which there are only two points of entry into government employment, entry-level and senior political level—an approach increasingly at odds with the expectation held by young people of working in many organizations.[74]

2. Government can hire nonprofit organizations,[75] or even contractors (other than those doing the work contracted for), to provide needed functional expertise. It is easy to ironize about this. Such ironization doesn't render this solution less sensible. Even if government employed its own in-house technical experts—say, software programmers—there are so many subspecializations and idiosyncratic areas of expertise within a functional domain that for any specific effort, the in-house people would still be likely to lack technical skills in the specific area. Thus, in-house expertise frequently does not obviate the need for outside expertise. Indeed, in areas such as information technology, it is common for private sector customers to use independent third-party information sources (such as the Gartner Group) to help them develop requirements and evaluate vendors. Government has done this for many years in a number of areas, including weapons systems, even when it had far more "doers" with technical skills on staff.

3. Although it needs to be careful about how it does this, government can make judicious use of contractors who will, or may, be doing the work to provide some of the technical expertise needed for developing requirements for the work that will be done.

As will be discussed below, there are situations—because of the government pay structure and temporary or surge requirements—where work is contracted out even though the government's requirements are highly changeable, uncertain, and difficult to measure using performance metrics. In these situations, contract administration often means in effect treating the contractor as an employee subject to hierarchy-like direction.[76] "Technical direction" clauses generally appearing in cost-reimbursement contracts allow such treatment.[77] Indeed, contractors frequently complain that government "micromanages" details of how they do the work.[78] However, absent specific statutory authority, agencies are prohibited from entering so-called personal services contracts,[79] where government employees directly supervise contractor employees. This prohibition, often skirted de facto, probably does not make sense in situations where contracting should be occurring even though they do not correspond to TCE theory.

Public Law Issues

Various contributions to this volume make clear to a reasonable observer that, at least on occasion, government contracting raises public law issues involving due process or other rights of citizens, as well as transparency and decision-making accountability. It is at the same time important to realize that these examples represent a tiny proportion of government contracting, lest there be established a new legal regime to ensure respect for such values that applies to contracts in general. This could easily engender enormous burdens on the ability of the procurement system to achieve its goals, especially in an environment where the new regime would be exploited by organizations seeking to use it for reasons unrelated to promotion of public law values—with major impacts on the ability of contracts to be expeditiously awarded and successfully administered, without in most cases even creating any benefits in terms of the constraints that administrative law scholars value.

Sometimes public law issues are raised by the very decision to contract out a function rather than perform it in-house, because the functions—say, legitimately applying force to people other than in self-defense, making policy, or issuing legally binding determinations of general applicability—are seen as legitimately belonging only to government. These are activities known in government contracting as "inherently governmental." As early as 1989, it was uncovered during Senate hearings that at the Environmental Protection Agency (EPA) contractors were drafting budget documents, overseeing field investigators, drafting responses to public comments during the rulemaking process and writing regulation preambles, and organizing and conducting public hearings.[80] At the Department of Energy, contractors were drafting congressional testimony, conducting hearings on challenges to security clearance decisions, and giving advice on decisions on nuclear technology export.[81] Many object on philosophical grounds to prison privatization.[82] Other times—as with protections of civil rights or government transparency and accountability issues (such as Freedom of Information Act (FOIA) provisions)—the objection is not so much to contracting per se as to the status of various public law protections, for citizens or for democracy, when functions are contracted.

Issues about contracting out inherently governmental functions have been frequently raised in the context of Iraq, regarding the notorious participation of contractors in prison interrogation at the Abu Ghraib prison and, more generally, to the large presence in Iraq of private security companies such as Blackwater.[83] As far as private security companies go, the discussion has been marred by a serious misunderstanding of their role. These companies overwhelmingly are used to provide security for U.S. *contractors* undertaking economic, social, and infrastructure reconstruction projects in Iraq, *not* to engage in military operations against Iraqi insurgents, a task that is the job of the Army.[84]

Still, it is important to raise these questions. But it is also important to ask how commonly they occur in government contracting, lest overly restrictive remedies be adopted to deal with them. To provide some idea of the extent to which government contracts raise public law issues with which this volume is concerned, a random sample of one hundred solicitations in *FedBizOpps,* the daily publication presenting government contracting opportunities, for a single recent day (July 6, 2006) was examined.[85] Of these, only two can be viewed as even potentially raising any public law issues. Contracts include solicitations for "manufacturing of security pallets for ammunition," "purchase of a ball nut actuator for power transmission in aircraft," "reconstruction of a forest road . . . and removal of dangerous trees," "270,000 fiberboard boxes," "janitorial services for air traffic control center in Indianapolis," "transcription services for the Department of the Army Inspector General," "remove miscellaneous debris from Pinhook Bog within Indiana Dunes National Lakeshore," and "weekly on-site dermatology clinic services at a VA medical center."[86]

As noted, at most two of the hundred solicitations even arguably raise public law issues, in both cases limited to fear of policymaking inappropriately being contracted out.[87] The closest among the hundred to being problematic is the solicitation for development of planning documents, including holding a public meeting, for the "byway corridor plan regarding Mt. Hood and Willamette National Forest." And there is a solicitation by the Bureau of Public Debt of the Treasury Department for contracted auditing services for Haiti, which might conceivably involve making policy decisions in Haiti, conceivably in turn affecting the U.S. government.[88] Additionally, the list includes a solicitation by EPA for a sole-source contractor to prepare draft agency comments on air emission provisions in a standard being developed by a nonprofit standardization organization (American Society for Testing and Materials) for hydronic heater emissions; however, the organization doing the work for the agency is an association of six northeastern state clean air government agencies. None of these solicitations appears to raise questions that, considering the scope of problems of American governance, are anything but trivial. Furthermore, while chapters in this volume raise questions about inappropriately contracting out inherently governmental functions, it is relevant to note that just as there may be inappropriate decisions to contract out jobs that should be kept inside government, the opposite mistake may occur as well, and not necessarily to a minor degree. The 1998 Federal Activities Inventory Reform (FAIR) Act[89] required agencies to develop an annual "inventory" of their civil service jobs that indicated which of them were "commercial" activities.[90] Office of Management and Budget (OMB) regulations require that commercial activities be further divided into those that, although commercial, are adjudged inappropriate for potential outsourcing, for reasons such as to preserve a core capability (defined as involving the agency's ability to accomplish its unique mission), to have program personnel available to provide contract or program management, to permit rotation of personnel for career growth or to maintain maximum productivity. Government-wide, the first such set of inventories produced the conclusion that, of 1.8 million federal civilian employees,[91] a full 765,000 were listed as commercial, of whom about 390,000 were deemed appropriate for public-private competition pursuant to OMB Circular A-76. This represents over 20 percent of existing federal jobs.[92]

To gain an idea of what these commercial jobs might be, inventories for the most recently available year[93] were examined for DOD and the Department of Health and Human Services (the civilian agency with the largest budget), to see the five largest commercial job categories listed. The 2005 DOD inventory listed 168,207 jobs (of 572,402 total positions) as commercial and appropriate for public-private competition. Examples included 12,246 civil servants providing financial/accounting services, 8,322 operating DOD commissaries (stores), 7,320 providing minor building construction/maintenance/repair, 5,524 in computing services/database management, and 5,396 providing administrative management/correspondence support. The Health and Human Services inventory listed 22,256 such jobs (of 66,669 total positions), including 3,589 civil servants providing nursing services, 2,606 providing administrative support, 1,432 in medical records/transcription, 1,040 in medical services, and 881 in computing services/database management. All in all, these inventories remind us that potential "misclassification" is not a one-way street.

If one wishes to limit situations where government inappropriately contracts out functions that should be performed in-house, including functions that could or should be seen as inherently governmental, it is important first to understand why this occurs. Donahue's analysis[94] is trenchant. He argues—consistently with the previous discussion—that there are there are two kinds of misclassification, not only decisions to contract out activities that should be kept in-house but also decisions to keep in-house work that should be contracted. Both kinds of misclassification, he argues, relate to the relatively more egalitarian wage structure of the federal government, compared with the private sector. This means that high-end professional and managerial government jobs tend to be paid less than comparable ones in the private sector, while low-end blue-collar type jobs tend to be paid more. This produces decisions to contract out high-end work inappropriately, including work involving quasi-policymaking or authoritative legal decisions as well as other high-end work that may involve an agency's core competencies, because it is difficult to attract good people to perform the work at salaries the government pays.[95] One could deal with this problem by creating a more market-adapted wage structure in government. Here, government has tied its own hands. If the public law community wishes to reduce inappropriate contracting for policymaking, there is probably no more important step it could take than to lobby for reforms in the government's wage structure. However, people should be advised that the idea of paying already well-paid "bureaucrats" more money— particularly salaries higher than those of members of Congress—like the idea of hiring more "bureaucrats" to manage contracts, wins no political appeal contests. At a minimum, public law scholars should understand the dynamic—and it is not the narratives the community commonly adopts—of what is occurring.

Along with wage structure considerations, by far the most common reason for contracting for quasi-policymaking or other activities troubling the public law community is the need for temporary or surge capacity, a consideration distinct from the TCE tradition. Take the infamous example of contractors being used for prison interrogation at Abu Ghraib, and consider the Army's problem. It needed a stable of people fluent in Arabic for questioning prisoners (or translating between interrogator and prisoner). But this need came up suddenly, and it lasted for a limited time. There are countless other languages (Urdu? Spanish? Serbo-Croatian? Chinese?) for which similar demands might unpredictably appear. Surely it doesn't make sense for the Army to employ stables of language experts to wait around for the time when they might (hypothetically) be needed. Should the Environmental Protection Agency keep on staff an expert on hydronic stoves, waiting around to comment on proposed standards for them? If an agency needs to develop a new financial management information technology system every ten years, does a make sense to employ staff expert at this, waiting for the once-in-a-decade event?

Again, this wound is partly self-inflicted. Taking the Abu Ghraib translators as an example, the contractor did not have on staff a bevy of Arabic speakers suitable for this work any more than the Army did. The contractor went out and recruited them when it received the contract.[96] The Army could not do this because it is difficult (though not impossible),[97] once they are hired, to get rid of civil servants because there is no further demand for their work, and difficult to hire temporary employees, particularly to hire them quickly. Again, the public law community could accomplish more to reduce inappropriate contracting by advocating reform of the civil service hiring and dismissal system than through many of its other proposals—though, one more time, the prospects for such changes, which are strongly opposed by government employee unions, are small.

More broadly, in de facto hierarchy situations where government managers significantly direct work by contractor employees, these managers frequently prefer "supervising" contractors to civil servants, oddly (from a TCE perspective) because they believe they have more control over contractor employees than in-house ones. One federal manager with a mixed civil service/government workforce recounts a situation when a contractor and a civil servant were both suspected of a security breach at the workplace; the contractor employee was gone from the workplace within a day, while the civil servant was still present several months later.[98] This set of events occurred because civil service rules are so different from the standard TCE environment. Under these circumstances, one remedy for inappropriate decisions to contract would be to increase the flexibility of the civil service system, so that poorly performing employees could be removed from the workforce more easily and employees assigned in more flexible ways. Opposition to civil service reform, then, implies creating more situations where government becomes inclined to contract rather than producing in-house.

Sometimes whether it makes substantive sense to contract out work requiring temporary skills depends on a judgment about whether specialized knowledge exists in the private sector or how easy it would be for the government to develop the temporarily needed skills in-house through real-time training or self-education. Take the EPA hydronic heater emissions issue. Without knowing exactly how arcane the knowledge of hydronic heater emissions is and to what extent such knowledge exists in the private sector, one cannot make a judgment about whether it is appropriate, from a temporary capacity perspective, to contract out comments.

Sometimes it is hard to draw a line between "policy advice" and "policymaking." On the one hand, it would seem self-defeating for the government to deprive itself of good outside policy advice; outside advice can add fresh perspectives that might not exist inside the organization. But there are two objections. One, from a perspective of contracting theory, is that the ability to weigh policy proposals in-house should be a core competency, suggesting that outside advice should at most occur at the margins of the policymaking process, not at the center. The second is that advice may become de facto decision making, with "recommendations" rubber-stamped by the people inside.

It should be noted that from a public law perspective, where development of documents or advice that may involve policy or value issues is contracted out, there is normally no reason to believe the contractor would have any self-interest reducing its ability to provide disinterested advice. In cases where policy or value issues are relatively minor—as is probably true, for example, for the byway corridor plan for the national forest discussed earlier—the least restrictive way to deal with public law issues would be for the government simply to explain to the contractor the relevant legal or policy context for the advice the contractor is being asked to give. One can, however, imagine situations where a contractor might have a self-interest in providing biased advice—as when an economic research unit of a company producing sulphur dioxide emissions provides a report to EPA on the economic consequences of sulphur dioxide regulation, or an information-technology company selling security software provides a business case regarding agency purchase of security software. Here, the least restrictive way to deal with the problem is to invoke existing "organizational conflict of interest" rules[99] either to prevent a firm with a conflict from bidding on a contract or to prevent a firm that does an underlying study from bidding on work growing out of the study.

Losing Individual Rights by Contracting?

If one is afraid that the individual rights protected if a service is delivered in-house would be lost by contracting, the least intrusive way of dealing with this is through contract clauses incorporating public law protections. There is ample precedent for contract clauses imposing public policy objectives generally (going beyond statutory requirements for firms in general) on those contracting with the government, a practice launched when President Franklin D. Roosevelt signed an executive order in 1941 prohibiting defense contractors from discrimination based on race. Currently, many such requirements are imposed through contract clauses on contractors in general, such as additional workplace affirmative action requirements not applied to businesses in general[100] and special efforts to maintain a "drug-free workplace,"[101] although inclusion of such clauses on a case-by-case basis is more unusual.

Such clauses are not unproblematic, as they establish obligations going beyond general statute that firms may avoid by refraining from contracting with government in the first place, meaning that such clauses tend to limit competition to contractors specializing in government work rather than those for whom this would be a small portion of their business.[102] For this reason, the FASA eliminated requirements for a number of such special clauses when government purchases commercial items.[103]

Use of such clauses to provide public law protections already occurs. For example, Bureau of Prisons requests for proposals for their prison management contracts have a section called "inmate rights," which states, *inter alia:* "All services and programs shall comply with . . . the U.S. Constitution; all applicable federal, state and local laws and regulations; applicable Presidential Executive Orders (E.O.); all applicable case law; and Court Orders. Should a conflict exist between any of the aforementioned standards, the most stringent shall apply."[104] Furthermore, in addition to requiring the contractor to establish a prisoner grievance procedure, solicitations also state that the contractor must allow prisoners to make complaints through the Bureau of Prisons' own procedures. Solicitations specifically state that "[t]he contractor shall stock and provide inmates with [Bureau of Prisons] administrative remedy forms" and use the Bureau's complaint-tracking system "to facilitate the administrative remedy process." Additionally, "[w]hen relief is granted upon appeal, the contractor shall take corrective action as indicated in the response." Although one may still object that the legitimate exercise of force other than in self-defense is inherently governmental, it would be hard to argue that the Bureau of Prisons has removed human rights protections for prisoners that would apply if the prison were being run in-house.

For Medicare benefits, a statutory requirement for private parties (insurance carriers and fiscal intermediaries) in §§1869 and 1879 of the Social Security Act[105] mandates establishment of an appeals procedure for beneficiaries denied treatment. Center for Medicare and Medicaid Services regulations prescribe a five-step review process for private-party treatment denials, involving two steps of appeals to government ALJ's and further appeal to federal courts.[106]

A number of federal agencies contract for debt collection. A representative example is the Department of Education (ED), which has contracted out debt collection activities for college student loans since 1981. An examination of DOE's most recent solicitation for these services again suggests significant attention to public law issues.[107] The solicitation states that the contractor must not only obey all debt collection statutes and the Privacy Act, but must also follow the more stringent government-unique Federal Claims Collection Standards and the Education Department Debt Collection Regulation. All debt collection letters must be approved by ED. Each contractor employee must certify in writing that they have received training regarding the Privacy Act before they begin collection activities. ED runs a complaint system for borrowers, and if two apparently valid complaints are received against any contractor employee, that employee must be removed from work on the contract; complaints are also one of the factors in determining the fee the contractor receives. Finally, private debt collectors have no enforcement authority—the government must bring any enforcement actions.

For Medicaid and food stamps, federal law prohibits contractors from making eligibility determinations, though no such prohibition appears in other benefit programs such as Temporary Assistance for Needy Families and the Child Health Insurance Program.[108] Federal law requires an appeals process, including affirmative notice to the applicant of the right to appeal, for all programs involving federal funds, whether eligibility decisions are made by government employees or contractors. Some states also offer judicial review.

Freedom of Information Act?

Some have argued that FOIA should be applied to contractors.[109] General applicability of FOIA to all government contractors would be a devastating policy that would almost certainly cause the wholesale withdrawal of firms not completely dependent on government business from the government marketplace. IBM, Kraft Foods, or General Motors would surely be unwilling to accept the idea that their sales of computers, cookies, or cars to the government rendered a large number of internal business documents related to production of those items subject to public release. They would react to such a policy by ceasing to sell to the government.

A less intrusive alternative would be the application of FOIA, through contract clauses, to some or all activities under a given contract where FOIA-type issues are considered to be important. It is unlikely large defense contractors, for example, would refrain from contracting with government if a FOIA clause were added, though such a clause would probably stop predominantly commercial firms from competing with them for business where they might otherwise be able to do so, creating a barrier to entry in the government marketplace.

Those (defense) contractors accepting a FOIA clause would likely, even in a competitive environment, raise their prices considerably for work including such a provision, increasing taxpayer costs in a way likely to be highly disproportionate to any benefits to the public. The reason is contractors' horror at the possibility that, unlike individual government employees, they might be subject to enormous monetary liability in a lawsuit if a recommendation they made in a document eventually released under FOIA turned out to have created catastrophic liability.[110] These fears would not only cost the government money; they would also inhibit honest communication from contractors, one value contractors bring to the government in the first place.[111]

Finally, FOIA clauses in individual contracts would create a large burden on the government, which would need to determine whether a given document was subject to FOIA release (presumably companies would not be trusted to make such determinations themselves). It is naïve to expect that the only, or even the major, requests for FOIA documents would come from public-spirited individuals or groups seeking greater democratic accountability. Contractors have business competitors interested in obtaining proprietary or other information about rivals. Currently, the major FOIA requesters in the domain of government contracting are rivals seeking information from bids submitted to the government. Proprietary information is exempt from FOIA, but competitors nonetheless hope to learn from information not classified as proprietary. Meanwhile, it is time-consuming for both the government and the contractor to reach decisions about what information is proprietary. Furthermore, there are groups opposed to contracting on ideological or interest-based grounds having little or nothing to do with public law issues—such as employee unions—that would welcome the opportunity to make contracting less effective and thus less attractive to the government compared to in-house production. It is likely that such groups would frequently file FOIA requests with the aim of burdening the government or discouraging firms from contracting with the government. With the shortage of contracting employees available to do core contracting work—and with few prospects of unlimited increases, or indeed any increases, in these resources—it is hard to imagine that the contracting workforce would do more good for society dealing with FOIA requests than doing mainstream contracting work.

When contractors produce publicly available (or FOIA-discoverable) reports for the government, as with the planning documents for the byway corridor plan for a national forest discussed earlier, public accountability regarding the content of such documents can be achieved via the government agency that receives, and might use, the documents, since contractor documents submitted to the government are subject to FOIA.

The desirability of such clauses should be carefully considered on a case-by-case basis, where the strength of any public interest in FOIA applicability should be weighed against the public interest in robust competition among vendors. My general conclusion is that including such clauses would normally be undesirable.

Applying the APA to Solicitations?

The most far-reaching proposal for dealing with public law issues in contracting is to apply notice and comment procedures of the Administrative Procedure Act to (presumably draft) notices or solicitations, at the time the government announces its intention to contract.[112] As I understand it, the purpose of the notice and comment would be to solicit public comment on public law issues connected with the work to be contracted; for example, what kinds of procedures a contractor should follow (or be prohibited from following) in doing the work, what kinds of remedies members of the public should have for adverse contractor decisions, what general government policies (such as applicability of FOIA) should apply to the contract.

Given the minute proportion of contracting actions that raise public law issues, this proposal can only be described as using a nuclear weapon to kill a gnat. It would add significant time to the contracting process for obtaining comments, and, where comments were received, analyzing them, developing responses, getting these approved through an internal hierarchy, and sometimes defending responses against litigation. The harm to the public's interest in effective contracting would not just involve delays. It would also require diversion of part of government's overstretched contracting workforce to deal with these issues. As with FOIA requests, given the shortage of contracting employees, this hardly seems like a priority for using limited resources.

One response to this objection might be that if there are no public law interests at stake in a contract, there will be no public comments and thus no increased burden on the agency. This argument would be incorrect. First, even if there are no comments, the notice and comment procedure delays the contracting process and thus makes contracting less able to serve agency missions. Second, one cannot assume that absence of any legitimate public law interests would protect the government from having comments filed. As with FOIA requests, notice and comment provisions would be introduced into a world where there are groups that welcome the opportunity to make contracting less effective. It is likely that such groups would frequently file comments and even initiate lawsuits, especially for larger or more controversial contracts, even though the objections raised had nothing to do with public law–related issues. Comments and lawsuits might also come from incumbent contractors hoping to have their contract extended without competition beyond the contractual period through delays whose length the government cannot easily predict. In both kinds of cases, lawsuits would not be deterred by the unlikelihood of judicial victory, since the main goal is delay, either to make contracting less attractive ex ante for the agency or to extend an incumbent's period of performance.

One might propose dealing with these various problems by subjecting only certain solicitations to notice and comment. For example, the requirement could be limited to larger contracts. But even that is a significant number of contracts, and thus a significant increase in burdens on agencies: in fiscal year 2006, the government awarded 22,189 contracts and task orders of $1 million or more, and 2,312 of $10 million or more. The magnitude of this additional burden is suggested by the comparison that in 2005 all federal agencies published for public comment only 139 proposed new and 524 proposed revised rules that make changes in the Code of Federal Regulations.[113] Furthermore, I suspect there is little if any correlation between the dollar value of a contract and the likelihood it raises significant public law issues. To take an obvious example, the Iraq interrogator contract was very modest in value, as contracts to write drafts of agency testimony before Congress would be.

One might alternatively state in law that only contracts determined to raise, say, "significant" public law issues (however defined) would require notice and comment. One might establish a notice and comment exception for urgent contracts. However, conclusions that a contract raised no significant public law issues, or raised such issues but merited an urgency exception, would themselves need to be justified at the buying office level and approved at a higher level. Such activities would themselves take up significant agency resources and delay the process. They could presumably also be challenged in court by the same contracting opponents or incumbent contractors, again adding delay.

Finally, many of the kinds of public law issues that might be raised in an APA notice and comment requirement for contracts—involving impacts of an organization's procedures on the rights of the public—are not subject to notice and comment procedures when work is performed in-house; the APA does not apply to "rules of agency organization, procedure, or practice" (§553(b)) (although there has been litigation regarding the scope of this provision, and sometimes agencies voluntarily subject such procedures to APA notice and comment). Thus, for example, Occupational Safety and Health Administration or EPA handbooks outlining standard operating procedures for inspectors to use in inspecting plants are not submitted for notice and comment. APA notice and comment would thus sometimes put a greater administrative law burden on contracting than on in-house production.

Given the rare occurrence of these kinds of issues and the disproportionate burden APA provisions would create, surely a better route is simply to raise the awareness of the contracting community that public law issues may arise in certain limited contracting situations, so that it becomes more likely that the government considers them when appropriate. Groups concerned with public law issues that may arise in certain situations can meet with agencies to raise the issues. If necessary, congressional intervention can be sought. Surely these approaches make more sense than the nuclear option of the APA.

This is no utopian proposal. Even without educational efforts, government has shown concern for public law–related issues, as the examples given earlier suggest. Other evidence of the openness of the procurement community to efforts voluntarily to promote public law values is adoption by the Federal Acquisition Council, which develops the Federal Acquisition Regulations (FAR), of a self-imposed obligation to use notice and comment procedures for regulations governing operation of the procurement system (as opposed to individual contracts); even though the APA explicitly excludes matters "relating to" public contracts from notice and comment rulemaking requirements,[114] the FAR imposes requirements of notice and comment for "significant revisions" to regulations.[115]

Some Concluding Observations

If the public law community wishes to see government contracts be generally well-managed (including management of public law issues they raise), its members need to worry about contracting issues they don't normally consider. I have suggested earlier that two causes of "excessive" contracting are government's unwillingness to pay higher salaries to professionals and features of the traditional civil service system. Both of these are hard to change, but support of the public law community would be welcome in both cases.

It should also be obvious from the previous discussion that good contract management is not a job for drones. There is increasing concern about a "human capital crisis" in the federal government, centering around problems government is having in recruiting or retaining bright, committed people needed to accomplish its work.[116] Although this issue was not on the agenda when procurement reform began, we can now see reform as part of a strategy to deal with that crisis. It is hard to attract talented young people into a bureaucratic system, weighed down by rules and hierarchy, that does not allow them to use their minds. Redesigning the jobs of contracting professionals to make them less bureaucratic is a crucial part of any strategy for dealing with the government's human capital crisis.

If members of the public law community care about the overall performance of the procurement system, they actually also have an interest in allowing the system to pay attention to its goals—though this is asking more of legal scholars, both given law's focus on constraints in general and given the animus in the profession towards official discretion in particular. Maintaining a focus of the procurement system on goal attainment is a constant challenge, as experience during the Bush administration illustrates.[117] The most serious challenge to procurement reform has come from a desire to use procurement abuse, real or alleged, as a partisan political issue. The political system, of course, never lost its interest in abuse, though attention to it had declined during the height of reform. But during the Bush administration the issue of abuse took a partisan edge. Partly, this came as an unintended consequence of efforts to increase public-private competitions; the understandably vociferous opposition of federal employee unions to this created a situation where an important organized group had a vested interest in a procurement system that worked poorly (or appeared to work poorly), because a badly functioning procurement system makes contracting less attractive. So unions began to oppose procurement reform, which had been trying to improve the system, and to play up allegations of abuse that made the system look bad. Democrats, in opposition, toed the unions' line. Then, in the run-up to the 2004 presidential campaign and the debate over Iraq policy, Democrats discovered an issue in allegations regarding Halliburton, the company Vice President Cheney had headed that had received large Iraq contracts. Democrats claimed procurement abuse: Halliburton had been awarded contracts improperly, and the company was cheating the government. Similar allegations were made with regard to awards of large emergency contracts after Hurricane Katrina to so-called crony contractors to the Republican Party. Virtually every procurement expert dismissed these claims.[118] But they brought abuse to the center of attention.

Some of procurement reform's wounds were self-inflicted. In their eagerness to switch the system's focus from abuse to mission accomplishment, reformers did not pay enough attention to combating abuse problems. Reports emerged of abuses related to procurement reform itself—examples of government employees misusing government-provided credit cards, contracts for information technology services under streamlined procurement vehicles made with only one bid, and situations where, in the name of commercial item buying, defense contractors providing weapons systems (such as a new-generation military aircraft) had been excused from providing traditional cost data. There were several instances of postemployment abuses involving procurement officials going to work for contractors. All this allowed reform opponents to cast procurement reform itself as a source of abuses, either for policies it developed or for insufficient attention paid to, say, postemployment abuses. Procurement reformers were mistaken not to act more forcefully from the beginning to tend the system's boundaries. Thus, while many of the specific changes reform instituted were still on the books a decade later, the spirit of frontline innovation basic to the movement had vanished, replaced by a fear of becoming the object of scandal and investigation.[119]

The public law community has performed a service in identifying issues that need the attention of the contracting community. Most of the contracting community wants to continue down a path of seeking better attainment of contracting goals. In some areas—such as the need for more and better people to manage government contracts—the perspectives of the two communities merge. More generally, with good will on both sides, I would hope solutions can be crafted that take the concerns of each community into account in a way that pays attention to legitimate public law values while honoring the value of getting public business accomplished in an efficient and effective manner.

Public law scholars face a choice. They can ally themselves with those (unfortunately including many in the public contracts bar) who wish to return the procurement system to a preoccupation with constraints[120] and seek only a contracting system that manages constraints well, including those the public law community has identified. That path will provoke bitter opposition from most of the procurement community. Or public law scholars can ally themselves with those who wish to see procurement well managed in general, including managing appropriate public law concerns. The latter path allows cooperation and, one hopes, furthers aims of both groups.

CHAPTER EIGHT

Federal Contracting in Context

What Drives It, How to Improve It

STAN SOLOWAY

ALAN CHVOTKIN

Introduction

Over the last two decades, government outsourcing has become an increasingly common trend. Today, total federal spending on contracts for goods and services of all kinds exceeds $450 billion, representing nearly 40 percent of the total discretionary budget of the federal government.[1] Of that total spending, nearly 60 percent is spent on services, often referred to as "outsourcing." While often presumed to be driven by political ideology, recent government outsourcing is much more a reflection of three key trends: a fundamental shift in the role and ownership of technology, nearly revolutionary change in the management of businesses and institutions of all kinds, and difficulties on the part of the government in recruiting and retaining the talent necessary for technologically driven service delivery. Outsourcing is the natural outgrowth of these conditions and is essential to help government achieve its mission. It is, in simple terms, reflective both of major change in the general economy and of the new "face of government." Even as the government must identify and pursue new and innovative means of attracting and retaining critical skills, this "new face" is almost certain to be a permanent feature of government into the decades ahead.

Today, all federal procurement is underpinned by a broad regime of statutory, regulatory, and policy strictures. And there is no evidence or any other reason to believe that additional layers of laws or rules, including the overlay of additional administrative law precepts, would do anything to improve the process or its outcomes. Such additions would likely hamstring the process, reduce the government's needed flexibility, interfere with the government's ability to access the full range of available solutions, and upset the existing delicate balance between the very real and legitimate interests of the public (whose dollars are being expended) and the equally legitimate requirements of a business relationship. As articulated so well by Steve Kelman in Chapter 7, that balance is essential; moreover, many of the basic principles of administrative law are already present throughout the federal procurement process.

At the macro level, the federal procurement regime is specifically designed to lead the government to decisions that are in its, and the taxpayers', best interests. While critical aspects of the federal outsourcing and procurement regime—like the highly regulated treatment of competitors—already reflect some fundamental tenets of administrative law, protection of the public interest will not be served by adding yet more layers. For example, the current process is widely transparent—procurements are publicly advertised, winners are publicly announced, and any study focused on the possible "conversion" of work currently being performed by federal employees to private sector performance must be announced to Congress in advance—and subject to extensive oversight. Further, as is true in other elements of governance, the government has specially trained and licensed "agents" (contracting officers) who are the sole individuals authorized to commit public dollars via contract.

Of course, no one can objectively argue that improvement is not needed—clearly there are challenges that must be addressed in a system this large and complex. But those changes must be targeted to where and how real and meaningful improvement can be made. As such, the changes pursued should begin with the recognition that acquisition management and contract administration must be a core competency of the government; change thus must be focused on ensuring that government acquisition professionals are fully trained, empowered, and best prepared to handle the challenges of today's procurement needs. This would include not only a renewed emphasis on acquisition but a careful review of and emphasis on the broader personnel policies and structures that today often inhibit the government's ability to attract and retain the requisite skills. There is a growing recognition that this is where the real payoff will be found, but to date it has been the subject more of rhetoric than meaningful action.

Nonetheless, some aspects of the outsourcing trend generate important questions relating to how the government can best manage its missions and protect the public interest. To what extent does the federal procurement process contain adequate safeguards and incentives to ensure that activities performed by private contractors are being done in the government's best interest? Is the government abdicating its responsibilities for determining requirements and managing cost, schedule, and performance?

Most experts agree that when properly managed, outsourcing, and perhaps more specifically the competitive marketplace that underpins it, can and generally does drive higher performance and improve service delivery. They also recognize that the government has increasing mission and skills gaps that cannot otherwise be filled. Some reject those conclusions. They see outsourcing as an intentional "replacement" strategy; that is, outsourcing is the purposeful replacement of federal employees with contractor employees, done primarily to make government look smaller. Still others recognize the reality of outsourcing but remain concerned about issues of accountability, transparency, and the protection of the public interest and democratic principles.

As with all policy debates, there are also some for whom the issue is essentially one of philosophy, from those who automatically presume that the private sector does everything better than the government to those who believe the introduction of profit and loss pressures into the government sphere creates a set of untenable tensions. And, of course, there are those for whom the issue is essentially and simply one of addressable markets—the numerous constituencies with large stakes in the outsourcing controversy, like public employee unions, whose membership levels are directly tied to the number of civil servants, or the private sector, whose profits are tied to government business opportunities.

Parsing the underlying motivations and interests associated with this important policy debate can be difficult. Clearly, one must be able to distinguish between, and understand the foundational reality of, principally parochial points of view and those of substance. And in order to objectively consider the many issues involved, one must step back and assess the environment in which the federal government now functions.

Unfortunately, the public debate has largely centered on the wrong issues and been founded on a set of assumptions that are often incorrect. This is increasingly true of the current discussion on outsourcing and procurement taking place in Congress, the media, and even in other chapters in this volume. The debate fails to recognize the changing dynamics of professional management and the role—and, perhaps more importantly, ownership—of technology and technology-driven business processes. The debate also tends to overstate the role of contractors, and confuses and misuses terminology. All told, these assumptions generate a debate that all too often misses the essential points.

Thus, the first steps in any serious discussion of the contemporary role of outsourcing in the federal market are to establish a factual baseline and framework, correct existing misperceptions and mythology, and address the existing regimes of law and regulation that guide the current outsourcing process.

Federal Outsourcing Today

Outsourcing vs. Privatization

Among the many areas of confusion is the difference between "outsourcing" and "privatization," which are very different in nature and impact, yet are too often presumed to be synonymous. Understanding the critical differences is essential to the broader discussion in this book and beyond.

"Outsourcing" is, in simple terms, little more than contracting for a given service. In an outsourcing arrangement, the seller retains all ownership and control of the function(s) involved. Outsourcing is, in effect, a temporary business relationship, based on competitive processes and designed to develop and implement a needed mission solution, fill an immediate gap in skills or other aspects of the organization, or improve performance and efficiency.

On the other hand, "privatization" involves circumstances in which the private sector invests private capital in existing or planned government assets and in return assumes ownership of the asset or function. In these cases, the private sector assumes the financial and infrastructure risk in return for the opportunity to have a long-term business relationship with the government—a relationship ultimately determined by the private owner's performance and adherence to pre-negotiated standards of performance. For example, in the case of military housing privatization, private sector developers invest private capital in the development of housing for soldiers, and the soldiers then pay rent to the private owners. While the private owners must commit in advance to maintaining rents at a certain level (generally tied to the housing allowance given to soldiers), the owners must also maintain the housing at a certain standard or risk financial and other penalties. Similarly, the privatization of utilities at military bases also involves private investment in base utilities, and the ensuing transfer of ownership to the private sector, in return for which the private entity then contracts with the base to provide utility service. Given the often strained fiscal realities facing governments at all levels, such strategies can be critical to helping the government meet mission and infrastructure needs without having to identify and dedicate large amounts of public funds in advance.

In some countries, particularly Great Britain, where industries had historically been largely nationalized, "privatization" has been a steady trend for decades. For example, British Airways was formerly the British Overseas Aircraft Company and was owned by the U.K. government. In the United States, however, true privatization is actually significantly more limited and is generally driven by some combination of financial pressures (particularly the availability to the government of investment capital) and a desire to put in place a competitive alternative to activities that are believed to be poorly functioning.

For example, the privatization of military housing reflects a recognition that the military does not have, and likely will not have in the foreseeable future, adequate resources to repair, upgrade, or maintain its hundreds of thousands of housing units, huge percentages of which were, or still are, in remarkable disrepair. As such, the reliance on private capital is logical and necessary. The experiments around "privatized" education being conducted in some localities are typically more reflective of the second driver—establishing a competitive alternative to poorly performing public schools. When limited to infrastructure rather than the actual delivery of education, however, it is principally or equally a financial decision.

Clearly, depending on the function to be privatized, the issues can be very complex—and are often more complex than those associated with outsourcing, particularly given the increased level of risk for the private owner. However, under both "outsourcing" and "privatization" arrangements, the government customer can and should continue to exercise significant control. The terms and conditions in both types of arrangements are generally structured to include not only the traditional financial terms and conditions but also the government's expectations and rights, and they should be so structured. Thus, as will be discussed later in this chapter, even when a function or activity is "privatized," the government can and does determine performance parameters and generally has, or should have, a range of remedies available in the event performance is inadequate.

For the purposes of this chapter, our discussion will focus on the issues associated with outsourcing rather than privatization. On some levels, the issues and drivers are very similar. But there are distinct aspects to both.

Outsourcing: Two Tracks, One Set of Rules

It is important to recognize that there are two parallel tracks of outsourcing in government. Outsourcing is sometimes an intentional act arrived at through a deliberative, governmental "make or buy" decision made on the basis of cost efficiency or higher performance. The increased reliance on contractors to support military operations is one good example. The Army recognized more than a decade ago that it needed to focus its available resources on its strategic mission—warfighting—and thus could not afford to have soldiers performing basic support functions, such as logistics or providing basic life support (for example, food, housing, and hygienic facilities). Thus, the growth in contractor support on the battlefield has been the result of a deliberate manning and strategic decision by the Army in particular. Even with the substantially higher direct short-term costs (when compared to military salaries) associated with its contractors, the military recognized that the lifecycle costs (recruitment, training, and, not insignificantly, short- and long-term benefits) of active duty military significantly outstrip the costs associated with contractor personnel, who are engaged for only a limited period of time and for whom the military has no lifetime responsibility.

The decision by the National Security Agency (NSA) a decade ago to outsource its network and information technology functions was driven by similar considerations—the agency determined that its mission needs were best served by focusing its resources on its core workforce and mission—intelligence analysis—rather than managing its internal computer systems. The NSA realized that it never would be able to adequately resource and support noncore functions.

The NSA example is instructive as well because the agency also committed itself to ensuring that the outsourcing was not done "on the backs" of the existing workforce. In fact, one of the key source selection criteria revolved around the extent to which bidders would support and transition the existing workforce. In the end, the entire affected workforce was offered positions with the winning company, in many cases coupled with pay raises and signing bonuses. For the bidding companies, the NSA workforce represented a potential new asset in an environment in which the technical skills they possessed were (and remain) in short supply—after all, the issue was never the "quality" of the people; it was the agency's strategic mission. Thus, the NSA decision was good for the agency, good for the workforce—they went from performing a support function in an organization to being part of an entity's core mission—and good for industry as well.

However, strategic decision making such as that done by the NSA becomes eminently more difficult when it is subjected to the vicissitudes of the political arena, even when the decision is clearly in the interests of the taxpayer and the agency, and does not disadvantage the incumbent federal workforce. That is entirely consistent with the basic goal of all federal acquisition. However, as discussed earlier, for some, outsourcing is essentially a parochial and political issue. Thus, to the extent those interests hold sway in the immediate political environment, strategic decisions will be trumped by politics rather than the public's interest, as they routinely are today. As discussed below with regard to competitive sourcing, this troubling dynamic has contributed greatly to the competitive sourcing program's struggles. But it also offers an important caution to those who advocate extensive "public" engagement in the procurement process. Since much of that engagement is exercised through Congress, decisions can ultimately be determined not by the broad public interest but by the relative political muscle of special interests. This raises real challenges to the delicate balance between Congress's appropriate oversight role and the twin need for federal agencies to conduct objective procurements and incentivize performance-improving change.[2] As suggested by Stephen Goldsmith and William Eggers, even in the best and most innovative institutions change can be brutally painful and difficult.[3] In a public, often inertial, and ultimately political institution like the government, it is even harder.

The second outsourcing track is more often based in strategic and human capital realities, and although the financial implications are always considered, in some cases they may pale in comparison to the fundamental mission issues. While some are fond of arguing against outsourcing because contractor employees are sometimes more expensive than government employees, the truth is that comparing private and public sector compensation levels tells only a portion of the story.

Facing seminal changes to the economy and to the role and ownership of technology, a generally losing competition with the broader private sector for talent, and a significantly graying workforce, agencies have had little choice but to turn increasingly to the private sector. It is also true that, as evidenced by the so-called pay gap between the government and the private sector, an issue that has long been a centerpiece of the federal employee union legislative agenda, in some cases the private sector workforce is more expensive than the government workforce. This is particularly true for workers with critical skills for which there is far less global supply than demand. The market has set a value on those skills, and while companies have little choice but to meet the market's demands, government compensation levels for those skills continue to lag behind that market value. Thus, the outsourcing decision sometimes comes down to a simple question: pay more for the right skills or risk mission performance. And the government is, first and foremost, mission focused.

This mission-driven outsourcing is an acute illustration of the changing face of government. As the government seeks to modernize and "transform" while remaining distanced from the broader marketplace of technology and skills, to the degree to which it organically performs and executes its missions it is also changing.

While the forces—efficiency and mission focus—driving these two tracks are somewhat different, the procurement process is the same for both. Rules governing competition, what functions can or cannot be outsourced, and the government's oversight and management of those contracts are all essentially the same. The only significant exceptions involve public/private competitions conducted under Office of Management and Budget (OMB) Circular A-76.[4]

Understanding the Existing Regime for Oversight and Accountability

Federal law treats the ability to bid for U.S. government contracts as a privilege, not a right.[5] Fundamentally, the federal procurement process is designed to be entirely neutral as to who "wins" a competition, as long as the winning side will do what is best for the government and the taxpayers. In striving for that neutrality, the law requires that the government's actions be fair to all parties.

Thus, the process strives to be highly open and transparent. There are two basic methods to ensure fairness: accountability through contracting rules and the terms of the contract itself, and accountability through oversight conducted by contracting officers, program managers, auditors, and others.

The contracting process is replete with public disclosures and announcements, strict rules of engagement, and post-award insight and control. For every potential contract with a value over $25,000, the government is required to post the opportunity publicly so that any qualified firm has the opportunity to bid.[6] While this public disclosure requirement does not apply to every incremental task order awarded under existing indefinite delivery contracts, the creation of those contract vehicles is subject to the same notice requirements. Furthermore, for every contract award in excess of $25,000, basic information—including the nature of the contract, total contract value, identity of the winning firm, and so on—is made available to the public via the Internet. Certain contracts also include provisions for additional performance time, financial rewards, and more that are intended to incentivize quality performance. While there is some disagreement and even confusion surrounding the appropriate use of incentives or award fees, including how, if at all, to measure contractor performance when major program factors (shifting requirements, funding instability, security issues, and more) are outside the contractor's control, there is broad agreement that the appropriate use of such tools is very effective.[7]

In addition, companies wishing to pursue federal government business must meet basic requirements. For example, every company must first register in the Central Contractor Registration (CCR) database and, in so doing, document that it is a legitimate business with a legitimate business bank account, a federal tax identification number, and a business address.[8] All offerors are also subject to a business responsibility determination, made by the contracting officer, in which the company's basic business ethics and legal status are affirmed.[9]

For their part, and consistent with contract law, contractors have responsibility for executing their work according to the terms and conditions of the contract. The primary responsibility for oversight of contracts rests with the contracting entity. In fact, the Federal Acquisition Regulation treats "contract administration" as an essential element of the total contracting process.[10]

The contracting officer is the federal official who solely controls and directs all aspects of contract execution. Indeed, unlike the commercial sector, the federal procurement process operates under a concept of "actual" authority rather than "implied" authority.[11] In the commercial world, it would not be uncommon for a contractor to perform work slightly outside of the scope of the contract or out of sequence with the requirements of a contract, provided that doing so was at the direction of an appropriate "implied" authority, such as the company CEO. In such a circumstance, the contractor would rightly expect to be paid—and almost certainly would be. In government contracting, by contrast, only the contracting officer with "actual" authority can direct the performance of work. No agency head, military commander, or other government official can direct work under a contract without the express approval of the contracting officer.[12] Contracting officers also have a variety of tools and techniques, such as approval of contract deliverables, program reviews, and payment approvals, to ensure that contractors are performing according to the contract terms.

Under most contracts, the government must affirmatively approve payment for work performed. Payment is only made at the end of the period of performance and only after the contractor submits an invoice and supporting documentation to demonstrate that the work was performed. Only under special circumstances, and with advance government approval, will a contractor be provided interim or progress payments as work is accomplished.[13] The rationale behind such financing flexibility is fairly simple: where significant investment is required, particularly on a long term or high risk (for example, war zone, complex systems development) contract, the cost of invested capital (for example, interest on borrowed money, which is itself based on the relative risk associated with a project) is significant enough that it is in the government's best fiscal interest—and a business necessity—to ameliorate a portion of those costs with advance or progress payments.

When a contractor fails to comply fully with the terms and conditions of a contract, the government has numerous administrative tools available to take appropriate remedial action. For example, the award of an option period under a contract is solely at the discretion of the contracting officer,[14] as long as the decision is rationally based. The government can also suspend or debar a contractor from doing future business with the federal government, hold the contractor financially responsible for the failure to perform, and charge the contractor for any additional costs of reperformance.[15] Despite suggestions to the contrary, the government does, in fact, utilize the suspension and debarment procedures when violations are significant enough to warrant it— witness Enron, MCI/Worldcom, and Arthur Andersen. There is also a panoply of substantial civil and criminal penalties for certain behaviors, including those contained in the civil False Claims[16] and False Statements Acts,[17] which are extremely potent and often invoked.[18]

Many government organizations play an integral part in the payment process, including the Defense Finance and Accounting Service (DFAS) and the General Services Administration, each of which has expertise in the regulations and procedures governing payments to contractors. To further assist the contracting officer, there are agencies, most notably the inspectors general or independent audit functions within various departments of the government (such as the Defense Contract Audit Agency within the Department of Defense), that have expertise in the intricacies of government accounting rules and regulations. Moreover, to assist contracting officers in performing contract administration, particularly for larger, more complex programs, several agencies, such as the Defense Department (DOD)'s Defense Contract Management Agency (DCMA) and civilian agency inspectors general, use their special expertise to monitor and report contractor performance. These agencies also perform periodic inspections of contractor facilities.[19]

Despite these procedural protections, individual violations occur. In 2004, Air Force procurement official Darleen Druyun pled guilty to defrauding the government and to making biased procurement decisions that cost the government billions of dollars.[20] Her plea was followed by an admission of guilt by a senior executive of the Boeing Company. A year earlier, the DOD's top small business officials were convicted of extorting money from companies seeking to participate in the government's "Mentor-Protégé Program," under which small firms are assisted and mentored by larger government contractors.[21] In the aftermath of those two high-profile cases, a fierce debate over ethics in government, and ethics in government contracting, ensued. That debate was further fueled by the guilty plea of former Congressman Randy Cunningham, who admitted to receiving bribes from a government contractor in return for using his influence—and the congressional "earmarking" process—to secure work for the contractor.[22]

The questions raised following the Druyun, Neal (the former DOD small business official), and Cunningham cases have been the same: How could this happen? How did they get away with it? What laws need changing?

In truth, despite the publicity that has swirled around government contracting in recent years, it is notable that virtually every case of contractor misbehavior—or alleged misbehavior—has been uncovered through existing oversight and investigative procedures. In few cases, if any, has a gap in the law been identified. Cunningham, Druyun, the Boeing executive, and the small business officials all knew what they were doing was illegal. They did not believe or attempt to claim that their actions were allowable under even the most liberal interpretation of law or regulation. For example, every government employee knows it is illegal to be negotiating for *any* personal benefit with any entity that might benefit from the official's position or powers. While the behavior of these individuals was reprehensible and intolerable, it occurred because of their own lack of integrity and not due to a gap in law. In the Druyun case, the investigation did reveal an environment in which one government official was able to operate with too few checks and balances—a problem the Air Force has begun to address. But while structure and process improvement is always important to guard against future violations, it is not at all clear that additional ethics laws or restrictions would have any effect in these types of cases.

Beyond a few, albeit visible, cases of individual ethics violations, many of the most difficult, and equally visible, contracting challenges have occurred in the context of nontraditional environments, such as the war in Iraq and the aftermath of Hurricane Katrina. As explained elsewhere in this chapter, emergency environments create situations that require more flexibility and government discretion. While there have clearly been cases of contractor or government employee abuse of the process, overall the effects of emergency or wartime environments on contracting are stark but widely misunderstood. As a result, all too often issues associated with contracting, particularly contracting in Iraq, have been viewed through traditional prisms and expectations about cost, performance, and more, that are designed for routine environments, rather than with the requisite perspective. Indeed, despite the contrary perception of many in Congress and likely the general public, the Special Inspector General for Iraq Reconstruction (SIGIR) has repeatedly testified that "fraud has not been a significant component of the U.S. [contracting] experience in Iraq." The SIGIR identified numerous problems, prominently including substantial waste (driven by security and other environmental factors, inadequate staffing, poor planning by the government customer, and so on) that have emerged; but as his testimony (reiterated in an October 2007 speech) suggests, given the dollars and the scope of activities involved, actual fraud has not been as common as some assert.[23]

Even more recently, the report of the Commission on Army Acquisition and Program Management in Expeditionary Operations[24] stressed the need for much greater attention to the front end of the acquisition process (structure, people, skills, and so on) rather than additional ex post facto oversight, since such oversight only identifies problems after they have occurred and does little, per se, to help prevent them.

This is not to say that the system does not face substantial challenges or that violations of procedures or laws do not occur. They clearly do. But on balance, viewed objectively, and given the 30 million transactions and $450 billion spent by the government annually for all goods and services, the system is far from fundamentally dysfunctional. Thus, while it is entirely appropriate to review existing legal and practical regimes to ensure that the government's best interests are being served, there is no evidence that substantial overhauls of procurement law, or the addition of new regulatory or statutory requirements, will meaningfully improve the process.

Federal Outsourcing Today: How Far Have We Gone?

In his widely cited book, former Brookings Institution scholar Paul Light argues that the majority view—that the size of government has shrunk—is wrong.[25] Fundamentally, Light argues that although the civil service is smaller than it was fifteen years ago, the size of the government cannot merely be measured by the number of federal employees, but must include the private contractors who perform work on behalf of the government. Simply put, the true size of government must be measured by budget and mission, and on that score the government has been steadily growing. On that point Light is clearly correct.

Budget displays provided by the Office of Management and Budget support Light's contention. The federal budget has two primary categories: discretionary spending and mandatory spending. The discretionary portion of the budget is the source of funding for all agency operations, including contracted work, federal personnel (military and civilian) and more. Mandatory spending, as the term suggests, funds entitlement programs (Social Security, Medicare, Medicaid, child health programs, and so on) and interest on the federal debt. Mandatory spending now accounts for approximately 62 percent of the federal budget—a total expected to rise to 68 percent or more by 2012.[26]

Between 1995 and 2004, the discretionary budget of the federal government grew by approximately 81 percent.[27] Indeed, from the period immediately following 9/11 through fiscal year 2006 alone, the discretionary budget grew by nearly two-thirds.[28] In other words, as Light argues, despite claims by each of the last four administrations, the government's mission, and thus "government" itself, continues to grow.

Light further argues that we have witnessed a quiet revolution in government, during which the size of the federal workforce has been slashed while the actual size of government has grown. He argues that a "shadow workforce" of employees in the for-profit and nonprofit communities now dwarfs the organic federal workforce. By Light's latest estimate, that shadow workforce now numbers nearly eight million strong, as compared to a federal civilian workforce of 1.8 million.

This is where Light's analysis becomes far more problematic, although it is unfortunately becoming accepted as gospel. Light's estimate is widely misinterpreted and analytically flawed.

First, Light includes in his analysis all spending on contracts, including goods (which amount to 45 percent of total contract spending and include every product—from laptops to weapons systems to pencils—the government buys). Of course, the government does not manufacture, and never has manufactured, laptops, pencils, computers, or virtually any product. As such, in assessing the "role of contractors" in the federal government, it is only really relevant to base the comparative analysis on data associated with the acquisition of services—work performed by individuals that might have been or at least theoretically could be performed by government employees.

Total spending on service contracting in fiscal year 2006 was approximately $240 billion.[29] This should be the analytical baseline. Moreover, that $240 billion reflects far more than salaries; it also includes benefits, equipment, overhead, and profit.[30] And while the cost elements of service contracts are, by definition, widely varied, most experts agree that overhead accounts for a minimum of 25 percent, and almost certainly 30 percent or more, while the portion devoted to equipment costs (such as the laptops provided in the course of managing an agency's information technology needs) varies dramatically, and can in some circumstances account for over half (and in some cases as much as 80 percent) of the total costs. In short, of the $240 billion spent on service contracting, only a portion goes directly to contractor employee salaries.

From an analytical perspective, this is an important point because the salary and benefits alone of the federal civilian workforce, which consists of fewer than 2 million people, are approaching $180 billion.[31] And as noted earlier, it is widely accepted that, particularly in high skill, high-demand professions, government salaries significantly lag behind the private sector. Thus, if one accepts the contention that the "shadow workforce" now amounts to 8 million people, one would also have to accept the contention that for substantially less money (given the percentage of contract dollars spent on infrastructure, overhead, and equipment), the private sector is providing the government with four times as many people. Obviously, this could not be the case.

Light's research relies on a highly regarded econometric model, the U.S. Department of Commerce's Regional Input-Output Modeling System (RIMS), which measures both direct and indirect employment generated by the expenditure of a dollar. For example, RIMS is often used to estimate the impact of a new plant or other industrial facility on a local community, and measures not just the employment at that facility but also the ancillary work that is likely to result from the increased economic base. Light's figures thus include not only the direct employment effect—the number of contractors directly working on behalf of the government—but also the indirect employment effect—the number of positions, such as teachers, store clerks, and other broader employment, stimulated by the expenditure on the contract. While Light acknowledges this fact, and in his 1999 book makes clear that the "shadow workforce" includes "direct and indirect employment," many critics ignore this critical distinction.[32] Light's work has thus become a rallying point for those who assert that the government has "outsourced" itself.

But has government done so? Light's research and the misinterpretation that too often accompanies it aside, how much has the role of contractors grown?

There is no question that that role has grown and that it is likely to continue to do so. It is also clear that the scope of work now being outsourced by the government is broader than before. In fact, the amount of federal funds being committed to service contracts has nearly doubled just since 9/11.[33] But that alone does not answer the more pertinent question: how much has the *proportional role* of contractors actually grown?

Prior to 9/11, about 21 percent of the federal discretionary budget was being devoted to service contracts versus organic (agency) performance. In the five years following 9/11, while total spending on service contracts nearly doubled, the discretionary budget grew approximately 65 percent.[34] Thus, although service contracting grew at a more rapid pace, *as a proportion of the federal budget it grew to only about 24 percent—a 15 percent proportional increase.*

Further, despite very rapid growth for a few years immediately following 9/11 (largely resulting from the war in Iraq and the advent of new, highly sophisticated and complex missions associated with homeland security), service contract growth has actually been remarkably steady for more than a decade, increasing at a compound annual rate of slightly more than 6 percent[35]—only slightly more than the rate of inflation. Unfortunately, some look only at the gross dollar expenditure without the requisite context and proportion, and thus claim that government contracting has skyrocketed.[36] The complete data, however, show that relative to the government's overall mission, the growth in service contracting, while significant and continuing, has been less than is generally assumed.

Technology, the Workforce, and the New Economy

What is the real driver of the increased spending on government service contracting? Many believe the increase has resulted from deliberate political and policy pressure, but we disagree. While employment ceilings and cost-cutting goals have perhaps fed this growth to some degree, their contribution has been relatively minor. Instead, the government's increased use of private sector providers is at its core a reflection of the government's demography, the changing dynamics of professional management, and the role and ownership of technology and technology-driven business processes.

In his January 2006 State of the Union Address,[37] President George W. Bush pledged to increase the federal budget for basic research substantially. He thus became the latest in a line of Presidents who have recognized the importance of the government's role in research and development. What is largely ignored, however, is the fact that over the last several decades the government's role as a progenitor of new technology has diminished.

It is only in the last thirty or so years that the private sector has invested more in research and development than the government. Before that, federally funded research and development in national security, space exploration, and other fields outstripped total private investment in research and development and provided the essential seed capital and intellectual firepower for most major technological developments. That is no longer the case.[38] Federal investments in research and development have been flat or declining in recent decades, while private sector investments, particularly in applied research, have steadily increased. Even accounting for the variations just prior to and following the dot-com crash, private sector investment in new technology now dwarfs that of the federal government. By some estimates the ratio is now almost four to one.[39] Much of that development has built on earlier federally driven and funded development, and has fueled the technology revolution that now drives the global economy. The impacts of this change have been enormous.

In other words, in a world now driven by an unprecedented, rapid pace of technological change, the government, once the predominant source of new technology and principal "owner" of the technology workforce, is now a follower. Moreover, where much of the current technology revolution fed off government-funded and government-driven programs, just the reverse is often true today, as government requirements, even in seemingly specialized areas like security, are increasingly derived from commercial technology applications. Further, given the dominance of technology of all kinds throughout the economy, the government is often not the biggest customer in the marketplace or even a customer at the table helping drive commercial research and development priorities.

The intelligence arena is an excellent example. In November 2006, the Defense Science Board issued an internal assessment that found that the government's lack of influence over and lack of involvement in technology innovation has had "an enormous impact. [That] makes it more likely that our adversaries can employ the very same—or perhaps even more advanced" solutions than the United States. The report further noted that "[t]he government now has far less control than before over the problems addressed, the selection of personnel to perform the work, and the locations where the work is carried out, and less knowledge than ever before of what work is actually being done [in technology development]." As reporter Shane Harris noted, "today, the private sector directs almost all new research."[40]

The Defense Science Board report is notable not only because of the stark picture it paints for U.S. intelligence activities, but also because it is essentially a reiteration of what has been one of the most significant drivers in the growth of the federal professional services market: the dominance of the private sector in technology development and ownership and the corollary human capital reality that technology workers go where the technology work—and technology ownership—is.

Even as the digital revolution has emerged, the government has been exceedingly slow to respond. In 2003, this point was driven home by the National Commission on Public Service, headed by former Federal Reserve Board Chairman Paul Volcker (the Volcker Commission).[41] In its report, the commission described the dramatic changes that have taken place in the "work of government"—changes that the commission argued have not been reflected in either organizational structure or personnel policy adjustments. Discussing the changes since 1950, the time of the last major governmental reorganization, the Volcker Commission reported:

> Nearly every aspect of government became more technically complex. A space program emerged and quickly became a significant federal activity. Foreign aid and foreign trade became important components of foreign relations. Ensuring the safety of food and drugs, of travel, and of the workplace loomed larger in importance. Science and technology research, complex litigation, rigorous analysis, and innovation in service delivery became critical responsibilities in agency after agency. Financial regulators became hard pressed by the competitiveness of modern capital markets. Increasingly, government operations were contracted to the private sector.[42]

As technological change has dramatically transformed the landscape and hastened the elimination of hierarchical communications and management, it has also hastened a fundamental revolution in the way high-performing businesses and institutions are run. Most importantly, for government, the new management structure brought about by technology is multidimensional and multipronged. As Goldsmith and Eggers said in their 2004 book:[43] "Modern technologies allow organizations to share data and integrate their business processes with partners outside the four walls of the organization, enabling them to share information in real time about supply and demand and customers' preferences."[44]

Thus, the digital business revolution has resulted in high-performing businesses tearing down traditional hierarchical structures in order to facilitate access to and partnerships with a wide array of outside allies—the "network." This less hierarchical structure allows for faster exchange of information and more efficient delivery of services. Here, unlike in the past, the government is a follower, not a leader. Government struggles to shed its hierarchical, bureaucratic method of decision making precisely because it is driven by public policy values first and cost savings, or even performance improvements, second.[45]

That is not to say that the government is not focused on either efficiency or performance improvement. It is. And the government has made many attempts to respond to the reality of technological change, through initiatives like the Clinton-era "National Performance Review" and the Bush II administration's "e-government" and related activities. Like a growing number of governments at all levels in many countries, it is slowly and out of necessity seeking to shed that traditional structure to take advantage of the efficiencies, higher service quality, and greater agility offered by technology. But the process has been exceedingly slow, and, as the Defense Science Board, the Volcker Commission, and others have noted, the government struggles not only to keep pace with technology change, but also to recruit, train, and retain the requisite workforce in this new environment.

Instructively, the first four recommendations of the Volcker Commission center on major organizational reform that, at its heart, would enable the government to manage in the new and connected network more effectively.[46] As both the Volcker Commission and Goldsmith and Eggers pointed out, citizens now demand levels of service from their government that are the norm in their daily lives. Faced with unavoidable and seemingly endless resource constraints, governments must now access the full range of new capabilities that enable a more agile and rapid response to change and demand

Beyond organizational change, however, the growth in government outsourcing is driven by the growing scarcity of the skills needed by the government to implement its missions, particularly in professional and technology positions. Interestingly, the professional and technical fields are the largest categories of federal employment—as well as the fastest growing and largest categories of federal outsourcing. However, despite the rapid growth in missions that require such a highly skilled workforce, the government has been able to increase its total professional workforce only 3 percent and actually reduced its technology labor force 2 percent over the last five years, a time during which overall government missions (as measured by the discretionary budget) have grown by some two-thirds. In other words, the government is locked in a competition for talent with the global economy at large—and, as the Volcker Commission stated, it struggles to compete effectively. As a result, agencies increasingly have little choice but to adopt the "Willie Sutton"[47] approach to management—they are going where the people are, increasingly turning to private sector partners.

Virtually every task performed by the government depends on technological innovations to improve the quality of service; thus, advances in technology practically mandate that the government increasingly rely on organizations whose employees have expertise and experience in the relevant field. This is particularly true in functional areas that are most dependent on the dramatic pace of change in technology and in the role of technology as a management tool. In fact, according to the Federal Procurement Data System (FPDS), the growth in outsourcing over the last decade has been almost exclusively in the areas of professional and administrative services and information technology, while the market for equipment repair, facilities maintenance, and other traditional blue-collar functions has been flat. Information and communications technology has grown at more than twice the rate of overall services contracting, and professional and administrative services outsourcing has grown at a rate nearly 50 percent higher than the overall outsourcing growth.[48]

This trend is consistent with broader trends in the general economy, in which the role of traditional blue-collar positions has been shrinking for many years. It is also entirely consistent with federal government hiring trends. In 2004, blue-collar positions in the federal government accounted for just 11 percent of the total federal workforce, a drop from 16 percent in 1994.[49] During that same period, professional, administrative, and technical workers grew from 58 percent of the workforce to nearly 76 percent. In other words, even as the government has moved more toward an outsourcing model, it has also increased its hiring in those same outsourced functional areas—as has been the case throughout the general economy.

For the government today, the primary challenge is one of recruiting and retaining employees with critical management-level skills, to enable appropriate oversight and to ensure the achievement of cost, schedule, and performance objectives by an increasingly external delivery system (the "network"). It is, by almost any objective measure, and as the Volcker Commission suggested, unrealistic to think—and therefore unreasonable to expect—that the government could or should fully rebuild its organic capabilities of the past. But it clearly must aggressively address its fundamental skills needs. Most immediately, even as it faces unprecedented market competition for talent, the government also faces some uniquely daunting and disturbing demographic challenges.

In the federal workforce today, there are nearly two and one-half times as many federal employees over the age of fifty as there are employees under thirty.[50] This graying of the federal workforce portends a retirement wave that is inevitable and unprecedented. Perhaps even more significant is the fact that employees in junior- to middle-management levels are exiting the government faster than the government is hiring new entry-level employees.[51] When the retirement wave hits, which it must, the already pronounced skills gaps and recruitment shortfalls, particularly in management, will be even more evident and critical.

Furthermore, as the Volcker Commission observed:

Far too many talented public servants are abandoning the middle levels of government, and too many of the best recruits are rethinking their commitment, either because they are fed up with the constraints of outmoded personnel systems and unmet expectations for advancement or simply lured away by the substantial difference between public and private sector salaries in many areas. . . . For too many, even their best efforts to be responsive and creative end up in organizational oblivion.[52]

The July 2007 report of the Partnership for Public Service highlighted that the federal government will need nearly 200,000 "mission critical" new hires over just the next two years to keep pace with the rising need for national security, evolving agency needs, and expected federal workforce retirements.[53] There are scores of positions unfilled at the Department of Homeland Security, including the Federal Emergency Management Agency (FEMA), raising questions about FEMA's preparedness.[54] In short, the government is clearly struggling to hire and retain its next-generation workforce. Most of all, the struggle is about recruiting and maintaining critical skills in technology and management, and about people having access to the tools to manage service delivery, cost, schedule, and performance.

This situation does not necessarily suggest that there is nothing the government can do to improve and address its human capital challenges. However, rather than focus on the supposed evils of outsourcing, reform must focus on why "far too many talented public servants are abandoning the middle levels of government, and too many of the best recruits are rethinking their commitment."[55]

The civil service system is in dire need of reform.[56] And reform mandates that the government look at its competition (the broader commercial marketplace) to determine what they do differently that enables them to win the battle for people generally. For example, most high-performing companies manage, compensate, develop, and support their core workforce differently than they do other important but noncore elements of their workforce. They recognize that their greatest competitive discriminators are found in that core workforce because, by definition, its work is most directly related to the organization's success.

This is anathema to the current civil service structure, where very little such segmentation occurs. Indeed, this very dichotomy is at the heart of some current debates over the possibility that the government has "outsourced its brain."[57] The issue is not the broader trend to partner with the private sector; it is the atrophy of some core capabilities—in systems engineering, program management, and acquisition, among other areas. The trend toward more use of private sector capabilities in these areas is not entirely reversible. Thus, it is clear that the government must find strategies to compete more effectively for the critical skills needed to ensure its ability to manage its requirements and performance. Unfortunately, it is not clear that the leadership and political will exists to make the requisite changes to the federal personnel system. Many proposals for change have been put forth, but none has been fully executed, due in large part to some combination of missteps by their proponents and vehement opposition from federal employee unions.

Nowhere is this more evident than in acquisition. If 40 percent of the discretionary budget is spent on goods and services, acquisition clearly must be a core mission of government. This mission becomes even more critical due to the fundamental irreversibility (with some limited functional exceptions) of the outsourcing trend. However, as the Government Accountability Office (GAO)—formerly the General Accounting Office—and others have repeatedly found, the acquisition workforce remains undermanned, underresourced and often undertrained.

In the final analysis, the trend toward outsourcing is a reflection of individual government activities at their Darwinian best—adapting to the world around them in order to meet growing mission demands. Indeed, Darwin's lesson, that the species most likely to survive is that which is most adaptable to change, is very apt in this case. Despite attempts over two administrations to incentivize or even force agencies to consider the outsourcing option, the growth in outsourcing has principally been a reflection of market realities: the private sector has made massive investments in and continually seeks to capitalize on emerging technologies to improve service delivery of all kinds. The government has not.[58] Moreover, as a result of investment trends and budget priorities, the capital, technology, and skills required to apply that technology are increasingly being developed in the private, rather than public, sector.

The government's and the public's best interests are therefore served by recognizing and adjusting to these new realities while meeting the important objectives of transparency, accountability, and access to the full range of existing and emerging solutions. As the Defense Science Board report suggested, however, the government is still too handicapped by bureaucratic processes, excessive regulation, and a lack of flexibility, preventing it from performing its wide-ranging mission tasks.

A Strategy of Replacement?

On a macro scale, the data also show that outsourcing has, by and large, not been used as a tool to displace federal employees. Indeed, the idea that outsourcing is reflective of an overt "replacement" strategy is unsupported by the data.

From 1986 to 2001, the federal workforce was reduced by 27 percent.[59] Almost all of those reductions came in DOD and resulted from factors entirely unrelated to outsourcing. Reductions in the workforce were primarily the result of changes in national security requirements after the dissolution of the Soviet Union and the end of the cold war.[60] Those changes drove broad downsizing throughout DOD, including both military and civilian personnel reductions and several rounds of base closures and realignments. During those same years, *total* civilian agency employment actually increased by about 1.6 percent.[61]

Despite those personnel trends, from 1992 to 2001, the period most often cited by those who believe outsourcing is at its core a replacement strategy, spending on contracted services actually grew much faster in the civilian agencies (28 percent), where the personnel reductions were much less pronounced, than in DOD (18 percent), where the personnel reductions were almost entirely experienced.[62] Taking into account the post–9/11 years, spending on contracted services between 1995 and 2005 did grow much more slowly in the civilian agencies (73 percent) than in DOD (126 percent), although much of that spending was related to changed priorities following 9/11 and the wars in Iraq and Afghanistan.[63] And in the years since 9/11, government agencies, especially DOD and the Department of Homeland Security, have clearly been seeking to add to, and not reduce, the civil service. In other words, if the strategy of replacement was as prominent as some suggest, one would expect to see far greater growth in contracting in those agencies where the personnel reductions have been greatest. Instead, the opposite has occurred.

In addition, current government statistics show that the areas of most rapid growth in services contracting (for example, engineering and program management) are *also* areas in which the government has been adding, or trying to add, organic workforce capabilities.

There were, and in some cases still are, employment ceilings that constrain agency hiring. Such ceilings almost certainly drive at least some additional outsourcing. Employment ceilings, however, are not a new phenomenon, and were not instituted in order to justify additional outsourcing opportunities.[64] Moreover, while arbitrary employment ceilings are no more defensible than arbitrary outsourcing goals or restrictions, it is not at all clear that if those ceilings were lifted, the government could hire the people it needs to perform its mission. Just look at the hundreds, if not more, of contracting positions alone that, as of August 2007, were open and unfilled in government.[65] Or look more broadly at the more than 100,000 federal government positions that were open and unfilled as of June 2008.[66] Indeed, between the loss of talent to the private sector—a loss driven principally, according to various surveys, by the better compensation, opportunities for professional development, and work-life quality that exist in the private sector—and the government's resultant difficulties competing for talent, there is little reason to believe that the ceilings themselves are, broadly speaking, significantly affecting the levels and degrees of outsourcing. Ironically, it is often true that the most vocal opponents of outsourcing are also often the most vocal opponents of the kinds of reforms recommended by the Volcker Commission and others.

Competitive Sourcing as a Management Tool

In the federal system the conversion of work from organic federal performance to private sector performance is governed by a policy called "competitive sourcing," in which potential private sector providers compete with government entities for that work. In other words, "competitive sourcing" is not "outsourcing," in that it does not presume that work currently performed by the government will or should be performed by a contractor. The process for such competitions is set forth in OMB Circular A-76 and was created in 1976 to give federal employees the opportunity to compete.[67] Under the process prescribed in Circular A-76, when a private contractor wins a public/private competition, that contractor is required to provide a right of first refusal to the affected federal employees for any positions for which those employees are qualified. As a result, when work is converted to private performance under A-76, a very low proportion—approximately 5 percent—of affected federal employees are ultimately involuntarily separated (meaning that they end up unemployed because they opt to not accept positions with the contractor, do not take other federal positions, do not retire, and do not find other outside employment).[68] Moreover, only a fraction of the work being performed by contractors today has been converted from performance by government civilians to the private sector.

During the Clinton administration, the National Performance Review led DOD to focus on serious reforms to its business management practices and, under Secretaries William Perry and William Cohen, to pursue an aggressive competitive sourcing agenda.[69] In 2001, the Bush Administration made competitive sourcing one of five "pillars" of the President's Management Agenda.[70]

Despite the senior-level focus of two consecutive administrations on using competition as a management tool, the effect has been minimal—almost all of the work reviewed or competed under the process (sometimes referred to as "competitive sourcing studies") has remained in house, particularly since 2001. In 2005 and 2006, OMB reports show that when competitions were held, over 80 percent of the commercial activities identified as suitable for competition continued to be performed by federal employees.[71] The ability of the government to adequately and accurately assess and project its total program costs for purposes of comparison to a private sector bid (which must contain all cost elements based on rigid accounting standards) remains an area of substantial dispute. As well, the studies themselves are often structured in ways that most private sector bidders consider suboptimal. Moreover, Congress has layered the process with requirements that tend to discourage competition, and almost always demands the chance to review, or even overturn, those few competitive sourcing studies that do result in a decision to award a contract. As a result, in an increasingly significant number of cases (half or more, according to the 2007 OMB Competitive Sourcing Report), one or zero private sector bidders participate.

Two recent cases offer instructive insights into the current state of the competitive sourcing agenda. In 2007, controversy erupted over the substandard conditions in a portion of the Walter Reed Army Medical Center (WRAMC). At about the same time the controversy arose, a private contractor began work at WRAMC. Immediately, accusations were leveled that outsourcing and the contractor's poor performance were the cause of the problem. However, it quickly became evident (although not widely reported) that the contractor arrived on site *after* the discovery of the substandard conditions and that the facility in question was not even part of the original work plan awarded to the contractor (it was in fact a later addition). The WRAMC debacle resulted from mismanagement by the Army and was in no way related to outsourcing. Nonetheless, building off the emotions, mythology, and politics created by the controversy, Congress passed, without debate or discussion, a broad prohibition on any DOD outsourcing at any of its medical facilities.

Similarly, a small minority-owned (so-called 8(a)) firm was awarded a contract through a competitive sourcing study to provide administrative support for various elements of the Labor Department. About 20 percent of the work was to be done for the Mine Safety and Health Administration (MSHA). Without debate or discussion as to whether inspection functions were actually a part of the contract, West Virginia Senator Robert Byrd declared that mine safety inspection should be "inherently governmental" and shepherded an amendment through Congress to an unrelated bill that imposed a complete ban on outsourcing of *all* functions (even support services, janitorial work, and so on) at MSHA—not just the inspection activities. Faced with the new amendment, the Labor Department had no choice but to respond. However, instead of simply removing the MSHA portion of the work from the contract, the Labor Department decided to avoid any further political opposition and canceled the entire contract. Remarkably, the department even refused to compensate the small company that had been awarded the contract for its invested costs, including its bid and proposal costs, saying that such costs were simply a "risk" of doing business with the government.

These are but two of many examples of how competitive sourcing through the A-76 process, designed as a management tool to enhance efficiency and performance through the use of competition, has been effectively neutralized by opponents of outsourcing who utilize the political, rather than procurement, process to achieve their goals. This troubling dichotomy was in fact recognized by the congressionally created Commercial Activities Panel, chaired by the Comptroller General (the head of GAO). The panel recommended that the A-76 process be viewed and managed as a procurement process, complete with the competition, transparency, rights, and accountability that undergird the federal acquisition system. That recommendation was only partly implemented by the Bush Administration, and even that partial implementation has been steadily attacked and diluted by Congress at the behest of anti-outsourcing special interests.

In simple terms, despite the occasional success (defined as an effective and meaningful competition, regardless of whether it is won by the government or a company), the A-76 process has been virtually eliminated as a management tool by excessive restrictions, ineffective execution, and politically inspired source selections made not by the agency but by Congress. Thus, despite both the Clinton- and Bush-era initiatives, less than 2 percent of the $250 billion federal market for contracted services has been awarded through the competitive sourcing process,[72] and there is little reason to believe the role of competitive sourcing will grow significantly any time soon. If anything, the credibility of the process is at an all-time low. Fair criticisms can be leveled at both administrations for the manner in which they sought to energize and incentivize the use of competitive sourcing; however, the substance and goals of the process have now largely been lost to much broader political battles over union politics and government management. Nevertheless, it is equally fair to note that even as Congress appropriately demands transparency in the process, its own decision making with regard to specific legislative provisions and restrictions has been largely closed to discussion, debate, or substantive legislative hearings.

As a final note on competitive sourcing, the lessons learned here provide insight into the broader application of administrative law tenets within federal procurement. In simple terms, the competitive sourcing debate and process offer an important cautionary tale about involving the political arena in sourcing and procurement decisions.[73]

Competition

Is competition really present in federal outsourcing? Some believe, and the press has widely reported, that there has been a recent and dramatic growth in noncompetitive contracting within the federal procurement process, which would in turn suggest that the benefits derived by the government from competition are not being attained.[74] While it is appropriate to demand that competition be the norm and not the exception, the claims tend to be based either on the wrong data or on a misunderstanding or misuse of terminology.

On one level the allegations are generally based on the total amount of dollars awarded without competition. But the real issue is one of proportion. After all, if total contract spending is increasing then one would expect some similar increase in the total dollars awarded non-competitively. While it may be true that in some areas competition may not have been as robust as one might hope, when looked at as a *percentage* of total federal procurement spending, competition in federal contracting is, proportionally, at about the same level as it was ten years ago.[75]

Additionally, "full and open competition" has a very specific meaning in government contracting, although it is often incorrectly assumed to be synonymous with "competitively awarded." Many contracts that are not coded as "full and open" are, nonetheless, highly competitive. For example, current law provides a 23 percent government-wide goal for small business and additional goals for other preference programs, such as 8(a) firms, firms owned by women, service-disabled veterans' firms, and HUBZone firms.[76] When these contracts are awarded through predetermined "set-asides" (meaning they are reserved for firms qualifying under the appropriate socioeconomic categories), the competitions are not "full and open" because, by definition, they are limited solely to those companies that qualify for the programs. Yet the contracts are "competitively" awarded within the set-aside categories.

Similarly, a significant percentage of work performed under services contracts is awarded as task orders under indefinite-delivery, indefinite-quantity multiple-award contracts. In these cases, the overarching contract is generally awarded through full and open competition to a select number of winning companies, and the actual work is defined and performed incrementally through individual, competitively awarded task orders. Just as with contracts set aside for small or small disadvantaged businesses, those task orders do not qualify as awarded under "full and open" competitions, but they result from not just one but two levels of competitive procedures.

Finally, in the services sector most contracts are awarded for one year with several, often four or five, "option" years (principally because agencies cannot commit funds prior to appropriations being made available). As such, a five-year contract for services typically consists of one "base year" and four separate "option years," with the option exercised at the sole discretion of government (based on performance to date, the availability of funds, and, of course, a continued need for the work). Thus, by definition, while every option is treated as a separate contract award, it is not, nor is it expected to be, "competitive."

Competition is a fundamental premise of federal contracting. The public has a right to expect that to be the case. Understanding these definitions and terms is essential to understanding whether competition is being achieved. A failure to use them correctly can lead one to conclusions that are simply incorrect and to even broader erroneous assumptions about federal contracting in general.

Legal Limits on Outsourcing

Is Anything "Inherently Governmental"?

As outsourcing inexorably grows, and the realities of networked management take hold, it still holds true that certain government functions, like policymaking, law enforcement, or substantial decision making, are reserved for performance by appropriate federal employees.

Defining what are known as "inherently governmental" functions is essential to any broader discussion of the boundaries of the public-private relationship.

During the 1980s, then-Chairman of the Senate Governmental Affairs Committee David Pryor (D-AR) held a series of hearings into the ways various agencies were utilizing private contractors. In his book "The Shadow Government," Daniel Guttman, once Pryor's top staffer, defined the progression of the hearings and the concerns they raised, principally that contractors were performing significant policy functions including writing testimony and more.[77] The hearings eventually led to the government promulgating formal policy defining "inherently governmental" functions in 1992. The new policy, embodied in Office of Federal Procurement Policy Letter 92-1 (92-1), sought to provide guidance on those functions that must be performed by government employees.[78]

The policy helped to clarify the critical separation between "governance"—the setting of policy, the commitment of resources—and "government"—the act of executing the government mission. Among other things, the policy clarified that the setting of policy, the direct enforcement of law, the commitment of government funds, and actions which otherwise bind the government or involve substantial decision making discretion are reserved for performance by appropriate federal employees.[79] While it is possible to identify discrete cases in which the policy has been intentionally or inadvertently violated, 92-1 remains the standard against which such decisions are typically measured. There have been periodic attempts to review or revise 92-1, but each of those reviews has concluded that the policy letter presents a clear set of guiding principles.

While 92-1 remains a central line of demarcation between governance and government, it is augmented by the Federal Activities Inventory Reporting Act (FAIR Act),[80] under which all agencies are required to publish annually an inventory of all government positions and to categorize each position as noncommercial (i.e., inherently governmental), commercial but not available for outsourcing, or commercial and suitable for competitive sourcing. The inventories are publicly released, fully appealable by an interested party,[81] and apply to all work currently performed by government employees.

Neither 92-1 nor the FAIR Act has the last word. As noted earlier, often that last word lies with the political process. Agencies sometimes opt to deem functions appropriate for outsourcing that some, usually those affected by the decision, question. And Congress often gets involved on behalf of affected constituencies. For example, when the Department of Homeland Security coded the work of its Immigration Information Officers (IIOs) as commercial, the federal employee unions appealed to Congress, claiming that the work of the IIOs should be considered inherently governmental. Although the administration pointed out that the IIOs are only first-line information resources and exercise no decision-making discretion, Congress sided with the federal employee unions and barred any competitive sourcing initiative involving IIOs (but did not reclassify the positions).[82] Similarly, when in 2005 the Federal Aviation Administration sought to compete its flight services stations, members of Congress unsuccessfully sought to reclassify the functions as inherently governmental.[83]

These are but two of many examples in which congressional action brought an additional layer of politics into agency management decisions. In fact, congressional interference now reaches beyond the federal government and has included numerous attempts, again at the behest of public employee unions, to prohibit states from utilizing private sector providers to modernize, streamline, and integrate their public assistance programs.[84]

Have We Crossed the "Inherently Governmental" Divide?

Despite the existing policies and the built-in checks and balances, we are today entering a new debate over the nature of inherently governmental functions. The outsourcing debate has raised new issues about how the government can best manage its missions and retain control of its own technical and mission destinies, as well as protect the public interest.

It is true that the lines separating functions that are close to but not clearly inherently governmental from those that might be outsourced are becoming more blurred. Here, there are really two issues at play: the degree to which expanded outsourcing is a necessity driven by growing skills gaps within the government, and the degree to which some outsourcing involves work that is so closely tied to fundamental responsibilities of the state that it should not be performed by private contractors.

As to the first issue, that trend is in large part a reflection of the hemorrhaging of the government's management core, one result of which is to require agencies to fill critical skills gaps and tap outside sources for program, financial, technology, and other management functions. The trend is also a reflection of the shift in technology and in workforce ownership. After all, if the bulk of requisite technology skills are resident in the private sector, it only follows that the government will increasingly have to rely on the private sector not only for the performance of technology-driven functions but also for the design, evaluation, and overall management of such functions.

It is a given that certain functions should be retained by government employees. And the growing role of the private sector in the provision of government services logically requires that we explore how the government's management of outsourcing can ensure that entities and individuals involved adhere to existing safeguards and continue to serve the public's interest.

Likewise, it can fairly be argued that the government actually has more insight into and control over its contracted activities than its own organic functions. Every contract payment is predicated on an approved invoice; contractors performing poorly can be, and often are, either terminated by the government or unable to win further work.[85] In short, the role of contract administration and management has never been more central to the right functioning of the government—for it is through the contract vehicle that the government can best protect its interest. Inadequate contract management impairs the government's ability to do its job.

Some of these issues become more pronounced in particularly sensitive areas, such as prison management and battlefield contracting for security services. There, the functions involve much more than routine service delivery and touch upon the most fundamental of governmental responsibilities, and therefore are often the subject of public and scholarly criticism.

The scandal at Abu Ghraib prison is one example of the prominence of these issues. The very existence of contract interrogators has itself fueled a strong debate over whether such roles—specifically, directing or conducting actual interrogations—are appropriate for contractors.[86] Similarly, some, such as Professor Dolovich in this volume, have raised questions about the propriety of outsourcing or privatizing domestic prison operations. They too are concerned with the blurring of lines, recognizing that a prison environment represents one of the most basic and critical intersections between the state, its citizens, and social values. Thus, the argument goes, outsourcing cannot merely be viewed strictly through a prism of economics or management flexibility.

WARFIGHTING: WHERE ARE THE LINES?

For some, the use of contractors in Iraq and Afghanistan has been inextricable from a broader antipathy for the war or its prosecution. Clearly, the two issues must be separated and analyzed on their own terms. Parsing the real issues involved, therefore, requires a dispassionate assessment of how, why, and where contractors are engaged.

For example, the Army has clearly determined that, in the long run, it makes better financial sense to utilize private contractors for logistical support and for the technical skills needed to manage and maintain increasingly complex communications technologies. Further, in Iraq in particular, the number and scope of contractors "on the battlefield" has been driven by the early decision to conduct three concurrent missions (military operations, construction, and development). Tens of thousands of contractor employees from for-profit and not-for-profit entities and from numerous nations (the majority of these employees are Iraqi nationals) are heavily engaged in initiatives around massive infrastructure construction, economic development, health care systems, education, agriculture, democracy, governance, and more, for which such contractors have a longstanding and well-established expertise.

Beyond the provision of technical, logistical, maintenance, and other military-related support, as well as the construction and development roles almost always performed by nongovernment entities, debate has emerged over the use of private contractors to provide security in theaters of military operations. While a substantive debate over whether future missions should be adjusted to reduce the need for private security may be perfectly reasonable, the realities on the ground today in Iraq and Afghanistan are just that: realities. And those mission realities create the need for private security.

After all, Iraq is a country that is roughly the size of California. And the Army, with its broad and complex missions in Iraq as well as Afghanistan, simply does not have the manpower to provide facility and personal security for the literally thousands of construction and development projects—and their thousands of employees—now under way across both countries. Moreover, many of the most experienced international development professionals prefer to rely on qualified private security (often consisting of host country nationals) rather than to be closely tied to the military. Thus, as Iraq has evolved into the largest sustained military operation since Vietnam and the most expansive national reconstruction and development undertaking since the Marshall

Plan, it should come as no surprise that there are increasing numbers of contractors involved, and more private security requirements.

Critics of battlefield contracting have argued that massive outsourcing has drawn civilian contractors into military work without cost controls or assurance of contractual compliance, led to military abuses, and jeopardized civilian safety and democratic accountability. However, while there assuredly have been instances of poor performance, there is little or no evidence to support the rather extreme suggestions some have made. Indeed, as noted above, the Special Inspector General for Iraq Reconstruction has said there was actually little evidence of widespread fraud or abuse in Iraq contracting. Likewise, while there have been cases of both military and civilian personnel engaging in unlawful activity, there is little to no evidence that such activity was widespread.

The military can also articulate metrics to support its reliance on private contractors. As one example, the Navy has concluded that it brought over 60 percent of its firepower to the early phases of the Iraq conflict, but used only 20 percent of its manpower. As a result, recognizing the enormous, essentially permanent costs of recruiting, training, and retaining a standing force, the Navy is modestly reducing its permanent manpower so as to ensure that the bulk of the force is wholly focused on the strategic mission while outsourcing more of its support to a nonpermanent, flexible "as needed" contractor core. This move is an example of an outsourcing strategy driven by the need for flexibility and cost savings.

Many have raised concerns about the accountability of contractor (and federal) employees overseas. And to be sure, while *contract accountability* is and always has been clearly delineated in the contract document, gray areas have persisted regarding the ability to prosecute individuals for crimes committed in country. Congress recognized this problem when in 2000 it enacted the Military Extraterritorial Jurisdiction Act (MEJA),[87] providing federal criminal jurisdiction for contractor acts on U.S. military facilities overseas.[88] Subsequent to U.S. involvement in Iraq, Congress acted to expand MEJA coverage to contractors performing under any DOD contract overseas, whether the offense occurred on base or off. As of September 2007 the Department of Justice was prosecuting at least a half dozen cases under the still relatively new MEJA provision.

In addition, in 2006, Congress passed an amendment to the defense authorization bill, holding contractor civilians "serving with or accompanying an armed force in the field" subject to the Uniform Code of Military Justice (UCMJ) even if Congress has not declared war.[89] That provision has generated substantial concern among civil liberties groups (the American Civil Liberties Union has opposed the legislation) and industry alike, who believe it raises significant constitutional and other issues (the right to trial by a jury of one's peers, observance of the federal rules of evidence, personal interviews, consideration of the federal sentencing guidelines, and so on). The imposition of the UCMJ—which itself is a broad set of laws—could also create conflicts with the separate sets of procurement laws. For instance, federal contract law clearly states that only a contracting officer has the specific authority to direct the contractor to perform on a contract.[90] On the other hand, under the UCMJ, authority is based on rank: a senior officer has the authority to direct those of lower rank. Which is the controlling statute?

Moreover, while U.S. government contractor employees in Iraq were granted immunity from prosecution under *Iraqi* law (by agreement between the then-dissolving Coalition Provisional Authority (CPA) and the incoming Iraqi government—an agreement that extended the immunity that had existed under the CPA), primarily due to the embryonic and unstable nature of the Iraqi justice system, there was general agreement in the contracting industry that clear lines of accountability needed to be established, and that individual criminal acts should not go unpunished. In the wake of a shooting incident in a Baghdad square involving employees of the security firm Blackwater, as of May 2007 Congress appeared poised to approve legislation—supported by the contracting industry, including the security sector—to expand MEJA coverage to all contractor employees performing on U.S. government projects overseas. It could be fairly argued that addressing this critical issue has taken far too long; indeed, the proposal to expand MEJA is not a new one. That notwithstanding, it is clear that tools exist for the government to hold contractors accountable and that those tools are continually being reviewed and, where necessary, revised.

PRIVATIZATION OF DOMESTIC PRISONS

The issues are slightly different when it comes to the privatization of domestic prisons and related governmental functions. The privatizing of those activities has fundamentally been driven by economics (the lack of capital for the construction of new facilities) and a belief that, given the poor performance of the traditional prison system, some form of competition—accompanied by appropriate metrics—would serve the prison system better than the rigid monopolies that have characterized its past. The principal argument against prison privatization has been that a prison represents the most basic of intersections between the state and its citizens; thus, ethical and societal mores might be threatened by decisions made on a purely economic or strategic basis.

Yet it is also true that the symbols of those mores and ethical principles, such as the way in which prisoners are treated, educated, fed, and otherwise supported, can be built into the contract vehicle itself and are often among the critical performance metrics that must be met by the private provider. Under a contract, the government has full leverage to require the contractor to adhere to whatever performance metrics it wishes to specify. The same is true in cases where the facility has been privatized—the government has every right to demand that the facility meet its performance requirements as a condition for its using the facility's services. Some private prisons have successfully met these goals and, in so doing, have adhered to public values as defined in their contract with the government. Thus, the question still comes back to management and administration—the effective use of the contract vehicle to drive the appropriate and desired outcomes and behaviors.

Because the contract vehicle is essential to maintaining procedural safeguards, it is even more important that any reform focus on effective contract management to ensure that critical performance metrics are met by the private provider. Moreover, although one could argue that the large majority of the public knows little about contracting or even about the treatment of prisoners, thus making political accountability for the mishandling of prison contracts minimal, prison privatization and outsourcing certainly take place in the public eye. As with competitive sourcing at the federal level, virtually every significant effort to privatize or outsource such functions has been the focus of significant public comment and legislative debate.[91] And it is the fundamental responsibility of the state to ensure that its values and mores are enforced in any event, be it by civil or merit systems employees or private contractors. Contracts do nothing to lessen that responsibility and, if properly constructed, can and should fully address it. In many cases, especially given the nature of the civil service or merit employee systems involved, the government can actually exercise more direct and immediate control over the actions and behaviors of individuals performing on a contract than it can with its own organic workforce.

In sum, then, decisions as to which functions of government can or should be outsourced are often driven by a plethora of sometimes competing factors. And while political ideology plays a role in determining the extent to which outsourcing and privatization are considered, it has rarely been determinative. Moreover, while the government's contract management and administration weaknesses have often been the focus of heated discussion and debate, and issues and problems with contracting have burst onto the public stage in recent years, it remains true that the regime governing federal contracting is both exacting and extensive. While sometimes imperfect and imperfectly executed, the process reflects many of the most basic principles of smart management, fair play, transparency, and accountability.

Proper Management for Proper Government

Checks and Balances: The Role of the Government Accountability Office

The federal procurement process is designed not only to ensure the fairness of competition between businesses for the government's mission, but also to serve the public and to ensure adherence to democratic norms, by assuring that the highest-quality products and services are chosen.

The Government Accountability Office (GAO, formerly the General Accounting Office) is a legislative branch agency that plays an important role in providing checks and balances on the federal contracting process. GAO performs two core functions in the contracting area: analysis and adjudication.

In its analysis role, GAO is well known for its reports to Congress on how agencies spend money and execute programs. GAO has a long history and unique experience reviewing contracts by federal agencies and each month issues dozens of reports on its work. In fact, GAO has annually issued a list of "high risk" areas of federal operations, and, not surprisingly, has included government contracting of individual agencies and government-wide programs on that list.[92] The Comptroller General of the United States, the head of GAO, has special statutory authority to review the books and records of contractors.[93]

In addition, GAO serves a quasi-judicial function through its adjudication of "bid protests" of certain federal agency contracting actions, pursuant to a grant of congressional authority under the Competition in Contracting Act.[94] While these bid protest "decisions" are usually advisory only,[95] federal agencies historically follow the recommendations and GAO is required to notify Congress when a federal agency does not do so.[96] Likewise, the federal courts have jurisdiction to hear pre-award and post-award challenges to agency procurement actions[97] and additional authority to resolve claims from contractors resulting from their contract performance.[98]

In addition, while GAO historically hears bid protests brought by private sector offerors competing under an A-76 competition, prior to 2007 it had been precluded from hearing challenges to an agency competitive sourcing action raised by federal employees or their representatives.[99] Federal courts have also been precluded from hearing protests from federal employees or their union representatives challenging an agency competitive sourcing action, determining that they are not "interested parties" in the legal sense of the term.[100]

Moreover, important issues of unitary government also arise when agency officials, acting on behalf of government employees, take legal action against the government itself. In part to address a perceived imbalance in the rights of private sector offerors versus government "bidders" under the May 2003 revised OMB Circular A-76,[101] in 2004 Congress amended the Competition in Contracting Act to provide authority for GAO to hear a challenge to an agency's competitive sourcing action made by the representative of the federal employees "bidding" on such action.[102] That right was intentionally not extended to the courts although legislation is under consideration to give them that power.

Checks and Balances: The Role of Congress

Beyond its responsibility for setting policy and appropriating funds to support government operations, Congress has a significant oversight responsibility for the management of federal agencies and for the roles of both contractors and civil servants in meeting evolving agency needs. In recent years, Congress has spent significant time debating and sometimes passing legislation related to the types of activities that can be considered for outsourcing and the procedures that should govern doing so. Congress also routinely reviews and occasionally tightens or modifies federal procurement law to address perceived or real problems, such as inadequate competition. While there are issues with Congress's level of involvement in this process, the work of the House Select Bipartisan Committee to Investigate the Preparation for and Response to Hurricane Katrina, the House Committee on Homeland Security, and the Senate Homeland Security and Governmental Affairs Committee[103] demonstrates the capabilities of Congress to address national issues.

At the same time, while there have been numerous hearings in the Armed Services Committees in the House and Senate on U.S. policies and military actions in Iraq, the congressional hearings focusing primarily on contracting practices and experiences relating to Iraq have been principally dominated by partisan wrangling and, regrettably, have reflected the ways in which procurement issues are increasingly the surrogate for other political agendas.[104] Indeed, there can be no question that the debate over outsourcing, as well as the overall debate about federal contracting, has unfortunately been fueled by broader passions about the conduct of the war in Iraq, as well as the government's poor handling of the disaster created by Hurricane Katrina and even the debacle at WRAMC, none of which was, or is, itself related to outsourcing.

The House Armed Services Committee has used its annual DOD Authorization Act as a forum for raising issues relating to the role of contractors on the battlefield. For example, in 2004 the enacted version of the fiscal year 2005 National Defense Authorization Act included provisions requiring DOD to issue updated guidance and policy statements regarding contractors supporting deployed forces in Iraq.[105] In 2005, the House's approved version of the fiscal year 2006 National Defense Authorization Act included several provisions under Title XVI, known as the "Contractors on the Battlefield Regulatory Act," providing additional direction to the department in addressing the roles of contractors on the battlefield both accompanying and not accompanying the force.[106]

*Separating the Routine from the Emergency—Lessons
Learned from Iraq and Katrina*

Contracting problems in Iraq and in New Orleans after Hurricane Katrina are extreme manifestations of common phenomena and serve to illustrate the difficulty of ensuring adherence to contracting procedural safeguards. Iraq and Katrina bring to bear situational forces that exacerbate the management and personnel problems inherent in the procurement process—problems that cannot be resolved through additional law. At the same time, circumstances present in Iraq and in post–Katrina New Orleans require more contractor discretion than other circumstances. Thus, difficulties in Iraq are not illustrative of flaws in the procurement system in general. Understanding how and why outsourcing and contract management challenges played out in these nontraditional environments is essential to understanding the broader context of federal procurement oversight and performance. Indeed, the lessons of Iraq and Katrina are essential to understanding current gaps in the management of the federal procurement process.

IRAQ—THE TOTAL FORCE

From the outset of the federal government's modern planning for military activities, it has recognized that contractors are an integral element of the "total force" that it brings to the battle space.[107] Contractors have been on the battlefield since the Revolutionary War, and have been accompanying the force in significant numbers for decades. The April 2007 report of U.S. Central Command identified more than 128,000 civilians supporting and funded by DOD entities in Iraq.[108] Of those civilians, more than half are Iraqi nationals and another third are third-country nationals (many from coalition partner nations). Only about 16 percent are American citizens. Firm data are not yet available regarding a similar measure of civilian contractors supporting nondefense activities (such as those of the United States Agency for International Development (USAID) or the Departments of State, Treasury, and so on), or activities funded and managed through United Nations or Iraqi auspices. But the sheer size, scope, and labor intensity of the nation-wide reconstruction and development efforts suggest strongly that the figure could be as high, or close to as high, as the 128,000 supporting the DOD. It is estimated that today, 80 percent or more of that work-force are Iraqi nationals.[109]

In the weeks leading to the first deployment of U.S. troops into Iraq, the Army tasked its logistics support contractor, Kellogg, Brown & Root (KBR), to prepare for work in Iraq under their competitively awarded LOGCAP III contract. KBR won the LOGCAP contract when it was first competed in the 1990s, later lost a recompetition for it, and won it back during its third competitive cycle. Many of the so-called no-bid contracts discussed with regard to Iraq contracting were actually task orders directed under the competitively awarded LOGCAP contract. And while there may be some reasonable criticisms of the Army's broad use of that contract, it is not correct to deem it "no bid." Similarly, the Army Corps of Engineers conducted a limited competition and awarded a contract to KBR to prepare to extinguish any fires that might be started in the vast Iraqi oil fields.[110] In addition, USAID made its only sole source award to International Resources Group (IRG) to provide infrastructure support to USAID mission personnel in Iraq in the first days following the fall of the Saddam Hussein regime.[111]

It is clear that DOD specifically, and the federal government generally, could not fulfill its mission requirements without substantial reliance on contractors. Moreover, longstanding federal personnel policies that limit the government's ability to deploy employees, and that limit the time that those who are deployable can be in harm's way, also drive these kinds of strategic personnel decisions. Indeed, while some have criticized the use of private contractors in Iraq to assist federal acquisition and contracting personnel, no one has yet proposed or been able to move forward the kind of personnel policy reforms that would be necessary to outsource functions that the government would rather not outsource.

Nonetheless, necessary and important questions remain as to whether adequate planning was done to ensure that the requisite government workforce was available to provide important planning, management, oversight, and operational capabilities. At Abu Ghraib, where there was a shortage of qualified linguists, one can fairly ask if adequate planning was done relative to the available linguistic force. To the extent that the requirement for interpreters could be foreseen, it is also fair to ask whether the deployment of available personnel was appropriately prioritized so that government personnel were first assigned, or transferred when needed, to those linguistic and interpreting tasks that are particularly sensitive, such as in a prison.

Moreover, as noted elsewhere in this chapter, work remains in terms of defining the legal status of contractors working on a battlefield and of determining whether or not the same restrictions should apply to those doing armed security work as to those performing more traditional functions. But those are issues that can and should be resolved with proper attention to and consultation with all interested parties, including the Justice Department, the agencies, and industry, and not by the unilateral implementation of new federal procurement regulations or policies.

The same is true in acquisition. USAID took on the initial responsibility for some of the early Iraq deployment contracts, but had to divert resources from its ongoing global developmental assistance mission to do the work.[112] DOD did not deploy large numbers of contracting officers into the Iraq theater in the early phases of the war, preferring to rely on U.S.–based resources to support activities eight time zones from the U.S. east coast.[113] In fact, during the height of the conflict in Iraq, there were more audit and oversight personnel working in Iraq than there were warranted federal contracting officers.

In late 2005 and into 2006, the contracting situation stabilized, and the nature of contracting requirements moved from emergency and contingency support into longer-term sustainment mode; thus, the frenetic pace of contracting has slowed significantly, and controversies have been far fewer. Yet, as the DOD's 2006 Quadrennial Defense Review acknowledged,[114] the federal government's unavoidable reliance on contractors to support and fulfill its deployed missions brings to the forefront the importance of developing and maintaining doctrine, policies, and contracting provisions to meet the widely varied challenges facing both the government and contractors. The unique requirements of an active military theater, let alone one in which two other enormous and complex missions were concurrently being executed, created unique contracting challenges for which the government, and in some cases, its contractors, was ill prepared. It is important to note that it was not just the government contracting community, or in some cases, even its contractors, that struggled with this unique environment. The oversight process, as documented by the SIGIR and others, has been extensive, but too often rooted in traditional assumptions about procurement and accounting in normal environments rather than reflective of realities on the ground.[115] While easy to critique from afar, it is far more difficult to address in an active military theater. Fundamentally, this poses an issue of planning and coordination of the kind that has plagued the prosecution of the Iraq mission, as reported in 2006 by GAO and the SIGIR, among others.[116]

Here again, the report of the Commission on Army Acquisition and Program Management in Expeditionary Operations is instructive. That report identified a range of structural and personnel shortfalls within the Army acquisition system that inhibited effective contract management and performance. Moreover, the report addressed more than the numbers of government acquisition personnel available (although it did recommend that the Army hire 1,000 additional civilian contracting professionals and add some 400 military contracting positions). Much of its critique centered on the Army's acquisition structure, including the fact that the Army managed many of the Iraq and Afghanistan contracts from U.S. locations. The Commission's principal message—that the Army is not structured or resourced properly to manage its contemporary mission—is one that can also easily be applied to the Hurricane Katrina situation and even to more routine aspects of federal procurement as well.

Finally, when all is said and done, some of the harshest criticisms of the performance of contractors in Iraq resulted in substantially more smoke than fire. While there clearly have been issues with performance and in some cases accountability, not all is as it appeared from initial reports. For example, final audit reports on the work done in the early phases by KBR, the official "bogeyman" in Iraq, have shown that the problems were far less sweeping than initially proclaimed. As the SIGIR report on KBR's food service contract said, while some problems did occur, "overcharges" were not nearly as significant as previously alleged, the company's performance was exemplary, and its response to identified problems was rapid and appropriate. Needless to say, in a business dominated by the instant reporting of dramatic bad news stories, that final report did not qualify for any headlines.

KATRINA—A DISASTER WITHIN A DISASTER

In August 2005 Hurricane Katrina caused more significant damage to the U.S. mainland than any other natural disaster in the nation's history. While the response and recovery is still active, even the initial analyses of the federal, state and local response show failures on virtually every level and every segment.[117] This is also true of FEMA's preparation for and response to the disaster.

While state and local jurisdictions bear the primary and initial responsibility for addressing disaster response and recovery, the federal government is frequently called on to provide resources to respond to significant damage.[118] Katrina was a powerful hurricane that covered a wide swath of the Gulf Coast, but FEMA, the Department of Homeland Security, and apparently the entire federal apparatus were ill prepared for its arrival or its aftermath.[119]

Congress reacted quickly in the aftermath of Katrina. Through two emergency appropriations acts, Congress provided over $68 billion in relief funds. In addition, Congress promptly provided for an increase in the threshold for using small-purchase contracting procedures for federal contracts awarded to help recover from Katrina.[120] The controversy over the executive branch utilization of special congressional authority, such as the President's waiver of the Davis-Bacon Act[121] drew much political and public attention to Katrina contracting practices and mistakes.

Local government activities form an important part of the overall disaster response; however, the preponderance of the response to significant disasters is provided by private firms working under contracts awarded by FEMA or other federal agencies. While FEMA had previously competed and awarded a limited number of contingency contracts, these contracts could not fulfill the enormous needs that arose in the hours and days immediately following Katrina's devastation. As a result, FEMA and other federal agencies had to immediately award massive emergency contracts for housing, food, blue tarps, pumping and construction materials, and other supplies and services—sometimes without a sufficient and sufficiently trained contracting staff and without the time needed for normal competition and the use of traditional regulations and practices to meet rapidly escalating needs. Where FEMA had only forty contracting officers available to meet the immediate needs of the pre- and post-Katrina response, a year later the Department of Homeland Security's Inspector General proclaimed that more than 450 auditors and investigators were reviewing the contracts for "fraud, waste and abuse."[122]

Moreover, it is clear that some negative perceptions of the FEMA-awarded contracts were themselves based on erroneous information. For example, Congress at first excoriated FEMA for a contract awarded to Carnival Cruise Lines (to use one or more cruise ships for emergency shelter). Initially, some in Congress were led to believe that Carnival was charging the government $1500 per week for staterooms that normally cost $750 per week when the ship is under way. However, the price to the government was based not just on the stateroom costs, but on the cruise line's average daily per-passenger revenue rate (room, plus food, plus liquor, plus gambling). After all, if the ships were to be taken out of service, the company had a reasonable right to compensation for the revenues it would lose. In that sense, the contract was "revenue neutral."

FEMA did make mistakes; and some of the special authorities in place for just this kind of circumstance may well have been misused, albeit despite good intent. But here, as with contracting in Iraq, it is vital to recognize that traditional contracting—including traditional expectations—is not feasible during times of emergency. And while that reality should not lead us to ignore problems, it must inform the way we think about the specific problems that emerged.

IRAQ AND KATRINA—TOO MANY SIMILARITIES AND
SEVERAL KEY DIFFERENCES

While the long-term stories about Iraq and Katrina are still being written, it is already eminently clear that, in both cases, the federal government and the responsible lead federal agencies were unprepared for the magnitude of the requisite responses, including the level of needed contractor support and the extent of contract administration and management challenges. In both cases, federal agencies lacked access to the necessary contracting resources to meet basic federal acquisition requirements—even under emergency conditions. Furthermore, in both cases, the doctrine, planning, and regulations for promptly and properly using contractors to respond to such contingency operations were out of date, insufficient, and not well communicated among all essential government and industry players.

Yet there also some notable differences that must be taken into account. After Katrina, there was no lack of qualified domestic companies and personnel capable of responding to evolving needs in the Gulf Coast, while support in Iraq required significant travel, so that the government could only draw on a limited pool of contractor resources or qualified personnel able to transition quickly. In New Orleans, there was no special personnel security requirement imposed on companies and the workforce, and the firms working there did not have to perform in a life-threatening, hostile environment; in Iraq, the physical and national security challenges significantly affected the ability of contractors to travel to and perform their work. Finally, the initial emergency response and recovery to Katrina was of short duration with a definable transition to sustainment needs and long-term recovery. In Iraq, the emergency contracting phase extended over many months and various repetitive cycles based on the changing security posture.

If anything, the common lessons of Iraq and Katrina highlighted the abject failure of coordination and communication not only among the responsible lead agencies and their contractors, but also among the agencies, the oversight communities, and the legislature. These lessons also demonstrate that initiatives designed to improve performance and accountability the next time must be focused on systemic and personnel weaknesses, rather than the addition of more law to the procurement process.

Conclusion: Do We Need More Law?

Prominent scholars of administrative law and related fields, including many who are writing in this volume, have proposed subjecting contractors to document disclosure requirements, broadening False Claims Act coverage, and generally more broadly applying principles of administrative law to contract management. While the contracting process certainly needs improved management and substantial investment in the federal acquisition workforce, more law is not the answer to current contracting challenges.

It is true that the federal government was ill prepared for dealing with the magnitude of the contracting forces it used in Iraq and post-Katrina New Orleans. And it is true that responses to emerging or identified challenges are often too slow to come. For example, DOD acknowledges that its doctrine and contract regulations are out of date and inadequate.[123] While the Army took limited action to update its contract provisions applicable to "contractors accompanying a force deployed,"[124] it was not until March 23, 2004 that DOD issued department-wide proposed rules for all DOD contractors. It was more than two years after the first troop and contractor deployment into Iraq that DOD finalized its contract regulations.[125] DOD has not yet finalized an update of its internal Joint Staff doctrine and requirements, even with the prompting of Congress twice in the last two years.[126] Despite recommendations dating from early in the Iraq conflict (and in some cases, prior to it) for meaningful government-wide acquisition regulations,[127] as of August 2007 no such regulations had been finalized. Similar delays have been experienced in the establishment of standards and qualifications for private security firms employed in Iraq, despite industry recommendations in June 2003 that such steps be taken. But these bureaucratic challenges themselves do not warrant the overlay of additional and potentially conflicting statutory constructs.

Nor can critics' concerns with the ethical aspects of outsourcing be resolved by additional law. Individuals and companies involved in the various contracting scandals profiled in media reports and legislative hearings did not take advantage of legal loopholes; what they did was patently illegal—and they knew it when they did it. Thus, to the extent such cases raise questions about ethics and ethics laws, the focus rightly belongs on individual behavior and the balance of law versus personal ethics.

The same is true of federal contracting at large. There have certainly been questions raised and evident problems identified in recent years—almost all of them, as the SIGIR, GAO, and others have made clear, related to unstable or uncertain requirements, inadequate human capital investments and support, poor planning and more. There has also been a wide range of statutory and regulatory proposals in recent years purportedly designed to improve accountability and transparency and protect the government. But it is not always clear what substantive "problems" the proposals have been designed to fix, or whether they would have any salutary effect at all.

For example, to improve perceived gaps in transparency and contractor accountability, several proposals would require creation of an integrated database to track and align contractor performance on contracts as well as every aspect of a contractor's corporate behavior. While this sounds fairly reasonable, it mistakenly assumes that corporate behavior or performance are not now considered—or supposed to be considered—in source selection decisions. They are, and the law clearly requires that they be.

Moreover, none of the proposals put forward provide a fundamental, objective set of criteria, and a framework therefor, that would provide meaningful assessments of not only a company's record, but also of the relative severity of violations identified, the difference between civil, criminal, and relatively routine administrative disputes; steps the company has taken to mitigate future violations; whether the violations were individual or reflective of a broad corporate culture, and so on. Furthermore, such proposals ignore the fact that our system of laws establishes appropriate punishments for violations of every stripe, from fines to jail time. To the extent contractors have already paid fines or served a suspension, do the additional penalties associated with a denial of federal work conflict with fair competition or amount to an unreasonable expansion of established remedies? In some cases, where patterns are clear and violations significant, such steps may well be warranted; that is precisely the purpose of the responsibility determination that must be made by a contracting officer. And no one argues that scofflaws should benefit from public contracts. But such distinctions require deep analysis, broad legal expertise, and adherence to established precepts of due process, much of which is lacking in current discussions or in the kinds of legislative proposals described above.

The legal framework for determining what can be outsourced, how the outsourcing is to be conducted, and how performance under a contract is to be overseen is fundamentally sound, quite public, and replete with layers of oversight, checks, and balances. Adding more layers to it will serve little purpose and achieve few results.

Instead, the real question is one of people and tools. The reality is that both government and society are undergoing a transformation. This transformation can be sped up or slowed down by ideological initiatives at either end of the spectrum, but it cannot be stopped or reversed. Problems that have already emerged, as well as problems that will surface in the future, are mostly traceable to the government's failure not only to recognize but also to address the human capital dimension meaningfully. Because more than a third of the discretionary budget is spent on contracts, acquisition is among the government's most critical, core responsibilities. And it is on the contracting, program management, and business management skills, which will require increased funding and an aggressive effort to develop the government acquisition workforce further, that we should focus our attention and our resources.

In the 1990s, the focus in government contracting was on improving the federal acquisition process so that the government would have access to the broadest possible array of solutions and capabilities to meet its mission and improve outcomes. As Steve Kelman extensively explains elsewhere in this volume, it was broadly recognized then that the existing procurement regime was far too burdensome, contained far too many layers of non-value-added requirements and rules, and was keeping significant portions of the broad commercial marketplace out of the government's sphere. The results of that focus were a series of bipartisan bills and regulatory changes that focused on process improvement. To a great extent, however, there was simply not a concomitant focus on the people responsible for that process, particularly in the federal acquisition workforce. Our energies should be focused on people, who deserve and need proper training and resources, and on providing contractors with clear guidelines and appropriate oversight. That is how the public interest, as well as the government interest, can best be served, protected, and fulfilled.

B. Use Existing Tools

CHAPTER NINE

Six Simple Steps to Increase Contractor Accountability

NINA A. MENDELSON

Introduction

The legal framework pertaining to government contractors is patchy at best. Nonetheless, agency purchases of sophisticated professional services, such as research and information technology, are on the rise.[1] This chapter primarily focuses on the issues raised by such services contracts, or in Ruth Hoogland DeHoog and Lester Salamon's words, "purchase-of-service contracting."[2] As detailed elsewhere in this volume, agencies are increasingly relying on the private sector to perform not only commercial services but also what might be traditionally viewed as "governmental" or even, by some, "inherently governmental" functions.[3] For example, contractors may not only supply aircraft and maintenance services, but may also administer airports, libraries, and prisons, operate immigration detention facilities, collect income taxes, and supply security services.[4] As the Comptroller General of the United States recently observed, "[t]he [Department of Defense] is now buying launch services, rather than rockets"[5] and flight simulator training services for Air Force pilots rather than flight simulators themselves.[6] As contractor tasks become more related to what we consider critical government functions, the contractor workforce is increasingly blending with the civil service, and contractors are exercising decision-making power in new contexts. For an example of this extended contractor authority, in 2006 the Department of Homeland Security signed a $30 billion contract with Boeing to "conceptualiz[e], design[], build[], and operat[e]" a comprehensive border security plan known as SBInet, aimed at securing northern and southern U.S. land borders, including the Great Lakes. According to an analysis prepared by U.S. Senate staff, private contractors bear responsibility not only for building and operating the border security project, but also for much of the *oversight* of the contract itself.[7] For another example, the Department of Energy spends over 90 percent of its budget on contracts, including contracts to operate research laboratories, maintain nuclear weapons stockpiles, and clean up radioactive and hazardous wastes resulting from weapons production.[8]

Contractors that supply sophisticated services over long periods of time can end up with significant discretion to set policy. Contractors safety-testing helicopters may have significant control over what tests to perform, for example.[9] In the border security project, Boeing's responsibilities include devising and providing the "*optimum* mix of personnel, technology, infrastructure, and response platforms" to detect and classify border breaches.[10] Such policy decisions have the potential to serve public goals for the particular program—or to undermine them. As the responsibility and discretion of contractors increases, contractor activities can present greater risks for national security, human health and the environment, and public safety. In implementing their contracts, government contractors may attend to—but may also disregard—other legal obligations, such as employee rights or environmental compliance. Reports of agency contractors violating other applicable laws, including worker safety laws, are widespread.[11] The contractor that operates the Department of Energy Pantex nuclear weapons facility has repeatedly been fined for safety violations, including one instance when the contractor's technicians improperly sealed a crack in the high explosives surrounding the plutonium sphere of the hydrogen bomb, causing an even bigger crack and "increas[ing] the potential for a violent reaction."[12]

Government agencies can also be afflicted with problems of poor performance, cost overruns, or legal violations. However, government agencies are constrained by a number of laws that keep their functions open to public view and make the agencies legally accountable for underperforming or causing harm. Contractors, by comparison, can bypass many of these constraints. They function under a patchwork of laws and doctrines, many of which were designed primarily for other purposes. At best, the current laws governing contractors amount to a makeshift legal framework.

Close agency supervision of a contractor could, in theory, provide a functional substitute for other forms of public and legal accountability. The contract could guide and constrain the contractor's discretion, and the prospect of supervision (and reductions in contract payments) by an agency motivated to serve the public interest might prompt better performance by the contractor. The government contract, however, may simply be inadequate to guide a contractor or constrain its functions. Especially for service contracts, such as the hiring, administration, planning, and operating contracts described above, agencies can face great challenges in adequately specifying terms, including "defining requirements, establishing expected outcomes, and assessing contractor performance."[13] Lack of competition among qualified private entities and limited contract supervision can increase the chances of poor contract performance. Federal agency supervision of contract performance is widely recognized as inadequate.[14] As several authors in this volume observe, these problems call for greater contractor accountability as well as more transparency and public involvement in the contracting process.[15]

Reforms to the legal framework governing contractors should accordingly be aimed at increasing contractor accountability and responsibility. That may mean that a contractor may more often be liable in court for harm the contractor has caused or for problems in contract performance. However, litigation should not be the sole means of increasing contractor accountability. Any legal reforms should also help the mechanisms of government function better. Ideally, legal reforms should prompt agencies to draft contract terms more carefully and to monitor government contractors more thoroughly. Agencies likely will have superior access to information about the public's needs, project demands, contractor qualifications, and contractor performance. Compared with a private plaintiff, agencies will also be more publicly accountable for supervising government contracts. It thus makes sense to encourage effective agency supervision of contracting wherever possible. One way to prompt greater agency involvement is to enlist contractors in seeking, rather than avoiding, agency supervision and involvement in key decisions.

Looking at federal law and federal contracting activities, this chapter offers several simple steps that could be taken to increase the accountability of federal contractors, especially those supplying services, and to increase agency involvement in contractor supervision. I will not advocate abandoning contracting either completely or for some large category of activities (such as battlefield actions or intelligence gathering).[16] Nor will I advocate the overhaul of the state action doctrine, which defines when private party activities may be attributed to the state, thus subjecting them to constitutional constraints.[17] Further, the chapter does not focus on special issues presented by contracting abroad. Instead, I propose six paths to change existing statutes and contracting practice. Rather than suggest an entirely new legal framework, the purpose here is to identify straightforward reform opportunities in the context of existing law. The changes would be aimed at ensuring that a contractor does not face significantly fewer incentives than the agency itself to perform its job properly and comply with the law. While any statutory change that increases contractor responsibility could, of course, bring controversy, these changes could make contractors more appropriately responsible within the framework of existing laws.

In later sections this chapter identifies and compares major laws that constrain government agencies and government contractors, and summarizes some possibilities for reform.

Federal Agency Responsibility Compared with Government Contractor Responsibility

This section briefly overviews the existing legal structure governing federal agency activities and federal agency contracting. The analysis focuses on important disparities in treatment of agencies and contractors, as well as areas in which a relatively small legal change might significantly increase contractor accountability.

Federal agencies are subject to an array of requirements aimed at ensuring transparency in decisionmaking, public accountability, and accountability in court. The Administrative Procedure Act (APA) requires public participation in informal rulemaking through the notice-and-comment process. Federal agency actions are subject to judicial review under the APA, as well as other statutes.[18] Federal agencies also are subject to public disclosure requirements under the Freedom of Information Act (FOIA).[19] Because many of these legal requirements are explicitly aimed at government agencies or instrumentalities, however, a contractor performing services under a government contract may have no parallel responsibility. That may be so even when the contractor exercises discretion closely resembling that of a public agency.[20]

Federal agencies also are subject to political oversight from Congress, the White House, and indirectly via elections, the public at large. Sometimes this political oversight is formally structured by statutes that, for example, call for reporting to congressional committees. Federal contractors, like federal agencies, are subject to congressional and presidential oversight. Congressional committees may hold hearings, and members of Congress exercise further oversight of agency contracting, by requesting U.S. Government Accountability Office (GAO) reports. As with oversight of administrative agencies, however, oversight of contractors is often reactive and ad hoc rather than systematic.[21] Halliburton's contracting performance in Iraq has received significant attention in congressional oversight hearings, but less attention has been paid to systematic cost overruns by Federal Aviation Administration (FAA) contractors[22] or to substantial overbilling by a contractor hired by the Transportation Security Administration to set up high-speed computer networks linking federal airport employees to security centers.[23]

Unlike federal agencies, contractors have comparatively limited obligations to disclose information to the public, and the APA applies only to agencies, thereby excluding contractors.[24] Thus, the primary *judicial* oversight of a contractor's activity is likely to be through the adjudication of a contract claim when the contractor seeks payment, when an agency seeks relief under a contract or for a contract breach, or when the contractor is alleged to have violated the False Claims Act (FCA) by presenting a false or fraudulent claim.[25] The contracting agency may also elect to seek exclusion of the contractor from procurement activities in debarment or suspension proceedings.[26] A contractor also may face private tort liability or a private claim under the False Claims Act, though both types of liability are limited. In short, then, it is primarily up to the contracting agency to hold a contractor accountable; government contractors currently have relatively little accountability in court to private parties.[27] The following section examines in greater detail different types of liability that contractors, agencies, or both may face, together with the limitations of that legal responsibility.

Contract Liability to the Agency

An agency may bring a claim against a contractor for failure to perform the contract itself. The claim can address the contractor's overcharging or provision of substandard services, as well as failure to conform to other particular contract requirements. Such a claim (like a contractor's claim for nonpayment under the contract) is covered by the Contract Disputes Act.[28] Contract liability surely can be used to hold contractors accountable, but its effectiveness depends on the availability of agency resources to monitor contract performance and to pursue claims where necessary. Besides those resources, holding contractors accountable in this manner critically depends on having enforceable contract terms that are well specified. Yet contract terms are not always sufficiently specific to support a claim of breach when contractors violate their obligations. For example, contracts may not clearly require compliance with other applicable laws.[29] As the United States Acquisition Advisory Panel found, "the government's difficulties in defining requirements are well documented."[30]

Tort Liability

Tort liability applies to some degree to both agencies and contractors whose actions cause harm. Under the Federal Tort Claims Act (FTCA), federal agencies have waived sovereign immunity to state tort claims for a "negligent or wrongful" act or omission or particular intentional torts of "investigative or law enforcement officers." An agency is not, however, liable if the claim is based on the agency's exercise or failure to exercise a "discretionary function or duty" within the meaning of the Act.[31] Such discretionary functions include determinations in "establishing plans, specifications, or schedules of operations. Where there is room for policy judgment and decision there is discretion."[32] Straightforward examples of such discretion might include decisions on whether to launch a space shuttle or what type of security to provide in airports. An agency's exercise of such judgment may be immune from judicial second-guessing in the form of tort liability. However, as discussed in greater detail below, the agency decision still may be subject to judicial review and invalidation under the APA if it is arbitrary, capricious, or illegal.

For government contractors, tort liability also may be limited and, in some cases, unduly so. Courts recognize a government contractor defense to tort liability, which a contractor may assert when the federal government has approved reasonably precise specifications, the equipment or service provided conformed to those specifications, and the contractor warned the government about known dangers.[33] Consequently, if the United States has approved precise specifications, as with, for example, the manufacture of an aircraft part, the contractor will not face tort liability for conforming to those specifications. That seems reasonably consistent with holding the government and not the contractor responsible for key policy decisions. It also is consistent with deferring to government decisions that weigh concerns differently than civilian judges might, consistent with the "discretionary function" exception to government tort liability.[34] Indeed, courts have expressly noted the link between the government contractor defense and the discretionary function exception to the FTCA. Where the contractor has acted at variance with the contract specifications, however, tort liability may be available.[35]

However, in some settings, the government contractor defense could excessively limit the tort liability of contractors. Injured parties might be forced to "bear the costs of contractor negligence."[36] This is especially the case when an agency does not completely specify the terms of a contract, a particular risk for longer-term or complex contracts. For example, in a long-term contract for prison administration, the agency may not anticipate the range of circumstances that will require a contractor response. Some such responses might cause injury—imagine a contractor's decision not to make medical treatment available to inmates suffering particular illnesses not itemized under the prison administration contract. Similarly, one could imagine the contractor that operates a nuclear weapons facility failing to go beyond the particular safety requirements identified in a contract, even if a reasonable investigation might suggest that more safety measures are required.

In the best case scenario for contractor accountability, a court could conceivably decline to apply the government contractor defense in a tort case unless the government had specifically required particular actions (or nonactions) on the part of the contractor.[37] The contractor would then face tort liability for harm caused by any actions not directed by the government. On the other hand, in cases in which the government contract does not specifically address the contractor's action, some courts have more broadly allowed contractors to claim the defense to tort liability that would otherwise obtain. As long as contract terms are, overall, "reasonably precise," these courts have allowed the government contractor defense if the contractor conformed to existing contract terms, even if the injury arose from contractor activities *not* specifically directed by the government.[38] In one recent case involving a fatal accident that occurred when an Army helicopter's tail fin broke off, the maintenance contractor argued that it was not liable even though its employees had not inspected the fin. Although the contractor was not barred from conducting a thorough inspection of the fin and was aware of a Federal Aviation Administration advisory regarding it, the contractor was nevertheless held not liable because the Army had not *required* the contractor to perform this particular inspection. The contractor was still allowed to benefit from the government contractor defense to liability.[39]

This sort of overbroad application of the government contractor defense clearly reduces a contractor's incentive to exercise reasonable care—even though the contractor may well be the most knowledgeable party involved and better able than potential victims to bear risk.[40] The chance of overbroad application of the defense is significantly increased in a services contract, especially one that covers a long period of time. Because such a contract is not likely to anticipate every situation that may arise, the contractor may end up, as a practical matter, with substantial discretion. At the same time, a court might be more willing to conclude, in view of a long contract term, that contract terms are "reasonably precise" under the circumstances, thus permitting the contractor to escape otherwise applicable tort liability. Again, this diminishes the contractor's incentive to use reasonable care. Moreover, because greater detail in a contract could reduce the contractor's discretion and thus potentially reduce the scope of the government contractor defense, the contractor also would have little incentive to seek out more detailed contract specifications from the agency or ongoing agency monitoring and approval of its actions.

Further, although the government contractor defense can become unavailable if a contractor fails to disclose "known" dangers to the government, it still generally remains available if a contractor has declined to reasonably investigate possible risks arising after the execution of the contract or to seek additional agency monitoring of the contract's performance.[41] Over long periods of time, a service contractor will be uniquely positioned to investigate potential risks inherent in the implementation of the contract, but this aspect of the government contractor defense doctrine further reduces the incentive to do so.

In short, although tort liability could serve as a significant incentive for a contractor to exercise reasonable care, the overbroad application of the government contractor defense undermines it, especially in the context of long-term service contracts.

APA Review

An agency action, including a rulemaking, may be set aside under APA review if it is "arbitrary, capricious, an abuse of discretion, or contrary to law."[42] Courts may also grant other forms of injunctive relief, but not money damages, under the APA.[43] APA review provides an avenue for assessing claims not only of statutory violation, but also of constitutional violation. Through the "arbitrary and capricious" review standard, the APA also provides a plaintiff who has proper standing with an opportunity for judicial review of conduct that would be immune from tort liability under the FTCA's "discretionary function" exception.[44]

Finally, the APA provides for public involvement in agency rulemaking through notice and comment procedures and requires publication of both "substantive rules of general applicability and statements of general policy."[45]

However, these requirements do not apply to agency contracting decisions or to decisions of contractors. Although courts have occasionally held that agency decisions governing an entire category of contracts must be made through rulemaking, for the overwhelming majority of individual contracts notice and comment requirements do not apply.[46] Consequently, there may be no public involvement in a particular agency decision to outsource functions or to set the terms on which the agency will do so.

Nor do APA requirements apply to contractors; the APA, by its terms, applies only to an "agency," which is defined to include only an "authority of the Government of the United States."[47] The APA's definition of "agency" does not include government contractors.[48] Procedural requirements for broad decisions accordingly do not apply. Nor are contractor decisions subject to outside review in court, even those functional and policy decisions that, if made by an agency, would clearly be subject to APA review as "arbitrary, capricious . . . or not in accordance with law."[49] For example, an agency's decision that inspection of helicopter tailfins is unnecessary, including one made despite an FAA advisory on easily cracked helicopter tailfins, would be subject to APA review. Similarly, an agency's decision to require that nuclear weapons facility security guards work over seventy hours per week, even if there are employee complaints that exhausted employees cannot effectively protect security, would be subject to APA review. Although it might have the same effects on employee and public safety and public resources, a similar decision made by a contractor would not be subject to review.

Freedom of Information Act Disclosure Requirements

Under the Freedom of Information Act, federal agencies must make written information promptly available on request, subject to some limited exceptions, such as for national security, predecisional materials, and trade secrets.[50] As with the APA, however, federal agency contractors are considered private parties that are not covered by the statute.[51] Moreover, FOIA's exemption for confidential "trade secrets and commercial or financial information" could preclude federal agency disclosure of some information about contractors, even if the agency had possession of the information.[52] As Rosenbloom and Piotrowski describe, a contractor that operated much of the space shuttle fleet and was "integrally involved" in the decisions of the National Aeronautics and Space Administration relating to the disastrous Columbia space shuttle mission had documents that were nonetheless not covered by FOIA.[53] Similarly, this exemption has been applied to protect contractor information about design, test results, and compliance with other laws, such as equal employment laws.[54]

The concern here is that the public does not possess a clear entitlement under these statutes to information concerning decisions made by a contractor, even important ones such as operational decisions involving the space shuttle or a prison operator's devising of directives to individual guards. That reduces decisionmaking transparency and accountability.

Bivens-*Type Actions*

So-called *Bivens* claims are special claims for money damages that courts have implied under particular provisions of the Constitution.[55] Although the Constitution itself does not provide a remedy for violating, for example, the Fourth Amendment right not to be subjected to unreasonable search or seizure, the courts have reasoned that money damages are sometimes appropriate to redress the injury to an individual who has suffered such a search. Such damages awards can also deter further constitutional violations. *Bivens* claims can be brought against individual federal officers (though not the employing agency) for damages for violating the Fourth, Fifth, and Eighth Amendments' protections of individual liberties, and possibly others as well.[56] Congress made clear when it amended the FTCA in 1974 that it viewed the statute, which imposes liability on federal agencies, and the *Bivens* doctrine, which imposes liability on individual agency employees, as "parallel, complementary causes of action."[57]

A government contractor's employee might conceivably face direct liability for violating an individual's constitutional rights under *Bivens* or related cases.[58] However, the Supreme Court has barred *Bivens* claims against the employing corporate entity.[59] The Supreme Court held that such claims were barred against a prison operator, despite strenuous arguments from the Legal Aid Society that without direct *Bivens* liability imposed on the contractor, private prison operators were hiring (and would continue to hire) inadequate numbers of guards, increasing the chance of uncontrolled violence and constitutional violations.[60]

Even if individual employees may face *Bivens* liability for violating the constitutional rights of an individual, they could be judgment proof. This worsens the moral hazard faced by the contractor. The contractor accordingly may have little incentive to supervise its employees with the goal of preventing constitutional deprivations or other injuries.

The lack of *Bivens* liability, combined with the available defenses to tort liability, means that a contractor will be accountable for poor contract performance primarily to the contracting agency. And if agency oversight is inadequate or contract terms are not well specified, that accountability too will be limited.[61]

False Claims Act Liability for "False Certification"

The False Claims Act allows a private person to bring a *qui tam* suit in the name of the United States to recover penalties from a person who knowingly presents a false or fraudulent claim to the government.[62] A special feature of the act is that any private individual may bring such a claim; no showing of direct injury need be made.[63] Although previous law barred a plaintiff from bringing such an action if the suit was "based upon evidence or information in possession of the United States . . . at the time such suit was brought,"[64] the FCA was amended in 1986 to globally authorize such suits with very limited exceptions; the most important bars to suit are a previously filed government civil action or the public disclosure of allegations or transactions in a public hearing, congressional, administrative or GAO report, or by the news media.[65] Such suits have been brought, for example, to expose the fraudulent obtaining of federal grants and false certification of compliance with contract terms.[66] Claims may be focused on a contractor's overcharging or based on theories of supplying substandard products or services.[67] A contractor will face liability if it knowingly and falsely certifies its compliance with an applicable contract term, statute, or regulation.[68]

The FCA may thus enable a private party to hold a contractor responsible for statutory or regulatory noncompliance even where the government has not discovered the issue or pursued the contractor itself for noncompliance. For example, in *United States ex rel. Holder v. Special Devices, Inc.*,[69] the relator successfully argued that the contractor had falsely certified compliance with environmental and health and safety regulations. The court held that the contractor's failure to comply with the regulations, as warranted in its contract with the government, had caused pollution, resulting in government losses and giving rise to a FCA claim.[70]

However, not every act of regulatory or statutory noncompliance will serve as the basis of a FCA claim against a contractor. Instead, regulatory compliance must have been falsely represented to the government and also have been relevant to the government's disbursement decision—again, generally meaning that the contract must require or reference it.[71] Further, although the FCA also provides a cause of action for "worthless services," that claim is aimed at truly deficient conduct—where "services literally are not provided or the service is so substandard as to be tantamount to no service at all."[72] Such claims are rarely successful.[73]

In addition, the FCA requires a plaintiff to show that a contractor "knowingly" presented such a false or fraudulent claim, which the statute defines to mean that the contractor either possessed actual knowledge of the information or acted in deliberate ignorance or reckless disregard of the truth or falsity of the information.[74] A negligent failure to investigate a safety risk or an issue of legal compliance, for example, may not serve as the basis for liability.

In short, current law provides some avenues toward holding contractors accountable. However, those avenues are limited in some important ways. For example, although an agency may hold a contractor responsible for inadequate contract performance, the effectiveness of that remedy depends on the agency drafting well-specified contracts and on the investing of agency resources in contract enforcement actions, something an overtaxed agency may not have the will to do, especially in the context of a longer-term service contract. Meanwhile, contractor responsibility to third parties is also limited. Contractor "policy decisions" may not be subject to disclosure or outside review, even if equivalent agency actions would be, under the APA or FOIA. Contractor liability for failure to exercise reasonable care may be limited, especially in the context of service contracts, by an overbroad application of the government contractor defense. Finally, contractor liability under the False Claims Act for substandard performance may be too limited or too difficult to establish, especially if contract terms are not well specified or because the contractor's presentation of a false claim cannot be shown to be "knowing."

Importantly, a number of the shortcomings in the current legal regime are exacerbated by inadequate contract terms. Clearer specification by federal agencies of contractor responsibilities would unquestionably increase contractor accountability. Accordingly, any proposed reforms should not only clarify contractor responsibility, but also encourage agencies to define specific contractor responsibilities more carefully and to monitor contractor activities closely.

Six Avenues for Increasing Contractor Accountability

This section offers six relatively straightforward suggestions for amending the governing statutes discussed above or addressing the government contractor defense. They are straightforward in the sense that they work within the context of existing law, without requiring the creation of a broad new legal framework. Some suggestions are modest; others may be viewed as controversial or not easily accomplished.

At a minimum, the hope here is to generate a broader discussion about possible legal changes to the existing regime governing contractors. In particular, more information should be made available to the public regarding essential aspects of contracts and contractor supervision. In addition, legal changes should increase the accountability of contractors for their implementation of contracts. A contractor should face more appropriate incentives both to perform a particular contract properly and to use reasonable care in exercising its contractual discretion. Enhancing opportunities for private enforcement of contract terms could help prompt better contractor performance by supplementing agency oversight and enforcement.

One risk of increasing contractor liability to private parties, however, might be that the prospect of lawsuits brought by a few highly motivated groups or individuals could drive contract performance priorities, rather than government agency decisions. Compared with private parties, government agencies are better able to weigh competing social priorities, are more publicly accountable for those decisions, and may well possess better information about how a contractor can best serve the needs of the public. Accordingly, if opportunities for private enforcement are increased, they should be structured as a supplement to, rather than a substitute for, agency enforcement. One way of doing so would be to supply contractors with defenses to some private claims if the contractor can show that the agency adequately specified

the contractor's responsibilities and monitored the contractor's performance. Such a defense further might lead contractors to seek out better-specified contracts and more agency supervision. This would more closely align the incentives of contractors and the general public. It also is likely to prompt agencies to monitor contractors more closely or to specify contractual terms more clearly.

Six possibilities for change follow.

Subject Contractors to Document Disclosure Requirements

Requiring contractors to publicly disclose documents relating to the performance of their contracts, at a minimum, would increase transparency in contract performance. For example, unless it is specified in a contract, a contractor operating a private prison is under no particular obligation to release to the public a directive to individual prison guards, even though that directive may significantly influence the way inmates are treated. Similarly, a contractor operating a government laboratory or other facility is under no general obligation to publicly release safety directives issued to employees. Greater transparency in turn could evoke greater agency supervision of contractor performance and other forms of oversight, including political oversight. Of course, a contractor is likely to resist the disclosure of trade secrets or sensitive financial information, and appropriate exceptions could be drafted for this type of information.

One possible way to increase transparency is to require, as a matter of statute, regulation, or agency practice, that government contracts provide that critical documents, such as operating procedures related to contract execution, be supplied to the agency. From there, the documents would be under agency control and hence subject to public disclosure under FOIA.[75] Alternatively, FOIA could be amended to make such contractor documents directly subject to disclosure without requiring transmittal to the agency.

Clarify the Government Contractor Defense to Tort Claims

As discussed above, the contractor defense, as interpreted by some courts, appears to insulate a contractor from tort liability as long as there are reasonably precise contract specifications with which the contractor has complied (and the contractor has notified the government of particular dangers known to the contractor). The difficulty is that a contractor may escape tort liability for a particular harmful decision even if the agency neither required nor approved that decision.

One possible solution is to enact a statute limiting the availability of the government contractor defense unless the contractor shows not simply that it has not violated the contract, but also that the events giving rise to the tort claim either amounted to its *required* compliance with particular contract terms or that the agency knew of and approved (or, less stringently, had an opportunity to disapprove) the particular decision or action that gave rise to the tort claim.

Relatedly, Congress has recently enacted provisions in the Homeland Security Act (HSA) that modify the government contractor defense. In some respects, the modification is problematic in its reduction of government contractor accountability. Apparently aimed at design defect claims,[76] the modification provides a "rebuttable presumption" that the government contractor defense applies to tort claims arising out of the sale of qualified antiterrorism technologies.[77] Moreover, that defense is available even when the contractor is selling its products directly to private parties.[78]

Despite its apparent expansion of protections for contractors, the modification nevertheless appears to increase contractor accountability relative to the current form of the government contractor defense in two relevant respects: First, the defense is only available if the Secretary of Homeland Security has specifically *approved* the technologies after a comprehensive review of their design to assure that they are "safe for use as intended."[79] Second, the seller has an independent obligation to conduct "safety and hazard analyses" and to supply that information to the Secretary. In short, the agency has a specific obligation to review the design, while the seller has an independent obligation to investigate safety and supply that information to the secretary.[80]

This aspect of the HSA language might serve as a model for modifying the government contractor defense to tort claims. For example, legislation might clearly specify that for a contractor to invoke the defense, the contractor would need to show that an agency actually did approve (or at least had an opportunity to disapprove) the action that is the basis for the tort claim. Moreover, to provide the greatest incentive to a contractor to disclose available safety information to the agency, an amendment should clarify that a contractor's negligent failure to disclose relevant information to an agency would also bar assertion of the defense.

Such a modification would make clear that a contractor would face tort liability for its own implementation decisions not specified or required by an agency. That would give a contractor more appropriate incentives to exercise reasonable care in performing a contract, while prompting it to seek greater agency supervision of its critical decisions.

Broaden False Claims Act Coverage

Broadening the range of claims available under the FCA might increase a contractor's incentive to comply with widely applicable laws, such as environmental or safety laws. As mentioned above, from the perspective of empowering "private attorneys general," the FCA has a great advantage over the other laws imposing legal responsibility on contractors: a broad plaintiff class. Under the FCA *qui tam* provisions, any plaintiff can have standing under Article III of the Constitution, based only on the assignment of the United States' interest in the contract.[81]

As currently written and interpreted by the courts, the FCA's primary limitation is that it is predicated on contract specifications. Inadequate specification of a contract will pose an obstacle to an FCA claim. Meanwhile, a contract probably must require a warranty of compliance with particular laws to serve as the basis for a FCA challenge to a contractor's failure to comply with those laws. Finally, for a plaintiff to prevail, the plaintiff must show that the contractor's certification is knowingly false or in reckless disregard of truth or falsity. Again, these limitations present particular problems in the context of purchase-of-services contracts, which are likely to be complex and incompletely specified compared with supply contracts.

One possible solution is to amend the FCA to provide liability for noncompliance with applicable laws in the course of contract performance, even when a services contract includes no explicit warranty that the contractor has complied with the law in question. Alternatively, Congress could require that a services contract include a warranty that the contractor is complying with applicable laws. As with citizen suits under environmental laws,[82] individuals could function as private attorneys general to hold a contractor responsible for performing the contract or for complying with applicable legal regimes, particularly when there is no government enforcement action.

Authorizing additional FCA suits could increase the cost of contracting, perhaps significantly. Moreover, government contractors could be exposed to a greater risk of third-party enforcement actions than their counterparts that contract only with private parties. This disparity in responsibility seems justified, however, by the more public nature of many functions a government contractor will undertake, together with the contractor's receipt of public funds.

Such an amendment could clarify that such private enforcement is meant to supplement, rather than substitute for, agency supervision and enforcement. Accordingly, an FCA amendment could provide a defense to a claim if the contractor can show that contract terms have been adequately specified and that the agency has adequately supervised the contract's performance, including the contractor's compliance with applicable laws.

An FCA regime modified along these lines would increase a contractor's accountability for contract implementation and encourage it to investigate the possibility that its activities are not in compliance with applicable laws or are otherwise creating dangers to the public. Meanwhile, the availability of the defense would ensure that private FCA suits serve primarily as an adjunct to active contract supervision by publicly accountable federal agencies.

Authorize Claims for Violating Constitutional Rights

Congress might also specifically authorize *Bivens*-type claims against federal contracting entities, thereby reversing the Supreme Court holding in *Correctional Services Corp. v. Malesko*.[83] This would put federal contractors on the same footing as their state-level counterparts, who may bear responsibility for constitutional violations undertaken "under color of" state law.[84] More to the point, it would give private contracting entities market-based incentives to honor—and to ensure their employees honor—the constitutional rights of individuals.

Subject Agency Contracts to APA Rulemaking Procedures

Alfred Aman has already sensibly proposed an APA amendment to clarify that agency contracting should be open to the public through an "unadorned form of informal notice and comment proceedings. The contracts should be published for comment on the policy-making aspects inherent in the duties to be undertaken."[85]

Judicial review of contracts in which contractors receive significant discretion would render the contracting process more transparent and participatory, although it would clearly increase the upfront cost of contracting and potentially slow it down if judicial review of every such contract were sought. It likely would create an incentive for agencies to develop more completely specified contracts and to supervise contract performance more thoroughly. Concerns regarding delays and litigation could potentially be addressed with fee-shifting provisions for meritless challenges or with deadlines for the conclusion of a notice-and-comment process.

Subject Federal Contractor Policymaking to the APA

The APA could be amended to encompass contractors to a limited extent by, say, amending the statute's definition of "agency action" to include a policymaking action by a contractor engaged in the performance of a federal contract. This would enable private entities to challenge contractor actions as "arbitrary, capricious, an abuse of discretion, or contrary to law."[86]

Subjecting every action taken by a contractor—including even hiring and purchasing decisions—to judicial review would be costly and excessive. However, contractors often possess discretion to make a range of broader decisions implicating significant policy concerns. With each such area of broad discretion comes an increased potential for abuse. These broader decisions should be subject to review.

For example, Guttmann has described an internal "health and safety plan" adopted by a contractor managing the cleanup of an Energy Department site that instructed nuclear weapons workers not to tell government health and safety inspectors of " 'possible/probable problem areas,' [or] 'any alleged violations' or to 'volunteer any information or make admissions.' "[87] This type of "policymaking" has obvious implications for how well public goals will be served by the contractor's performance. If such a policy were issued by an agency, it generally would be subject to judicial review as "arbitrary and capricious" or not "in accordance with law."[88] Subjecting contractors to similar review under the APA would appropriately increase a contractor's accountability for its exercise of broad discretion.

Admittedly, such an amendment could raise the prospect that a contractor might be held responsible for an action that should truly be imputed to the contracting agency, such as carrying out an instruction not to conduct a particular safety inspection. Accordingly, as with some of the earlier proposed reforms, such an amendment should be coupled with a new defense that the contractor's decision was directed by the agency or was reached subject to direct agency supervision. The presence of such a defense would encourage contractors to seek out active agency supervision, rather than to avoid it, and ideally, would also result in agencies identifying inappropriate contractor actions before they are implemented.

Such a proposal might face two difficulties, however. First, a court reviewing an agency action under the APA to ensure that it is not arbitrary, capricious, or contrary to law generally understands that standard to mean the agency must comply with and be guided by the purposes of the statute authorizing the action at hand (though of course the agency must also comply with other applicable laws). This review framework may not translate neatly to the contractor context, both because a contractor must comply with the contract itself and because of broader concerns about contractor compliance with a wide range of relevant laws.[89] In the contractor context, amendments to the APA might clarify that the contractor should be guided both by the concerns of the contracting agency's authorizing statute and by the contract's purposes. The contractor's obligations might also be defined with reference to the purposes of other centrally relevant statutes. For example, for the contractor's "health and safety plan" described above, judicial review should focus on whether the contractor adequately considered the contract's purposes, presumably including achieving a protective cleanup and safe work environment. A court could also consider the goals of the environmental laws the cleanup contractor was being asked to carry out.

Second, and more practically, new APA claims against contractors, like APA claims against agencies, would be subject to constitutional restrictions on standing. Thus, only a comparatively narrow class of plaintiffs, such as a plaintiff with a concrete injury reasonably traceable to the challenged action and redressable by a remedy sought in the lawsuit,[90] could challenge contractor actions. For example, it is unclear who might possess standing to seek judicial review of inadequate provision of security services at American embassies or poor cleanup by an Energy Department contractor. A group of taxpayers or an organization ideologically interested in the issues clearly would lack such standing.[91] On the other hand, embassy employees not yet endangered by negligent security service provision—or employees working on an Energy Department cleanup site—might have standing to seek judicial review without yet having suffered the injury that would give rise to a tort claim.

Despite these shortcomings, creating an avenue under the APA to review policy decisions made by contractors would represent an important step in the direction of greater accountability.

Conclusion

As agencies have increasingly chosen to rely upon contractors to perform complex services, holding contractors accountable for their performance has also become increasingly difficult. Much of the relevant
legal regime assumes that critical policy decisions will be in the control
of federal agencies, rather than recognizing the extent to which these
tasks are now being contracted out to private entities. Meanwhile, however, contractors are being enlisted in numerous activities that call for
policy judgment, including decisions about program design, preparation of critical risk analyses, intelligence gathering, and the operation of
government facilities or programs. Contractors have not been held fully
accountable for this increase in functions, either through the legal regime or through oversight by the contracting agency. That has led to
poor contracting decisions, cost overruns, and decisions in some settings that harm the rights of individuals. The preceding proposals are
suggestive of steps we might take—without radically changing the
framework of existing law—to render contractors significantly more
accountable for their performance of important government contracts.
The suggested reforms are neither foolproof nor uncontroversial.
Nonetheless, they represent concrete suggestions for possible legal
choices that would result in greater transparency and accountability in
government contracting and contractor performance.

CHAPTER TEN

Privatization and Democracy

Resources in Administrative Law

ALFRED C. AMAN, JR.

Governing by contract in the United States today should be understood as integral to the processes, both political and economic, that made privatization a major domestic response to as well as a driver of globalization. Faced with increased competition in global markets, the "Reagan revolution" responded with a domestic political program aimed, in part, at curtailing market regulation and other government functions in favor of "privatization."[1] Globalization as we understand it today in the United States is inseparable from its domestic politicization as neoliberal reform because these phenomena were, and are, interrelated as mutual cause and effect. Democratic and Republican administrations over the past two decades have claimed electoral mandates for government reforms under the banner of (in successive eras) "privatization," "contracting out," and "competitive sourcing," as well as other means of "disembedding" the state from the market.[2] The eventual bipartisan consensus around such reforms was evidence of the wide credence lent to the binary zero-sum distinction between the public and the private sectors at their core. The reforms themselves institutionalized that binary distinction as a pragmatic reality, reinforcing the key terms of proponents' idealized appeals, such as "efficiency" and "market freedom."

Today, the dominance of the public/private distinction as a feature of governance and contemporary political vocabulary makes it difficult for us to recognize these frames as something other than common sense categories, and their effects as anything other than a rational response to the natural operation of the global economy. It also makes it difficult to conceptualize alternatives.[3] Alternatives are necessary if we are to repair the democracy deficit attendant on the commonsense view that markets and government operate in separate spheres, such that markets belong to a global sphere, while government is domestic.

In this chapter, I propose that administrative law is a resource for ameliorating this democracy deficit, as well as deepening our understanding of the realities of the relationship of local politics and global markets (that is, beyond the conventional binary), by expanding the public's participation in the contracting-out process. My main premise is that the public interest is qualitatively different from market functions, since the most vulnerable populations—children, the elderly, the poor, and those in confinement for reasons of health or imprisonment—are almost by definition excluded from participation in the market as well as political life.[4] Fundamental state responsibilities involving services for marginal groups such as prisoners and the poor were among the earliest government services to be contracted out to private entities, and thus they remain central to any understanding of how neoliberal reform was presented to the public as a necessary response to globalization—that is, as cost-cutting efficiency in the national interest.[5]

The creation of the privatization movement's key terms is recent, and their promulgation well choreographed.[6] Robert Poole, founder of the Reason Foundation (the leading think tank of the privatization movement), has been credited with inventing the term "privatization"[7] in the 1960s. As director of the Office of Management and Budget (OMB), Mitch Daniels coined "competitive sourcing" as a more neutral proxy term, after "privatization" became laden with partisan political associations.[8] The George W. Bush administration—a leading proponent of "public-private competitions" compared to preceding administrations[9]— seems to prefer the even more neutral-sounding term "management," as in the President's Management Agenda (PMA).[10]

It would seem that no neutral term exists, as critics of the policies mandating privatization under any of these rubrics use a different language altogether. Scholars among the critics have generally followed the early proponents of "privatization" in adopting that term and its root as the antonym for government action even though they do not share the ideological claims of those proponents.[11] I do the same for the sake of convenience, but part of my project in this chapter is to encourage some reconsideration of this language and its implications for public participation in the privatization process. When we imagine public and private as complements to each other in a single field, we make them alternatives, or at some level fungible through the commercial sector. Yet, the evidence from current debates points to elements of the public interest that resist incorporation into the private commercial sector. Cast in binary opposition, the terms fail to account for both the current diversity of public-private arrangements and the breadth of the current debate in relation to privatization and the public interest.

More fundamentally, the sharp distinction between the public and private sectors popularized by early proprivatization advocates presents obstacles to the wider concept of democracy I advocate in this chapter. Administrative procedure offers a corrective in the form of another configuration of democratic values and an alternative set of key terms (e.g., notice, participation, public interest) appropriate to the contemporary situation. I am not suggesting that neoliberalism and privatization are inherently objectionable, or that administrative law and neoliberalism are somehow inherently opposed. Nor am I proposing that administrative law can solve every problem related to privatization and contracting out. Rather, I use administrative law because its principles clarify the relationship between government and markets, and yield a more nuanced sense of democratic possibility where these intersect. They do so through their focus on administrative values rather than on the a priori distinction between public and private that tends to conceal as much as it reveals of the complexities and stakes in contemporary governance.[12]

I suggest that administrative law can remedy many democracy-deficit concerns by furthering regulatory efficiency while ameliorating the tension between this efficiency and responsiveness to social needs, especially those for which there is little or no political or commercial support. It is this tension that has consistently been the focus of those who defend privatization as a means of enhancing the nation's (or state's or municipality's) position in relation to the challenges of global competition.

While globalization as such is beyond the scope of this chapter, contemporary analyses of globalization offer insight into the nature of the democracy deficit that is my concern. The institutional developments known in common parlance as "globalization" are conventionally understood as involving broadly transnational processes of market-oriented governance and their accompanying homogenizing effects.[13] Notwithstanding the importance of globalization's international aspects, limiting discussion to the extraterritorial tends to obscure the domestic processes through which globalization was and continues to be institutionalized. Specifically, given the executive's constitutional responsibilities in foreign affairs, globalization places disproportionate emphasis on the power of the executive branch.

The impact of globalization on "homefront" governance includes increased needs—or rationalizations as need—for rapid deployment of government action that stretches beyond the ready capacity of domestic governments. Hence, not only the federal executive but also other branches and levels of government play roles in privatization, and in a politics of privatization, that makes it appear to be the rational response to global competition. The politicization (and polemicization) of this particular construction of globalization—as a foreign economic threat coupled to a golden opportunity—is most evident in the legislative arena and at the state level. The inclusion of the domestic "face" of globalization thus improves the analysis of its causes and effects, and is a necessary (if insufficient) step in addressing the democracy deficit inherent in the neoliberal response to globalization.[14]

As I have already indicated, my primary interest is in exploring how administrative law can mitigate the democracy deficit, especially when it is the direct delivery of services to vulnerable populations that has been privatized.[15] Administrative law can reduce the democracy deficit by exposing delegations to the private sector to a transparent political process rather than subsuming them under the managerial prerogative of agency heads. Administrative law can and should be a principal resource for debates over privatization and government responsibility— as administrative law affirms both the relevance of public values and the urgency of public participation whenever the state seeks reform through privatization. Such reform would affect public participation in relation to federal contracts as well as in relation to state and local governments, which also have their own diverse privatization statutes requiring or restricting privatization in general or in relation to specific government services.[16] Various state privatization statutes deal mainly with three phases in the privatization process. The first phase involves the fundamental decision to outsource to private actors. This decision entails a wide range of rationales and checks. The second phase involves the terms and conditions under which the private actor agrees to perform this task. The third phase involves the contract's implementation, which also includes monitoring.

In what follows, I argue that administrative law provides a means to reconceptualize procedures appropriate to privatized contexts without the limitations of the public/private distinction in the jurisprudential sense. Expanding the use of administrative law could expand the political process that negotiates the public-private divide by involving the public past the point of the legislative decision to authorize outsourcing. Indeed, this could extend past the point of an agency's own decision to outsource, all the way to the contracting process, including contract implementation and monitoring.

My argument in favor of extending administrative law to government contracts with the private sector, particularly where the contract involves direct services to a vulnerable population, rests primarily on three sets of interrelated issues. The first involves assumptions about competition among potential providers of the particular service in question. The desire to resort to private providers of certain services does not ensure that they exist and, if they do, that there is, in fact, healthy competition among them. Moreover, even if more than a handful of potential competitors exist, one must evaluate their past performance. Related to such concerns is the nature of the competition involved and what precisely was delivered aside from cost reductions. For example, in the area of private prisons, one could hold out a distinctive and successful approach towards reducing recidivism rates as a criterion for obtaining a contract.

Quite apart from the existence and nature of the service and service providers involved, one must account for the intended beneficiaries. Vulnerable populations, such as children, the elderly, the poor, or prisoners, are not likely to have much or any market or political power, almost by definition. Furthermore, inadequate service delivery to them may jeopardize their individual civil and human rights. Thus, for example, outsourcing health care for prison populations likely to have a much higher incidence of serious health problems such as AIDS requires a greater financial commitment than health care for a more health-diverse population.[17] Leaving it solely to the market or to politics writ large will not be enough.

Finally, and closely related to the nature of the issues involved for vulnerable populations, is the ability of contracting processes to depoliticize the kinds of issues raised above. Focusing almost exclusively on the bidding process that usually accompanies such contracts tends to obviate the more fundamental question of the adequacy of the market in any particular area of service need, and, more fundamentally still, the question whether the market is subject to a democratic process as to priorities and trade-offs. Vulnerable populations often need more resources and not fewer, so a contract process dedicated to finding a low cost, if not the least-cost, provider risks obscuring and minimizing what should be a major political decision. But my attention to the needs of marginal groups (particularly prisoners, in the extended examples below) is not meant to draw attention to their special needs but rather to make a more general case for attending to the democracy challenges of the privatization process that their condition makes vivid.

The following discussion is in three parts. The first begins with a discussion of traditional conceptions of administrative law, including the public/private distinction that forms much of its foundation. The public/private binary often predetermines the procedure employed. State actors trigger constitutional and statutory protections; nonstate actors usually do not.[18] However, as I show, this can mislead as a guide to the interests of the contracting parties and stakeholders. Private contracts and public/private hybrid arrangements intended to carry out the public's business should all be subject to administrative law. The range of positions that can be taken and compromises that can be made in determining whether and how a contract should be entered into, what the contract should say, and how it should be implemented and monitored is far wider than what can be captured by a binary approach to the public/private distinction. Thus, a mechanical application of the public/private distinction can easily exclude voices and viewpoints that are relevant and necessary if privatized or public/private hybrids are to reach legitimate and practicable substantive outcomes.

The second part of this chapter further develops the limitations of the public/private discourse by exploring these terms *as they are used* for their multiple differences in the configuration of power in relation to the institutions of government. This helps us understand part of the range of state privatization statutes, as well as opportunities for new approaches. As we shall see, most statutes deal with only the initial decision to privatize, consonant with public/private binary structure. Indeed, a relatively narrow conception of the public/private distinction underlies many of these statutes, especially in their early forms, and only recently do some explicitly provide for direct citizen input. I explore some of these legislative proposals in this section.

The third part of the chapter goes on to explore some of the implications of these proposals in terms of their potential to expand the applications of administrative law. The new legislative proposals place strong certification requirements on agencies prior to issuing contracts or finalizing their award. In particular—especially when states require agencies to provide for "pull-back" or "step-in"[19]—delegations to private firms in a sense create temporary agencies.

Administrative law is above all relevant to framing and meeting the demands of what I think of as *democratic challenges*—that is, the challenges of sustaining core democratic values—across the array of these public/private configurations. These values are articulated in administrative law, as involving transparency, accountability, information, and participation. Executing government by contract should take these values into account across the horizon of public/private configurations. Democracy should not rest on a priori distinctions between state and society, but on active political engagement and communication—in the context under discussion here, over questions of public need, as well as both the power and the limits of commerce in relation to their fulfillment.

Thinking Past the Public/Private Binary

U.S. administrative and substantive regulatory law has traditionally served as a bridge between two sets of relationships: those of individuals to the state, and those of states to markets.[20] The market realm and the state realm have historically stood for different concepts. Markets are said to stand for private ordering *as opposed to* state regulation; free markets *as opposed to* government bureaucracies.[21] An important constitutionally based version of the public/private distinction derives from these differences. The state action doctrine is based on the explicit text of the Constitution imposing various restrictions on the exercise of state power: "Congress shall make no law . . ."[22] nor shall "any state . . . deprive any person of life, liberty, or property without due process."[23] American administrative law, created primarily for public bodies, [24] has followed these broad constitutional outlines. For the most part, both administrative and constitutional law incorporate a discursive distinction between public and private actors and draw a bright line between them.[25] Even so, under the state action doctrine, some private entities might be considered "state actors" for some purposes.[26] The constitutionally based procedures triggered by this designation are limited in comparison to the procedures required of governmental entities under statutes such as the Administrative Procedure Act or the Freedom of Information Act (FOIA). This is the major area in which the bright-line distinction between public and private actors is unnecessarily restrictive.

Private actors and federal corporations have always played an important role in the regulatory process, but the recourse to the market has become increasingly favored as a regulatory approach and is now very much a part of the present landscape.[27] The Clinton administration surpassed Reagan's in terms of privatization, and the George W. Bush administration has made privatization one of the main tenets of federal management.[28] The relationship of individuals to the state is demonstrated in analyses of the procedures used by administrative agencies to carry out their statutory duties. Various theories of procedure abound, but the fundamental questions of administrative law are essentially constant, centered on the adequacy of the processes: Do they protect the rights of the regulated while still making it possible for the agency to act without unnecessary delays or procedural costs? Are they fair and transparent, and do they allow for appropriate levels of citizen participation? The same kinds of questions should be asked in the various private contexts. If they are, then administrative law cannot remain statecentric.

Historically, the legitimacy of the state's intervention in the market to correct specific problems served as the basis of the relationship of states to markets. These rationales for state intervention usually identify certain kinds of market failure (such as natural monopoly) that in turn trigger certain regulatory responses. Legitimacy was predicated on the understanding that the market did not always work even on its own terms. For example, the New Deal era debates that elaborated these points of tension and mediation between states and markets were grounded in the realities of the Great Depression. These debates did not begin as philosophical or political commitments in the abstract, but as answers to concrete questions of the reach of federal powers in relation to the urgent need to revive markets.[29] The resulting initiatives were not a new application of federal power in and of itself, but an extension of the scope of federal power. Proponents justified this extension as a means of curing the market of its most pressing ills for the sake of the public's overwhelming interest in economic recovery.[30] The regulations that followed, up to and including the development of the administrative state in the 1960s and 1970s, were not put forward as a preferable alternative to the private sector as such, but rather as a means of protecting the public interest while simultaneously managing other aspects of market failure. The main actor during the New Deal era through the environmental era of the 1960s was the legislative branch. It passed a host of statutes and created many new agencies during this period.[31]

By contrast, the Reagan administration's deregulatory stance rewrote these developments in highly ideological terms that shifted the starting point and frame of reference from the government to the market. Advocates of deregulation lumped the layered and somewhat fragmented ad hoc history of regulation together as "big government," and rhetorically constructed it as the foil of the market. This was a significant historical revision of regulation. But the Reagan-era rhetoric (and deregulatory agenda) created the impression—indeed the illusion—of a zero-sum relation between regulation and market values. The antiregulatory discourse that developed not only met with ready acceptance on the part of the public at the time, but also remains deeply entrenched today—through the public/private binary—as a commonsense notion about how markets and law work. No politician today can afford to contest this paradigm, despite its overstatement of the opposition between government and markets, and its understatement of the implications for democracy in this polarization.[32]

Today, for some proponents of privatization, government is presumed to be inefficient in terms of costs.[33] These proponents define the relationship of states to markets in general terms, as a form of accountability to the government's "clients,"[34] the citizenry defined as "the government's customer, the taxpayer."[35] OMB Circular A-76 (revised) states this compact as follows: "The longstanding policy of the federal government has been to rely on the private sector for needed commercial services. To ensure that the American people receive maximum value for their tax dollars, commercial activities should be subject to the forces of competition."[36] Proponents present competition as a driver for efficiency, cost saving,[37] and improved ratios of cost and quality,[38] as well as a mechanism to enhance the performance of current government-run enterprises.[39] The private sector may be key to the "freeing of trapped value from an underperforming asset" (i.e., state property),[40] providing state government with an income stream, and curtailing the flow of state resources (in the form of mandatory contributions from wages) to state employees' unions.[41] The benefit of off-loading risk is also cited as a point in favor of privatization[42] At the federal level, too, privatization is favored by some in the George W. Bush administration as a means of bypassing federal employees' unions, traditionally pro-Democratic.[43] Advocates also tout the private sector's relative degree of specialization and access to expert knowledge, including expertise in pricing and business operations.[44] The opening pages of the PMA refer to "the Administration's commitment to market-based government, where competition drives improved performance and efficiency of federal programs."[45] State privatization statutes differ widely in their initial presumptions as to the inherent desirability of privatization.[46] At any rate, these formulations are far removed from the traditional approach that sought corrective measures to specific forms of market failure. Privatization is nowadays presented by most proponents as a generalized social contract between the state and its citizen-customers. And for its most partisan adherents, its binarism remains important as the template for merging the state's roles as service provider and employer, especially where unions are involved.[47]

The rhetoric of public/private that presents these terms as complements or as opposite ends of a single spectrum implicitly concedes the perspective of an antiregulatory ideology, crediting the market with particular values more or less as an article of faith.[48] Competitive markets do not necessarily preexist privatization,[49] however, and the benefits *claimed* for the market are not necessarily *restricted* to the market. The benefits of competition might also be found in inter-agency competition,[50] since improved business expertise is not precluded for civil servants. In reality, the availability of the private sector for public functions opens regulation to a wide variety of models within the government itself. In sum, it would seem that one cannot be simply "for" or "against" privatization, or "for" or "against" government on the basis of any of the rationales cited above.

The contemporary binary positions have been in play for a long time. Classical New Deal and environmental era advocates of administrative procedure and regulation now want to use procedure as a means of limiting privatization, or at least holding it accountable to public values.[51] Classical deregulators who tried to set up procedural obstacles to regulation now emphasize the affirmative benefits of privatization.[52]

The contemporary dominance of privatization (and perhaps even more so the key terms of its discourse) does not cancel the relevance of the earlier history of the institutions transformed or swept away by privatization, even if those institutions and the alternatives to privatization have been largely erased from political memory. Therefore, the substantive effects of procedural reform do not allow us to consider the preference for government or privatization to be merely the effect of pendulum swings; the effects of such preferences are cumulative. Thus, today's proponents of privatization might not be so much opposed to government as they are skeptical that government provision of services represents a viable political option. Additionally, modern critics of privatization might be the counterparts to its defenders in an earlier era, to the extent that their common preference might be to streamline the contracting process and encourage private actors to take on particular functions formerly reserved for government. Thinking of these positions in historical terms helps keep their complexities in view, whether as potential for compromise and innovation or for new forms of opposition.[53]

Except for those who are ideologically committed to privatization on philosophical grounds, contracting out is a means to an end—a set of regulatory tools that will enable the state to deliver services more efficiently and effectively, even if it means enlisting the private sector to do so. These categories of combinations are, of course, themselves internally diverse. Yet these are not merely differences of degree along the same spectrum but points of contention over the nature and limits of the public interest.

Meeting Democracy's Challenges

In this section, I argue for an approach to contracting out that moves beyond the public/private binary to the use of administrative law to address democracy challenges. My own assessments turn primarily on the democratic criterion of citizen participation: Do the procedures in question enable a political process to develop around the issues involved in the contract under consideration? To lay the groundwork for this discussion, this section examines state approaches to privatization, noting the degree to which various state statutes are driven largely by opposing conceptions of the usefulness of the process.[54]

A few words are in order about these statutes: most date from the late 1980s and 1990s. In this first generation of privatization statutes, states take diverse approaches to privatization, legislatively requiring different degrees of process by certain key actors involved and subjecting private service providers to differing degrees of public accountability. For example, many states have statutes that allow the privatization of prisons while others ban it altogether.[55] A number of states also have statutes that privatize procurement and services in some or all state agencies.

The statutes differ in the extent to which they specify why and how privatization should occur. They do not usually address questions that involve the implementation and continued oversight (and the monitoring of oversight) of contracts. Moreover, public participation is limited to legislative representatives; most early statutes do not require (or allow) citizens' input. Under most statutes, these contracts are viewed, in effect, as if they were extensions of the statutes involved, rather than rules in the making (in which case they would be subject to direct citizen participation, transparency, and amendment). In order to maximize the democratic value of the procedures adopted, the process should accommodate multiple positions in the determination of whether a particular agency responsibility should be outsourced. Diverse viewpoints and stakeholders must enter into the dialogue.

State Legislative Approaches to Privatization

In examining these statutes, I emphasize the criteria they use to determine whether and how to privatize a particular governmental function or service. General privatization statutes tend to be strongly binary in their approach to the public/private distinction. There seems to be a built-in assumption about the efficiency of private actors as opposed to governmental providers. If the statutes emphasize efficiency goals, as most do, they encourage the selection of private providers for the purpose of advancing these ends. Even so, they leave room for interpretations that accommodate a more flexible approach on such issues. For example, Colorado's privatization statute assumes a unitary purpose behind privatization, namely efficiency. The statute provides that "it is . . . the policy of this state to encourage the use of private contractors for personal services to achieve increased efficiency in the delivery of government services."[56] Yet, the statute does not specify precisely the nature of the required efficiency that private providers are expected to achieve. Some later statutes specify measures of quality, for example, that were omitted from earlier legislation.

Other statutes are more skeptical of the likely benefits provided by privatization. They, too, are binary in nature, but contain language that reinforces the status quo, at least with respect to the public character of the service providers involved. The Massachusetts privatization statute, for example, uses multiple rationales for privatizing, and seeks to elicit the reasons and goals of the privatization proposal under consideration prior to authorization. The statute states that the legislature "hereby finds and declares that using private contractors to provide public services formally provided by public employees does not always promote the public interest."[57] This scenario for cooperation is premised on a strong public service sector that is open to private providers for service delivery.

Privatization Statutes: Costs and Savings

Most early privatization statutes present the choice as one between the market and the government. In opting for or encouraging the market, they do so primarily in cost terms. They are focused on saving money and usually assume that recourse to the market will lower costs. Like Colorado's general privatization statute, some but not all of these laws have a unified underlying sense of purpose—to increase efficiency. But statutes differ over the degrees of efficiency required as conditions for authorization of privatization. In the area of private prisons, for example, some of these statutes require a showing of a minimum-percentage cost savings from private prison operators.[58] This implies an understanding that there would be little point in privatizing if some savings were not realized, even though privatization might impinge upon citizens' rights if the costs-savings bar is set too high. It thus becomes incumbent upon policymakers to ascertain what precisely the cost savings are.

Accordingly, some statutes specify what expenses private providers may or may not reduce. The Colorado statute, for example, explicitly allows private providers to adjust worker wages and benefits: "The general assembly recognizes that such contracting may result in variances from legislatively mandated pay scales and other employment practices that apply to the state personnel system."[59] In contrast, Washington, D.C., requires a private provider to offer displaced workers a right of first refusal for jobs with the private company, and further requires that the private company comply with the government pay scale for six months.[60] The D.C. statute restricts a private provider's ability to meet cost targets by hiring more efficient workers or changing incentive structures; any required efficiency gains must therefore come through the reduction of other costs. The Colorado statute, like many others, provides that "privatization of government services may not result in diminished quality in order to save money."[61] When privatizing prisons, however, or for that matter, other governmental responsibilities, one must set out what kinds of accountability mechanisms exist for different groups to assert their ideas of what quality might mean, and how quality will be measured.

The creation of zones of public participation for debate and compromise becomes critical in the resolution of these concerns. But such arenas are not easily accessible if concerns with cost factors alone automatically commit the process to the private sector. Nor are they rendered irrelevant if the legislature discusses some costs and not others. Costs are not just expenses on the part of a service provider, but distributions relative to values, monetary and otherwise, among the public at large, requiring an understanding of various relationships in the management process. Therefore, the social values that inform our judgments about costs should be central issues for public debate. The selection of cost reductions is a political concern of broad public relevance even if the service provider is a private entity. This question of which cost reductions should have priority is best resolved at the contractual *and* legislative stages of the privatization process.

Privatization as Economic Efficiency

Since the Reagan administration, privatization advocates have pointed to cost efficiency as the primary reason for shifting government functions to the commercial sector.[62] The earliest privatizations involved services for vulnerable populations, corrections being a leading area of contracting out since the early1980s. Prison populations have grown astronomically over the last twenty years, and the "skyrocketing" prison population with its resulting costs has been a major impetus towards privatization.[63] New crimes, drug laws, "three strikes and you're out" legislation, and a general toughening of criminal law penalties have pushed the number of inmates ever upward.[64] The need for prisons coincides with low tax policies in most jurisdictions, thus creating difficult political issues when it comes to financing new construction and to servicing existing prisons.[65]

By the 1990s, the cost-saving rationale for private prisons was well established, and this—along with the history mentioned above—makes prison privatization a useful window onto the wider terrain of privatization. In 1996 alone, twelve states legislated authorization for private facilities, private programs within state prisons, and the contractual leasing of prison space to other states for prisoners from out-of-state facilities.[66] This trend continued throughout the 1990s.

But "efficiency" was not simply a matter of streamlining operations or more aggressively seeking economies in sourcing. State legislators dealt extensively with inmates themselves as potential income streams in public or private facilities by requiring them to pay many of their own costs, and for costs associated with inmate litigation. Some states required inmates to be responsible for the general costs of their "room and board," including insurance co-pays and other contributions for medical care.[67] Inmate litigation was also made partially recoverable as revenue potential: inmates bore the costs of civil actions they might file—in some cases with additional penalties in the form of deductions of work credits.[68] Subsequent legislative trends suggest that the conversion of the inmate to a revenue *resource* involved further controls on inmate litigation beyond payments and cost sharing. For example, in 1997 ten states established time limits, disciplinary actions, and other sanctions against inmates deemed to have filed "false, frivolous, malicious or harassing actions."[69]

In general, the productivity of inmates became increasingly prominent as a legislative issue. Prison work programs expanded with prison privatization; in 1997, ten states created mandatory work programs for inmates.[70] Some states placed checks on the "return" on investment represented by inmates—for example, in the form of requirements of wage parity with the nonprison labor market and in barring the displacement of nonprisoner labor within prisons.[71] Additional legislative issues relevant to prison privatization involved the privatization of juvenile prisons,[72] transfers of out-of-state or foreign prisoners to private facilities,[73] and cost-related thresholds on crowding (mandating release of prisoners deemed not to be dangerous, or whose care was excessively costly).[74]

Privatization in the prison context—even when presented to the public in stark cost-savings terms—involves far more than an economy of savings, or some straightforward transfer of public functions to the private sector. Through these legislative trends, privatization would seem to be associated with a broader transformation of the status of inmate, from a unit of cost to a commodity (e.g., in contractual transfers) and to a revenue source. As this shift occurred, states established checks on inmates' access to legal proceedings, converting even complaints into revenue. Legislative responses to this transformation focused on the protection of local labor markets against unfair competition from prison labor and on the exchange value of the goods prisoners produced. In the prison context, then, terms such as "cost efficiency" or even "privatization" capture only the bottom line on a state budget, and not at all the repositioning of the inmate and the private prison system in relation to the commercial sector. These issues are examples of the sorts of democratic challenges that are erased when analysis is limited to the terms of the public/private distinction.

Accountability and Information

The new state privatization statutes also consider methods of holding private entities accountable. Here, too, the situation of private prisons yields more general insights—in this section, as to how states' management of the accountability of private providers, in the absence of public participation, tends to be guided by concerns that are more managerial than performance related. For example, one way to increase the accountability of private operators is to limit the length of the privatization contract. The U.S. Supreme Court recognized this form of accountability in *Richardson v. McKnight*.[75] In analyzing the differences between public and private prisons, the Court noted that a Tennessee statute that applied to private prison providers limited a contract's term to three years. It would thus seem that the majority assumed that the firm's "performance is disciplined . . . by pressure from potentially competing firms who can try to take its place."[76] Many states, however, do not specify a maximum contract length; and some statutes explicitly allow for long term contracts. Arkansas, for example, states that contracts with private prisons "may be entered into for a period of up to twenty (20) years."[77] By contrast, Ohio provides that a contract "shall be for an initial term of not more than two years, with an option to renew for additional periods of two years."[78] Shorter contracts increase the potential frequency of public input into the process, which would ideally be encouraged before contract renewal takes place.

A problem with the Court's preference for the short-term contract requirement provided by Tennessee law is that it assumed that a number of firms would be available if the private provider involved in this case fell short in its performance. But the privatized-prison industry is largely oligopolistic. As of December 31, 1998, over 76 percent of private prison capacity was controlled by just two companies: Wackenhut Corrections Corporation (now Geo) and Corrections Corporation of America. Since then, little of significance has changed with regard to their market dominance.[79]

In other ways, too, privatization may precede the development of a full-fledged competitive market. When states privatize, they must realize that the benefits of any marketlike effects are concentrated in the period before a contract is entered into: "The distinctive feature of contracting out is the element of ex ante competition—competition for the market as opposed to in it."[80] The imposition of long-term contracts between states and prison providers is likely to concentrate the industry further by providing fewer opportunities for new companies to enter a market with a very limited number of potential customers.

In addition to the accountability-increasing feature of having a short contract period, Tennessee also provides that any private prison "must agree that the state may cancel the contract at any time after the first year of operation, without penalty to the state, upon giving ninety (90) days' written notice."[81] This provision encourages the state to oversee the running of any private prison more closely, as the delegation can easily be revoked. Private groups interested in the privatization of prisons also have an incentive to monitor the private provider more closely, because at any time after the first year, they can lobby the state to rescind the contract if it becomes apparent that a different provider (either public or private) would be preferable.

Another important issue for accountability purposes involves the actors who actually negotiate the privatization contract. To the extent that contracts become (in effect) immutable, often even to later legislatures, it is important that the participation of the public and the public's representatives be maximized as early in the contracting process as possible. Again, it might be most interesting to think about this issue in the context of private prisons, because of the increased difficulty of involving the affected population directly.

While several privatization statutes, such as Tennessee's, provide for some participation by the legislative branch in the contracting phase, few suggest any method for direct involvement by the public. For example, Tennessee's statute provides a complex contract approval procedure involving several individuals and entities, but makes no provisions for the direct input of the public.[82] All proposed or renewable contracts must be approved by the state building commission, the attorney general, and the commissioner of corrections.[83] Additionally, all contracts are reviewed by two legislative oversight committees that can make comments to those responsible for approving contracts before such approval takes place.[84] The contracts are also sent to the state and local government committees of both the Tennessee Senate and the House, which may also make comments to the authorities.[85] While this procedure involves various members of the legislative and executive branch, it does not provide opportunities for the public to comment directly on the decision to outsource. States have addressed this issue in various ways. For example, the privatization procedure in Tennessee involves members of both the executive and legislative branches, and includes legislators themselves, who usually are open to public input. In Idaho, however, the decision to enter into a contract with a private prison provider is left solely to the state board of correction.[86]

One of the few states to call specifically for a public hearing is Montana. Montana law requires an agency to form a privatization plan before any program, not just prison-related programs, can be privatized.[87] Public hearings produce little benefit, however, if the public is not provided with adequate information with which to make informed suggestions about the quality and value of privatized services. Kentucky law requires the production of this information, at least in the correctional facility context:

> The private provider shall develop and implement a plan for the dissemination of information about the adult correctional facility to the public, government agencies, and the media. The plan shall be made available to all persons. All documents and records, except financial records, maintained by the private provider shall be deemed public records.[88]

Kentucky does not rely solely on voluntary disclosure by the provider to amass information on the functioning of privatized prisons. The legislature has also required that "[t]he department shall annually conduct a performance evaluation of any adult correctional facility for which a private provider has contracted to operate. The department shall make a written report of its findings and submit this report along with any recommendations to the private provider and the Legislative Research Commission."[89]

While private corporations may be more cost-sensitive than public entities, this does not necessarily translate into incentives that produce publicly desirable results. For example, an oft-cited criticism of private prisons is that they may have an incentive to actually increase recidivism or at least forego initiatives that would reduce recidivism, such as education. Michigan addresses this problem by mandating that private companies require prisoners without high school degrees to earn a general education certificate (GED).[90] Colorado requires that private providers guarantee education services (and other services including dental, medical, psychological, diet, and work program) of at least as high quality as public prisons.[91] As noted above, however, the problem with Colorado's provision is that it does not specify any performance measures to aid in analysis and comparison. The prison privatization provisions create large amounts of data that are eventually transmitted to the public. But they do not provide a mechanism for the public to participate in the privatization decision, limit the length of any contract, or impose requirements (at least to any great degree) for the actual running of the prisons. From the standpoint of how the public might be constructively engaged in these issues, the prison context is not so specialized as it might seem at first, given the exclusion of inmates from the public sphere. In the prison context, the relevant public is not restricted to prisoners, but might also include family members, potential employers, and representatives of the communities where they are housed. Thus, as in the previous section, the prison context is illustrative of how the rationales for efficiency and accountability operate in practice more broadly in the absence of substantial public participation.

Democracy Challenges at the Public/Private Divide

Democracy challenges are not limited to the prison context; they emerge whenever the equation of citizen and consumer (or client, or customer) comes into question. Today, the most avid proponents of privatization seem to be struggling to hold onto the binary opposition of public versus private, even as they seek alternative terms to avoid the polemicized aura of "privatization."[92] Their persistent use of the public/private opposition at the same time demonstrates the limiting framework of the binary concept, and hints at their claim of functional equivalence of the public and the private sectors—a claim that demonstrates the expendability of certain government services. In equally strong terms, privatization's strongest opponents invoke the binary distinction to insist on the sectors' nonequivalence (for example, during the Massachusetts debate over the privatization of water and sewage services, discussed below).[93] In the aggregate then, "public/private" cannot capture the entire scope of the privatization debate. That debate has more than two sides; it is a composite field of contention divided by potentially deep disagreements over the extent to which the commercial sector can serve the public interest—and whether citizens should be defined as "clients" or "customers." The opponents of the early privatization efforts in the 1980s articulated their criticisms in these and related terms—the difference between markets in theory and practice, the inadequacy of commerce to provide services for those at the social and economic margins, and the adverse implications for the working class of the emphasis on cost savings.[94]

Thinking about the issue this way gives us a chance to approach privatization as an intersection of administrative, economic, and social practices—that is, reconnecting what neoliberalism tends to treat as separate spheres. The public/private binary structure tends to suppress discussion of how privatization can coincide with a vision of democracy that demands more than the accomplishments of a free market. Let us therefore explore a conception of contracting out that responds more fully to democracy challenges. In this section, I present a series of examples to show the specificity of public/private engagements, highlighting their different starting points relative to the public interest. Once again, the examples are drawn primarily from state-level legislation. For our purposes, the pending and even the failed bills are as relevant as those that are successful, since the purpose is to show something of the range and substance of political debate as it is currently developing.

Statutory Requirements of Procedure

Recent legislation and legislative proposals address the challenges of the democracy deficit primarily through procedural reforms of preexisting privatization authorizations. As such, they do not fundamentally challenge privatization and competitive sourcing as modern principles of government management. But contemporary legislative efforts in relation to privatization, contracting out, and competitive sourcing—primarily procedural in their content—are evidence of wide dissensus over the democratic implications of such efforts. Procedural debate—as is often the case—is a proxy for substantive debate. The contemporary politics of privatization is not so much engaged with the question of government versus private contractors as it is with the democracy challenges of *both* government *and* privatization.

While there appears to be widespread consensus as to the desirability of privatization (at least under some circumstances), a survey of procedural proposals suggests the extent of the divergence over the meaning of the public interest, and whether the public interest can be fulfilled by the private sector. The examples in this section are drawn from the 2005 and 2006 state legislative records.[95]

For some proponents of privatization, cost efficiency is in itself a requirement of the social contract between a government and its citizens; cost efficiency is automatically taken as a warrant for privatization (or public/private competition). In Virginia, a recent bill would have required all state agencies to turn to private providers for a wide range of procurement matters if they were on a list of commercial providers maintained by the state;[96] the operative provision was a paragraph inserted in a bill otherwise devoted to unrelated issues of procurement (computers, lighting) by particular agencies. In Florida, proponents of privatization supported legislation (later withdrawn) that would have encouraged private investment in public education through tax credits.[97] In Georgia, an environmental privatization study articulates the basic efficiency rationale in terms encompassing a broader concept of the public interest that stresses program effectiveness, increases in performance quality through competition, and agency flexibility.[98]

In an important contrast with earlier provisions, several state legislatures have considered bills that would make the decision to privatize (or contract with a private entity) subject to multiphase processes of public notice and comment, as well as detailed accountings of projected costs and cost savings. For Indiana, a leading "privatization" state under the leadership of Governor Mitch Daniels, a new proposed bill would require a notice, comment, and accounting process in every case of contracting out.[99] In New Jersey, too, the contracting process would be subject to a lengthy process of notice, comment, and accounting—including certification that the contract would not only result in "substantial aggregate cost savings," but that it would otherwise be "contrary to the public interest to have the function performed directly by the state."[100] In New York, the 2007 legislative calendar opened with a proposed bill that would ban private contracts for construction and repair of critical transportation infrastructure pending a study of the impact of privatization on the viability of infrastructure in terms of quality and cost.[101]

While the Reason Foundation characterizes such proposals as attempts to chill privatization, they do not go as far as some failed legislative efforts to ban privatization outright. For example, a Massachusetts bill entitled "An Act to Preserve Public Water and Sewer Systems" would have banned the privatization of water and sewer services.[102] The preamble stipulates that natural resources are outside the commercial sphere; it sets them within the jurisdiction of local government—explicitly distinguishing between local political processes and transnational commerce—on the grounds that local government has an electoral mandate. In this proposal, privatization is cast as the "sale" of municipal rights, and the bill seeks to enshrine the notion that "the very idea of turning such a basic resource as water . . . into a commodity should be repugnant to a democratic society."[103] The bill was heard twice in committee and was set aside for study in February 2006.

In Hawaii, which authorized privatization only in 2001,[104] a recently proposed revision of that authorization would require contracting agencies to demonstrate the proposed contract's potential impact on civil service employees, the nature of the service proposed to be privatized, whether a private contract for the service is in the public interest, and whether contracting with a private provider has the potential to increase cost savings when compared to the in-house resources already available to the contracting agency.[105] It also recognizes that adverse economic conditions might destabilize a private actor and asks the contracting agency to consider whether entering into a private contract for the particular service might "jeopardize the government's ability to provide the service if the private entity fails to perform."[106]

One distinctive legislative proposal from Massachusetts addresses privatization's democracy challenges by barring contracts with firms outside the United States.[107] This proposal contrasts with Indiana Governor Daniels's hopeful anticipation of a time when "antiforeign" sentiment might yield to the tangible benefits of transnational involvement in privatization.[108] The difference between these two orientations—both of which favor privatization—underscores the inadequacy of the public/private distinction in relation to the current politics surrounding democracy challenges. Still, it is clear that "privatization" and related terms retain a strong political valence, as these textual examples also suggest.

My aim in presenting these legislative efforts is to show how they respond to different understandings of democracy and different meanings of "public interest." The bills do not differ fundamentally in their acceptance of some private sector role as integral to government. They differ strongly in their starting points—requiring agencies to defend their decision either for or against contracting out. They also differ somewhat in the priority they give to public participation and in their efforts to create parity between private and public workforces in terms of wages, labor conditions, and security.

Administrative law provides a framework for navigating such differences in an open and democratic way. Such differences cannot be resolved as a matter of managerial technique. Administrative law requires basic democratic procedures including publicity, opportunities for participation, and the inclusion of dissenting community groups. A further point in common among these proposals is that they end with the award of the contract. In the privatization context, administrative law could (and should) be extended to provide the terms of the proposed contract to the public prior to negotiations with potential service providers, and the general public should have a role in those negotiations at least through a public commenting process. This is what I consider in the next section.

Toward a Model Statute

Drawing on some of the provisions in the statutes noted above, this section suggests elements that might be found in a model statute that takes more explicit account of democratic values as discussed above. It is important to keep in mind that the legislative phase is only one of the steps in most privatization processes. A second privatization phase occurs when the governmental body in charge of a particular service or regulatory task decides to outsource, and (in a third phase) selects a particular private entity according to whatever contract bidding processes are in force. Next, the agency negotiates a contract with that private provider. Finally, the contract must be implemented and monitored. As we have seen, each of these phases entails its own democracy challenges and its own potential for public participation through the political process.

Accommodating the democracy needs of various groups and interests need not require massive amounts of procedure. Rather, the statutes involved could draw on the best of those already in place and make needed additions. The statutes should not assume that public providers are inherently superior to private ones or vice versa. They should be neutral in this regard, and accordingly they should require an agency wishing to privatize or pull back to give notice of its intentions as well as the basis for its proposed action. Contracts with private providers should be of relatively short duration and information should be provided to the public on the performance of the contractor, as well as on any proposed changes to the contract.

Legislators should concentrate on the most urgently needed reforms, giving priority to agency contracts involving primary governmental functions. Few statutes among the first generation discussed above allow for direct involvement of citizens in the contracting process. Once an agency decides to contract out its primary functions, the proposed contract should be noticed to the public on the agency web site as if it were a rule promulgated for public comment. The public should have a chance to comment on the goals of the contract, its mode of enforcement, the monitoring of its implementation (including what shall constitute monitoring), and all other issues deemed relevant. As with a rule in a regulatory proceeding, the agency need not adopt all or any of the suggestions made, but it should provide its own reasons for accepting the ultimate contract.

Given the importance of communication in democratic procedure, agencies should accommodate these interests with a process that allows participants to communicate with one another as well as with the ultimate decision maker. Once a contract is entered into, these discussions should occur with some frequency. The nature of the enterprise requires ongoing monitoring of the contract terms, as well as opportunities to comment on its administration, and provision for amendments regarding the duties of the private actor. Procedurally speaking, the privatizing agency should be willing to:

- treat the proposed contract more like a rule than a contract negotiated between two parties. It can be put up on the agency's web site with a call for public comments, suggestions, alternative language, and ways to achieve its substantive reform goals from whomever wishes to comment including affected parties and their representatives. In our extended example of private prisons, this would include prisoners and their representatives as well;

- provide extensive information on the track records of firms competing for the contract;

- ensure fair competition among the bidders. All of them should agree that if they are chosen, they will be subject to regular reporting requirements and a modified FOIA requirement that allows interested members of the public to make relevant inquiries about their operation while the contract is in place. That contract should be subject to renewal, but only after another round of competitive bidding occurs. Renewals should be scheduled to give adequate time for planning and implementation on the part of the provider, yet also to keep external assessment in the foreground—on a three-year cycle, for example.

Notice and comment procedures make transparency feasible and meaningful. Transparency need not impose undue impediments to the bargaining process on prospective providers. A presumption in favor of the bargains struck in such contracts can be written into the governing statutes. Indeed, the purpose of these citizen-oriented procedures is to ensure that the diverse views and voices involved in such public-regarding private arrangements are heard. This does not merely acknowledge a public dimension; it underscores the existence of genuine public values that require debate and contest. Such contests would articulate different formulations of democracy—as inherent in the operations of the market, or external to the market as a larger framework of critique and reform—thereby enriching our democratic culture.

Moving beyond the public/private distinction broadens the potential role for administrative law in relation to contemporary democracy challenges posed by globalization on the domestic front. It does so by bringing the essence of the domestic-global relation—the privatization contract—into public view through a domestic political process. The role of administrative law procedure is not to settle the question of privatization but to support a political process around the complex public/private combinations that typify privatization today. Specifically, its role relates to two main goals: expanding opportunities for public participation and expanding decision makers' accountability in the form of an obligation to acknowledge the substance of public input in their decision-making processes.

Conclusion

Historically, the administrative law process was an alternative to private law dispute resolution, tending to widen the variety of interests and actors in decision-making contexts.[109] Today, that bright line between public and private would be difficult to sustain. Decisions to privatize, as well as the administration of outsourced programs, offer creative alternatives to some forms of traditional regulation to the extent that they are covered by administrative law. Privatized and deregulated contexts introduce additional bargaining currencies beyond traditional adjudicatory or legislative policymaking procedures. When private providers carry out government responsibilities, or when market incentives are introduced to achieve certain regulatory outcomes, these approaches are not substitutes for regulation, but are the means of accomplishing regulatory ends. In other words, they are not merely outcomes of regulation, but part of the regulatory process itself. Private actors, private incentive structures, and markets in general are not necessarily (and certainly not categorically) opposed to state-based approaches from the standpoint of efficient service to the public interest. Numerous efforts to align the wage structures, job security, labor conditions, performance standards, and public interest needs of the public and private sectors have accompanied the privatization movement, especially in recent years.[110]

In fashioning procedures for the creation and ongoing implementation of such new democratic arrangements, administrative law is a crucial resource. It can provide the legal architecture necessary for democratic input on questions of privatization, accountability, and transparency, as contracts are negotiated and implemented. To realize the full potential of administrative law in privatized contexts, some adjustments of perspective are in order. Administrative law is traditionally statecentric in its focus, its procedures designed to control the exercise of state power by governmental agencies. By contrast, in privatization contexts, the primary actors are private contractors.

As we have seen, privatization statutes vary widely across the states, and over time. The first generation of statutes—sent aloft by strong commitments on the part of the Reagan, Bush I, and Clinton administrations—concentrated on opening government to wider participation by the commercial sector when this idea was still new to most agencies at the federal and state levels. The strongest opposition between proponents and critics of privatization followed lines of tension developed over other issues, especially between agencies and government employees' unions, and government and public interest groups.[111] In addition, the binary opposition between government and privatization advocates was sustained by partisan politics and more general attitudes toward government.[112] The politics of privatization in its most partisan forms appears to both fuel and draw energy from the "popular intuition" as to the nature and significance of the public/private distinction.[113] The second generation of statutes now emerging appears to be filling in at least some of the differences between these positions.

The new proposals along these lines underscore the point that privatization and government were never on an entirely continuous spectrum of alternatives, given their different constructions of the "public interest" (as fulfilled in a free market or by other means), "citizens" (as taxpayers or rights-bearing individuals in some broader sense) and "institutional procedures" (as business operations or in more public terms). While "publicization"[114] of the commercial sector is important to the current legislative efforts (e.g., to achieve parity between governmental and private workers), norms of privatization also suffuse the government, particularly along the broad horizon where the immediate constituency is not in a position to generate a return on investment (e.g., inmates, welfare recipients, and others). Reducing the costs of serving those constituencies was (and remains) central to the development of privatization and its political promotion—and so have been my main concern in this chapter. But it is not just in those cases that statutes should clearly provide throughout the life of the contract for ongoing monitoring, opportunities for public input, and accountability on the part of agencies and contractors.[115] In general, adopting such provisions would be a significant and needed revision of most privatization statutes, which end at the point where the contract is awarded.

Extending administrative law into government contracts with the private sector might seem like a radical expansion of its province; however, it would be consistent with the direction of some current reforms, which reinsert and hold onto a notion of the public interest that is not fully reducible to the operations of the market. These reforms do so primarily by layering the contracting process with procedures designed to expose it to public scrutiny. Particularly in such contexts, where the government acknowledges its ongoing responsibilities even in areas that are not inherently governmental, it seems consistent with democratic values, and therefore appropriate, to extend its role into the life of the contract itself. When the private sector is not able to sustain a competitive market for needed services, privatization is best understood as a temporary or provisional delegation of government agency; administrative law values and procedures would be as appropriate in these contexts as they are in conventional government agencies. To the extent that legislative oversight represents an alternative approach to the one I propose, administrative law procedures would offer the further advantage of obviating some of the problems of legislative oversight noted by Professors DeShazo and Freeman in their study of Congress, in particular "disjointed majoritarianism" and legislative lag.[116]

Improving the engagement of the private sector with interested citizens on these fronts, supported by the accountability measures discussed above, would be a significant step towards reviving a political process around the public interest in terms broader than the prevailing neoliberal discourse. That discourse draws bright lines between the public sector and the private sector—that is, between government and business—and makes these bright lines central not only to national economic security but also to personal liberty.

In the contemporary milieu, such formulations rest in large part on taken-for-granted notions as to the nature of globalization. Specifically, imagining "the global" as something apart from "the local" fails to capture the extent to which privatization was (and continues to be) driven by domestic politics. It was that framing, linked to national economic security in the face of global competition, that made cost-efficiency arguments broadly compelling. This is not to dismiss such arguments as partisan, but to point to their embeddedness in a particular view of the world and the institutional reforms that worldview deemed rational. While it might seem intuitively true that "the commercial environment is now global, but legal sovereignties are still territorial,"[117] such bright-line distinctions divert attention from the actualities of the production of "the global" through particular understandings of commerce, and the ways these are put into practice through domestic law. It is at the interface between understandings and practices that administrative law is an important resource for government by contract.

C. Press Constitutional Restrictions

CHAPTER ELEVEN

Private Delegations, Due Process, and the Duty to Supervise

GILLIAN E. METZGER

It is clear that increasing reliance on private entities in lieu of direct government action is a consistent and major dynamic of modern governance. It is also clear that constitutional law has had little to say about privatization, even as privatization is fundamentally reshaping government.[1] Few instances of privatization result in the private entities involved being found to be "state actors" under current doctrine and thus subject to constitutional controls. Meanwhile, constitutional prohibitions on delegation of government power to private hands exist more in theory than in fact, with the courts sustaining broad private delegations of rulemaking and adjudicatory authority. To the extent constitutional law plays a role, it is often the counterproductive one of creating incentives *against* close government oversight and supervision of private delegates.

I have argued elsewhere that the current constitutional approach to privatization is fundamentally inadequate, and that instances of privatization should instead be subjected to a reformulated private delegation analysis. Under such an analysis, the constitutionality of delegating power to a private entity to act on the government's behalf would turn on the presence of adequate accountability mechanisms to ensure that government power is exercised in conformity with constitutional constraints.[2] In what follows, I first briefly restate my arguments in favor of such a private delegation analysis, and then turn to examining what the approach would mean in practice by focusing on the types of mechanisms needed to ensure that privatized programs comport with procedural due process demands. Procedural due process poses a particular challenge for this private delegation approach. On the one hand, preserving adequate constitutional controls requires that the basic due process norms of regularity and fairness apply notwithstanding the switch to privatized governance; on the other, these norms are in tension with privatization's goals of harnessing private flexibility and self-interest to improve government programs. Resolving this tension requires adjusting due process requirements to reflect the realities of privatized governance. More fundamentally, it may entail reconceiving due process as imposing, at least in some privatization contexts, a duty on the government to actively supervise its delegates.

The Failure of Current Constitutional Analysis of Privatization and the Need for a Reformulated Private Delegation Doctrine

The two prisms through which constitutional law currently approaches privatization, state action doctrine and private delegation doctrine, are in fact converses of one another. Ordinarily, the Constitution applies only to the actions of government actors. State action doctrine asks whether ostensibly private parties nonetheless should be considered government actors for constitutional purposes and thereby subject to the Constitution's strictures. A finding of state action is, in essence, a judicial determination that for constitutional purposes a challenged action either could not be truly privatized, because of the function it represents, or was not privatized enough to remove the action from the Constitution's purview. Private delegation doctrine takes over where state action leaves off. It accepts the ostensible private status of the actors at issue, and asks instead whether the Constitution prohibits delegating certain powers to private hands.

Though analytic opposites in this sense, these two doctrines are subject to much the same limitations. Both have been applied too narrowly, perhaps because both are blunt instruments that offer courts little flexibility in addressing concerns raised by privatization. I believe these flaws necessitate a new form of constitutional analysis, one that combines private delegation doctrine's focus on how private grants of power are structured with state action's concern to ensure that exercises of government power remain subject to constitutional strictures.[3]

The Inadequacies of Current State Action and
Private Delegation Doctrine

Perhaps the most salient point about current state action and private delegation doctrine is their lack of practical impact on instances of privatization. The most logical basis for finding state action in privatization contexts—namely, that private entities are performing a public function—is virtually precluded by the Supreme Court's restriction of the public function test to functions traditionally and exclusively performed by government.[4] Taken literally, this formulation excludes most tasks commonly performed by government today. More importantly, private provision of services on behalf of the government constitutes a public function under this test only if the services are ones that the government is required to provide directly, which is rarely the case.[5]

As a consequence, the only grounds realistically available for finding state action will be the government's connections or interaction with the private entity. Here, the obstacle to finding state action is the general requirement that government participation must be present in the specific act being challenged; absent such participation, only government compulsion or formal control of the private actor will suffice.[6] Although in a recent decision a divided Court was willing to find state action based on the government's background involvement, it emphasized that the extent of involvement rose to the level of "pervasive entwinement"—as well as that government officials extensively participated in the private entity at issue, performing the acts by which it "exist[ed] and function[ed]."[7] Neither public control of a private entity, nor participation in specific actions, nor a background of extensive public involvement is likely to be present in a great many instances of privatization. Quite to the contrary. Private providers regularly make a myriad of day-to-day decisions on their own; indeed, allowing private actors such implementation discretion and flexibility is one of privatization's central aims. Public involvement is limited to issuing general requirements that providers must meet and conducting periodic reviews.[8]

What frequently is present in instances of privatization is a formal delegation of authority from the state to the private entity, whether by contract or by governing statutes and regulations.[9] Yet such delegations have little significance under current state action doctrine. In fact, a broad delegation of power actually provides the basis for denying the existence of state action, because a private delegate's exercise of independent judgment and discretion is taken as strong evidence that significant government control and involvement is lacking.[10] To the extent private delegations are considered, courts evaluate them under the rubric of private delegation doctrine. But private delegation doctrine has little practical bite in its present form.[11] Although nominally adhering to decisions from the early New Deal (and before) holding that the Constitution prohibited delegating legislative power to private hands, the Supreme Court has not since invalidated any such private delegation. Instead, it has found that provision for government review of private decision making was sufficient to meet constitutional prerequisites, without investigating whether such review was more than perfunctory in practice.[12] Perhaps most importantly, no attempt has been made to link the constitutionality of a private delegation to the risk that it will place government power outside of constitutional limits; instead, enforcing constitutional limits on exercises of government power has been left entirely to state action doctrine.

The net result of these developments is evident: current constitutional law has little relevance to privatization. Private contractors providing government services or programs are rarely found to be state actors other than in a few discrete contexts, such as private prisons.[13] Even rarer still—in fact, never—is a private delegation found to illegitimately transfer regulatory power in violation of federal constitutional requirements.[14]

Of course, this lack of relevance does not necessarily indicate failures in these doctrines as they are currently posited. Indeed, the desuetude of constitutional prohibitions on private delegations seems largely appropriate. This is not to deny that, increasingly, private groups are being given the power to set government policy, whether through direct delegation of oversight functions,[15] control over standard setting,[16] or grants of broad authority over program implementation.[17] Nor is it to deny that some such delegations are normatively problematic.[18] But prohibiting private delegations altogether is too blunt a response to the legitimate concerns that they raise. Given the Court's acceptance of economic and social legislation that realigns private groups' rights and powers vis-à-vis one another,[19] a categorical constitutional bar on all private delegations of government power is no longer feasible. Efforts to erect narrower prohibitions, such as targeting unduly broad private delegations or private involvement in core government functions, involve the Court in difficult line-drawing quandaries.[20] What this means is that the political branches must necessarily bear primary responsibility for guarding against inappropriate involvement of private actors in public decision making.[21]

The absence of state action under privatization is, however, more of a concern. A central dynamic of government privatization is the way in which it transfers power over government programs and program participants to private hands. Perhaps the most significant inadequacy of current state action doctrine is its failure to appreciate that the control private entities thereby acquire over third parties' access to government benefits and services is fundamentally government power. A prime example of this failure of recognition was the Supreme Court's decision in *Blum v. Yaretsky*, where the Court acknowledged that private nursing homes' determinations controlled Medicaid beneficiaries' access to skilled nursing services, but denied that this effect made a difference to the state action inquiry: "That the State responds to [the homes' decisions to discharge or transfer patients to lower levels of care] by adjusting benefits does not render it *responsible* for those actions."[22] More generally, the Court's insistence upon specific government involvement as an essential prerequisite for finding state action is fundamentally misguided. Such involvement is a very poor litmus test for determining when a private entity should be viewed as wielding government power. On the contrary, the extent of government power exercised by private actors is likely to vary inversely rather than directly with government involvement. Some minimal government involvement in the form of delegation of responsibilities to private actors is needed; but beyond that, the less the government is involved, the more discretion and power private entities have.

Hence, as a means of enforcing constitutional controls on government power, current state action doctrine is seriously underinclusive. This criticism goes to the heart of state action principles, because one of the central purposes of the doctrine as it has developed over time is to ensure the vibrancy of constitutional limits notwithstanding that private entities are wielding government power.[23] Moreover, the recent trend of granting private contractors more discretion over program implementation and greater responsibilities should give pause, as it suggests that the range of private exercises of government power that fall outside constitutional protections is expanding.

At the same time, however, state action doctrine is also notably overinclusive. Under standard analysis, if a private entity is found to be a state actor, then not only can the government be sued based on its actions, but the private entity itself is directly subject to constitutional requirements.[24] Yet when the government can be charged with responsibility for private acts, imposing constitutional constraints on the private entity as well is unnecessarily intrusive. The biggest culprit in creating this overkill aspect is the fact that state action is treated as an all-or-nothing affair; current doctrine does not allow separating government responsibility for private actions that may violate constitutional requirements from direct private liability for constitutional violations. State action decisions take scant account of the presence of alternative accountability mechanisms that render the application of constitutional constraints to private actors unnecessary.[25] The all-or-nothing character of state action doctrine also reinforces its underinclusiveness, by creating a bright-line distinction between instances when private actors are held to be wielding government power and those when they are not. The effect is to increase the harm done by inadequate tests for government power, since failure to recognize the roles played by private actors and the ways by which government can influence their behavior serves to put many instances of privatization wholly outside of constitutional controls.

Finally, the combined effect of the doctrine's underinclusive and overinclusive characters means that current state action doctrine creates indefensible obstacles to effective and accountable use of privatization. Government gains perverse incentives to privatize without close supervision, since by doing so it may place day-to-day implementation of programs outside of constitutional controls. Yet several scholars studying privatization emphasize the importance of close government involvement and cooperation with private entities. Such involvement allows the government to benefit from private expertise and innovation, while preserving public control of government programs and guarding against self-interested private decision making. Close oversight is particularly important where market failure and abuse of power are most likely: where providers hold a monopoly on provision of particular services, the services at issue are complex and difficult to specify ab initio, competitive pressures are minimized by difficulties in exit or lack of information, or recipients are relatively powerless.[26]

Some might question whether the incentive effects of current state action doctrine have any noticeable impact on the ground. It seems fair to say that privatization decisions are fueled more by efforts to shed employees and by ideology regarding the appropriate role of government than by constitutional doctrine.[27] Even so, that does not mean that escaping restrictive constitutional strictures (both to gain operational flexibility and to avoid financial liability) might not be seen as an additional reason to privatize in a hands-off fashion, particularly in regard to politically unpopular programs. In any event, what seems clear is that current state action doctrine does not encourage governments to engage in active oversight or provide protections to ensure that their private delegates do not abuse their delegated powers.

Reformulating Private Delegation Doctrine

The challenge is to address state action doctrine's too limited application and ensure that private exercises of government power conform to constitutional requirements, without thereby worsening its overinclusive character. The solution to this problem, I have argued, is to rethink state action in a private delegation framework. While constitutional prohibitions on private delegations are difficult to justify, it does not follow that governments should be able to delegate such power with impunity, given that the effect of such delegations is often to place exercises of authority beyond the scope of constitutional controls. Under my reformulated private delegation approach, the crucial constitutional question is whether adequate accountability mechanisms exist by which to ensure that private exercises of government power comport with constitutional requirements. Requiring that the government create such mechanisms is thus the constitutionally imposed price of allowing it to delegate government power to private hands. Nonetheless, the government still retains some flexibility in structuring its private delegations, because a number of mechanisms are available by which to meet constitutional demands. For example, the government can itself review private decision making, or instead impose independently enforceable procedural and substantive constraints on its private delegates. A third alternative is to grant program participants substantial choice among private service providers, thereby limiting any single provider's control over a participant's access to government benefits or services.

A central feature of this proposed private delegation analysis is that it casts aside current state action doctrine's insistence that constitutional requirements apply directly to private parties exercising government power. Nothing in our constitutional structure or history mandates that constitutional accountability be achieved by such direct application, as opposed to enforcement of constitutional requirements through other means. To the contrary, the core insight of the Court's private delegation decisions is that the structure of a private delegation should matter more in determining a private delegation's constitutionality than the simple fact that private actors are exercising government power. More specifically, these decisions recognize, in their emphasis on the need for formal government supervision, that nonconstitutional accountability mechanisms can adequately address the constitutional concerns that private delegations might otherwise create.

Subjecting all private delegations to this analysis is not feasible, given the extremely broad scope of what could qualify as a private delegation of government power.[28] But heightened scrutiny is particularly appropriate for those instances in which private delegates are granted powers not simply for their own advantage, but to enable them to act—and more specifically, to interact with third parties—on the government's behalf. A workable proxy, which allows the private delegation approach to take advantage of an existing body of law, is to focus on delegations that create an agency relationship between the private entity and the government.[29] It is this characteristic of acting on behalf of government that makes private delegations particularly threatening to the principle of constitutionally constrained government. By effectively stepping into the government's shoes in its dealings with third parties, private entities are more likely to have access to powers that are distinctly governmental, such as the ability to exert coercive powers on a nonconsensual basis and control over access to government resources and government programs.

Of course, working out what this reformulated approach would entail in practice remains a significant challenge. One critical issue concerns determining when accountability mechanisms are adequate to render a private delegation of this sort constitutional. To ensure constitutional accountability, the protections provided third parties must be equivalent to those that would result if the private entities in question were directly subject to constitutional constraints. But "adequate" in this context does not necessarily mean "protections and constraints identical to those that would apply to public officials." Instead, involvement of private entities may well affect the substance of the applicable constitutional norms.[30] As a result, part of the constitutional discussion triggered by privatization needs to address the ways in which participation of private entities in implementing government programs should—and should not—alter the substantive content of constitutional norms.

Private Due Process

Time now to bring constitutional theory to the ground and look at what this reformulated private delegation analysis means in practice. This section seeks to do so by examining the implications of this approach for private due process. What types of accountability mechanisms are necessary to ensure that the demands of procedural due process are met in privatized contexts? How should the participation of private entities alter our understanding of what due process requires? Although little judicial precedent exists providing concrete guidance on these questions—unsurprisingly, given the restrictive approach to state action—determining what procedural due process requires in contexts of private decision making is getting attention from nonjudicial quarters.[31]

Several reasons exist to focus on due process. One is its historic importance as a guarantor of basic procedural regularity and fairness in how government operates. To be sure, current doctrine limits the scope of procedural due process in significant ways. Prime among these is the rule that due process is triggered only by deprivation of property interests that amount to entitlements, not deprivation of discretionary benefits, privileges, and the like.[32] Even when an entitlement is at stake, under the *Londoner–Bi-Metallic* divide due process imposes few (if any) procedural requirements on rule making.[33] But in the sphere of adjudication, when government makes binding decisions that determine specific individuals' access to services and benefits to which they can make a claim of entitlement, due process demands the basic procedural protections of notice and some opportunity to be heard before an impartial adjudicator.[34] Moreover, with expanding privatization, private entities increasingly are undertaking adjudications on behalf of the government. Examples include determinations by private insurance carriers or HMOs regarding whether specific medical services are covered under Medicaid or Medicare, decisions by private associations to revoke institutions' accreditation and thus their eligibility to receive federal funds, and assignment by private arbitrators of rights to Internet domain names.[35]

Determining what procedural due process demands in contexts of privatized adjudication is thus of growing practical relevance. In addition, due process concerns—specifically, the fear of misuse of government power for private ends outside of the requirements of fairness and procedural regularity applicable to government—generate much of the disquiet that privatization provokes.[36] Ensuring that delegations to private adjudicators are structured to conform to basic due process norms is thus crucial to securing the legitimacy of privatized governance. But structuring private delegations to accord with due process is not a simple matter. A real tension exists between due process's demands of regularity and impartiality, on the one hand, and privatization's frequent reliance on private flexibility and self-interest on the other.

Navigating this tension requires a careful assessment of what due process requires in different privatization contexts. Not all instances of privatization raise problems of self-interest or bias polluting private delegates' decision making, nor do all contexts demand the same degree of procedural regularity. The *Mathews v. Eldridge* balancing test, which governs judicial assessments of whether particular procedures comport with due process, is well designed to take this variation into account.[37] Under *Mathews,* in assessing what process is due a court weighs the private and government interests involved, the risk of an erroneous decision under current procedures, and the benefits of additional protections.[38] As applied to private adjudication, such balancing demands greater procedural protections where dangers of financial self-interest and bias are acute, but fewer protections—potentially, even fewer than apply in analogous public contexts—when involvement of private decision makers is likely to improve the fairness of decision making.

In what follows, I first discuss in detail different dimensions of private bias and how best to balance the need for impartial decision making with the impact that procedural restrictions have on private flexibility and autonomy, both important values if the government is to reap the putative benefits of privatization. My aim here is to work largely within the scope of existing due process doctrine, but I also demonstrate how procedural requirements applicable to public adjudications might need to change to take into account the realities of privatized programs. I then turn to suggesting ways in which due process doctrine might need to be more radically revised to address the challenges of privatization.

Demands of Impartiality, Notice, and Some Opportunity to Be Heard

The clearest due process concern raised by privatization is the problem of the financially interested decision maker. Financial interest is a factor in many privatization contexts where private entities implement government programs and provide government-funded benefits or services. Contracts may pay a set amount for provision of services regardless of what the services actually cost; an excellent illustration here is Medicaid and Medicare HMOs. Alternatively, contracts may tie part of a private contractor's reimbursement to its performance; for example, job training and work placement contracts frequently make full payment dependent on beneficiaries being placed in jobs for a minimum period of time. In both cases, the aim is to use private companies' financial interest to benefit government programs, either by improving services or limiting costs. An additional effect, however, is to give a private contractor financial incentives at odds with the interests of program participants—to limit provision of costly services, force out participants who require extensive services, are hard to place, and so on.[39] Indeed, even where a contractor is paid a set amount independent of its performance or the cost of services provided, simply the desire to win renewal of a contract could be said to give it a financial interest in keeping the cost of the program down by denying claims and services.[40] While these financial incentives may be particularly powerful in the case of for-profit contractors, nonprofits face them as well, particularly if their financial situation is tenuous or they are financially dependent on government contracts.[41]

Existing precedent is clear in holding that adjudication by some financially interested decision makers violates due process, even absent evidence of actual bias.[42] Interestingly, precedent exists specifically on the question of private adjudication and private involvement in adjudication. In *Gibson v. Berryhill* the Supreme Court ruled that due process was violated when private optometrists serving as members of a state board in license revocation proceedings might benefit financially if the licenses at issue were revoked.[43] In *Schweiker v. McClure*, by contrast, the Court upheld the use of private insurance carriers to issue final rulings on certain Medicare claims. In so holding, the Court emphasized that the carriers paid all the claims with "federal, and not their own, funds" and that the federal government paid the salaries of the carriers' hearing officers.[44]

Schweiker suggests that a mere desire to win contract renewal is too indirect an influence to create disqualifying bias—at least where regulations exist imposing obligations of impartiality. *Gibson*, meanwhile, suggests that due process is violated when a private decision maker acting on the government's behalf has a personal pecuniary stake in the decision at issue. What about the situation in between these poles, where a private adjudicator has no personal financial stake in the decision she is making, but her employer does: Is such general financial interest on the part of the decision maker's employer too remote to violate due process? *Schweiker* avoided answering this question, holding that "in the absence of proof of financial interest on the part of the carriers, there is no basis for assuming a derivative bias among their hearing officers."[45]

Precedent from the public adjudication context—most notably a series of challenges to criminal convictions under Ohio's system of mayor's courts—establishes that general and indirect financial interests can but do not always create unconstitutional bias.[46] As enunciated in the mayor's court cases, the relevant inquiry for impermissible bias is whether "the [decision maker's] situation is one 'which would offer a possible temptation to the average man as a judge.' "[47]

It seems fair to conclude that such possible temptation exists when a private adjudicator's employer stands to gain financially from her decisions. This is particularly true if the adjudicator may suffer financial loss as a result of her decisions; indeed, in such a situation the adjudicator herself could be said to have a direct financial interest in the decision at issue, in addition to her employer.[48] Similarly, a basis for inferring bias clearly exists when the adjudicator has substantial executive responsibilities, as occurs when the employee charged with resolving claims for denied services or benefits is also responsible for supervising initial claims handlers.[49] But even when the adjudicator has no other responsibilities or enjoys contractual or regulatory promises of independence, it seems quite possible that concern about financial impact on her employer—and derivatively, to her employment prospects—could tempt her to deviate from impartiality in decision making.[50] While separation of function protections, such as segregating prosecutorial and adjudicative functions and guaranteeing the independence of adjudicators, often suffice to guard against impermissible bias in public adjudications,[51] in private contexts these protections may not be as reliable. Policing against abuse of such protections may be more difficult in private settings, given such factors as the greater openness of government[52] and the frequent presence of administrative mechanisms by which government employees can challenge adverse employment actions.[53] Private contractors often have greater flexibility in constructing workplace rules and greater ability to influence their employees' actions indirectly.[54] In addition, the small size and relative informality of many private contractors means that private adjudicators may lack the insulation enjoyed by their public counterparts and be more exposed to ex parte pressure from their employers.[55]

As a result, at least where private adjudicators' decisions regarding third-party claims can have a significant financial impact on their employers, the presumption should be that even insulated private adjudicators would face too great a temptation to advance their employers' financial interests. The central question then posed is whether concerns that financial interest may bias private adjudications can be adequately addressed through provision for subsequent independent review. Decisions addressing public adjudication contain language insisting that an initial decision maker be financially disinterested,[56] although subsequent case law has not developed this requirement further, and if anything the Court appears increasingly skeptical of predeprivation hearing requirements.[57] What is clear enough, though, is that requiring an initially impartial decision maker would preclude many forms of privatization today. Indeed, one commentator has argued that the requirement of an initially impartial decision maker precludes use of managed care organizations under Medicare and Medicaid.[58]

The draconian effects of prohibiting *any* financially interested decision makers militate against imposing such a requirement. True, a real danger exists that individuals will not seek independent review, making the initial decision final. Nonetheless, the possibility of independent review should provide some protection against abuse, and the prohibition on financially interested decision making is after all a prophylactic rule—what ultimately violates due process is actual, not potential, bias.[59] Perhaps more importantly, private financial interest may yield benefits as well as abuses; managed care organizations' financial self-interest, for example, may lead them to put a premium on preventive medicine and on ferreting out fraud or excessive treatments.[60] Thus, a categorical prohibition on any financially interested decision making seems unwarranted. Instead, timely independent review of service and claim denials should generally suffice to meet due process concerns about biased decision making.[61] Put in terms of the private delegation approach, without such provisions these grants of adjudicatory power would be unconstitutional.[62]

Further complexity comes from considering how to treat claims of policy bias in private adjudications. Privatization allows government to draw upon private professionals and others with specialized knowledge in a field. But with expertise often comes substantive policy commitments that affect how disputes are viewed. Individuals participating on educational accreditation committees, for instance, are likely to have preset ideas regarding the requirements of adequate educational programs, and accrediting organizations incorporate certain programmatic minima into their accrediting standards. Of course, some critique accreditation standards as little more than self-interest, charges raised recently regarding ABA accreditation of law schools.[63] The more significant point is that even when their motives are pure, private adjudicators chosen because of their expertise will come to accreditation decisions with precommitments. As the Second Circuit once remarked regarding arbitration, "parties agree to arbitrate precisely because they prefer a tribunal with expertise regarding the particular subject matter of their dispute," yet "[f]amiliarity with a discipline often comes at the expense of complete impartiality. Some commercial fields are quite narrow, and a given expert may be expected to have formed strong views on certain topics, published articles in the field and so forth."[64]

Such policy or programmatic bias similarly exists in the context of public adjudication, and has encountered little judicial resistance. Courts require substantial evidence of prejudgment in a particular case—an "irrevocably closed" mind—with substantive familiarity seen as contributing to expertise and informed administration rather than bias.[65] But should policy or programmatic bias be as tolerated in regard to private adjudication? As is true in public contexts, private expertise may often enhance the quality and accuracy of decision making. For example, nonprofit professional and ideological commitments may operate to the benefit of program participants, leading nonprofit caseworkers to avoid abusive practices and oppose government policies they view as harsh.[66] Inclusion of private actors chosen because of their partisan views can even lend legitimacy to some regulatory schemes, by guaranteeing that all affected interests are represented.[67] But particularly given open government requirements and separation-of-function protections that insulate initial decision makers, the programmatic commitments of public adjudicators are more likely to be overt and to reflect publicly chosen policies than those of their private counterparts.[68] As a result, participants in private adjudications may have difficulty determining the extent of policy bias and successfully countering it.

One possible means of addressing the problem of hidden policy biases without sacrificing the benefits of private substantive expertise would be to target instead the closed environment of private decision making. Basic due process principles would seem to require that individuals have notice of the rules and policies being applied to them and be provided with a statement of the basis for decision. Similarly, due process would seem to demand that individuals be given an opportunity to contest the application of such rules and policies to their specific case.[69] Thus, the government may need to impose notice and minimal hearing requirements as a condition for constitutionally delegating adjudicatory authority to private actors. An example here comes from the Higher Education Act. Under the Act, for an accreditation to limit an educational institution's eligibility to participate in government programs, the accrediting agency must, among other things, use procedures that comply with due process. Due process is defined in the Act to include adequate specification of deficiencies at the institution or program being examined and notice of an opportunity for a hearing; the Act also requires that the agency make public a summary of any review action on request.[70]

Yet limits exist on the level of openness that due process can be said to mandate. Does due process require that private adjudicators reveal their decisions in analogous contexts, even if those decisions are not relied on or invoked in the case at hand? To reveal more general policies and guidance manuals governing how a private entity operates? Although individuals may be able to demand discovery of such material in a lawsuit, under current case law due process does not impose such general disclosure requirements on government.[71] That alone is not decisive, as due process may entail greater disclosure in private adjudicatory contexts. Making public a privatized program's operating procedures and substantive scope yields significant benefits. It limits the extent to which private entities can avoid expenses simply by not informing participants that they are eligible for certain benefits and services.[72] In addition, evidence from analogous cases is plainly important support for an individual's claim, as well as a significant means of enforcing regularity and consistency in decision making. But fashioning a broad disclosure requirement for privatization contexts is not without costs. Private entities may become unwilling to deviate from general policies in specific cases for fear they will have to do so in future cases as well; they may also become unwilling to issue general guidance if the effect of doing so is to render their internal operations more public. Moreover, forcing openness also exacts a cost in private autonomy—not perhaps an overwhelming concern, given that private entities always have the option of foregoing participation in government programs, but a cost that deserves acknowledgment nonetheless. A closed environment is more conducive to private self-definition and control, candid interactions, and operational flexibility.

In short, determining the extent of impartiality and disclosure demanded by private due process requires balancing competing values of fairness, transparency, flexibility, and private autonomy. In many ways, therefore, the concerns raised by private adjudication can be addressed through application of *Mathews* balancing, particularly if the individual and government interests at stake are viewed somewhat expansively.[73] Indeed, the requirements of notice, explanation, and independent review articulated so far fit fairly easily within the established due process lexicon, even if the specific procedural protections mandated for private and public adjudicatory contexts differ.

The Government's Duty to Supervise

Yet due process in private adjudication contexts also has dimensions that are less easily encompassed within standard due process analysis. Most significantly, many of the decisions being given over to private hands involve discretionary benefits to which individuals can make no claim of statutory, regulatory, or contractual entitlement. Decisions by private welfare contractors regarding which individuals get to participate in particularly desirable work or training programs are an example; while some welfare programs may grant entitlements to participate in training programs, the choice of which program a beneficiary is assigned is highly likely to be left to the contractors' discretion. Such discretionary decisions, albeit adjudicatory in the *Londoner–Bi-Metallic* sense, do not trigger procedural due process protections at all under current analysis, given its restriction of due process to entitlement contexts.[74] Thus, for example, procedural due process requirements of impartiality and independent review simply do not apply.

Similarly, current doctrine precludes using due process to demand that private entities engage in rulemaking, even regarding benefits and services that qualify as entitlements. Instead, well-established case law grants agencies broad power to set policy through general rules or instead through case-by-case adjudication; due process at most provides protection against some instances of retroactive application of new policies.[75] Hence, even if in privatization contexts due process is read to require extensive disclosure of private rules and policies regarding government benefits and services, program participants would still lack the ability to demand that private actors formulate such rules in the first place. Moreover, given the general exemption of rulemaking from procedural due process requirements under *Bi-Metallic,* were a private entity to issue standards to govern its implementation of a government program, program participants would have no right to express their views or demand an explanation of why a particular approach was chosen.

That is not to say that individual procedural protections *should* apply in these contexts. Requiring individual notice and opportunity for a hearing for all private discretionary decisions could be extremely burdensome and intrusive on private autonomy, as could forcing private entities to provide a role for public participation when they establish operational rules.[76] Both arguably create poor incentives, such as encouraging private entities to forego rulemaking altogether or to operate in an unduly rigid and rule-bound fashion. Individual procedural rights also seem a poor paradigm for analyzing the systemic concerns in these contexts. Given the discretionary nature of the decisions at stake, the issue is less achieving a correct result in a particular case than it is ensuring that the private entity is considering relevant factors and adhering to norms of consistency and equality across its decisions as a whole. Nonetheless, wholly exempting private discretionary decision making from procedural requirements is troubling, given that private decision makers are not publicly accountable and often have a financial interest in their decisions.

In short, significant gaps exist in the extent to which tweaking current due process rules can address the concerns with self-interested abuse of power as well as the lack of accountability and transparency in privatized governance. Instead, a more fundamental revision of current doctrine may be needed. One change that appears particularly warranted is the development of a due process–based duty to supervise, under which the government must actively oversee decision making by its private delegates, at least when that decision making directly affects third parties. Imposing such a duty to supervise offers a means of checking the potential for arbitrary action and abuse of power that privatization presents, without unduly limiting private flexibility in specific cases. It also reflects the private delegation emphasis on the responsibilities that ensue as a result of the government's decision to transfer power to private hands. Stated in private delegation terms, the justification for a duty to supervise is that only government supervision can adequately guard against self-interested decision making and ensure that due process demands of regularity and fairness are met in contexts of privatized governance. Government supervision is also essential to ensure that public officials remain ultimately responsible for exercises of government power.

Some precedent exists for viewing due process as incorporating such a duty to supervise. Notably, even current private delegation doctrine, weak as it is, underscores the importance of government supervision, as it requires that the government retain formal oversight powers over its private delegates.[77] Yet imposing a duty to supervise goes beyond existing private delegation doctrine, because it requires that the government not simply provide formal oversight but further take an active role in monitoring its private delegates and their implementation of government programs.[78] The Supreme Court has also emphasized the importance of government supervision in two of its recent encounters with privatization, although it has not indicated the extent required for such supervision to be legally relevant.[79] Interestingly, a similar emphasis on government supervision of privatization is arising from other, nonconstitutional quarters. Public administration and public contracts scholars are strikingly united on the importance of government management of its private contractors if privatization is to succeed as a tool of modern governance—as well as on the government's frequent failure to perform its oversight responsibilities adequately.[80] The focus of this scholarship is management- and policy-based, but the same conclusion results: increasing privatization demands greater recognition of government's oversight and supervision responsibilities.[81] One advantage of developing a due process–based duty to supervise is that doing so adds the force of constitutional law to these efforts at managerial reform, with the potential for constitutional invalidation giving both the government and its private contractors an incentive to ensure adequate oversight.

A central question facing any effort to construct such a duty to supervise, however, is: How active must the government's supervision of its private delegates be to satisfy its constitutional obligations? The current exemption of public discretionary decision making from procedural due process constraints makes it hard to read a duty to supervise as demanding government review of all discretionary private decisions; mandating such a degree of government involvement would likely render many instances of privatization infeasible. But requiring the government to impose and enforce a general prohibition on bias on all private adjudications, even those involving discretionary benefits, seems not unduly intrusive.[82] The duty to supervise could also be used as a basis for requiring private entities to promulgate standards and procedures to govern their decision making, on the logic that such measures help ensure government oversight by rendering private policy choices more transparent. Alternatively, courts could calibrate the degree of active oversight required for specific instances of private decision making with the extent to which the government has imposed requirements of procedural regularity and transparency on its private delegates. Under such an approach, government would retain the ability to leave its private delegates procedurally unencumbered, but at the price of having to review those delegates' decisions and activities more carefully. Another factor that seems appropriate for courts to take into account is the importance of the private decision at stake; greater oversight is needed when the powers exercised by private delegates are significant than when private delegates' impact on third parties is more minimal.[83]

A second and related query is: Even if such a duty to supervise exists, to what extent should it be judicially enforced? Separation of powers and federalism concerns, as well as recognition of limited judicial competency in assessing management strategies, surely caution courts against too vigorous enforcement. As the Court once remarked, administrative agencies are "far better equipped than the courts to deal with the many variables involved in the proper ordering of [their] priorities."[84] But these concerns do not justify wholesale judicial deference to the government's oversight choices. Under such limited review, requirements of government supervision and oversight cease to have real meaning, and the potential constitutional abuses associated with private delegate decision making go unaddressed. Particularly in a time of increasing privatization, greater judicial enforcement of government oversight obligations serves to preserve our constitutional scheme rather than undermine it.[85] Moreover, the above discussion of what a duty to supervise might require suggests that it should be possible to enforce such a duty in a way that leaves the government substantial flexibility.

Of course, if understood as imposing only minimal oversight obligations, the constitutional duty to supervise may offer little protection against potential private abuses of government power. And even if more robust in its demands, such a duty—like the private delegation analysis on which it is based—is limited to instances where a private contractor is interacting with third parties on the government's behalf.[86] Hence, establishing meaningful and widespread government oversight of all the government's private delegates requires more than reconceiving due process as embodying a duty to supervise. Positive law reforms are equally if not more essential. In this regard, Nina Mendelson's proposals to link contractor legal immunity to the presence of active supervision seem particularly worth exploring, given their potential to turn government contractors into advocates of greater government oversight.[87] Perhaps most basically, achieving adequate government supervision depends upon the political branches recognizing that such supervision is essential if privatization is to yield its promised improvements in the performance of government programs.

CHAPTER TWELVE

Outsourcing and the Duty to Govern

PAUL R. VERKUIL

Introduction

This chapter explores the duty to govern as a dimension of state authority. It seeks a positive role for government in what Leslie Green sees as a neglected aspect of the theory of authority.[1] It also complements Gillian Metzger's chapter in this volume on the relationship of privatization to the nondelegation doctrine.[2] Professor Metzger argues for a nondelegation rule that requires government to structure authority transferred to the private sector. The nondelegation doctrine postulated here argues not just that transfers of power to private hands must be accompanied by procedural standards, but that in some settings the transfer of governmental power should not occur at all. If the President cannot transfer the executive power to the Vice President, then the Secretary of Defense cannot transfer his authority to RAND, nor can the Assistant Secretary at the Environmental Protection Agency transfer her power to make reasoned decisions to contractors. The nondelegable duty doctrine is both a harder and easier argument to sustain under the traditional theory; harder because it potentially forbids delegations; easier because it does not require a search for ascertainable standards.[3] This nondelegation theory poses prudential limits like standing and justiciability[4] that may limit the role of the courts. But the judiciary does not have the last word. All political officials take oaths to uphold the Constitution. The delegation and rule of law theories offered here are the responsibility of each of the branches.

The chapter also explores statutory and administrative requirements that are clearly enforceable and reinforce the constitutional arguments. It then considers recent developments in airport security as a case study and analyzes the public and private dimensions of the services there provided. From that experience, a definition of nondelegable duties emerges.

Downsizing and Governance

The federal government is in the midst of a long-term downsizing of its civilian workforce.[5] This has been a bipartisan effort, beginning in the Reagan and Bush I administrations, spurred on by the "reinventing government" movement in the Clinton administration, and firmly embraced by the Bush II administration, with its commitment to further reduce civilian payrolls.[6] If President Bush achieves his personnel goals the federal civilian workforce will be reduced to about one million non-postal[7] employees. While the civilian workforce is not always reduced in favor of private service provision—the Transportation Security Agency (TSA) recently added over 60,000 government employees to maintain airport security, a function that was previously privatized—downsizing is clearly the trend.

This trend can adversely affect the provision of government services by targeting some essential (policy) jobs for outsourcing, and by leaving inadequate numbers of staff to oversee the private sector employees who assume the outsourced jobs. It is difficult to know how many government officials are needed for oversight purposes, but when the number of private contractors grows to more than twelve times the number of government employees,[8] control issues arise. When policy positions are outsourced or those in policy positions are stripped of adequate staff, essential government functions may be neglected. And when the number of service contracts grows exponentially,[9] the government's ability both to govern and to oversee outsourced service providers can be severely tested.

Defining Policy Officials

To some extent all government officials, down to the cop on the beat or the private in Iraq, engage in acts of judgment and discretion that define the policymaking function. But policy level officials of government hold others accountable; they have been selected, in John Rohr's phrase, to "run a Constitution."[10] At the federal level, these officials are appointed as Officers of the United States or selected as members of the Senior Executive Service ("SES"). The number of presidential appointments has been estimated at around 3,300 and the SES at about 7,700 members.[11] These roughly 11,000 officials have the primary responsibility for managing 1 million government employees and over 12 million contractors. Their responsibilities have grown dramatically with a downsizing government.

In addition, the ratio of political appointees to career officials has grown during this period of downsizing.[12] Political officials have the confidence of the party in power. However, there is evidence that political appointees are less effective managers than the career officials they replace.[13] For example, FEMA's inability to manage disaster relief in the aftermath of Hurricane Katrina is partially attributable to the number of political appointees in its senior leadership.[14] The increase in presidential appointees, the added responsibilities of all policy officials due to downsizing, and the resulting reliance upon contractors left FEMA in an untenable position.[15] Most studies have concluded that the hurricane disaster relief effort suffered acutely from inadequate public management, preparation, and control.[16]

In the military setting, operations in Iraq have exposed serious leadership deficiencies that can also be partially attributed to outsourcing and downsizing.[17] The creation of what amounts to a "privatized military"[18] as a sophisticated provider of security services to the United States shows how shorthanded the military is in these critical theaters of operation. While private contractors have existed for a long time,[19] the George W. Bush administration vastly expanded their responsibilities. Private services are now performed on the battlefield,[20] where contractors are involved in military functions as interrogators[21] and security guards. In fact, the recent investigation of Blackwater's activities as a contractor for the State Department reveals how much lethal force its employees have exercised since the Iraq war began.[22] But given the difficulty in meeting recruitment goals during the war in Iraq,[23] this unprecedented level of military outsourcing will be hard to rein in.

Downsizing of the civilian workforce affects the military independently of the size of our "public" armed forces. The military is subject to civilian control through the President as Commander in Chief, so civilian policymakers ultimately are responsible for military policy. The Pentagon has been hard hit by civilian retirements and personnel cutbacks, even as the defense budget has expanded. The growing shortage of civilian contracting officers at the Pentagon, noted by the Government Accountability Office (GAO),[24] is one consequence.

This shortage comes precisely when contractual oversight is most needed as private contractors operate in Iraq largely under single-sourced, noncompetitively bid, multibillion-dollar contracts.[25] Deficiencies in contract performance have been embarrassing, costly, and pervasive.[26] Fixing this problem, or even stemming it, rests on experienced public officials who are increasingly in short supply. Thus, government has started to outsource the duty to oversee those outsourced activities.[27] When the contractor oversight function is outsourced, policymakers are further compromised and accountability of the government is frustrated.

Oversight and Policymaking

When the response to the GAO's report on inadequate oversight[28] is to delegate that function to private contractors, the Department of Defense (DOD) exacerbates the accountability problem rather than solving it. If government does not have adequate personnel to oversee its outsourcing, it does not have adequate personnel to read the reports on outsourcing submitted by its private overseers. Moreover, when the Vice President is the former CEO of a primary contractor in Iraq (Halliburton),[29] the oversight role is essential. DOD should ensure that the lack of adequate personnel at the policy level does not hinder the government's ability to decide objectively whether to outsource in the first place.

All firms, including government, confront the classic choice of whether to perform functions directly (in-house) or indirectly (through contractors).[30] In government, to properly exercise the "make or buy choice," however, both the function and the choice must be objectively examined. If the function involves policymaking there is no choice to make—government officials must perform it. David Walker, the Comptroller General of the GAO, puts it: "War fighting, judicial, enforcement, regulatory, and *policy-making* functions should never be privatized."[31] Yet these functions are increasingly delegated to private hands.

In the disaster relief and military settings, "tactical privatization"[32] now gives private contractors the authority to perform enforcement and policymaking functions. Private contractors can now be seen not only on the streets of Baghdad, but also in New Orleans. It has long been thought by conservatives and liberals alike that the public provision of security and protection against disasters are public goods.[33]

Actions to protect the commons often require a "special public trust."[34] When public duties are outsourced in this setting, that trust is compromised. Thus, delegating the oversight function both diminishes the public role and raises constitutional concerns.

The Case for Constitutional Governance

Policymaking is reserved to the political branches of government through the separation of powers doctrine. Inevitably, the structural Constitution is about governance or, more precisely, democratic governance.[35] Separation of powers helps to ensure democratic governance in two ways: it assigns governing duties to separate branches, and it prevents those branches from transferring or reassigning those duties to others. Much of the duty to govern is assigned to the Executive under Article II, where the Executive power combines with the commander-in-chief power.[36] But all three branches are crucial players.

Structural Controls on Administration

Executive control over the administrative branch, that branch not mentioned in the Constitution,[37] is assured in several ways. The President works through a network of constitutionally defined deputies designated "Officers of the United States."[38] Presidential control of these officers is ensured through the ability to require "the Opinion, in writing, of the principal Officer in each of the executive Departments"[39] and by the President's responsibility to "take Care that the Laws be faithfully executed."[40]

But it is another clause—the Appointments Clause[41]—that does the most to protect against improper delegations of policymaking authority to private parties. The President appoints "Officers of the United States." Congress, through the Senate, advises and consents to those appointments. This clause provides several significant protections: it protects the Executive against Congress; it protects both branches against the "administrative" branch, and it also protects against the delegation of authority to private parties. The Justice Department's Office of Legal Counsel (OLC) usefully defines these protections as the horizontal and vertical dimensions of the Appointments Clause.[42] The horizontal protections prevent the legislative branch from aggrandizing power by limiting its appointment and removal of executive officials to positions outlined in the Appointments Clause.[43] The vertical effect is triggered when the Executive delegates power to outsiders. It is this dimension of the Appointments Clause that is least well understood and will be elaborated upon in this chapter.

In sum, if the President or a cabinet secretary were to assign duties to private contractors that are normally performed by either principal or "inferior"[44] officers, that official would be delegating duties to those not covered by the Appointments Clause. Officers of the United States are said to exert "significant authority," which is inherent in, and exclusive to, the executive function.[45] When the President appoints military officers, for example, their duties fall within the constraints of this requirement.[46] Even junior officers (for example, second lieutenants or ensigns) are subject to this requirement, though their command authority is limited.[47] When they exercise command authority in conflict situations or assert force (including, for example, the interrogation of prisoners in Iraq) they perform significant duties in the sense required by *Buckley v. Valeo*.[48]

When these duties devolve to private contractors, constitutional responsibilities have been transferred without congressional approval. Combat military actions, "warfighting," by Comptroller General Walker's description,[49] are thus nondelegable actions and the phrase "private military"[50] describes a function offensive to the Constitution. If constitutional duties of this dimension are viewed as nondelegable, Congress may not provide power to the Executive to hire "private" officers of the United States. But such a stringent rule may not be necessary. If one mediates between the formalist and functionalist views of cases like *Myers* and *Humphrey's Executor*,[51] a middle ground emerges where Congress can expressly exercise delegating authority.

In this way, the executive branch's private delegations can be given legitimizing effect. Through congressional authorization, the branch participation goals of the Appointments Clause can be satisfied. Just as Congress cannot add restrictions to the Appointments Clause (by applying it to removal of officials), the President cannot frustrate Congress's power under the Appointments Clause by delegating officers' duties to private contractors without congressional concurrence. Congress's interests under the appointments process are twofold: they include the power to oversee and, if necessary, to impeach the officers involved. The power to impeach is lost when certain functions are exercised by private contractors. But if Congress consents to a transfer of public power to private hands, that is, if it approves contracting out certain functions, it effectively accepts the loss of control such transfers imply. Of course, this argument sidesteps the question whether

Congress can effectively waive its appointments powers. A strong view of the nondelegation doctrine stands as a barrier to such waivers. But since Congress has not specifically authorized private military activities at this stage, the approval of such activities remains a central issue.

Moreover, another constitutional provision appears to contemplate private military action under some circumstances, providing that Congress gives its approval. At one time, the Marque and Reprisal Clause[52] anticipated private military activities through the employment of privateers. But the Executive could employ these contractors only *if* Congress approved. Thus, even this clause provided a constitutional safeguard against the unilateral use of military power by the executive branch.

On the civilian side, the OLC memorandum mentioned above cites only two "vertical" cases, neither of which is directly applicable to the contractor situation.[53] The paucity of case law is not surprising. It may be due to several factors: the absence of any instances of policy delegations to private hands, the assumption that such delegations are within the executive power, or, more likely, procedural limitations like justiciability and standing[54] that limit the prospects of such cases.

As a result, a constitutional principle requiring public responsibility for public acts has not been adequately developed. Such a principle would depend on the courts embracing a corollary to the horizontal "antiaggrandizement" principle that limits one branch's ability to usurp the authority of the other.[55] An "antidevolution principle" would prevent the President from aggrandizing power at the expense of Congress by privatizing executive functions subject to the Appointments Clause. To illustrate, consider that, in overseeing delegations of military authority to private hands, President Bush acts sometimes with, and sometimes without, congressional authorization. On occasion, he may even be acting in the face of congressional restrictions (such as those posed by the Subdelegation Act,[56] which limits delegations to officers of the United States). When he does so, according to the principle just described, his authority would be at its "lowest ebb."[57]

The executive branch's delegation of public power to private hands also occurs frequently in the domestic context. Privatized actions are often not transparent in that setting, due to the vagaries of the contracting process and the inapplicability of the Federal Advisory Committee Act (FACA)[58] and the Freedom of Information Act (FOIA),[59] which publicize meetings and documents submitted to government. If applicable, these statutes would help condition the President's transfer of civilian policymaking authority to private hands and also protect Congress and the public from loss of democratic responsibility.

But there are other constitutional provisions that can potentially challenge private delegations.

Due Process Limits on Private Delegations

The nondelegation doctrine has been largely unenforced by courts since the New Deal period. However, the principle still attracts loyal adherents who would like to see it revitalized.[60] If the doctrine were to reemerge, it could be reformulated to limit executive as well as congressional delegations. At first glance, it might seem inappropriate to extend the traditional nondelegation doctrine to the contracting context. As Professor Vikram Amar has suggested,[61] delegations become more problematic when they are harder to reclaim. Outsourced power can always, in theory, be reclaimed through contractual restrictions. The contracts themselves can become instruments for structuring the delegated power. Of course when contracts are open ended, single sourced, and long term, as they have been in Iraq, delegated power is not so easily retrievable. Thus, nondelegation theory alone may not be a sufficient instrument for constraining pervasive outsourcing. Other constitutional provisions are available, however.

The Due Process Clause may be invoked to constrain privatization. One of the most famous nondelegation cases, *Carter v. Carter Coal*,[62] raised both nondelegation and due process concerns.[63] Under the Bituminous Coal Conservation Act,[64] district boards elected by coal operators and unions set wages binding on all coal producers. The Supreme Court set aside this grant of decision-making power to private parties on both grounds. So even if use of the nondelegation doctrine remains problematic when applied to contracting, due process considerations might lead courts to limit such delegations.[65] What offended the *Carter Coal* Court was that the public interest was nowhere represented in a delegation that authorized private lawmaking. As Professor Tribe has noted, "[t]he judicial hostility to private lawmaking ... represents a persistent theme in American constitutional law."[66] Of course, privatization is not exactly private lawmaking—the vertical delegations of governmental power to private contractors usually involve policymaking, not private decision making in the *Carter Coal* sense. But when due process requires a decision maker, it usually requires a public actor.[67] To this extent, when the grant of power has a public dimension, it can be viewed as "publicized" for due process purposes.[68]

Appointments Clause Limits on Private Delegations

As noted above, the Appointments Clause could also serve as a deterrent to private delegations of significant government authority. The clause identifies those public officials who must conduct the policy-making business of government: officers of the United States. The Constitution divides those who work for the government into three categories: principal officers, inferior officers, and employees.[69] The first two categories ought to be subject to Appointments Clause limitations on the outsourcing of authority,[70] whereas the jobs of employees are of lesser constitutional importance and may be outsourced.

Officers of the United States exercise "significant authority"[71] under the Supreme Court's decision in *Buckley,* which established three criteria for officer status: exercise of significant authority, duration of employment, and permanent nature of the duties assigned.[72] Since the case itself involved members of the Federal Election Commission, all three criteria were clearly satisfied. The question for Appointments Clause purposes is whether these criteria are independent or alternative.

This led to a debate between two presidential administrations. The administration of George H. W. Bush adopted the "alternative criteria" view[73] in arguing for the unconstitutionality of *qui tam* actions (private law enforcement).[74] By asserting that significant authority under the Appointments Clause was both necessary and sufficient, the Bush I Office of Legal Counsel concluded that the private relator who initiated an action on behalf of the government would be exercising authority constitutionally reserved to the Attorney General.[75]

Adopting this strict reading would make it more likely that outsourcing decisions could be held to violate the Appointments Clause. That is, if the exercise of significant authority were the sole *Buckley* criterion, many contractors would fall within its terms. The Appointments Clause question would become simply whether private contractors exercised significant authority or "insignificant" authority—that is, whether they performed the duties of officers or those of employees. Private contractors delegated "significant authority" would, like *qui tam* relators, ipso facto become unconstitutional actors.[76]

To illustrate, consider the extensive government contracting undertaken by the administration of George W. Bush in the context of the Iraq war. If all devolution of "significant authority" is forbidden, much of this contracting is constitutionally suspect: the private military cannot engage in warfighting on the battlefield, nor can contractors make policy for agencies.

This argument, based on the OLC interpretation of *Buckley* embraced by the Bush I administration, has weaknesses which were revealed by the competing interpretation embraced by the Clinton administration. President Clinton's Office of Legal Counsel expressly disavowed the earlier Bush OLC opinion and argued instead for the independent status of each of the three Appointments Clause criteria considered by *Buckley*.[77] In so doing, the opinion primarily sought to preserve *qui tam* actions,[78] not to opine on private delegations.[79] Yet its conclusions are instructive for our inquiry here. Because *qui tam* actions would not fail the second and third *Buckley* criteria, they would be constitutional under the Appointments Clause, so long as Congress expressly consents (as it did in the False Claims Act). This consent is vital as a normative matter because it protects Congress's role in the appointments process. But if Congress has expressly not acted (as, for example, in the private contractor context), or if it can be shown that Congress has acted to restrict delegations, then the Appointments Clause can still operate.

Moreover, the Appointments Clause not only requires significant authority to be exercised by officials, it also requires these officials to take oaths to uphold the Constitution.[80] The oath requirement is no mere formality: it is the way the Constitution separates public from private actors.[81] Government officials, like Supreme Court justices, the President and members of Congress, take oaths to uphold the Constitution.[82] While not all oath takers may exercise significant authority, the Constitution ensures that no one who exercises significant authority is not an oath taker. Moreover, these officers, once confirmed, are also subject to the impeachment power, a power Congress uses to oversee the executive branch. If duties of executive branch officials are transferred to private hands, these delegatees become "unimpeachable" and Congress loses a constitutionally designed accountability mechanism.

It is interesting to ask whether the unitary theory of the Executive[83] would accept this view of the Appointments Clause. Recent commentary by Professor Sai Prakash, a well-known unitarian, reinforces the Clinton OLC position in the *qui tam* context.[84] As a matter of original constitutional intent, if congressionally authorized *qui tam* actions survive, the Appointments Clause retains its controlling power absent specific delegations.

For those concerned about pervasive outsourcing, of course, the single-criterion view staked out by the first Bush administration would make it easier to sustain a constitutional claim. All the President (or a Department head) would have to do to run afoul of the Constitution under this approach is to delegate the duties of an officer of the United States to a private contractor.[85] In the military setting, such delegations occur with regularity, because the term "officers" includes those who carry out battlefield assignments frequently delegated to security contractors. Yet because *qui tam* actions have survived constitutional review,[86] the Bush I single-criterion view is less convincing. This makes private contractor delegations less vulnerable, since the other two criteria established by *Buckley* (duration and established roles) are rarely satisfied by delegations to private contractors.[87]

Still, even if delegations to contractors were to pass constitutional muster under *Buckley*'s nondelegation test, they might nevertheless run afoul of the Appointments Clause if Congress has not authorized them. Statutes that authorize delegations of significant authority, such as the False Claims Act, are hard to find, arguably because Congress values its oversight prerogatives. In the absence of authorizing statutes,[88] delegations should be subject to challenge under the Appointments Clause.

This leaves principal officers, if not the President, at risk when they delegate significant authority to private hands. In the civilian setting, consultants to agencies who do policymaking work may be delegates of significant authority. For example, consultants who advise FEMA officials to contract for services actually make payments in disaster relief situations and prepare hurricane evacuation plans.[89] Contractors may also conduct peer review processes for agencies and may review, summarize, and prepare agency responses to submissions in rulemaking. These seem like policymaking roles. If so, the work these contractors do is potentially significant in the constitutional sense, and subject to Appointments Clause challenges.

To be sure, government officials employ these contractors. But these arrangements still raise some difficult questions: When contractors exercise "authority" is it "significant" or even "governmental" when it is submitted for formal approval to an official of government? The official who approves is presumably exercising governmental authority. Yet if the contractor does all the substantive work—for example, the contractor prepares a policy letter and a government official signs it without change—can we be confident that he or she has exercised the constitutionally requisite authority?[90] In a recent study of Department of Homeland Security (DHS) outsourcing, GAO concluded that in using management support contracts supporting the performance by agency officials of inherent government functions, DHS did not assess the risk that government decisions "may be influenced by, rather than independent from, contractor judgments."[91] In other words, contractors at DHS are coming close to displacing government deciders. This raises the hard management question: does a rubber stamp satisfy the Constitution?

The Distinction between "Significant" and "Authority"

Even if we show that private contractors do "significant" work, do we have to show that they exercise the constitutionally requisite "authority"? The decisions made by contractors cannot usually take effect until a public official, who has sworn an oath of office, approves them. It is the government official who makes the decision governmental. Yet what precisely is required of such an official? Surely the exercise of meaningful authority by officers of the United States must involve more than simply endorsing the work of private contractors, and in many cases it does. But some actions of officials in agencies like FEMA and DHS suggest that public officials are not always in charge. The question is whether such failures are simply poor oversight and execution, or whether they rise to the level of unconstitutionally delegated authority. Bad management may not be unconstitutional governance.

At one time the Supreme Court said that to *exercise* significant authority the government official must actually do the work. By calling the Secretary of Agriculture to account when significant work was delegated to a lesser government official, the Court in *Morgan v. United States*[92] (*Morgan I*) created a formidable legal accountability standard. The Court's reasoning established a legal principle that he (or she) who decides must hear the evidence. Of course, the Secretary's delegates in *Morgan I* were public officials—either employees or "inferior" officers[93]—not private contractors. Had the Secretary delegated power instead to a private actor, the Court surely would have disapproved.[94] Moreover, the Secretary was acting in a judicial capacity when he delegated decision-making power to a hearing officer. Had he let a private decision maker exercise that power, the delegation might have also raised the due process concerns expressed in *Carter Coal*.[95]

Although the requirement from *Morgan I* that those who decide must hear was later abandoned by the Court,[96] the principle it established has inherent appeal in situations where decisions are delegated not to subordinates but to private parties. It is one thing to use consultants to help set priorities or provide analysis. It is another to recommend management changes that are implemented uncritically. Moreover, in some decision contexts like rule making, record and analysis requirements place an enhanced duty to decide on the agency official.[97]

The Court imposes a "hard look" requirement on agency decision makers in this context.[98] Perhaps delegations to private contractors of the record compilation and analysis functions may be permissible, but delegations of additional authority—for example, analysis and drafting of the concise statement of basis and purpose—seem to outsource decisional authority. Transfers of intellectual and decisional powers to private hands, even if the final signature remains with the government official, offend the appointments power and frustrate the principles underlying hard look review (which assume that the *agency* has an obligation to take a hard look before deciding). It is hard to see how these actions do not cross the significant-authority requirement of *Buckley.*

For separation of powers reasons, the courts may be reluctant to call the agency to account. The Supreme Court is not anxious to embarrass the Executive, and it uses the "rule of regularity" to presume decision maker good faith.[99] Yet the presumption of regularity, which can allow broad subdelegations to subordinates, only makes sense if it is limited to government officials. Under the Subdelegation Act, "[t]here is no such presumption covering subdelegations to outside parties."[100] A federal agency may turn to outside entities "provided the agency makes the final decision itself."[101] And in no event may an agency "merely 'rubber-stamp' decisions made by others under the guise of seeking their 'advice. . . .'"[102] In *U.S. Telecom Association v. FCC,* the District of Columbia Circuit limited the use of outside advice because it saw "the risk of policy drift inherent in any principal agent relationship"[103] as interfering with its role on judicial review. The judicial review function is pointless unless it contemplates agency officials who themselves consider alternatives before deciding to take significant actions like promulgating rules.[104]

In addition, the *Chenery* principle,[105] which requires that courts uphold agency actions based solely on the reasons given, connects the validity of agency action to the reasoning process.[106] Agencies, unlike Congress, are bound on judicial review by the reasons they assert.[107] And, of course, insistence upon a reasons requirement justifies the deference accorded agency actions under *Chevron v. National Resources Defense Council.*[108] When agencies choose among reasonable statutory interpretations under step two of *Chevron,* reviewing courts must defer to their expertise. If the expertise is a function not of agency insights but of outsiders' views uncritically adopted by the agency, the deference principle is frustrated and should not apply.

Of course, it may be difficult to detect the influence of contractors on an agency decision, in part because not all agency contracts are easily accessible to the public, or to courts. But where such agency contracts become known, and where the contracts authorize private actors to provide significant analysis, the decisions that result are surely deserving of judicial skepticism rather than deference. Deference is earned by agencies that engage in thorough analysis.

The delegation of significant authority may have become an inevitable consequence of the privatization movement. As argued above, the single-criterion Bush I view of *Buckley* is more hospitable to nondelegation challenges than are the independent Clinton OLC requirements of duration and scope of appointment.[109] In situations where agencies employ private contractors on a regular basis to prepare, draft, and reason out decisions, the contractors ought to be viewed as presumptively exercising significant authority. The Appointments Clause, which forbids delegations of significant authority without congressional authorization, and the Court's role in judicial review both demand that reasoned decision making remain a nondelegable duty of agency governance.

Control of Privatization by Statutory and Regulatory Means

From the early years of the republic, the necessity for the President to act through subordinates in the exercise of statutory powers was judicially accepted.[110] The Supreme Court was reluctant even to determine whether the actions taken were themselves legal.[111] While the Court had more difficulty with the executive delegation of adjudicatory powers, that too has come to be accepted practice.[112] Responsibility for adjudicatory actions has now largely been placed in the hands of administrative delegates who are not under direct presidential control.[113]

Congress has an interest in controlling how the President delegates executive power to subordinates. Conflicts between the political branches over how to control subordinate executive actors have long existed.[114] Dean Elena Kagan has articulated a broad constitutional role for executive administration and management that reads statutes as giving the President ultimate control.[115] But Congress regularly places statutory responsibility in subordinates, in particular Department heads, rather than in the President directly. According to Professor Kevin Stack, however, this creates both a constitutional and a "statutory" Executive.[116] In the latter case, Congress retains a significant role in assigning decision responsibility that can rein in expansive notions of executive control over subordinates.

But Congress also supports delegations directly to the Executive. Congress has, for example, vindicated presidential acts that were initially taken without statutory authority.[117] And in general, Congress has cooperated with the President in permitting subdelegations of executive power to subordinates. Through reorganization acts, Congress has recognized the realities of the modern administrative state by accommodating the President through express grants of subdelegation power.[118] These subdelegations, however, were to executive officials rather than private contractors, who under *Carter Coal* were not thought to be appropriate delegates.

Convincing rationales for limiting delegations to private contractors in the policymaking arena can also be drawn from both the Subdelegation Act and the Office of Management and Budget's (OMB) practice under Circular A-76.[119]

The Subdelegation Act and Private Contracting

The Subdelegation Act[120] makes delegations to the President's subordinates presumptively valid. The Act reflects the pragmatic understanding of presidential management that the Commission on Organization of the Executive Branch of the Government (the Hoover Commission) endorsed.[121] The Commission's goal was to make government management flexible by allowing agencies to behave more like private employers.[122] The Subdelegation Act supports that goal by granting presumptive power to the President to transfer duties to officials. It was designed to aid presidential management, not to limit the President's powers.[123] The Act does not address delegations to private contractors, even though the Hoover Commission sought to give government more of the powers of a private employer.[124] In fact, by limiting delegations to officers or high government officials, it implied limits on outside delegations, rather than encouragement of them.[125]

It made sense for Congress to limit delegations to officers of the United States. These are officials the Senate has in most cases preapproved under the Appointments Clause and over whom it retains some control through the impeachment process. Delegations by the President to those outside this category are forbidden by the Act unless they are expressly provided for by statute. This approach ensures Congress's continuing oversight of the delegation process, consistent with the flexibility granted the executive under the Hoover Commission.[126]

But the Act also helps set constitutional limits. If no statute grants the President or a Department head the power to subdelegate policymaking authority to private contractors, the Subdelegation Act stands as an implicit bar. If the President acts in the face of the statute, his power, while still perhaps constitutionally exercised, is greatly weakened.[127] Administration interpretations have been consistent with this view. Even where a delegating statute exists,[128] it is not used to justify the delegation of inherent government functions. Thus when Attorney General Ashcroft sought to contract out forty-eight program analyst and program manager positions responsible for grant activities, the OLC had to decide whether the delegation of those activities was statutorily and constitutionally permissible. In determining that employees, not officers, held these positions, the OLC reviewed *Buckley*'s "significant authority" requirements.[129] The Attorney General concluded that these were not policymaking positions and permitted them to be contracted out.[130]

This exercise in responsible administration makes two essential points. First, the executive branch honors the Subdelegation Act in its decisions to privatize. Second, the executive branch assumes the duty to police the significant authority requirements of *Buckley*. In exercising this responsibility, the President is fulfilling his oath to uphold the Constitution. Were he to privatize policy positions he could violate that oath. Additionally, if the Executive violated the Subdelegation Act by delegating significant duties to private parties without statutory authority, that decision could be reviewed by the courts.[131] Assuming a proper plaintiff,[132] the Subdelegation Act would support judicial review. In fact, when read as both limiting and granting authority for presidential delegations, the Act assumes a central role in supervising the devolution of public power to private hands.

OMB's Circular A-76 Process

The outsourcing process established by Congress is actively pursued by the executive branch. The President controls the contracting out of policymaking functions through the OMB. OMB's Circular A-76 process[133] establishes a framework for evaluating contracting decisions, which Mathew Blum explains in detail in this volume.[134] Under the Federal Activities Inventory Reform Act (FAIR Act),[135] agencies submit biannual inventories of jobs that can be competitively sourced to private contractors. Circular A-76 sets up the process for determining whether jobs may be competitively sourced.[136] Government officials whose jobs are listed for outsourcing can challenge the agency decision by establishing the superiority of their services, but judicial review has been restricted by arguments concerning standing.[137] This competition between the private and public sectors has been encouraged and expanded by the Bush administration.[138]

The A-76 process has clear limits that reflect the constraints of the Appointments Clause and Subdelegation Act: competitive sourcing excludes "inherently governmental activities." Though rarely connected, the phrase invites comparison to the exercise of "significant authority" under the *Buckley* case; the definition of "inherently governmental activities" gives concrete dimensions to the concept of "significant authority." Circular A-76 defines these activities as:

(1) Binding the United States to take or not to take some action by contract, policy, regulation, authorization, order, or otherwise;

(2) Determining, protecting, and advancing economic, political, territorial, property, or other interests by military or diplomatic action, civil or criminal, judicial proceedings, contract management, or otherwise;

(3) Significantly affecting the life, liberty, or property of private persons; or

(4) Exerting ultimate control over the acquisition, use, or disposition of United States property (real or personal, intangible), including establishing policies or procedures for the collection, control, or disbursement of appropriated and other federal funds.[139]

The use of private military contractors such as Blackwater clearly fails this test, since their activities involve actions "significantly affecting life, liberty, or property of private persons." The *Buckley* requirement is worth comparing to this definition. The two criteria that the Clinton Administration felt were independent in the "Officer of the United States" designation (duration and permanent position) do not appear in the A-76 definition. Both the Clinton and Bush I OLC opinions recognized this discrepancy and sought to resolve it by agreeing that the "inherently governmental activities" requirement may be broader than the *Buckley* requirements.[140] That the executive branch (through OMB) has in place a process that can be more strict than the significant authority requirement in limiting delegations to private hands is itself significant. It reflects a willingness to protect significant government functions, such as policymaking, from being contracted out. And it shows that the requirement can be made operational from a management perspective.

The following example helps show how the process works.

THE SEAFOOD INSPECTOR CHALLENGE

While government employees often prevail in A-76 contests,[141] they usually do so by showing that they are more competitive than the private alternative. Thus, the focus is on the competitive outsourcing side of the ledger, not the initial inherently governmental activities determination. Sometimes, however, affected individuals successfully challenge the agency's initial decision to designate a function for competitive sourcing rather than preserving it as an inherent function. When the National Oceanic and Atmospheric Administration (NOAA) decided to list the position of seafood inspector for competitive challenge rather than exempt it as an inherently governmental function, the government inspectors whose jobs were at stake challenged the agency's competitive sourcing designation.[142] NOAA denied their objections.

However, on appeal to the Department of Commerce (which oversees NOAA), the employees successfully asserted the inherently governmental status of their positions.[143] The Department accepted their argument that inspectors were public officials who wielded discretionary authority under A-76 and were not just employees. Interestingly, its position also garnered the support of the private fishing industry, which might have been expected to favor privatization. The industry, which paid for the inspection process, feared that private inspectors might not have the same credibility with customers in the European Union and China, where they exported much of their product.[144] In their view, inspector credibility and wearing the badge of a public official go "hand in hand."[145] Thus, inherently governmental functions were equated with those that government must perform not only to be legal, but also to be credible.

This credibility argument has resonance. It helped lead Congress to make airport security personnel public officials under the Transportation Security Act. This change is an important counterexample to the trend toward privatization. It shows that sometimes public solutions are widely seen as both more reliable and more credible by the public and Congress.

Case Study: The Role of Government in Airline Security

Before September 11, 2001, private airlines operating under FAA oversight screened passengers and baggage at airports as part of their overall service responsibility, which included providing ticket agents, pilots, flight attendants, and maintenance personnel.[146] The airlines did not actually employ the screeners as they did flight and maintenance staff; instead they entered into contracts with private security firms.[147] Not surprisingly, these contracts went to the lowest bidders, who often provided personnel lacking language skills and other qualifications (some were even convicted felons).[148] The Department of Transportation Inspector General found that in the years prior to 2001 undercover agents could readily penetrate security at most airports.[149] Indeed, just days after September 11, seven of twenty people carrying knives passed through security at Dulles Airport.[150]

It was against this background that Congress confronted the need to improve airport security. Senators John McCain and Ernest Hollings introduced a bill to federalize the airport security workforce that passed the Senate unanimously.[151] The bill required public employee screeners and also reformed the way law enforcement personnel were stationed at airport checkpoints.[152] After initially supporting the Senate bill, President Bush shifted to an alternative House bill designed to limit the federal role.[153] This bill would have installed federal supervisors at baggage and passenger screening checkpoints, but left the security workforce itself—the inspectors of passengers and baggage—in private hands.[154] Ultimately, support for complete federalization was so overwhelming[155] that the President relented.

The New Consensus

The Aviation and Transportation Security Act (ATSA) was passed by Congress and signed by the President on November 19, 2001.[156] ATSA created a new department, the Transportation Security Administration (TSA), within the Department of Transportation, and gave the TSA responsibility for aviation security.[157] The TSA was to federalize airport security screeners within one year. Screeners were required to speak and read English, be U.S. citizens, have no criminal record, and be high school graduates.[158] Screeners were also required to complete forty hours of classroom instruction and sixty hours of on-the-job instruction.[159] The act also provided for a pilot program to test private security personnel in up to five airports across the country.[160] In addition, airports were to be allowed to apply to reprivatize (as part of the Security Screening Opt-out Program) after November 19, 2004.[161]

The public employment status of airline security personnel counters the trends toward privatization of government functions discussed above. It is a prominent counterexample in a world of outsourced services. Democrats and Republicans realized the need for some changes in the status of airport security personnel, but the scope of those changes led to contentious debate. The Senate Democrats pushed for full federal employment.[162] The House Republicans responded by proposing a bill that only partially deprivatized the security personnel.[163] The White House sought to avoid what it saw as a needless increase in bureaucracy.[164] Given the Bush administration's commitment to privatization[165] and opposition to unions,[166] it is not surprising that it disfavored full federal employment.

But that is what it got—in passing a public employment bill that added 64,000 new federal employees,[167] Congress was swayed by arguments that U.S. airports, like borders, should be patrolled by federal personnel. The notion of private contractors conducting safety inspections struck both legislators and the public as a distortion of government responsibilities. By equating airport security officials with customs officials, Congress in effect endorsed the values of oath taking, badges, and public service itself.[168] But the public status of TSA's employees ran counter not only to the privatization trend in the United States, but to that in other countries with seemingly greater commitments to public sector solutions.[169]

The Values of Public Employment

The preference for public security officials at airports reflects unease about private contractors. Some members of Congress even raised questions about the loyalty of those employed by private firms to perform the inspection task.[170] The statutory requirements of absence of a criminal record and higher educational and training levels were meant to assure more reliable employees, and the requirement for U.S. citizenship was presumably meant to enhance loyalty.[171]

Yet these conditions could have been required of contract employees.[172] Since the privatization trend has already encompassed prison guards, military contractors, and others who are as much a part of the security network as TSA employees,[173] why curtail privatization in this instance? Something more was at work. President Bush, in his signing message, noted that "[f]or the first time, airport security will become a direct federal responsibility, overseen by [a] new undersecretary of transportation for security."[174] This uncharacteristic support for public solutions by a President committed to outsourcing can only be explained by the need to assure the public that airlines were secure. A similar phenomenon was at work in the seafood inspector setting described earlier.[175]

But public status itself does not assure superior performance. And carefully supervised private employees can be capable of effective inspections.[176] The government might have approached the issue differently. A careful analysis might have examined the nature of the jobs involved to determine whether they were "inherently governmental" or eligible for "competitive sourcing."[177] The OMB A-76 competitive sourcing process could have been employed to designate those jobs that were necessarily governmental and those that were eligible to be contracted out.[178] The airport security function could have been divided into separate components that would isolate jobs appropriate for private contractors. Inspectors with limited and nondiscretionary roles, such as those who check passenger baggage, would likely have been eligible for outsourcing. Those who supervised (and exercised judgment and discretion) would have retained governmental status.

Yet without requiring these "competitive" functions to be governmental, the goal of public reassurance might not have been achieved. Public status enhances credibility. The presence of an inspector with government authority calmed the public and achieved the overall goal of the program.[179] Government status reflects values that transcend the individual nature of the jobs being analyzed. There is something in our democratic system that puts symbolic as well as practical value on public service. It is what John Donahue calls "fidelity to the public's values."[180]

Privatization and Airport Screeners in Europe

During the debate over the airport security bill it was observed that European countries used private inspectors at airports.[181] European countries are known to be more public–sector oriented and comfortable with statist solutions than the United States.[182] Yet privatization of government jobs is a significant development in Europe. In the European Union (EU), the choice to employ public or private airport security personnel varies by state and the EU limits its role to setting common standards for airport security.[183] These standards require public oversight but permit the employment of private contractors in the airport security setting.

The standards cover use of airport security equipment, the requirement of background checks for security personnel, and provision for unannounced inspections of individual airport security arrangements.[184] The choice between public or private providers of security is not dictated by these standards. Thus, the function of baggage and passenger inspections can be delegated to private actors. German law, for example, embraces a concept of "functional privatization" which allows entities to receive assistance from private parties.[185] This delegation to private hands is not absolute, however. Under German law, the delegation must be supervised by a public official, administrative procedures necessary to protect individuals must remain in place, and decisions that affect individuals must be made by public officials.[186]

These procedural protections assure public oversight of the airport inspection process, but they also permit employment of private screeners at many European airports. Member state and EU common control standards help determine when public officials should be required to perform "public" functions. They are reminiscent of OMB's A-76 inherent government activities standards.[187]

Reconciling the Use of Public and Private Officials in Airport Security
The United States has set limits in the kind of government jobs that can be privatized, not the kind that can be made public.[188] Functions that are "inherently governmental" are explicitly excluded from outsourcing. The distinction between competitive and inherent functions is not easy to apply, however. Indeed, the A-76 process shares some of the ambiguities surrounding public service jobs under EU law.[189]

Suppose TSA were to put public inspectors up for competitive sourcing under A-76, as it might do if more airports sought exemptions from the current rules. TSA employees would likely argue that they performed inherently governmental functions, but would they prevail?

Security is a core role of government, yet government still delegates aspects of that function to private hands, as the use of private security in Iraq dramatically demonstrates. It is the level and degree of the delegation that must be analyzed. The act of screening passengers or baggage is a limited assignment; properly supervised, it does not seem to require a government presence.[190] Certainly it does not in Europe. And Congress could have voted the other way on TSA officials here— at least as to the inspection function performed by those officials.[191] So the inspection function itself seems not to be inherently governmental.

However, placing public oversight and control in private hands (outsourcing the entire process) is a different matter. The Undersecretary of Homeland Security is required to perform these functions. They are inherently governmental and thus nondelegable. This would be true under A-76 and also under statutory and constitutional principles.

The need for supervision and control are indicators of inherent functions. While the actual inspections are relatively limited and discrete assignments that may be delegated,[192] the responsibility to ensure proper performance by such personnel remains a governmental one. European countries permit private airport inspectors but only if they are controlled, trained, and overseen by public officials. We seem to have reached the same conclusion. In the limited opt-out context for five airports that were exempted from the Act, the Undersecretary of Homeland Security still must oversee the private contractors.[193] In this context, expanding the number of airport opt-outs would not be problematic from a public-private responsibility perspective.

ESTABLISHING PUBLIC REQUIREMENTS FOR AIRPORT SECURITY

If one were doing a simple make-or-buy choice,[194] outsourcing airport security could be competitively bid to determine which provider would perform better and at what cost. So long as the elements of the service could be measured and priced in advance, the case for privatization could be made. Indeed, in terms of inspector quality, airport security studies do not reveal a performance edge on government over private inspectors.[195]

The private advantage, if there is one, is confined to the actual inspection process, however. Determining how privatized employees are supervised and trained remains a governmental function. In the United States and Europe these jobs are placed in government hands in order to protect the public. Public officials perform oversight duties that involve matters of judgment, control, and responsibility. The harder their jobs are to describe in contractual terms, the harder they are to privatize. At some level, they may even be nondelegable.

Consider the earlier argument about the nondelegability of significant authority by officers of the United States. In the military setting, those officers (lieutenants and above) perform functions that cannot be delegated but their subordinates (privates and noncommissioned officers) may, like airport inspectors, have their duties delegated to private contractors.

The EU's airport security directives addressed these issues,[196] and Congress did as well in establishing the TSA. Should decisions be made to privatize the airport security function, oversight remains the function of government. Whether or not public oversight is effective can still be debated, but there is no doubt where the responsibility lies.

APPLYING THEORIES OF PUBLIC CONTROL

Assuming that airport screeners perform delegable duties, how far up the chain of command can the public role be delegated without abandoning the government's responsibility to govern? John Donahue views this question from the dual perspective of efficiency and public management.[197] He argues that government should choose the best structure (public or private) necessary to assure accountability.[198] In so doing, he grants the accountability criterion priority over efficiency in public decisionmaking.[199]

Accountability, in the form of process and oversight, has long been recognized as the necessary condition for effective privatization.[200] Delegations to private hands that ignore the accountability criterion are inherently suspect, whatever their efficiency advantage. But that broad proposition must be focused on the tasks at hand. Since security is an essential public function, privatization must be integrated into the framework of security, not the other way around. In terms of airport security, this requires a careful analysis of the various functions performed by the officials involved. The crucial accountability/efficiency question is not whether specific arrangements are outsourced, but whether those performing the inspection functions are properly supervised. As long as the delegated assignments are clearly defined and limited by contract,[201] and the oversight function is publicly performed, the private delegation can be accommodated.

Conclusion

This chapter has addressed questions about the threat privatization poses to democratic governance. The examples provided raise concerns about a practice that sometimes ignores limits set by statute, administrative rules, and even the Constitution. The constitutional case reminds us that the government service is built into our democratic system. The courts are involved because of the significant authority requirement *Buckley* placed upon "Officers of the United States." Across the last three administrations the executive branch has interpreted significant authority and related criteria of duration and permanency to be constitutional necessities.

Congress has a constitutional stake in this determination as well, since it participates in the process that creates officers of the United

States. The Appointments Clause is the relevant constitutional requirement. And Congress's role is also seen in terms of the Subdelegation Act, which tracks the constitutional arguments by statute. The Act can be interpreted as a limitation on the power of the executive to delegate. It supports a constitutional theory of nondelegation of inherently governmental functions to private hands.

Privatization is also constrained under OMB's Circular A-76. The A-76 process not only fosters competitive sourcing, but also addresses the inherent nature of government activities. Properly applied, the process can help restore balance to the movement toward private delegation. Competitive sourcing surely adds a valuable dimension to government, and outsourced services are often in the interests of efficient public management. But the limits upon competitive sourcing are constitutionally based—*Buckley*'s significant authority requirement is connected to the concept of inherently governmental functions. The challenge for government is to judge these delegations from the perspective that preserves the duty to govern. This is no easy sell in an era of privatization. Leslie Green has stated, "The idea that our leaders might have a fundamental duty to govern and to bear responsibility for doing so seems quaint."[202] We are in need of some quaintness in this regard.

The story is not only about erroneous delegations of significant authority—as may be happening, for example, with the use of private security firms in Iraq or contractors employed by FEMA or other agencies. Sometimes the public solution is chosen when it need not be. The airport security experience cuts in the other direction. After September 11, 2001, Congress and the President created over 60,000 governmental positions. The reasons for doing so are important to understand as a political matter. But they may have represented an overreaction to legitimate needs for public oversight and control. The TSA stands as a reminder that our political leaders sometimes see public solutions as more reliable and defensible in times of stress.

Still, the pressures are more in the direction of excessive outsourcing of government functions. Ultimately, government cannot function effectively if it fails to retain and adequately staff those positions that assure public control of public functions. The burden of this chapter is to alert us to these changes and restore more balance in the public provision of services. And it concludes that some duties are nondelegable or are delegable only with Congress's participation. In sum, governance is too important to be left to the private sector.

CHAPTER THIRTEEN

Public Values / Private Contract

Laura A. Dickinson

Domestic law scholars and policymakers have long debated the question of whether privatization undermines core public law values in the United States.[1] Yet with both nation states and international organizations increasingly privatizing foreign affairs functions, privatization is now as significant a phenomenon internationally as it is domestically. Indeed, even beyond the military outsourcing addressed elsewhere in this volume, states and international organizations are entering into more and more agreements with private nonprofit and for-profit entities to deliver all forms of aid, including humanitarian relief, development assistance, and post-conflict reconstruction.[2] Private actors, in conjunction with governments and international organizations, are even undertaking diplomatic tasks such as peacekeeping negotiations.[3]

Although widespread privatization in the international sphere potentially threatens a variety of what we might call public law values—human rights norms, norms against corruption and waste, and democratic process values[4]—traditional forms of public international law are unlikely to offer mechanisms that would provide an effective response. First, many international law norms, like domestic constitutional norms, apply primarily to states. Second, even if such norms were expanded (either through formal amendment or through judicial interpretation) to apply to government contractors, the apparatus of international law enforcement is sufficiently weak that only a very small handful of bad actors are likely ever to be held to account. Accordingly, those nongovernmental organizations (NGOs), policymakers, activists, lawyers, and scholars most interested in assuring accountability in an era of privatization might profitably turn their attention toward alternative paths.

And ironically, the very government contracting that is the engine of privatization itself opens the space for an intriguing set of accountability mechanisms. These contracts could be reformed to include many provisions that would help to create standards of behavior, performance benchmarks, and a means of enforcement in domestic courts. This chapter sets forth nine such provisions, arguing that contracts be drafted to (1) explicitly extend relevant norms of public international law to private contractors, (2) specify training requirements, (3) provide for enhanced monitoring both within the government and by independent third-party monitors, (4) establish clear performance benchmarks, (5) require accreditation, (6) mandate self-evaluation by the contractors, (7) provide for governmental takeovers of failing contracts, (8) include opportunities for public participation in the contract negotiation process, and (9) enhance whistleblower protections and rights of third-party beneficiaries to enforce contractual terms.

Together, such provisions may help to ensure that private contractors are accountable both to the publics they serve and to those who are most affected by their work. In some cases, implementing these proposals would merely require government actors to better fund existing contract programs and to better enforce statutory and regulatory terms now in force. For example, there is no question that simply providing better monitoring of existing contractual provisions would significantly enhance accountability. But as this chapter makes clear, the reform task cannot stop there. Thus, many of the proposals I suggest would involve important changes both to the language of the contracts themselves and the way that they are supervised. Such proposals draw on reforms that have already been implemented to a large degree in domestic privatization contracts.

In discussing these various reform possibilities, I will use Iraq as a case study, and I will examine all of the publicly available contracts the U.S. government has negotiated to support the U.S. military or to provide for foreign aid to Iraq. In some ways, of course, Iraq presents a particularly hard case for these reform proposals because of the heightened security concerns that accompany wartime contracting. Although such security concerns might make some reforms more difficult, most of these proposals could plausibly be adopted in ways that would not compromise security. And of course, many contracts negotiated by states or international organizations with contractors providing a variety of foreign-affairs functions do not involve such wartime exigencies.

Although the contract-based approach to accountability that I propose is obviously not a panacea, it may be at least as effective as the relatively weak enforcement regime of public international law. Moreover, the contractual mechanisms I discuss are particularly important in the foreign affairs context because many of these contracts are negotiated in secret, without competition, on a "no-bid basis," based on exceptions to the normal requirements of the Federal Acquisition Regulations (FAR).[5] For example, with respect to the U.S. government's foreign affairs contracts in Iraq, in many cases it is impossible for the public or a watchdog group even to obtain the texts of the contracts, either because government officials have kept them secret for security reasons[6] or because the contractors have exercised what is essentially a veto, under the Freedom of Information Act (FOIA), on the release of certain types of commercial information.[7] Problems posed by secrecy are reinforced by conflict-of-interest problems because many of the contracts are awarded to firms run by former government personnel. A recent study by the Center for Public Integrity reports that 60 percent of the companies that received contracts in Iraq or Afghanistan "had employees or board members who either served in or had close ties to the executive branch for Republican and Democratic administrations, for members of Congress of both parties, or at the highest levels of the military."[8] Thus, it is essential that, at the very least, the contracts themselves incorporate public values.

Of course, one might think that any proposal to reform the government contracting process is unrealistic because one of the main reasons governments privatize is precisely to avoid the kind of accountability I propose. Yet governments are not monolithic, and there are undoubtedly many people within bureaucracies, such as contract monitors, who honestly wish to do their jobs well and would therefore welcome (and lobby for) contractual mechanisms that increase accountability.[9] In addition, sometimes contractors themselves seek greater oversight. For example, the International Peace Operations Association (IPOA), a U.S.-based industry group, has developed a code of conduct that requires companies to accept that they will be bound by international humanitarian and human-rights-law norms.[10] Indeed, many private military companies are eager for more regulation and accreditation requirements, in part because they want to distinguish themselves from what they view as "rogue" outfits that give the industry as a whole a bad name, or because they wish to create higher barriers to entry for new firms. Finally, and perhaps most importantly, NGOs and international organizations can adopt some of the reforms I propose (such as creating accreditation standards) even *without* government action, and their work can sometimes pressure states to adopt more comprehensive oversight regimes. The problem is that policymakers and scholars have not sufficiently focused on privatization or the possible accountability mechanisms that could be embodied in contracts. Thus, the primary aim of this chapter is to raise awareness about the ways in which contractual provisions might embody public law values and to stimulate a broader-ranging debate about the best way to respond to privatization in the international context.

Contracts between governmental entities and the private organizations providing services can themselves serve as vehicles to promote public law values. Contractual terms can specify norms and structure the contractual relationship in ways that spur contractors to implement those norms. Thus, although typically conceived as the quintessential private law form, contracts used in this way can be a tool to "publicize" the privatization relationship.[11]

Administrative law scholars have explored this insight in the domestic context. Most notably, Jody Freeman has suggested that states "could require compliance with both procedural and substantive standards that might otherwise be inapplicable or unenforceable against private providers" and could mandate that personnel receive training equivalent to that of analogous state actors.[12] Contracts could also require compliance with specific performance standards and include performance benchmarks, graduated penalties, oversight by contract managers or independent observers, and reporting requirements.[13] Along with these front-end contractual terms to enhance accountability, contracts could also encourage back-end enforcement in the courts when these mechanisms fail. For example, contracts could explicitly permit third-party beneficiary suits and even allow relevant interest groups to bring suit in some contexts.[14]

Despite this extensive work in the domestic setting, however, few if any international law scholars, policymakers, or NGOs have considered the possibilities of using contractual terms in the international context. This lack of attention is due largely to the fact that international law scholars have not focused on privatization specifically. Instead, they have usually conceptualized the problem as one involving nonstate actors more generally. As a result, with the rise of each new category of nonstate actor, international law scholars, practitioners, and sometimes judges have primarily responded by seeking to bring that nonstate actor within the ambit of formal international legal instruments. Accordingly, they have argued either that the law should expand to reach each type of nonstate entity,[15] or that courts should impose liability on nonstate actors linked to the state.[16] And though literature on corporate responsibility,[17] NGOs,[18] soft law,[19] and transnational networks[20] has attempted to address some informal modes of accountability, the failure to discuss contract is notable.

Accordingly, I seek to bridge the gap between domestic administrative law and international law scholarship by addressing specific contractual mechanisms that might be used to extend public law values to privatized foreign affairs. Building on domestic scholars' insights, I discuss nine possible types of provisions that could be incorporated into government contracts in the foreign affairs context.

Incorporating Public Law Standards in Contractual Terms

First, of course, the contracts could explicitly require that the contractors obey the norms that implement public law values. Specifically, the terms of each agreement could provide that private contractors must abide by relevant legal rules applicable to governmental actors. Contractual terms would thus eliminate any ambiguity created by the state action requirement in existing domestic and international legal regimes.

In the domestic setting, such provisions are commonplace. As a term in their contracts with privately run prisons, for example, many states require compliance with constitutional, federal, state, and private standards for prison operation and inmates' rights.[21] In addition, contractual agreements may require contractors to provide for hearings and review of contractor actions.[22]

The U.S. government's military and foreign aid contracts in Iraq, by contrast, are woefully inadequate on this score. To be sure, a 2005 Department of Defense (DOD) document providing general instructions regarding contracting practices does state that contractors "shall abide by applicable laws, regulations, DOD policy, and international agreements."[23] Yet, of the sixty publicly available Iraq contracts,[24] none contains specific provisions requiring contractors to obey human rights, anticorruption, or transparency norms. The agreements between the U.S. government and CACI International, Inc., to supply military interrogators starkly illustrate this point. The intelligence personnel were hired pursuant to a standing "blanket purchase agreement" between the Department of the Interior and CACI, negotiated in 2000.[25] Under such an agreement the procuring agency need not request specific services at the time the agreement is made, but rather may enter task orders as the need arises. In 2003, eleven task orders worth $66.2 million, none of which was the result of competitive bidding, were entered.[26] The orders specify only that CACI would provide interrogation support and analysis work for the U.S. Army in Iraq, including "debriefing of personnel, intelligence report writing, and screening/interrogation of detainees at established holding areas."[27] Significantly, the orders do not expressly require that the private contractor interrogators comply with international human rights or humanitarian law rules such as those contained either in the United Nations Convention on Torture or the Geneva Conventions. Likewise, although the contractors are subject to international and domestic laws prohibiting the bribery of government officials,[28] none of the contracts specifically prohibits the contractors themselves from accepting bribes, an area that remains ambiguous in domestic and international law. Similarly, the contracts do not provide terms specifying the applicability of FOIA, which would help make contractor activities more transparent.

Requiring That Private Contractors Receive Training

Foreign affairs contracts could also explicitly require that contractors receive training in activities that would promote public law values. Such training, as a contractual requirement, could help instill a sense of the importance of these values in contractor employees. At the same time, training could provide employees with concrete recommendations about how to implement these values in specific, challenging situations.

Again, in the domestic setting such training provisions are commonplace. A standard term in state agreements with companies that manage private prisons, for example, requires companies to certify that the training they provide to personnel is comparable to that offered to state employees.[29] Such training would normally include instruction concerning legal limits on the use of force and examples of what those limits mean in circumstances likely to arise in the prison setting.

Yet while the 2005 DOD instructions require documentation of training concerning appropriate use of force,[30] none of the publicly available Iraq contracts appears to require such training. Indeed, although a few of the agreements require that contractors hire employees with a certain number of years' experience,[31] none specifies that the contractor must provide any particular training at all. For example, the U.S. government's agreement with Chugach McKinley, Inc., to screen and hire a broad range of military support personnel—from doctors to "special mission advisers"—says nothing about whether such personnel will receive training in applicable international law standards, even though they may be in a position to commit abuses.[32] The U.S. government's agreements with CACI to provide interrogators are likewise completely silent on whether interrogators will receive education in international humanitarian and human rights law, training that U.S. military interrogators would normally receive.[33] It is not surprising, then, that an Army Inspector General report on the conditions that led to the Abu Ghraib scandal concluded that 35 percent of CACI's Iraqi interrogators did not even have any "formal training in military interrogation policies and techniques," let alone training in international law norms.[34] This omission is particularly glaring given the highly volatile Iraq environment.

Anticorruption training would also be useful for foreign affairs contractors generally, and for contracts in Iraq specifically. Iraq ranks among the worst countries in the world on Transparency International's corruption index,[35] and it is no surprise that such corruption reaches U.S. contractors operating there. For example, one former Coalition Provisional Authority (CPA) official, Alan Grayson, has asserted that lack of employee screening, training, and internal oversight mechanisms led to shocking abuses committed by Custer Battles, a company that was awarded two $16 million contracts by the U.S. Agency for International Development (USAID) to provide security for the Baghdad airport and to distribute Iraqi dinars.[36] Custer Battles employees reportedly chartered a flight to Beirut with $10 million in new Iraqi dinars in their luggage,[37] set up sham Cayman Islands subsidiaries to submit invoices, and regularly overcharged for materials—in one case billing the United States $10 million for materials that it purchased for $3.5 million.[38] Yet aid contracts, like the one with Custer Battles, generally say nothing about training for contractors in how to screen and monitor employees so as to avoid corruption. And while training requirements undoubtedly would increase the cost of the contracts, the fraud and waste that could be deterred with better training might well offset such increases.

Enhancing Contractual Monitoring, Both by Internal Governmental Actors and by Third Parties

Provisions could also be made for increased contract monitoring, which could provide an important check on abuses. Such monitoring should include, to begin with, sufficient numbers of trained and experienced governmental contract monitors. At the same time, governmental ombudspersons—leaders of independent offices charged with providing enhanced oversight—could serve as an important supplement to the contract monitors. Thus, at a minimum, it is essential that government agencies devote enough resources to ensure that these requirements are implemented in a meaningful way. In addition, outside independent NGOs, both for-profit and nonprofit, can serve an important function by monitoring contracts.

Contracts for services in the domestic context regularly include this three-tiered monitoring structure: government personnel assigned as contract monitors, supplemented by agency actors such as ombudspersons, further supplemented by independent outside groups. In the privatized health care context, for example, where private nursing homes receive Medicaid funding and private hospitals receive Medicare and Medicaid support, the trend is toward agreements that require a state-appointed contract manager.[39] Federal agencies such as the Department of Health and Human Services (whose inspector general issues reports on contracts with private hospitals that receive public funding)[40] and the Health Care Financing Administration (which exerts fairly tight control over private nursing homes receiving Medicaid funding)[41] also have significant oversight authority. In addition, third-party independent organizations play an important role. For example, the Joint Commission on Health Care and Accreditation of Health Organizations (JCAHO), certifies health care institutions for compliance with federal regulations and state licensure laws.[42]

Foreign affairs contracts currently provide for far less monitoring. To be sure, the statutory and regulatory scheme includes provisions for governmental contract monitors, supplemented by inspectors general of the respective agencies responsible for the contracts,[43] as well as for auditing of contracts by independent private accounting firms.[44] Yet the work of these monitors focuses primarily on whether the contractors are keeping adequate accounts and refraining from fraud and bribery. Contracts say little about human rights norms, and governmental contract monitors and ombudspersons are not ordinarily focused on these values when scrutinizing contractors.[45] To the extent that independent third-party groups are empowered to monitor under the contract, these third parties tend to be auditing firms that are better equipped to offer expertise in financial matters than in international human rights or humanitarian law. Foreign affairs contracts rarely, if ever, provide for monitoring by independent groups with expertise in this area.[46]

Moreover, in practice, foreign affairs contracts tend to escape even this limited oversight. This is because many of the monitoring requirements tend not to apply in emergency situations, which are, of course, precisely the occasions when military intervention or humanitarian relief efforts and post-reconstruction aid are most likely. Thus, ordinary contracting procedures, such as competitive bidding, are often waived.[47] In addition, many of the contracts are written as cost reimbursement contracts—often termed "cost plus" agreements—under which the government reimburses the contractor for costs incurred in providing a service, plus a fee that is calculated as a percentage of the cost.[48] Though often criticized as leading to waste and abuse,[49] such contracts become the norm in emergency situations, rather than the exception. At the same time, too few contract monitors are appointed, those who are appointed lack expertise, and ombudspersons are not given the resources they need to do an effective job.

The monitoring of the Iraq contracts, or virtual lack thereof, provides a salient example. The government agencies with responsibility for the contracts—primarily USAID, DOD, and the now-dismantled Coalition Provisional Authority—devoted extraordinarily minimal resources to monitoring.[50] For example, USAID has responsibility for approximately $3 billion in reconstruction projects,[51] but the agency had only four contract monitoring personnel on the ground as of March 2003.[52] In fact, due to the difficulties of monitoring contracts with so little staff, USAID determined to contract out the monitoring function itself.[53] Likewise, a DOD Inspector General study concluded that more than half of the Iraq contracts had not been adequately monitored.[54] This fact is not surprising given that DOD's acquisition workforce was reduced by more than half between 1990 and 2001, while the department's contracting workload increased by more than 12 percent. In addition, those who were assigned to monitor contract performance were often inadequately trained.[55] Finally, in an ironic twist, private contractors themselves are often hired to write the procedures governing contracting rules and monitoring protocols, thus leading to further conflict-of-interest problems. Indeed, the DOD handbook on the contracting process was drafted by one of its principal military contractors.[56]

The CPA was plagued with similar problems. A recent report notes that the CPA hadn't kept accounts for the hundreds of millions of dollars of cash in its vault, had awarded contracts worth billions of dollars to American firms without tender, and had no idea what was happening to the money from the Development Fund for Iraq which was being spent by the interim Iraqi government ministries.[57]

One former CPA official has observed that, as a result of poor oversight, "contracts were made that were mistakes, and were poorly, if at all, supervised [and] money was spent that could have been saved, if we simply had the right numbers of people."[58] For example, even devoting a single staff person to the two $16 million Custer Battles contracts that gave rise to multiple instances of fraud and abuse[59] would have saved at least $4 million.[60]

Finally, the dispersal of authority to issue foreign affairs contracts across multiple agencies creates interagency communication problems and conflicts of interest that impede oversight.[61] For example, officials at different agencies use different methods to calculate the costs of contracts, and these methods may also vary from those used by the companies themselves.[62] In addition, because agencies can earn fees for facilitating other agencies' contracts but are not adequately held to account for monitoring those contracts, agencies have incentives to sponsor other agencies' contracts but little incentive to supervise them.[63] These arrangements can lead to abuse, as occurred in the case of the Department of the Interior sponsorship of DOD's task orders for intelligence services at Abu Ghraib prison under an existing contract between CACI and the Interior Department.[64]

In short, foreign affairs contracts could provide far better protections for public law values through greater monitoring. Although the statutory and regulatory regime contemplates a combination of supervision by contract monitors, independent agency oversight through inspectors general, and limited financial auditing by third-party entities, these provisions have not worked well in practice due to insufficient staffing and resources, combined with the large number of contracts. To be sure, statutory and regulatory reforms could address these problems. But, alternatively, the contracts themselves could remedy these deficiencies to some extent, by specifying greater numbers of monitors and requiring that they possess a certain degree of training, as well as by allowing for independent oversight by third-party groups such as the International Committee of the Red Cross (ICRC).

One might, at first blush, think that greater monitoring would be difficult amidst the exigencies and security concerns of a wartime mobilization. Yet part of the solution is simply to realize that, in an era of private military contracting, DOD and similar agencies must keep an adequate number of contract monitors permanently on staff and provide them with ongoing training in order to help them spot abuses relating both to costs and to substantive problems like human rights violations. Moreover, to the extent that new monitors must be hired at the time of mobilization, such hiring is not so difficult given the huge amounts of money flowing to these contracts. Indeed, simply ensuring that a small percentage of each contractual fee gets allocated to monitoring would go a long way towards relieving the monitoring deficiency. Both these monitors and the independent inspectors general discussed above are already agency employees and therefore would (or easily could) possess adequate clearances to address potential security concerns. Third-party monitors are, of course, more difficult from a security perspective, but certainly the ICRC has a long history of monitoring prisons during wartime and has effectively preserved secrecy. Thus, there is no reason to think that adequate monitoring is an impractical goal.

Laying Out Clear Performance Benchmarks

Of course, increased contract monitoring can only be fully effective to the extent that the contracts have clear benchmarks against which to measure compliance. In the domestic context, commentators and policymakers have long urged that contracts include benchmarks, and rigorous performance standards regularly appear in contracts.[65] Scholars have argued that, ideally, performance-based contracts should "clearly spell out the desired end result" but leave the choice of method to the contractor, who should have "as much freedom as possible in figuring out how to best meet government's performance objective."[66]

These ideas have been implemented most notably in contracts with private prisons. For example, under the model contract for private prison management drafted by the Oklahoma Department of Corrections, contractors must meet delineated standards for security, meals, and education.[67] They must also certify that the training provided to personnel is comparable to that offered to state employees.[68] In Texas, contractors must abide by similar terms and, in addition, must "establish performance measures for rehabilitative programs."[69] In addition, the American Correctional Association (ACA) is revising its accreditation standards to include performance measures, and the Office of Juvenile Justice and Delinquency Prevention is developing performance-based standards for juvenile correctional facilities.[70] Commentators have noted, further, that performance measures for private prison operators could include both

> process measures such as the number of educational or vocational programs, or outcome measures such as the Logan quality of confinement index, the number of assaults, or the recidivism rate. Because no single statistic adequately captures 'quality,' and because focusing on any single measure could have perverse effects, performance-based contracts should tie compensation to a large and rich set of variables.[71]

Privatized welfare programs have also experimented with performance measures as a means to improve quality. In 1996, Congress authorized the implementation of welfare programs "through contracts with charitable, religious, or private organizations."[72] Since then, states have increasingly contracted with such organizations,[73] and many of these contracts contain performance benchmarks and output requirements.[74] For example, under a performance-based system, a welfare contractor might receive financial rewards for increasing the percentage of program participants who receive job placements.[75]

Foreign affairs contracts tend to be notably less rigorous in providing for performance measures. Although military service contracts are difficult to evaluate because so many of them are not publicly available, contract officers familiar with these contracts have remarked on their generally vague terms.[76] And the fact that they are often indefinite delivery/indefinite quantity contracts adds to their open-ended quality.[77] Under this structure, the government awards a contract that does not specify how many services or goods will be necessary or the dates upon which they will be required.[78] These additional details are specified in subsequent task orders, which themselves are often vague because they need not pass though the same degree of supervision as the initial contract award.[79] Of course, such contracts may sometimes be necessary, because the government cannot know in advance precisely what will be required or for how long.[80] Yet the lack of any administrable standards in these contracts can lead to significant abuses.[81]

Of the publicly available Iraq contracts for military services, it is striking that none contains clear benchmarks or output requirements. Instead, they are phrased in amorphous language that provides little opportunity for compliance evaluation. For example, a contract between the U.S. government and MPRI, Inc., to provide translators for government personnel, including interrogators, simply states that the contractors will supply interpreters.[82] The agreement says nothing about whether the interpreters must be effective or how effectiveness might be measured.[83] Similarly, the CACI task orders for interrogators specify only that CACI will provide interrogation support and analysis work for the U.S. Army in Iraq, including "debriefing of personnel, intelligence report writing, and screening/interrogation of detainees at established holding areas."[84] Other than these broad goals, the task orders say little more. To be sure, security concerns may require some degree of vagueness. Nonetheless, the task orders could be much more specific about training requirements, standards of conduct, supervision, and performance parameters.

Turning to the foreign aid context, agencies tend to promote the use of results-based agreements, under which contractors must demonstrate specific, tangible results that are to be evaluated by the agency.[85] Yet in practice many such agreements do not actually contain any results-based requirements, often because the aid, particularly in emergency relief settings, is provided on an expedited basis to organizations with very small staffs. With regard to Iraq, for example, a review of the publicly available USAID agreements reveals that only a few set forth specific performance benchmarks or requirements.[86]

To be sure, performance benchmarks that are too strict can pose problems. As scholars of domestic privatization have noted, discretion can serve useful goals; indeed, discretion is in part what makes privatization desirable, as private contractors have more flexibility than rule-bound bureaucratic actors to pursue innovative approaches.[87] Output requirements that preserve flexibility about the means to achieve results are therefore the most effective.[88] But even carefully tailored output requirements can go awry, as when, for example, private welfare providers "cream" those accepted into their programs in order to increase the percentage of those who receive job placements.[89] Moreover, output requirements can sometimes give contractors tunnel vision, leading them to focus only on the benchmarks, thereby missing opportunities to achieve wider benefits. A recent study of the enhanced "auditing" that accompanied privatization in Thatcherite Britain, for example, suggests that narrow output requirements steered organizations and individuals away from broader, more diffuse, social goals.[90]

In addition, by their very nature, results-based contracts raise difficult questions about how best to measure output. Creating benchmarks may be relatively straightforward if the project at issue involves simply building a bridge or dam, but it is very difficult to measure intangibles, such as fostering human development or building civil society.[91] Likewise, short-term results, such as whether food aid was delivered, are much easier to measure than longer-term systemic efforts to alleviate poverty, provide education, and so on. As a consequence, results-based contracts tend to put more emphasis on short-term delivery of services rather than longer-term impact.[92] Finally, of course, contractual output requirements do not necessarily ensure compliance, because contractors may simply fail to meet their goals. In addition, even the most detailed performance requirements and standards inevitably leave considerable discretion to the contractor.

Nonetheless, despite problems with overly rigid performance benchmarks, the foreign affairs contracts (at least those that are publicly available) appear to fall at the opposite end of the spectrum. Indeed, they possess so few benchmarks and output requirements that they contain no meaningful evaluative criteria whatsoever. In such circumstances, enhanced performance benchmarks could be a useful contractual tool.

Requiring That Contractors Receive Accreditation from Independent Organizations

Another contract-based tool for promoting public law values is accreditation. Independent organizations, often consisting of experts or professionals in the field, can evaluate and rate private contractors. These ratings can then be used in the contracting process because agreements can require that contractors receive certain rankings. Or governmental entities or international institutions, such as the United Nations, could develop accreditation regimes.

Again, the domestic context offers a particularly rich set of examples that could provide useful lessons in the foreign affairs setting. For example, in the field of publicly funded, privately provided health care, JCAHO accredits hospitals receiving Medicare and Medicaid funding. Indeed, such accreditation is required by statute as well as by contract.[93] State laws or contractual terms also often specify that health maintenance organizations must receive accreditation by the National Committee for Quality Assurance (NCQA), an independent non-profit organization, before receiving public funding.[94] Until recently, NCQA certification was primarily voluntary, offering health maintenance organizations an advantage when competing for lucrative health-care delivery contracts. When states became managed care purchasers, however, they adopted NCQA as a benchmark of quality.[95]

Similarly, many contracts with private prison operators require companies to receive accreditation by the American Correctional Association.[96] An organization of correctional professionals that has existed for over a century, the ACA accredits prisons and provides training for prison personnel while also setting standards that apply to virtually every aspect of prison operation.[97] Not only has ACA accreditation become a standard contract requirement,[98] but federal courts have used ACA standards to interpret constitutional and statutory provisions.[99] Even private investors look to accreditation as an indication of quality.[100] Thus, the accreditation requirement creates significant compliance incentives.

Privatized education regimes such as charter schools have also considered accreditation by independent organizations as a means of ensuring quality.[101] The focus of many independent organizations on facilities and administrative processes over underlying educational quality has led some critics to charge that educational accreditation is relatively ineffective.[102] Nonetheless, commentators have advocated improved accreditation procedures and greater use of such accreditation to promote public law values.[103]

Indeed, domestic administrative law scholars have noted that these independent, private accrediting entities are effectively setting the standards that give meaning to public law values.[104] In that regard, the relative insularity of the standard-setting and accreditation process may undermine the ability of broader groups, including consumers and the public at large, to participate in the process.[105] There is also the concern that private accreditors in some cases might be too close to the contractors, and therefore too lenient.[106] Nevertheless, even critics agree that the standards are often much better than those that would be developed by agency bureaucrats, and despite the imperfections, accreditation has served as an important check on the contracting process.[107]

In contrast, accreditation is glaringly absent in the foreign affairs context.[108] Human rights organizations, governments, and the United Nations have begun to encourage corporations, particularly those in the extraction industries, to comply with voluntary labor, environmental, and human rights standards.[109] A consortium of NGOs that deliver humanitarian relief has initiated the Sphere Project, which is an effort to set standards for the provision of humanitarian aid, including specific guidelines for field operations, training, and self-evaluation.[110] And, as discussed previously, an industry-founded association of private security companies, IPOA, has constructed a comprehensive code of conduct that includes human rights standards.[111] Nevertheless, neither the United Nations nor domestic governments nor outside groups concerned with potential abuses by foreign affairs contractors has so far undertaken serious efforts either to harness these nascent accreditation initiatives or to promote other accreditation projects.[112]

This failure is particularly striking in the Iraq context. Not one of the publicly available contracts for aid or military services requires that the entities receiving the contracts be vetted or accredited by independent organizations. For example, unlike domestic prison contracts, which routinely require accreditation by ACA and compliance with a comprehensive set of standards, the contracts with CACI to provide interrogators at Abu Ghraib contain only the most basic guidelines and make no mention of human rights compliance or accreditation requirements.[113] The contract between the U.S. government and Dyncorp International to provide law enforcement advisers to train Iraqi police similarly contains no provision mandating that Dyncorp be accredited,[114] even though Dyncorp employees were implicated in sex abuse when performing under a similar contract in Bosnia.[115] Likewise, although contracts could require that humanitarian aid organizations agree to the Sphere guidelines, no such requirement has been imposed.[116]

Yet such accreditation would seem to be particularly important in the foreign affairs area, where, as discussed previously, security concerns and special considerations often eliminate competition in the contracting process, resulting in contracts that are structured without the usual market controls. Significantly, the problem is not only that international organizations and domestic governments neglect to require accreditation in their contracts, but also that NGOs and other independent groups have not sought a robust accreditation role. After all, more NGOs could, as the Sphere Project has done in humanitarian aid, begin to rate military contractors independently, regardless of whether the government contracts require such accreditation. These ratings might then become an industry standard that the government could be persuaded to use as a contracting factor—a situation that occurred with NCQA in the domestic health-care context. And even if agency officials negotiating contracts choose not to impose accreditation requirements, the ratings could serve as a point of pressure in Congress and with the public at large. Thus, NGOs should spend at least as much energy developing accreditation regimes as they do pursuing transnational litigation under various formal international law instruments. International organizations could also seek to create accreditation regimes. Such accreditation would likely be influential over time, even if states at first refuse to implement accreditation requirements into their contracts formally.

Mandating Contractor Self-Evaluation

Contractors could also be required to perform self-evaluations as a way of enhancing accountability. Presented with an internal self-evaluation, an outside monitor, whether governmental or third party, can often scrutinize the contractor's performance more quickly and efficiently. Of course, self-evaluation gives the contractor discretion to massage the data and can, indeed, be subject to outright manipulation and abuse. Nonetheless, it can be a useful starting point for outside monitors, who at least can make a faster assessment at the outset as to whether the contractor has met the contract goals. In addition, self-evaluation can encourage more effective internal policing by the contractor.

Due to these potential benefits, self-evaluation has emerged as a frequently used tool in the domestic context. In the world of private prisons, for example, contractors regularly are subjected to self-evaluation requirements. In Texas, prison contractors must "establish performance measures for rehabilitative programs and develop a system to assess achievement and outcomes."[117] Likewise, in the field of health care a health maintenance organization must conduct continuous "quality improvement," in an ongoing internal self-evaluation process, if it is to receive accreditation.[118] Contracts that require accreditation thus effectively mandate such self-evaluation.

In the foreign affairs context, private foreign aid providers operating under agreements with USAID are regularly required to perform self-evaluation, but neither the foreign aid contracts provided through other agencies nor the military contracts more generally seem to contain such provisions. Again, taking the publicly available Iraq contracts as an example, none requires the private contractor to file self-evaluation reports, develop internal assessment practices, or otherwise engage in self-evaluation.[119] And while self-evaluation on its own is unlikely to improve contract compliance significantly, such self-evaluation can be useful in combination with some or all of the other contractual provisions discussed in this chapter.

Enhancing Governmental Termination Provisions and Allowing for Partial Governmental Takeover of Contracts

Contracts could also include terms allowing the relevant government (or international organization) to take over the contract by degrees before ultimately terminating the agreement for failure to observe provisions implementing public law values. Currently, most contracts allow, either implicitly or explicitly, only for outright termination for noncompliance. On its face such an outright termination provision seems as if it would provide a strong incentive for contractor compliance. In actual practice, however, outright termination is such an extreme measure that governments are often reluctant to invoke it, and because contractors know that termination is so unlikely, the provisions have almost no disciplining effect.

Thus, it would be better if such termination provisions were supplemented with more graduated penalties, such as provisions permitting the partial governmental takeover of contracts. Because graduated penalties are less extreme than outright termination, they are far more likely actually to be invoked by contract monitors, making them a more effective enforcement mechanism than the harsher, but rarely invoked, termination provisions. Moreover, if partial takeover fails to stem the abuses, outright termination still remains a penalty of last resort. In the domestic context, states are increasingly turning to mechanisms such as graduated penalties—to increase oversight of private nursing homes receiving public funding, for example.[120] Scholars and practitioners have also called for the use of such penalties in the private prison setting.[121]

Turning to foreign affairs, while some contracts do contain termination provisions, they are rarely exercised and are not supplemented by lesser, graduated penalties. As a result, the government has little leverage over contractors. The Iraq contracts provide a notable demonstration of this problem. When CACI employees were implicated in abuses at Abu Ghraib prison, for example, the U.S. government did not terminate its contract. Indeed, although the particular employees implicated in the abuse charges no longer work at CACI,[122] it is unclear whether government actors even so much as stepped up their supervision of the contracts. To the contrary, CACI actually received a contract *extension* for interrogation services.[123]

Obviously, governments (and international organizations) should be encouraged to invoke termination provisions when contractors fall short. But even without full termination of the contracts, graduated government (or international organization) takeover could provide an added incentive for contractors to promote public law values.

Allowing for Beneficiary Participation or Broader Public Involvement in Contract Design

Contracts could also permit beneficiaries or the broader public to help shape contract terms and evaluate performance. In the domestic context, commentators have suggested that such beneficiary participation or public involvement could greatly enhance the extent to which contractors fulfill public law values.[124] Indeed, as Alfred Aman has argued, precisely because privatization contracts are difficult to terminate and sometimes become "immutable," it is "important that the participation of the public and the public's representatives be maximized as early in the process as possible."[125] He thus advocates allowing the broader public to play a role in the design of the contracts themselves.[126]

Some state and local governments have begun to expand the public's role. For example, Wisconsin's contracts with managed care organizations to provide health care to Medicare and Medicaid recipients include provisions for participation by community groups.[127] Other states have gone even further and now require broad public involvement in virtually all privatization decisions. In Montana, for example, any privatization decision must be made subject to a plan available to the public and open to public comment.[128] Other states have similar provisions.[129]

Foreign affairs contracts might benefit from this approach. Indeed, such participation may be particularly important to promote public law values, because the ordinary democratic process open to those experiencing the effects of privatization in the domestic context is essentially unavailable for noncitizens outside the United States who are affected by the activities of contractors. To be sure, even in the domestic context, there has long been a worry that privatization removes a crucial democratic check on government. The link between those affected by government action and the government actors is attenuated when that activity is farmed out, first from legislatures to agencies and then from agencies to private contractors. Scholars and policymakers worry that this form of delegation reduces transparency, which in turn reduces the ability of those affected to vote their preferences when things are not going well.[130] But when governments turn to private contractors to perform foreign affairs functions, the problem increases exponentially because many of the people affected by the contracts in question do not belong to the U.S. democratic polity or indeed any democratic polity at all. Moreover, U.S. citizens may be less inclined to use the democratic process to voice their views when the effects of contracting are felt mainly overseas.

While it may make less sense to allow involvement of those noncitizens affected by military contractors overseas, due to obvious security concerns, beneficiary involvement or broader public participation in the design and evaluation of foreign aid contracts might be particularly useful. Governments providing long-term development aid through private organizations have to some degree already begun to adopt this approach. In the United States, USAID has allowed local beneficiaries and NGOs to help design development aid agreements, usually on an informal basis, and most frequently when such agreements are negotiated through field offices.[131] Agencies other than USAID, however, are less likely to engage in such consultation.[132] Humanitarian aid and postconflict reconstruction assistance are also less likely to incorporate such an approach, though recently the United Nations High Commissioner for Refugees has begun to explore the possibility of evaluation of humanitarian aid by refugees and internally displaced persons.[133]

It must be left for another day to provide a more detailed discussion of how best to maximize opportunities for those affected by a foreign aid project to participate in the design of that project.[134] Certainly, the idea raises a whole host of practical problems. For example, it will be difficult to determine who exactly can speak for an affected population. Is NGO participation sufficient? How does one determine which civil society actors are most representative? What if different sectors of the population disagree as to the efficacy of a proposed project? Even assuming one determines the appropriate voices, what form should the feedback take? Is informal consultation enough? Or should there be a more formal notice and comment period? Is it necessary to establish an independent tribunal with the power to quash the project altogether? And should such a tribunal be governmental or private? While these questions certainly must be addressed, it seems that if we are asking them, we will already have advanced the debate quite a bit. The important point for now is that we must at the very least begin to explore ways of involving those affected by foreign affairs agreements in the contracting process itself. Explicit contractual requirements would go a long way toward facilitating consultation with beneficiary populations, thereby effectuating through contract a broader form of public participation.

Strengthening Enforcement Mechanisms

Finally, contracts could provide for enhanced enforcement mechanisms. Contracts could, for example, give beneficiaries the opportunity for privatized administrative hearings. Additionally, contracts might include third-party beneficiary suit provisions, empowering contract beneficiaries or other interested parties to sue in domestic courts for breach of contract. And whistleblower protections might be enhanced. All of these measures would likely increase compliance with contractual terms.

In the domestic context, governments and policymakers have begun to implement such measures, though private grievance procedures remain more prevalent than broader third-party beneficiary suit provisions and whistleblower protections. Commentators regularly call for an expansion of third-party beneficiary suit provisions[135] (which must be clearly specified in the contract because courts generally refuse to impute them),[136] but such provisions remain rare. Many private contractors providing aid, however, do offer individual complaint mechanisms for affected beneficiaries.[137] Although these aid providers are not state actors and would therefore generally be immune from constitutional review, such contractual provisions do allow for notice and opportunity to be heard, thereby incorporating elements of constitutional due process. These private grievance systems are perhaps most evident in contracts with private prison operators, which typically require such mechanisms.[138] But they appear in other contexts as well, such as health care. For example, the Medicare statute requires that health maintenance organizations receiving federal funding to cover their treatment of Medicare beneficiaries "provide meaningful procedures for hearing and resolving grievances between the organization . . . and members enrolled."[139]

Governments might experiment with similar measures in the foreign affairs arena.[140] The World Bank has taken steps in this direction, by enabling aid beneficiaries to bring grievances before special tribunals challenging gross abuses.[141] Third-party beneficiary suit provisions, however, are virtually nonexistent, and none of the Iraq contracts contains such a provision. Contracts could also enhance whistleblower protections in order to strengthen enforcement. U.S. government officials currently receive whistleblower protection for reporting abuses in the negotiation or management of contracts, but employees of private companies are not protected under the general Whistleblower Protection Act.[142] In specific statutes, however, Congress has at times extended whistleblower protection to private employees, and the False Claims Act does protect private sector employees working for a government contractor from retaliation for providing information concerning the unlawful performance of the contract.[143] The Act also provides for *qui tam* actions to encourage such employees to come forward.[144] Significantly, however, the False Claims Act only applies to fiscal fraud and abuse by contractors; it does not protect employee whistleblowers who might report human rights or other abuses committed by contractors. Thus, the False Claims Act's whistleblower protections (and possibly its *qui tam* provisions as well) should be expanded in the foreign affairs context either by statute or as a default contractual provision. Such a change, combined with the availability of third-party beneficiary suits, would go a long way towards making sure that any contract-based efforts to provide accountability will have back-end enforcement to encourage compliance. Short of that, contractors could at least be required to provide their own private grievance mechanisms, which would afford some opportunity for those affected by a contract to complain about its design or implementation.

International law scholars, policymakers, and advocates can no longer afford to ignore privatization. Indeed, if anything the scope and pace of privatization in the international arena is increasing. Moreover, it will not be sufficient merely to tweak existing international law treaties or doctrines (or even invent new ones) in order to bring state actors within the ambit of formal international law. After all, even if international or domestic courts could be convinced that private contractors should be treated as state actors (which is far from certain), international and transnational public law litigation will never be able to hold more than a handful of people accountable. Accordingly, those who seek to preserve or expand the values embodied in public international law will need to look elsewhere to find mechanisms for ensuring accountability in a privatized world.

In this chapter, I have suggested one such mechanism: the government contract that creates the privatized relationship in the first place. Drawing on the far more extensive domestic administrative law literature on the subject, I have identified a variety of provisions that could be incorporated into such contracts. These provisions seek to encourage compliance with and enforcement of human rights and humanitarian law, to ensure transparency and democratic accountability, and to promote norms against corruption, waste, and fraud. Taken together, the suggested provisions provide a menu of options for regulators, activists, policymakers, and scholars who are concerned about the potential for abuse in our current contracting processes.

Of course, governments may be hesitant to insist on some of these contractual provisions. For example, officials may fear that such requirements could unduly increase the costs of privatization both to the contractor and to the government entity overseeing the contract.[145] Or to take a more cynical view, resistance might stem from the fact that governments actually benefit from a more opaque process with less public oversight. In any event, one seeming difficulty with relying on contractual provisions is that the increased oversight will be included in contracts only as a matter of legislative or executive grace, and therefore can be rescinded or limited at any time.[146]

Yet such objections do not render a contractual approach unrealistic. To begin with, concerns about the cost of additional contractual requirements may well be overstated. As the Custer Battles fiasco makes clear, in many cases better oversight could actually save the government far more money than it costs. And as to concerns that added contractual provisions will cause contractors to walk away or prohibitively raise their rates, the short answer is that far more empirical work must be done to assess whether such dire predictions are accurate. After all, it seems quite unlikely that contractors bidding for these extraordinarily lucrative contracts with governments such as the United States will pull out of the process just because of some added contract requirements. To the contrary, the government should, by all rights, have tremendous leverage in the contracting process because there are unlikely to be competing customers similarly able to offer billions of dollars in contract awards. Indeed, while government contractors in the past have often objected to enhanced contractual oversight by raising concerns about increased compliance costs,[147] at least one commentator has challenged such claims, noting the absence of compelling evidence that increased oversight (for example, through *qui tam* suits) has resulted in a significant number of firms refusing to do business with the government.[148]

In addition, while some governmental officials surely would prefer a more opaque process, governments are not monolithic entities, and proposals such as the ones outlined in this chapter may be taken up and championed by members of the bureaucracy, even without the imprimatur of higher-level executive branch officials or the legislature. Moreover, it is incorrect to think that more robust contractual monitoring can only come about through official executive branch or legislative action. First of all, some of the proposals for monitoring of contracts and accreditation or rating of contractors could be undertaken by NGOs or other groups without any official action whatsoever. While such evaluations might not initially have the power of the state behind them, the example of NCQA indicates that, over time, governments can be convinced to adopt a previously unofficial rating system as their own. Second, even if governments never adopted the standards, the mere process of evaluating and accrediting contractors would provide a rich source of public information about privatization that could be used to bring popular political (or economic) pressure to bear on noncompliant contractors. Such public reporting might also allow citizen watchdog groups (or even competing contractors) to monitor the effectiveness of particular contracts, publicize deficiencies, and lobby government officials for change.[149] Third, advocacy at the international level could result in treaties or other international regimes that actually require governments to include oversight provisions in certain categories of contracts, thus creating increasing pressure for change. In any event, as the domestic examples demonstrate, governments and agencies can, at least at times, be mobilized to require meaningful contractual oversight.

In the end, whatever the drawbacks of a contractual approach, they are certainly no greater than the weaknesses of the existing formal transnational/international court system. Indeed, the use of contractual provisions carries the benefits of opening up the possibility of legal enforcement whether or not there is state action and of providing the foundation for legal action in domestic, as well as international, fora. Thus, international law scholars, activists, and advocates should spend at least as much time studying and lobbying for contract-based compliance regimes as they do seeking further openings for international or transnational litigation.

Perhaps most importantly, we must remember that the proper management of privatization will almost certainly require a variety of approaches, and we need not choose one to the exclusion of others. My aim here is simply to focus attention on privatization in the international realm as a crucial field of study, to call for dialogue among international and domestic scholars, advocates, and policymakers concerning appropriate responses, and to suggest that more attention be paid to the possibility of using contractual provisions to provide accountability. None of these aims requires that contract become the only response to privatization. To the contrary, in the coming years we will need to think broadly and creatively about how best to respond to the threats posed by the outsourcing of governmental functions to nongovernmental entities. Only through such efforts will we be able to find ways to protect crucial public law values in the era of privatization that is already upon us.

Notes

List of Contributors

Index

Notes

Introduction

Thanks to Warren Postman and Lena Konanova for research assistance and comments.

1. American outsourcing is often referred to as "privatization," but that label is somewhat misleading. The term "privatization" historically refers to the selling of state assets, whereas in the contemporary context the term incorporates the practice of government outsourcing of tasks to private actors. This outsourcing may proceed through a variety of mechanisms, including contract, vouchers, public-private "partnerships," tax incentives, and government-sponsored private enterprise. The defining feature of outsourcing is that in each instance, functions or activities that were at one time handled by government employees are now instead supplied by private actors, many of whom are organized as for-profit entities. See generally U.S. Government Accountability Office (GAO), *Terms Related to Privatization Activities and Processes* (GGD-97-121) (July 1997), available at www.gao.gov/special.pubs/gg97121.htm. The authors in this volume alternatively use the terms privatization, outsourcing, and contracting to refer to all of these practices.

2. While the number of federal civil servants has decreased, the number of private contractors in the employ of the government has increased dramatically since the beginning of the George W. Bush administration. See Paul C. Light, "Fact Sheet on the New True Size of Government" (Washington, DC: Brookings Institution, 2003), p. 4, available at www.brookings.edu/dybdocroot/gs/cps/light20030905.pdf.

3. See generally Martha Minow, "Outsourcing Power: How Privatizing Military Efforts Challenges Accountability, Professionalism, and Democracy," 46 *Boston College Law Review* 989 (2005).

4. See Chapter 13 below (analyzing CACI work orders for debriefing of personnel, intelligence report writing, and screening and interrogation of detainees); Patrick Radden-Keefe, "Don't Privatize Our Spies," *New York Times,* June 25, 2007, at A23 (discussing outsourced design of surveillance systems and managing case officers in CIA stations overseas); Chapter 9 below (discussing the $30 billion DHS contract with Boeing to "conceptualiz[e], design[], build[], and operat[e]" a comprehensive border security plan aimed at securing northern and southern American land borders); Chapter 5 below (discussing outsourcing of target selection and general military support).

5. As the GAO recently observed, "[t]he [Department of Defense] is now buying launch services, rather than rockets," and flight simulator training services for Air Force pilots rather than flight simulators themselves. See GAO Testimony before the Subcomm. on Defense of House Comm. on Appropriations, *Contracting for Better Outcomes,* GAO-06-800T (September 7, 2006) (statement of David M. Walker, Comptroller General of the United States); GAO, *Contract Management: Service Contract Approach to Aircraft Simulator Training Has Room for Improvement,* GAO-06-830 (September 2006), p. 1. Thanks to Nina Mendelson for these examples.

6. Dan Guttman, "Contracting United States Government Work: Organizational and Constitutional Models," 3 *Public Organization Review* 281, 281 (2003).

7. Major General George R. Fay, *AR 15-6 Investigation of the Abu Ghraib Detention Facility and 205th Military Intelligence Brigade* (2003), p. 7, available at http://fl1.findlaw.com/news.findlaw.com/hdocs/docs/dod/fay82504rpt.pdf; see also Chapter 13 below.

8. See U.S. Senate Democratic Policy Committee, *An Oversight Hearing on Contracting Abuses in Iraq,* 108th Cong., 1st sess., 2004 [hereinafter Dorgan Hearing] (discussing the administration's decision to award Halliburton a $7 billion sole-source, no-bid contract for oil infrastructure work).

9. For example, even if the public requests information under FOIA regarding terms of contracts with private firms, "the contractors essentially have a veto over the release of contract terms if they contain 'trade secrets and commercial or financial information obtained from a person and [are] privileged or confidential.'" Laura Dickinson, "Government for Hire: Privatizing Foreign Affairs and the Problem of Accountability Under International Law," 47 *William and Mary Law Review* 135, 192 (2005) (citing 5 U.S.C. §552(b)(4) (2000)).

10. There were only 37 "oversight" hearings during the 108th Congress in 2003–2004, as compared with 135 in 1993–1994, when Congress was last dominated by Democrats. See Norman J. Ornstein and Thomas E. Mann, "When Congress Checks Out," *Foreign Affairs* (November/December 2006), p. 71 (arguing that "since George W. Bush has become president, oversight has all but disappeared").

11. See Special Inspector General for Iraq Reconstruction, *Lessons Learned in Contracting and Procurement* (July 2006), p. 94, available at www.sigir.mil/

reports/pdf/Lessons_Learned_July21.pdf; U.S. House of Representatives Committee on Government Reform—Minority Staff, Special Investigations Division, *Dollars, Not Sense: Government Contracting under the Bush Administration* (June 2006) pp. 7–9, available at oversight.house.gov/Documents/20060711103910-86046.pdf (noting the increase in no-bid and noncompeted contracts).

12. GAO Testimony before the Subcomm. on Defense of the House Comm. on Appropriations, *Improved Management and Oversight Needed to Better Control DOD's Acquisition of Services*, GAO-07-832T (May 10, 2007) (statement of John P. Hutton, Director Acquisition and Sourcing Management).

13. See, e.g., GAO, *Competitive Sourcing: Greater Emphasis Needed on Increasing Efficiency and Improving Performance*, GAO-04-367 (February 2004); see also Committee on Government Reform—Minority Staff, Special Investigations Division, *Waste, Fraud, and Abuse in Hurricane Katrina Contracts* (August 2006), available at oversight.house.gov/Documents/20060824110705-30132.pdf (describing nineteen Katrina contracts collectively worth $8.75 billion that have been plagued by waste, fraud, abuse, or mismanagement due to poor planning, inadequate oversight, and reliance on noncompetitive contracts).

14. GAO, *Contract Management: Opportunities to Improve Surveillance on Department of Defense Service Contracts*, GAO-05-274 (March 2005), p. 1 (finding that officers believe they do not have enough time to carry out their surveillance duties)

15. See, for example, "Contractor, Army Office Fell Short, Audit Finds," *Washington Post*, April 23, 2005, at E1 (explaining how Aegis, a large contractor of the government, was in charge of overseeing ten other primary providers of security).

16. See, e.g., Dorgan Hearing (examining instances of abandoned $85,000 trucks, contractors staying at five-star hotels, companies charging $45 for a case of soda, and other instances of waste in Iraq).

17. See Chapter 8 below.

18. See Chapter 5 below.

19. Ibid.

20. See GAO Testimony Before the Subcomm. on Defense of the House Comm. on Appropriations, *Conditions in Iraq Are Conducive to Fraud, Waste, and Abuse*, GAO-07-525T (April 23, 2007) (statement of David M. Walker, Comptroller General of the United States).

21. See Laura Dickinson, "Legal Regulation of Private Military Contractors, the New Mercenaries," in Jordan J. Paust et al., eds., *International Criminal Law*, 3d ed. (Durham, NC: Carolina Academic Press, 2007); Laura Dickinson, "Contract as a Tool for Regulating Private Military Companies," in Simon Chesterman and Chia Lehnardt, eds., *Mercenaries to Market* (New York: Oxford University Press, 2007).

22. See, e.g., GAO, *Department of Homeland Security: Improved Assessment and Oversight Needed to Manage Risk of Contracting for Selected Services*,

GAO-07-990 (September 2007) (finding that Department of Homeland Security has not assessed the risk associated with contractors closely supporting inherently governmental functions and that the oversight provided "did not always ensure accountability for decisions or the ability to judge whether the contractor was performing as required").

23. As Novak points out, the dominant meanings given to the distinction between "public" and "private" are themselves products of late nineteenth- and twentieth-century history, making comparisons over the time vulnerable to confusions.

24. See Federal Procurement Data System, Trending Analysis Report since Fiscal Year 2000, available at www.fpdsng.com/downloads/top_requests/FPD SNG5YearViewOnTotals.xls; see also Minority Staff of Committee on Government Reform, *Dollars, Not Sense*, 3–4.

25. See Jody Freeman, "Extending Public Law Norms through Privatization," 116 *Harvard Law Review* 1285 (2003).

26. While this book focuses on contracting by the federal government, some state and local governments may embrace outsourcing in pursuit of efficiency gains, due to resource constraints or as part of an effort to stimulate local economic development. Chapter 4 below—detailing state licensing of private hazardous waste cleanup regulators—illustrates patterns of outsourcing at the state level.

27. When mechanisms such as vouchers and partnerships are used, the demands on government to specify and evaluate private performance are no smaller and potentially even greater than with contracting.

28. See, e.g., Airline Deregulation Act of 1978, Pub. L. No. 95–504, 92 Stat. 1705 (codified at 49 U.S.C. §§1301–1389).

29. See Al Gore, National Performance Review, "From Red Tape to Results: Creating a Government That Works Better and Costs Less" (September 7, 1993), available at www.ipo.noaa.gov/About/npr.html.

30. President William Jefferson Clinton, State of the Union Address (January 23, 1996).

31. See Robert E. Moffit, "Taking Charge of Federal Personnel" (Heritage Foundation, 2001). See also "The Green-Zoning of America," *New York Times*, February 5, 2007, A21.

32. Guttman, "Contracting United States Government Work," at 291.

33. Minority Staff of Committee on Government Reform, *Dollars, Not Sense*, at 1.

34. Note that what might be considered "inherently governmental" has shifted over time. As government has grown in both size and reach in the last century, however, it has come to be responsible for many more functions and services than in the nineteenth century. The size of government has grown sharply in the twentieth century. After rising from about 2 percent of the gross national product in 1789 to about 8 percent in 1902, federal expenditures grew to approximately 40 percent of GNP by the 1980s. See Jeremy Atack and Peter Passell, *A New Economic View of American History* (New York: Norton,

1994), p. 653. The number of federal civilian employees per citizen nearly tripled from 1900 to 2000, an absolute increase of 1,051 percent. See Susan B. Carter et al., eds., 5 *Historical Statistics of the United States* (New York: Cambridge University Press, 2006), pp. 5–127. If one counts outsourced work in the tally of "government" work (a controversial move, in terms of the themes of this book) the number of federal jobs has grown about 70 times and could be as high as 17 million. See Light, "Fact Sheet on the New True Size of Government."

35. See Administrative Procedure Act, 5 U.S.C. §§553, 706 (2000). Government contracts are, importantly, an exception to the rulemaking provisions, ibid. at §553(a)(2).

36. See Freedom of Information Act, 5 U.S.C. §552 (2000).

37. Private contractors fall outside FOIA's guarantees of public access to information about governmental operations. See Chapter 6 below. In addition, management of information about government contracts has itself become a function outsourced by the federal government to private companies that charge fees and otherwise control the relevant information. See Chapter 5 below.

38. See "Contractors Outnumber Troops in Iraq," *Los Angeles Times,* July 4, 2007, at A1 (putting the number at more than 180,000 but detailing various inconsistencies and uncertainties in arriving at that number).

39. Pippa Norris, *A Virtuous Circle: Political Communications in Postindustrial Societies* (Cambridge: Cambridge University Press, 2000), p. 309.

40. Philip Shishkin, "Blackwater Shooting Crisis Rallies Baghdad," *Wall Street Journal,* September 24, 2007, at A3.

41. Contracting out for food, office supplies, and other goods regularly available in the commercial market raises fewer problems for most observers of government outsourcing. Many outsourced contracts are mundane in the sense that they purchase goods or services that are already produced for the commercial market (office supplies, laundry service, information technology services, etc.). Government contracts for such goods and services simply place the government in the same role as any other purchaser of a product that is fungible in a market with many other consumers. The goods and services are not distinctive and the fact of their origin in private commerce does not alter the quality or behavior of government functions. Contracting with private providers for such goods can raise concerns about possible fraud and waste, but for the most part it does not deeply implicate democratic values.

42. See generally "Is Government Outsourcing Its Brain?" *Wall Street Journal,* March 30, 2007, at A1.

43. This OMB document defines "inherently governmental" to include those activities that require the exercise of substantial discretion in applying government authority and/or in making decisions for the government. See U.S. Office of Management and Budget, Circular No. A-76 (Revised), May 29, 2003, p. A-2; see also L. Elaine Halchin, "Circular A-76 Revision 2003: Selected Issues" 5–6 (Congressional Research Service, January 7, 2005), available at

www.opencrs.com/rpts/RL32017_20050107.pdf. In 2002, the Comptroller General reported that warfighting, judicial, enforcement, regulatory, and policymaking functions fall within the inherently governmental category. Minow, "Outsourcing Power," at 1015 (quoting GAO, *Commercial Activities Panel: Improving the Sourcing of the Federal Government*, GAO-02-847T (September 2002), p. 21). See also Guttman, "Contracting United States Government Work," at 293 (citing to GAO, *Government Contractors: Are Service Contractors Performing Inherently Governmental Work*, GAO 92-11 (November 1991), p. 4 (noting that the "concept of 'governmental functions' is difficult to define")).

44. Such departures from the regular process can also prompt suspicions of "giveaways" to favored companies, especially when a relatively small number of companies—with close ties to the incumbent administration—benefit disproportionately from contracts worth billions of dollars. One recent government investigation reported that five companies received 21 percent of total federal contract dollars in 2005. See Minority Staff of Committee on Government Reform, *Dollars, Not Sense*, at 6. In 2004, the Center for Public Integrity similarly found that between 1998 and 2003, 1 percent of the biggest contractors won 80 percent of all defense contracting dollars. Center for Public Integrity, *Outsourcing the Pentagon* (September 29, 2004), available at www.publicintegrity.org/pns/report .aspx?aid=385 ("One of the biggest contracts awarded in the war in Iraq went to Kellogg Brown & Root, a key subsidiary of Halliburton Co., the firm Vice President Dick Cheney ran as CEO before he stepped into the White House and became one of the prime movers urging the president to invade Iraq. Of the $4.3 billion in defense contracts Halliburton won in fiscal 2003 only about half were awarded based on competitive bidding.").

45. Congressional and media investigations concluded that Halliburton overcharged $61 million worth of gasoline (see "U.S. Sees Evidence of Overcharging in Iraq Contract," *New York Times*, December 12, 2003, at A1) and $186 million for meals not actually served (see "$1 Billion Misspent in Iraq," *Detroit Free Press*, June 16, 2004) and could not account for an estimated 43 percent of its billing. Under the contract, all costs were incurred by the government, while Halliburton received substantial profits.

46. For a discussion of critical accountability terms, see James Jay Carafano and Alane Kochens, "Engaging Military Contractors in Counterterrorism and Security Operation," in James J.F. Forest, ed., 1 *Countering Terrorism and Insurgency in the 21st Century: International Perspectives* (Westport, CT: Praeger Security International, 2007), pp. 190, 199–201.

47. Ibid., 205.

48. Ibid.

49. See Dina Rasor and Robert Bauman, *Betraying Our Troops: The Destructive Results of Privatizing War* (New York: Palgrave Macmillan, 2007), pp. 13, 16, 17, 182, 187, 234.

50. See Jerry L. Mashaw, "Accountability and Institutional Design: Some Thoughts on the Grammar of Governance," in Michael Dowdle, ed., *Public Accountability* (Cambridge: Cambridge University Press, 2006), pp. 115, 119.

51. See, e.g., Department of Defense, *Quadrennial Defense Review Report* (February 2006), available at www.defenselink.mil/qdr/report/Report20060203 .pdf

52. See Guttman, "Contracting United States Government Work," 285 (citing Bureau of the Budget Circular A-49, issued in the 1950s, as the precursor to today's OMB Circular A-76).

53. Members of Congress must know full well that downsizing government will not relieve the need to provide the services the public demands. Yet Congress tends to be unresponsive to reports of contract fraud, abuse, and mismanagement, even when they occur on a rather massive scale and are documented by its own investigative agency, the Government Accountability Office.

54. Mashaw, "Accountability and Institutional Design," 118.

55. Ibid. at 120–122.

56. Martha Minow, *Partners, Not Rivals: Privatization and the Public Good* (Boston: Beacon Press, 2002); Jody Freeman, "Extending Public Accountability Through Privatization: From Public Law to Publicization," in Dowdle, *Public Accountability.*

57. Mashaw, "Accountability and Institutional Design."

58. Caratano and Kochems, "Engaging Military Contractors," at 205.

59. Benedict Kinsbury, Nico Krisch, and Richard B. Stewart, "The Emergence of Global Administrative Law," 68 *Law and Contemporary Problems* 15 (2005).

60. See Nico Krisch and Benedict Kingsbury, "Introduction: Global Governance and Global Administrative Law in the International Legal Order," 17 *European Journal of International Law* 1 (2006).

61. In some cases, there will be unsolvable conflicts between a private company's interest in minimizing costs in order to maximize profit, and the government's obligation to see that statutory mandates are complied with, even if they cost more. See Guttman, "Contracting United States Government Work," 290.

1. Public-Private Governance

Epigraph: Justinian, *Digest*, ed. Theodor Mommsen and Paul Krueger, trans. Alan Watson (Philadelphia: University of Pennsylvania Press, 1985), 2.14.38.

1. Francis Fukuyama, *The End of History and the Last Man* (New York: Free Press, 1992); Frederic Jameson, *Postmodernism, or, The Cultural Logic of Late Capitalism* (Durham, NC: Duke University Press, 1991); Jacques Derrida, *Specters of Marx: the State of the Debt, the Work of Mourning, and the New International,* trans. Peggy Kamuf (New York: Routledge, 1994); Daniel Bell, *The Coming of Post-Industrial Society: A Venture in Social Forecasting* (New York: Basic Books, 1973); Jean Comaroff and John L.

Comaroff, eds., *Millennial Capitalism and the Culture of Neoliberalism* (Durham, NC: Duke University Press, 2001).

2. For some excellent discussion of recent trends, see Martha Minow, *Partners, Not Rivals: Privatization and the Public Good* (Boston: Beacon Press, 2002); Paul Pierson, *Dismantling the Welfare State? Reagan, Thatcher, and the Politics of Retrenchment* (New York: Cambridge University Press, 1994); Daniel Yergin and Joseph Stanislaw, *The Commanding Heights: The Battle between Government and the Marketplace That Is Remaking the Modern World* (New York: Simon & Schuster, 1998).

3. I owe this perspective on the idea of contingency and history to the teachings of Morton Horwitz. See, for example, Morton J. Horwitz, "History and Theory," *Yale Law Journal* 96 (1987): 1825; Horwitz, "Comment: The Historical Contingency of the Role of History," *Yale Law Journal* 90 (1981): 1057; Horwitz, "Comment: The History of the Public/Private Distinction," *University of Pennsylvania Law Review* 130 (1982): 1423.

4. See, for example, the essays in Rexford G. Tugwell, ed., *The Trend of Economics* (New York: F. S. Crofts, 1930); Tugwell, *American Economic Life and the Means of Its Improvements* (New York: Harcourt, Brace, 1930), 581, 737; see also the work of Walton Hale Hamilton, including Walton H. Hamilton and Helen R. Wright, *A Way of Order for Bituminous Coal* (New York: Macmillan, 1928); Hamilton, *The Politics of Industry* (New York: Knopf, 1957).

5. Jason Scott Smith, *Building New Deal Liberalism: The Political Economy of Public Works, 1933–1956* (New York: Cambridge University Press, 2006); Alan Brinkley, *The End of Reform: New Deal Liberalism in Recession and War* (New York: Alfred A. Knopf, 1995); Colin Gordon, *New Deals: Business, Labor, and Politics in America, 1920–1935* (New York: Cambridge University Press, 1994); Ellis W. Hawley, *The New Deal and the Problem of Monopoly: A Study in Economic Ambivalence* (Princeton, NJ: Princeton University Press, 1966); William E. Leuchtenberg, *Franklin D. Roosevelt and the New Deal, 1932–1940* (New York: Harper & Row, 1963).

6. L. P. Hartley, *The Go-Between* (London: H. Hamilton, 1953), 3.

7. This has not precluded theorists and philosophers from trying to articulate a third sphere somewhere between the public and the private. One important example includes theories of "civil society" as a distinct sphere of associative relationships somewhere between the public state and the private family. See for example, Adam Ferguson, *An Essay on the History of Civil Society,* ed. Fania Oz-Salzberger (Cambridge: Cambridge University Press, 1995); G.W.F. Hegel, *The Philosophy of Right,* trans. T.M. Knox (Oxford: Clarendon Press, 1942). The other important and more recent example is Jürgen Habermas's theory of the public sphere. See Habermas, *The Structural Transformation of the Public Sphere: An Inquiry into a Category of Bourgeois Society,* trans. Thomas Burger (Cambridge, MA: MIT Press, 1989); Habermas, *Between Facts and Norms: Contributions to a Discourse*

Theory of Law and Democracy (Cambridge, MA: MIT Press, 1996), especially 329–446.

8. Norberto Bobbio, "The Great Dichotomy: Public/Private," in *Democracy and Dictatorship: The Nature and Limits of State Power,* 1–21 (Minneapolis: University of Minnesota Press, 1989).

9. See for example the work of Edward S. Corwin, *Liberty against Government: The Rise, Flowering and Decline of a Famous Juridical Concept* (Baton Rouge: Louisiana State University Press, 1948); Louis Hartz, *The Liberal Tradition in America: An Interpretation of American Political Thought since the Revolution* (New York: Harcourt, Brace, 1955), 60–62; Richard A. Epstein: *Takings: Private Property and the Power of Eminent Domain* (Cambridge, MA: Harvard University Press, 1985). For a fuller discussion, see William J. Novak, "The Pluralist State: The Convergence of Public and Private Power in America," in Wendy Gamber, Michael Grossberg, and Hendrik Hartog, eds., *American Public Life and the Historical Imagination* (South Bend: University of Notre Dame Press, 2003), 27–48.

10. See for example, Charles A. Beard, *An Economic Interpretation of the Constitution of the United States* (New York: Macmillan, 1919); Arthur M. Schlesinger, Jr., *The Age of Jackson* (Boston: Little, Brown & Co., 1945); Sean Wilentz, *Chants Democratic: New York City and the Rise of the American Working Class, 1788–1850* (New York: Oxford University Press, 1984).

11. John R. Commons, *Legal Foundations of Capitalism* (New York: Macmillan, 1932); Harold J. Laski, *Liberty in the Modern State* (New York: Faber & Faber, 1930); Adolf A. Berle and Gardiner C. Means, *The Modern Corporation and Private Property* (New York: Harcourt, Brace & World, 1968); V.O. Key, *Politics, Parties, and Pressure Groups* (New York: Thomas Y. Crowell, 1942); Grant McConnell, *Private Power and American Democracy* (New York: Alfred A. Knopf, 1966); Joseph Schumpeter, *Capitalism, Socialism, and Democracy* (New York: Harper & Brothers, 1942); John Kenneth Galbraith, *The Affluent Society* (Boston: Houghton Mifflin, 1958); Theodore J. Lowi, *The End of Liberalism: Ideology, Policy, and the Crisis of Public Authority* (New York: Norton, 1969); Morton S. Keller, *Affairs of State: Public Life in Late Nineteenth Century America* (Cambridge, MA: Harvard University Press, Belknap Press, 1977); Theda Skocpol, *Protecting Soldiers and Mothers: The Political Origins of Social Policy in the United States* (Cambridge, MA: Harvard University Press, Belknap Press, 1992).

12. Frederick Pollock and Frederic William Maitland, *The History of English Law before the Time of Edward I,* 2nd ed., 2 vols. (Washington, DC: Lawyers' Literary Club, 1959); Frederic William Maitland, *Township and Borough* (New York: Cambridge University Press, 1898); H.D. Hazeltine, G. Lapsley, and P.H. Winfield, eds., *Maitland: Selected Essays* (Cambridge: Cambridge University Press, 1936).

13. Frederic William Maitland, *The Constitutional History of England: A Course of Lectures* (Cambridge: Cambridge University Press, 1908), 45.

14. Charles M. Andrews, *The Colonial Period of American History*, 2nd ed., 3 vols. (New Haven, CT: Yale University Press, 1964); Francis Newton Thorpe, *The Federal and State Constitutions, Colonial Charters, and Other Organic Laws of the States, Territories, and Colonies Now or Heretofore Forming the United States of America* (Washington, DC: Government Printing Office, 1909); Christopher L. Tomlins, "The Legal Cartography of Colonization, the Legal Polyphony of Settlement: English Intrusions on the American Mainland in the Seventeenth Century," *Law and Social Inquiry* 26 (2001): 333.

15. "The First Charter of Virginia," April 10, 1606, the Avalon Project at Yale Law School, www.yale.edu/lawweb/avalon/states/va01.htm (accessed 8/01/06).

16. According to Bernard Bailyn, the distinctive tradition of mixed public and private power embodied in the colonial charters led, over time, to the creation of an equally distinctive political tradition in the new world. Bernard Bailyn, *Origins of American Politics* (New York: Vintage Books, 1969). See also Jack P. Greene, *Peripheries and Center: Constitutional Development in the Extended Polities of the British Empire and the United States, 1607–1788* (Athens: University of Georgia Press, 1986); Daniel J. Hulsebosch, *Constituting Empire: New York and the Transformation of Constitutionalism in the Atlantic World, 1664–1830* (Chapel Hill: University of North Carolina Press, 2005). For specific examples of the public-private traditions in the American colonies, see, e.g., Bailyn, *The New England Merchants in the Seventeenth Century* (Cambridge, MA: Harvard University Press, 1955); Christine L. Heyrman, *Commerce and Culture: The Maritime Communities of Colonial Massachusetts, 1690–1750* (New York: Norton, 1984).

17. Hendrik Hartog, *Public Property and Private Power: The Corporation of the City of New York in American Law* (Chapel Hill: University of North Carolina Press, 1983), 58, 66.

18. J. Willard Hurst, *The Legitimacy of the Business Corporation in the Law of the United States, 1780–1970* (Charlottesville: University of Virginia Press, 1970); Hurst, *Law and Economic Growth: The Legal History of the Lumber Industry in Wisconsin, 1836–1915* (Madison: University of Wisconsin Press, 1984); Louis Hartz, *Economic Policy and Democratic Thought, Pennsylvania, 1776–1860* (Cambridge, MA: Harvard University Press, 1946), Herbert Hovenkamp, *Enterprise and American Law, 1836–1937* (Cambridge, MA: Harvard University Press, 1991); Naomi R. Lamoreaux, *Insider Lending: Banks, Personal Connections and Economic Development in Industrial New England* (New York: Cambridge University Press, 1994); E. Merrick Dodd, Jr., *American Business Corporations until 1860* (Cambridge, MA: Harvard University Press, 1954); John W. Cadman, Jr., *The Corporation in New Jersey: Business and Politics, 1791–1875* (Cambridge, MA: Harvard University Press, 1949); Oscar and Mary F. Handlin, "Origins of the American Business Corporation," in Frederic C. Lane and Jelle C. Riemersma, eds., *Enterprise and Secular Change* (Homewood, IL: R.D. Irwin, 1953), 102–124;

Pauline Maier, "The Revolutionary Origins of the American Corporation," *William and Mary Quarterly* (3rd Ser.), 50, no. 1 (1993): 51–84.

19. Ernst Freund, *The Police Power, Public Policy, and Constitutional Rights* (Chicago: Callaghan & Company, 1904), 358–359. If one doubts the inherent public and regulatory nature of the original corporate charters, Freund lists the following as typical statutory restrictions placed on nineteenth-century corporations: "The objects for which corporations may be organized; conditions as to minimum number of organizers, and sometimes as to their residence; conditions as to denomination of shares and their transferability; manner of organization, name, subscription and payment of capital, and preliminary contracts; regarding officers and members rights, including general meetings, right to vote, qualification and number of directors, their election, term of office, and removal, the power to make and alter bye-laws; the management of corporate business, including payment of dividends, acquisition and disposition of real estate, and the contracting of loans; liability and power to assess; increase and reduction of capital; change of name and purposes; duration, extension, liquidation, consolidation; registration of officers and shareholders; and requirement of accounts and reports."

20. William J. Novak, *The People's Welfare: Law and Regulation in Nineteenth-Century America* (Chapel Hill: University of North Carolina Press, 1996), 106; Berle and Means, *The Modern Corporation and Private Property*, 11; Joseph S. Davis, *Essays in the Earlier History of American Corporations*, 2 vols. (Cambridge, MA: 1917), 2: 24–27; Hurst, *Legitimacy of the Business Corporation*, 14–15; Hartz, *Economic Policy and Democratic Thought*, 38.

21. See Harry N. Scheiber, *Ohio Canal Era: A Case Study of Government and the Economy, 1820–1861* (Athens: Ohio University Press, 1968); Oscar Handlin and Mary Flug Handlin, *Commonwealth: A Study of the Role of Government in the American Economy. Massachusetts, 1774–1861* (New York: New York University Press, 1947); Carter Goodrich, *Canals and American Economic Development* (New York: Columbia University Press, 1961); John Lauritz Larson, *Internal Improvement: National Public Works and the Promise of Popular Government in the Early United States* (Chapel Hill: University of North Carolina Press, 2001).

22. Allen Steinberg, *The Transformation of Criminal Justice: Philadelphia, 1800–1880* (Chapel Hill: University of North Carolina Press, 1989).

23. *Laws of New York* (1813), c. 86 (R.L.); Novak, *People's Welfare*, 58.

24. Lawrence M. Friedman, *Crime and Punishment in American History* (New York: Basic Books, 1993); Michael Willrich, *City of Courts: Socializing Justice in Progressive Era Chicago* (New York: Cambridge University Press, 2003); David S. Tanenhaus, *Juvenile Justice in the Making* (New York: Oxford University Press, 2004). The complicated role of public-private governance in the construction and maintenance of Jim Crow segregation has also been explored in the work of Barbara Welke, *Recasting American Liberty: Gender, Race, Law, and the Railroad Revolution, 1865–1920* (New York: Cambridge University Press, 2001); and A.K. Sandoval-Strausz, "Travelers,

Strangers, and Jim Crow: Public Accommodations and Civil Rights in America," *Law and History Review* 23 (2005): 53–94.

25. Jacob S. Hacker, *The Divided Welfare State: The Battle over Public and Private Social Benefits in the United States* (New York: Cambridge University Press, 2002); Jennifer Klein, *For All These Rights: Business, Labor, and the Shaping of America's Public-Private Welfare State* (Princeton, NJ: Princeton University Press, 2003); Christopher Howard, *The Hidden Welfare State: Tax Expenditures and Social Policy in the United States* (Princeton, NJ: Princeton University Press, 1999).

26. For the best discussion, see the work of Gail Radford, e.g., Radford, "From Municipal Socialism to Public Authorities: Institutional Factors in the Shaping of American Public Enterprise," *Journal of American History* 90 (2003): 863–890; Radford, *Modern Housing for America: Policy Struggles in the New Deal Era* (Chicago: University of Chicago Press, 1996). See also David A. Moss, *When All Else Fails: Government as the Ultimate Risk Manager* (Cambridge, MA: Harvard University Press, 2002).

27. John Kenneth Galbraith, *American Capitalism: The Concept of Countervailing Power* (White Plains, NY: M.E. Sharpe, 1980).

28. James Willard Hurst, "Problems of Legitimacy in the Contemporary Legal Order," *Oklahoma Law Review* 24, no. 2 (May 1971): 225; Hurst, *Justice Holmes on Legal History* (New York: Macmillan, 1964), 29, 31. For more on Hurst and the constitutional balance of power, see Novak, "Law, Capitalism, and the Liberal State: The Historical Sociology of James Willard Hurst," *Law and History Review* 18 (2000): 97–145.

29. Hannah Arendt, *On Revolution* (New York: Penguin Books, 1963), 154. Arendt's fundamental insight about the revolution and the Constitution leading to the creation of a new power center in the United States has been pursued more recently by Max Edling in *A Revolution in Favor of Government: Origins of the U.S. Constitution and the Making of the American State* (New York: Oxford University Press, 2003).

30. Gordon Wood, *Creation of the American Republic* (Chapel Hill: University of North Carolina Press, 1969), 3–91; J. G. A. Pocock, *The Machiavellian Moment: Florentine Political Thought and the Atlantic Republican Tradition* (Princeton, NJ: Princeton University Press, 1975), especially chapter 15, "The Americanization of Virtue." See generally James T. Kloppenberg, "The Virtues of Liberalism: Christianity, Republicanism, and Ethics in Early American Political Discourse," in *The Virtues of Liberalism* (New York: Oxford University Press, 1998), 21–37; Daniel T. Rodgers, "Republicanism: The Career of a Concept," *Journal of American History* 79, no. 1 (June 1992): 11–38.

31. For one of the best statements on this theme, see Richard L. McCormick, "The Discovery that Business Corrupts Politics: A Reappraisal of the Origins of Progressivism," *American Historical Review* 86 (1981): 247–274. See also Daniel T. Rodgers, *Atlantic Crossings: Social Politics in a Progressive Age* (Cambridge, MA: Harvard University Press, 1998); James T. Kloppenberg, *Uncertain Victory: Social Democracy and Progressivism in European and*

American Thought, 1870–1920 (New York: Oxford University Press, 1986); Morton Keller, *Regulating a New Economy: Public Policy and Economic Change in America, 1900–1933* (Cambridge, MA: Harvard University Press, 1990); Keller, *Regulating a New Society: Public Policy and Social Change in America, 1900–1933* (Cambridge, MA: Harvard University Press, 1994).

32. For further development of this theme, see Novak, "The Legal Origins of the Modern American State," in Bryant Garth, Robert Kagan, and Austin Sarat, eds., *Looking Back at Law's Century: Time, Memory, Change* (Ithaca, NY: Cornell University Press, 2002), 249–283; Novak, "The Not-So-Strange Birth of the Modern American State," *Law and History Review* 24 (2006): 193–200.

33. Brooks Adams, *The Law of Civilization and Decay: An Essay on History* (New York: Macmillan, 1895); Henry Adams, *The Degradation of the Democratic Dogma* (New York: Macmillan, 1919); Roscoe Pound, "The New Feudalism," *American Bar Association Journal* 10 (1930): 553; Pound, "Liberty of Contract," *Yale Law Journal* 18 (1909): 454–487; Morris R. Cohen, "Property and Sovereignty," *Cornell Law Quarterly* 13 (1927): 8–30; Robert L. Hale, "Coercion and Distribution in a Supposedly Non-Coercive State," *Political Science Quarterly* 38 (1923): 470–494; Hale, *Freedom through Law: Public Control of Private Governing Power* (New York: Columbia University Press, 1952).

34. Comaroff and Comaroff, *Millennial Capitalism.*

35. Sheldon S. Wolin, *Politics and Vision: Continuity and Vision in Western Political Thought* (Princeton, NJ: Princeton University Press, 2004), xx.

36. Bobbio, "The Great Dichotomy," 2–3.

37. James Kent, *Commentaries on American Law*, 4 vols. (1826; New York: Da Capo Press, 1971), 2: 265.

38. For a full discussion of *salus populi* and the police power, see Novak, *People's Welfare.*

39. In Chicago alone recently Millennium Park has been closed for the exclusive use of Toyota and Allstate, the Chicago Skyway has been leased to a private company for ninety-nine years, and there is serious discussion of the privatization of Midway Airport.

40. Commonwealth v. Rush, 14 Pa. 186, 191 193 (1850); State v. Woodward, 23 Vt. 92, 99 (1850); Commonwealth v. Bowman and Duncan, 3 Pa. 202 (1846). The legal ideas of public nuisance and purpresture were particularly important legal defenses of public rights in the nineteenth century. See Novak, *People's Welfare,* especially chapter 4.

41. Max Weber, *Economy and Society,* ed. Guenther Roth and Claus Wittich, 2 vols. (Berkeley: University of California Press, 1978), 1: 56.

2. The Transformation of Government Work

This chapter is adapted from material published in Donahue, *The Warping of Government Work* (Cambridge, MA: Harvard University Press, 2008), chapter 5. This adaptation has benefited greatly from suggestions by Lena Konanova.

1. R.H. Coase, "The Nature of the Firm," 4 *Economica* (n.s.) 386 (1937).
2. For a useful discussion of this theme see Naomi R. Lamoreaux, Daniel M.G. Raff, and Peter Temin, "Beyond Markets and Hierarchies: Toward a New Synthesis of American Business History," 108 *American Historical Review* 404 (2003).
3. Relevant books include E.S. Savas, *Privatization: The Key to Better Government* (Chatham, NJ: Chatham House, 1987); E.S. Savas, *Privatization and Public-Private Partnerships* (New York: Chatham House, 2000); John D. Donahue, *The Privatization Decision: Public Ends, Private Means* (New York: Basic Books, 1989); and Elliott D. Sclar, *You Don't Always Get What You Pay For: The Economics of Privatization* (Ithaca, NY: Cornell University Press, 2000). On the Bush administration's competitive sourcing campaign, see Commercial Activities Panel, *Improving the Sourcing Decisions of the Federal Government: Final Report* (Washington, DC: General Accounting Office, 2002).
4. Paul Light commissioned a heroically ambitious but less than fully convincing effort to estimate the headcount of nongovernmental personnel delivering federally funded services. Paul C. Light, *The True Size of Government* (Washington, DC: Brookings Institution Press, 1999).
5. The most frequently cited empirical reference on local privatization is the series of surveys undertaken in 1982, 1988, 1992, 1997, and 2002–2003 by the International City/County Management Association. Each year more than 3,000 local governments and some 1,500 county governments were queried about their service delivery practices, with a response rate ranging between 36 and 46 percent for cities and roughly half that for counties. At the state level, a similarly respectable but limited survey effort has been undertaken by the Council of State Governments. Keon S. Chi and Cindy Jasper, *Private Practices: A Review of Privatization in State Government* (Lexington, KY: Council of State Governments, 1998).
6. Stephen Minicucci and John D. Donahue, "A Simple Estimation Method for Aggregate Government Outsourcing," 23 *Journal of Policy Analysis and Management* 489 (2004).
7. Michael E. Motley, "U.S. Postal Service: A Look at Other Countries' Postal Reform Efforts" (testimony before the Senate Subcommittee on Post Office and Civil Service and House Subcommittee on the Postal Service, January 25, 1996), General Accounting Office, GAO/T-GGD-96-60.
8. Background on this quiet splitting of postal functions can be found in Mary S. Elcano, R. Andrew German, and John T. Pickett, "Hiding in Plain Sight: The Quiet Liberalization of the United States Postal System," in Michael A. Crew and Paul R. Kleindorfer, eds., *Current Directions in Postal Reform* (Boston: Kluwer, 2000), pp. 337–352, and in General Accounting Office, "U.S. Postal Service: A Primer on Postal Worksharing," GAO-03-927 (2003).
9. President's Commission on the United States Postal Service, *Embracing the Future: Making the Tough Choices to Preserve Universal Mail Service* (2003): 110.
10. Ibid., 35–51.

11. These figures are from the Census Bureau's electronic data files maintained by the Governments Division, "State and Local Government Employment and Payroll" series, for 2002 available at www.census.gov.

12. These comparisons are based on 2005 data from Bureau of Labor Statistics, Occupational Employment Statistics database, available at www.bls.gov/OES.

13. Department of Education, National Center for Education Statistics, *Digest of Education Statistics 2002,* Table 80, "Staff employed in public elementary and secondary school systems, by functional area, 1949–1950 to fall 2000."

14. The figures on the breakdown of internal versus external service delivery in this paragraph were calculated from Department of Education, National Center for Education Statistics, *Digest of Education Statistics 2002,* Table 164, "Total expenditures for public elementary and secondary education, by function and subfunction: 1990–1991 to 1999–2000."

15. These comparisons are based on 2003 data from Bureau of Labor Statistics, Occupational Employment Statistics database, available at www.bls.gov/OES/.

16. Kirsten Lundberg, "Private Food Service in Houston's Public Schools?" Kennedy School of Government Case C-15-01-1622.0 (2001).

17. Federal Procurement Data Center, "Federal Procurement Report, Fiscal Year 2002," p. 2. The FPDC has more recent data posted for other categories, but as of 2006 was behind schedule in posting its usual tallies of top contractors.

18. Ibid.

19. Ibid. See also Bernard Wysocki, Jr., "Private Practice: Is U.S. Government 'Outsourcing Its Brain'?" *Wall Street Journal,* March 30, 2007, at A1.

20. See M. Bryna Sanger, *The Welfare Marketplace: Privatization and Welfare Reform* (Washington, DC: Brookings Institution Press, 2003).

21. Federal Procurement Data Center, "Federal Procurement Report, Fiscal Year 2002," at 7–9.

22. For instance, American Management Systems, which concentrates on state and local rather than federal contracting, announced a major strategic shift in 2003 to focus on the burgeoning demand for outsourced information technology services in the public sector. Anitha Reddy, "Fairfax's AMS Sets Sights on Outsourcing," *Washington Post,* December 4, 2003, at E5.

23. Corporate IT outsourcing raises its own set of concerns. Much of the debate centers on shifting work overseas to take advantage of a divide in the working world related to, but different from, the one at issue here. Security anxieties arise as well, as related in John Schwartz, "Experts See Vulnerability as Outsiders Code Software," *New York Times,* January 5, 2003, at C1.

24. Harvard's Kennedy School of Government, where I teach, contracts out much of the routine work of installing hardware, maintaining servers, and extricating clueless faculty from the messes we get ourselves into. But a formidably competent IT director and her crack staff form the core of the operation.

25. This trend is discussed in a (generally enthusiastic) study by Yu-Che Chen and James L. Perry, *IT Outsourcing: A Primer for Public Managers* (IBM Endowment for the Business of Government, 2003), 9.

26. A team led by Nobel laureate Joseph Stiglitz produced a crisp application of classic economic principles to underscore that there are many domains that government should stay out of as IT reshapes the options. But the report specifies that employing technology to "improve the efficiency with which public services are provided" is an entirely appropriate public task. Joseph E. Stiglitz, Peter R. Orszag, and Jonathan M. Orszag, *The Role of Government in a Digital Age* (Computer and Communications Industry Association, 2000).

27. R. Jeffrey Smith and Joe Stephens, "Safety an Issue since '90s; Experts Critical of Shuttle Program's Budget Cuts," *Washington Post,* February 3, 2003, at A1.

28. The Bureau of Labor Statistics' Occupational Employment Statistics reports suppress much of the information on avionics technicians in the industry that includes the United Space Alliance—probably to preserve confidentiality, because USA constitutes all or most of the avionics technicians employed in that industry. Avionics technicians earn about $43,000 in government, about $47,000 in transportation equipment manufacturing, about $52,000 in air transportation, and about $39,000 in air transport support. The average salary for aerospace engineers is nearly the same in business and government, though in government it is lower on the high end and higher on the low end.

29. My familiarity with the shuttle operations contract dates from work I did in 2001–2002 with the RAND Corporation, but all facts cited are from publicly available documents, including the report of that task force: Space Shuttle Competitive Sourcing Task Force, *Alternate Trajectories: Options for Competitive Sourcing of the Space Shuttle Program* (RAND Corporation, 2002). Relevant press reports include R. Jeffrey Smith and Joe Stephens, supra note 27, and Greg Schneider and Ariana Eunjung Cha, "Cost-Conscious NASA Relies on Contract Firms," *Washington Post,* February 3, 2003, at A17.

30. Lockheed's largest customer, accounting for roughly $25 billion, was the U.S. public sector, primarily but not exclusively the federal government. Another $5 billion was for sales to foreign governments. Much of this, of course, was for the aircraft and other hardware that nobody would expect governments to make for themselves. But a large and growing share was for information technology services, consulting, and other functions that could be done internally. Lockheed Martin, *2003 Annual Report,* p. 68.

3. The Federal Framework for Competing Commercial Work

Any opinions expressed in this document are solely those of the author and do not necessarily represent the views of OFPP, OMB, or the United States government.

1. Office of Management and Budget, *The President's Management Agenda, Fiscal Year 2002* (Washington, DC: Executive Office of the President, 2001), pp.17–18, available at www.whitehouse.gov/omb/ (accessed 9/13/07).

2. Agency estimates suggest that over one-fifth of all federal employees (i.e., manpower equating to roughly 390,000 federal positions) perform commercial tasks that potentially could be performed by the private sector.

3. However, the PMA does not stand as the only example where an administration has emphasized the need to compare the cost of in-house performance against performance by the private sector. For example, in 1987, the Reagan administration issued an executive order requiring agencies to "conduct annual studies of not less than 3 percent of the department or agency's total civilian population, until all identified potential commercial activities have been studied [to determine whether they could be performed more economically by private industry]." Executive Order No. 12,615, 52 *Federal Register* 44,853 (November 19, 1987).

4. For a list of reports that OMB cites as confirmation that public-private competition is beneficial, see Office of Management and Budget, *Competitive Sourcing: Conducting Public-Private Competition in a Reasoned and Responsible Manner* (Washington, DC: Executive Office of the President, July 2003), 9 n.2 [hereinafter OMB's July 2003 report], available at www.whitehouse.gov/omb/ (accessed 9/13/07), and Office of Management and Budget, *Competitive Sourcing: Report on Competitive Sourcing Results, Fiscal Year 2003* (Washington, DC: Executive Office of the President, May 2004), 13 n.9 [hereinafter OMB's May 2004 report], available at www.whitehouse.gov/omb/ (accessed 9/13/07). The list includes studies conducted by the Center for Naval Analysis, the RAND Corporation, the IBM Endowment for the Business of Government, and the Government Accountability Office (GAO).

5. For a comprehensive discussion on the differences among competitive sourcing, outsourcing, and privatization, see Jacques S. Gansler, *Moving toward Market-Based Government: The Changing Role of Government as the Provider* (Arlington, VA: IBM Endowment for the Business of Government, 2003), available at www.businessofgovernment.org (accessed 9/13/07).

6. For examples of privatizations, see Gansler, *Market-Based Government*, 28–30.

7. As discussed in this chapter, federal policies have been modified in recent years to ensure both sectors are routinely considered before work is converted to private-sector performance. In particular, a long-standing policy principle that discouraged the government from competing with the private sector has been eliminated, along with the practice of allowing work to be directly converted to the private sector without evaluating in-house capabilities and costs. In addition, agencies are evaluated under the PMA based on whether they are using competition in a reasoned manner and whether the competitions are producing cost savings and improved performance—not whether work has been outsourced. In fact, every agency that has successfully used competitive sourcing under the PMA continues to rely on federal employees for a substantial amount of the work competed under restructured operations that are projected to save taxpayers billions of dollars.

8. This paper primarily addresses actions associated with commercial activities currently performed by federal employees. Based on 2006 data from agency workforce inventories, the federal government devoted approximately 390,000 full-time employee equivalents (FTEs) to the performance

of commercial activities that could be considered for performance by the private sector. Assuming the government paid roughly $97,000 per civilian FTE annually in salary and benefits in FY 2006, this equates to roughly $38 billion per year.

9. Competitive sourcing may be applied to work that is currently being performed in-house, work that is being performed by a contractor, or even new work (i.e., work that is required by a federal agency but is not currently being performed for the agency by either sector). The PMA has focused on work that is currently being performed in-house. When the PMA was launched, the administration explained that "[b]y rarely subjecting commercial tasks performed by the government to competition, agencies have insulated themselves from the pressures that produce quality service at reasonable cost." *President's Management Agenda,* 17. This focus notwithstanding, Congress recently instructed the Department of Defense (DOD) to develop guidelines and procedures for ensuring that special consideration is given to using federal employees for work that is currently being performed under contracts that, among other things, were not awarded on a competitive basis or have been determined by a contracting officer to be poorly performed due to excessive costs or inferior quality. National Defense Authorization Act for Fiscal Year 2006, Pub. L. No. 109–163, §343, 119 Stat. 3136, 3200–01 (2006) (codified at 10 U.S.C. §2461 note).

10. Office of Management and Budget, *Performance of Commercial Activities,* Circular No. A-76 (Revised) (Washington, DC: Executive Office of the President, May 29, 2003) [hereinafter Circular], available at http://www.whitehouse.gov/omb/ (accessed 9/14/07).

11. Pub. L. No. 105–270, 31 U.S.C. §501 note (2000) [hereinafter FAIR Act].

12. See, e.g., Office of Management and Budget, *2005 Inventories of Commercial and Inherently Governmental Activities,* Memorandum M-05-12 (Washington, DC: Executive Office of the President, May 23, 2005) [hereinafter OMB's 2005 inventory guidance], available at www.whitehouse.gov/omb/ (accessed 9/14/07), and Office of Management and Budget, *Development of "Green" Plans for Competitive Sourcing,* Memorandum for the President's Management Council (Washington, DC: Executive Office of the President, December 22, 2003) [hereinafter OMB's Green Plan memo], available at www.whitehouse.gov/omb/ (accessed 9/14/07). A number of statutory requirements also impose obligations or restrictions on individual agencies' use of public-private competition. See below.

13. For a comprehensive case study evaluating the decision-making steps taken by the Internal Revenue Service in its application of competitive sourcing to its area distribution centers (which are responsible for processing customer orders for tax-related forms and publications) and the use of information technology at tax processing centers, see Willima Lucyshyn and Sandra Young, "Case Study 2: Competitive Sourcing—The IRS Improves Performance and Modernizes Operations," in Jacques S. Gansler and William Lucyshyn, eds., *Implementing Alternative Sourcing Strategies: Four Case Studies* (Washington, DC:

IBM Center for the Business of Government, 2004), 31–45 [hereinafter *Four Case Studies*], available at www.businessofgovernment.org (accessed 9/14/07).

14. The FAIR Act requires executive agencies to prepare annual inventories of activities performed by their employees that, in the judgment of the agency, are not inherently governmental functions. §2(a). Circular A-76 further requires agencies to identify activities that are inherently governmental. Attachment A, §A. Inventories must identify (1) the specific activities being performed by "function codes" established by OMB, (2) the manpower (stated as full-time equivalent employees (FTEs)) required to perform the activity in each location the work is performed, (3) the place of performance, (4) the organizational unit performing the work, and (5) a point of contact. Commercial inventories must also assign a reason code to each activity, identifying whether the activity is suitable for competition. The reason codes are prescribed by the Circular. Ibid. §C.

15. FAIR Act §5(2)(A), (B).

16. OMB calculates these figures based on each agency's FAIR inventory submission. See "FAIR Act Inventory Releases," www.whitehouse.gov/omb/ (accessed 10/17/07).

17. Individual agency inventories are made available to the public. Points of contact are identified in notices published by OMB. The Federal Acquisition Regulation (FAR), which codifies uniform policies and procedures that executive agencies must follow when acquiring goods and services, includes an illustrative list of inherently governmental functions that mandate performance by government personnel. See 48 C.F.R. §7.503(c) (2006).

18. FAIR Act §§5(2)(C)(i), (B), (B)(i) & (B)(v).

19. Attachment A §B(1)(b).

20. 48 C.F.R. §7.503(d).

21. See also Ronald W. Reagan National Defense Authorization Act for Fiscal Year 2005, Pub. L. No. 108-375, §804, 118 Stat. 1811, 2007 (2004) (codified at 10 U.S.C. §2383) (addressing the award of contracts for performance of the acquisition functions closely associated with inherently governmental functions that are listed in FAR 7.503(d)). The Act states that DOD may enter into a contract for a performance of one of these activities only if (1) the contracting officer determines that the appropriate military or civilian DOD personnel (A) cannot reasonably be made available to perform the functions, (B) will supervise contractor performance of the contract, and (C) will perform all inherently governmental functions associated with the functions to be performed under the contract; and (2) the contracting officer ensures that the agency addresses any potential organizational conflict of interest of the contractor in the performance of the functions under the contract.

22. Attachment A §B(1).

23. The Circular defines an "interested party" as "(1) a private sector source that is an actual or prospective offeror for a contract or other form of agreement to perform the activity and has a direct economic interest in performing the activity that would be adversely affected by a determination not to procure

the performance of the activity from a private sector source; (2) a representative of any business or professional association that includes within its membership private sector sources referred to in (1) above; (3) an officer or employee of an organization within an executive agency that is an actual or prospective offeror to perform the activity; (4) the head of any labor organization referred to in section 7103(a)(4) of title 5, United States Code, that includes within its membership officers or employees of an organization referred to in paragraph (3)." Circular, attachment D, at D-6.

24. FAIR Act §3.

25. Circular, Attachment A, §C. The Circular provides "reason codes" for agencies to indicate the rationale for continued government performance of a commercial activity. For example, the activity may be undergoing an agency-approved restructuring (e.g., closure or realignment), a statute may prohibit performance by the private sector, or the agency may determine that private sector performance is otherwise inappropriate.

26. OMB's July 2003 report, 3. See also Office of Management and Budget, Competitive Sourcing: Reasoned and Responsible Public-Private Competition, Agency Activities, A Supplement to the July 2003 Report (Washington, DC: Executive Office of the President, September 2003), 6 [hereinafter OMB's September 2003 report], available at www.whitehouse.gov/omb/ (accessed 9/17/07). ("Even those [agencies] who have had the greatest success with competitive sourcing would readily acknowledge that public-private competition is not appropriate for all commercial activities.")

27. See Attachment to OMB's 2005 inventory guidance, 1.

28. See Attachment to OMB's 2005 inventory guidance, 3. The Circular requires agencies to prepare justifications to explain why an activity has been designated as unsuitable for competition. The justifications must be made available to the public upon request. See Circular, Attachment A, §C(2).

29. Interested parties may challenge an agency's determination that an activity is or is not suitable for competition as part of the inventory challenge process described above. See Circular, Attachment A, §D(2).

30. For a list of Web sites containing individual agency FAIR inventories, see "FAIR Notices of Availability," www.whitehouse.gov/omb/ (accessed 9/17/07).

31. See OMB's Green Plan memo. See also OMB's September 2003 report, 6–7.

32. OMB's September 2003 Report, 7.

33. See OMB's Green Plan memo, 2.

34. See Office of Management and Budget, Competitive Sourcing: Report on Competitive Sourcing Results, Fiscal Year 2004 (Washington, DC: Executive Office of the President, May 2005), 17 [hereinafter OMB's May 2005 report], available at www.whitehouse.gov/omb/ (accessed 9/17/07); OMB's May 2004 report, 12–14; OMB's September 2003 report, 4.

35. "Agencies may . . . determine that pursuit of competition is premature and that a better means to improve the operational efficiency of a commercial activity performed by government personnel is to internally reengineer prior to undertaking a public-private competition." OMB's September 2003 report, 4.

36. Congress requires agencies to report how competitive sourcing efforts are coordinated with human capital considerations. Consolidated Appropriations Act, 2004, Pub. L. No. 108–199, div. F, §647(b)(9), 118 Stat. 3, 361 (2004) (codified at 31 U.S.C. §10, note). Joint steps identified by agencies include (1) developing accurate definitions of activities performed by the workforce, (2) timing competitions to minimize workforce disruptions, (3) involving a human resource advisor to assist employees as they reorganize their operations as part of a competition, and (4) exploring opportunities to provide soft landings for directly affected employees. See OMB's May 2004 report, 16–17. See also Office of Management and Budget, *Competitive Sourcing: Report on Competitive Sourcing Results, Fiscal Year 2005* (Washington, DC: Executive Office of the President, April 2006) [hereinafter OMB's April 2006 report], available at www.whitehouse.gov/omb/ (accessed 9/17/07);Office of Management and Budget, *Competitive Sourcing: Report on Competitive Sourcing Results, Fiscal Year 2006* (Washington, DC: Executive Office of the President, May 2007) [hereinafter OMB's May 2007 report], available at www.whitehouse.gov/omb/ (accessed 9/17/07). The Circular expressly requires that every most efficient organization (MEO) be assisted by a human resource expert (referred to as a human resource advisor, or HRA) to assist the team in addressing issues related to the potential reorganization of their operations (e.g., classifying positions, determining training needs, assisting in the development of the cost estimate, and preparing soft landing options). See Circular, attachment B, §A(8)(d).

37. See U.S. General Accounting Office, *Competitive Sourcing: Greater Emphasis Needed on Increasing Efficiency and Improving Performance,* GAO-04-367 (Washington, DC, February 2004), 38–40 [hereinafter GAO's February 2004 report] available at www.gao.gov (accessed 9/17/07).

38. See GAO's February 2004 report, 37–38.

39. See OMB's May 2004 report, 12. DOE's "Competitive Sourcing Executive Steering Group" includes the Deputy Secretary, the Under Secretary for Energy, Science and Environment, the Under Secretary for Nuclear Security, and the Director, Office of Management, Budget and Evaluation/Chief Financial Officer. Advisory members may include representatives from General Counsel, Congressional and Intergovernmental Affairs, Public Affairs, affected line organizations, and representatives from the National Headquarters' offices of employee unions. See U.S. Department of Energy, Competitive Sourcing Executive Steering Group, *Competitive Sourcing Program Operating Guidelines,* CS-OG-01 (Washington, DC, July 1, 2004), 2, available at management.energy.gov (accessed 9/17/07). See generally U.S. Department of Energy, *Competitive Sourcing Program Feasibility Review Charter* (Washington, DC, May 2005), available at www.cfo.doe.gov (accessed 9/17/07).

40. Baseline costs include in-house personnel costs, overhead, contract support costs and, in some cases, other costs (e.g., cost of capital, leases, supplies and materials). OMB's April 2006 report, 26.

41. Circular, attachment B, §A(8).
42. Circular, attachment B, §A. In addition, DOD officials are required to consult monthly with affected employees. 10 U.S.C. §2467(b) (2000).
43. Office of Management and Budget, "Performance of Commercial Activities," 68 *Federal Register* 68, 32,134 (May 29, 2003) at 32,139.
44. These procedures apply both to potential conversions of work from the public to the private sector and to conversions of work from the private sector to the public sector.
45. Standard competitions accounted for 84 percent of the activities competed in fiscal years 2004–2006 (measured in terms of FTEs).
46. Circular, attachment B, §§B(1), D(1).
47. See 48 C.F.R. subpart 6.1. Other federal agencies, in addition to the agency currently performing the work, may compete to perform on a fee-for-service or reimbursable basis. See Circular at §4(c) (speaking in terms of using competition to determine if "government personnel" should perform the work, as opposed to just the incumbent agency provider, which is usually an organization internal to the agency competing the work).
48. Performance-based work statements are structured around desired mission outcomes rather than how the work is to be performed. This strategy fosters the creativity and initiative of providers and encourages them to come forward with their best innovative solutions. For additional background on performance-based acquisitions, see "Seven Steps to Performance-Based Acquisition," acquisition.gov (accessed 9/17/07).
49. See Circular, attachment B, §D(4)(a)(1)(a).
50. Attachment B, §A(8)(a).
51. OMB's May 2007 Report, 13. For further discussion on the results of competitive sourcing, see below.
52. Circular, attachment B, §D(5)(c)(4)(a).
53. See Circular, attachment C, §A(1).
54. Agencies are required to use a prescribed costing software, COMPARE, which incorporates the costing procedures of the Circular. See www.comparea76.com (accessed 9/17/07).
55. See Circular, attachment C, §B(2)(f).
56. See Circular, attachment C, §B(5).
57. Circular, attachment C, §C(4).
58. Circular, attachment C §C(6).
59. Circular, attachment C §A(11).
60. Circular, attachment C, §D.
61. The Circular also provides a streamlined process that agencies may use at their option for competitions of activities performed by sixty-five or fewer FTEs. Unlike standard competitions, which involve head-to-head competition, streamlined competitions may be performed using a paper analysis where the cost of private sector performance is based on documented market research and then compared to the cost of in-house performance. The lack of head-to-head competition and the smaller size of the activity being studied

generally result in smaller savings, though many agencies have successfully reduced the cost of small support functions through streamlined competitions, largely by allowing their employees to develop MEOs. On average, agencies project savings of about $11,250 per FTE competed under a streamlined competition in FY 2006. OMB's May 2007 report, 35. Circular A-76 does not envision application of a conversion differential, as is required for standard competitions. However, pursuant to section 842(a) of Pub. L. No. 109–115, 119 Stat. 2396, 2506 (2005), Congress precluded most agencies from converting work to private sector performance using FY 2006 appropriations if the activity was performed by more than ten FTEs, unless conversion to private sector performance would result in 10 percent savings (or savings of $10 million) as documented through an actual competition. This requirement was extended to FY 2007 appropriations by Pub. L. No. 109–289, div. B, 120 Stat. 1257, 1311 (2006), as amended by Pub. L. No. 110–5, 121 Stat. 8 (2007).

62. Circular, attachment B, §F.
63. Circular, attachment D; Office of Management and Budget, *Clarification of the Term "Directly Interested Party"* (Washington, DC: Executive Office of the President, March 25, 2005), available at www.whitehouse.gov/omb/ (accessed 9/19/07).
64. 31 U.S.C. §3551(2)(B) (2000 & Supp.2004). Section 329 of the House National Defense Authorization Act for Fiscal Year 2008 would expand the definition of "interested party" to include "any one individual who, for the purpose of representing the Federal employees engaged in the performance of the activity or function for which the public-private competition is conducted . . . has been designated as the agent of the Federal employees by a majority of such employees," H.R. 1585, 110th Cong., 1st sess., 2007.
65. 31 U.S.C. §3552(b) (2000 & Supp.2004).
66. See generally Circular, attachment B §E.
67. Office of Management and Budget, Attachment to *Competition Framework for Financial Management Lines of Business Migrations* (Washington, DC: Executive Office of the President, May 22, 2006), 6 [hereinafter OMB's Competitive Migration Framework], available at www.whitehouse.gov/omb/ (accessed 9/19/07).
68. Ibid.
69. See also Office of Management and Budget, *Performance Periods in Public-Private Competitions,* Memorandum M-04-12 (Washington, DC: Executive Office of the President, April 30, 2004), available at www.whitehouse .gov/omb (accessed 9/19/07).
70. The panel, consisting of a diverse group of high-level officials from the public sector, private sector, and academia, was created by Congress "to study the policies and procedures governing the transfer of commercial activities for the Federal Government from Government personnel to a Federal contractor." Fiscal Year 2001 National Defense Authorization Act, Pub. L. No. 106–398, §102, 114 Stat. 1654, 1654A-221 (2000). The panel's

analysis and recommendations are published in Commercial Activities Panel, *Improving the Sourcing Decisions of the Government: Final Report* (2002) [hereinafter Commercial Activities Panel Report].

71. Commercial Activities Panel Report, 47.

72. See Commercial Activities Panel Report, 37–43.

73. Commercial Activities Panel Report, 39.

74. Performance of Commercial Activities, 68 Fed. Reg. 32,134 (May 29, 2003). These changes were arrived at after OMB solicited and evaluated public comment on proposed revisions. See Performance of Commercial Activities, 67 Fed. Reg. 69,769 (November 19, 2002).

75. Performance of Commercial Activities, 68 Fed. Reg. at 32,136.

76. In eliminating direct conversions, OMB noted that agencies "may be foregoing opportunities to reap savings and make better economic decisions through public-private competitions when they undertake a direct conversion." Ibid., 32,137.

77. Bureau of the Budget, *Commercial-Industrial Activities of the Government Providing Products or Services for Governmental Use.* Bulletin No. 55–4 (Washington, DC: Executive Office of the President, January 15, 1955).

78. See Office of Management and Budget, Cost Comparison Handbook, Supplement No. 1 to OMB Circular No. A-76: Policies for Acquiring Commercial or Industrial Products and Services Needed by the Government (Washington, DC: Executive Office of the President, March 1979). The handbook states: "The American people have a right to expect economical performance of Federal activities. Some activities are inherently governmental functions or, for other reasons, must be performed by Federal employees. Many activities, however, may be performed either by contract or by Federal employees. The choice between these alternatives must be based on a finding as to which method of performance would be more economical." See p. 1.

79. Circular A-76 has traditionally limited agencies' ability to make best value decisions by prohibiting agencies from trading off cost and quality considerations when evaluating the federal employees' tender. When the Commercial Activities Panel reviewed the Circular and the competitive sourcing process, it recommended that these restrictions be removed. It concluded that while cost must always be a factor, agencies should also be allowed to structure competitions to take into account the government's need for "high-quality, reliable, and sustained performance, as well as cost efficiencies." Commercial Activities Panel Report, 9. Despite the panel's recommendation (endorsed by a supermajority of its participants), Congress limited the use of tradeoffs in fiscal year 2006. Agencies are required to choose between an incumbent in-house government provider and the private sector solely based on lowest cost even if the agency can demonstrate that private sector performance would provide a superior solution, considering both cost and quality. Transportation, Treasury, Housing and Urban Development, the Judiciary, the District of Columbia, and the Independent Agencies Appropriations Act, 2006, Pub. L. No. 109–115, §842(a), 119 Stat. 2396, 2506 (2005).

80. For example, the ATO and private sector offerors must respond to a solicitation within the same timeframes, and offerors from both sectors are to be evaluated by the same officials. Circular, attachment B §§D(4)(a)(1), D(5)(c)(1).

81. The Commercial Activities Panel found that competitions routinely took two and a half to three years to complete under the old Circular. Commercial Activities Panel Report, 23, table 4. The revised Circular generally allows agencies one year to complete a standard competition from the date it is publicly announced and ninety days to complete a streamlined competition. Circular, attachment B §§C(2), D(1). (According to OMB's May 2007 report, these time frames are generally being met.) As described above, the Circular imposes no timeframes on preliminary planning leading up to the announcement of competition. See Circular, attachment B §A (giving substantive steps, not timelines, for preplanning). According to OMB, this approach helps to ensure that competitions are adequately and properly planned.

82. For example, the revised Circular separates the team formed to write the performance work statement from the team formed to develop the government's tender and "most efficient organization" (MEO) plan. In addition, the MEO team, directly affected personnel and their representatives, and any individual with knowledge of the MEO or agency cost estimate in the agency tender will not be permitted to be advisors to, or members of, the source selection evaluation board. Circular, attachment B, §D(2)(c).

83. The solicitation will require offers and agency tenders to include a quality control plan for self-inspection, and the performance of the selected provider—public or private—will be measured based on a quality assurance surveillance plan. Circular, attachment D, §E(4). Performance agreements with agency providers will be documented in letters of obligation. For additional discussion, see above.

84. U.S. General Accounting Office, *Competitive Sourcing: Implementation Will Be Challenging for Federal Agencies*, GAO-03-1022T (July 24, 2003), 4, available at www.gao.gov (accessed 9/19/07).

85. New Century, New Process: A Preview of Competitive Sourcing for the 21st Century; Hearing before the House Committee on Government Reform, 108th Cong., 1st sess., 44–45 (2003) (statement by Philip W. Grone, Principal Assistant Deputy Under Secretary of Defense for Installations and Environment).

86. OMB's May 2007 Report, 18.

87. See also OMB's May 2007 Report, 18–19; OMB's April 2006 Report, 5–8; OMB's May 2005 Report, 3–5. In addition, OMB announced that agencies would be expected to use public-private competition when planning "to upgrade to the next major release of [their] current core financial management system or modernize to a different core financial management system." OMB's Competitive Migration Framework, 1. Competitions would take place between public shared service centers and private providers with a demonstrated capability and capacity to provide efficient and effective service. These migrations are a component of the PMA's E-Government initiative

to help agencies eliminate redundant investments in "in-house" solutions that might be provided more effectively by another public or private sector source. Ibid at 1–2.

88. OMB's May 2007 Report, 8–9 tbl.4.

89. Letter from the Honorable Paul A. Denett, administrator for Federal Procurement Policy, to the Honorable Nancy Pelosi, Speaker of the House of Representatives (May 2, 2007), available at http://www.whitehouse.gov/omb/procurement/comp/src/transmittal_house.pdf. Competitive sourcing figures presented in this section generally reflect data on public-private competitions completed between fiscal years 2003 and 2006. Since this chapter was prepared, OMB has issued a report on fiscal year 2007 activities and five-year trends. See Office of Management and Budget, *Competitive Sourcing: Report on Competitive Sourcing Results, Fiscal Year 2007* (Washington, DC: Executive Office of the President, May 2008), available at http://www.whitehouse.gov/omb/procurement/reports/comp_sourc_fy2007.pdf (accessed 6/9/08). The fiscal year 2007 figures do not significantly change the analysis in this section.

90. OMB's May 2007 Report, 16. This rate assumes the government paid roughly $90,000 per civilian FTE annually in salary and benefits in FY 2003–2006.

91. Ibid.

92. President's Management Council, *Giving the American People More for Their Money* (Washington, DC: Executive Office of the President, October 13, 2006), attachment F, available at http://www.whitehouse.gov/results/ (accessed 10/17/07).

93. See, for example, Steven L. Schooner, "Competitive Sourcing Policy: More Sail Than Rudder?" 33 *Public Contract Law Journal* 263 (2004).

94. OMB's May 2007 Report, 2.

95. DOD reported that only 2 percent of the service contracting dollars it awarded in FY 1999 resulted from the application of competitive sourcing. Commercial Activities Panel Report, 21 (quoting U.S. Department of Defense, Report to the Senate on Completed DOD A-76 Competitions (2000)). The balance of contract dollars represents work that typically has been in the private sector (e.g., research and development, technical services, operation and maintenance of government facilities, medical services, transportation services, and construction or maintenance of real property).

96. OMB's April 2006 Report, 12. The historical average is roughly 50 percent. OMB's July 2003 Report, 2.

97. OMB's May 2007 Report, 12.

98. Jacques S. Gansler and William Lucyshyn, *Competitive Sourcing: What Happens to Federal Employees* (Washington, DC: IBM Center for the Business of Government, 2004). From 1995 through early 2004, competitions conducted at DOD resulted in position reduction of about 38 percent, which breaks down as follows: 16 percent transferred to other government jobs, 11 percent retired, 5 percent involuntarily separated, 3 percent temporary employees

that were terminated, and 2 percent unfilled positions that were eliminated. Ibid., 25 table 5.

99. OMB's May 2007 Report, 6. In fact, only 2.3 percent of the civilian positions in DOD competitions reaching final decision between FY 2003–2006 were subject to involuntary separation. Ibid. Generally speaking, the term "involuntary separation" refers to employees who were involuntarily separated from government service after receiving a reduction-in-force (RIF) notice and were not eligible for retirement. The term does not include individuals who took early retirement or transferred to another government job. It also does not include the termination of temporary employees or the elimination of unfilled positions. Agencies are making concerted efforts to provide soft landings for affected employees. In addition to retraining and reassignment, many employees are offered buyouts and early retirements. See OMB's May 2007 Report, 13; OMB's April 2006 Report, 12–13.

100. See OMB's May Report, 12–13.

101. Excluding core work allows an agency to focus its consideration of public-private competition on repetitive, routine, work that is purely commercial and not core to the agency. Examples of noncore work could include installation, operation, testing and maintenance of desktops and servers, building and grounds maintenance, administrative support services, payroll processing, and workforce training. While noncore work may be essential to daily agency operations, its potential conversion to contract performance based on cost savings and performance improvements should not, with effective contract management, expose the agency to substantial risk. The principle of ensuring that federal agencies have the competencies and capacity to perform core work is echoed in other OMB management policies. For example, OMB guidance on information technology (IT) activities emphasizes that qualified federal IT project managers are the government's "first line of defense against the cost overruns, schedules slips, and poor performance that threaten agencies' ability to deliver efficient and effective services to citizens." Office of Management and Budget, *Information Technology (IT) Project Manager (PM) Qualification Guidance,* Memorandum M-04-19 (Washington, DC: Executive Office of the President, July 21, 2004), available at www.whitehouse.gov/omb/ (accessed 9/19/07). The Chief Information Officers Council has identified the appropriate competencies, experiences, and training for federal employees to effectively manage IT projects at various complexity levels. Agencies have developed plans to close IT skill and competency gaps. Plans include additional workforce training, mentoring, development of Communities of Practice, skills incentive programs, increased emphasis on the retention of staff, and expanded recruitment activities. Agency progress is being measured on the scorecard for the PMA's human capital initiative. See Office of Management and Budget, *Analytical Perspectives: Budget of the U.S. Government, Fiscal Year 2007,* 154–155 (Washington, DC: Executive Office of the President), available at www.whitehouse.gov/omb/ (accessed 9/19/07).

102. OFPP is responsible for setting the overall direction of government-wide procurement policy. 41 U.S.C. §404 (2000). As part of its general responsibilities, OFPP manages the competitive sourcing initiative.

103. Office of Management and Budget, *Skills Assessment of Contracting Professionals* (Washington, DC: Executive Office of the President, March 7, 2007), available at www.whitehouse.gov/omb/.

104. See "DOD Studies Its Procurement Capabilities," *Federal Computer Week,* September 4, 2007, available at www.fcw.com/ (accessed 9/19/07).

105. See Office of Management and Budget, *The Federal Acquisition Certification for Program and Project Managers* (Washington, DC: Executive Office of the President, April 25, 2007), available at www.whitehouse.gov/omb/ (accessed 9/19/07). OFPP has also issued guidance that standardizes training and experience requirements for contracting officer technical representatives, i.e., the officials designated by contracting officers to perform contract administration in regard to technical issues. See Office of Management and Budget, *The Federal Acquisition Certification for Contracting Officer Technical Representatives* (Washington, DC: Executive Office of the President, November 26, 2007), available at http://www.whitehouse .gov/omb/procurement/memo/fac-cotr.pdf (accessed 6/10/08). In addition, OFPP has issued guidelines to help agencies conduct more thorough and complete reviews of their acquisition functions to determine if they have the internal controls, structure, and staffing they need to support agency missions in a timely and cost-effective manner. See Office of Management and Budget, *Conducting Acquisition Assessments under OMB Circular A-123* (Washington, DC: Executive Office of the President, May 21, 2008), available at http://www.whitehouse.gov/omb/procurement/memo/a123 _guidelines.pdf.

106. Pub. L. No. 109–313, 120 Stat. 1734 (2006).

107. Ibid., §4.

108. Office of Management and Budget, *Plans for Hiring Reemployed Annuitants to Fill Acquisition-Related Positions* (Washington, DC: Executive Office of the President, September 4, 2007), 1, available at www.whitehouse .gov/omb/ (accessed 10/17/07). For a number of years, OMB has recognized the need to preserve a core competency in contract administration and has recognized agency actions to exempt contracting officer representatives who assist with contract administration from public-private competition. See OMB's May 2005 Report, 14.

109. OMB, Plans for Hiring Reemployed Annuitants, 1.

110. U.S. Department of Homeland Security, *Ongoing Challenges in Creating an Effective Acquisition Organization,* GAO-07-948T (June 7, 2007), 8–10, available at www.gao.gov/ (accessed 9/19/07).

111. Hearing before the Subcommittee on Oversight of Government Management, the Federal Workforce and the District of Columbia of the Senate Committee on Homeland Security and Governmental Affairs, 110th Cong., 1st sess., 5–6 (2007), available at hsgac.senate.gov (accessed

9/19/07) (testimony of Paul A. Schneider, Under Secretary for Management, Department of Homeland Security).

112. See GAO, *Department of Homeland Security: Improved Assessment and Oversight Needed to Manage Risk of Contracting for Selected Services,* GAO-07-990 (September 2007). The GAO's recommendations include establishing strategic-level guidance for determining the appropriate mix of government and contractor employees to meet mission needs; assessing the risk of contractor services as part of the acquisition planning process; defining contract requirements to clearly describe roles, responsibilities, and limitation of contractor services as part of the acquisition planning process; assessing program office staff and expertise necessary to provide sufficient oversight; and reviewing contracts as part of acquisition oversight. Ibid.

113. 48 C.F.R. §37.114 (2005).

114. Ibid.

115. In describing weaknesses of the pre–May 2003 version of the Circular, OMB acknowledged that "even where competition is used to transform a public provider into a high-value service provider, few steps are routinely taken to ensure this potential translates into positive results." Performance of Commercial Activities, 67 Fed. Reg. 69,769, 69,771 (November 19, 2002).

116. Circular, attachment B §E(2).

117. Consolidated Appropriations Act, 2004, Pub. L. No. 108–199 §647, 118 Stat. 3, 361 (2004). Pursuant to §647 of the Act, agencies report on the number of federal employees studied under competitions, incremental costs, savings, the number of federal employees to be studied in the coming fiscal year, and how the agency aligns competitive sourcing decisions with its strategic workforce plan.

118. DOD, the largest user of public-private competition, developed guidelines to standardize how DOD calculates baseline costs for commercial activities that are selected for competition. See OMB's April 2006 Report, 16. This guidance should help to improve consistency and transparency in calculating savings.

119. Office of Management and Budget, *Report to Congress on FY 2004 Competitive Sourcing Efforts,* Memorandum M-05-01 (Washington, DC: Executive Office of the President, October 15, 2004), 5–6, 9–10 [hereinafter OMB Memorandum M-05-01], available at www.whitehouse.gov/omb/ (accessed 9/19/07); Office of Management and Budget, *Report to Congress on FY 2003 Competitive Sourcing Efforts,* Memorandum M-04-07 (Washington, DC: Executive Office of the President, February 26, 2004) [hereinafter OMB Memorandum M-04-07], available at www.whitehouse.gov/omb (accessed 9/19/07).

120. OMB's April 2006 Report, 18.

121. See OMB's April 2006 Report, 19. Where the MEO is selected to perform, agencies will also seek to separate MEO performance efficiencies or

inefficiencies from differences in cost that simply reflect assumptions made by the Circular A-76 costing factors used to compare costs between the public and private sectors during competition (e.g., an agency is experiencing slightly higher costs because the Circular assumes labor costs at a fixed rate and employees are actually getting paid at a slightly higher level).

122. OMB's May 2004 Report, 18.

123. Agency success in the use of competitive sourcing is also tracked by OMB through use of a management scorecard. The management scorecard is used to evaluate an agency's status—as measured against government-wide standards for success—and progress in achieving customized agency milestones for the competitive sourcing initiative and other major initiatives that comprise the PMA. See *The Federal Government Is Results-Oriented: A Report to Federal Employees* (August 2004), 4, available at www.whitehouse.gov/ (accessed 9/19/07). See also *Giving the American People More for Their Money: A Report from the President's Management Council* (July 2005), 8–13, available at www.whitehouse.gov/. An agency's status and progress are assessed using a three-color traffic light system. Green signifies success; yellow signifies mixed results; red signifies unsatisfactory results. For a copy of PMA agency status scores, see www.whitehouse.gov (accessed 9/19/07). For a copy of the PMA success standards for competitive sourcing, see www.whitehouse.gov (accessed 9/19/07).

124. See Executive Office of the President, Office of Management and Budget, *Validating the Results of Public-Private Competition* (April 13, 2007), available at www.whitehouse.gov/omb/ (accessed 9/19/07).

125. See OMB's April 2006 Report, 17–18.

126. A general comparison of the number of positions agencies initially projected for competition to that which they report as having been competed suggests that agencies opt not to compete a considerable portion of positions that were initially under consideration for competitive sourcing. For example, agencies tentatively planned to announce competitions involving almost 74,000 positions in FY 2004, 2005 and 2006, but competitions completed during this time or announced and pending at the end of FY 2006 totaled around 39,000 positions. OMB's May 2007 Report, app. A-1 at 27, app. A-2 at 28; OMB's April 2006 Report, app. A-1 at 28, app. B at 30; OMB's May 2005 Report, app. A-1 at 33, app. C at 37; OMB's May 2004 Report, app. F. Some of the difference may be due to employee movement to other activities or general attrition prior to public announcement of the competition. Congressional prohibitions may also be a factor if the agency did not anticipate the restriction, but once a legislative restriction is imposed, agencies adjust their projections accordingly.

127. According to data in the Federal Procurement Data System, agency expenditures on service contracting have essentially doubled between FY 2000 and FY 2006, from approximately $128 billion to about $250 billion. See FPDS, *Electronic Standard Report on Service Codes*, available at www.fpds

.gov (generated 07/19/07). This increase is largely attributable to new commercial work or segregable expansions of commercial work which, under the Circular, may be competed among private sector sources without considering agency performance, if the work is suitable for private sector performance. See Circular, §5.d. During this same period, the workforce also expanded to take on new responsibilities, with civilian executive branch salaries and expenses increasing from about $130 billion to $180 billion. See *Analytical Perspectives, Budget of the United States Government,* FY 2002 (Washington, DC: Executive Office of the President, 2001), 217, and *Analytical Perspectives, Budget of the United States Government,* FY 2008 (Washington, DC: Executive Office of the President, 2007), 367. As discussed above, the Circular requires inherently governmental work to be performed by federal employees and anticipates that core commercial work will also be performed in-house without consideration of the private sector.

128. Transportation, Treasury, Housing and Urban Development, the Judiciary, the District of Columbia, and the Independent Agencies Appropriations Act, 2006, Pub. L. No. 109–115, §842(a), 119 Stat. 2396, 2506 (2005). OMB's April 2006 and May 2007 reports express concerns with restrictions that force agencies to choose between the government and private sector solely based on lowest cost. While cost-only comparisons generally work well for competitions that involve routine needs, such as building or lawn maintenance, OMB finds that "[s]olutions prepared with the expectation of being evaluated only on cost typically perpetuate the status quo and rarely offer innovation or capital investment when it is needed." Office of Management and Budget, *Competitive Sourcing: Report on the Use of Best Value Tradeoffs in Public-Private Competitions* (Washington, DC: Executive Office of the President, April 2006), 6, available at www.whitehouse.gov/omb/ (accessed 9/19/07).

129. See Consolidated Appropriations Act, FY 2008, Pub. L. No. 110-161, Division E, §515.

130. See Consolidated Appropriations Act, FY 2008, Pub. L. No. 110-161, Division A, §730.

131. See Consolidated Appropriations Act, FY 2008, Pub. L. No. 110-161, Division F, §415(a)(1).

132. See Consolidated Appropriations Act, FY 2008, Pub. L. No. 110-161, Division F, §415(a)(2).

133. See Consolidated Appropriations Act, FY 2008, Pub. L. No. 110-161, Division C, §103.

134. See Consolidated Appropriations Act, FY 2008, Pub. L. No. 110-161, Division G, §111.

135. See Duncan Hunter National Defense Authorization Act for Fiscal Year 2009, H.R. 5658, 110th Cong. §325 (engrossed as agreed to or passed by House, May 22, 2008).

136. See U.S. Troop Readiness, Veterans' Care, Katrina Recovery, and Iraq Accountability Appropriations Act, 2007, Pub. L. No. 110–28, §§6201,

6602, 121 Stat. 112, 171, 178 (2007) (deeming all Department of Energy employees at the National Energy Technology Laboratory and all Department of Labor employees at the Mine Safety and Health Administration to be inherently governmental).

137. See, e.g., S. Rep. 110–127, at 103–104 (2007) ("The Committee fails to see any evidence of cost savings or increased efficiency by undergoing these expensive competitions."); H. Rep. 110–207, at 10 (2007) ("A-76 competitions potentially outsource Federal workforce responsibilities and result in the loss of technically skilled Federal workers, institutional knowledge and effective oversight over worker performance.").

138. See, e.g., National Defense Authorization Act for FY 2008, Pub. L. No. 110–181, §324 (2007), requiring the Department of Defense to develop guidelines on insourcing new and contracted out functions.

139. See 10 U.S.C. 2463(c), as added by §324 of Pub. L. No. 110-181. This provision builds on a requirement Congress imposed on DOD in the National Defense Authorization Act for Fiscal Year 2006, Pub. L. No. 109–163, §343, 119 Stat. 3136, 3200–01 (2006) to create guidelines and procedures for ensuring that consideration is given to using federal government employees for work that is currently performed, or would otherwise be performed, under contract. DOD issued guidelines in July 2007. Under Secretary of Defense, *Implementation of Section 343 of the 2006 National Defense Authorization Act* (Washington, DC, July 27, 2007), available at competitivesourcing.navy.mil (accessed 10/17/07).

140. Through the third quarter of fiscal year 2008, only competitive sourcing activity was officially tracked under the PMA.

141. Section 5(c) of the Circular acknowledges the development of high-performing organizations as an alternative to standard and streamlined competitions. In May 2008, the PMA's "competitive sourcing" initiative was renamed the "commercial services management" (CSM) initiative to recognize that agencies improve the operation of their commercial functions using a variety of techniques, including competitive sourcing and internal business process reengineering. Internal reengineerings, which may lead to the establishment of HPOs, generally do not entail public-private competition or the potential conversion of work from the public sector to the private sector. However, reengineerings with the greatest chance for success are likely to use the same types of disciplined management practices as competitive sourcing, but for competition, such as baselining, benchmarking, human capital planning, and tracking of results against a clear performance agreement. OMB's CSM initiative will track reengineerings of commercial services that rely on these disciplined skills. See Office of Management and Budget, *Plans to Address Management Challenges for July 1, 2009 and 2010*, Memorandum to the President's Management Council (Washington, DC: Executive Office of the President, May 22, 2008), available at http://www.mainet.com/PTBIVCoverMemoandAttachmentA1_1 .pdf.

4. Rent-a-Regulator

This chapter is adapted from an article published in *Ecology Law Quarterly* Vol. 33, No. 4 (© 2006) by permission of the Regents of the University of California. I thank Jody Freeman and Martha Minow for generous assistance and valuable advice. All errors are mine alone.

1. On military privatization, see Peter W. Singer, *Corporate Warriors: The Rise of the Privatized Military Industry* (Ithaca, NY: Cornell University Press, 2003); Martha Minow, "Outsourcing Power: How Privatizing Military Efforts Challenges Accountability, Professionalism and Democracy," 46 *Boston College Law Review* 989 (2005); Jon D. Michaels, "Beyond Accountability: The Constitutional, Democratic, and Strategic Problems with Privatizing War," 82 *Washington University Law Quarterly* 1004–1005 (2004); on private police, see Heidi Boghosian, "Applying Restraints to Private Police," 70 *Missouri Law Review* 191 (2005); David A. Sklansky, "The Private Police," 46 *UCLA Law Review* 1165 (1999); on private prisons, see Sharon Dolovich, "Legitimate Punishment in Liberal Democracy," 7 *Buffalo Criminal Law Review* 433–434 (2004); and on privatization of port management, see "Under Pressure, Dubai Company Drops Port Deal," *New York Times,* March 10, 2006, at A1.
2. See Jody Freeman, "Extending Public Law Norms through Privatization," 116 *Harvard Law Review* 1285, 1286–1287 & n.6 (2003). Cf. Jody Freeman and Daniel A. Farber, "Modular Environmental Regulation," 54 *Duke Law Journal* 795, 799 (2005) (describing, in the context of environmental regulation, how tools and governance structures "can be built, unbuilt, and rebuilt," in a process of "configuring and reconfiguring the component parts of the regulatory system, and deploying the actors operating within it, without necessarily replacing existing structures with something wholly new").
3. See generally Lester M. Salamon, "The New Governance and the Tools of Public Action: An Introduction," in Lester M. Salamon, ed., *The Tools of Government: A Guide to the New Governance* (New York: Oxford University Press, 2002), pp. 1–47.
4. Compare David Osborne and Ted Gaebler, *Reinventing Government: How the Entrepreneurial Spirit Is Transforming the Public Sector* (Reading, MA: Addison-Wesley, 1992), and Jeff Jacoby, "Bill Weld's Revolution That Wasn't," 6 *City Journal* 49 (1996), with American Federation of State, County and Municipal Employees (AFSCME) "Privatization: The Public Pays" (on file with author) ("Despite everything you do, public officials may still decide to privatize public services. When that happens, you need to fight back on every front."). Although less dogmatic, Elliot Sclar also provides forceful arguments against far-reaching privatization. See Elliot D. Sclar, *You Don't Always Get What You Pay For: The Economics of Privatization* (Ithaca, NY: Cornell University Press, 2000).
5. The U.S. Environmental Protection Agency defines brownfields as "real property, the expansion, redevelopment, or reuse of which may be complicated by

the presence or potential presence of a hazardous substance, pollutant, or contaminant." U.S. Environmental Protection Agency (EPA), "Brownfields Cleanup and Redevelopment," www.epa.gov/swerosps/bf/index.html (last accessed September 25, 2007). Brownfields law and policy encompasses the economic and environmental benefits and challenges that come from redeveloping contaminated properties rather than merely remediating them.

6. See Kris Wernstedt, "A Broader View of Brownfield Revitalization," in Richard D. Morgenstern and Paul R. Portney, eds., *New Approaches to Energy and the Environment: Policy Advice for the President* (Washington, DC: RFF Press, 2004), pp. 82–86 (noting that estimates of the number of brownfield sites in the nation range from 130,000 to 1 million).

7. See Martha Minow, "Public and Private Partnerships: Accounting for the New Religion," 116 *Harvard Law Review* 1229, 1242–1243 (2003) (describing the failures of public schools, prisons, and social services).

8. Jacoby, "Bill Weld's Revolution," 49.

9. See §49–153, Ariz. Rev. Stat. (Arizona's Greenfields Pilot Program, repealed effective 2008); §22a–133v, Conn. Gen. Stat. Ann. (Connecticut's Licensed Site Professional Program); "Cleanup Star Program Guidance Document," www.state.nj.us (accessed 11/03/06) (New Jersey "Cleanup Star" program, created as agency policy); N.C. Admin. Code 15A, r. 13C.0300 (North Carolina "registered environmental consultant" program); Ohio Rev. Code Ann., §3745-300-05 (Ohio's "certified professionals" in its Voluntary Action Program). The sixth state program, that in Massachusetts, is the subject of this chapter. Other states certify licensed professionals to perform more minimal functions and require state approval before action is taken. See Heidi Gorovitz Robertson, "Legislative Innovation in State Brownfields Redevelopment Programs," 16 *Journal of Environmental Law and Litigation* 62–63 (2001) (describing cleanup programs in Colorado, Delaware, Kansas, Maine, and Missouri).

10. See Donald F. Kettl, *Sharing Power: Public Governance and Private Markets* (Washington, DC: Brookings Institution, 1993), pp. 99–129 (describing EPA's use of contractors). In addition, the federal EPA now requires a landowner to retain a private consultant as part of the due diligence required to qualify as an innocent purchaser under the "all appropriate inquiries" provision of the Comprehensive Environmental Response, Compensation, and Liability Act. See U.S. EPA, "Final Rule, Standards and Practices for All Appropriate Inquiries," 70 *Federal Register* 66,070 (November 1, 2005), codified at 40 C.F.R. Part 312 (2007).

11. Different states have different names for the licensed professionals who oversee cleanups. For example, in Massachusetts they are Licensed Site Professionals (LSPs); in Connecticut they are Licensed Environmental Professionals (LEPs); in North Carolina there are both Registered Environmental Consultants (RECs) and Registered Site Managers (RSMs); in Ohio they are Licensed Consultants (LCs); and in New Jersey they are Cleanup Stars. This chapter focuses on the Massachusetts program and thus uses the term "LSP."

12. See Minow, "Outsourcing Power," 1001 ("[d]o contractors do what they are asked to do—and not do what they are not asked to do?"). The question is slightly more nuanced where, as here, the private decision makers are not actually contractors, but the concept of an agent's execution of a principal's goals remains the same.

13. See Martha Minow, *Partners, Not Rivals: Privatization and the Public Good* (Boston: Beacon Press, 2002), p. 44 (arguing that public values must be upheld even when government contracts out services).

14. See DEP memorandum to author on MassDEP privatized waste site cleanup program (October 18, 2005) (on file with author) (compiling audit results) [hereinafter "DEP Memorandum"]. The audit results are discussed below.

15. See Daniel A. Farber, "Taking Slippage Seriously: Noncompliance and Creative Compliance in Environmental Law," 23 *Harvard Environmental Law Review* 301–311 (1999) (defining positive and negative slippage).

16. DEP Memorandum.

17. Sclar, *The Economics of Privatization*, 129.

18. See Minow, "New Religion," 1246–1248 (cautioning that privatization may dilute public values). A similar argument might point out that if privatizing environmental regulation grants discretion to the private decision maker, it could obstruct the formation of a continuous set of environmental standards and values across communities. Cf. ibid., 1253 (warning that privatization in schooling may lead to a set of "disparate activities" lacking "common purpose" and thus frustrating "shared goals").

19. An Office of Management and Budget (OMB) document defines "inherently governmental" to include those activities that "require the exercise of substantial discretion in applying government authority and/or in making decisions for the government." See U.S. Office of Management and Budget, Circular No. A-76 (Revised), May 29, 2003, p. A-2.

20. See Dan Guttman, "Governance by Contract: Constitutional Visions; Time for Reflection and Choice," 33 *Public Contract Law Journal* 339 (2004) (stating that in the "real-world context," "the question is not whether contractors perform regulatory, war-fighting, or law enforcement functions," but instead how to determine the legitimacy of such contracting).

21. In the Massachusetts program, for example, the estimated DEP staffing requirement for the publicly administered program was 519 full-time equivalent (FTE) staff, compared to 324 for the privatized program. The actual staffing as of September 2005 was 165. For a candid discussion by the DEP commissioner of the pressure imposed by depleted agency resources, see Robert W. Golledge, "Effective Regulation in Lean Times: A State View," *ABA Trends* 35, no. 5 (2004): 2. See also Freeman, "Extending Public Law Norms," 1295–1301, 1317 (describing agencies as "already frequently underfunded to carry out their basic regulatory and adjudicative tasks).

22. Even states that publicly oversee hazardous waste cleanups utilize a pay-to-play model. States use various cost recovery mechanisms, including application fees, sliding scales, or flat fees per phase, to recoup their expenditures on

oversight and related costs. For a list of states that use such cost recovery mechanisms, see Joel B. Eisen, "Brownfields of Dreams? Challenges and Limits of Voluntary Cleanup Programs and Incentives," 1996 *University of Illinois Law Review* 966 n.353 (1996). See also E.I. Du Pont de Nemours & Co. v. New Jersey Department of Environmental Protection, 661 A.2d 1314 (Sup. Ct. N.J. 1995) (upholding New Jersey's authority to recover oversight costs). See also Interview with Dale Desnoyers, Director of Environmental Remediation, New York Department of Environmental Conservation (September 1, 2005) (characterizing state cost recovery as "the polluter pays concept carried over to the brownfields arena").

23. See generally Amy L. Edwards, ed., *Implementing Institutional Controls at Brownfields and Other Contaminated Sites* (Chicago: American Bar Association, 2003).

24. See generally New York Department of Conservation, Division of Remediation, Draft Brownfield Cleanup Program Guide, www.dec.state.ny.us (accessed 11/27/06), p. 7.

25. See, e.g., "A Cleanup That's Easier Legislated Than Done," *New York Times,* December 4, 2005, p. B1.

26. Cf. Minow, "New Religion," 1242–1243 (describing the failures of public schools, prisons, and social services).

27. The MCP is codified at Mass. Regs. Code 310, §40.0000 (2006).

28. Mass. Gen. Laws, ch. 21E §3A(o) (2002).

29. See Mass. Regs. Code 309, §§7.00–7.15 (2006) (procedures governing disciplinary actions of the LSP Board); see also ibid., §7.03 (pertaining to initiation of complaints and permitting "any person or any member of the Board" to file a complaint against an LSP).

30. See Mass. Gen. Laws ch. 21E, §19 (2002) (defining waste site cleanup activity opinion); §40.006, Mass. Regs. Code 310 (2006) (defining LSP opinion).

31. See Mass. Regs. Code 310, §40.009 (2006) (listing actions that require professional opinion).

32. At the limit, an LSP's lack of involvement in a project can violate the Code of Professional Conduct. See Mass. Regs. Code 309, §4.03 (2006) (proscribing issuance of LSP opinion if the LSP has not, at a minimum, "periodically reviewed and evaluated the performance by others" of the task in question).

33. DEP Memorandum.

34. Interview with John Fitzgerald, Director of Response and Remediation, Bureau of Waste Site Cleanup, Massachusetts DEP (September 12, 2005).

35. See "Conducting Feasibility Evaluations under the MCP" (Policy #04-160, July 2004), www.mass.gov/dep/cleanup/04-160.pdf (accessed 11/04/06) [hereinafter "Feasibility Evaluations"]; see also Interview with Deborah Gevalt, Senior Vice President, Haley & Aldrich, Inc., and Licensed Site Professional (January 13, 2006) (noting that DEP has given "very clear guidance" that LSPs should strive to achieve background conditions).

36. See Mass. Regs. Code 310, §40.1050 (2006).

37. As defined in the regulations, "background" means

> those levels of oil and hazardous material that would exist in the absence
> of the disposal site of concern which are either: (a) ubiquitous and consis-
> tently present in the environment at and in the vicinity of the disposal site
> of concern; and attributable to geologic or ecological conditions, or at-
> mospheric deposition of industrial process or engine emissions; (b) attrib-
> utable to coal ash or wood ash associated with fill material; (c) releases to
> groundwater from a public water supply system; or (d) petroleum
> residues that are incidental to the normal operation of motor vehicles.

Mass. Regs. Code 310, §40.0006(12) (2006). See also "Feasibility Evaluations."
38. See "Feasibility Evaluations."
39. See Mass. Dep't Envtl. Prot., Waste Site Cleanups Notifications and Status,
available at http://www.mass.gov/dep/cleanup/sites/sdown.htm (follow "re-
lease.zip" hyperlink; then open "release.dbf" icon) [hereinafter "Mass.
Waste Site Cleanups"]. The percentages in this section were calculated by
sorting DEP's database by category of site and class of Response Action Outcome (RAO). These calculations are based on sites in the 120-day notification category, which excludes spills but includes longer-term brownfields redevelopment.
40. See generally Ned Abelson et al., "Activity and Use Limitations in Massachusetts," in Edwards, *Implementing Institutional Controls*, 189–202.
41. See Salamon, *The Tools of Government*, 1–47; Stephen Goldsmith and
William D. Eggers, *Governing by Network: The New Shape of the Public
Sector* (Washington, DC: Brookings Institution Press, 2004); Jody Freeman,
"The Private Role in Public Governance," 75 *New York University Law Review* 636–665 (2000).
42. See John D. Donahue, *The Privatization Decision: Public Ends, Private
Means* (New York: Basic Books, 1989), pp. 58–68.
43. Sclar, *The Economics of Privatization*, 29–44 (discussing privatization of
highway maintenance in Massachusetts).
44. To be sure, although less common than plain-vanilla contracting out of tasks
like garbage collection, the LSP program is not a rarity in delegating aspects of
the regulatory process to private actors. See Sidney A. Shapiro, "Outsourcing
Government Regulation," 53 *Duke Law Review* 389 (2003). Moreover, the
dichotomy between service provision and regulation is often a matter of
form—see Gillian E. Metzger, "Privatization as Delegation," 103 *Columbia
Law Review* 1367 (2003)—especially when complex functions like schooling,
prisons, and warfare are involved. See sources cited in notes 1–6 above.
45. For an explanation of various versions of capture theory, see generally
Richard A. Posner, "Theories of Economic Regulation," 5 *Bell Journal of
Economics and Management Science* 341–344 (1974).
46. See Elliot Steinberg, "President's Message: Courts Chip Away at DEP Aggressive Enforcement Tactics," *LSPA Newsletter* (May 2005), www.lspa

.org/resources (accessed 11/04/06) (citing Superior Court Civil Action No. 04-5570-BLS (March 10, 2005)).

47. Ibid., 2.

48. Ibid. The conflicts of interest affecting LSPs are discussed below.

49. Allan R. Fierce, "The Accountability of Licensed Site Professionals to the LSP Board," p. 1 (on file with author).

50. Kettl, *Sharing Power,* 121.

51. See generally John R. Allison, "A Process Value Analysis of Decision-Maker Bias: The Case of Economic Conflicts of Interest," 32 *American Business Law Journal* 484 (1995) (listing five types of bias, including "a prejudgment about legislative facts" and "a prior commitment on adjudicative facts") (internal quotation marks omitted) (quoting Kenneth C. Davis, *Administrative Law Treatise,* vol. 2, 2nd ed. (San Diego, CA: K.C. Davis Publishing Company, 1978), §19:1, p. 371).

52. See Massachusetts DEP, "A Massachusetts Property Owner's Guide to Hiring a Licensed Site Professional," www.mass.gov/dep/cleanup/lsp.pdf (accessed 11/27/06) (urging property owners to "[s]hop around" for an LSP).

53. See Interview with John Fitzgerald, Director of Response and Remediation, Bureau of Waste Site Cleanup, DEP (September 12, 2005). That the LSP cannot afford to act as the client's "conscience" bears similarity, again, to a lawyer-client relationship. Compare Geoffrey Miller, "From Club to Market: The Evolving Role of Business Lawyers," 74 *Fordham Law Review* 1124 (2005) (noting that the competitive market for legal services and a client's ability to switch counsel makes it more difficult for lawyers to act as the client's conscience).

54. Interview with John Fitzgerald (September 12, 2005) (noting that LSPs have incentives to do a D+ job).

55. The dynamic is similar to that of in-house counsels, as the role of the in-house LSP involves loyalty and being "part of the team." See, e.g., Geoffrey C. Hazard, Jr., "Ethical Dilemmas of Corporate Counsel," 46 *Emory Law Journal* 1017 (1997).

56. Fierce, "Accountability of Licensed Site Professionals," 1. Compare Miller, "From Club to Market," 1114 (describing the legal profession as a "buyer's market in which clients call the shots" (quoting F. Leary Davis, "Back to the Future: The Buyer's Market and the Need for Law Firm Leadership, Creativity and Innovation," 16 *Campbell Law Review* 148 (1994) (internal quotation marks omitted)).

57. See Interview with Larry Schnapf, Schnapf Environmental Law Center, e-mail communication (August 10, 2005).

58. See, e.g., James M. Buchanan, "Markets, States, and the Extent of Morals," 68 *American Economic Review* 365 (1978).

59. Cognizant of the potential problems that contract structure can cause, the 1990 privatization report did envision that contractual structure would be regulated. The LSP Board, too, has discussed various means of regulating

contracts. The original regulations for professional conduct prohibited the use of contingency fees; if LSPs were only paid if they rendered a finding of no significant risk, they would obviously have increased incentives to slight the regulations in order to make such a finding. However, the Board subsequently decided against regulating contract structure at all, concluding that truly objectionable contracts would violate the broader prescription of professional responsibility and thus more specific regulation was not necessary. The new regulation, Mass. Regs. Code 309 §4.05, states, "An LSP shall not let his or her ownership interest, compensation, or continued employment affect his or her Professional Services to the extent that said Professional Services do not meet the standards set forth in" the LSP Code of Professional Conduct and the MCP. See Board of Registration of Hazardous Waste Site Cleanup Professionals, "Regulations Committee Meeting Minutes" (January 21, 1999) (agreeing to recommend replacing the contingency fee regulation with the current "accepting compensation" regulation).

60. See Joel Hirschhorn, National Governors Association Center for Best Practices, "Applying Pay for Performance Paper Techniques to Brownfields Cleanups" (on file with author). However, the difficulty in articulating performance standards has inhibited widespread use of these contracts. Cf. Steven J. Kelman, "Contracting," in Salamon, The Tools of Government, 282.

61. See Donald F. Kettl, "Managing Indirect Government," in Salamon, The Tools of Government, 491.

62. Donald Kettl phrased it this way: "The fundamental irony of privatization and its other third-party variants is that they require very, very strong public management to make them work well." Ibid., 500.

63. Massachusetts DEP, Interim Report: Waste Site Cleanup Program Improvements and Funding Requirements (November 30, 1990), pp. 5–6.

64. Ibid.

65. Interview with John Fitzgerald, Director of Response and Remediation, Bureau of Waste Site Cleanup, Massachusetts DEP (October 7, 2005).

66. Alfred C. Aman, Jr., "Privatization, Prisons, Democracy and Human Rights: The Need to Extend the Province of Administrative Law," 12 Indiana Journal of Global Legal Studies 534 (2005) (arguing, in the context of prison privatization, that "[t]he state must retain and be able actually to exercise 'step-in' rights—that is, to reclaim any privatized part of its prison system— and to do this it needs to have ongoing capacity and skill levels of its own") (quoting Richard Harding, "Private Prisons," 28 Crime and Justice 265 (2001)).

67. One needs to look no farther than FEMA's struggle to respond in the wake of Hurricane Katrina to recognize that transferring control to private providers may hamper government responsiveness when it is needed. See, e.g., FEMA after Katrina, Testimony of Albert Ashwood, Vice-President, National Emergency Management Association, Federal Document Clearing House Congressional Testimony (October 6, 2005) ("I'm not against privatizing or utilizing

the resources out there, but there is a point in which the federal government must accept some responsibility for ensuring that functions exist to respond and recover for whatever the disaster 'du jour' may be.").

68. See New Jersey Cleanup Star Program Guidance Document, www.state.nj.us (accessed 11/27/06). Properties involving groundwater contamination, for example, are ineligible for private oversight. Ibid.

69. Massachusetts DEP, *Interim Report,* 6.

70. Ibid., 32–33.

71. See Massachusetts DEP, Audit Fact Sheet, www.mass.gov (accessed 11/04/06).

72. Ibid.

73. 1998 Mass. Acts, ch. 206; Mass. Regs. Code 310, §40.1110 (2006).

74. Interview with John Fitzgerald (October 7, 2005).

75. See Massachusetts DEP, Audits—General Information, www.mass.gov/dep/cleanup/compliance/audinfo.htm (accessed 01/25/06).

76. Donald F. Kettl, "Foreword," in Goldsmith and Egger, *Governing by Network,* viii (discussing NASA's excessive reliance on contractors).

77. Margaret R. Stolfa, "Massachusetts' Activity and Use Limitations," in Edwards, *Implementing Institutional Controls,* 187 n.37.

78. Ibid.

79. See Minow, *Partners, Not Rivals,* 152–153.

80. See, e.g., Louis Lowenstein, "Financial Transparency and Corporate Governance: You Manage What You Measure," 96 *Columbia Law Review* 1335 (1996).

81. Notably, the agency has been taking an increasingly aggressive approach to enforcement in recent years, moving away from its previous, and more expensive, "compliance assistance" approach. See, e.g., Massachusetts DEP, *Compliance and Enforcement Annual Report, Fiscal Year 2004,* www.mass.gov (accessed 11/27/06) (describing a record year for enforcement actions). See also Interview with Mark Roberts, McRoberts, Roberts, & Rainer, LLP, former LSP Board member (January 14, 2006).

82. See Mass. Regs. Code 309, §§7.00–7.15 (2006) (procedures governing disciplinary actions of the LSP Board); see also ibid., §7.03 (pertaining to initiation of complaints and permitting "any person or any member of the Board" to file a complaint against an LSP).

83. "This is always the Board's prerogative—not to include a particular MCP violation in the formal disciplinary charges brought against an LSP after an investigation. In such instances, the Board simply finds that the MCP violation 'does not rise to the level of one warranting discipline.' If DEP wants the Board to take this particular MCP violation more seriously, it will have to take some action that demonstrates clearly to LSPs that DEP has made this interpretation." Allan Fierce, e-mail communication (October 27, 2005) (on file with author).

84. See, e.g., Mark Seidenfeld and Janna Satz Nugent, " 'The Friendship of the People': Citizen Participation in Environmental Enforcement," 73 *George*

Washington Law Review 298–302 (2005) (describing the role of citizens in environmental enforcement).

85. See Mass. Regs. Code 310, §40.1404 (2006) (Public Involvement Plan Site Designation).

86. See generally Mass. Regs. Code 310, §40.1403 (2006) (Minimum Public Involvement Activities in Response Actions).

87. However, the proposed MCP amendments would make notice more meaningful by transforming the newspaper notice from a legal notice to a readable advertisement in the news section of the paper. See *Final Amendments, Massachusetts Contingency Plan,* 310 CMR §40.0000, §40.1403, www.mass .gov (accessed 11/04/06). The amendments to Mass. Regs. Code 310, §40.1403 would still allow a traditional legal notice rather than an advertisement if the advertisement was more than 20 percent more expensive than the legal notice, or if the newspaper did not agree to run the advertisement. Ibid.

88. Cf. Freeman, "Extending Public Law Norms," 1285 (noting the government's ability to "exact concessions—in the form of adherence to public norms—in exchange for contracting out its work").

5. Outsourcing Power

Thanks to Robyn Bacon, Kristin Flower, Brishon Rogers, Mira Edmonds, and Amanda K. Edwards for research and editing assistance, and to the editors of the Boston College Law Review for assistance in editing a related earlier article, "Outsourcing Power: How Privatizing Military Efforts Challenges Accountability, Professionalism and Democracy," 46 *Boston College Law Review* 989 (2005).

1. The Talk of the Town: Comment—Rummyache, *New Yorker,* May 1, 2006, 33.

2. U.S. House of Representatives Committee on Government Reform— Minority Staff, Special Investigations Division, Dollars, Not Sense: Government Contracting Under the Bush Administration (June 2006), p. 3.

3. Ibid., 4.

4. Ibid., 5.

5. Spencer E. Ante with Stan Crock, "The Other U.S. Military," *Business Week,* May 31, 2004. See Peter W. Singer, "Warriors for Hire in Iraq," *Salon,* April 15, 2004, http://www.salon.com (estimating 15,000–20,000 contract workers in Iraq).

6. John M. Broder, "Filling Gaps in Iraq, Then Finding a Void at Home," *New York Times,* July 17, 2007, http://www.nytimes.com/2007/07/17/us/ 17contractor.html?_r=1&oref=slogin. Another estimate indicates more than 180,000 civilian contractors work alongside the 160,000 troops in Iraq. T. Christian Miller, "Contractors Outnumber Troops in Iraq," *Los Angeles Times,* July 4, 2007, http://articles.latimes.com/2007/jul/04/nation/na-private4.

7. See Jeremy Scahill, "Blackwatergate," *Nation,* October 22, 2007, p. 4 (private military contractor Blackwater USA drafted State Department report investigating alleged abuses by Blackwater employees).

8. Dan Guttman, "Commentary: The Shadow Pentagon, Private Contractors Play Huge Role in Basic Government Work—Mostly out of View," *Center for Public Integrity,* October 8, 2004; Dan Guttman, "Governance by Contract: Constitutional Visions: Time of Reflection and Choice," 33 *Public Contract Law Journal* 321–360 (2004). For an example of practices under the Clinton administration, see "Improving the Combat Edge through Outsourcing," 11 *Defense Issues* 30, http://www.defenselink.mil/speeches/1996/di1130.html.

9. Congress requires agencies to inventory what work should be understood as commercial and what instead is inherently governmental. See Federal Activities Inventory Reform (FAIR) Act of 1998, Pub. L. No. 105–270, 31 U.S.C. §501 note; see also Executive Office of the President, Office of Management and Budget, Circular A-76 (May 29, 2003). The 2003 revision of A-76 invites competitive source bids from both private sector and public agency providers. 68 Fed. Reg. 32134. For a fuller discussion of A-76, see Chapter 3 above.

10. By the very nature of the issue, the number of private contractors working for the federal government is difficult to obtain, although the trend toward increasing use of this labor force is widely reported. See Paul C. Light, "The True Size of the Government," *Government Executive,* January 1, 1999, http://govexec.com/features/0199/0199s1.htm; Christopher Lee, "Big Government Gets Bigger," *Washington Post,* October 6, 2006 (Paul C. Light estimates growth from 5.06 million contractors in 1990 to 7.63 million in 2005). For criticisms of Paul Light's estimates, see Chapter 8 below. Light's estimates have been corroborated by others. See, e.g., Jenny Mandel, Number of Federal Jobs Opened to Contractors to Jump This Year, *GovernmentExecutive.com,* April 20, 2006, http://www.govexec.com/dailyfed/0406/042006ml.htm.

11. Guttman, "Governance by Contract," 335.

12. Executive Office of the President, Office of Management and Budget (OMB), *The President's Management Agenda: Fiscal Year 2002,* p. 12, http://www.whitehouse.gov/omb/budget/fy2002/mgmt.pdf.

13. Remarks as Delivered by Secretary of Defense Donald H. Rumsfeld, "DOD Acquisition and Logistics Excellence Week Kickoff—Bureaucracy to Battlefield," The Pentagon (September 10, 2001), http://www.defenselink.mil/speeches/2001/s20010910-secdef.html.

14. Ibid.

15. Ken Silverstein, *Private Warriors* (New York: Verso, 2000), p. xv.

16. Dan Guttman, "Outsourcing the Pentagon: Commentary: The Shadow Pentagon: Private Contractors Play a Huge Role in Basic Government Work—Mostly out of Public View," http://store.publicintegrity.org/pns/report.aspx?aid+386 (Oct. 8, 2004)(The Center for Public Integrity).

17. "War-Mart," *St. Louis Dispatch,* October 18, 2003, at 30.

18. See Major Lisa L. Turner and Major Lynn G. Norton, "Civilians at the Tip of the Spear," 51 *Air Force Law Review* 1 (2001). "Never has there been such a reliance on nonmilitary members to accomplish tasks directly af-

fecting the tactical success of an engagement." Ibid., 3 (quoting Colonel Steven J. Zamparelli, "Competitive Sourcing and Privatization: Contractors on the Battlefield: What Have We Signed Up For?" *Air Force Journal of Logistics* 9–10 (Fall 1999)).

19. Turner and Norton, "Civilians at the Tip of the Spear."
20. "Debate on Military Contractors Heats Up," *San Diego Union-Tribune*, May 7, 2004, at A1; Daniel Bergner, "The Other Army," *New York Times Magazine*, August 14, 2005, at 29.
21. Singer, "Warriors for Hire."
22. Bernard Wysocki, Jr., "Is U.S. Government 'Outsourcing Its Brain'?" *Wall Street Journal*, March 30, 2007, A1, A10.
23. Guttman, "Outsourcing the Pentagon."
24. Ibid.
25. Ibid. These expenditures more than doubled recently. Ibid.
26. Current outsourcing uses fewer "foreign locals trained by the CIA" and more "high-ranking U.S. military officers fresh out of the armed forces." Silverstein, *Private Warriors*, 143.
27. Mercenaries helped give Alexander the Great his name; King Henry II of Britain banned the Flemish mercenaries that nearly kept him from the throne and hired his own mercenaries; and mercenaries worked for Rameses II and King David. See W. Scott Jesse, "Readers Companion to Military History," college.hmco.com/history/readerscomp/mil/html/mh_033800_mercenaries.htm; Serge Yalichev, *Mercenaries of the Ancient World* (London: Constable, 1996); Kenneth Fowler, *Medieval Mercenaries: The Great Companies*, vol. 1 (Malden, MA: Blackwell, 2001); Silverstein, *Private Warriors*, xv, 143.
28. Norse mercenaries worked for companies that helped the Byzantine Empire in 1032. Major Todd S. Milliard, "Overcoming Post-Colonial Myopia: A Call to Recognize and Regulate Private Military Companies," 176 *Military Law Review* 1 (2003). Free companies of mercenary troops became a familiar staple of medieval warfare. See Fowler, *Medieval Mercenaries;* Peter W. Singer, *Corporate Warriors: The Rise of the Privatized Military Industry* (Ithaca, NY: Cornell University Press, 2003), pp. 22–26; Milliard, "Overcoming Post-Colonial Myopia," 2.
29. "The Shadowy World of Guns for Hire," *Daily Yomiuri* (Tokyo), May 11, 2005, at 2; Singer, *Corporate Warriors;* Silverstein, *Private Warriors;* Major J. Ricou Heaton, "Civilians at War: Reexamining the Status of Civilians Accompanying the Armed Forces," 57 *Air Force Law Review* 155 (2005); Steven B. Hilkowitz, "Contractors on the Battlefield: An Overview of Federal Contracting Issues," 26 *Construction Lawyer* 20 (2006).
30. Deborah Avant, "Think Again: Mercenaries," *Foreign Policy* (July/August 2004), p. 20; Clifford J. Rosky, "Force, Inc.: The Privatization of Punishment, Policing, and Military Force in Liberal States," 36 *Connecticut Law Review* 912, 912–913 (2004); Janice E. Thomson, "State Practices, International Norms, and the Decline of Mercenarism," 34 *International Studies Quarterly* 23 (1990).

31. Thomson, "State Practices, International Norms," 26.
32. Ibid., 27.
33. "Need an Army? Just Pick Up Your Phone," *New York Times,* April 2, 2004, at A19 (quoting Peter W. Singer).
34. Milliard, "Overcoming Post-Colonial Myopia," 11 (describing fourteen-person team from Military Professional Resources, Inc.). Companies organized in the United Kingdom, South Africa, and Israel, as well as the United States, have built the modern privatized military industry. See Singer, *Corporate Warriors.*
35. See Heaton, "Civilians at War," 159–168; Hilkowitz, "Contractors on the Battlefield"; Jon D. Michaels, "Beyond Accountability: The Constitutional, Democratic, and Strategic Problems with Privatizing War," 82 *Washington University Law Quarterly* 1019 (2004).
36. James R. Davis, *Fortune's Warriors: Private Armies and the New World Order* (Vancouver, CA: Douglas & McIntyre, 2000).
37. John F. Burns, "The Deadly Game of Private Security," *New York Times,* September 23, 2007, at 3.
38. Ibid. See Martha Minow, *Partners, Not Rivals: Privatization and the Public Good* (Boston: Beacon Press, 2003); see "Inside the Army, Cost Figures Heavily in Debate over Contractor Use in Theater," 2007 WLNR 5169114 (March 19, 2007).
39. See "Tax Farmers, Mercenaries and Viceroys," *New York Times,* August 21, 2006, at A21 (civil fraud by private security contractor at Baghdad's airport). There are risks, too: with religious players providing services, there are risks of religious coercion, and exclusionary practices. See Martha Minow, "Public and Private Partnerships: Accounting for the New Religion," 116 *Harvard Law Review* 1229 (2003).
40. Silverstein, *Private Warriors,* at 167.
41. GAO, DOD Personnel: DOD Actions Needed to Strengthen Civilian Human Capital Strategic Planning and Integration with Military Personnel and Sourcing Decisions (March 2003), www.gao.gov/new.items/d03475.pdf.
42. Burns, "The Deadly Game."
43. Allison Stanger and Omnivore, "Foreign Policy, Privatized," *New York Times,* October 5, 2007, at A27 (reporting figures from the Federal Procurement Data System).
44. See S. 674: Transparency and Accountability in Military and Security Contracting Act of 2007, http://www.govtrack.us/congress/bill.xpd?bill=s110 -674&tab=summary (introduced by Senator Barack Obama); H.R. 369: Transparency and Accountability in Security Contracting Act of 2007, http://www.govtrack.us/congress/bill.xpd?bill=h110-369 (introduced by Congressman David Price).
45. "Contract and Fiscal Law Developments of 2003—The Year in Review: Appendix A: Department of Defense (DOD) Legislation for Fiscal Year 2004," 2004 *Army Lawyer* 199, http://www.loc.gov/rr/frd/Military_Law/pdf/01 -2004.pdf. The Deputy Secretary of the Department of Homeland Security

told potential bidders for the Secure Borders Initiative, " 'This is an unusual invitation. . . . We're asking you to come back and tell us how to do our business.' " Scott Shane and Ron Nixon, "In Washington, Contractors Take on Biggest Role Ever," *New York Times,* February 4, 2007 (quoting Michael P. Jackson).

46. U.S. Senate Democratic Policy Committee, *An Oversight Hearing on Contracting Abuses in Iraq,* 108th Cong., 1st sess., 2004 [hereinafter Dorgan Hearing], p. 17 (testimony of Steven Schooner).

47. U.S. House of Representatives Committee on Government Reform, *Dollars, Not Sense.*

48. Another company had equal, if not superior experience. Senate Democratic Policy Committee, Dorgan Hearing, 8.

49. Ibid., 8–10 (testimony of Sheryl Tappan, former Bechtel proposal manager).

50. Singer, "Warriors for Hire."

51. Senate Democratic Policy Committee, Dorgan Hearing, 6 (comments of Congressman Waxman).

52. "Panel to Hear of Halliburton Waste," *Washington Post,* July 22, 2004, at E1.

53. Share-in-savings contracts allow the contractor to share savings from its own system, yet these are difficult to measure, and without caps these contracts expose the government to potentially limitless demands for payment, made worse by questionable accounting practices. Jason Miller, "Former OFPP Head Warns Agencies about Risks of Share-in-Savings Contracts," *Post-Newsweek Information Inc. (Newsbytes),* November 12, 2004.

54. "Halliburton Back in the Fray; Kerry Alleging Cronyism over Contracts in Iraq," *Houston Chronicle,* September 18, 2004, at A26; Griff White, "Army Ceasing Contract with Halliburton," *Boston Globe,* July 12, 2006, p. A2; "Army, Halliburton Talk Settlement; A Deal Would Officially End Billing Disputes," *Houston Chronicle,* October 23, 2004, at 1. The company's leaders claim that they made little profit and would demand a much larger profit margin when rebidding. "Halliburton Weighs Options on Bidding for Iraq Work," *New York Times,* September 8, 2004, at C3. But see William D. Hartung, World Policy Institute, American News Women's Club, "Private Military Contractors in Iraq and Beyond: A Question of Balance," June 22, 2004, http://www.worldpolicy.org/projects/arms/updates/FPIFJune2004.html (alleging kickbacks and luxury expenditures). Halliburton settled separate charges of misleading financial statements. "Cheney's Years at Halliburton Under Scrutiny," *Dallas Morning News,* September 8, 2004, at 1A.

55. "Halliburton Accused of Not Justifying £1bn Army Bills," *Guardian* (London), August 12, 2004, at 17. See also Senate Democratic Policy Committee, Dorgan Hearing, 20. One subcontract administrator discovered that transportation prices were inflated by 500 percent, but no effort was made to recover these costs. Senate Democratic Policy Committee, Dorgan Hearing, 25–26. The Pentagon blocked congressional efforts to secure full information about Halliburton's billing under a $2.5 billion contract for oil site repairs

and fuel imports. "Lawmakers, Including Republicans, Criticize Pentagon on Disputed Billing by Halliburton," *New York Times,* June 22, 2005, at A10.

56. Griff White, "Army Ceasing Contract With Halliburton," *Boston Globe,* July 12, 2006, at A2.

57. U.S. House of Representatives Committee on Government Reform, *Dollars, Not Sense,* 29–30 (summarizing Department of Defense Inspector General, Report No. 2006-10, *Acquisition: Contract Surveillance for Service Contracts,* 2005). In some instances, the oversight is hampered by the lack of basic agreement about the very bases for billing. See Statement of William Solis, Director, Defense Capabilities and Management, Government Accountability Office, to the Committee on Senate Homeland Security and Governmental Affairs Subcommittee on Federal Financial Management, Government Information, Federal Services, and International Security, "Managing Contingency Contracting in Hostile Zones," *Congressional Quarterly,* January 24, 2008 (reporting contractor's bill for food service for 15.9 million soldiers when it had served only 12.5 million—more than 3.4 million fewer—and dispute over billing based on camp populations versus actual food served).

58. Guttman, "Governance by Contract" (quoting Angela Styles, former head of the Office of Federal Procurement Policy). The Army announced it is ending its logistical contract with Halliburton—but only after two-thirds of the contract fees had been spent, and over 90 percent contractually obligated. Griff White, "Army Ceasing Contract with Halliburton," at A2.

59. See "Army Calls Abuses 'Aberrations'; Report Cites 94 Detainee-Mistreatment Cases in Iraq and Afghanistan," *Washington Post,* July 23, 2004, at A01. See "No One, Not Even Bush, Is Above the Law," *Houston Chronicle,* July 2, 2004, at A36; "Forever Stained By Prison Abuse Scandal," *Pittsburgh Post-Gazette,* December 21, 2004, at A1; "4th Solider Guilty in Prison Scandal," *Los Angeles Times,* November 3, 2004, at A12. Yet in June 2005 Secretary of Defense Donald Rumsfeld contemplated promoting Lieutenant General Ricardo Sanchez, the commander in Iraq during the Abu Ghraib prison abuse scandal. "Ex-Top General in Iraq in Line for Promotion," *International Herald Tribune,* June 21, 2005, at 10.

60. Major General George R. Fay, "Contracting-related Issues Contributed to the Problems at Abu Ghraib Prison," *AR 15-6 Investigation of the Abu Ghraib Detention Facility and 205th Military Intelligence Brigade* (2003), p. 47, http://fl1.findlaw.com/news.findlaw.com/hdocs/docs/dod/fay82504rpt .pdf. See "Charges Behind the Barbed Wire," *Washington Post,* December 13, 2004, at E01. More than one-third of the abuse incidents involved contractor personnel. Steven L. Schooner, "Contractor Atrocities at Abu Ghraib: Compromise Accountability in a Streamlined, Outsourced Government," 16 *Stanford Law & Policy Review* 549 (2005). Civil suits against private contractors are pending. See "A Price Tag for Mistakes," *Newsweek,* December 31, 2007/January 7, 2008, p. 16.

61. See "Charges Behind the Barbed Wire," *Washington Post,* December 13, 2004 (quoting leaked internal army report by Major General Antonio

Taguba's internal investigation). CACI denied involvement by their employees in the abuse and also asserted that the individuals in question no longer worked for them. Ibid. Titan tried to distance itself from responsibility by noting that the individual traced to their operations actually worked for a subcontractor. Ante, "The Other U.S. Military."

62. U.S. House of Representatives Committee on Government Reform, *Dollars, Not Sense,* 20–22.

63. Schooner, "Contractor Atrocities."

64. Cited in Senate Democratic Policy Committee, Dorgan Hearing, 18 (Schooner testimony). See Guttman, "Outsourcing the Pentagon." See also Guttman, "Governance by Contract," 340.

65. "Managing Contingency Contracting in Hostile Zones," supra; see Schooner, "Contractor Atrocities."

66. Schooner, "Contractor Atrocities" (discussing the Fay report).

67. Reports document persistent problems with Los Alamos, the weapons facility run under contract by the University of California. Repeatedly losing classified and sensitive material and technology, more than three-quarters of the security personnel there also failed tests of required skills and security. See "Lapses at Labs Go Back Decades," *San Francisco Chronicle,* August 1, 2004, at A1.

68. Government Accountability Office, *Army Should Do More to Control Contract Costs in the Balkans* (2000), http://www.gao.gov/archive/2000/ns00225.pdf, cited in Rebecca Rafferty Vernon, "Battlefield Contractors: Facing the Tough Issues," 33 *Public Contract Law Journal* 385, 385–386 (2004).

69. See Guttman, "Governance by Contract," 323–324.

70. GAO, Department of Defense: Further Actions Are Needed to Effectively Address Business Management Problems and Overcome Key Business Transformation Challenges (November 2004), http://www.gao.gov/new.items/d05140t.pdf.

71. GAO, Military Operations: DOD's Extensive Use of Logistics Support Contracts Requires Strengthened Oversight (July 2004), http.//www.gao.gov/new.items/d04854.pdf.

72. GAO, DOD Business System Modernization: Billions Continue to Be Invested with Inadequate Management Oversight and Accountability (May 2004), http://www.gao.gov/new.items/d04615.pdf.

73. Senate Democratic Policy Committee, Dorgan Hearing, 19 (testimony of Danielle Brian, executive director of the Project on Government Oversight).

74. GAO, DOD Personnel Clearances: Additional Steps Can Be Taken to Reduce Backlogs and Delays in Determining Security Clearance Eligibility for Industry Personnel (May 2004), http://www.gao.gov/new.items/d04632.pdf.

75. GAO, Contract Management: DOD Needs Measure for Small Business Subcontracting Program and Better Data on Foreign Subcontracts (April 2004), http://www.gao.gov/new.items/d04381.pdf.

76. GAO, DOD Contract Payments: Management Action Needed to Reduce Billions in Adjustments to Contract Payment Records (August 2003), http://www.gao.gov/new.items/d03727.pdf.

77. GAO, Best Practices: Improved Knowledge of DOD Service Contracts Could Reveal Significant Savings (June 2003), http://www.gao.gov/new.items/d03661.pdf; GAO, Use of Value Engineering in Defense Acquisitions (February 2003), http://www.gao.gov/new.items/d03590r.pdf.

78. GAO, Military Operations: DOD's Extensive Use of Logistics Support Contracts Requires Strengthened Oversight (July 2004) www.gao.gov/new.items/d04854.pdf.

79. James Glanz, "Bechtel Meets Goals on Fewer Than Half of Its Iraq Rebuilding Projects," *New York Times,* July 26, 2007, http://www.nytimes.com/2007/07/26/world/middleeast/26reconstruct.html?_r=1&oref=slogin.

80. Inspector General Coalition Provisional Authority, *Report No. 04-013, Coalition Provisional Authority's Contracting Processes Leading Up to and Including Contract Award* (2004) (cited in Schooner, "Contractor Atrocities").

81. Commission on Army Acquisition and Program Management in Expeditionary Operations, "Urgent Reform Required: Army Expeditionary Contracting" (Gansler Commission Report on Contracting), October 31, 2007, p. 4, https://acc.dau.mil/CommunityBrowser.aspx?id=179150&lang=en-US.

82. The GAO and Inspectors General report that DOD fails to gather information to permit contract oversight. See GAO, *Best Practices: Improved Knowledge,* at 3; GAO, *DOD: Further Actions,* at 1; Guttman, "Governance by Contract."

83. Aegis was hired to coordinate more than fifty private security companies in Iraq. "Spicer Clear to Pursue Pounds 160M Iraq Contract," *Independent* (London), September 19, 2004 at 2. Aegis became a lightning rod because its head, Tim Spicer, commanded two soldiers charged and convicted of murder in Northern Belfast and previously directed a company selling arms to Sierra Leone in violation of a United Nations embargo. "Family Lobbies over U.S. Contract," *Irish Times,* June 18, 2004, at 8; "DynCorp Seeks to Overturn Iraq Security Contract," *Financial Times* (London), July 22, 2004, at 8.

84. Senate Democratic Policy Committee, Dorgan Hearing, 12.

85. See FAIR Act of 1998; OMB, *Circular A-76.*

86. Committee on Oversight and Government Reform, "Administrative Oversight, Waste, Fraud, and Abuse," http://oversight.house.gov/story.asp?ID=1202 (describing passage of H.R. 1362, the Accountability in Contracting Act).

87. David H. Laufman, "Congress Getting Tougher On Government Contracting," 15 *Metropolitan Corporate Counsel* 40 (December 2007) (summarizing Accountability in Government Contracting Act of 2007 (S. 680), which would require agencies to increase training for contract management and to increase use of competitive bidding and transparency in procurement).

88. Ann Markusen, "The Case against Privatizing National Security," 16:4 *Governance* 471–501 (2003).

89. Guttman, "Governance by Contract," 343.
90. The GAO changed its name from General Accounting Office to Government Accountability Office, just as the proliferating privatization of the military made government accountability newly elusive. "Answer Man: Name That Agency," *Washington Post,* March 14, 2005, at C11; "GAO Gets New Name," *Washington Post,* July 12, 2004, at B2.
91. Pub. L. 81–506, 64 Stat. 107.
92. See Michaels, "Beyond Accountability," 1073–1074; see U.S. Constitution, Article 1, section 8, clause 16.
93. See K. Elizabeth Waits, Note, "Avoiding the 'Legal Bermuda Triangle': The Military Extraterritorial Jurisdiction Act's Unprecedented Expansion of U.S. Criminal Jurisdiction over Foreign Nationals," 23 *Arizona Journal of International and Comparative Law* 493 (2006). Other potential sources include the International Criminal Court, ibid.(but the United States has not signed the treaty authorizing jurisdiction), and the Special Maritime and Territorial Jurisdiction, allowing jurisdiction over U.S. civilians in military bases, see Coyle, infra note 100. See also Heather Carney, Note, "Prosecuting the Lawless: Human Rights Abuses and Private Military Firms," 74 *George Washington Law Review* 317 (2006).
94. 18 U.S.C. §3261–3267. In 2004, the definition of "employee" covered by the Act was amended to include private contractors assisting the military mission, including those working for agencies other than the Department of Defense. See 18 U.S.C.S. § 3267: "As used in this chapter [18 U.S.C.S. §§3261 et seq.]:

  (1) The term "employed by the Armed Forces outside the United States" means—
  (A) employed as—
    (i) a civilian employee of—
      (I) the Department of Defense (including a nonappropriated fund instrumentality of the Department); or
      (II) any other Federal agency, or any provisional authority, to the extent such employment relates to supporting the mission of the Department of Defense overseas;
    (ii) a contractor (including a subcontractor at any tier) of—
      (I) the Department of Defense (including a nonappropriated fund instrumentality of the Department); or
      (II) any other Federal agency, or any provisional authority, to the extent such employment relates to supporting the mission of the Department of Defense overseas; or
    (iii) an employee of a contractor (or subcontractor at any tier) of—
      (I) the Department of Defense (including a nonappropriated fund instrumentality of the Department); or
      (II) any other Federal agency, or any provisional authority, to the extent such employment relates to supporting the mission of the Department of Defense overseas.

See Colonel Michael J. Davidson, "Ruck Up: An Introduction to the Legal Issues Associated with Civilian Contractors on the Battlefield," 29 *Public Contract Law Journal* 233 (2000).

95. Robert Capps, "Outside the Law: Pending Lawsuits Allege That U.S. Military Contractors on Duty in Bosnia Bought and 'Owned' Young Women," *Salon,* June 26, 2002, http://archive.salon.com/news/feature/2002/06/26/bosnia/ (part 1); Robert Capps, "Crime without Punishment, Investigators Knew Employees for U.S. Military Contractors in Bosnia Bought Women as Sex Slaves," *Salon,* June 27, 2002, http://archive.salon.com/news/feature/2002/06/27/military/.

96. Capps, supra.

97. Ibid.

98. A whistle-blower lost her job for exposing the scandal—and later won a British damages award. "Contractor Tries to Avert Repeat of Bosnia Woes, Sex Scandal Still Haunts DynCorp," *Chicago Tribune,* April 19, 2003, at C3.

99. A swift process follows unless there is a cover-up. At least one civilian officer in Bosnia was told by his military commanders to lie about the Dyn-Corp sexual scandal; he quit. "Military Should Not Investigate Itself," *Boston Globe,* May 5, 2004, at A10; "Bosnia Sex Trade Shames UN," *Scotland on Sunday,* February 9, 2003, at 24.

100. Marcia Coyle, "A Strategy for Blackwater: Three Key Legal Regimes to Rein in Iraq Contractors," *National Law Journal,* October 22, 2007, pp. 1, 17. "Who Investigates Private Interrogators in Iraq?" *Dallas Morning News,* May 7, 2004, at 22A.

101. "Contractors Fall through the Legal Cracks," *Los Angeles Times,* May 4, 2004, at A8. The one contractor subjected to a criminal trial arising from conduct in Afghanistan was convicted of beating a detainee who died in U.S. custody; a federal jury found David Passaro guilty under the USA PATRIOT Act, which extends to military bases overseas. Andrea Weigl, "Passaro Convicted of Assaulting Afghan," *News & Observer,* August 18, 2006, http://www.newsobserver.com/497/v<->print/story/476483.html. See also Estes Thompson, "Civilian Abuse Trial Starts Today," *Boston Globe,* August 7, 2006 (prosecutors used the USA PATRIOT Act because military justice would not apply to the contractor; USA PATRIOT Act permits charges against U.S. nationals for crimes committed on land or facilities designed for use by the U.S. government).

102. Associated Press, "House Passes Bill to Subject Iraq Contractors to U.S. Law," *Wall Street Journal,* October 5, 2007, at A6; August Cole and Evan Perez, "Blackwater Is Put on the Hot Seat," *Wall Street Journal,* October 2, 2007, at A4.

103. H.R. 2740, MEJA Expansion and Enforcement Act of 2007, October 4, 2007.

104. Elana Schor, "Report: US Fails at Enforcing Prosecution of Contractors," *Guardian Unlimited,* January 16, 2008. See 18 U.S.C.S. §3267 (quoted in note 94, supra).

105. Burns, "The Deadly Game"; Philip Shishkin, "Blackwater Shooting Crisis Rallies Baghdad," *Wall Street Journal,* September 24, 2007, at A3.

106. Burns, "The Deadly Game."

107. Marc Linderman, "Civilian Contractors under Military Law," *Parameters,* Autumn 2007, 83–94; William C. Peters, "On Law, Wars, and Mercenaries: The Case for Courts-Martial Jurisdiction over Civilian Contractor Misconduct in Iraq," 2006 *Brigham Young University Law Review* 367. See Peter W. Singer, "Frequently Asked Questions on the UCMJ Change and Its Applicability to Private Military Contractors," *Brookings,* January 12, 2007, http://www.brookings.edu/opinions/207/0112defenseindustry _singer.aspx.

108. Shishkin, "Blackwater Shooting." Blackwater was initially conceived as a training center serving civilian and military security needs on a 50–50 split, but as of 2006, 90 percent of its revenues came from the government. Joanne Kimberlin and Bill Sizemore, "Profitable Patriotism," *Virginia Pilot and Ledger-Star* (Norfolk, VA), July 24, 2006, 2006 WLNR 12799835.

109. Shishkin, "Blackwater Shooting."

110. David M. Herszenhorn, "House's Iraq Bill Applies U.S. Laws to Contractors," *New York Times,* October 5, 2007, at A1. A grand jury investigation could also proceed alongside investigation by the FBI and the Congress. See David Johnson and John M. Broder, "U.S. Prosecutors Subpoena Blackwater Employees," *New York Times,* November 20, 2007, at A10.

111. See Rod Powers, "Civilian Contractors Now Subject to UCMJ," http:// usmilitary.about.com/od/justicelawlegislation/a/civucmj.htm:

> Paragraph a (10) of Article 2 originally read, "(10) In time of war, persons serving with or accompanying an armed force in the field."
>
> In a Vietnam-era case, the Court of Military Appeals set aside the conviction of a civilian contractor in Saigon because it construed the old Art. 2(a)(10) to apply only in cases of declared war. *United States v. Averette,* 19 C.M.A. 363, 41 C.M.R. 363 (1970).
>
> The new provision changes this paragraph to read: "In time of declared war *or a contingency operation,* persons serving with or accompanying an armed force in the field."

112. See Peter W. Singer, "Frequently Asked Questions on the UCMJ Change and Its Applicability to Private Military Contractors," *The Brookings Institution,* January 12, 2007, http://www.brookings.edu/printme./wbs?page= pagedefs/e5392d64c76aff4080007b870a141.

113. See McElroy v. Guagliardo, 361 U.S. 281 (1960); Reid v. Covert, 354 U.S. 1 (1957).

114. Princeton University Program in Law and Public Affairs, "Princeton Problem-Solving Workshop Series in Law and Security: A New Legal Framework for Military Contractors?" 4 (June 8, 2007), lapa.princeton.edu/news-detail.php?ID=17.

115. Coyle, "A Strategy for Blackwater"; Schor, "Report: US Fails at Enforcing Prosecution."
116. See, e.g., Major Karen L. Douglas, "Contractors Accompanying the Force: Empowering Commanders with Emergency Change Authority," 55 *Air Force Law Review* 127 (2004); Major Mark R. Rupert, "Criminal Jurisdiction over Environmental Offenses Committed Overseas: How to Maximize and When to Say 'No,' " 40 *Air Force Law Review* 1 (1996); Turner and Norton, "Civilians at the Tip of the Spear," 95 (discussing lack of clarity over whether contractors, unlike military, are subject to the employment, tax, and customs laws of the host nation). See also Charles E. Cantu and Randy W. Young, "The Government Contractor Defense: Breaking the *Boyle* Barrier," 62 *Albany Law Review* 403 (1998) (exploring issues); "Debate on Military Contractors Heats Up," *San Diego Union-Tribune*, May 7, 2004, at A1. See Kateryna Rakowsky, Note, "Military Contractors and Civil Liability: Use of the Government Contractor Defense to Escape Allegations of Misconduct in Iraq and Afghanistan," 2 *Stanford Journal of Civil Rights and Civil Liberties* 365 (2006).
117. Guttman, "Governance by Contract," 336.
118. Whether civilian contractors would receive prisoner-of-war status is unclear. See Major Charlotte M. Liegl-Paul, "Civilian Prisoners of War: A Proposed Citizen Code of Conduct," 182 *Military Law Review* 106 (2004); Kristen McCallion, "War for Sale! Battlefield Contractors in Latin America and the 'Corporatization' of America's War on Drugs," 36 *University of Miami Inter-American Law Review* 317 (2005); Adam Sherman, "Forward unto the Digital Breach: Exploring the Legal Status of Tomorrow's High-Tech Warriors," 5 *Chicago Journal of International Law* 335 (2004); Turner and Norton, "Civilians at the Tip of the Spear"; Colonel Kenneth Watkins, "Controlling the Use of Force: A Role for Human Rights Norms in Contemporary Armed Conflict," 98 *American Journal of International Law* 1 (2004); Dieter Fleck, ed., *Handbook of Humanitarian Law in Armed Conflicts* (New York: Oxford University Press, 1999).
119. Recent draft rules indicate that a contract employee may seek permission to carry a weapon by asking the contracting officer to ask the combatant commander. See Hilkowitz, "Contractors on the Battlefield," 25–26 (discussing DFARS 252.225.7040, Draft Department of Defense Directive 4XXX.aa, Management of Contingency, Contractor Personnel during Contingency Operations, and Draft Department of Defense Instruction 4XXX.bb, Procedures for Management of Contingency Contractor Personnel).
120. See Sheri Qualters, "Second Front in Iraq War: Lawsuits," *National Law Journal*, March 12, 2007, at 7 (discussing suits brought under state fraud and wrongful death rules and defended in terms of political question doctrine and government-contractor defense).
121. Peter W. Singer, "Can't Win with 'Em, Can't Go to War without 'Em: Private Military Contractors and Counterinsurgency," September 27, 2007, www3.brookings.edu/fp/research/singer200709.pdf.

122. GAO, *Army Should Do More,* cited in Vernon, "Battlefield Contractors," 385–386.

123. Fay, *Investigation of Abu Ghraib;* Senate Democratic Policy Committee, Dorgan Hearing, 17.

124. Michaels, "Beyond Accountability," 1085–1087.

125. Unnamed former soldier, quoted in Burns, "The Deadly Game."

126. Vernon, "Battlefield Contractors," 407–408.

127. See Heaton, "Civilians at War," 195–197.

128. Private contractors probably cannot claim immunity from host-country laws under the Status of Forces Agreement where U.S. troops are stationed with the permission of a foreign country. See Hilkowitz, "Contractors on the Battlefield," 21–22.

129. Silverstein, *Private Warriors,* 145.

130. Nicole B. Casarez, "Furthering the Accountability Principle in Privatized Federal Corrections: The Need for Access to Private Prison Records," 28 *University of Michigan Journal of Law Reform* 249 (1995); Craig D. Feiser, "Privatization and the Freedom of Information Act: An Analysis of Public Access to Private Entities under Federal Law," 52 *Federal Communications Law Journal* 21 (1999).

131. Kristen Elizabeth Uhl, Comment, "The Freedom of Information Act Post–9/11: Balancing the Public's Right to Know, Critical Infrastructure Protection, and Homeland Security," 53 *American University Law Review* 261, 293 n. 188 (2003). See also Karen E. Jones, Comment and Casenote, "The Effect of the Homeland Security Act on Online Privacy and the Freedom of Information Act," 72 *University of Cincinnati Law Review* 787 (2003); Jack Beermann, "Privatization and Political Accountability," 28 *Fordham Urban Law Journal* 1507 (2001); Jody Freeman, "Extending Public Law Norms through Privatization," 116 *Harvard Law Review* 1285 (2003). See Freedom of Information Act, 5 U.S.C. §551 (1); 5 U.S.C. §552 (b)(4).

132. John Doe Agency and John Doe Government Agency v. John Doe Corporation, 493 U.S. 146 (1989). Another court allowed trial to proceed over requested disclosure of some contractor information. See TPS, Inc. v. Department of Defense, 330 F.3d 1191 (9th Cir. 2003).

133. McDonnell Douglas Corp. v. U.S. Dept. of Air Force, 375 F.3d 1182 (D.C. Cir. 2004); see ibid., at 1194 (Garland, J., dissenting in part).

134. 375 F.3d at 1193. Judge Garland's partial dissent notes that this nondisclosure interferes with public ability to evaluate "whether the government is receiving value for taxpayer funds, or whether the contract is instead an instance of waste, fraud, or abuse of the public trust." Ibid.

135. Jim Krane, "Private Firms Do US Military's Work," Associated Press, October 29, 2003, www.globalpolicy.org/security/peacekpg/training/1029private.htm.

136. More than 200 private contract employees may have been killed in Iraq. "Risk and Reward in Iraq," *Northern Territory News* (Darwin, Australia), May 7, 2005, at 15.

137. Light, "The True Size of the Government." See Schooner, "Contractor Atrocities"; "The Contract the Military Needs to Break," *Washington Post*, September 12, 2004, at B3; Singer, "Warriors for Hire."

138. Singer, "Warriors for Hire."

139. The Federal Procurement Data Center previously gave Internet access to information about defense contracts awards, yet the government outsourced this service and now charges for data access. Senate Democratic Policy Committee, Dorgan Hearing, 30–31.

140. U.S. House of Representatives Committee on Government Reform, *Dollars, Not Sense*, 12–14.

141. Ibid., 10–12. Seventy percent of expenditures through cost-plus contracts came through the Department of Defense. Ibid.

142. Jason Miller, "Former OFPP Head Warns Agencies" (comments of Angela Styles, former head of the Office of Federal Procurement Policy).

143. U.S. House of Representatives Committee on Government Reform, *Dollars, Not Sense*, 43–65; " 'Breathtaking' Waste and Fraud in Hurricane Aid," *New York Times*, June 27, 2006, at 1.

144. See John Terrence A. Rosenthal and Robert T. Alter, "Clear and Convincing to Whom? The False Claims Act and Its Burden of Proof: Why the Government Needs a Big Stick," 74 *Notre Dame Law Review* 1449–1458 (2000).

145. See Yochi J. Dreazen, "Contractor Admits Bribing a U.S. Official in Iraq," *Wall Street Journal*, April 19, 2006, at B1.

146. See "Tax Farmers" (describing judge's decision to throw out $10 million jury verdict against Custer Battles for defrauding the government because the company worked for the Coalition Provisional authority, not an instrumentality of the U.S. government).

147. Interview between Mira Edmonds and Lieutenant Colonel Margaret Stock, law professor at West Point, October 21, 2004 (e-mail summary to Martha Minow, October 22, 2004).

148. Burns, "The Deadly Game."

149. Walter Pincus, "U.S. Pays Steep Price for Private Security in Iraq," *Washington Post*, October 1, 2007, at A17.

150. Davidson, "Ruck Up," 266.

151. Ibid. See Vernon, "Battlefield Contractors," 393.

152. Senate Democratic Policy Committee, Dorgan Hearing, 12.

153. Ibid.

154. There is no settled definition of a mercenary in international law. See Milliard, "Overcoming Post-Colonial Myopia." For a thoughtful comparison of international law treatment of private military contractors with mercenaries, see E.L. Gaston, Note, "Mercenarism 2.0? The Rise of the Modern Private Security Industry and Its Implications for International Humanitarian Law Enforcement," 49 *Harvard International Law Journal* 221 (2008).

155. Niccolò Machiavelli, *The Prince*, ed. Quentin Skinner, trans. Russell Price (New York: Cambridge University Press, 1988), 42–47 (arguing that mercenaries are disloyal and cowardly).

156. Vernon, "Battlefield Contractors," 394–395 (private contractors fled Persian Gulf War for fear of chemical warfare).

157. See ibid.

158. Machiavelli, *The Prince*, 43. See Protocol Additional to the Geneva Conventions of 12 Aug. 1949, and relating to the Protection of Victims of International Armed Conflicts (Protocol I), June 8, 1977, 1125 U.N.T.S. 3.

159. See Burns, "The Deadly Game."

160. "Briton Jailed for Arms Dealings," *Washington Post*, September 11, 2004, at A16; "Why Those Dogs of War Are Still Barking," *Daily Telegraph* (Sydney), February 18, 2005, at 64.

161. "The Other Army," *New York Times Magazine*, August 14, 2005, at 29.

162. Burns, "The Deadly Game" (discussing Brigadier General Karl R. Horst's report to the *Washington Post* in 2005).

163. Thomas E. Ricks, *Fiasco: The American Military Adventure in Iraq* (New York: Penguin Press, 2006), 370–371.

164. Ibid., 371.

165. Deborah N. Pearlstein, "Finding Effective Constraints on Executive Power: Interrogation, Detention, and Torture," 81 *Indiana Law Journal* 1274–1279 (2005).

166. "Debate on Military Contractors Heats Up," *San Diego Union-Tribune*, May 7, 2004, at A1 (quoting Taguba report).

167. Senate Democratic Policy Committee, Dorgan Hearings (testimony of Marie DeYoung).

168. Michaels, "Beyond Accountability," 1083–1094, 1101–1106.

169. Burns, "The Deadly Game."

170. Heaton, "Civilians at War," 163–177, 184–197. Heaton argues that civilian contractors not identified as combatants are not entitled to prisoner-of-war status. Ibid., 173–174. But see supra note 118 for a different view.

171. See "Need an Army? Just Pick Up the Phone," *New York Times*, April 2, 2004, at A19; David Isenberg, "A Fistful of Contractors: The Case for a Pragmatic Assessment of Private Military Companies in Iraq," 46 (British American Security Information Council Research Report 2004.4) (September 2004), http://www.basicint.org/pub/Research/2004PMC.pdf.

172. David Ivanovich, "Labor Dept.: 1,001 Contractors Have Died in Iraq," *Houston Chronicle*, August 9, 2007 ("In response to a request from Rep. Jan Schakowsky, D-Ill., the Labor Department revealed that 1,001 civilian contractors had died in Iraq as of June 30, including 84 during the second quarter of the year. . . . Besides those killed, 4,837 workers in Iraq and 879 in Afghanistan suffered injuries severe enough to miss at least four days of work, the Labor Department said."; Aaron Wasserman, "Contractors Face Big Risks in Iraq," *Metro West Daily News* (Framingham, MA), December 16, 2007, http://www.metrowestdailynews.com/homepage/x60439429 ("917 contractors were killed in Iraq and about 10,500 had been injured there through March 2007, according to the federal Labor Department, Reuters reported in July"). Thanks to Steve Schooner for these sources.

173. James Risen, "Back from Iraq, Contractors Face Combat-Related Stress," *New York Times,* July 5, 2007, p. A1.

174. See Michaels, "Beyond Accountability"; "Risk and Reward in Iraq," supra note 136; "Private Armies Also Fight," *St. Louis Post-Dispatch,* October 30, 2003, at A8.

175. See James Glanz, "Auditor in Iraq Finds Job Gone after Exposes," *New York Times,* November 3, 2006, at A1 (lawyer who exposed failures by Halliburton and Parsons loses his job as his oversight agency—the Office of the Special Inspector General for Iraq Reconstruction—was eliminated during the conference committee drafting of a military authorization bill); Robert Burns, "Democrats Urge Probe in Demotion of Army Critic," *Boston Globe,* August 20, 2005 (senior civilian Army official demoted after publicly criticizing the award of a no-bid contract to Halliburton in Iraq).

176. See also "How the Allies Won the War, but Then Lost the Battle for Peace," *Independent* (London), January 28, 2005, at 4; Krane, "Private Firms Do US Military's Work."

177. E.g., Thomas Cusack, "On the Domestic Political-Economic Sources of American Military Spending," in Alex Mintz, ed., *The Political Economy of Military Spending in the United States* (New York: Routledge, 1992); Karl DeRouen, Jr., and Uk Heo, "Defense Contracting and Domestic Politics," 53 *Political Research Quarterly* 753–769 (2000).

178. Avant, "Think Again: Mercenaries," 20; Avant, "The Market for Force: Exploring the Privatization of Military Services," *Foreign Affairs,* March 21, 1999; Michaels, "Beyond Accountability," 1050–1082, 1115. See also Kateri Carmola, *Private Military Companies and New Wars: Risk, Law and Ethics* (forthcoming 2009).

179. Avant, "Think Again: Mercenaries" (private contractor receives U.S. assistance while advising Croatian government).

180. See Seymour M. Hersh, *Chain of Command: The Road from 9/11 to Abu Ghraib* 53 (2004); Jackson Nyamuya Maogto, "Subcontracting Sovereignty: The Commodification of Military Force and the Fragmentation of State Authority," 13 *Brown Journal of World Affairs* 160 (2006).

181. "U.S. Loan to Fund Bell Aircraft Deal," *Dallas Morning News,* October 31, 1996, at 12D.

182. In April 2005, Congressman David Price and other representatives introduced the Transparency and Accountability in Security Contract Act, which would require disclosure of such information by private military contractors doing business with the federal government and would also require allocation of sufficient resources to enable the contracting agency to "perform oversight of the performance of the contract." H.R. 2001, 109th Cong., 1st sess., sec. 2(a). It was reintroduced and is still pending as H.R. 369. The bill would also require the Department of Defense to adopt regulations setting standards for the training of private security company personnel and for the equipment, including body armor, used by such individuals. Ibid., sec. 2(b). See www.theorator.com.

183. August Cole, "Fresh Bid to Life Veil on Security Work," *MarketWatch,* May 16, 2005, www.marketwatch.com.

184. The British government pursues regulations of private military companies, and distinguishes mercenaries from servicemen in foreign armies and defense industrial companies. Ninth Report of the Foreign Affairs Committee, Private Military Companies, Session 2001–2002; Response of the Secretary of State for Foreign and Commonwealth Activities (October 2002); Return to an Address of the Honourable the House of Commons (Feb. 12, 2002), Private Military Companies: Options for Regulation, p. 7, http://www.fco.gov.uk/Files/kfile/mercenaries.0.pdf.

6. How Privatization Thinks

Epigraph: Mary Douglas, *How Institutions Think* (Syracuse: Syracuse University Press, 1986), p. 69.
I thank Matt Adler, Jody Freeman, Mark Greenberg, Martha Minow, and Rick Sander for helpful comments and suggestions, and Diana Varat for excellent research assistance.

1. This term is my own. See Sharon Dolovich, "State Punishment and Private Prisons," 55 *Duke Law Journal* 441 (2005). This framing is in theory consistent with any available method for calculating the efficiency of a given policy. For further discussion on cost-benefit and cost-effectiveness approaches to determining efficiency in the prison context, see below. Such approaches to analyzing efficiency are necessarily comparative. It thus may seem redundant to call the perspective I examine here *comparative* efficiency. I adopt this label nonetheless to call attention to the particular implications for the privatization debate of the comparative component of this perspective. I explore those implications below.

2. In this chapter, I approach the deliberative framework of comparative efficiency as a subject in its own right, distinct from the commentators who adopt and deploy it. This framing may lead to some perhaps jarring locutions. But it is consistent with my aim, which is to consider how the terms we use to talk about a given problem or phenomenon may operate as an independent force with tangible effects on the ultimate shape of the world.

3. Many private, for-profit penal facilities are not prisons but jails. For ease of reference, in this chapter I use the term "private prisons" to refer both to private, for-profit prisons and private, for-profit jails.

4. Douglas, *How Institutions Think,* 92.

5. See, e.g., Sarah Armstrong, "Bureaucracy, Private Prisons, and the Future of Penal Reform," 7 *Buffalo Criminal Law Review* 288 (2003).

6. It bears noting that, although the study of private prisons is somewhat out of fashion as a scholarly matter, this penal form continues to play a significant and ever-increasing part in corrections in the United States and worldwide. At the end of 2005, there were 107,447 inmates held in private prisons and jails in the United States, up from 98,628 the previous year. See U.S. Department of Justice, *Prisoners in 2005,* Bulletin No. NCJ 215092 (2006), p. 6, www.ojp

.usdoj.gov/bjs/pub/pdf/p05.pdf. Perhaps the clearest indication of the ongoing relevance of private prisons in American corrections may be seen in the enthusiasm expressed for the industry's prospects by Lehman Brothers investment analysts Jeffrey T. Kessler and Manav Patniak, who assert that they "continue to remain positive on the private prison industry, quite simply because the demand that exists for private prisons today is at an all-time high since we started coverage in 2001." Jeffrey T. Kessler and Manav Patniak, *Security Industry Annual Report 2006* (Lehman Brothers Global Equity Research North America, November 7, 2006), p. 253; see also ibid., 253–55 (including among their reasons for anticipating the private prison industry's intermediate-term growth: "continued growth in the overall prison population; the overcrowding, or "over-occupancy" issue; and the "baby boom echo," which means that the children of baby boomers are "increasingly entering an age range (mid-teens to twenty-four years old) "that is 'highest risk' with regard to potential incarceration (especially males)"). On the continued growth of prison privatization on the international front, consider just one recent issue of *Prison Privatisation Report International*, which features stories discussing existing private prisons or plans for privatization in Honduras, Chile, the Czech Republic, Hong Kong, Japan, Germany, France, the United Kingdom, the United States, South Africa, Australia, and Israel, among others. See Public Services International Research Unit, *Prison Privatisation Report International, No. 74* (University of Greenwich, England, October 2006), www.psiru.org/justice/PPRI74W.htm#CHILE.

7. See Dolovich, "State Punishment and Private Prisons," 440 n.4 (collecting citations to scholarly treatments of the issue of private prisons).

8. According to the June 2006 report of the Commission on Safety and Abuse in America's Prisons, there were over 34,000 reported instances of assault among prisoners and almost 18,000 reported instances of assault by prisoners against staff in state and federal facilities in 2000. And even these numbers, the Commission found, understate the pervasiveness of the violence. Vera Institute of Justice, Commission on Safety and Abuse in America's Prisons, *Confronting Confinement* (June 2006), pp. 24–25, www.prisoncommission.org (accessed 7/10/06). For anecdotal accounts of violence behind bars, see Sanyika Shakur, aka Monster Kody Scott, *Monster: The Autobiography of an L.A. Gang Member* (New York: Penguin Books, 1993) (describing truly horrific levels of violence in the high-security wing of the Los Angeles County Jail); Michael G. Santos, *Inside: Life behind Bars in America* (New York: St. Martin's Press, 2006) (recounting many extremely violent incidents in various federal penitentiaries, and characterizing this level of violence as routine in those facilities); K. C. Carceral, *Prison, Inc.: A Convict Exposes Life inside a Private Prison*, ed. Thomas J. Bernard (New York: New York University Press, 2006) (describing the slide toward systemic violence in a private prison in an unnamed southern state).

9. See Dolovich, "State Punishment and Private Prisons," 496 n.225, 526–528, 523 n.339.

10. See, e.g., Christine Bowditch and Ronald S. Everett, "Private Prisons: Problems within the Solution," 4 *Justice Quarterly* 451 (1987); see also Ira P. Robbins, "Privatization of Corrections: Defining the Issues," 40 *Vanderbilt Law Review* 826 (1987).

11. See, e.g., Charles H. Logan, *Private Prisons: Cons and Pros* (New York: Oxford University Press, 1990), pp. 155–158.

12. For an account of the lobbying efforts of the politically powerful California Correctional and Peace Officers Association (CCPOA), see Dolovich, "State Punishment and Private Prisons," 530–532.

13. See, e.g., J. Robert Lilly and Paul Knepper, "The Corrections-Commercial Complex," 39 *Crime and Delinquency* 154–155 (1993).

14. See Dolovich, "State Punishment and Private Prisons," 536–542.

15. For discussion, see ibid., 510–512.

16. Ibid., 502–505 (describing the elevated levels of violence in private prisons).

17. See Richard Harding, "Private Prisons," 28 *Crime and Justice: A Review of Research* 294, 296, 304 (2001); Sean McConville, "Aid from Industry? Private Corrections and Prison Crowding," in Stephen D. Gottfredson and Sean McConville, eds., *America's Correctional Crisis: Prison Populations and Public Policy* (New York: Greenwood Press, 1987), p. 240.

18. For further discussion of the innovation claim in the private prison context, see Dolovich, "State Punishment and Private Prisons," 476–477.

19. For an elaboration on the argument that private prisons function very much like public prisons, see Dolovich, "State Punishment and Private Prisons," 500–502 (arguing that the main practical differences between public and private prisons stem from the fact that private prisons systematically underinvest in labor).

20. "Rise of Private Prisons: How Much of a Bargain?," *New York Times,* March 27, 1989, A14 (quoting Bob Owens, internal auditor for the Texas Department of Corrections: "I'm an old state bureaucrat . . . I don't have any philosophies. If they can do it cheaper than the state can, more power to them."); see also "Private Prisons: A Question of Savings," *New York Times,* July 13, 1997, F5 (quoting Donal Campbell, Commissioner of the Tennessee Department of Corrections: "I think as long as it does not cost any more than it costs the state, then we should consider privatization. . . . We should compare and explore the options out there that would save the taxpayers money.").

21. See Sharon Dolovich, "Legitimate Punishment in Liberal Democracy," 7 *Buffalo Criminal Law Review* 385–419 (2004); Dolovich, "State Punishment and Private Prisons," 462–471, 515–518.

22. As this formulation suggests, the approach I adopt is a self-consciously Rawlsian one. For an elaboration of this argument, including detailed derivation of these two principles, see Dolovich, "Legitimate Punishment in Liberal Democracy."

23. The foundational or "baseline" liberal democratic values include a commitment to individual liberty, dignity, and bodily integrity; limited government;

the primacy and sovereignty of the individual; and the entitlement of all citizens to equal concern and respect. I assume that a liberal democracy is any democratic society with a stated commitment to these values. See Dolovich, "Legitimate Punishment in Liberal Democracy," 312 n.11, 313–314.

24. As Robert Frank puts it, "[s]carcity is a simple fact of the human condition. To have more of one good thing, we must settle for less of another." Robert H. Frank, "Why Is Cost-Benefit Analysis So Controversial?" 29 *Journal of Legal Studies* 914 (2000).

25. See Diana Fuguitt and Shanton J. Wilcox, *Cost-Benefit Analysis for Public Sector Decision Makers* (Westport, CT: Quorum, 1999), p. 36.

26. The conventional way to understand the aim of cost-benefit analysis is "Kaldor-Hicks" efficiency, which is achieved "if there is a hypothetical cost-less lump sum redistribution in the project world, from winners to losers, such that this amended project world is Pareto efficient relative to the status quo." Matthew D. Adler and Eric A. Posner, "Implementing Cost-Benefit Analysis When Preferences Are Distorted," 29 *Journal of Legal Studies* 1108 (2000). In contrast, Adler and Posner have a "revisionary take," which characterizes cost-benefit analysis "as a way to implement overall well-being." Matt Adler, personal communication (September 24, 2006); see also Adler and Posner, "Implementing Cost-Benefit Analysis," 1108–1116. Although I use the language of overall well-being here, I do so because it best captures the understanding of cost-benefit analysis that motivates my discussion. I do not intend thereby to take sides in the debate among economists as to the appropriate way to characterize the aims of cost-benefit analysis.

27. Even attempting to pin down a precise meaning of this concept would be a difficult enterprise. As Amartya Sen notes, "the term 'cost-benefit analysis' has considerable plasticity and various specific procedures have been called by that name." Amartya Sen, "The Discipline of Cost-Benefit Analysis," 29 *Journal of Legal Studies* 932–933 (2000); see also Adler and Posner, "Implementing Cost-Benefit Analysis," 1108–1116.

28. See Fuguitt and Wilcox, *Cost-Benefit Analysis,* 35.

29. See, for example, the essays in Ruth Chang, ed., *Incommensurability, Incomparability, and Practical Reason* (Cambridge, MA: Harvard University Press, 1997).

30. I assume that under the real-world conditions of partial compliance, *all* incarceration will be to some extent inconsistent with the demands of this principle. Full compliance is therefore unrealistic, and the best we can do is aim to be as compliant as possible.

31. For discussion as to whether cost-benefit analysis is necessarily consequentialist, see Martha Nussbaum, "The Costs of Tragedy: Some Moral Limits of Cost-Benefit Analysis," 29 *Journal of Legal Studies,* 1028–1030 (2000); Sen, "The Discipline of Cost-Benefit Analysis," 936–938.

32. Again, even this way of framing the issue may concede too much, since it implies the possibility of articulating the "cost" of violating a moral obligation in terms comparable with the financial cost of privatization.

33. See Nussbaum, "The Costs of Tragedy," 1017 (suggesting that systematically considering the possibility that no available alternative is morally justified "reinforces commitments to important moral values that should in general be observed, . . . motivates us to make appropriate reparations for conduct that, while in a sense inevitable, was also unethical, . . . and leads us to ask how the tragic situation might have been avoided by better social planning."). See also ibid. at 1011.

34. At least this is true of what Sen has called the "limited mainstream methodology" of cost-benefit analysis. See Sen, "The Discipline of Cost-Benefit Analysis," 945. Sen's work suggests that a more sophisticated version of cost-benefit analysis may transcend the concern just articulated. But for my purposes, it is enough that the limitation I identify is shared by "limited mainstream" versions of cost-benefit analysis. For one thing, my aim here is to sketch the broad concerns raised by the approach and not to demonstrate its inability to satisfy them on any conceivable version. Moreover, however appealing a sufficiently nuanced and sophisticated cost-benefit approach may be in theory, such an approach is unlikely to inform debate in the practical context of prison privatization even assuming an effort to incorporate broader normative concerns into the analysis.

35. This principle requires that criminal punishments not be gratuitously inhumane. Given the extremely limited circumstances under which this principle would authorize inhumane punishment—circumstances that in practice would be very rare indeed if they existed at all—the working assumption when applying this principle must be that *any* inhumane punishment would represent a violation. See Dolovich, "Legitimate Punishment in Liberal Democracy," 409–419; Dolovich, "State Punishment and Private Prisons," 469–470. An assessment in terms of this principle thus requires consideration of the relative humanity of a given facility.

36. See, e.g., Oliver Hart, Andrei Schleifer, and Robert W. Vishny, "The Proper Scope of Government Theory and an Application to Prisons," 112 *Quarterly Journal of Economics* 1127 (1997) (arguing against prison privatization on the grounds that the inevitably incomplete contracts that establish the scope of the contractor's responsibilities accord considerable discretion to private prison administrators and guards, discretion that allows scope for physical abuse against inmates). See also Dolovich, "State Punishment and Private Prisons," 478–79 (discussing the problem of incomplete contracts in the private prisons context).

37. Simon Dinitz, "Are Safe and Humane Prisons Possible?" 14 *Australian and New Zealand Journal of Criminology* 3–19 (1981).

38. See Robert P. Weiss, "Private Prisons and the State," in Roger Matthews, ed., *Privatizing Criminal Justice* (London: Sage, 1989), p. 43 (quoting John Mack, "Writing Off the Doomed," *The Progressive* (September 1984), p. 21): "The vast majority [of inmates] are what Saul Bellow refers to as the mindless 'superfluous population,' the 'doomed people' who have been 'written off.' ").

424 · Notes to Pages 137–140

39. See, e.g., Gary King, Robert O. Keohane, and Sidney Verba, *Designing Social Inquiry: Scientific Inference in Qualitative Research* (Princeton, NJ: Princeton University Press, 1994); Matthew D. Adler, "Fear Assessment: Cost-Benefit Analysis and the Pricing of Fear and Anxiety," 79 *Chicago-Kent Law Review* 977 (2004).

40. For discussion of these issues, see Dolovich, "State Punishment and Private Prisons," 515–42.

41. A rich literature exists that addresses the challenges and appropriate parameters of public debate on matters of value. See, e.g., John Rawls, *Political Liberalism* (New York: Columbia University Press, 1993); Amy Guttman and Dennis Thompson, *Democracy and Disagreement: Why Moral Conflict Cannot Be Avoided in Politics, and What Should Be Done about It* (Cambridge, MA: Belknap Press of Harvard University Press, 1996).

42. For a history of this process, which the author characterizes as the bureaucratization of American penal administration, see Armstrong, "Bureaucracy, Private Prisons, and the Future of Penal Reform," 288.

43. Discussing an emerging trend in corrections policy toward charging prisoners a daily fee for room and board, for example, a Michigan jail administrator recently asked "why law-abiding citizens should be burdened with the cost of incarceration *when they never use that service,* or why taxpayers should be further victimized by supporting inmates who have the wherewithal to pay." Michelle M. Sanborn, "The Pay-to-Stay Debate: Inmates Must Take Financial Responsibility," 65 *Corrections Today* 22 (2003) (emphasis added). See also E. S. Savas, "Privatization and Prisons," 40 *Vanderbilt Law Review* 899 (1987) (describing recidivists who have been imprisoned in multiple facilities as "comparison shopper[s]" whose opinion as to the virtues of various institutions might contribute to comparative assessments of public and private facilities).

44. See Armstrong, "Bureaucracy, Private Prisons, and the Future of Penal Reform," 302.

45. See, e.g., Eric A. Posner, "Transfer Regulations and Cost-Effectiveness Analysis," 53 *Duke Law Journal* 1069 (2003). Cost-effectiveness analysis may also allow the assessment of policies to determine which of the available options can "maximize effectiveness for a given budget or set of resources," although this alternative is not a focus of the private prisons debate. Fuguitt and Wilcox, *Cost-Benefit Analysis,* 277. For a brief explanation of the differences between cost-benefit and cost-effectiveness approaches, see infra.

46. See Joseph T. Hallinan, *Going up the River: Travels in a Prison Nation* (New York: Random House, 2001), p. 167 ("The success of private prisons . . . is driven by a single premise: They are cheaper than their public counterparts."); see also Harding, "Private Prisons," 310 (describing the interest in prison privatization in the United States as "less about doing a different job more innovatively than doing the same job less expensively").

47. Thus, even if a given proposal to privatize is defeated, to keep the debate focused on cost-minimization is still a victory for privatization because it signals

the official belief that no further normative issues relating to incarceration require attention, and that relative cost is the only thing that matters. And, it bears noting, once this belief is in place, any normative concerns that arguably remain are rendered invisible.

48. See, e.g., Henry M. Levin and Patrick J. McEwan, *Cost-Effectiveness Analysis: Methods and Applications,* 2nd ed. (Thousand Oaks, CA: Sage, 2001), pp. 14–19. See also supra note 34.

49. Fuguitt and Wilcox, *Cost-Benefit Analysis,* 274.

50. In health policy analysis, the net benefit of a given treatment is measured in "quality adjusted life years" or "QALYs." The term seeks to capture both the extent to which a given medical treatment extends life and the quality of life that would be experienced by those thereby kept alive. Levin and McEwan, *Cost-Effectiveness Analysis,* 204. On this approach, quality of life is measured as a number between zero (death) and one (perfect health) and is generally derived from one of a number of "stated preference format[s]," W. Kip Viscusi, "Monetizing the Benefits and Risks of Environmental Regulation," 33 *Fordham Urban Law Journal* 1014 (2006), including the "standard gamble, time trade-off and the use of rating scales." Certi Phillips and Guy Thompson, "What Is a QALY?," p. 2 www.jr2.ox.ac.uk/bandolier/booth/glossary/QALY.html (accessed 9/17/06). When the benefits of a particular treatment are measured in QALYs, the QALY figure represents the number of years of life the treatment's application is expected to save multiplied by the value of the quality of life (between one and zero) that is expected to result from this application. For example, if a treatment extends a person's life by four years at a quality of life of .75, then the QALY is equal to 3. Ibid. This approach allows doctors to use QALY values to compare various medical treatments and pursue the treatment that promises to save the most QALYs overall. And more importantly for our purposes, it also allows policymakers to use QALY values to compare various public health initiatives and to pursue the approach that saves the highest number of QALYs at the lowest possible cost. For further discussion on this approach, see Levin and McEwan, *Cost-Effectiveness Analysis,* 204–205.

51. Levin and McEwan, *Cost-Effectiveness Analysis,* 276–280.

52. This account necessarily oversimplifies the complex issues arising in the health policy context. For further discussion of these issues, see Erik Nord, *Cost-Value Analysis in Health Care: Making Sense out of QALYs* (New York: Cambridge University Press, 1999); John La Puma and Edward F. Lawlor, "Quality-Adjusted Life-Years: Ethical Implications for Physicians and Policymakers," 263 *Journal of the American Medical Association* 2917 (1990).

53. Note that these two considerations are the central concerns of parsimony and humanity, respectively.

54. The notion that comparative efficiency is apolitical, and its concerns value-neutral, is implicit in the private prisons literature. In that literature, it is a commonplace that issues relating to the "allocation" of punishment—i.e.,

who should be incarcerated, for what offense, and for how long—are necessarily distinct from and must be kept separate from those issues relating to
the "administration" of punishment—i.e., how the prisons should be run
and who should run them. The implication of this distinction is that questions of allocation are normative and thus necessarily require political determinations outside the scope of the private prisons debate, while questions of
administration are simply (value neutral) management issues that comparative efficiency can therefore appropriately resolve. See Richard Harding, *Private Prisons and Public Accountability* (New Brunswick, NJ: Transaction
Publishers, 1997), p. 22; see also Paul Moyle, "Separating the Allocation of
Punishment from Its Administration: Theoretical and Empirical Observations," 11 *Current Issues in Criminal Justice* 166–170 (1999).

55. On the early history of private involvement in American corrections, see
Dolovich, "State Punishment and Private Prisons," 450–454.

56. As is well known to any corrections official, overcrowding in penal facilities
raises stress levels, exacerbates interpersonal tensions, and creates endless
opportunities for the development of rancor and hostility among inmates
and between inmates and line officers. It thus makes the job of keeping order
more difficult and leads to increased violence. It also overtaxes prison services like health care, dental care, drug treatment, and other programming,
and burdens the physical plant in ways guaranteed to compromise living
conditions.

57. See Harding, *Private Prisons and Public Accountability*, 22 (describing the
authorization for, and realization of, overcrowding in private prisons that occurred in the United States, the United Kingdom, and Australia by the mid-
1990s, and stating that "the brief halcyon period when private sector prisons
were in effect quarantined from overcrowding has already come to an end").

58. The term is Feigenbaum and Henig's. Harvey B. Feigenbaum and Jeffrey R.
Henig, "The Political Underpinnings of Privatization: A Typology," 46
World Politics 195 (1994).

59. In positing an inherent difference between public and private, comparative
efficiency need not assume that this difference has any particular content. It
bears noting, however, that in the private prisons literature, the comparative
efficiency question plays out before an ideological backdrop that *does* give
particular content to the distinction. Specifically, it tends to regard state institutions as "bloated, wasteful, [and] ineffective," in contrast to the "more
flexible, more innovative, and more entrepreneurial" character of the competitive private sector. David Osborne and Ted Gaebler, *Reinventing Government: How the Entrepreneurial Spirit is Transforming the Public Sector*
(Reading, MA: Addison-Wesley, 1992), p. 12. From this ideological perspective, the private sector is presumed to be the better option. Theoretically,
comparative efficiency could exist independently of this ideological picture.
But where comparative efficiency is informed by this ideology—which in
practice it frequently is—the assumption of the inherent difference between
public and private invariably leads to arguments in favor of privatization.

60. See supra, "The Insistence on Comparison."
61. Douglas, *How Institutions Think*, 92.

7. Achieving Contracting Goals and Recognizing Public Law Concerns

I would like to acknowledge help on answering specific questions for this chapter from Alan Chvotkin, Jody Freeman, Matt Blum, Steve Schooner, and Stan Soloway. Michael Hoke and Greg Dorchak provided helpful research assistance.

1. One subset of these questions, regarding the proper limits for activities that may rightfully be contracted out in the first place, has received attention in the procurement community for some time. Office of Management and Budget (OMB), Circular A-76 (2003), www.whitehouse.gov/omb/circulars/1076/a76_incl_tech_correction.html (discussion of "inherently governmental" functions that may not be contracted out).
2. Ronald A. Coase, "The Nature of the Firm," 4 *Economica* 386 (1937).
3. Kenneth J. Arrow and Tibor Scitovsky, *Readings in Welfare Economics* (Homewood, IL: Published for the American Economic Association by R.D. Irwin, 1969), p. 48.
4. Oliver E. Williamson, *Markets and Hierarchies, Analysis and Antitrust Implications: A Study in the Economics of Internal Organization* (New York: Free Press, 1975); Williamson, "The Economics of Organization: The Transaction Cost Approach," 87 *American Journal of Sociology* 548 (1981); Williamson, *The Economic Institutions of Capitalism* (New York: Free Press, 1996); Williamson, *The Mechanisms of Governance* (New York: Oxford University Press, 1996).
5. C.K. Prahalad and Gary Hamel, "The Core Competence of the Corporation," *Harvard Business Review*, May–June 1990, at 79.
6. See John D. Donahue, *The Privatization Decision: Public Ends, Private Means* (New York: Basic Books, 1989).
7. For example, if there is uncertainty but no asset-specific investments, the contract can easily be recompeted if important changes occur and the contract cannot be renegotiated to mutual satisfaction.
8. Especially because the more that production is transaction-specific, the lower the production-cost advantages (economies of scale and of learning) from contracting.
9. Williamson notes, for example, that while contractual disputes may be taken to court, employees, or one division of a firm that supplies components to another division, generally cannot litigate disputes over directions from the employer or decisions about transfer prices. It is also generally easier to observe employee behavior directly than to observe the behavior of contractors in cases where effort is the only performance indicator.
10. I. Geyskens, J-BE.M. Steenkamp, and N. Kumar, "Make, Buy, or Ally: A Transaction Cost Theory of Meta Analysis," 49 *Academy of Management Journal* 519 (2006).

11. Trevor L. Brown and Matthew Potoski, "Transaction Costs and Institutional Explanations for Government Service and Production Decisions," 13 *Journal of Public Administration Research and Theory* 441 (2003).
12. For example, weapons system development in government.
13. Ian R. Macneil, "The Many Futures of Contracts," 67 *University of Southern California Law Review* 691 (1974).
14. See FAR 1.102, 60 Fed. Reg. 34,732 (July 3, 1995).
15. H.G. Rainey, R.W. Backoff, and C.H. Levine, "Comparing Public and Private Organizations," 36 *Public Administration Review* 223 (1976); Emanuel S. Savas, *Privatization and the Public Sector: How to Shrink the Government* (Chatham, NJ: Chatham House Publishers, 1982).
16. Savas, *Privatization and the Public Sector,* 134–135.
17. To take an extreme example, what should the State Department's metrics be? Should the Forest Service cut down trees for economic use or preserve them for wilderness lovers?
18. James Q. Wilson, *Bureaucracy: What Government Agencies Do and Why They Do It* (New York: Basic Books, 1989); R. Simons, "Control in an Age of Empowerment," *Harvard Business Review,* March-April 1995, at 80.
19. Linear programming or economics terminology speaks of maximizing goals subject to constraints.
20. Steven J. Kelman, "What Is Wrong with the Revolving Door?" in Barry Bozeman, ed., *Public Management: The State of the Art* (San Francisco: Jossey-Bass, 1993), pp. 224–251.
21. John W. Thibaut and Laurens Walker, *Procedural Justice: A Psychological Analysis* (Hillsdale, NJ: L. Erlbaum Associates, 1975); Tom R. Tyler, *Why People Obey the Law* (New Haven, CT: Yale University Press, 1990); Joel Brockner and Batia W. Weisenfeld, "An Integrative Framework for Explaining Reactions to Decisions: The Interactive Effects of Outcomes and Procedures," 120 *Psychology Bulletin* 189 (1996).
22. A helpful way to think about the difference between goals and constraints, although it does not apply perfectly, is in terms of the common distinction in moral philosophy between "negative" and "positive" duties. B. Russell, "On the Relative Strictness of Negative and Positive Duties," in Bonnie Steinbock, ed., *Killing and Letting Die* (Englewood Cliffs, NJ: Prentice-Hall, 1980), pp. 215–237; M. Tooley, "An Irrelevant Consideration: Killing versus Letting Die," ibid., 56–62), where the former are duties to refrain from some action (e.g., don't kill) and the latter to undertake some action (e.g., save people who are dying). Constraints can generally be respected if an organization does nothing; if an agency lets no contracts it will not violate the constraint that contracting officials shouldn't award contracts to relatives; if it has no program to combat terrorism it will not risk violating the due process rights of terrorist suspects. Meeting goals almost always requires action. Simons is explicit about this when he states, "If I want my employees to be creative and entrepreneurial, am I better off telling them what to do or telling them what not to do? The answer is the latter. Telling people what to do by

establishing standard operating procedures and rule books discourages the initiative and creativity unleashed by empowered, entrepreneurial employees. Telling them what *not* to do allows innovation, but within clearly defined limits . . . [B]oundary systems are stated in negative terms or as minimum standards." Robert Simons, *Levers of Control: How Managers Use Innovative Control Systems to Drive Strategic Renewal* (Boston: Harvard Business School Press, 1995), p. 84.

23. Wilson, *Bureaucracy*, 115.

24. R. Gregory, "Accountability in Modern Government," in B. Guy Peters and Jon Pierre, eds., *Handbook of Public Administration* (London: Sage Publications, 2003), pp. 557–568.

25. More broadly, greater attention is paid in government to mistakes than to achievements. Even in the 1920s, Leonard Dupree White observed that public officials perceive that "[w]henever we make a mistake, some one jumps on us for it, but whenever we do something well nobody pays any attention to us. We never get any recognition except when we get 'bawled out.' " *Introduction to the Study of Public Administration* (New York: 1926), pp. 243–244. A half-century later, Derek Rayner, the CEO of Marks & Spencer, brought into the British government under Prime Minister Margaret Thatcher, noted that in government "[f]ailure is always noted and success is forgotten." Quoted in Peter Hennessy, *Whitehall* (New York: Free Press, 1989), p. 595.

26. FAR 1.102 (emphasis added).

27. Max Weber, *The Methodology of the Social Sciences* (New York: Free Press, 1949).

28. The bureaucratic form that has become so associated with government that James Q. Wilson's classic book on government agencies is titled simply *Bureaucracy*, and political scientists working on government agencies generally refer to them by the generic name "the bureaucracy."

29. Herbert Kaufman, *Red Tape: Its Origins, Uses, and Abuses* (Washington, DC: Brookings Institution, 1977).

30. Theodore Roosevelt, *Works* (New York: C. Scribner's Sons, 1926).

31. Steven Kelman, *Procurement and Public Management: The Fear of Discretion and the Quality of Government Performance* (Washington, DC: AEI Press, 1990); Robert E. Klitgaard, *Corrupt Cities: A Practical Guide to Cure and Prevention* (Washington, DC: World Bank Institute, 2000); Susan Rose-Ackerman, *Corruption and Government: Causes, Consequences, and Reform* (New York: Cambridge University Press, 1999), pp. 59–68.

32. One of the earliest GAO decisions on this topic was U.S. Department of Agriculture (B-182337) (1975), which talked about "administrative expediency." See also National Customer Engineering (B-251135) (1993), which talked about "mere administrative convenience."

33. In the traditional system, people often referred—using a phrase that now seems anachronistic—to "buying a Cadillac rather than a Chevrolet."

34. This is called a "request for proposals" (RFP) for procurements with non-price evaluation factors and an "invitation for bids" (IFP) for sealed bids.

35. Many agencies, though never DOD, present exact numerical point weights for the various factors and subfactors, adding up to 100.

36. Kelman, *Procurement and Public Management.* Agencies sometimes looked at "past experience"—how *often* a company performed a certain kind of work before (something that could be placed in a proposal), but not at how *well* they had performed the contracts they completed; however, for those bid solicitations that included "past experience," it was seldom given more than a nominal weight in evaluating proposals.

37. Pub. L. 87–653, 76 Stat. 528–529 (codified as amended at 10 U.S.C. §2306a (2000)).

38. See Kelman, Procurement and Public Management.

39. Ibid.

40. "Military Specifications: Cookie Mix, Dry," *Harper's,* October 1985, p. 25.

41. Jeff Bingham et al., Integrating Commercial and Military Technologies for National Strength: An Agenda for Change; Report of the CSIS Steering Committee on Security and Technology (Washington, DC: Center for Strategic and International Studies, 1990).

42. In some cases, commercial firms established separate production lines for runs of products just for DOD, so that their extra costs of doing business with the government wouldn't hurt their commercial business. This deprived the government of economies of scale.

43. Keki R. Bhote, Strategic Supply Management: A Blueprint for Revitalizing the Manufacturer-Supplier Partnership (New York: American Management Association, 1989).

44. Roderick M. Kramer and Tom R. Tyler, *Trust in Organizations: Frontiers of Theory and Research* (Thousand Oaks, CA: Sage Publications, 1996); Dan Cohen and Laurence Prusak, *In Good Company: How Social Capital Makes Organizations Work* (Boston: Harvard Business School Press, 2001).

45. This argument is analogous to the view that government interventions each sought by one group add up to a system whose costs outweigh its benefits for everybody. See Barry Weingast et al., "The Political Economy of Benefits and Costs: A Neoclassical Approach to Distributive Politics," 89 *Journal of Political Economy* 642 (1981).

46. Pub. L. No. 103–355, 108 Stat. 3243 (1994) (codified in scattered sections of 10 U.S.C. and 41 U.S.C.).

47. FAR 42.1503(b)).

48. Under the previous regime, the prospect of a two-year wait to get on contract if one cut off a poorly performing contractor strongly inhibited ending unsatisfactory work, unless performance was catastrophic.

49. The canonical example is to require that the grass be kept at no more than 1/2 inch rather than stating the grass shall be mowed every two weeks.

50. See OMB, Office of Federal Procurement Policy, Best Practices for Performance-Based Contracting (1998).

51. The canonical example was elimination of the spec for chocolate chip cookie mix (along with all the other military-specified (milspec) food) and its re-

placement in 1996 by an entirely new way of buying food for the troops, whereby the government contracted with commercial food distributors who offered an electronic catalogue of commercial food items to mess sergeants.

52. "You've Come a Long Way," *Federal Computer Week*, April 17, 2000, at 3.

53. FAR 15.201.

54. Chip Mather and Ann Costello, "An Innovative Approach to Performance-Based Acquisition: Using a SOO," *Acquisition Directions Advisory* (May 2001), p. 1. Sometimes a contractor who will be, or may be, doing the work is in a better position than a third party to help an agency shape its requirement, because it has a stronger interest in eventual success than the third party does or because it may know the agency more intimately. If the contractor has already been chosen for the work, this creates conflicts of interest, but such contractor-influenced shaping can occur with fewer such risks in a limited competition where perhaps two suppliers are facing off to receive the final work.

55. See James G. March et al., *The Dynamics of Rules: Change in Written Organizational Codes* (Stanford, CA: Stanford University Press, 2000). In the context of an agency dealing with the public, and with elected officials, codifying good practice into rules has an additional advantage. "Making decisions in accordance with specific rules . . . helps repel attempts by politicians to reverse . . . decisions on behalf of irate . . . constituents." Eugene Bardach and Robert A. Kagan, *Going by the Book: The Problem of Regulatory Unreasonableness* (Philadelphia: Temple University Press, 1982), p. 36. More generally, when a government official has decision-making authority over a person, making the decision according to a rule reduces interpersonal tension involved in an unfavorable ruling—one can say, "The rule made me do it."

56. Donald F. Kettl, *Government by Proxy: (Mis?)managing Federal Programs* (Washington, DC: CQ Press, 1988); H. Brinton Milward, "What Does 'Hollow State' Look Like?" in Barry Bozeman, ed., *Public Management: The State of the Art* (San Francisco: Jossey-Bass, 1993); Milward, "Capacity, Control, and Performance in Interorganizational Settings," 6 *Journal of Public Administration Research and Theory* 193 (1996).

57. Shelley E. Taylor, *Positive Illusions: Creative Self-Deception and the Healthy Mind* (New York: Basic Books, 1989).

58. Constantly updated specifications for weapons and information technology projects can be a problem as well, making it difficult to stabilize requirements and thus to get a project actually defined, so one thing one tries to do in managing such projects is to create discipline in change requests. But again the point is that the costs of the final project include features not included in original cost estimates.

59. To be included in the study, projects needed to take at least four years and cost at least $1 billion.

60. Edward W. Merrow, *A Review of Cost Estimation in New Technologies: Implications for Energy Process Plants* (Santa Monica, CA: RAND Corporation, 1979).

61. Bill Kern, "Relief from Out-of-Control Projects," 41 *Contract Management* 32 (2001).
62. During the 1994–1998 period, aerospace/defense firms in the index averaged a 14 percent rate of return on equity, compared, for example, with 26 percent for chemical or diversified manufacturing firms and 17 percent for auto parts firms. Defense Science Board, "Impact of DoD Policies/Practices on the Health/Competitiveness of U.S. Defense Industry," *Task Force Report* (April 2000), p. 11.
63. Computer Sciences Corporation, Annual Report 2000, p. 63.
64. Trevor L. Brown and Matthew Potoski, "Contracting for Management: Assessing Management Capacity Under Alternative Service Delivery Arrangements," 25 *Policy Analysis and Management* 323 (2006).
65. Something similar occurred after Hurricane Katrina, where funds for large numbers of after-the-fact auditors and inspector-general personnel were appropriated—there ended up being many times the number of such personnel dealing with Katrina than there were contracting personnel.
66. Federal Acquisition Institute, *Annual Report on the Federal Acquisition Workforce-Fiscal Year 2005* (July 2006), pp. 8, 2.
67. Steven L. Schooner, "Fear of Oversight: The Fundamental Failure of Businesslike Government," 50 *American Law Review* 627 (2001).
68. A senior procurement official at a major civilian agency has estimated that at many civilian agencies, prior to the credit card 40 percent of procurement personnel were working on these small transactions (Robert Welch, personal communication).
69. Even between 1998 (the earliest year for which data are currently available) and 2006, the number of contract specialists/officers aged 35–39 has declined by about one-third, while the number over 55 has gone up by about two-thirds. U.S. Office of Personnel Management, *Employment Cubes* (2006), www.fedscope.opm.gov/employment.asp (accessed 11/3/06).
70. *Program* managers are the program customers for what is being bought; *contract* managers are the procurement officials responsible for business (and to some extent legal) elements of the contract.
71. Donald F. Kettl, *Sharing Power: Public Governance and Private Markets* (Washington, DC: Brookings Institution, 1993).
72. The activities of government program managers for weapons systems or for major agency projects that establish a program management organization come closest to the kinds of executive-type functions described above, although there are special features of the DOD weapons-system program management environment that make it difficult for the program manager to get sufficiently involved in these executive functions. Program managers are typically military officers on relatively short (two or three year) tours of duty, which makes it difficult for them to set and execute a program strategy. Weapons programs are in such competition with each other for budget funds that program managers, especially given their brief tenure, often have an interest in presenting wildly optimistic plans at the beginning of a project and,

later on, downplaying problems rather than confronting them,. The enormous hierarchy of the military services and the Office of the Secretary of Defense produces a situation where inordinate time is spent "briefing" superiors and preparing for reviews. Until recently, the culture of program offices played relatively modest attention to cost control. And, of course, there are inherent problems in keeping work on new weapons systems to cost, schedule, and performance targets. See generally Ronald J. Fox, *The Defense Management Challenge: Weapons Acquisition* (Boston: Harvard Business School Press, 1988).

73. H. Brinton Milward and Keith G. Provan, "Governing the Hollow State," 10 *Journal of Public Administration Research and Theory* 359 (2000).

74. Paul C. Light, *The True Size of Government* (Washington, DC: Brookings Institution Press, 1999).

75. Such as the so-called federally funded research and development companies (e.g., the RAND Corporation) that work only for the government.

76. Arthur L. Stinchcombe, *Information and Organizations* (Berkeley: University of California Press, 1990).

77. John Cibinic and Ralph C. Nash, *Cost-Reimbursement Contracting* (Washington, DC: George Washington University, 1994), pp. 975–976.

78. In defense of "micromanagement," at least in a cost-reimbursement environment where the contractor does not commit to achieving any particular results, government people might fear that otherwise the contractor will waste money going down unproductive paths.

79. FAR 37.104.

80. Light, *The True Size of Government,* 13–14.

81. Daniel Guttman, "Public Purpose and Private Service: The 20th Century Culture of Contracting out and the Evolving Law of Diffused Sovereignty," 52 *Administrative Law Review* 1111 (2000).

82. John J. DiIulio, "The Duty to Govern: A Critical Perspective on the Private Management of Prisons and Jails," in Douglas C. McDonald, ed., *Private Prisons and the Public Interest* (New Brunswick, NJ: Rutgers University Press, 1990).

83. P.W. Singer, *Corporate Warriors: The Rise of the Privatized Military Industry* (Ithaca, NY: Cornell University Press, 2003).

84. Contractors are generally responsible for providing security for themselves, and they hire these firms to do so. There are cases, particularly in much smaller outposts where there is a very small military presence alongside significant contractor presence, where private security may sometimes "protect" the military, but those are real exceptions. Private security also guarded the original senior officials of the Coalition Provisional Authority just after the invasion, but this was because they were seen as officials of a "coalition," not American officials, and it was considered inappropriate to have them guarded by U.S. soldiers.

85. A list of the entire one hundred solicitations is available from the author on request.

86. My personal favorite was a solicitation to "provide aerobics instructors at an Air Force base in Oklahoma."

87. More broadly, one might argue that public law issues could be raised if there turned out to be safety or other public policy concerns arising in connection with production or installation of even some of the simple manufactured products discussed here, or with operation, say, of the skin disease clinic or aerobics classes; these could be avoided if the products or services were manufactured in-house, which might subject information regarding their manufacture to the Freedom of Information Act (FOIA), or if FOIA applied to these contractors. However, while perhaps government employees might run skin clinics or aerobics classes, it is hard to imagine that it makes sense for the government to establish plants to manufacture fibreboard or to have government construction organizations build roads, and application of FOIA to suppliers of commercial products to the government is almost certainly a bad idea.

88. What can be determined from the solicitation is that the Inter-American Foundation contracted with the Bureau of Public Debt to provide such audit services, and the Bureau is in turn contracting them to a private firm.

89. Pub. L. No. 105–270, 112 Stat 2382 (codified as amended at 31 U.S.C. §501 note).

90. See Chapter 3 above.

91. This excludes the U.S. Postal Service.

92. If anything, agencies had an incentive to understate the presence of commercial jobs suitable for public-private competition, since outsourced jobs might reduce the "empires" of those currently managing them.

93. As of the time this chapter was written.

94. Chapter 2 above.

95. Still others have very high uncertainty and asset specificity, without huge cost advantages for the contractor. The supramarket salaries for blue-collar work in turn produce resistance against contracting out commercial-type jobs currently performed inside government—though both TCE and core competency analysis suggest they should be contracted—because incumbent employees (and their union representatives) correctly believe that contracting them out would likely lower the wages for them.

96. In other cases, contractors do indeed have a stable of people with certain skills on staff—say, experts on developing financial management information technology systems—that can readily be applied to individual assignments in agencies.

97. The government may undertake a "reduction in force" if positions are permanently not needed.

98. Steven Kelman, "Strategic Contract Management," in John D. Donahue and Joseph Nye Jr., eds., *Market-Based Governance: Supply Side, Demand Side, Upside and Downside* (Washington,: Brookings Institution Press, 2002), pp. 88–102.

99. FAR Part 9.5.

100. Exec. Order No. 11,246, 3 C.F.R. 339 (1964–1965), *reprinted as amended in* 42 U.S.C.A. §2000e (2003).
101. Drug-Free Workplace Act of 1988 §5152, 41 U.S.C. §701 (2000).
102. For example, Wal-Mart (which would be in a strong position, given its logistics capabilities throughout the country, to assist government in provision of emergency services after hurricanes or other disasters) refuses to contract with the government to avoid being subject to such clauses.
103. S. Rep. No. 103–259, at 7 (1994), *reprinted in* 1994 U.S.C.C.A.N. 2598, 2603–2604, said the statute "would encourage the acquisition of commercial end-items and components . . . by exempting commercial items from government-unique certifications and accounting requirements that serve as a disincentive for commercial companies to participate in government acquisitions."
104. U.S. Bureau of Prisons, *Criminal Alien Requirement* 7 (RFP-PCC-0011) (2006). This is boilerplate language used in all similar solicitations.
105. See 42 U.S.C. §1395ff (2000).
106. U.S. Centers for Medicare and Medicaid Services, "Medicare Claims Processing Manual Chapter 29—Appeals of Claims Decisions," www.cms .hhs.gov/manuals/downloads/clm104c29.pdf (accessed 11/21/06).
107. U.S. Department of Education, Draft Statement of Work Private Sector Collection Activity for Student Related Debts (2006).
108. This difference seems to result from Democratic Party control of Congress when the first two laws were passed, and Republican control at the time of passage of the latter two.
109. See, e.g., Guttman, "Public Purpose and Private Service" (citing, for example, situations such as the Columbia space shuttle accident where it is suggested that contracting out shuttle operations to the United Space Alliance made access to documents, and hence democratic accountability, more difficult than it would have been had the operations been performed in-house).
110. A senior government contracting official recounts a negotiation with a space contractor who wished to be indemnified from liability if the spacecraft returned to earth with the Andromeda Strain. When the official noted wryly that if this occurred all life on earth would be destroyed, the contractor manager responded, "With our luck, the lawyers would survive."
111. Deliberational documents are nondisclosable under FOIA (5 U.S.C. 552(b)(5)), but this provision has been extensively litigated, and is unlikely to assuage contractor fears about liability for advice. One might overcome this problem though legislation indemnifying contractors for liability from claims arising out of predecisional advice, but such a proposal would almost certainly face strong opposition.
112. Jody Freeman, "Extending Public Norms through Privatization," 116 *Harvard Law Review* 1305–1306 (2003).
113. U.S. General Services Administration, Regulatory Information Service Center, *Final and Proposed Rules through 2005 Including Agency* (2006).
114. APA §4(a), 5 U.S.C. §553(a) (2000).

115. FAR §1.501, 48 C.F.R. §1.501 (2005).
116. This phrase has been popularized by David Walker, Comptroller-General of the United States. E.g., General Accounting Office, *High-Risk Series: An Update* (2001).
117. Steven Kelman, *Unleashing Change: A Study of Organizational Renewal in Government* (Washington, DC: Brookings Institution Press, 2005).
118. For example, the founder and CEO of one of the four so-called crony contractors receiving emergency contracts after Hurricane Katrina is a lifelong Democrat and until the hurricane the chair of the Louisiana Democratic Party. Carola Hojos, "Boosted, Not Battered, in the Hurricane's Wake," *Financial Times*, October 5, 2005, p. 10.
119. The government sought agency volunteers to help with emergency contracting after Katrina; some who had volunteered withdrew after press coverage of alleged contracting scandals made them fear that going to New Orleans might end up destroying their careers.
120. Or even with interest groups that, for their own reasons, want to minimize contracting of any sort; such groups' efforts are most directed at nonprofessional commercial work that is least problematic to the public law community.

8. Federal Contracting in Context

1. See Federal Procurement Data System, "Trending Analysis Report Since Fiscal Year 2000," www.fpds.gov; see also *Historical Tables, Budget of the United States Government, Fiscal Year 2007,* www.gpoaccess.gov, p. 113 (total discretionary budget for 2006 is estimated to be $990 million).
2. See Chapter 7 above.
3. Stephen Goldsmith and William Eggers, *Governing by Network: The New Shape of the Public Sector* (Washington, DC, 2004).
4. See Chapter 3 above.
5. See Transco Sec., Inc. v. Freeman, 639 F.2d 318, 321 (6th Cir. 1981) (finding liberty interest in right to bid on government contracts).
6. See 48 C.F.R. pt. 5 (2007).
7. The Government Accountability Office (GAO), however, has found that award fees are often granted despite poor or incomplete performance. See GAO, "Defense Acquisitions: DOD Has Paid Billions in Award and Incentive Fees Regardless of Acquisition Outcomes," www.gao.gov.
8. 48 C.F.R. §52.204–7 (2007).
9. Ibid.
10. 48 C.F.R. §1.102–4 (2007); see also 48 C.F.R. §42.202 (2007).
11. 48 C.F.R. §42.302 (2007).
12. Ibid.
13. 48 C.F.R. §32.102 (2007).
14. 48 C.F.R. §1517.207 (2007).
15. See, e.g., 48 C.F.R. pt. 9.4 (2007).
16. 31 U.S.C. §3729 (2000).

17. 18 U.S.C. §1001 (2000).
18. See Andrew L. Hurst, "Civil False Claims Act of 2003," 51 *Federal Lawyer* 34 (January 2004) (explaining that "more than $12 billion since 1986, including more than $2.1 billion for the fiscal year ending Sept. 30, 2003," has been recovered under the Federal Civil False Claims Act damage provisions).
19. See generally 48 C.F.R.§42 (2007).
20. See "Boeing Ex-Officer Pleads Guilty in Hiring Case," *Wall Street Journal*, November 16, 2004, at A2.
21. See "2 Ex-Pentagon Officials Guilty in Fraud Scheme," *Washington Post*, July 11, 2003, at B05.
22. See "Representative Quits, Pleading Guilty in Graft," *New York Times*, November 29, 2005, at A2.
23. See, e.g., Hope Yen and Pauline Jelinek, "Audit: Millions Wasted in Iraq," *Chicago Tribune*, January 31, 2007, at C1.
24. Commission on Army Acquisition and Program Management in Expeditionary Operations, "Urgent Reform Required: Army Expeditionary Contracting" (October 2007), www.army.mil/docs/Gansler_Commission_Report_Final_071031.pdf.
25. Paul Light, *The True Size of Government* (Washington, DC: Brookings Institution Press, 1999).
26. Historical Tables, Budget of the United States Government, Fiscal Year 2006, 104–105, www.gpoaccess.gov.
27. Ibid.
28. Ibid.
29. See Federal Procurement Data System (FPDS), fiscal year 2006 reports, available at www.fpds.gov.
30. The bid rate is often misunderstood. This number is not reflective of only contractor salaries, but also includes benefits, bonuses, equipment, transportation, and other overhead. Furthermore, in setting their salary structures, companies must factor in the compensation levels for critical skills that are competitive with the broader marketplace.
31. See Office of Personnel Management, "Federal Civilian Workforce Statistics, The Fact Book 2005," at 62, www.opm.gov.
32. Steven L. Schooner, "Competitive Sourcing Policy: More Sail Than Rudder?" 33 *Public Contract Law Journal* 277 (2004) (arguing that "[o]utside of the public conscience, contractors have filled the gap, and the Government has grown").
33. See FPDS, FY 2006 reports, www.fpds.gov.
34. Historical Tables, Budget of the United States Government, Fiscal Year 2006, 104–105.
35. Center for Strategic and International Studies, "Structure and Dynamics of the U.S. Federal Professional Services Industrial Base, 1995–2004," www.csis.org., p. 10.
36. See, e.g., Scott Shane and Ron Nixon, "In Washington, Contractors Take on Biggest Role Ever," *New York Times*, February 4, 2007, at 1; House of

Representatives, Committee on Government Reform, "Dollars, Not Sense: Government Contracting under the Bush Administration," oversight.house.gov.

37. See President George W. Bush, State of the Union Address, January 31, 2006, www.whitehouse.gov.

38. With the notable exception of the National Institutes of Health, federal R&D spending has declined. See Michael E. Davey, "Federal Research and Development Funding: FY 2006," Congressional Research Service Report for Congress RL32799 (Washington, DC, February 2006).

39. See Brandon Shackelford, "Slowing R&D Growth Expected in 2002," www .nsf.gov, p. 3.

40. Shane Harris, "Intelligence Innovation Lags," *National Journal,* August 4, 2007.

41. See National Commission on the Public Service, "Urgent Business for America: Revitalizing the Federal Government for the 21st Century," www3 .brookings.edu.

42. Ibid., 4.

43. Goldsmith and Eggers, *Governing by Network.*

44. Ibid., 17.

45. See Chapter 7 above.

46. See National Commission on the Public Service, "Urgent Business for America," at 14–17.

47. When the notorious bank robber Willie Sutton was asked why he robbed banks, he replied, "Because that's where the money is." See Federal Bureau of Investigation, "Famous Cases: Willie Sutton," www.fbi.gov (accessed 9/29/07).

48. Center for Strategic and International Studies, "Structure and Dynamics of the U.S. Federal Professional Services Industrial Base, 1995–2004," pp. 10–11 (analyzing FPDS data).

49. See Office of Personnel Management, "The Fact Book 2005," p. 13.

50. Ibid., 58.

51. Based on unpublished research conducted by the authors.

52. National Commission on the Public Service, "Urgent Business for America," 8.

53. See Partnership for Public Service, "Where the Jobs Are: Mission Critical Opportunities for America," ourpublicservice.org/OPS/publications/view-contentdetails.php?id=118.

54. See "Job Vacancies at DHS Said to Hurt U.S. Preparedness," *Washington Post,* July 9, 2007, at A01.

55. National Commission on the Public Service, "Urgent Business for America," 8.

56. See Jeff McDermott, "A New Focus for Civil Service Reform," 53 *Federal Lawyer* 4 (July 2006) (arguing that the current system is "plagued by indecipherable job descriptions, outdated application methods, and extended delays").

57. "Private Practice: Is U.S. Government 'Outsourcing Its Brain'?" *Wall Street Journal,* March 30, 2007, at A1.

58. See Shackelford, "Slowing R&D Growth," 3.

59. See Office of Personnel Management, "Federal Civilian Workforce Statistics, The Fact Book 2002," www.opm.gov, p. 8.

60. See Commercial Activities Panel, "Improving the Sourcing Decisions of the Government," competitivesourcing.navy.mil, p. 24.

61. See Office of Personnel Management, "Fact Book 2002," at 8.

62. See FPDS, Federal Procurement Report (FY 1992), p. 5, available at www.fpdsng.com/downloads/FPR_Reports/FPR81_99/FEDPROCREPORT_FY1992.pdf; FPDS, Federal Procurement Report (FY 2001), p. 5, available at www.fpdsng.com/downloads/FPR_Reports/FPR2001a.pdf.

63. See FPDS, Federal Procurement Report (FY 2005), pp. 19–20, available at www.fpdsng.com/downloads/FPR_Reports/2005_fpr_section_I_total_federal_views.pdf; FPDS, Federal Procurement Report (FY 1995), p. 5 available at www.fpdsng.com/downloads/FPR_Reports/FPR81_99/FEDPROCREPORT_FY1995.pdf.

64. See, e.g., "Reagan Imposes New Ceilings on Government Employment," *Washington Post,* March 7, 1981, at A1.

65. See "Job Vacancies at DHS Said to Hurt U.S. Preparedness."

66. *California Job Journal,* June 8, 2008; *and Challenger, Gray & Christmas.*

67. See Chapter 3 above for a detailed description of the A-76 process.

68. See Office of Management and Budget (OMB), Report on Competitive Sourcing Results, Fiscal Year 2005 (Washington, DC: Executive Office of the President, April 2006) p. 12, available at www.whitehouse.gov/omb/procurement/comp_src/cs_annual_report_fy2005_results.pdf.

69. See Al Gore, National Performance Review, "From Red Tape to Results: Creating a Government That Works Better and Costs Less" (September 7, 1993), available at www.ipo.noaa.gov/About/npr.html.

70. See OMB, President's Management Agenda (2002), 17, available at www.whitehouse.gov/omb/budget/fy2002/mgmt.pdf.

71. See OMB, Report on Competitive Sourcing Results, Fiscal Year 2005, 3; see also Chapter 3 above.

72. OMB, "Report on Competitive Sourcing Results, Fiscal Year 2006 (Washington, DC: Executive Office of the President, May 2007) available at www.whitehouse.gov/omb/procurement/comp_src/cs_report_fy2006.pdf.

73. OMB notes the following legislative restraints on the competition process: restrictions on the process used to evaluate competitors (e.g., prohibitions on the use of best value tradeoffs when evaluating prospective providers), the activities competed (e.g., competitive sourcing precluded for rural development and farm loan programs at the Department of Agriculture and immigration information activities at the Department of Homeland Security), and resources available for competition (e.g., caps imposed on Department of Interior and Forest Service; reduced funding for the Corps of Engineers). See OMB, Report on Competitive Sourcing Results, FY 2005, 19; see also Chapter 3 above.

74. See House of Representatives, Committee on Government Reform, "Dollars, Not Sense: Government Contracting under the Bush Administration" (June

2006), pp. 7–9, available at oversight.house.gov/Documents/20060711103910 –86046.pdf (claiming that the amount of money spent on noncompetitive contracts increased from 33 percent of federal contract dollars ($67.5 billion) in 2000, to 38 percent ($145 billion) in 2005).

75. See Office of Federal Procurement Policy Office memorandum titled "Enhancing Competition in Federal Acquisition," May 31, 2007, available at www.whitehouse.gov/omb/procurement/memo/competition_memo_053107 .pdf.

76. See Small Business Act (SBA) (Pub. L. No. 85–536, 72 Stat. 384) (July 18, 1958) (codified at 15 U.S.C. §631 et seq.) §8(a).

77. Daniel Guttman and Barry Willner, *The Shadow Government* (New York: Pantheon Books, 1976).

78. See OMB, Office of Federal Procurement Policy Policy Letter 92-1, September 23, 1992, available at www.whitehouse.gov/omb/procurement/ policy_letters/92-1_092392.html.

79. Ibid.

80. Federal Activities Inventory Reform Act of 1998 (FAIR Act) (Pub. L. No. 105–270, 112 Stat. 2382) (October 19, 1998) (codified at 31 USC §§501).

81. See ibid., §§3(b), (e)(1).

82. See "House, Senate Trying to Place Curbs on Competitive Sourcing," *Washington Post,* July 22, 2005, at B2.

83. See "White House Wants More IT Security Funds for FAA," *Newsbytes,* October 20, 2005.

84. See, e.g., Farm, Nutrition, and Bioenergy Act of 2007, H.R. 2419, 110th Cong., 1st sess., 2007).

85. Streamlined procedures in the Federal Acquisition Regulation, FAR 42.1503, that made it easier to form contracts also made it easier to terminate contracts for poor performance. See Chapter 7 above.

86. See "Two Contractors Accused of Roles in Iraq Jail Abuse," *Wall Street Journal,* June 10, 2004,at A6.

87. Military Extraterritorial Jurisdiction Act of 2000 (Pub. L. No. 106–523, 114 Stat. 2488) (November 22, 2000), as amended (codified at 18 U.S.C. 3261 et seq. (2000)).

88. While some scholars, like Peter Singer, argue that the process is not practical because U.S.–based federal prosecutors cannot investigate contractor crimes committed overseas, prosecutors and military officials do in fact cooperate to bring contractors to justice.

89. See John Warner National Defense Authorization Act for Fiscal Year 2007 (Pub. L. No. 109–364, 120 Stat. 2083) (October 17, 2006), §552.

90. Federal Acquisition Regulation, 48 C.F.R. §42.302.

91. See "For the Record," *Washington Post,* December 13, 1996, at A22.

92. See GAO, Annual High Risk Series: An Update (January 2005), available at www.gao.gov/new.items/d05207.pdf.

93. See 31 U.S.C. §712 (2000).

94. See Competition in Contracting Act of 1984 (CICA) (Pub. L. No. 98–369, 98 Stat. 1175)) (July 18, 1984) (codified in scattered sections of 31 and 41 U.S.C.); see also 4 C.F.R. pt. 21 (2007) (GAO bid protest regulations).

95. See generally "Bid Protests at GAO: A Descriptive Guide," 8th ed., United States Government Accountability Office, Office of General Counsel (GAO-06-797SP; January 2006), available at www.gao.gov/decisions/bidpro/bid/d06797sp.pdf.

96. See 31 U.S.C.A. §3554(e)(1) (2000).

97. Tucker Act, 28 U.S.C. §1491(a) (2000).

98. Contract Disputes Act, 41 U.S.C. §601 (2000).

99. See Bid Protest Regulations, 70 *Federal Register* 19,679 (April 14, 2005); see also Commercial Activities Panel, "Improving the Sourcing Decisions of the Government" (April 2002), 86–89, available at competitivesourcing.navy.mil/reference_documents/regulations/circular/commercialactivities-panelreport_4_02.pdf.

100. See Am. Fed'n of Gov't Employees, AFL-CIO v. United States, 258 F.3d 1294 (Fed. Cir. 2001).

101. See OMB Circular A-76, particularly Part F at B-20.

102. The National Defense Authorization Act for Fiscal Year 2005 (Pub. L. No. 108-375, §326, 118 Stat. 1848) (2004) amended the definition of "interested party" for protests under CICA to include the "official responsible for submitting the Federal agency tender in a public-private competition" in certain cases. See also Bid Protest Regulations, Government Contracts, 4 C.F.R. §21 (2007) (permitting an intervention by individuals "representing a majority of the employees of the federal agency who are engaged in performance of the activity or function").

103. See generally hearings of the United States Senate Committee on Homeland Security and Governmental Affairs, available at www.access.gpo.gov/congress/senate/senate12sh.html.

104. See, e.g., House Appropriations Committee, Subcommittee on Defense, Hearing on Contracting in Iraq (May 10, 2007).

105. See Ronald W. Reagan National Defense Authorization Act for Fiscal Year 2005, Pub. L. No. 108-375 (October 28, 2004), §1205.

106. See Title XVI of H.R. 1815, National Defense Authorization Act for Fiscal Year 2006, as passed by the House (May 25, 2005). This title was not included in the final conference version but the statement of managers accompanying the conference report directed the DOD to undertake similar actions.

107. Department of Defense, Quadrennial Defense Review Report (February 2006), p. 75, available at www.defenselink.mil/qdr/report/Report20060203.pdf.

108. See "Contractors Outnumber Troops in Iraq," *Los Angeles Times,* July 4, 2007, at A1.

109. Ibid.

110. Letter from Lieutenant General Robert B. Flowers to Representative Henry A. Waxman (April 8, 2003).

111. See United States Agency for International Development, Memorandum, USAID's Compliance with Federal Regulations in Awarding the Iraq Personnel Support Services Contract (June 20, 2003), available at www.usaid .gov/oig/iraq_doc/memorandum_03–002_06–20–03.pdf.

112. See testimony of Joseph Farinella, Acting Assistant Inspector General for Audit, U.S. Agency for International Development, before the Committee on Government Reform, Subcommittee on National Security, Emerging Threats, and International Relations, U.S. House of Representatives, October 18, 2005, available at http://www.usaid.gov/oig/whoweare/Testimony _101805.pdf.

113. See Special Inspector General for Iraq Reconstruction (SIGIR), "Iraq Reconstruction: Lessons Learned in Contracting and Procurement" (July 2006), p. 48, available at www.sigir.mil/reports/pdf/Lessons_Learned_July21.pdf.

114. DOD, Quadrennial Defense Review Report, at 80.

115. See SIGIR, "Lessons Learned in Contracting," at 48.

116. Ibid.

117. See generally Select Bipartisan Committee to Investigate the Preparation for and Response to Hurricane Katrina, "A Failure of Initiative"; see also Frances F. Townsend, "The Federal Response to Hurricane Katrina: Lessons Learned" (February 2006), available at www.whitehouse.gov/reports/ katrina-lessons-learned.pdf.

118. Under the Stafford Disaster Relief and Emergency Assistance Act of 1974 (Pub. L. No. 93–288, 88 Stat. 143) (May 22, 1974) (codified at 42 U.S.C. §§5121 et. seq.) federal assistance is provided to state or local governments based on a declaration by the President. In 2005, the President made forty-eight declarations of major disasters and sixty-eight emergency declarations. See Federal Emergency Management Agency, 2005 Federal Disaster Declarations, available at www.fema.gov/news/disasters.fema?year=2005.

119. Select Bipartisan Committee to Investigate the Preparation for and Response to Hurricane Katrina, "A Failure of Initiative."

120. See Second Emergency Supplemental Appropriations to Meet Immediate Needs Arising from the Consequences of Hurricane Katrina (Pub. L. No. 109–62, 119 Stat. 1990, September 8, 2005), §101(2).

121. See "Jobs and Joblessness on the Gulf Coast," New York Times, November 2, 2005, at A28.

122. See "Homeland Security Is Faulted in Audit," Washington Post, December 29, 2005, at A1; "FEMA's Decline: An Agency's Slow Slide from Grace," GovExec.com (accessed Sep. 28, 2005).

123. See Department of Defense, Instruction, "Contractor Personnel Authorized to Accompany the U.S. Armed Forces" (October 3, 2005), available at www.dtic.mil/whs/directives/corres/pdf/302041p.pdf.

124. Foreign acquisition; contractors accompanying the force; deployment of contractor personnel in support of military operations, Interim regulation,

68 Fed. Reg. 66738 (November 28, 2003), available at http://edocket .access.gpo.gov/2003/pdf/03-29416.pdf.

125. See Defense Federal Acquisition Regulations System (revised September 13, 2007), available at www.acq.osd.mil/dpap/dars/dfars/html/current/tochtml .htm.

126. See Ronald W. Reagan National Defense Authorization Act for Fiscal Year 2005 (Pub. L. No. 108–375, §326, 118 Stat. 1848) (2004); National Defense Authorization Act for Fiscal Year 2006 (Pub. L. No. 109–163, 119 Stat 3136) (2006).

127. See, for example, January 27, 2004 letter from the Professional Services Council to Department of Army regarding interim acquisition rules published by the Department of Army on November 28, 2003 (see note 125, supra), available at http://www.pscouncil.org/pdfs/PSCArmy CAFCommentsJanuary27.pdf.

9. Six Simple Steps to Increase Contractor Accountability

Thanks to Andrea Delgadillo Ostrovsky for top-notch research assistance, to Riyaz Kanji for useful suggestions, and to the University of Michigan Law School's Cook Fund for generous research support.

1. The federal government is now spending close to $30 billion per year on professional services contracts alone and nearly $400 billion overall on procurement from private contractors, more than 60 percent of which is spending on services rather than goods. See David Rosenbloom and Suzanne Piotrowski, "Outsourcing the Constitution and Administrative Law Norms," 35 *American Review of Public Administration* 103, 117 (June 2005) ("Today, the federal government is spending almost $28 billion annually on professional services contracts—a 57 percent jump from 5 years earlier."); Chapter 8 above (citing services contracts statistics and noting that current contracts demand "increasingly sophisticated management skills"); Draft Report of the Acquisition Advisory Panel to the Office of Federal Procurement Policy and the United States Congress 1 (December 2006) ("[e]ach year Federal agencies spend nearly $400 billion a year for a range of goods and services"), available at www.acquisition.gov/comp/aap/index.html (last visited February 22, 2007); ibid., 2 ("spending on services accounts for more than 60 percent of total procurement dollars"). See also U.S. Government Accountability Office, Federal Procurement: Spending and Workforce Trends, Report to the House Committee on Government Reform and Senate Committee on Governmental Affairs, Rept. GAO 03-443 (2003), pp. 3, 5–6, 32 (noting that federal agencies procured more than $300 billion in goods and services during fiscal year 2001), available at www.gao.gov/new.items/d03443.pdf.

2. Ruth Hoogland DeHoog and Lester M. Salamon, "Purchase-of-Service Contracting," in Lester M. Salamon, ed., *The Tools of Government: A Guide to the New Governance* 319, 319 (Oxford: Oxford University Press, 2002).

3. In its Circular No. A-76, the Office of Management and Budget instructs agencies to contract out only "commercial" activities, rather than "inherently

governmental" ones. It defines the latter to include "an activity that is so intimately related to the public interest as to mandate performance by government personnel." These include activities binding the United States to take (or
not take) some action by order, regulation, or contract; activities determining,
protecting, and advancing economic or political interests through military or
diplomatic action, judicial proceedings, or contract management; and activities "significantly affecting the life, liberty, or property of private persons."
See Office of Management and Budget, Executive Office of the President,
OMB Circular A-76, Performance of Commercial Activities 1–3 (2003),
available at www.whitehouse.gov/omb/circulars/a076/a76_rev2003.pdf; e.g.,
DeHoog and Salamon, "Purchase-of-Service Contracting," 319, 328 (noting
appeal of contracting to provide human services to sidestep "long-standing
conservative opposition to government involvement in social welfare" and to
avoid "enlarging government bureaucracies").

4. See David A. Sklansky, "The Private Police," 46 *UCLA Law Review* 1165
(1999).

5. Statement of David M. Walker, Comptroller General of the United States,
Testimony before the Subcommittee on Defense, House of Representatives
Committee on Appropriations, "Contracting for Better Outcomes," GAO-
06-800T (September 7, 2006).

6. See U.S. Government Accountability Office, Contract Management: Service
Contract Approach to Aircraft Simulator Training Has Room for Improvement, Rept. GAO-06-830, September 2006, p. 1.

7. See Memorandum of Majority Staff, House Committee on Oversight and
Government Reform, to Members of the Committee, Feb. 8, 2007, at 1,
available at oversight.house.gov/Documents/20070208121519-64647.pdf.
The memorandum alleges that at least one contractor hired for oversight,
Booz Allen Hamilton, may have a conflict of interest due to its longstanding
relationship with Boeing. Ibid. at 3.

8. See U.S. Government Accountability Office, DOE Contracting: Better Performance Measures and Management Needed to Address Delays in
Awarding Contracts, Rept. GAO-06-722 (June 2006), p. 1 (noting that DOE
spent approximately $22.9 billion in fiscal year 2005, 90 percent of its an-
nual budget, on contracts for a variety of "mission-related activities," and
that 90 percent of those contracting dollars were directed to "facility management contractors").

9. E.g., Hudgens v. Bell Helicopters/Textron, 328 F.3d 1329, 1334 (11th Cir.
2003) (resolving dispute arising out of maintenance contractor's decision not
to monitor helicopter tail fin closely).

10. See U.S. Customs and Border Protection, Fact Sheet: SBInet: Securing U.S.
Borders (September 2006) (emphasis added), available at http://www.dhs
.gov/xlibrary/assets/sbinetfactsheet.pdf.

11. E.g., OMB Watch, Anti-Scofflaw Rule Proposed (1999) (describing repeated
workplace safety violations among successful government contractors), available at www.ombwatch.org/article/articleview/569/1/221?TopicID=1. The

Notes to Pages 242–244 · 445

Government Accountability has also documented extensive labor law and workplace safety violations among contractors. See U.S. Government Accountability Office, Federal Contractors: Historical Perspective on Noncompliance with Labor and Worker Safety Laws, Rept. T-HEHS-98-212, July 14, 1998, p. 4.

12. See Ralph Vartabedian, "Experts Fear Nuclear Facility Is Lax on Safety; Conditions at the Pantex Weapons Plant Draw Federal Scrutiny," *Los Angeles Times*, February 21, 2007, at A1 (quoting "federal safety inspectors"). In 2005, a contractor responsible for screening and hiring security guards for U.S. Army bases hired many guards with criminal records that included felony and domestic violence convictions; one guard had an active warrant and was arrested while on duty. See U.S. Government Accountability Office, Contract Security Guards: Army's Guard Program Requires Greater Oversight and Reassessment of Acquisition Approach, Rept. GAO-06-284, April 2006.

13. U.S. Government Accountability Office, Contracting for Better Outcomes, September 7, 2006, p. 15.

14. The U.S. Government Accountability Office has published countless reports documenting inadequate contract supervision by agencies. See, e.g., U.S. Government Accountability Office, Homeland Security: Contract Management and Oversight for Visitor and Immigrant Status Program Need to be Strengthened, Rept. GAO-06-404, June 2006; Testimony of Comptroller General David M. Walker, Defense Acquisitions: DOD Wastes Billions of Dollars through Poorly Structured Incentives, Rept. GAO-06-409T, April 5, 2006; U.S. Government Accountability Office, Federal Bureau of Investigation: Weak Controls over Trilogy Project Led to Payment of Questionable Contractor Costs and Missing Assets, Rept. GAO-06-306, February 2006; U.S. Government Accountability Office, Defense Inventory: Army Needs to Strengthen Internal Controls for Items Shipped to Repair Contractors, Rept. GAO-06-209, December 2005; see also DeHoog and Salamon, 326 (noting costs associated with agency monitoring of contracts); Dan Guttman, "Nuclear Weapon," *Environmental Forum*, November/December 2000, p 19 (noting Secretary O'Leary's 1993 admission that the Department of Energy "was unable to hold its contractors to account").

15. This issue has received extended attention by Lester M. Salamon in his 2002 book *The Tools of Government* (cited above) and in "The New Governance and the Tools of Public Action: An Introduction," 28 *Fordham Urban Law Journal* 1611 (2001).

16. E.g., Steven L. Schooner, "Contractor Atrocities at Abu Ghraib: Compromised Accountability in a Streamlined, Outsourced Government," 16 Stanford Law and Policy Review 549, 564–65 (2005) (critiquing "indefinite-delivery/indefinite-quantity" (ID/IQ) contracts).

17. E.g., American Manufacturers Mutual Insurance Co. v. Sullivan, 526 U.S. 40, 50–55 (1999) (applying "state action" doctrine to find that insurers' withholding of payment for medical benefits pending "utilization review" was not fairly attributable to State of Pennsylvania).

18. See 5 U.S.C. §702 (person "aggrieved by agency action" can seek judicial review). Agencies can, of course, also be subject to standards imposed under particular authorizing statutes.
19. 5 U.S.C. §552.
20. For example, "agency" under the Administrative Procedure Act and under the Freedom of Information Act refers to an "authority of the Government of the United States." 5 U.S.C. §551(1). See generally Jody Freeman, "Extending Public Law Norms through Privatization," 116 *Harvard Law Review* 1285, 1306 (2003) (identifying other laws that apply only to agencies, not contractors).
21. See, e.g., Mary M. Cheh, "Legislative Oversight of Police: Lessons Learned from an Investigation of Police Handling of Demonstrations in Washington, D.C.," 32 *Journal of Legislation* 1, 21 n.100 (2005) ("committees may not be fully motivated unless they can uncover a politically favorable scandal"); Bernard Rosen, *Holding Government Bureaucracies Accountable* 21 (New York: Praeger, 1989).
22. A Transportation Department inspector general's report, requested by Senator Charles Grassley, concluded that FAA contracting approaches cost the government "millions of dollars in [cost] overruns." See Del Quentin Wilber, "Probe of FAA Contracting Finds Waste; Mismanagement Blamed for Losses in Millions," *Washington Post,* September 23, 2006, at D1.
23. See Robert O'Harrow, Jr., and Scott Higham, "Contractor Accused of Overbilling U.S.; Technology Company Hired after 9/11 Charged Too Much for Labor, Audit Says," *Washington Post,* October 23, 2005, at A1.
24. See 5 U.S.C. §551(1) (defining "agency" as "each authority of the United States").
25. The government may also bring criminal charges under the Major Fraud Act for fraud in connection with large contracts (those exceeding a value of $1 million). See 18 U.S.C. §1031.
26. See generally 48 C.F.R. part 9 (describing suspension and debarment proceedings).
27. Besides the legal requirements summarized here, a host of other requirements that would apply to agencies also do not apply to private contractors. These include civil service hiring rules, including, for example, requirements of antinepotism in hiring (5 U.S.C. §2302(b)(6)–(7)), and adherence to ethics rules (5 C.F.R. 2635.101).
28. 41 U.S.C. §601 et seq. A contractor's claim for nonpayment would be brought under the Tucker Act, 28 U.S.C. §1491.
29. Government contracts covered by the Rehabilitation Act of 1973 represent a notable exception; they must require a contractor to employ or promote qualified handicapped individuals without discrimination based upon disability. E.g., American Airlines v. Herman, 176 F.3d 283, 284–85 (5th Cir. 1999) (discussing Act's requirements).
30. See Draft Final Report of the Acquisition Advisory Panel to the Office of

Federal Procurement Policy and the United States Congress (December 2006), at 6 (also noting findings of the Government Accountability Office and agency inspectors general that "orders under interagency contracts frequently contain ill-defined requirements"), available at www.acquisition .gov/comp/aap/documents/DraftFinalReport.pdf.

31. 28 U.S.C. §2680(a).

32. Dalehite v. United States, 346 U.S. 15, 34 (1953).

33. Boyle v. United Technologies Corp., 487 U.S. 504, 512 (1988). Some courts have required that the agency's approval be discretionary in the sense of the Federal Tort Claims Act, involving the "permissible exercise of policy judgment." See Lamb v. Martin Marietta Energy Systems, Inc., 835 F. Supp. 959, 966 (W.D. Ky. 1993). While case law applying the defense to service contracts is not extensive, research has not uncovered a case where a court has refused to apply the defense in tort cases on the ground that a service, rather than a product, has been provided to the government. See Yearsley v. W.A. Ross Construction Co., 309 U.S. 18 (1940) (applying defense and rejecting attempt by landowner to hold government contractor liable for erosion of property caused by contractor's work constructing dikes); Askir v. Brown & Root Services Corp., 1997 U.S. Dist. LEXIS 14494 (S.D.N.Y. September 23, 1997) (applying defense to private contractor providing logistical support to United Nations' peacekeeping operation in Somalia); Lamb v. Martin Marietta, 835 F. Supp. at 963 (finding defense available to government contractor operating uranium production plant for Energy Department); Richland-Lexington Airport Dist. v. Atlas Properties, Inc., 854 F. Supp. 400 (D.S.C. 1994).

34. E.g., In re Aircraft Crash Litigation, 752 F. Supp. 1326, 1334 (S.D. Ohio 1990) (recognizing that without government contractor defense, contractors held liable for design features might pass costs on to government, "imposing costs on the government which the FTCA['s discretionary function exception] was enacted to prevent").

35. E.g., Lamb v. Martin Marietta, 835 F. Supp. at 967 (refusing to let defendant assert government contractor defense in part because of conduct neither "approved" nor "condoned" by agency and because contractor "did not always follow DOE orders"). See generally Boyle, 487 U.S. at 504–07, 512 (noting that state law is preempted by federal contractor defense in recognition of "uniquely federal interests" in "getting the government's work done" and the exercise of significant discretion by governmental entities such that the application of state law would create "significant conflict" with federal policy).

36. Steven L. Schooner and Erin Siuda-Pfeffer, "Post-Katrina Reconstruction Liability: Exposing the Inferior Risk-Bearer," 43 Harvard Journal on Legislation 287, 326 (2006).

37. E.g., Correctional Services Corp. v. Malesko, 534 U.S. 61, 74 n.6 (2001) (commenting in dicta that defense applies "where the government has directed

a contractor to do the very thing that is the subject of the claim"); Densberger v. United Technologies Corp., 283 F.3d 110, 120 (2d Cir. 2002) (stating, in dicta, that "[i]n failure to warn cases, this means that the ultimate product users cannot sue the contractor for failure to warn if the government controlled which warnings the contractor was allowed to provide to those users, and thereby precluded the warnings at issue from being given"); New Jersey Department of Environmental Protection v. Exxon Mobil Corp., 381 F. Supp. 2d 398, 404 (D.N.J. 2005) (despite significant government control over operations, contractor could not assert defense with respect to improper hazardous waste disposal without evidence that government exercised control over disposal); Jama v. INS, 334 F. Supp. 2d 662, 688 (D.N.J. 2004) (refusing to apply government contractor defense unless challenged contractor activity actually directed by government).

38. E.g., Lambert v. B.P. Products North America, Inc., 2006 U.S. Dist. LEXIS 16756 (S.D. Ill. April 6, 2006) (defense in design defect case does not depend on government having exercised judgment with respect to "specific feature alleged to be defective;" reasonably precise specifications will suffice for contractor to assert defense).

39. E.g., Hudgens v. Bell Helicopters/Textron, 328 F.3d 1329, 1334 (11th Cir. 2003) (government contractor defense was available to maintenance contractor that failed to identify fatal cracks in helicopter tail fin, because government had precisely specified items for maintenance inspection and because contractor had "no duty" to go further than Army directed, despite FAA advisory on tail fin problems).

40. Schooner and Siuda-Pfeffer, "Post-Katrina Reconstruction Liability," 310 (based on least cost avoider/superior risk bearer arguments, arguing that "either the government or its contractors [should] bear the risk of their negligent decisions or actions").

41. See generally Ronald A. Cass and Clayton P. Gillette, "The Government Contractor Defense: Contractual Allocation of Public Risk," 77 *Virginia Law Review* 257 (1991).

42. See 5 U.S.C. §706.

43. Fidelity Financial Corp. v. Federal Home Loan Bank, 589 F. Supp. 885, 895 (N.D. Cal. 1983) (stating that "[t]he law on this issue is unambiguous: the APA does not confer upon federal courts the authority to assess and levy monetary relief").

44. See Franklin Savings Corp. v. United States, 180 F.3d 1124, 1140 n.21 (10th Cir. 1999) (noting that "[b]ecause review of bad faith may be available under the APA . . . a refusal to permit such inquiry in FTCA suits will not leave all plaintiffs without remedy").

45. See 5 U.S.C. §551(4) (defining "rule"); 5 U.S.C. §552(a) (imposing publication requirements); 5 U.S.C. §553 (setting forth rulemaking procedures).

46. See 5 U.S.C. §553(a) (rulemaking requirements do not apply to "a matter relating to . . . contracts"). Compare Brown v. Housing Authority, 471 F.2d 63 (7th Cir. 1972) (finding agency exempt from §553 requirements in re-

quiring local housing authorities to set up grievance procedures) with National Association of Psychiatric Treatment Centers for Children v. Weinberger, 658 F.Supp. 48 (D. Colo.), appeal dismissed and remanded, 909 F.2d 1378 (10th Cir. 1987) (refusing to apply exemption where agency proposed prescriptive changes in overall contents of all participation agreements with mental health treatment centers in manner that would affect calculation of congressionally established benefits).

47. See 5 U.S.C. §551(1) (defining "agency"); 5 U.S.C. §702 (providing right of review under APA of "agency action"); cf. FOIA, 5 U.S.C. §552 ("each *agency* shall make available to the public information as follows").

48. To date, no court has yet interpreted "agency" in the APA to include any nonfederal entity, even one with significant contractual obligations to the United States. See, e.g., International Brominated Solvents v. American Conference of Governmental Industrial Hygienists, Inc., 393 F. Supp. 2d 1362, 1379–80 (M.D. Ga. 2005) (refusing to find private occupational safety organization to be "agency" under APA despite allegations that entity was created by officials of federal government); The Organic Cow, LLC, v. Northeast Dairy Compact Commission, 164 F. Supp. 2d 412 (D.Vt. 2001) (holding that although compact that created commission had status of federal law, commission was not "agency" under APA, since it was an authority of six states, rather than the U.S.); Singleton Sheet Metal Works v. City of Pueblo, 727 F. Supp. 579 (D. Colo. 1989) (finding that city was not APA "agency" despite cooperation agreement with Army Corps of Engineers). See also Gilmore v. Department of Energy, 4 Supp. 2d 912, 918–919 (N.D. Cal. 1998) (refusing to find that con tractor was "government controlled corporation" under FOIA absent "substantial degree of federal control or supervision").

49. 5 U.S.C. §706(2)(A).

50. See generally 5 U.S.C. §552.

51. 5 U.S.C. §552(f) (defining "agency" for FOIA purposes); see, e.g., Forsham v. Harris, 445 U.S. 169 (1980) (federal grantees were not subject to FOIA disclosure requirements); Irwin Mem'l Blood Bank of San Francisco Medical Society v. American National Red Cross, 640 F.2d 1051, 1053 (9th Cir. 1981) (American Red Cross was not considered agency for purposes of FOIA despite Red Cross's receipt of money from government contracts and specific purpose grants and government's power to appoint eight of Red Cross's board of governors). On rare occasions, courts have concluded that private party documents can be subject to FOIA if an agency exercises extensive control over the documents and the documents were created on behalf of the agency. Burka v. United States Department of Health and Human Services, 87 F.3d 508 (D.C. Cir. 1996). Further, the Office of Management and Budget has now required that, as a condition of receiving a federal grant, hospitals, universities, and other nonprofits must agree that data produced under the award will normally be subject to FOIA access. See Office of Management and Budget, Final Revision: Circular A-110, 64 Fed. Reg. 54,926 (October 8, 1999).

52. See 5 U.S.C. §552(b)(4). See generally Chapter 13 below (noting that military contractors in Iraq have "exercised what is essentially a veto" under 5 U.S.C. §552(b)(4) to prevent public disclosure of contracts themselves); see also Critical Mass Energy Project v. Nuclear Regulatory Commission, 975 F.2d 871, 879 (D.C. Cir. 1992) (holding that exemption applied to voluntarily disclosed private information to agency because, among other things, disclosure would "jeopardize [agency's] continuing ability to secure such data" if information would not customarily be released from private party), cert. denied, 507 U.S. 984 (1993).

53. See Rosenbloom and Piotrowski, "Outsourcing the Constitution," at 106 (noting that fuller disclosure of contractor's activities was only possible through extraordinary inquiry by Columbia Accident Investigation Board).

54. See "Federal Procurement in the Federal Courts 1987–88: A Selective Review," 19 *Public Contract Law Journal* 14, 115 n.116 (1989) (listing cases).

55. See FDIC v. Meyer, 510 U.S. 471, 485 (1994).

56. Bivens v. Six Unknown Federal Narcotics Agents, 403 U.S. 388 (1971) (Fourth Amendment protection against unreasonable search or seizure); Davis v. Passman, 442 U.S. 228 (1979) (Fifth Amendment due process clause); Carlson v. Green, 446 U.S. 14 (1980) (Eighth Amendment). These claims, however, are subject to qualified "good faith" immunity, see Harlow v. Fitzgerald, 457 U.S. 800 (1982).

57. Carlson v. Green, 446 U.S. at 19–20.

58. See Sarro v. Cornell Corrections, Inc., 248 F. Supp. 2d 52, 58–59 (D.R.I. 2003) (citing cases).

59. Correctional Services Corp. v. Malesko, 534 U.S. 61 (2000).

60. See Amicus Brief of Legal Aid Society in Correctional Services Corp. v. Malesko, 2001 WL 826705 (U.S., July 20, 2001).

61. See generally Clayton P. Gillette and Paul B. Stephan, "Richardson v. McKnight and the Scope of Immunity after Privatization," 8 *Supreme Court Economic Review* 103, 108 (2000) (discussing issues). Gillette and Stephan suggest that corporate *Bivens* liability may be consistent with *Bivens* liability for government employees but not government agencies on the following theory: government agencies can be presumed to act in the public interest, but simply may not supervise employees very well. Imposing liability on individual employees will make them properly consider constitutional rights, while imposing liability on agencies may overdeter them and make them overly timid in pursuing the public interest. Whether this is plausible or not, *Bivens* liability surely seems appropriate for the private contracting entity to ensure that employees are supervised in a way that minimizes constitutional violations.

62. 31 U.S.C. §§3729–31.

63. The Supreme Court confirmed that False Claims Act plaintiffs bringing *qui tam* claims would meet constitutional standing requirements in Vermont Agency of Natural Resources v. United States ex rel. Stevens, 529 U.S. 765 (2000).

64. See 31 U.S.C. §232(c) (1976).

65. See 31 U.S.C. §3730(e). In addition, an FCA plaintiff must file a complaint in camera, and the complaint is held under seal for sixty days to permit a government decision to intervene in the suit and proceed with the action. 31 U.S.C. §3730(b). However, if the government does not act, the plaintiff may pursue the claim.

66. E.g., Cook County v. United States ex rel. Chandler, 538 U.S. 119 (2003) (regarding fraudulent obtaining of grant); United States ex rel. Hendow v. University of Phoenix, 461 F.3d 1166 (9th Cir. 2006) (holding that *qui tam* relator's complaint alleging university falsely certified that it did not pay recruiters on per-student basis stated False Claims Act claim), cert. denied, 127 S. Ct. 2099 (2007).

67. E.g., United States ex rel. Lee v. SmithKline Beecham, Inc., 245 F.3d 1048, 1053 (9th Cir. 2001) (discussing "worthless services" theory).

68. See United States ex rel. Quinn v. Omnicare Inc., 382 F.3d 432, 441 (3d Cir. 2004)

69. 296 F. Supp. 2d 1167 (C.D. Cal. 2003). See also El Dorado Irrigation District v. Traylor Brothers, 2005 WL 3453913 (E.D. Cal. 2005) (discussing "implied certification" theories of FCA liability).

70. United States ex rel. Holder, 296 F. Supp. 2d at 1178.

71. Mikes v. Straus, 274 F.3d 687, 696 (2d Cir. 2001); see also United States ex rel. Fallon v. Accudyne Corp., 880 F. Supp. 636, 638 (W.D. Wis 1995) ("it is not the violation of environmental laws that gives rise to an FCA claim but the false representations to the government that there has been compliance"); Shaw v. AAA Engineering and Drafting, Inc., 213 F.3d 519, 530 (10th Cir. 2000).

72. See In re Genesis Health Ventures, Inc., 112 F. App'x. 140 (3d Cir. 2004).

73. See, e.g., Mikes v. Straus, 274 F.3d at 703; United States ex rel. Swan v. Covenant Care, Inc., 279 F. Supp. 2d 1212, 1221 (E.D. Cal. 2002); In re Genesis Health Ventures, Inc., 112 F. App'x at 143.

74. See 31 U.S.C. §§3729(a)(1), (2); ibid. §3729(b).

75. See, Nicole Casarez, "Furthering the Accountability Principle in Privatized Federal Corrections: The Need for Access to Private Prison Records," 28 *University of Michigan Journal of Law Reform* 249, 293 (1995) (advocating that model prison contracts require contractors to provide documents to agency).

76. See 107 Cong. Rec. S11,405 (November 19, 2002) (comments of Sen. Chafee).

77. See 6 U.S.C. §442(d).

78. In addition, even when the defense does not apply, the Act does away with punitive damages completely and with joint and several liability for noneconomic damages in tort claims arising out of the sale of antiterrorism technologies. See 6 U.S.C. §§442(b)(1), (2).

79. See 6 U.S.C. §442 (emphasis added). This mirrors some of the most stringent applications of the government contractor defense. E.g., Kerstetter v. Pacific

Scientific Company, 210 F.3d 431, 435 (5th Cir. 2000) (discussing when agency has conducted adequate "substantive review" to make defense available), cert. denied, 531 U.S. 919 (2000).

80. On the other hand, once eligibility is established, the seller may lose the defense only for failure to submit information to the secretary that amounts to "fraudulent[]" behavior or "willful misconduct." 6 U.S.C. §442(d). That implies, perhaps, that a negligent failure to submit the prepared safety and hazard information to the secretary will not deprive a seller of the defense. A better approach would clearly bar a seller from asserting the defense if the failure to submit information were negligent.

81. Vermont Agency of Natural Resources v. United States ex rel. Stevens, 529 U.S. 765 (2000).

82. E.g., 33 U.S.C. §1365 (authorizing Clean Water Act citizen enforcement actions).

83. 534 U.S. 61 (2000).

84. See 42 U.S.C. §1983.

85. Alfred C. Aman, Jr., "Privatization and the Democracy Problem in Globalization: Making Markets More Accountable through Administrative Law," 28 *Fordham Urban Law Journal* 1477, 1501–02 (2001). Aman also argues that citizens should have the opportunity to petition an agency to amend a contract even before the contract expires.

86. 5 U.S.C. §706.

87. Guttman, "Nuclear Weapon," at 23.

88. 5 U.S.C. §706.

89. A possible argument is that Congress meant for a contractor's violation of relevant laws to be remedied through the mechanisms provided in the laws themselves.

90. See, e.g., Lujan v. Defenders of Wildlife, 504 U.S. 555 (1992).

91. E.g., Sierra Club v. Morton, 405 U.S. 727 (1972) (refusing to recognize "ideological" standing).

10. Privatization and Democracy

I wish to thank Carol J. Greenhouse for her comments on this manuscript. I am also deeply grateful to my research assistant, Ed Livingston, Indiana '07, for all of his splendid help.

1. The presidency of Ronald Reagan shifted the dynamic of national power from the then-entrenched Democratic Party. Yet the "Reagan Revolution" involved not only a shift in political fortunes, but a deliberate and sustained focus on economic reforms that included "deregulation, privatization, free market philosophy, and a reduced role of government." Joe Martin, "The Next Ten Years—A White Knuckle Decade with Nowhere to Hide; A Prospective on Management Trends," *Business Quarterly*, March 22, 1989, 51. A concerted attempt to move toward increased privatization of government was always central to the revolution's ideological goals; however, movement toward privatization proved more difficult, and met with more re-

sistance than advocates had anticipated. Privatization efforts by the Reagan administration met with consistent opposition, and prompted the Republican Party and other privatization advocates to move toward less confrontational tactics and to adopt less explicit language in an attempt to embed a privatization ideal in the political psyche. See Margaret E. Kriz, "Slow Spin-Off," *National Journal,* May 7, 1988, 1184 (describing privatization advocates as seeking to put forward ideas that would "continue to germinate" in future administrations, even if they were not Republican-controlled). For a current perspective on the long-term effects on outcomes of the Reagan Revolution on the modern political, social, and economic landscape, see Dick Meyer, "Reagan's Revolution Plus 25," December 1, 2005, www.cbsnews .com/stories/2005/12/01/opinion/meyer/printable1088888.shtml.

2. David Harvey has noted that for modern privatization advocates the meaning of the word "privatization" carries with it references to the political ideals of individual dignity and individual freedom that were deliberately incorporated into the founding of the modern neoliberal movement. See David Harvey, *A Brief History of Neoliberalism* (Oxford: Oxford University Press, 2005), pp. 5–6. "Contracting out" refers to the practice of government contracting with a private employer for the delivery of some good or service, where the ultimate responsibility for the success of the service or good delivery technically remains with the contracting government body. See Geoffrey F. Segal, Testimony to the Utah Law Enforcement and Criminal Justice Interim Committee, *Contracting Out Force Prisons to Focus on Results, Performance,* Reason Foundation (September 21, 2005), www.reason.org/ commentaries/segal_20050921.shtml. "Competitive sourcing" calls for the identification of government activities that are "commercial" and therefore able to be performed by the private sector, and the institution of a competitive bidding process to assign such activities to their most "efficient and effective" source. Geoffrey F. Segal, *Competitive Sourcing: Driving Federal Government Results,* Reason Foundation, www.reason.org/commentaries/ segal_compsourcing.pdf (last visited January 24, 2007).

3. See Chapter 6 above (arguing that the question of "comparative efficiency" has reframed the privatization debate so as to obscure alternatives or improvements to current options of public and private correctional facilities). On the taken-for-granted validity of "laissez-faire ideology," see Margaret Jane Radin R. Polk Wagner, "The Myth of Private Ordering: Rediscovering Legal Realism in Cyberspace," 73 *Chicago-Kent Law Review* 1295 (1998); see also Paul Schiff Berman, "Cyberspace and the State Action Debate: The Cultural Value of Applying Constitutional Norms to 'Private' Regulation," 71 *University of Colorado Law Review* 1278 (2000).

4. It is precisely the services to these populations that were among the earliest government functions to be outsourced to private contractors. See, e.g., Richard W. Harding, *Private Prisons and Public Accountability* (Rutgers, NJ: Transaction Publishers, 1997), p. 3 (documenting the rise of private prisons in the last two decades); Matthew Diller, "The Revolution in Welfare

Administration: Rules, Discretion, and Entrepreneurial Government," 75 *New York University Law Review* 1121 (2000).

5. For references to early privatization efforts at the state level affecting prisoners and the poor, see archived National Consortium of State Legislatures LegisBriefs, available at lexis.com.

6. See note 1 and accompanying text. In addition, the Republican Party's economic agenda, illustrated in part in the 1994 Contract with America, authored by Newt Gingrich, can be seen as an extension of this push to reconceptualize and reinforce a binary public/private divide. See Republican National Committee, "Contract with America" (2005), www.house.gov/house/Contract/CONTRACT.html. While the language used to promote the economic aims of the Contract with America appears to have contentiously avoided specific references to privatization, Newt Gingrich's more recent writings have been much more explicit. In a recent book Gingrich promotes what he calls the "principles of entrepreneurial public management" and unequivocally states that the government should "[p]rivatize more government functions. Many agencies or government services could be turned over to private companies that can deliver services more efficiently and at lower costs." Newt Gingrich, *Winning the Future: A 21st Century Contract with America* (Washington, DC: Regnery, 2005), pp. 170–73.

7. Reason Foundation, "Experts: Robert Poole" www.reason.org/poole.shtml (last visited October 12, 2007).

8. Indeed, Daniels claims to have coined the term, adding: "Personally, I never use the word 'privatization,' because it connotes an orthodoxy of its own...." Mitchell Daniels, "Reforming Government through Competition," in *Annual Privatization Report 2006* (Reason Foundation). Proponents of privatization also hailed the early efforts of the George W. Bush administration to expand the use of "competitive contracting" in order to "open more federal positions involving commercial activities to competition from the private sector." Ronald D. Utt, "Improving Government Performance through Competitive Contracting" (Heritage Foundation, June 25, 2001), available at www.heritage.org/Research/GovernmentReform/BG1452.cfm. The aggressive competitive sourcing strategies were pitched as a way to save $10 to $14 billion a year in program costs while improving basic public services. Ibid.

9. Robert Poole, "Reflections on 30 Years of Promoting Privatization," in *Annual Privatization Report 2006* (Reason Foundation), p. 23.

10. See Office of Management and Budget, *President's Management Agenda: Competitive Sourcing; Conducting Public-Private Competition in a Reasoned and Responsible Manner* (Executive Office of the President, July 2003), www.whitehouse.gov/results/agenda/competitive-sourcing20030724.pdf.

11. See Jody Freeman, "Extending Public Law Norms through Privatization," 116 *Harvard Law Review* 1285 (2003); see also Ellen Dannin, "Red Tape or Accountability: Privatization, Publicization, and Public Values," 15 *Cornell*

Journal of Law & Public Policy 101 (2005); Gillian E. Metzger, "Privatization as Delegation," 103 *Columbia Law Review* 1367 (2003); Chris Sagers, "CyberPersons, Propertization, and Contract in the Information Culture: Monism, Nominalism, and Public-Private in the Work of Margaret Jane Radin," 54 *Cleveland State Law Review* 219 (2006); Paul R. Verkuil, "Public Law Limitations on Privatization of Government Functions," 84 *North Carolina Law Review* 397 (2006).

12. By "public" and "private" I am referring to the colloquial (often zero-sum) distinction between government and the commercial sector in relation to privatization, not the *public-private divide* theorized by legal scholars concerned with the relationship of the state to private ordering. On the latter, see Berman, "Cyberspace," 1279–1281 (noting that those who criticize the legal distinction between public and private in constitutional adjudication argue that the "conceptual categories" that underlie the distinction are the result of "cultural constructions that tend to reflect dominant players in society"). Another scholar has noted that the majority of published academic opinion rejects "the premise that legal doctrine can rest on a supposed distinction between public and private actions," since "[e]ven in conduct in which no state official participates, it is possible to discern some decision of the state." Richard S. Kay, "The State Action Doctrine, the Public-Private Distinction, and the Independence of Constitutional Law," 10 *Constitutional Commentary* 334 (1993).

13. For a discussion and critique of how globalization has been constructed in this manner, see Alfred C. Aman, Jr., *The Democracy Deficit: Taming Globalization through Law Reform* (New York: New York University Press, 2004), pp. 1–14, 93–103, 129–140.

14. Ibid., 2–7.

15. For an analysis of privatization and various forms of the democracy deficit in the context of globalization, see Aman, *Democracy Deficit*.

16. The OMB estimates that approximately 26 percent of federal government positions are subject to competitive sourcing under the President's Management Agenda. OMB, *President's Management Agenda*, 3. For a detailed description of the federal policy for the competition of commercial activities as laid out by the Office of Management and Budget, see Verkuil, "Public Law Limitations," 402–421.

17. See Alfred C. Aman, Jr., "An Administrative Law Perspective on Government Social Services Contracts: Outsourcing Prison Health Care in New York City," 14 *Indiana Journal of Global Legal Studies* 301 (2007).

18. This is the general and accepted rule based upon the notion that a "[c]areful adherence to the 'state action' requirement preserves an area of individual freedom by limiting the reach of federal law." Lugar v. Edmondson Oil Co., 457 U.S. 922, 936 (1982). Various cases have drawn the line between state and private action fairly strictly. For example, in Blum v. Yaretsky, 457 U.S. 991 (1982), the Court held that nursing home patient defendants that had been denied Medicaid assistance by New York City officials had not

demonstrated that a sufficient "nexus between the State and the challenged action of the regulated entity so that the action of the latter may be fairly treated as that of the State itself." Ibid., 1004. Justice Rehnquist stated in the opinion of the Court that "a State normally can be held responsible for a private decision only when it has exercised coercive power or has provided such significant encouragement, either overt or covert, that the choice must in law be deemed to be that of the State." Ibid. Seven years later, Chief Justice Rehnquist drew the line even more sharply in DeShaney v. Winnebago County Dept. of Soc. Serv., 489 U.S. 189 (1989), in which the Court held that the county's social service department could not be sued under the Due Process Clause for failure to protect a child under their care. In order to trigger due process protections, there must be some affirmative action by the state to restrain an individual's liberty and not just a "failure to act to protect [an individual's] interests against harms inflicted by other means." Ibid., 200. However, one must be careful not to minimize the complexity involved in the jurisprudence of this area. The Fourteenth Amendment, for example, is premised to a certain extent on the contrary idea that "an extension of federal law [is] essential to the preservation of individual rights." Geoffrey Stone et al., *Constitutional Law* (Gaithersburg, MD: Aspen, 2001) at 1502; see also Ronald J. Krotoszynski, Jr., "Civil Rights and Civil Liberties: A Remembrance of Things Past? Reflections on the Warren Court and the Struggle for Civil Rights," 59 *Washington & Lee Law Review* 1062–1067 (2002) (detailing the Warren Court's efforts to "expand[] the scope of the doctrine to reach more ostensibly 'private' conduct" in order to more effectively enforce Fourteenth Amendment protections, and the subsequent pullback of this expansion by later Court bodies). Further, it would be wrong to conclude that private actors are not important players in the administrative process, or that the extension of administrative law principles should not seriously be considered when private actors carry out tasks for the public good. Alfred C. Aman, Jr., *Administrative Law and Process* 177 (2nd ed. 2006).

19. These terms refer to government action reclaiming services from the private sector, "pulling back" or "stepping in" under circumstances that compromise or preclude successful service delivery by a private provider (e.g., bankruptcy).

20. Administrative procedures are necessary to enable administrative agencies to carry out their statutory duties, while protecting those regulated from unfairness by the state; substantive regulation is necessary for the state to correct various kinds of market failures. "Regulatory mismatches," however, can alter the appropriate relationship between states and markets when, for example, the substantive regulation involved produces either too little or too much regulation in a particular instance. See Stephen Breyer, *Regulation and Its Reform* (Cambridge, MA: Harvard University Press, 1982), pp. 189–284.; see also Stephen Breyer, "Analyzing Regulatory Failure: Mismatches, Less Restrictive Alternatives, and Reform," 92 *Harvard Law Review* 547 (1979).

There can also be too much procedure. See Paul Verkuil, "The Emerging Concept of Administrative Procedure," 78 *Columbia Law Review* 264–265 (1978) (discussing procedural laissez faire).

21. See Milton Friedman, *Capitalism and Freedom* (Chicago: University of Chicago Press, 1962), pp. 2–4. The binary relationship between these two realms remains quite distinct for many who retain a view of the private sector and markets as being fundamentally virtuous and governments and regulatory frameworks as being fundamentally undesirable. Margaret Thatcher, the former Prime Minister of the United Kingdom, recently stated that "[s]tate control is fundamentally bad because it denies people the power to choose and the opportunity to bear responsibility for their own actions," and that "a system of free enterprise has a universal truth at its heart: to create a genuine market in a state you have to take the state out of the market." Margaret Thatcher, "Rebuilding an Enterprise Society through Privatisation," in *Annual Privatization Report 2006* (Reason Foundation). As part of this same report, Indiana Governor Mitch Daniels makes the case for what he characterizes as "judicious private contracting," and states that "[a]nything that strengthens the private sector vs. the state is protective of personal freedom." Daniels, "Reforming Government."

22. U.S. Const. amend. I.

23. U.S. Const. amend XIV.

24. See Administrative Procedure Act, 5 U.S.C. §551(1) (2000) (defining administrative agencies as authorities of the Government of the United States).

25. Several commentators have noted the persistence of the public/private divide in spite of its rejection by legal scholars. See generally Berman, "Cyberspace"; Radin and Wagner, "The Myth of Private Ordering"; Sagers, "Cyberpersons."

26. See, e.g., Metzger, "Privatization as Delegation," 1437–1439.

27. See ibid. A recent article in the *New York Times* noted that while contracting has been on the rise for decades, it has accelerated substantially during the Bush administration, rising from $207 billion in 2000 to $400 billion in 2006. "Without a public debate or formal policy decision, contractors have become a virtual fourth branch of government . . . fueled by the war in Iraq, domestic security and Hurricane Katrina, but also by a philosophy that encourages outsourcing almost everything government does." Scott Shane and Ron Nixon, "In Washington, Contractors Take On Biggest Role Ever," *New York Times,* February 4, 2007, at A1.

28. See Poole, "Reflections," 23.

29. For a detailed discussion of the New Deal and the administrative law and structures it spawned, see Aman, *Democracy Deficit,* 15–50.

30. See generally Franklin Delano Roosevelt, "The Second Inaugural Address (January 20, 1937)," reprinted in *The Public Papers and Addresses of Franklin Roosevelt,* ed. Samuel Rosenman (New York: Random House, 1941), pp. 1–6. The rhetoric evinces a deep commitment to addressing what was viewed as an immediate and widely shared threat to the broad public

good, and not that of an ideological power play; a problem-solving orientation, rather than an ideological one. The National Industrial Recovery Act (NIRA), ch. 90, 48 Stat. 195 (1933) (invalidated in A.L.A. Schechter Poultry Corp. v. United States, 295 U.S. 495 (1935)), for example, spoke of a "national emergency productive of widespread unemployment and disorganization of industry, which burdens interstate and foreign commerce, affects the public welfare, and undermines the standards of living of the American people...." Ellis Hawley has written about how the NIRA and the other administrative and governmental interventions of the time were designed to "appeal[] to the hopes of a number of conflicting pressure groups." Ellis Hawley, *The New Deal and the Problem of Monopoly: A Study in Economic Ambivalence* (Princeton, NJ: Princeton University Press, 1966), p. 33.

31. For a comparison of the growth of the Administrative State noting that the Environmental era dwarfed the New Deal when it came to the number and breadth of the law and regulations passed, see Alfred C. Aman, Jr., *Administrative Law in a Global Era* (Ithaca, NY: Cornell University Press, 1992), pp. 82–84.

32. For an extensive discussion of this history, see Aman, *Democracy Deficit*, 16–44.

33. See, e.g., David E.M. Sappington and J. Gregory Sidak, "Competition Law for State-Owned Enterprises," 71 *Antitrust Law Journal* 479 (2003) (arguing that government-run enterprises, like the U.S. Postal Service, value expansion of services and output over profit maximization and therefore are "less averse to the higher costs associated with expanded output and revenue," which may incentivize government enterprises to engage in anticompetitive behavior against privately owned enterprises). Ibid., 480. The cost inefficiency argument is also at the heart of the ongoing arguments against the current Social Security system. See, e.g., Daniel J. Mitchell, "The Social Security Trust Fund Fraud" (Heritage Foundation, February 22, 1999), available at www.heritage.org/Research/SocialSecurity/BG1256.cfm (stating that if the program were a private pension fund it would be forced to declare bankruptcy and that the "[p]romised retirement benefits are meager compared with the record level of payroll taxes that workers put into the system"). Advocates of Social Security privatization favor the implementation of "personal investment accounts," which in theory would allow individual workers to invest a portion of their payroll taxes in personal accounts tied to the stock market in order to garner a greater rate of return than the current pay-as-we-go system is said to provide. See Gingrich, *Winning the Future*, 25–41, which argues that the current Social Security system is no longer a "good deal for working people today." Ibid., 33.

34. "Our 'clients,' the American people" is the phrase of Mary Joy Jameson, associate administrator for the GSA; www.whitehouse.gov/results/agenda/howtheydidit-firstgov.html (last visited October 12, 2007).

35. "It is the cost-reducing, service-enhancing power of competition that we seek to capture for the government's customer, the taxpayer." See Daniels, "Reforming Government," 11.

36. Office of Management and Budget, Circular No. A-76 (Revised), *Performance of Commercial Activities* (Executive Office of the President, May 29, 2003), www.whitehouse.gov/omb/circulars/a076/a76_rev2003.pdf. Circular A-76 provides guidelines for government contracts with private providers. Paul Krugman, a regular critic of the economic policies of the George W. Bush administration, has observed that "[c]onservatives look at the virtues of market competition and leap to the conclusion that private ownership, in itself, is some kind of magic elixir." Paul Krugman, "Outsourcer in Chief," *New York Times,* December 11, 2006, at A27.

37. See, e.g., Daniels, "Reforming Government"; Adrian T. Moore, *Private Prisons: Quality Corrections at a Lower Cost* 1–2, available at www.reason.org/ps240.pdf.

38. See, e.g., Moore, *Private Prisons*. The cost versus quality argument is also quite prevalent in the debate over school privatization; see Thomas Toch, *Whittling Away the Public School Monopoly* (Washington, DC: Brookings Institution, 1999), www.brook.edu/views/op-ed/toch/19991115.htm.

39. See Brian M. Riedl, *Ten Guidelines for Reducing Wasteful Government Spending* (Heritage Foundation) www.heritage.org/Research/Budget/bg1622 .cfm (last visited March 7, 2007) ("There is little economic justification for the government's running businesses that the private sector can run itself.... Government failures are often larger than market failures; and anyone who has dealt with the post office, lived in public housing, or visited the local Department of Motor Vehicles understands how wasteful, inefficient, and unresponsive government can be.") The "candidates for privatization" offered by the report included air traffic control operations, the Corporation for Public Broadcasting, the postal service, Amtrak, and aerospace technology research and development. Ibid.

40. See, e.g., Daniels, "Reforming Government," 12. This idea that privatization of state industry would allow better and more efficient management of a high value asset was also given as an explicit motivation for the privatization of the Iraqi oil industry following the U.S. invasion in 2002. Proponents of privatization in Iraq stated that "structural economic reform and comprehensive privatization of government assets [would be] necessary to stimulate recovery and provide stability after years of disastrous economic policies under Saddam Hussein." Ariel Cohen and Gerald P. O'Driscoll, Jr., Achieving Economic Reform and Growth in Iraq (Heritage Foundation, 2003), www.heritage.org/Research/Iraq/wm236.cfm

41. See Daniels, "Reforming Government."

42. Risk shifting may be one reason for the quite broad privatization of military functions in the current Iraq war. Privatization has been used extensively in the current Iraq conflict and concerns have been raised over what critics see as the outsourcing of "purely military functions" to private contractors. Paul Krugman, "Battlefield of Dreams," *New York Times,* May 4, 2004, at A29. In 2003, employees of private corporations totaled over 10,000 contractors on the ground, making them the second largest contributor to coalition

forces in Iraq after the Pentagon, beating out all other allied forces. Ian Traynor, "The Privatization of War," *Guardian* (London), December 10, 2003, www.guardian.co.uk/print/0,3858,4815701-103681,00.html (noting that the ratio of contracted security personnel to servicemen and -women had increased from 1 to 100 in the first Gulf war to 1 in 10 in the current Iraq conflict). While most of these private contract employees are not working directly as security personnel some do, including jobs that involved the training of the Iraqi police force and the Iraqi army; the provision of security to community and political leaders, other private contractors, and contracting projects; and the operation of certain U.S. military weapons systems such as unmanned Predator drones. Ibid. Traynor notes that while civilian employees are subject to the same rules of engagement as foreign troops, they are not subject to the same oversight or legal codes, since civilian employees are subject to the law of the country they are in, not military authority, and that the legal system of the host country may not be in a position to effectively pursue legal recourse against violators. Ibid.

43. Paul Verkuil, "The Publicization of Airport Security," 27 *Cardozo Law Review* 2243, 2246 (2006).

44. Such claims are especially prevalent in recent public administration literature. For example, "network" public management theory often emphasizes delivery of government services through private contracts and maintains that such private sector arrangements deliver advantages over government delivery mechanisms including specialization, innovation capacity, speed, and flexibility. See, e.g., Stephen Goldsmith and William D. Eggers, *Governing by Network: The New Shape of the Public Sector* (Washington, DC: Brookings Institution Press, 2004). See also Daniels, "Reforming Government"; Moore, *Private Prisons*.

45. Office of Management and Budget, *President's Management Agenda* (2003), p. 1, www.whitehouse.gov/omb/procurement/comp_sourcing_072403.pdf.

46. See *Annual Privatization Report 2006* (Reason Foundation)(providing a sampling of this broad range, including a Connecticut bill (H.B. 5684), which would have barred contracting out and public/private partnerships had it not been vetoed by Governor Jodi Rell; a Virginia bill that would have required justification as to why a service has *not* been privatized; a Florida bill (C.S.C.S.S.B. 2518), requiring a separate "business case for each initiative"; and a Louisiana bill (H.B. 632), that, if passed, will require privatization of all adult correctional facilities by 2016).

47. This view of privatization as a way to circumvent what its proponents characterize as the corrosive effects of established unions is perhaps most clear in the education context. Calls for K–12 school privatization often explicitly lay blame for any observed deterioration of the public school system at the feet of teachers' unions and the centralization of school districts. See, e.g., Milton Friedman, *Public Schools: Make Them Private* (Cato Institute June 23, 1995), www.cato.org/pubs/briefs/bp-023.html (calling for the privatization of a–substantial fraction of all educational services" as a way to "de-

stroy" or "greatly weaken the power of the current educational establishment" as a "necessary precondition" to the improvement of the educational system). Other commentators have referred to the public school system as a "monopoly" that itself will benefit from school privatization as it is forced to compete with private, for-profit education companies like Edison Schools, Inc. See Toch, *Whittling Away* (arguing that "outside catalysts" are necessary to force local teachers' unions to "bring about real change" within the school system).

48. See Moore, *Private Prisons* ("Unless we assume that the decision makers in all the governments that contract with private prison firms are wilfully stupid, we have to believe that cost savings are being achieved").

49. For example, when the city of New York sought a new health care provider for its prison system in 2000, it received bids from only three bidders, two of which were local to the New York municipal area: Capital Health Management, based in Queens; St. Vincent's Hospital and Medical Center, based in Manhattan; and the Tennessee-based Prison Health Services, which was awarded the contract. Eric Lipton, "Company Selected for Rikers Health Care," *New York Times,* September 19, 2000, at B3. Trends toward consolidation of private providers may also have a negative effect on competition. In the prison health context, government prison systems may drop a provider due to dissatisfaction with the medical care provided, only to find themselves being stuck with the same provider again after a merger or acquisition of the new provider by the previously dropped company. In 1999, Prison Health Services purchased EMSA Government Services, a large competitor which had replaced PHS as the provider in Polk County, Florida prior to the acquisition. The purchase had the effect of returning inmate medical care back to PHS, much to the displeasure of the county. Paul von Zielbauer, "Harsh Medicine: Dying behind Bars; As Health Care in Jails Goes Private, 10 Days Can be a Death Sentence," *New York Times,* February 27, 2005, at A1.

50. There is also increasing skepticism as to how truly competitive the contracting process is in practice. Recent evidence indicates that "[c]ompetition, intended to produce savings, appears to have sharply eroded [with] fewer than half of all . . . new contracts and payments against existing contracts . . . subject to full and open competition. Just 48 percent were competitive in 2005, down from 79 percent in 2001." Scott Shane and Ron Nixon, "In Washington, Contractors Take On Biggest Role Ever," *New York Times,* February 4, 2007, at A1.

51. See, e.g., Mass. Gen. Laws Ann. Ch. 7, §52 (West 2003). Concerns about the effects that "competitive contracting" practices might have on current publicly employed workers has prompted several attempts at the federal level to enact legislation that would require new federal contracts to show a benefit, or at least no harm, to existing federal employees. For example, in 2001, Representative Albert Wynn, a Democrat from Maryland, introduced the Truthfulness, Responsibility, and Accountability in Contracting Act, H.R. 721, 107th Cong. (2001), which sought to suspend federal service contracting temporarily until

agencies "(A) established comprehensive and reliable reporting systems to track the costs of service contracting; (B) prevented work from being given to contractors without public-private competitions; and (C) subjected work performed by Federal contractors to the same level of public-private competition as that experienced by Federal employees." Ibid., §2(b)(2).

52. These categories are not static. Advocates of increased process may also be motivated by a distrust of government, leading them to advocate process as an obstacle to government involvement. Similarly, pro-privatization advocates may prefer public service if the state is enabled to deliver services more efficiently, even if it means enlisting the private sector for help.

53. As an example of the latter, those who advocate a limited conception of the proper role of government in society might nonetheless be willing to utilize government process mechanisms as a means to erect obstacles to government involvement already approved. An example of this orientation might be seen in Reynolds v. Giuliani, 35 F. Supp. 2d 331 (S.D.N.Y. 1999), in which the district court addressed a complaint from plaintiffs who alleged that the city of New York had deliberately designed the application program for its food stamp, Medicaid, and cash assistance programs in such a way as to prevent otherwise eligible individuals from obtaining aid. The plaintiffs' argument essentially amounts to a claim that their due process rights were being violated because of an imposition of *too much* process, imposing "unreasonable requirements" on individuals seeking aid. Ibid., at 333. While acknowledging that recent welfare changes meant that the administrative process implemented by the city of New York was still in flux, the district court nonetheless sided with plaintiffs, finding that the procedures in place at the time posed a potential threat of irreparable harm to plaintiffs and granting a preliminary injunction against the practices at issue. Ibid., at 347.

54. I focus on states since they are more varied, yielding a clearer (if still highly selective) picture of the politics surrounding privatization—especially in the first six years of the George W. Bush administration, when the White House and Congress were held by the same party, and Congress was strongly held to consensus.

55. Compare N.Y. Correct. Law §72 (1) (McKinney 2003) (requiring the department to maintain custody for all inmates) with Ark. Code. Ann. §12-50-106(a) (Michie 2002) (authorizing contracts for the construction, financing, and operation of facilities).

56. Colo. Rev. Stat. Ann. §24-50-501 (West 2003).

57. Mass. Gen. Laws Ann. ch. 7, §52 (West 2003).

58. See, e.g., Ky. Rev. Stat. Ann. §197.510(13) (Banks-Baldwin 1998) (requiring at least 10 percent savings); Tenn. Code An. §41-24-104(C)(2)(B) (2002 Supp.) (requiring at least 5 percent savings); Ohio Rev. Code Ann. §9.06(A)(4) (West 2002) (requiring at least 5 percent savings); Fla. Stat. Ann. §957.07 (West 2003 Supp.) (requiring at least 7 percent savings).

59. Colo. Rev. Stat. Ann. §24-50-501 (West 2003).

60. See D.C. Code Ann. §2-301.05b(d)(2)–(4) (2003).

61. Colo. Rev. Stat. Ann §24-50-501 (West 2003).
62. Sharon Dolovich has labeled this focus on monetary cost "comparative efficiency," and written extensively about the problematic nature of its application in the debate of whether or not to privatize state prison facilities. See Chapter 6 above. Dolovich notes that a pursuit of "efficiency" need not necessarily exclude a "realization of society's moral obligations," but that the tendency to frame the privatization question in terms of which actor, public or private, can provide the good or service *as it is already currently being provided by the public sector* at a lower cost "obscures troubling features" that may be common to both sectors given the current level of funding and the degree to which other social values are recognized.
63. See Moore, *Private Prisons*, 1.
64. See Harding, *Private Prisons*, 17–18; see generally Jonathan Simon, "Refugees in a Carceral Age: The Rebirth of Immigration Prisons in the United States," 10 *Public Culture* 577 (1998).
65. For a discussion of the various cost and political factors affecting privatization, see Harding, *Private Prisons*, 16–31. See also Chapter 6 above (noting that the cost savings and efficiency gains that were expected to result from the privatization of prisons were "seen as a means through which states could continue to imprison convicted offenders at prevailing levels while at the same time reversing the deterioration in prison conditions").
66. 1996 Alaska H2; Act of May 29, 1996, 1996 Fla. Sess. Law Serv. ch. 96–270(C.S.H.B. 2469) (codified as amended at Fla. Stat. Ann §946.502 (2001)); Act of April 8, 1996, 1996 Ga. Laws Act 817 (S.B. 675)) (codified at Ga. Code Ann. §42-2-8, §42-2-11 (1996)); Act of April 15, 1996, 1996 Ga. Laws Act 962 (S.B. 751) (codified as amended in scattered sections of Ga. Code. Ann. §42 (1996)) 1996 Ky. Laws Ch. 27 (H.B. 372) (approved February 28, 1996); 1996 Miss. I11728; 1996 Okla. Sess. Law Serv. Ch. 169 (H.B. 2937) (approved May 14, 1996); Or. H3489 (special session 1996); 1996 Va. Laws Ch. 795 (II.B. 563) (approved April 6, 1996); 1996 Va. Laws Ch. 632 (H.B. 1378) (approved April 6, 1996), 1995 Wis. Legis. Serv. Act 344 (1995 S.B. 602) (effective June 4, 1996); and 1996 Wyoming S86. For original source and additional information regarding 1996 state bills in notes 66–68, see National Conference of State Legislatures, *State Anti-Crime Legislation in 1996* (December 1, 1996), vol. 21, no. 14.
67. 1996 Del. Laws Ch. 410 (S.B. 376) (approved June 21, 1996); 1996 Ga. Laws Act 951 (S.B. 587) approved April. 15, 1996); 1996 Ill. Legis. Serv. P.A. 89-767 (S.B. 1604) (effective August 14, 1996); 1996 Il. Legis. Serv. P.A. 89–659 (H.B. 3451 (effective August 14, 1996); 1996 Ky. Laws Ch. 61 (H.B. 144) (approved March 14, 1996); 1996 Mich. Legis. Serv. P.A. 234 (H.B. 4947) (approved June 5, 1996); 1996 Minn. Sess. Law Serv. Ch. 508 (S.F. 2856) (approved by Governor in selected part April 2, 1996); 1996 Minnesota H3242; 1996 Ohio Laws File 202 (H.B. 480) (effective October 15, 1996); 1996 Okla. Sess. Law Serv. Ch. 109 (H.B. 2901) (effective November 1, 1996); 1996 Pa. Legis. Serv. Act 1996–40 (S.B. 856) (approved May 16,

1996); 1996 Tenn. Laws Pub. Ch. 871 (H.B. 2010) (approved May 13, 1996); 1997 Ohio Laws File 202 (H.B. 480) (approved July 17, 1996); 1997 Tenn. Laws Pub. Ch. 871 (H.B. 2010) (approved May 13, 1996); 1997 Wash Legis Serv. Ch. 177 (S.S.B. 6315) (approved March 29, 1996); 1996 Fla. Sess. Law Serv. Ch. 96–278 (C.S.H.B. 1165) (approved by Governor May 29, 1996); 1996 Hawaii H 3542; 1996 Ill. Legis Serv. P.A. 89–532 (S.B. 1268) (effective July 19, 1996); 1996 Md. Laws Ch. 621 (H.B. 467) (approved May 23, 1996); 1996 Mich. Legis. Serv. P.A. 286 (H.B. 4955) (approved June 15, 1996); 1996 Minn. Sess. Law Serv. Ch. 508 (S.F. 2856) (approved by Governor in selected part Apr. 2, 1996); 1996 Minnesota H3242; 1996 Wyoming H6.

68. In 1996, ten states assigned costs to litigant-inmates: 1996 Cal. Legis. Serv. Ch. 852 (A.B. 881) (approved by Governor Sept. 23, 1996); 1996 Cal. Legis. Serv. Ch. 886 (A.B. 2563) (approved by Governor Sept. 24, 1996); 1996 Del. Laws Ch. 411 (S.B. 377) (approved June 28, 1996); 1996 Fla. Sess. Law Serv. Ch. 96–106 (C.S.H.B. 37) (approved by Governor April 9, 1996); 1996 Fla. Sess. Law Serv. Ch. 96–248 (C.S.H.B. 211) (approved by Governor May 28, 1996); 1996 Ill. Legis. Serv. P.A. 89–656 (H.B. 3048) (effective January 1, 1997); 1996 Ky. Laws Ch. 118 (H.B. 323) (approved March 28, 1996); 1996 Miss. Laws Ch. 395 (S.B. 2668) (approved March 19, 1996); 1996 Miss. Laws Ch. 538 (S.B. 2872) (approved April. 12, 1996); 1996 New Jersey A897; 1996 S.C. Laws Act 455 (H.B. 4472) (approved July 3, 1996); 1996 Tenn. Laws Pub. Ch. 995 (H.B. 3082); 1996 Utah H214.

69. National Conference of State Legislatures, State Legislative Reports, *State Crime Legislation 1997*, vol. 23, no. 4 (1997).

70. Ibid.

71. See National Conference of State Legislatures, State Legislative Reports, *State Crime Legislation 1998*, vol. 23, no. 19 (November 1, 1998) (Colorado and Utah were among those states).

72. See, e.g., Act of July 1, 1996, 1996 Fla. Sess. Law Serv. ch. 96–422 (H.B. 2721) (West)(codified as amended at Fla. Stat. Ann. §957.04 (2006)).

73. E.g., Act of May 14, 1996, 1996 Okla. Sess. Law Serv. Ch. 168 (H.B. 2735) (West) (codified as amended in 57 Okla. Stat) (allowing the state department of corrections to turn over foreign nationals in detention to the U.S. Department of Justice for deportation, and to assist the Department of Justice in identifying noncitizens in state detention so as to facilitate their deportation).

74. Crowding yielded a variety of cost-based rationales for prisoner release, notably for elderly and infirm inmates. National Conference of State Legislatures. State Legislative Reports, *Significant State Juvenile Justice Enactments in 1996*, vol. 21, no. 13.

75. 521 U.S. 399 (1997).

76. Ibid., 410.

77. Ark. Code Ann. §12-50-106(d) (Michie 2002).

78. Ohio Rev. Code Ann. 9.06(A)(1) (West 2002).

79. See James Austin and Garry Coventry, U.S. Dep't of Justice, *Emerging Issues on Privatized Prisons* (2001), p. 4, available at www.ncjrs.gov/pdffiles1/bja/181249.pdf. Recent statistics show that Corrections Corporation of America has a capacity of approximately 71,000 beds and that Geo (the spin-off from Wackenhut) has a capacity of about 51,000 beds. The nearest competitor to either company, Cornell, has a capacity of only 19,500 beds. Palash R. Ghosh, "Private Prisons Have a Lock on Growth," *Business Week Online,* July 6, 2006, www.businessweek.com/investor/content/jul2006/pi20060706_849785.htm.

80. Simon Domberger and Paul Jensen, "Contracting Out by the Public Sector: Theory, Evidence, Prospects, 13 *Oxford Review of Economic Policy* 68 (1997).

81. Tenn. Code Ann. §41-24-104(a) (2002 Supp.)

82. Ibid.

83. Ibid.

84. Ibid.

85. Ibid.

86. Idaho Code §20-241A (Michie 1997).

87. The statute additionally requires release of the privatization plan to the public and affected employees, a public hearing on the proposed plan, and a subsequent public report of hearing results by the legislative audit committee. Any subsequent recommendations made by the committee are advisory only. Mont. Stat. Ann. §2 8 302 (2005).

88. Ky. Rev. Stat. Ann. §197.510(7) (Banks-Baldwin 1998).

89. Ibid. at §197.515 (Banks-Baldwin 1998).

90. Mich. Comp. Laws. Ann. §791.220g (11) (West 2001).

91. Colo. Rev. Stat. Ann. §17-1-202(f) (West 2003).

92. See Daniels, "Reforming Government,".11.

93. See, e.g., *NCSL State Legislative Report On Managed Care,* vol. 20, no. 12; Elizabeth Tedrow, "Social Security Privatization in Other Countries—What Lessons Can Be Learned for the United States," 14 *Elder Law Journal* 42 (2006) (on Hawaii and New Jersey state legislatures passing resolutions against federal privatization of social security); Nathaniel J. McDonald, "Ohio Charter Schools and Educational Privatization: Undermining the Legacy of the State Constitution's Common Schools Approach," 53 *Cleveland State Law Review* 467 (2005) (arguing for the invalidation of education privatization in Ohio).

94. See, e.g., Paul Starr, "The Limits of Privatization," in Steve H. Hanke, ed., *Prospects for Privatization* (New York: Academy of Political Science, 1987); Robert Kuttner, "Going Private: The Dubious Case for Selling Off the State," *New Republic,* May 29, 1983, 29–33.

95. LexisNexis State Capital.

96. H.B. 1122, 2006 Gen. Assem., Reg. Sess.(Va. 2006).

97. S.B. 2518, 2005 Sess. (Fla. 2005).

98. S.R.469, 151th Gen. Assem., Reg. Sess. (Ga. 2005) (passed Senate, pending in the House).

> "WHEREAS, the introduction of public-private competition into the delivery of environmental protection programs, services, and activities may result in improvements in the effectiveness, efficiency, and costs of such programs, services, and activities; and
>
> WHEREAS, it may be advantageous to identify disincentives toward efficiency and cost effectiveness in government enforcement and implementation of environmental laws and regulations and how the introduction of private sector competition or incentives may result in higher quality performance and more effective implementation of such policies and programs; and
>
> WHEREAS, there is a perceived need to focus on areas where new legislation may give the Environmental Protection Division and the Department of Natural Resources more flexibility to choose or "shop" and negotiate among private sector providers for the highest quality and lowest cost performance...."

Ibid.

99. S.B. 53, 2007 Gen. Assem., Reg. Sess. (Ind. 2007).
100. S.B. 1600, 212 Leg., Reg. Sess. (N.J. 2006). The Reason Foundation's 2006 Annual Report states that the bill, if enacted, will create a "chilling effect" on privatization initiatives throughout the state. See *Annual Privatization Report 2006* (Reason Foundation), 63.
101. A.B. 1021, 230th Ann. Leg. Sess. (N.Y. 2007)
102. H.B. 1333, 184th Gen. Ct., Reg. Sess. (Mass. 2005).
103. Ibid., §1.

> SECTION 1. Whereas, multinational private water companies are currently going from town to town in Massachusetts attempting to convince municipalities that they will save money and provide better service by privatizing their water and sewer systems in the face of mounting evidence to the contrary; and
>
> Whereas, the very idea of turning such a basic resource as water—and one absolutely necessary for human existence—into a commodity should be repugnant to a democratic society.
>
> Whereas, the policy of the Commonwealth should be to prevent the sale of every Massachusetts resident's right to a reasonably priced, publicly administered supply of clean water.
>
> Whereas, the commonwealth should defend the principle of water as a public trust as the debate over this resource heats up around the globe.

Therefore, the Great and General Court hereby approves this bill which will ban the privatization of public water and sewer systems in the Commonwealth of Massachusetts.

104. Act of May 3, 2001, 2001 Haw. Sess. Laws, Act 90 (S.B.1096) (codified as amended at Haw. Stat. Ann. §27-1) (Michie 2006).

105. Ibid.; see also S.B. 942, 23d Leg. (Haw. 2005), which provides in relevant part:

> c) In the determination made pursuant to this chapter, the state or county official shall consider whether contracting with the private entity will:
>
> (1) Jeopardize the government's ability to provide the service if the private entity fails to perform, or the contract becomes unprofitable or impossible for a private entity to perform;
>
> (2) Impact on any employee covered by civil service laws; provided that the impact shall not prevent the procurement of services pursuant to this chapter;
>
> (3) Affect the nature of the service the agency needs, including whether:
>
> > (A) The service is self-contained or part of a larger service delivery system;
> >
> > (B) The service is geographically dispersed;
> >
> > (C) The service is a core or ancillary government service and if in-house resources are available or needed;
> >
> > (D) Government control is necessary;
> >
> > (E) Government accountability can be shared, ...
> >
> > (F) Governmental authority will be diluted; ...
> >
> > (G) The Proposed privatization contract is in the public interest
>
> (4) Increase the potential for achieving cost savings . . . when compared to in-house resources, including:
>
> > (A) The need to abandon or repurchase capital improvements or equipment that are not fully depreciated;
> >
> > (B) The extent to which the service is available in the private sector marketplace; and
> >
> > (C) The extent to which federal or state restrictions may reduce private sector interest in providing or performing the needed or required service; and the extent to which the savings for the contracting agency are substantial enough to be sustained through any private sector or state cost fluctuations that could normally be expected during the contracting period. The cost savings shall clearly justify the size and duration of the contracting agreement; and
>
> (5) Affect the extent to which the services are needed or required, and how the criteria to select a service provider can be described in objective specifications."

S.B. 942, 23d Leg. 1st Sess. (Haw. 2005) (carried over to the next session) (uppercase indicates insertion to original legislation).

106. Ibid. at (c)(1).
107. S.B. 1742, 184th Gen. Ct., Reg. Sess. (Mass. 2005)
108. See Daniels, "Reforming Government," 13 (referencing the leasing of the Indiana Toll Road to an Australian-Spanish partnership).
109. See Richard B. Stewart, "The Reformation of American Administrative Law," 88 *Harvard Law Review* 1669–1670 (1975).
110. Jody Freeman has written on the potential for "expanding government's reach" into the private sector through incorporation of public interest values into private contracts; Freeman, "Extending Public Law Norms," 1285. The most recent revision of OMB Circular A-76, in 2003, was positively received by the U.S. Chamber of Commerce in these terms; see www.uschamber.com/issues/comments/1999_2003/021219a76comments .htm.
111. See, e.g., Public Citizen's campaign against water privatization under the banner "Water for All"; Public Citizen, Water for All, www.citizen.org/ california/water (last visited Mar. 08, 2007) (claiming that privatization of water resources may result in "corruption . . . rate hikes, inadequate customer service and a loss of local control and accountability").
112. Munger suggests that the privatization of welfare feeds on broader dissatisfaction with government. Frank Munger, "Dependency by Law: Poverty, Identity, and Welfare Privatization," 13 *Indiana Journal of Global Legal Studies* 391 (2006). See also Jennifer Arnette-Mitchell, "State Action Debate Reborn Again: Why the Constitution Should Act as a Checking Mechanism for ICANN's Uniform Dispute Resolution Policy," 27 *Hamline Journal of Public Law & Policy* 307 (2006); David Barnhizer, "Waking from Sustainability's 'Impossible Dream': The Decisionmaking Realities of Business and Government," 18 *Georgetown International Environmental Law Review* 595 (2006); Jack M. Beermann, "Privatization and Political Accountability," 28 *Fordham Urban Law Journal* 1557 (2001); Carol M. Rose, "Privatization—The Road to Democracy?" 50 *St. Louis Law Journal* 691 (2006).
113. "[D]espite repeated attacks on the public/private distinction, it survives both as a matter of constitutional doctrine and popular intuition." Berman, "Cyberspace," 1278.
114. See Freeman, "Extending Public Law Norms."
115. Beermann notes the importance of developing "substitute" accountability procedures for contractors performing government functions when they are in direct contact with the public. See Beermann, "Privatization," 1556. See also Laura A. Dickinson, "Public Law Values in a Privatized World," 31 *Yale Journal of International Law* 383 (2006) (proposing an extension of international law into government contracts, including whistle-blower protections re contract fulfillment).
116. J.R. DeShazo and Jody Freeman, "The Congressional Competition to Control Delegated Power," 81 *Texas Law Review* 1443 (2003).
117. See Radin and Wagner, "The Myth of Private Ordering," 1296.

11. Private Delegations, Due Process, and the Duty to Supervise

1. The same point is true of administrative law. To take a well-known example, core administrative statutes, such as the Administrative Procedure Act (APA) and Freedom of Information Act (FOIA) at the federal level, apply only to "agency" action, with "agency" being defined as a part of the government. See, e.g., 5 U.S.C. §551 (defining agency as "each authority of the Government of the United States"). See generally Jody Freeman, "The Private Role in Public Governance," 75 *New York University Law Review* 545 (2000) ("Administrative law, a field motivated by the need to legitimize the exercise of governmental authority, must now reckon with private power, or risk irrelevance as a discipline.").

2. See Gillian E. Metzger, "Privatization as Delegation," 103 *Columbia Law Review* 1367 (2003).

3. The discussion in this section is a condensed version of arguments I made previously in Metzger, "Privatization as Delegation," especially Parts II and IV.

4. See, e.g., Brentwood Acad. v. Tenn. Secondary Sch. Athletic Ass'n, 531 U.S. 288, 302–303 (2001); Blum v. Yaretsky, 457 U.S. 991, 1011–1012 (1982).

5. See *Blum,* 457 U.S. at 1011–1012 (rejecting claim that nursing homes were performing a public function in providing services states were required to provide under Medicaid because statute did not require states to provide the services themselves; moreover, "decisions made in the day-to-day administration of a nursing home are [not] the kind of decisions traditionally and exclusively made by the sovereign for and on behalf of the public"); Rendell-Baker v. Kohn, 457 U.S. 830, 842 (1982) (rejecting claim that private schools were performing a public function in providing education to special needs students on behalf of school districts because public funding "in no way makes these services the exclusive province of the State").

6. Am. Mfrs. Mut. Ins. Co. v. Sullivan, 526 U.S. 40, 50–55 (1999); see also Skinner v. Ry. Labor Executives' Ass'n, 489 U.S. 602, 614 (1989) ("Whether a private party should be deemed an agent or instrument of the Government for Fourth Amendment purposes necessarily turns on the degree of the Government's participation in the private party's activities....").

7. *Brentwood Acad.,* 531 U.S. at 300; see also ibid., 300–301 (noting that State Education Board members served as ex officio members of key association committees and that the board reviewed and approved association rules). Moreover, *Brentwood Academy* went out of its way to indicate that less extreme forms of government involvement might not suffice, stating that government purchases of contract services "do not convert the service providers into public actors." Ibid., 299.

8. See Metzger, "Privatization as Delegation," 1377–1394.

9. See, e.g., *Brentwood Acad.,* 531 U.S. at 300–301; San Francisco Arts & Athletics, Inc. v. U.S. Olympic Comm., 483 U.S. 522, 542–543 (1987); *Blum,* 457 U.S. at 994–995, 1007–1010, 1008 n.18.

10. For example, in *Blum,* the Court gave little weight to the way that the government had delegated responsibility to nursing homes to ensure that Medicaid beneficiaries received the appropriate level of care. See 457 U.S. at 1006–1008. Similarly, the only reference to the way that local school committees had delegated their statutory responsibilities to the private school in *Rendell-Baker v. Kohn* came in a footnote stating there was no evidence that the committees had done so to avoid constitutional constraints. 457 U.S. at 842 n.7. The one occasion on which the Court emphasized the significance of delegation per se is National Collegiate Athletic Association (NCAA) v. Tarkanian, where the Court stated that the ultimate question in state action analysis is "whether the State provided a mantle of authority that enhanced the power of the harm-causing individual actor." 488 U.S. 179, 192 (1988). But the Court ultimately found no state action in *Tarkanian,* ibid., 199, and it has not developed this suggestion that delegation matters in subsequent cases.

11. For similar conclusions, see, e.g., David M. Lawrence, "Private Exercise of Governmental Power," 61 *Indiana Law Journal* 647 (1986); George W. Liebmann, "Delegation to Private Parties in American Constitutional Law," 50 *Indiana Law Journal* 652–654 (1975).

12. See, e.g., Thomas v. Union Carbide Agric. Prods. Co., 473 U.S. 568, 592–593 (1985) (sustaining requirement of private arbitration of compensation claims notwithstanding that government limited to reviewing for fraud, misconduct, misrepresentation, and constitutional error); Sunshine Anthracite Coal Co. v. Atkins, 310 U.S. 381, 399–400 (1940) (emphasizing Secretary's power to review privately derived regulations but not inquiring into whether meaningful review occurred).

13. See, e.g., West v. Atkins, 487 U.S. 42, 50–51 (1988) (holding physician employed by state prison to be state actor); see also Street v. Corr. Corp. of Am., 102 F.3d 810, 814 (6th Cir. 1996) (holding private prison guard and private company managing prison to be state actors). Another interesting deviation from the general pattern is that several lower courts have found private entities controlling access to government-subsidized medical services to be state actors. See, e.g., Grijalva v. Shalala, 152 F.3d 1115, 1120 (9th Cir. 1998), vacated, 526 U.S. 1096 (1999); Catanzano v. Dowling 60 F.3d 113, 119–120 (2d Cir. 1995). However, these decisions are somewhat hard to square with the Supreme Court's precedent, particularly *Blum v. Yaretsky.* See infra text accompanying note 25.

14. More frequently, delegations may be read narrowly to avoid a constitutional problem. See, e.g., Cass R. Sunstein, "Is the Clean Air Act Unconstitutional?" 98 *Michigan Law Review* 357–359 (1999). In addition, state constitutional restrictions on private delegations are more potent. See, e.g., Bush v. Holmes, 919 So.2d 392, 405–411 (Fla. 2006) (holding that Florida's system of state-funded school vouchers for use at a private school violates the state constitution); Lawrence, "Private Exercise of Governmental Power," 649–651.

15. See, e.g., Richard L. Stone and Michael A. Perino, "Not Just a Private Club: Self Regulatory Organizations as State Actors When Enforcing Federal Law," 1995 *Columbia Business Law Review* 456–458 (discussing delegation of "primary responsibility for enforcing the Exchange Act" to private securities exchanges, and accompanying procedural protection requirements). Another example is the Public Company Accounting Oversight Board (PCAOB, colloquially known as Peekaboo), created by the recent Sarbanes-Oxley Act, which is statutorily denominated a nonprofit corporation yet given regulatory authority over accounting firms. As the members of PCAOB are appointed by the SEC, however, it is more akin to a public agency for constitutional purposes, leaving aside the question of whether its regulatory powers would render it a state actor. See Lebron v. Nat'l RR Passenger Corp., 513 U.S. 374, 378, 400 (1995); Donna M. Nagy, "Playing Peekaboo with Constitutional Law: The PCAOB and Its Public/Private Status," 80 *Notre Dame Law Review* 1036–1043, 1058–1059 (2005).

16. See, e.g., Lawrence A. Cunningham, "Private Standards in Public Law: Copyright, Lawmaking, and the Case of Accounting," 104 *Michigan Law Review* 312–314 (2005) (describing private involvement in setting accounting standards); Steven L. Schwarcz, "Private Ordering," 97 *Northwestern University Law Review* 319–329 (2002) (describing different forms of private involvement in regulation); Sidney A. Shapiro, "Outsourcing Government Regulation," 53 *Duke Law Journal* 401–404 (2003) (same).

17. See, e.g., Jocelyn M. Johnston and Barbara S. Romzek, "Contracting and Accountability in State Medicaid Reform: Rhetoric, Theories, and Reality," 59 *Public Administration Review* 383 (1999) (describing Kansas's transfer of Medicaid case management services for the elderly to regional nonprofit organizations); Rick Lyman, "Florida Offers a Bold Stroke to Fight Medicaid Cost," *New York Times,* January 23, 2005, at A25 (discussing Florida's plan to give private HMOs broad control over implementation of Medicaid).

18. As Paul Verkuil has argued, some instances of private policysetting may violate the fundamental norm, reflected in statutory and regulatory prohibitions on delegating inherently governmental functions as well as constitutional doctrines, that it is public officials who must govern. See generally Chapter 12 below.

19. See, e.g., New Motor Vehicle Bd. v. Orrin W. Fox Co., 439 U.S. 96, 109 (1978); see also Williamson v. Lee Optical, 348 U.S. 483, 486–489 (1955) (sustaining legislation advantaging ophthalmologists and optometrists at the expense of opticians against due process and equal protection attacks); Louis Jaffe, "Law Making by Private Groups," 51 *Harvard Law Review* 220–221 (1937).

20. In other delegation contexts, the Court has made clear its reluctance to police how much discretion on the part of a delegate is too much. See, e.g., American Trucking Ass'n v. Whitman, 531 U.S. 457, 473–76 (2001).

21. The Federal Activities Inventory Reform (FAIR) Act, P.L. 105–270, 112 Stat. 2382 (1998) (codified as 31 U.S.C. §501 note), and Office of Management

and Budget, Circular No. A-76, which prohibit contracting out of "inherently governmental functions" but leave determination of what constitutes an inherently governmental function to the executive branch, accord with this view. On the FAIR Act and Circular A-76, see Paul R. Verkuil, "Public Law Limitations on Privatization of Government Functions," 84 *North Carolina Law Review* 436–448, 452–459 (2006).

22. Blum v. Yaretsky, 457 U.S. 991, 1005 (1982); see also Rendell-Baker v. Kohn, 457 U.S. 830, 832 n.1, 842 (1982) (analogizing school providing educational services to special needs students on government's behalf to contractors who build roads and bridges for the government). The one occasion where the Court did stress a private actor's control over individuals' access to government services is *West v. Atkins,* where it emphasized that a state prisoner could not obtain medical care except through the private doctor who had contracted to provide medical care for the prison. 487 U.S. 42, 55–56 (1988). But *West* is distinguishable from most privatization contexts both because of its institutional setting—the doctor worked at the state prison—and because the constitutional duties the doctor fulfilled are exceptional in attaching directly to the state.

23. As the Court recently stated: "The judicial obligation is not only to preserve an area of individual freedom by limiting the reach of federal law and avoid the imposition of responsibility on a State for conduct it could not control, but also to assure that constitutional standards are invoked when it can be said that the State is responsible for the specific conduct of which the plaintiff complains. If the Fourteenth Amendment is not to be displaced, therefore, its ambit cannot be a simple line between States and people operating outside formally governmental organizations." Brentwood Acad. v. Tennessee Secondary School Ass'n, 531 U.S. 288, 296 (2001) (internal quotations, alterations, and emphasis omitted).

24. See, e.g., West v. Atkins, 487 U.S. 42, 54–58 (1988) (upholding prisoner's right to sue private physician found to be state actor for violations of Eighth Amendment obligation to provide adequate medical care).

25. See, e.g., *Brentwood Acad.,* 531 U.S. at 302–303 (rejecting private association's claim that alternative protections obviated need to subject private association to constitutional scrutiny without examining whether mechanisms offered adequate protection). One recent exception is *Logiodice v. Trustees of Maine Central Institute,* where the First Circuit put great weight on the fact that students expelled from private contract schools had "alternative means of redress"—specifically, the ability to enforce their rights to free education against their school districts in state court—in finding the private schools were not state actors. 296 F.3d 22, 29–30 (1st Cir. 2002), cert. denied, 537 U.S. 1107 (2003).

26. See Freeman, "The Private Role in Public Governance," 608, 623–625, 634–636 (noting value of close government supervision through contract managers and detailed contractual provisions as protections in privatization contexts); see also Elliott D. Sclar, *You Don't Always Get What You Pay For:*

The Economics of Privatization (Ithaca, NY: Cornell University Press, 2000), p. 121–129 (emphasizing importance of government adopting collaborative approach where goals of privatization are carefully specified); Donald F. Kettl, *Sharing Power: Public Governance and Private Markets* (Washington, DC: Brookings Institution, 1993), 39–40, 179–211 (stressing need for close government monitoring of its private partners but also noting that too much interdependence undermines government's ability to control its private partners).

27. The desire to shed personnel is particularly evident at the federal level. See Richard Stephenson, "Government May Make Private Nearly Half of Its Civilian Jobs," *New York Times,* November 15, 2002, p. A1 (reporting on President Bush's proposal to privatize 850,000 out of 2 million remaining federal civil service jobs); Steven L. Schooner, "Contractor Atrocities at Abu Ghraib: Compromised Accountability in a Streamlined, Outsourced, Government," 16 *Stanford Law & Policy Review* 561–564 (2005) (discussing the federal government's increased reliance on contracting for augmenting its personnel); see also Paul C. Light, *The True Size of Government* (Washington, DC: Brookings Institution, 1999), p. 1 (noting that the number of full-time federal government employees increases by nearly 11 million if employees of private contractors and grantees are included).

28. Licenses, corporate charters, and rights of property and are "delegations" of government power to private actors, as are government contracts with private service providers or statutes authorizing private regulation. See, e.g., Jaffe, "Law Making by Private Groups," 214, 220–21.

29. Despite being limited in this fashion, the private delegation approach would still encompass much of contemporary privatization. But one effect of focusing on agency relationships is that private delegations where the private contractors' services and activities are primarily for the government's own direct use may not receive heightened scrutiny. See Restatement (Third) of Agency § 1.01 cmt. c (Tentative Draft No. 2, 2001). Of course, distinguishing between instances where private contractors are primarily providing services and interacting with third parties and those where their services and products are primarily for the government's own use is no doubt easier in theory than in practice. Moreover, some instances of privatization are ineluctably both, with perhaps the paradigm example being the current use of private military contractors to provide security for U.S. facilities and civilian personnel in Iraq. See Daniel Bergner, "The Other Army," *New York Times Magazine,* August 15, 2005, 29.

30. Compare Michael L. Wells, "Identifying State Actors in Constitutional Litigation: Reviving the Role of Substantive Context," 26 *Cardozo Law Review* 100, 111–118 (2004) (arguing that whether or not state action is found should turn on the substantive constitutional values at stake in particular cases).

31. One example is the development, through negotiation among core interest groups, of due process protocols to govern private arbitration of certain types

of disputes. See, e.g., National Consumer Disputes Advisory Committee, Due Process Protocol for Mediation and Arbitration of Consumer Disputes (1998) [hereinafter Consumer Disputes Due Process Protocol]; Due Process Protocol for the Resolution of Health Care Disputes, contained in Commission on Health Care Dispute Resolution, Final Report 14–17 (1998) [hereinafter Health Care Disputes Due Process Protocol]. Another is executive agency efforts to craft appeal and review rights in contexts where government programs are privately administered. See, e.g., 42 C.F.R. §§423.560–423.638 (2005) (outlining grievance and appeal rights of Medicare participants receiving prescription drug coverage through private entities). Moreover, state courts have developed common law fair procedure requirements, often amplified by state statutes, that apply in some private contexts. See Jack M. Beermann, "The Reach of Administrative Law in the United States," in Michael Taggart, ed., *The Province of Administrative Law* (Oxford: Hart Publishing, 1997), 186–191; see generally Paul R. Verkuil, "Privatizing Due Process," 57 *Administrative Law Review* 963 (2005) (discussing common law fair procedure requirements and other examples of procedural requirements on private actors).

32. See Board of Regents v. Roth, 408 U.S. 564, 577 (1972).

33. Compare Londoner v. Denver, 210 U.S. 373, 385–386 (1908) (holding oral hearing with opportunity to present evidence and argument required before costs for road improvement imposed on surrounding properties) with Bi-Metallic Investment Co. v. State Bd. of Equalization, 239 U.S. 441, 445–446 (1915) (holding no predeprivation hearing required "where a rule of conduct applies to more than a few people" and distinguishing *Londoner* as an instance where "a relatively small number of persons was involved, who were exceptionally affected, in each case upon individual grounds"). *Bi-Metallic* is read as generally exempting rulemaking from due process, although additional procedural constraints apply to instances of rulemaking that single out particular entities for regulation, such as ratemaking. See United States v. Florida East Coast Ry. Co., 410 U.S. 224, 243–246 (1973).

34. See, e.g., Cleveland Bd. of Educ. v. Loudermill, 470 U.S. 532, 542–543 (1985) (describing "the root requirement" of the Due Process Clause as being that an individual be given notice and an opportunity to be heard and specifying that the shape of that hearing is determined under *Mathews v. Eldridge* balancing analysis); Mathews v. Eldridge, 424 U.S. 319, 324 (1976) (holding that type of predeprivation hearing required is determined by considering private interests affected, risk of an erroneous deprivation under existing procedures and benefit of additional procedural safeguards, and government's interests in avoiding additional procedures). For the requirement of an impartial decision maker, see sources cited infra note 43.

35. Whether the private actors in these examples should be viewed as acting on behalf of the government or instead as acting in a purely private capacity is a matter of dispute. See Metzger, "Privatization as Delegation," 1462–1470 & n.355, 1487–1492 (discussing when private actions should be viewed as undertaken on behalf of the government and arguing that HMOs and accredi-

tation organizations are so acting when their decisions affect access to government benefits); see also Michael Froomkin, "Wrong Turn in Cyberspace: Using ICAAN to Route around the APA and the Constitution," 50 *Duke Law Journal* 93–105, 93–105 (2000) (arguing that grant to private corporation of authority to regulate Internet domain name system should be viewed as a delegation of governmental policymaking and regulatory functions).

36. See Lawrence, "Private Exercise of Governmental Power," 659–662, 682–686; Jody Freeman, "Extending Public Law Norms through Privatization," 116 *Harvard Law Review* 1301–1311 (2003) (describing opposition to privatization rooted in public law norms that require government decision making to be "open, accountable, rational, and fair"); Texas Boll Weevil Eradication Found. v. Lewellyn, 952 S.W.2d 454, 469 (Tex. 1997) (arguing that private delegations should receive "more searching scrutiny than their public counterparts" because of concerns about private delegates' "personal or pecuniary interest[s]" and the potential for compromising democratic rule "when public powers are abandoned to those who are neither election by the people, appointed by a public official or entity, nor employed by the government").

37. Mathews v. Eldridge, 424 U.S. 319 (1976).

38. *Mathews,* 424 U.S. at 334–335; see Gilbert v. Homar, 520 U.S. 924, 931–932 (1997); Logan v. Zimmerman Brush Co., 455 U.S. 422, 434 (1982).

39. See, e.g., Metzger, "Privatization as Delegation," 1380–1394; see also Dru Stevenson, "Privatization of Welfare Services: Delegation by Commercial Contract," 45 *Arizona Law Review* 105–111 (2003) (describing financial incentives for-profit companies administering welfare benefits have under different contract approaches).

40. This last potential for bias is increasingly attracting attention in the arbitration context, where the concern is that the repeat-player status of one of the parties may incline the arbitrator to rule in that party's favor, so as to secure future business. See Margaret M. Harding, "The Limits of the Due Process Protocols," 19 *Ohio State Journal on Dispute Resolution* 452–453 (2004); Stephen Landsman, "ADR and the Costs of Compulsion," 57 *Stanford Law Review* 1614–1618 (2005).

41. See, e.g., Johnston and Romzek, "Contracting and Accountability," 390 (discussing how financial incentives and contractual responsibilities affected nonprofits providing Medicaid case-management services). For a discussion of moves to for-profit contractors and effects on nonprofits in the welfare context, see M. Bryna Sanger, *The Welfare Marketplace: Privatization and Welfare Reform* (Washington, DC: Brookings Institution Press, 2003), p. 55–69.

42. See Ward v. Village of Monroeville, 409 U.S. 57, 60–61 (1972); see also Tumey v. Ohio, 273 U.S. 510, 523 (1927) (holding due process violated where judge "has a direct, personal, substantial, pecuniary interest" in a certain result); Marshall v. Jerricho, 446 U.S. 238, 243 (1980) (emphasizing due process requires appearance of justice and thus may "bar trial by judges who have no actual bias") (internal quotations omitted). Involvement

by financial self-interested individuals in rulemaking and investigation is, however, more tolerated. See, e.g., Friedman v. Rogers, 440 U.S. 1, 18 (1979) (upholding statutory requirement that majority of board administering ban on commercial optometry be members of association that lobbied for the ban and in which commercial optometrists are ineligible for membership).

43. Gibson v. Berryhill, 411 U.S. 564, 578–580 (1973). The Court subsequently indicated that due process does not impose the same impartiality requirements when private actors are involved in government rulemaking, distinguishing *Gibson* on the ground that it involved adjudication of discipline charges. Friedman v. Rogers, 440 U.S.1, 18–19 & n.19 (1979). The contrast between *Gibson* and *Friedman* thus parallels the adjudication-rulemaking divide evident in procedural due process doctrine generally. See supra note 33 and accompanying text.

44. Schweiker v. McClure, 456 U.S. 188, 196–197 (1982). Although hearing officers' salaries were paid through a federal fund, they were "appointed by and served at the will of" the private carriers, leading the district court in the case to conclude that the carriers nonetheless controlled the hearing officers' incomes and therefore that the hearing officers had a pecuniary interest in their decisions. Ibid., 192–193.

45. Ibid., 197.

46. Compare *Ward,* 409 U.S. at 60–61 (holding due process violated when mayor exercised wide executive powers over village and a major part of village income came from monetary penalties imposed by mayor in mayor's court) with Dugan v. Ohio, 277 U.S. 61, 62–63 (1928) (finding no due process violation where mayor exercised primarily judicial functions and salary was fixed); see also DePiero v. City of Macedonia, 180 F.3d 770, 777–782 (6th Cir. 1999) (discussing mayor's court cases).

47. *Ward,* 409 U.S. at 60 (quoting Tumey v. Ohio, 273 U.S. 510, 532 (1927)).

48. An example is doctors who risk financial penalties or being dropped from managed care plans for recommending too costly care. See Jennifer L. Wright, "Unconstitutional or Impossible: The Irreconcilable Gap between Managed Care and Due Process in Medicaid and Medicare," 17 *Journal of Contemporary Health Law & Policy* 170–172 (2000).

49. See ibid., 61.

50. See *Schweiker,* 456 U.S. at 192 (noting district court finding that private contractor can control income of hearing officers even when officers are paid independently by controlling how often particular officers are used).

51. See Marshall v. Jerricho, 446 U.S. 238, 247–49 (1980) (upholding system where agency charged with enforcing Fair Labor Standards Act receives civil penalties obtained through enforcement actions and emphasizing that claims of violation are reviewed and decided in first instance by an ALJ whose salary is separately paid); see also Dugan v. Ohio, 277 U.S. 61, 64 (1928) (emphasizing that mayor's salary is guaranteed regardless of whether defendants were convicted is rejecting claim of bias).

52. See Metzger, "Privatization as Delegation" (noting FOIA's inapplicability); Daniel Guttman, "Public Purpose and Private Service: The Twentieth Century Culture of Contracting Out and the Evolving Law of Diffused Sovereignty," 52 *Administrative Law Review* 901–905 (2000) (discussing case law on private contractors' exemption from Freedom of Information Act). In addition to their exemption from open government requirements, private adjudicators often attach confidentiality requirements to their decisions. See, e.g., Timothy Stoltzfus Jost, "Confidentiality and Disclosure in Accreditation," 57 *Law & Contemporary Problems* 171, 174–182 (1994) (describing trend toward greater disclosure of accreditation information but noting some limits on public disclosure of such information); Landesman, "ADR and the Costs of Compulsion," 1628–1629 (describing closed nature of ADR proceedings and arguing for greater transparency).

53. See, e.g., 5 U.S.C. §554(a)(2) (providing that disputes over selection and tenure of ALJs are governed by formal adjudicatory procedures); 5 U.S.C. §§1201–1204 (creating independent Merit Systems Protection Board to adjudicate employees' claims of unlawful employment actions); 5 U.S.C. §§1221, 2302(b)(8) (federal employees whistleblower protection and right of action before the board).

54. See Richardson v. McKnight, 521 U.S. 329, 409–411 (1997) (emphasizing private prison companies' freedom from civil service requirements and greater ability to affect the behavior of their employees through incentives in holding that private prison guards do not qualify for the qualified immunity enjoyed by public prison guards under 42 U.S.C. §1983); see also Michael J. Trebilcock and Edward M. Iacobucci, "Privatization and Accountability," 116 *Harvard Law Review* 1423–1430, 1435–1436 (2003) (arguing in defense of privatization that "[p]rivate organizations are generally more effective than governments in motivating agents to act in ways that maximize a firm's profits").

55. See, e.g., Suzanne Lynn, *Complaint Resolution in the Context of Welfare Reform: How W-2 Settles Disputes* (New York: MRDC, November 2001), p. 13–17 (detailing pressures from colleagues felt by private employees performing reviews of denials of welfare benefits and services under Wisconsin's privately administered welfare program); see also Daniel J. Gifford, "Federal Administrative Law Judges: The Relevance of Past Choices to Future Directions," 49 *Administrative Law Review* 8–9, 20–30 (1997) (describing insulation of ALJ and large-scale and formality of adjudications under major federal benefits programs).

56. *Ward*, 409 U.S. at 61–62 (holding litigants are "entitled to a neutral and detached judge in the first instance" and that availability of subsequent trial de novo before an impartial adjudicator did not suffice); see also *Marshall*, 247 n.9 (noting *Ward*'s insistence on an impartial initial decision maker).

57. See, e.g., Lujan v. G&G Fire Sprinklers, 532 U.S. 189 (2001) (holding that due process clause does not require hearing before state can withhold payments to subcontractors for failure to comply with prevailing wage rules).

58. See Wright, "Unconstitutional or Impossible," 167–175.
59. Others have also emphasized the importance of review as a check on private financial bias, although with significant qualifications. See David Kennedy, "Due Process in a Privatized Welfare State," 64 *Brooklyn Law Review* 288–290, 302–03 (1998) (arguing that given potential biases of private welfare contractors, due process mandates fair hearing rights to challenge "every decision of import made by a private provider"); Warren L. Ratliff, "The Due Process Failure of America's Prison Privatization Statutes," 21 *Seton Hall Legislative Journal* 398–403 (1997) (arguing that "private contractors should be able to manage day-to-day prison operations so long as their decisions concerning individual rights are subject to plenary review," but maintaining that private prison operators should have no authority to determine release dates, impose discipline, classify prisoners, or award work credits).
60. See Metzger, "Privatization as Delegation," 1382–1383; see also Sidney A. Shapiro, "Matching Public Ends and Private Means: Insights from the New Institutional Economics," 6 *Journal of Small & Emerging Business Law* 52–53 (2002) (noting danger that an economically motivated private contractor will "resolve policy issues in a manner that maximizes its profit" yet noting that in some contexts the risks from such "potential opportunistic behavior" are lessened because . . . "the private actor's interests are aligned with the agency's interests").
61. This accords with the regulatory regime that governs decisions by Medicare HMOs, under which beneficiaries can obtain de novo internal review of service denials, if urgent, within 72 hours, with further denials being forwarded for review by an independent entity within 24 hours. See 42 C.F.R. §§422.590–592. The Medicare HMO regime also illustrates that independent review need not entail review by the government; there, the independent review is performed by an "independent, outside entity that contracts with" the government. Ibid., §422.592.
62. Some narrow exceptions may exist; for example, where professional norms are strong, reading due process to mandate review by an entirely separate entity might impose costs and inflexibility not justified by the interest in more accurate or fair decision making.
63. See Massachusetts Sch. of Law v. American Bar Ass'n, 107 F.3d 1026 (3d Cir. 1997) (upholding, on antitrust state action and petitioning immunity grounds, dismissal of lawsuit challenging denial of accreditation and ABA standards as anticompetitive); see also United States v. American Bar Ass'n, 934 F. Supp. 435 (D.D.C. 1996) (setting out settlement agreement between the U.S. Department of Justice and the ABA under which the ABA agreed, inter alia, to drop faculty and administrative salary standards and to change the composition of its accrediting committees so that law school representatives constituted no more than 50 percent of their membership); see generally Marina Lao, "Discrediting Accreditation? Antitrust and Legal Education," 79 *Washington University Law Quarterly* 1035 (2001).

64. Morelite Constr. Corp. v. N.Y.C. District Council Carpenters Benefit Fund, 748 F.2d 79, 83 (2d Cir. 1984).

65. See FTC v. Cement Inst., 333 U.S. 683, 701–02 (1948); see also Ash Grove Cement Co. v. FTC, 577 F.2d 1368, 1376–77 (9th Cir. 1978); Texaco v. FTC, 336 F.2d 754, 760 (D.C. Cir. 1964) (disqualifying hearing officer where "a disinterested reader . . . could hardly fail to conclude that he had in some measure decided [the outcome] in advance").

66. See Janna J. Hansen, "Note, Limits of Competition: Accountability of Government Contracting," 112 *Yale Law Journal* 2477–2478, 2495–2496 (2003) (discussing role of professional norms in child welfare contracting); Johnston and Romzek, "Contracting and Accountability," 389–394 (discussing accountability issues that arose when nonprofits took over case management of Kansas's Medicaid services for the elderly). Some argue, however, that the dynamics of government contracting relationships may erode nonprofits' independence. See Stephen Rathgeb Smith and Michael Lipsky, *Nonprofits for Hire: The Welfare State in the Age of Contracting* (Cambridge, Mass. : Harvard University Press, 1993), p. 72.

67. See United Farm Workers v. Arizona Agricultural Employment Bd., 727 F.2d 1479, 1477, 1480 (9th Cir. 1984) (upholding regulatory scheme under which agricultural board with adjudicatory as well as rulemaking and enforcement responsibilities contains two employer and two labor representatives as a legitimate effort to balance partisanship and private expertise).

68. See, e.g., 5 U.S.C. §557(b) (providing that findings and conclusions of law are part of the record and requiring that the employee who presides over a hearing issue a recommended decision even if the ultimate decision is made by the agency head); C & W Fish Co., Inc. v. Fox, 931 F.2d 1556, 1565 (D.C. Cir. 1991) (rejecting, in rulemaking context, claim of bias based on administrator's previously expressed substantive views and noting " '[a]n administrator's presence within an agency reflects the political judgment of the President and the Senate' ") (quoting Ass'n of Nat'l Advertisers v. FTC, 627 F.2d 1151, 1174 (D.C. Cir. 1979)); see also Gifford, "Federal Administrative Law Judges," 33 (noting reliance on regulations, directives, and the like to set policy rather than adjudication in large-scale public benefit programs).

69. See, e.g., Wilkinson v. Austin, 125 S. Ct. 2384, 2396 (2005) (noting that revised prison policy "provides that an inmate must receive notice of the factual basis leading to consideration for [supermax] placement and a fair opportunity for rebuttal. Our procedural due process cases have consistently observed that these are among the most important procedural mechanisms for purposes of avoiding erroneous deprivations."); Fuentes v. Shevin, 407 U.S. 67, 80 (1972) ("For more than a century the central meaning of procedural due process has been clear: Parties whose rights are to be affected are entitled to be heard; and in order that they may enjoy that right they must first be notified.") (internal quotations omitted). Recognition of these requirements is evident in the most recent due process protocols for health care and consumer disputes, which provide for hearings with adequate

notice, opportunity to present evidence and argument, and a written explanation of the basis for decision at a party's request. See Consumer Disputes Due Process Protocol, supra note 31, principle 12 §1, principle 15 §3; Health Care Disputes Due Process Protocol, supra note 31, principle 7 §1, principle 9 §2 (1998).

70. See 20 U.S.C. §§1099b(a)(6), 1099b(j). Moreover, accreditation associations are often required by common law to "conform [their] actions to fundamental principles of fairness," and thus have developed modes of decision making that are likely to meet due process demands. See Medical Inst. v. National Ass'n of Trade & Tech. Schs., 817 F.2d 1310, 1314 (8th Cir. 1987).

71. This lack of precedent no doubt reflects in part the fact that such disclosure requirements are imposed through the APA, FOIA, and similar enactments at the state level. See 5 U.S.C. §552(a)(1) (requiring publication in the Federal Register of agency "substantive rules of general applicability, and statements of general policy or interpretations of general applicability" and prohibiting using such measures to adversely affect any person if not published and actual notice is lacking). It also reflects the restriction of procedural due process to applying when protected liberty interests or entitlements are at stake; individuals are more able to assert such an interest in regard to rules and policies being applied to them directly than in regard to disclosure of program policies more generally.

72. See Matthew Diller, "The Revolution in Welfare Administration: Rules, Discretion, and Entrepreneurial Government," 72 *New York University Law Review* 1200–1202 (2000) (noting problem of caseworkers not informing beneficiaries of possible benefits and programs as an obstacle to fair treatment in public welfare programs, as administration has become more discretionary); Susan T. Gooden, "All Things Not Being Equal: Differences in Caseworker Support towards Black and White Welfare Clients," 4 *Harvard Journal of African-American Public Policy* 28–29 (1998) (reporting lower level of assistance offered to black welfare recipients by county caseworkers in Virginia).

73. For example, the government's interest is less in avoiding its own fiscal and administrative burdens than in avoiding having such burdens imposed on its private delegates, with the loss in innovation and flexibility for government programs that may result. Contra Kennedy, "Due Process in a Privatized Welfare State," 284–85 (arguing that "[i]n a privatized system of welfare administration, the governmental interest is dramatically minimized"). In addition, as indicated by decisions emphasizing that the potential for bias is enough to disqualify and stressing the need for a system of adjudication to *appear* just, see supra notes 41–46 and accompanying text, the concerns raised by financially interested decision makers include not just accuracy but also norms of fair treatment. But *Mathews* balancing is less well suited to addressing the private autonomy concerns raised by application of due process in privatization contexts; simply including the private entity's autonomy interests as a fourth balancing factor risks undervaluing either these interests or those of the affected individual when both have merit.

74. See Sidney A. Shapiro and Richard E. Levy, "Government Benefits and the Rule of Law: toward a Standards-Based Theory of Due Process," 57 *Administrative Law Review* 138 (2005) ("Under an entitlement approach, unconstrained discretion could not violate due process because the existence of unconstrained discretion means that there is no entitlement and due process therefore does not attach."). Some decisions issued before the Court established its entitlement analysis in *Roth* held that administrative exercises of standardless discretion per se violated procedural due process. See, e.g., Holmes v. New York Public Housing Auth., 398 F.2d 262, 265 (2d Cir. 1968). Although this requirement of standards regarding even discretionary benefits appears inconsistent with the Court's current procedural due process analysis, substantive due process analysis—rooted in liberty interests rather than property—still offers some protection against purely arbitrary action. See William Van Alstyne, "Cracks in 'The New Property': Adjudicative Due Process in the Administrative State," 62 *Cornell Law Review* 487–489 (1976). However, the Court's analysis of such a substantive due process claim is extremely deferential and only precludes purely irrational government action. See Flemming v. Nestor, 363 U.S. 603, 612 (1960) ("Particularly when we deal with a withholding of a noncontractual benefit under a social welfare program such as this, we must recognize that the Due Process Clause can be thought to interpose a bar only if the statute manifests a patently arbitrary classification, utterly lacking in rational justification.").

75. See NLRB v. Bell Aerospace Co., 416 U.S. 267 (1974) (holding agency choice of procedures subject to an abuse of discretion standard); SEC v. Chenery Corp., 332 U.S. 194 (1947) (same); Epilepsy Found. v. NLRB, 268 F.3d 1095 (D.C. Cir. 2001) (precluding retroactive application of new policy to require payment of damages for unlawful termination, finding such application would constitute a "manifest injustice"). Other constitutional constraints that might be read to demand the government formulate standards to guide its actions, such as the nondelegation doctrine, also impose little restriction in practice. See American Trucking Ass'n v. Whitman, 531 U.S. 457, 472–476 (2001) (rejecting claim that whether agency has adopted standards to guide its exercises of discretion is relevant to a nondelegation challenge and noting that very broad congressional delegations have been found to contain sufficient "intelligible principle" to meet nondelegation requirements).

76. The legitimacy of such claims of burden, however, turn on the extent of procedural protections demanded. For example, subjecting discretionary adjudicatory decisions to minimal procedural requirements such as the APA's requirement of "prompt notice" of an agency's denial of a request and "brief statement of the grounds for denial" seems unlikely to prove that onerous. See 5 U.S.C. §555; see also Alfred C. Aman, Jr., "Privatization and the Democracy Problem in Globalization: Making Markets More Accountable through Administrative Law," 28 *Fordham Urban Law Journal* 1501–1503 (2001) (arguing for extension of the APA to address privatization contexts); Verkuil, "Privatizing Due Process," 991–992 (proposing a new private

administrative procedure act with minimal notice, comment, and explanation requirements).

77. Additional support for imposing a duty to supervise arguably comes from the Appointments Clause, in that absence of supervision may influence whether an individual is found to exercise such significant discretion that she qualifies as at least an inferior officer, as opposed to being just an employee and thus exempt from the clause's purview. However, the types of decisions that many private delegates are making—whether or not to cover certain medical procedures under Medicare, for example—seem too limited in scope to be reserved for officers, even if the delegate is unsupervised. On the distinction between inferior officers and employees, see Chapter 12 below. But see Neil Kinkopf, "Of Devolution, Privatization, and Globalization: Separation of Powers Limits on Congressional Authority to Assign Federal Power to Non-Federal Actors," 50 *Rutgers Law Review* 340–344 (1998) (arguing that the Appointments Clause does not apply to private contractors as they are not government employees).

78. See supra note 15 and accompanying text. For rare instances when lower courts have required the government to exercise meaningful oversight of its private delegates, see Todd & Co. v. SEC, 557 F.2d 1008, 1014–1015 (3d Cir. 1977) (holding that government must independently review private securities associations' determinations and ensure compliance with governing rules); Gen. Elec. Co. v. N.Y. State Dep't of Labor, 936 F.2d 1448, 1458–1459 (2d Cir. 1991) (holding that government's acceptance without review of wages set by private collective bargaining agreements as prevailing wages would create an unconstitutional delegation).

79. See Correctional Services Corp. v. Malesko, 534 U.S. 61, 74 (2001) (emphasizing that inmates in private facilities could access the Bureau of Prisons' administrative complaint system and from there obtain judicial review in denying a *Bivens* action for constitutional violations against the private prison operators); Richardson v. McKnight, 521 U.S. 399, 412–413 (1997) (holding that individual guards at private prisons generally do not enjoy qualified immunity against constitutional claims under 42 U.S.C. §1983, but expressly reserving question of whether such immunity would be available to private individuals "acting under close official supervision").

80. See, e.g., Phillip J. Cooper, *Governing by Contract: Challenges and Opportunities for Public Managers* (Washington, DC: CQ Press, 2003) 8, 44–49, 102–104 (discussing importance of contract management and what adequate contract management entails); Kettl, *Sharing Power*, 37–40, 193–197 (arguing that privatization threatens accountability unless government invests in capacity to evaluate private contractor performance); Kevin Lavery, *Smart Contracting for Local Government Services* (Westport, CT: Praeger, 1999), 71–74, 203–204 (emphasizing importance of streamlined and professional contract management); Steven Kelman, "Strategic Contracting Management" in John D. Donahue and Joseph S. Nye, eds., *Market-Based Governance: Supply Side, Demand Side, Upside and Downside* (Washington,

DC: Brookings Institution Press, 2002), 88, 89–90, 92–93 (terming contract administration "the neglected stepchild" of strategic contract management); Dan Guttman, "Governance by Contract: Constitutional Visions; Time for Reflection and Choice," 33 *Public Contract Law Journal* 330–331 (2004) (arguing that the federal government lacks the capacity to oversee its contracted workforce); Schooner, "Contractor Atrocities at Abu Ghraib," 558–560 (same); Chapter 7 above.

81. See Schooner, "Contractor Atrocities at Abu Ghraib," 557 ("If the government plans to rely heavily upon contractors, it must maintain, invest in, and apply appropriate acquisition professional resources to select, direct, and manage those contractors.")

82. Compare Schweiker v. McClure, 456 U.S. 188 (1982) (emphasizing regulations requiring unbiased decision making by private hearing officers).

83. In similar vein, I have suggested that private delegations do not raise constitutional accountability concerns when program beneficiaries enjoy real choice over the services they receive or individuals can meaningfully participate in constructing the rules to which they are subject. See Metzger, "Privatization as Delegation," 1477–1479.

84. Heckler v. Chaney, 470 U.S. 821, 831–832 (1985); see also Rizzo v. Goode, 423 U.S. 262, 377–379 (1976) (invoking separation of powers and federalism principles in rejecting injunctive relief ordering city to improve its oversight of police).

85. For similar conclusions, see Guttman, "Governance by Contract," 349 (arguing "the nondelegation doctrine may experience a revival as a doctrine that focuses on fairness"); Chapter 12 below (arguing that the Appointments Clause and nondelegation doctrine support judicial intervention when a basic level of oversight is lacking).

86. See supra notes 28–29 and accompanying text.

87. See Chapter 9 above.

12. Outsourcing and the Duty to Govern

Some of the ideas presented here are explored in Paul R. Verkuil, *Outsourcing Sovereignty* (Cambridge: Cambridge University Press 2007).

1. Leslie Green, "The Duty to Govern," 13 *Legal Theory* 165, 165–166 (2007) (viewing the duty to govern as a "neglected aspect of a theory of legal and political authority": compared to the right to govern and the duty to obey). See also Leslie Green, *The Authority of the State* (Oxford: Clarendon Press 1988) (describing the nature of political authority).

2. See Chapter 11 above; see also Gillian Metzger, "Privatization as Delegation," 103 *Columbia Law Review* 1441–1443 (2003).

3. See Thomas W. Merrill, "Rethinking Article I, Section 1: From Nondelegation to Exclusive Delegation," 104 *Columbia Law Review* 2109–2112 (2004) (asking of the delegation doctrine only whether Congress has delegated, not whether it has accompanied the delegation with ascertainable standards).

4. The standing issues are particularly difficult in the military or foreign affairs settings. See, e.g., United States v. Richardson, 418 U.S. 166 (1974).
5. There are fewer than 1.95 million civilian federal employees (excluding the post office). In 1990 there were over 2.25 million. At the Department of Defense, civilian employment was cut in half during this period. See Office of Personnel Management, *Federal Civilian Workforce Statistics: The Fact Book* (2004), pp. 8-9 [hereinafter *Federal Civilian Workforce Statistics*].
6. In 2002, President Bush announced that the White House intended to let the private sector compete for 850,000 of the fewer than 2 million civilian federal jobs. See Richard W. Stevenson, "Government May Make Private Nearly Half of its Civilian Jobs," *New York Times*, November 15, 2002, at A1.
7. The percentage of postal employees has grown in proportion to total federal civilian employment. See *Federal Civilian Workforce Statistics*, at 7. The Postal Service, which could be a legitimate candidate for privatization, represents an increasingly larger percentage of the civilian government workforce.
8. Consider Paul C. Light, *The True Size of Government* (Washington, DC: Brookings Institution Press, 1999), p1 (private contractors provided 12.7 million full-time-equivalent government jobs in 1996).
9. See United States House of Representatives, Commission on Government Reform, Minority Staff Special Investigations Division, *Dollars, Not Sense: Government Contracting under the Bush Administration—New Findings* (prepared for Henry A. Waxman) (June 2006) (reporting that the value of sole source and other noncompetitive contracts awarded by the Bush administration has increased by 115 percent from $67.5 billion in 2000 to $145 billion in 2005, resulting in 38 percent of contract dollars being awarded without full and open competition).
10. See John A. Rohr, *To Run a Constitution* (Lawrence: University Press of Kansas, 1986), pp. 180–185 (Rohr uses the phrase, attributed to Woodrow Wilson, to describe those government officials—officers and SES members—whose job is to manage the government).
11. From 1987 to 2003 the number of SES positions has remained largely constant at about 7,800. From 1993 to 2003 the total work years of executive branch agencies has gone down from 2.18 million to 1.97 million as downsizing occurred. See *Federal Civilian Workforce Statistics*, 64, 73.
12. Paul Volcker notes that in 1960 President Kennedy had 286 political appointments to fill; President Clinton had 914 such positions by the end of his administration and President George W. Bush now has 3,361 political appointees. See National Commission on the Public Service (Volcker Commission), "Urgent Business for America: Revitalizing the Federal Government for the 21st Century," in Robert Klitgaard and Paul C. Light, eds., *High Performance Government* (Washington, DC: Rand Corporation, 2005), p36.
13. See generally David E. Lewis, "Staffing Alone: Unilateral Action and the Politicization of the Executive Office of the President, 1988–2004," 35 *Presidential Studies Quarterly* 496 (2005) (discussing presidents' decisions to politicize and their consequences). Professor Lewis also found that "politi-

cally appointed bureau chiefs get systematically lower management grades than bureau chiefs drawn from the civil service." David E. Lewis, "Political Appointments and Federal Management Performance," Policy Brief (September 2005), www.wws.princeton.edu/policybriefs/lewis_performance.pdf.

14. Weak political leadership at FEMA left many crucial policy decisions, such as the preparation of hurricane evacuation plans, to the private sector. See Jennifer Steinhauer and Eric Lipton, "FEMA, Slow to the Rescue, Now Stumbles in Aid Effort," *New York Times,* September 17, 2006, at A1 (documenting FEMA's inability to get more people out of shelters, provide services, or coordinate private efforts).

15. See Griff Witte and Charles R. Babcock, "A Major Test for FEMA and Its Contracting Crew," *Washington Post,* September 13, 2005, A1 (describing the loss of high-level talent at the agency, particularly in its acquisition personnel).

16. FEMA insiders and some who have worked with the agency say it has grown increasingly reliant on contractors in recent years not just for help in responding to disasters, but for planning and policymaking as well. It is a trend that has been augmented, they say, by the departure of FEMA's top civil servants and the arrival of political appointees with little disaster management experience. See generally Vicki Bier, "Hurricane Katrina as a Bureaucratic Nightmare," in Ronald J. Daniels, Donald F. Kettl, and Howard Kunreuther, eds., *On Risk and Disaster—Lessons from Hurricane Katrina* (Philadelphia: University of Pennsylvania Press, 2006), pp 243–254.

17. The war in Iraq has been understaffed from the outset, as several in the military tried to warn the Secretary of Defense. See Thomas E. Ricks, *Fiasco* (New York: Penguin Books, 2006), pp 41–43.

18. See P.W. Singer, *Corporate Warriors: The Rise of the Privatized Military Industry* (Ithaca, NY: Cornell University Press, 2003) (citing the use of military contractors in Africa, Eastern Europe and Latin America, in addition to Afghanistan and Iraq).

19. See ibid. at pp 115–136 (documenting examples and showing how the end of the cold war provided opportunities for private contractors).

20. RAND has provided advice on when and how the Army should use private contractors on the battlefield. Frank Camm and Victoria A. Greenfield, "How Should the Army Use Contractors on the Battlefield?: Assessing Comparative Risk in Sourcing Decisions" (2005), www.rand.org/pubs/monographs/2005/RAND_MG296.sum.pdf (accessed 11/17/06). Similarly, the Transportation Security Agency recently commissioned Lockheed Martin to determine whether public or private officials performed better security services at airports, a function Lockheed could itself perform if it were contracted out. See Chris Strohm, "TSA Examines Conflict of Interest Charges against Contractor," *GovExec.com,* May 23, 2005, www.govexec.com/dailyfed/0505/052305c1.htm.

21. The use of private contractors for interrogation at Abu Ghraib prison near Baghdad in addition to military officers has been noted. See Final Report

of the Independent Panel to Review Department of Defense Detention Operations, summarized in "Findings on Abu Ghraib Prison: Sadism, 'Deviant Behavior' and a Failure of Leadership," *New York Times,* August 25, 2004, at A1, A10. See generally Steven L. Schooner, "Contractor Atrocities at Abu Ghraib: Compromised Accountability in a Streamlined, Outsourced Government," 16 *Stanford Law & Policy Review* 549 (2005). The most dramatic use of private contractors in the civilian setting involves the use of Blackwater security personnel by FEMA after Hurricane Katrina. See Jeremy Scahill and Daniela Crespo, "Blackwater Mercenaries Deploy in New Orleans," *Truthout Report* (September 10, 2005), www.truthout.org (accessed 11/17/06).

22. See John M. Broder, "Report Says Firm Sought to Cover Up Iraq Shootings," *New York Times,* October 2, 2007, A1.

23. See Editorial, "America's Army on the Edge," *New York Times,* October 1, 2006, at 9 (discussing shortfalls in active duty troops and the necessity to expand the use of National Guard units in Iraq).

24. Government Accountability Office (GAO), *Contract Management: Opportunities to Improve Surveillance on Department of Defense Service Contracts,* GAO-05-274, March 2005, p 1 (noting that at the Pentagon contract surveillance is not a priority, there is no evaluation of surveillance personnel, and officers believe they do not have enough time to carry out their surveillance duties).

25. See, e.g., Dan Briody, *The Halliburton Agenda: The Politics of Oil and Money* (Indianapolis, IN: Wiley, 2004) (Kellogg Brown & Root's contracts to restore Iraq oil fields exceed $7 billion).

26. See, e.g., Erik Eckholm, "The Conflict in Iraq: Corruption Accusations; Memos Warned of Billing Fraud by Firm in Iraq," *New York Times,* October 23, 2004, at A1 (describing Air Force contract fraud action against Custer Battles); Erik Eckholm, "Judge Limits Statute's Ability to Curb Iraq Contractor Fraud," *New York Times,* July 12, 2005, at A6 (discussing district court ruling that False Claims Act does not apply to Coalition Provisional Authority).

27. See Dan Guttman, "Governance by Contract: Constitutional Visions. Time for Reflection and Choice," 33 *Public Contract Law Journal* 321 (2004) (describing deficiencies in oversight by contracting officials).

28. See GAO, *Contract Management.*

29. The Vice President's relationship to his former employer Halliburton and its former subsidiary Kellogg, Brown & Root is well documented. See Briody, *The Halliburton Agenda.* It reflects a mind-set that sees private providers as a preferable alternative to public ones.

30. See Oliver E. Williamson, "Public and Private Bureaucracies: A Transaction Cost Economics Perspective," 15 *Journal of Law, Economics, & Organization* 308–326 (1999) (favoring outsourcing if transaction costs are reduced).

31. See David M. Walker, "The Future of Competitive Sourcing," 33 *Public Contract Law Journal* 299, 304 (2004) (emphasis added).

32. See Jon D. Michaels, "Beyond Accountability: The Constitutional, Democratic, and Strategic Problems with Privatizing War," 82 *Washington University Law Quarterly* 1008–1010 (2004) (labeling as "tactical privatization" the trend toward making military policy outside the democratic constraints of governance).

33. F.A. Hayek, *The Road to Serfdom* (Chicago: University of Chicago Press, 1944), pp 133–134 ("Nor is there any reason why the state should not assist the individuals in providing for those common hazards of life . . . [including] such 'acts of God' as earthquakes and floods. Whenever communal action can mitigate disasters against which the individual can neither attempt to guard himself nor make provision for these consequences, such communal action should undoubtedly be taken.")

34. See Michael J. Lippitz, Sean O'Keefe, and John P. White, "Advancing the Revolution in Business Affairs," in Ashton Carter and John White, eds., *Keeping the Edge* (Cambridge, MA: MIT Press, 2001), p 176 (comparing DOD functions that do and do not require "special public trust").

35. See Stephen Breyer, *Active Liberty: Interpreting Our Democratic Constitution* (New York: Knopf, 2005), pp 3–4 (public liberty means more than freedom from despotic governments; it means active participation in our governing institutions).

36. See U.S. Const. art. II, §2.

37. See Jerry L. Mashaw, "Recovering American Administrative Law: Federalist Foundations, 1787–1801," 115 *Yale Law Journal* 1269–1270 (2006) (describing the Constitution's "missing" administrative branch).

38. See Myers v. United States, 272 U.S. 52 (1926) (defining executive officials); Williams v. United States, 42 U.S. (1 How.) 290, 296–97 (1843) (settled usage that Secretary of the Treasury may act for the President).

39. U.S. Const. art. II, §2, cl. 1.

40. Ibid., at §3.

41. Ibid., at §2, cl. 2.

42. See William P Barr, Assistant Attorney General, Office of Legal Counsel (OLC), *Constitutional Limits on "Contracting Out" Department of Justice Functions under OMB Circular A-76*, 14 Op. O.L.C. 94, 98 (April 27, 1990) (describing horizontal and vertical effects of Appointments Clause).

43. See Buckley v. Valeo, 424 U.S. 1 (1976) (per curiam) (limiting Congress's power to appoint officers); Myers v. United States, 272 U.S. 52 (1926) (limiting Senate's power to participate in removal of officers); see also Weiss v. United States, 510 U.S. 163 (1994) (deciding whether congressional addition of duties for military judges is within Appointments Clause); Humphrey's Executor v. United States, 292 U.S. 602 (1935) (approving congressional limit on presidential removal of independent agency commissioners for cause).

44. See U.S. Const. art. I, §2, cl. 1 (permitting Congress to vest the appointment of inferior officers "in the President alone, the Courts of Law, or in the Heads of Departments"). It is under this power that Congress placed some officials under the protection of the civil service. See United States v. Perkins, 116 U.S. 483

(1886) (civil service law constitutional); Myers v. United States, 272 U.S. 52, 162 (1926) (explaining inferior officer limitations under civil service). See also Freytag v. C. I. R., 501 U.S. 868, 884 (1991) (defining heads of departments).

45. See *Buckley*, 424 U.S. at 125–126. Admittedly, "significant authority" is not a self-defining phrase. One way to give it meaning is to analogize it to OMB's "inherently governmental activities" requirement. See discussion below.

46. The President appoints all military officers including second lieutenants and the Senate confirms them. See *Weiss*, 510 U.S. at 169 (all military officers are "Officers of the United States"). Such officers are required to be appointed by the President. See *Perkins*, 116 U.S. at 484 (cadet engineer appointed by Secretary of the Navy).

47. Of course, junior officers in battlefield conditions can be asked to assume policymaking duties normally performed by their superiors.

48. 424 U.S. 1 (1976).

49. See Walker, "The Future of Competitive Sourcing."

50. See Deborah D. Avant, *The Market for Force: The Consequences of Privatizing Security* (Cambridge: Cambridge University Press, 2005), pp 38–40 (describing various private military contracts).

51. See supra note 42.

52. U.S. Const. art. I, §8, cl. 11. The clause, which has not been used as a policy option since the presidency of Andrew Jackson, permits Congress, not the President, to "privatize" war to some limited degree. It does not allow the President to do so directly and it does not contemplate the payment of federal funds since, historically, privateering was a business financed by the privateers. See generally C. Kevin Marshall, "Putting Privateers in Their Place: The Applicability of the Marque and Reprisal Clause to Undeclared Wars," 64 *University of Chicago Law Review* 963–964 (1997).

53. See Barr, *Constitutional Limits on "Contracting Out,"* citing as examples of forbidden verticality Northern Pipeline Constr. Co. v. Marathon Pipeline Co., 458 U.S. 50 (1982) and A.L.A. Schechter Poultry v. United States, 292 U.S. 495 (1935). Since *Northern Pipeline* involved forbidden delegations of Article III power to magistrate judges (who are, if not Article III judges, at least federal employees) and since *Schechter* involved forbidden delegation by Congress to the President, neither example directly addresses private parties or contractors. A better case than *Schechter* would have been Carter v. Carter Coal, 298 U.S. 238 (1936) (delegation to private groups).

54. Compare Flast v. Cohen, 392 U.S. 83, 105–106 (1968) (taxpayer standing to challenge expenditures to parochial schools) with Lujan v. Defenders of Wildlife, 504 U.S. 555 (1992) (raising separation of powers objections to delegation of private authority to sue under the Endangered Species Act).

55. The antiaggrandizement principle emerges from the Framers' concern with congressional hegemony (Congress being then the most dangerous branch). See Bowsher v. Synar, 478 U.S. 714, 726 (1986) (holding that Congress cannot reserve for itself the power of removal of an officer charged with the execution of the laws except by impeachment); *Buckley*, 424 U.S. at

122–123 (same); compare Mistretta v. United States, 488 U.S. 361, 411 n. 35 (1989) (holding that presidential removal power over members of Sentencing Commission does not pose a special danger because, unlike in *Bowsher,* the President does not retain control over the "constitutionally assigned mission of another Branch").

56. Subdelegation Act, Pub. L. No. 82–248, 65 Stat. 710, 713 (1951) (codified at 3 U.S.C. §§301–303 (2000)). Under §301, the President has the broad power to delegate authority to "the head of any department or agency in the executive branch, or any official thereof who is required to be appointed by and with the advice and consent of the Senate."

57. See Youngstown Steel & Tube Co. v. Sawyer, 343 U.S. 579, 635–637 (1952) (Jackson, J., concurring) (if the President has congressional authorization for his actions judicial deference is granted). Attorney General Gonzales's memo justifying the President's national security intercept program also relies on *Youngstown.* See Department of Justice, *Legal Authorities Supporting the Activities of the National Security Agency Described by the President* (Washington, DC, 2006), pp 19–20.

58. 5 U.S.C.App. §2 (2000). See Cheney v. U.S. District Court, 542 U.S. 367 (2004), *remanded sub nom.* In re Cheney, 406 F.3d 723 (D.C. Cir. 2005) (en banc) (strictly construing FACA because of separation of powers considerations and holding that a presidentially convened committee consisting of federal officials and private industry members is exempt from the Act if only the public officials have voting power). Of course, failure to include the private sector in policymaking has also been criticized. See Association of American Physicians & Surgeons, Inc. v. Clinton, 997 F.2d 898 (D.C. Cir. 1993) (holding that the First Lady is a de facto employee of government and exempting the Health Care Task Force, which contained no private industry members, from FACA). FACA's application to advice given to the President raises sensitive interbranch issues. See Public Citizen v. Department of Justice, 491 U.S. 440, 467–468 (1989) (FACA does not apply to advice on judicial appointments given to the President by the ABA; three judges concurred in the proposition that the statute was unconstitutional in this regard). But the narrow reading of FACA leaves it less effective to constrain or (after *In re Cheney*) even to provide information about influence of the private sector, as long as private contractors do not participate in collective judgment under the Act. For a thorough analysis of FACA's scope and purpose, see Steven P. Croley and William F. Funk, "The Federal Advisory Committee Act and Good Government," 14 *Yale Journal on Regulation* 452 (1997).

59. 5 U.S.C. §552 (2000).

60. See, e.g., Larry Alexander and Saikrishna Prakash, *Delegation Really Running Riot* (2006), pp 15–22 (applying nondelegation theory to Articles II, III, and IV), ssrn.com/abstract—921743.

61. See Vikram David Amar, "Indirect Effects of Direct Election: A Structural Examination of the Seventeenth Amendment," 49 *Vanderbilt Law Review*

1378–1379 (1996); see also George W. Liebmann, "Delegation to Private Parties in American Constitutional Law," 50 *Indiana Law Journal* 650, 659 (1975) (issue is whether delegation "calls into question the future operation of the political process").

62. 298 U.S. 238 (1936).

63. Professor Jaffe, writing at the time of *Carter Coal,* thought the nondelegation aspect was unnecessary to the decision and would have relied on due process alone. See Louis L. Jaffe, "Law Making by Private Groups," 51 *Harvard Law Review* 248 (1937).

64. 49 Stat. 991 (1935), 15 U.S.C. §§801 et seq.(1935).

65. The coal company and union representatives were not only private adjudicators, but they were also private parties with an interest in the outcome. See Dr. Bonham's Case, 8 Coke Rep. 107 (1610) (defining natural justice as including interest in the outcome).

66. Laurence H. Tribe, *American Constitutional Law,* 3d ed. (New York: Foundation Press, 2000), p 993.

67. But see Thomas v. Union Carbide Agricultural Products Company, 473 U.S. 568 (1985) (no Appointments Clause problem with the government's use of private panel of arbitrators). Also, due process challenges to biased tribunals are made on an as applied, rather than direct, basis. Compare Gibson v. Berryhill, 411 U.S. 564 (1973) (optometrists biased against new competitors) with Friedman v. Rogers, 440 U.S. 1 (1979) (no direct challenge to a state board of independent optometrists).

68. This is the intent of Gillian Metzger's use of the nondelegation doctrine as a process control over private contractors. See Gillian Metzger, "Privatization as Delegation." See also Jody Freeman, "Extending Public Law Norms Through Privatization," 116 *Harvard Law Review* 1285 (2003) (urging a "publicization" view of privatized activities).

69. Chief Justice Marshall observed that "[a]lthough an office is 'an employment,' it does not follow that every employment is an office." United States v. Maurice, 26 Fed. Cas. 1211, 1214 (C.C.D.Va. 1823) (No. 15,747). The distinction between officers and employees has been the subject of numerous cases. See, e.g., Burnap v. United States, 252 U.S. 512, 516–519 (1920) (landscape architect was an employee, not an officer).

70. See Morrison v. Olson, 487 U.S. 654, 671–672 (1988) (describing the difference between principal and inferior officers and labeling the independent counsel "inferior").

71. See *Buckley,* 424 U.S. at 125–126. In contrast, "[e]mployees are lesser functionaries subordinate to Officers of the United States." Ibid. at 160 n. 162.

72. *Buckley* (supra note 48) cites with favor decisions that have excepted employees with intermittent and temporary duties from the definition of "officer." See Auffmordt v. Hedden, 137 U.S. 310 (1890) (merchant appraiser hired for special case); United States v. Germaine, 99 U.S. 508 (1878) (surgeon appointed to examine applicants for pensions in special cases not an officer).

73. See William Barr, Assistant Attorney General, Office of Legal Counsel, *Constitutionality of the Qui Tam Provisions of the False Claims Act,* 13 Op. O.L.C. 249 (July 18, 1989).

74. See False Claims Act, 31 U.S.C. §§3729 et seq (2000). *Qui tam* actions permit private relators to bring actions on behalf of the government for fraud unless the Department of Justice intervenes. A relator resembles a private contractor "hired" to help bring those committing fraud against the government to justice.

75. This argument created a split within the Administration: OLC argued that this criterion rendered the *qui tam* provision unconstitutional; this position was contested by the Solicitor General's office. Barr, *Constitutionality of the Qui Tam Provisions.* The opinion also argued that the *qui tam* actions violated Article III standing requirements and the separation of powers doctrine.

76. The Supreme Court has largely upheld the constitutionality of *qui tam* actions, relying on the long tradition of such actions and Congress's express acceptance of them under the False Claims Act. See Vermont Agency of Natural Resources v. United States ex rel. Stevens, 529 U.S. 765 (2000) (discussing the Article III challenges to the *qui tam* inquiry but reserving the question as to its Article II dimensions).

77. See Walter Dellinger, Acting Assistant Attorney General, Office of Legal Counsel, *Memorandum for the General Counsels of the Federal Government: The Constitutional Separation of Powers Between the President and Congress* (May 7, 1996), p 15 n. 66, www.usdoj.gov/olc/delly.htm ("We now disapprove the Appointments Clause analysis and conclusion of an earlier opinion of this Office.").

78. The debate, which arose in the context of the independent counsel, was over whether prosecution is an inherently executive function. Compare Lawrence Lessig and Cass Sunstein, "The President and the Administration," 94 *Columbia Law Review* 15–16 (1994), with Stephen L. Carter, "The Independent Counsel Mess," 102 *Harvard Law Review* 105 (1988). See Morrison v. Olson, 487 U.S. 654 (1988) (upholding the constitutionality of independent counsel statute).

79. Indeed, the Clinton OLC Memorandum, while denying the appointments power is implicated in private contractor situations, expressly reserves challenges to those actions under "the non-delegation doctrine and the general separation of powers principle." Dellinger, *The Constitutional Separation of Powers,* p 15 and nn. 61–63.

80. See U.S. Const. art. II, §1.

81. Cf. *Lujan* v. Defenders of Wildlife, 504 U.S. 555 (1992) (emphasizing importance of public officials, and the oath requirement, in the enforcement of public law).

82. See U.S. Const. art. 6; Akhil Reed Amar, *America's Constitution: A Biography* (New York: Random House, 2005), pp 62–63 (describing the importance the Constitution places on oaths and affirmations).

83. See, e.g., Christopher S. Yoo, Steven G. Calabresi and Anthony J. Colangelo,

"The Unitary Executive in the Modern Era, 1945–2004," 90 *Iowa Law Review* 601 (2005); Steven G. Calabresi and Saikrishna B. Prakash, "The President's Power to Execute the Laws," 104 *Yale Law Journal* 541 (1994) (President must control prosecutions). Those who believe in the unitary nature of executive power could be potential allies against the delegation of policy-making to private hands. If the executive power resides in the President, then it is he who must exercise it, not congressionally assigned officials, and certainly not privately contracted ones.

84. See Saikrishna Prakash, "The Chief Prosecutor," 73 *George Washington Law Review* 575–577, 590–591 (2005) (arguing that even though the President must exercise the prosecutorial power, *qui tam* and other private prosecution schemes (e.g., special prosecutors) can be constitutional so long as the President has the power to terminate these actions, even if by exercising the pardon power over those subject to private suits).

85. One way to avoid the Appointments Clause limitations on private contractors is to designate such delegatees as employees rather than officers. Under the independent three-criteria view urged by the Clinton Administration this would pass muster easily. See Dellinger, *Constitutional Separation of Powers*, at 15 n. 61, for further inquiry into the "significant authority" dimension of the delegation.

86. See *Vermont Agency*, 529 U.S at 778.

87. The contract process provides limits on scope and duration of delegations that would satisfy these criteria and negate the excessive delegation implication.

88. A possible "authorizing" statute might be the Fair Activities Inventory Reform (FAIR) Act, Pub. L. No. 105–70, 112 Stat. 2382, §2(a) (1998), but that Act incorporates OMB's A-76 process, which forbids the contracting out of inherent government functions. If no statute can be found to authorize the delegation, the executive's delegation is at a low ebb in *Youngstown Steel* terms.

89. See "A Major Test for FEMA"; see also Press Release, IEM Inc., "IEM Team to Develop Catastrophic Hurricane Disaster Plan for New Orleans and Southeast Louisiana" (June 3, 2004), available at www.ieminc.com/Whats_New/Press_Releases/pressrelease060304_Catastrophic.htm; "Homeland Security Chief Outlines FEMA Overhaul," *New York Times*, October 20, 2005, at A22 (describing FEMA's failures to respond to the Katrina disaster and proposing more public controls).

90. See Dan Guttman, "Inherently Governmental Functions and the New Millenium [*sic*]: The Legacy of Twentieth-Century Reform," in Thomas H. Stanton and Benjamin Ginsberg, eds., *Making Government Manageable* (Baltimore, MD: Johns Hopkins University Press, 2004), p. 54 (describing situations where a government official signs off on a contractor-drafted rule).

91. See GAO, Department of Homeland Security, Risk Assessment and Enhanced Oversight Needed to Manage Reliance in Contractors, GAO-08-142T, Oct. 17, 2007, p. 1 (GAO recommended that DHS "ensure govern-

ment control over and accountability for . . . [contractor] services that closely support inherent government functions"). Inherent functions are defined in the text and at note 137.

92. 298 U.S. 468 (1936).

93. The line between employees and inferior officers is not easily drawn. See Freytag v. Commissioner, 501 U.S. 868 (1991) (determining that a "special trial judge" is an inferior officer appointed by the Tax Court, which the majority found to be a "court of law" under the Appointments Clause). See also Landry v. FDIC, 204 F.3d 1125 (D.C. Cir. 2000) (determining administrative law judges at Federal Deposit Insurance Corporation to be employees rather than inferior officers).

94. The decision in Carter v. Carter Coal, 298 U.S. 238 (1936), which objected strenuously to delegating powers to private parties, appeared in the same volume as *Morgan I.*

95. See text accompanying notes 59–60 supra.

96. United States v. Morgan *(Morgan IV),* 313 U.S. 409 (1941).

97. See Richard J. Pierce, Sidney A. Shapiro and Paul R. Verkuil, eds., *Administrative Law and Process,* 4th ed. (New York: Foundation Press, 2004), §6 4 6; see also Citizens to Preserve Overton Park, Inc. v. Volpe, 401 U.S. 402, 420 (1971).

98. See Motor Vehicle Manufacturers Association v. State Farm Mutual Automobile Insurance Co., 463 U.S. 29 (1983) (describing hard look review).

99. See Daniel J. Gifford, "The Morgan Cases: A Retrospective View," 30 *Administrative Law Review* 237, 238 (1978) (*Morgan IV* "places a veil of secrecy over the 'mental processes' of the decisionmakers"); see also, e.g., U.S. Postal Service v. Gregory, 534 U.S. 1 (2001) (describing presumption of regularity).

100. See U.S. Telecom Ass'n. v. FCC, 359 F.3d 554, 566 (D.C. Cir.), *cert denied,* 125 S. Ct. 345 (2004) (holding a state commission to be a private party (contractor) in relationships to a federal agency).

101. *U.S. Telecom,* 359 F.3d at 568; see also Shook v. District of Columbia Fin. Resp. & Mgmt. Assistance Auth., 132 F.3d 775, 783–784 (D.C. Cir. 1998).

102. See Assiniboine & Sioux Tribes v. Bd. of Oil and Gas, 792 F.2d 782, 795 (9th Cir. 1986).

103. *U.S. Telecom,* 359 F.3d at 566.

104. One function of judicial review is to ensure that the agency officials who decide on a policy have actually reviewed the record before them. See, e.g., *Motor Vehicle Manuf. Ass'n,* 463 U.S. at 43 (1983) (agency required to consider alternatives to proposed rule). Indeed "hard look" review makes no sense unless it assumes that the "look" must be the agency's.

105. See SEC v. Chenery *(Chenery I),* 318 U.S. 80, 95 (1943).

106. Professor Stack has characterized the reasons requirement of *Chenery* as a fundamental principle rising to constitutional levels. See Kevin M. Stack, "The Constitutional Foundations of *Chenery,*" 116 *Yale Law Journal* 952, 958 (2007).

107. See ibid. at 967.
108. See Chevron U.S.A. Inc. v. NRDC, Inc., 467 U.S. 837, 842–844 (1984). "*Chevron* deference" leaves policy questions to the agencies, not the courts. It ensures political accountability by deferring to agency expertise, not "contractor expertise." See Stack, "Constitutional Foundations," at 1007.
109. The opinion also notes the requirement of oath taking by executive branch officials, which further distinguished them from private contractors. See Dellinger, *Constitutional Separation of Powers,* p 5, n. 10.
110. See *Williams v. United States,* 42 U.S. (1 How.) 290, 296–297 (1843) (Court unanimously rejected argument that President was personally required to dispense all monies from the treasury).
111. In Murray v. The Schooner Charming Betsy, 6 U.S. (2 Cranch) 64, 112 (1804), Justice Chase was reluctant to read President Jefferson's instructions, since "if they go no further than the law, they are unnecessary; if they exceed it, they are not warranted."
112. See Runkle v. U.S., 122 U.S. 543, 557 (1887) (as Commander in Chief he has the duty to review courts martial; requires it to be "his own judgment, and not that of another"). Compare U.S. v. Page, 137 U.S. 673, 680 (1891) (orders issued by President are presumed to be his).
113. See Morgan v. United States, 298 U.S. 468 (1936)(reversing and remanding); 304 U.S. 1 (1938) (reviewing case after remand).
114. See *Humphrey's Executor* v. United States, 295 U.S. 602 (1935) (holding for cause removal provision constitutional).
115. Elena Kagan, "Presidential Administration," 114 *Harvard Law Review* 2245 (2001); See Myers v. United States, 272 U.S. 52, 133 (1926) (heads of departments are the President's "alter ego"). Dean Kagan's view that statutory delegations to subordinates should be interpreted as channeling but not limiting presidential control has to be squared with the mixed statutory delegations where Congress clearly gives the President and his subordinates separate duties. See Kevin M. Stack, "The Statutory President," 90 *Iowa Law Review* 539 (2005).
116. See Stack, "The Statutory President" (describing the president's exercise of statutory powers); see also Kevin M. Stack, "The President's Statutory Powers to Administer the Laws," 106 *Columbia Law Review* 263 (2006) (arguing that the "President has statutory authority to direct the administration of the laws only when statutes expressly grant power to the President in name").
117. See Glendon A. Schubert, Jr., "Judicial Review of the Subdelegation of Presidential Power," 12 *Journal of Politics* 684–687 (1950) (discussing Congress's subsequent legislative approval of President Roosevelt's 1942 order interdicting Japanese Americans and citing other examples of this practice).
118. Congress had long made statutory grants of subdelegation power to the President in specific situations. In the aftermath of Panama Refining Co. v. Ryan, 293 U.S. 388 (1935), for example, Congress in the Conally Act of February 22, 1935, 49 Stat. 33 (1935) (codified at 15 U.S.C. 715j), granted the President or any agency officer or employee the power to interdict "hot

oil" under the Act. See Schubert, "Judicial Review of the Subdelegation of Presidential Power," at 682.

119. OMB, Circular A-76, Attachment A, Part B.

120. Supra note 56.

121. The Commission on Organization of the Executive Branch of the Government, *General Management of the Executive Branch* (Washington, DC: Government Printing Office, 1949). See Kenneth Culp Davis, *Administrative Law* (St. Paul, MN: West Pub. Co. 1951), pp 79–80.

122. "[T]he Government can no longer be treated as a single employer; but . . . to the extent consistent with the economy and the protection of the merit system, the individual agencies must be allowed to serve themselves as does a private employer, subject to supervision and guidance from a strong, progressive central personnel agency." The Commission on Organization of the Executive Branch of the Government, *Task Force Report on Federal Personnel* (Washington, DC: Government Printing Office, 1949), p viii.

123. See S. Rep. No. 81–1867, *reprinted in* 1950 U.S.C.C.A.N. 2931, 2932. Specifically, the Senate report stated, "The President now performs functions which have no reasonable claim upon his time or attention." Ibid., 2932. On its face, the 1950 Act related only to delegations by the President to appointed subordinates: "This bill will enable the President to direct the head of any department or agency in the Executive Branch of the Government, or any official thereof, appointed by and with the advice and consent of the Senate, to perform and exercise any function including any duty, power, responsibility, authority, or discretion vested in the President." Ibid., 2931. The language of the report made clear that the bill did not seek to proscribe any delegation power inherent in the presidency: "It does not limit any existing right of the President to delegate functions." Ibid. Under the theory of this bill, unilateral executive delegations of significant authority to contractors could only be excepted from the Subdelegation Act if such delegations were shown to be inherent, a proposition that the appointments clause itself contradicts.

124. Ibid.

125. See *U.S. Telecom,* 359 F.3d at 565 (preventing an agency delegation of power to a state agency and equating state entities with "outside parties"); see also Cudahy Packing Co. v. Holland, 315 U.S. 357, 367 (1942) (holding that Administrator of the Wage and Hour Division of the Department of Labor did not have authority to delegate his statutory power to sign and issue a subpoena duces tecum to regional director).

126. See Commission on Organization of the Executive Branch, *Task Force Report on Federal Personnel.*

127. Youngstown Steel & Tube Co. v. Sawyer, 343 U.S. 579, 646 (1952) (Jackson, J., concurring).

128. One such statute is 5 U.S.C. §301, which allows each head of department to prescribe regulations for "the general conduct of its employees." This provision has been interpreted to grant the Attorney General the power to

contract out. See Barr, *Constitutional Limits on "Contracting Out."* See also Touby v. United States, 500 U.S. 160 (1991) (upholding delegation by the Attorney General to Drug Enforcement Agency).

129. See Barr, *Constitutional Limits on "Contracting Out,"* pp 95–96 (citing *Buckley*).

130. Ibid., p 96 ("private individuals may not determine the policy of the United States"). Under the Debt Collection Act Amendments of 1986, 31 U.S.C. §3718(b), the Department of Justice must supervise and approve all the work of private counsel. In the course of this opinion, OLC also noted that the retention by the Attorney General of private counsel to assist in the collection of nontax debts owed the United States did not violate the Constitution. See ibid.

131. See *Youngstown Steel,* 343 U.S. at 646.

132. A government employee whose job is lost would be in a position to challenge the delegations under a relevant statute, such as 5 U.S.C.§301. However, the Federal Circuit, which has exclusive jurisdiction over bid protests, has not been hospitable to employee appeals. See AFGE v. U.S., 258 F.3d 1294 (Fed. Cir. 2001) (denying employee standing under relevant statutes).

133. OMB, Circular A-76, Attachment A, Part B.

134. See Chapter 3 above

135. Pub. L. No. 105–270, 112 Stat. 2382, §2(a) (1998).

136. The circular applies when a competitive challenge is permitted to a contracting out process. The vast majority of outsourcing is outside the scope of A-76 since competitive sourcing is not involved.

137. See Am. Fed'n of Gov't Employees v. Babbitt, 46 Fed.App'x 254, 256–57 (6th Cir. 2002) (per curiam) (civilian employees who lost jobs at Air Force bases lacked standing under the APA).

138. In May 2004, OMB issued a report on competitive sourcing for the prior year that indicated that agencies had completed 662 "competitive assessments" with a net estimated savings of $1.1 billion (over 3 to 5 years), or about $12,000 per FTE competed with a total cost avoidance of about 15 percent. See generally OMB, *The President's Management Agenda* (2002), pp 17–18, available at www.whitehouse.gov/omb/budget/fy2002/mgmt.pdf (discussing intention to outsource government jobs).

139. OMB Circular A-76, Attachment A, Part B, Section 1(a).

140. See Barr, *Constitutional Limits on "Contracting Out,"* p 99 n. 5 (describing A-76 as broader than *Buckley*).

141. See GAO, Commercial Activities Panel, *Improving the Sourcing Decisions of the Federal Government: Final Report* (2002), pp 19–20 (government employees prevailed in 50 percent of twenty-two challenges).

142. See James McCullough et al., "Feature Comment, Year 2003 OMB Circular A-76 Decisions and Developments," 46 *Government Contractor* (West) ¶ 27 at 259 (January 21, 2004).

143. Ibid.

144. Ibid.

145. Ibid.

146. 14 C.F.R. §108.9 (2001) (specifying airlines' security responsibilities).

147. See Paul Stephen Dempsey, "Aviation Security: The Role of Law in the War against Terrorism," 41 *Columbia Journal of Transnational Law* 649, 721 (2003).

148. See Andrew Hessick, "The Federalization of Airport Security: Privacy Implications," 24 *Whittier Law Review* 43, 46 (2002).

149. Ibid. (referring to a 1999 Department of Transportation Inspector General report).

150. See Dempsey, "Aviation Security," at 721.

151. See Aviation and Transportation Security Act, S. 1447, 107th Cong. (2001).

152. Ibid.

153. See "Bush Offers Compromise on Aviation Security Bill; It Stalls on Provision to Make All Screeners Federal Employees," *St. Louis Post-Dispatch*, October 4, 2001, at A7.

154. Airport Security Federalization Act of 2001, H.R. 3150, 107th Cong. (2001). The House bill did permit private screeners, but §3 stated that "all screeners must be supervised by uniformed federal employees of the TSA." 147 Cong. Rec. H7631-01 (November 1 2001), p 2 (remarks of Rep. Young of Alaska).

155. A *Washington Post* poll found 82 percent of Americans in favor, along with the U.S. Conference of Mayors and the entire U.S. Senate. See Hessick, "The Federalization of Airport Security: Privacy Implications," 51.

156. Aviation and Transportation Security Act (ATSA), Pub. L. No. 107-71, 115 Stat. 597 (2001) (codified as amended at 49 U.S.C.A. §114).

157. See Tara Branum and Susanna Dokupil, "Security Takeovers and Bailouts: Aviation and the Return of Big Government," 6 *Texas Review of Law and Politics* 431, 459 (2002).

158. See Hessick, "The Federalization of Airport Security: Privacy Implications," 53. The U.S. citizen requirement essentially disqualified rehiring of former airport security personnel, many of whom were immigrants. And it imposed a hiring requirement that does not even apply to the U.S. military. See Michael Hayes, "Improving Security through Reducing Employee Rights," 10 *IUS Gentium* 55, 60–61 (2004) (viewing the TSA as an anti labor bill).

159. Baggage screeners were subjected to extensive background checks by TSA, which it had difficulty implementing. See Department of Homeland Security, Office of Inspector General, *A Review of Background Checks for Federal Passenger and Baggage Screeners at Airports*, OIG 04–08 (January 2004).

160. The public employment requirement permitted five airports to opt out: San Francisco, Kansas City, Rochester, Jackson Hole, Wyoming, and Tupelo, Mississippi. See Department of Homeland Security, Transportation Security Administration (TSA), "Background on PP5 Airports," www.tsa.gov/what _we_do/optout/editorial_1719.shtm (accessed 11/27/06).

161. Branum and Dokupil, "Security Takeovers and Bailouts," 461.

162. See Aviation Security Act, S. 1447, 107th Cong. (2001).

163. See Airport Security Federalization Act of 2001, H.R. 3150.

164. See Press Release, White House Office of Communications, Congressional Debate on Federalizing Airport Security Personnel (November 6, 2001), available at www.whitehouse.gov/news/releases/2001/11/20011106-8 .html ("the best system is a mix of public and private screeners, so long as the federal government plays a very vigorous role in enforcing standards and setting much higher standards").

165. See supra note 135.

166. See National Public Radio (NPR), "Federalizing Airport Security Personnel," *Talk of the Nation* (October 25, 2001), 2001 WLNR 11940177 (Senator McCain justifies full federal employment under the TSA by the President's right to fire the federal employees at will).

167. See Hayes, "Improving Security," at 61.

168. See Paul R. Verkuil, "Public Law Limitations on Privatization of Governmental Functions," 84 *North Carolina Law Review* 397, 428–431 (2006) (discussing the historical importance of oath requirements). A third symbolic requirement, U.S. citizenship, was also added. See supra note 155.

169. The Administration initially sought to counter the full public employment requirement by referring to the use of private contractors at European airports. See NPR, "Federalizing Airport Security Personnel" (comments by Representative Roy Blunt (R-MO)).

170. Ibid.

171. See Clifford J. Rosky, "Force, Inc.: The Privatization of Punishment, Policing, and Military Force in Liberal States," 36 *Connecticut Law Review* 879, 979–981 (2004) (connecting the problem of loyalty to the choice between the public and the private use of force).

172. Indeed, in the private opt-out program which is part of the Act, qualified private screening companies are defined as those that employ the same contractual requirements for screeners as are applied to public employees. See 49 U.S.C.A. §§44919–44920. Qualified companies must also be owned and controlled by U.S. citizens. Ibid., §44920(d)(2).

173. See generally Rosky, "Force Inc.," (describing the private use of force and comparing it to public use, including airport security).

174. See "George W. Bush Signs the Aviation Security Bill," Federal Document Clearing House (November 19, 2001), 2001 WL 1458372.

175. See text accompanying note 139 supra.

176. The TSA employees do not always meet expectations. See "El Al Asks U.S. to Let It Do Extra Screenings at Newark," *New York Times,* May 12, 2006, at B2 (Israeli airline El Al inspectors received permission from TSA to do a second screening of baggage entering its planes).

177. OMB, Circular A-76, at A-2. See ibid., Part IV.B. See also Verkuil, "Public Law Limitations," 436–439 (describing OMB's A-76 process in detail).

178. This decision is close to what the House bill imposed. See Airport Security Federalization Act, H.R. 3150.
179. We cannot discount the consequences of September 11 on the public's opinion of public servants. In New York City, for example, police and fire officials have enjoyed the unlikely status of heroes. See National Commission on Terrorist Attacks upon the United States, *The 9/11 Commission Report* (Washington, DC: Government Printing Office, 2004), §9, "Heroism and Horror."
180. John D. Donahue, *The Privatization Decision: Public Ends, Private Means* (New York: Basic Books, 1989) at 12.
181. See supra note 166.
182. See Mark Freedland, "Law, Public Services, and Citizenship—New Domains, New Regimes?" in Mark Freedland and Silvana Sciarra, eds., *Public Services and Citizenship in European Law* (Oxford: Clarendon Press, 1998), pp 2–10 (describing the privatization and third way (public/private) movements in Europe).
183. See European Parliament and Council Regulation (EC) 2320/2002 establishing Common Rules in the Field of Civil Aviation Security, 2002 O.J. (L 355) 1–21.(Dec. 16, 2002).
184. See ibid., arts. 7–9.
185. See Emanuel Metz, "Government Perspective: Simplification of the Public Administration. The 'Lean State' as a Long-Term Task," 4 *Columbia Journal of European Law* 647, 651–654 (1998) (describing the role of privatization in Germany's Lean State program).
186. Ibid. These requirements also apply to a variety of other privatized activities, such as motor vehicle inspections, individual safety inspections, and traffic control. See Freedland and Sciarra, *Public Services and Citizenship*.
187. See OMB, Circular A-76, at A-2.
188. See generally Freeman, "Extending Public Law Norms."
189. Of course, in the United States, inherent government functions may not be delegated to private contractors, whereas EU law would seem to permit jobs designated as public service to be delegated to private contractors if the member state prefers.
190. It does not, for example, involve the search or restraint of passengers; that function is still performed by public officials.
191. Indeed, Congress did approve of private inspectors at five airports. See TSA, "Background on PP5 Airports."
192. Searches are intrusive and privacy-depriving. We ordinarily expect police officials to do searches and seizures. But they do so in criminal contexts, whereas most airport searches do not occur in such contexts. Nevertheless, when drugs are found during an airport search, it can become a criminal matter. See, e.g., United States v. Ramsey, 81 Fed. App'x 547 (6th Cir. 2003).
193. See TSA, "Background on PP5 Airports."
194. See Williamson, "Public and Private Bureaucracies," at 308–326.

195. See Verkuil, "Public Law Limitations," at 439 n. 233 (discussing study of comparative performance at airports including opt outs and finding no discernible differences in inspection quality).
196. See Freedland and Sciarra, *Public Services and Citizenship;* Regulation (EC) No. 2320/2002; Metz, "Government Perspective."
197. Donahue, *The Privatization Decision,* 79–81 (limiting private solutions to those that can be effectively contracted for and describing the need for accountability by public officials).
198. Ibid., 38.
199. Donahue describes accountability as "fidelity to the public's values." Efficiency is defined so as to incorporate these values. Ibid., 12. Donahue's premise is that privatization decisions are not made simply by comparing private and public forms' behavior, but by recognizing that "[p]ublic tasks are different, and mostly harder." Ibid., 215.
200. See Verkuil, "Public Law Limitations"; Metzger, "Privatization as Delegation," 103 (requiring procedures to accompany private delegations).
201. See Donahue, *The Privatization Decision,* 78 ("[A] well specified contract in a competitive context can enforce accountability . . .").
202. Leslie Green, "The Duty to Govern," 13 *Legal Theory* 166.

13. Public Values/Private Contract

For an extended version of the argument presented here, see Laura A. Dickinson, "Public Law Values in a Privatized World," 31 *Yale Journal of International Law* 384 (2006).

1. A recent symposium in the *Harvard Law Review* sums up the state of the debate. See Symposium, "Public Values in an Era of Privatization," 116 *Harvard Law Review* 1211 (2003).
2. See, e.g., Thomas G. Weiss, ed., *Beyond U.N. Subcontracting: Task-Sharing with Regional Security Arrangements and Service-Providing NGOs* (New York: St. Martin's Press, 1998); Ian Smillie, "At Sea in a Sieve? Trends and Issues in the Relationship between Northern NGOs and Northern Governments," in Ian Smillie and Henny Helmich, eds., *Stakeholders: Government-NGO Partnerships for International Development* (London: Earthscan Publications, 1999), p 7.
3. See, e.g., James L. Taulbee and Marion V. Creekmore, "NGO Mediation: The Carter Center," in Henry F. Carey and Oliver P. Richmond, eds., *Mitigating Conflict: The Role of NGOs* (Portland, OR: F. Cass, 2003), p 156.
4. To be sure, as I have argued elsewhere—see Laura A. Dickinson, "Government for Hire: Privatizing Foreign Affairs and the Problem of Accountability under International Law," 47 *William and Mary Law Review* 135 (2005)— these gaps may not be as significant as they first appear. To begin with, the baseline of accountability for state actors performing foreign affairs functions is not that great. Such actors are not held accountable for violating the norms that effectuate public law values very often. After all, international law has often been criticized for having relatively weak enforcement mechanisms.

See, e.g., Louis Henkin, "Politics of Law-Making," in Charlotte Ku and Paul F. Diehl, eds., *International Law: Classic and Contemporary Readings* (Boulder, CO: L. Rienner Publishers, 1998), pp 18–20. And while this fact may not be cause for celebration, it does serve to remind us that the shift to private actors does not represent a dramatic decline in accountability—certainly not as great a decline as in the domestic setting, where state actors are more often held accountable for failing to uphold public law values. In addition, alternative avenues of legal accountability may exist under private law. As in the domestic privatization context, immunities applicable to governmental employees arguably do not apply, thereby opening up potential private law actions such as tort claims. Thus, in some ways private contractors may face a greater risk of legal liability than governmental actors.

5. See Megan A. Kinsey, Note, "Transparency in Government Procurement: An International Consensus?" 34 *Public Contract Law Journal* 161–162 (2004).

6. 5 U.S.C. §552(b)(c)(1) (2000).

7. 5 U.S.C. §552(b)(c)(4) (2000).

8. See Maud Beelman, *Winning Contractors: U.S. Contractors Reap the Windfalls of Post-war Reconstruction* (October 30, 2003), Center for Public Integrity, http://www.publicintegrity.org/Content.aspx?src=search&context=article&id=65.

9. For example, I have spoken with several State Department and Defense Department employees who have expressed support for contractual reforms of the sort I propose here and have themselves been lobbying for such reforms within their organizations in recent years.

10. See International Peace Operations Association (IPOA), "Code of Conduct," http://ipoaonline.org/php/index.php?option=com_content&task=view&id=205&Itemid=172 (viewed June 9, 2008).

11. See, e.g., Jody Freeman, "Extending Public Law Norms through Privatization," 116 *Harvard Law Review* 1285, 1300 (2003).

12. Jody Freeman, "The Private Role in Public Governance," 75 *New York University Law Review* 543, 634 (2000).

13. Ibid., 635.

14. Ibid., 636.

15. See, e.g., Sylvie Junod, "Additional Protocol II: History and Scope," 33 *American University Law Review* 29, 30–33 (1983) (discussing guerrillas and insurgents); Math Noortman, "Non-State Actors in International Law," in Bas Arts et al., eds., *Non-State Actors in International Relations* (Burlington, VT: Ashgate, 2001), pp 71–72 (discussing NGOs); Steven R. Ratner, "Corporations and Human Rights: A Theory of Legal Responsibility," 111 *Yale Law Journal* 443, 524–530 (2001) (discussing corporations).

16. See, e.g., Allison Marston Danner and Jenny S. Martinez, "Guilty Associations: Joint Criminal Enterprise, Command Responsibility, and the Development of International Criminal Law," 93 *California Law Review* 75 (2005).

17. Ratner, "Corporations and Human Rights," 531–534; David Kinley and Junko Tadaki, "From Talk to Walk: The Emergence of Human Rights

Responsibilities for Corporations at International Law," 44 *Virginia Journal of International Law* 952 (2004).

18. Leon Gordenker and Thomas G. Weiss, "Pluralizing Global Governance: Analytical Approaches and Dimensions," in Leon Gordenker and Thomas G. Weiss, eds., *NGOs, the U.N., and Global Governance* (Boulder, CO: Lynne Rienner, 1996), pp 40–43.

19. See Dinah Shelton, ed., *Commitment and Compliance: The Role of Non-Binding Norms in the International Legal System* (New York: Oxford University Press, 2000).

20. See, e.g., Anne-Marie Slaughter, *A New World Order* (Princeton, NJ: Princeton University Press, 2004).

21. For example, under the model contract for private prison management drafted by the Oklahoma Department of Corrections, contractors must comply with constitutional, federal, state, and private standards, including those established by the American Correctional Association. See Oklahoma Department of Corrections, Correctional Services Contract, art. 1, www.doc.state.ok.us/Private%20Prisons/98cnta.pdf [hereinafter "Oklahoma Contract"]. Other states' contracts with companies that manage private prisons contain similar provisions. See, e.g., Florida Correctional Privatization Commission, Correctional Services Contract with Corrections Corporation of America, §5.1 [hereinafter "Florida Contract"]; Freeman, "Private Role," 634 (citing Texas Department of Criminal Justice model contract); see also J. Michael Keating, Jr., "Public over Private: Monitoring the Performance of Privately Operated Prisons and Jails," in Douglas C. MacDonald, ed., *Private Prisons and the Public Interest* (New Brunswick, NJ: Rutgers University Press, 1990), pp 138–141.

22. See Freeman, "Private Role," 608 (discussing contractual hearing and oversight mechanisms in the nursing home context).

23. Department of Defense Instruction No. 3020.41, §6.1 (October 3, 2005).

24. Center for Public Integrity, "Contracts and Reports" (providing text of contracts), www.publicintegrity.org (accessed 8/18/05).

25. See Agreement between the Department of the Interior and CACI Premier Technology, Inc., No. NBCHA010005 (2000) [hereinafter "DOI-CACI"].

26. Work Orders Nos. 000035D004, 000036D004, 000037D004, 000038D0004, 000064D004, 000067D004, 000070D004, 000071D004, 000072D004, 000073D004, & 000080D004, issued under DOI-CACI, www.publicintegrity.org/docs/wow/CACI_ordersAll.pdf.

27. Work Order No. 000071/0001, issued under DOI-CACI.

28. See, e.g., OECD Convention on Combating Bribery of Foreign Public Officials in International Business Transactions, art. 1, Dec. 18, 1997, 37 I.L.M. 1; False Claims Act, 31 U.S.C. §3729 (2000).

29. See, e.g., Oklahoma Contract, §6.4; Florida Contract, §6.5; Freeman, "Private Role," 634 (describing model contract for private prison management drafted by the Texas Department of Criminal Justice).

30. Department of Defense Instruction No. 3020.41, §6.3.5.3.4.

31. See, e.g., Work Order No. 000071/0001 issued under DOI-CACI, statement of work (requiring that human intelligence advisor must have at least "10 years of experience" and must be "knowledgeable of Army/Joint Interrogation procedures"). Notably, this work order does not require the contractor to provide any training. See ibid.

32. See Agreement between USDOD and Chugach McKinley, Inc., Professional Skills, No. DASW01-03-D-0025 (2003), www.publicintegrity.org/docs/wow/ChugachMcKinley-Iraq.pdf.

33. See DOI-CACI.

34. Department of the Army, Inspector General, *Detainee Operations Inspection* (2004), pp 87–89, www4.army.mil/ocpa/reports/ArmyIGDetaineeAbuse/DAIG%20Detainee%20Operations%20Inspection%20Report.pdf.

35. Out of 145 countries (with 145 as the worst), Iraq ranks 129th. Transparency International Corruption Perceptions Index 2004, www.transparency.org/news_room/latest_news/press_releases/2004/2004_10_20_cpi2004.

36. See Senate Democratic Policy Committee (SPDC), *An Oversight Hearing on Waste, Fraud, and Abuse in U.S. Government Contracting in Iraq,* 109th Cong., 1st sess., Feb. 14, 2005, p 4 [hereinafter SPDC, *Oversight Hearing*].

37. Ibid., 1–2 (statement of Alan Grayson).

38. Ibid., 2 (statement of Alan Grayson). These allegations resulted in a private enforcement suit under the federal False Claims Act, 31 U.S.C. §3730 (2000). See Yochai J. Dreazen, "Contractor Admits Bribing a U.S. Official in Iraq; Lawyer Uses Civil War-Era Law to Go after Firms for Corruption, but Administration Won't Help," *Wall Street Journal,* April 19, 2006, at B1. Indeed, in March 2006 a jury ordered Custer Battles to return $10 million in ill-gotten funds to the government. See ibid. Yet, though the district court judge in that case had permitted the suit to proceed, United States ex rel. DRC, Inc. v. Custer Battles, LLC, 376 F. Supp. 2d 617 (E.D. Va. 2005), it is unclear whether the verdict will ultimately hold up on appeal and whether such False Claims Act suits will be deemed sustainable in this context.

39. Freeman, "Private Role," 608–609.

40. See Department of Health and Human Services, Office of Inspector General, *The External Review of Hospital Quality: A Call for Greater Accountability* (1999), pp 1–2, oig.hhs.gov/oei/reports/oei-01-97-00050.pdf; see also Department of Health and Human Services, Office of Inspector General, *The External Review of Hospital Quality: The Role of Accreditation* (1999), pp 6–7, oig.hhs.gov/oei/reports/oei-01-97-00051.pdf (detailing lack of accountability and quality oversight in accredited hospitals).

41. See, e.g., Department of Health and Human Services, *Nursing Home Compare,* www.medicare.gov/NHCompare/Home.asp (database includes information on nursing homes certified by Medicare or Medicaid).

42. See Eleanor D. Kinney, "Private Accreditation as a Substitute for Direct Government Regulation in Public Health Insurance Programs: When Is It Appropriate?," 57 *Law and Contemporary Problems* 52 (1994).

43. Inspector general oversight arises from the Inspector General (IG) Act, codified as amended at 5 U.S.C. app. 3, §§1–12 (1994). "The IG Act authorized the creation of offices whose mission is to detect and prevent fraud, waste, and abuse in their respective departments and agencies across the executive branch." Michael R. Bromwich, "Running Special Investigations: The Inspector General Model," 86 *Georgetown Law Journal* 2027 (1998). For an analysis of the role that inspectors general play in various agencies, see ibid.

44. See U.S. Agency for International Development, Office of Inspector General, *Semiannual Report* (2004), p 13, www.usaid.gov/oig/public/semiann/sarc0409.pdf.

45. After a scandal, however, such as the uproar surrounding revelations of abuse at Abu Ghraib prison, ombudspersons may be enlisted to investigate such problems.

46. A model for this type of oversight might be the role that the International Committee on the Red Cross (ICRC) currently plays in monitoring the conduct of governmental actors during armed conflict. The Geneva Conventions require states parties to allow ICRC representatives to visit military detention centers to ensure that detainees are treated in accord with the principles of international human rights and humanitarian law. Geneva Convention Relative to the Treatment of Prisoners of War art. 126, Aug. 12, 1949, 6 U.S.T. 3316, 75 U.N.T.S 135; Geneva Convention Relative to the Protection of Civilian Persons in Time of War, Aug. 12, 1949, 6 U.S.T. 3516, 75 U.N.T.S. 287. Yet it is at best ambiguous whether the ICRC would be empowered to play a similar role with respect to private security contractors. The contracts could make this role explicit.

47. In practice, one way these requirements are avoided is through the use of blanket purchase order agreements, in which task orders can be issued under preexisting contracts. See Beelman, *Winning Contractors*. For criticism of the lack of open bidding on the Iraq contracts, see Center for Responsive Politics, *Rebuilding Iraq—The Contractors*, www.opensecrets.org/news/rebuilding_iraq/index.asp. For an opposing view, see Jeffrey Marburg-Goodman, "USAID's Procurement Contracts: Insider's View," 39 *Procurement Law* 10 (2003).

48. Federal Acquisition Regulation (FAR), Parts 16.301–16.307 {2006} Code Fed. Reg. 48.

49. Under the cost-plus system, companies have an incentive to inflate the costs of services so that their fee, typically measured as a percentage of this cost, is as high as possible, see Laura Peterson, Center for Public Integrity, "Outsourcing Government: Service Contracting Has Risen Dramatically in the Last Decade" (October 30, 2003), www.publicintegrity.org, although such contracts do contain a cost ceiling that cannot be exceeded without the contracting officer's approval. Part 16.301–1 (2005) Code Fed. Reg. 48. Under the FAR, these contracts can only be utilized when costs cannot be estimated with sufficient accuracy. Ibid., Part 16.301–2.

50. For a searing indictment of the government's failure to oversee military contractors and that failure's role in the Abu Ghraib atrocities, see Steven L.

Schooner, "Contractor Atrocities at Abu Ghraib: Compromised Accountability in a Streamlined, Outsourced Government," 16 *Stanford Law and Policy Review* 549 (2005).

51. See U.S. Agency for International Development, "Assistance for Iraq: Acquisition and Assistance Activities," www.usaid.gov/iraq/activities.html (accessed 11/27/06).

52. See Shane Harris, "AID Plans to Contract Out Oversight of Iraq Contracts," *GovExec.com,* May 20, 2003, www.govexec.com/dailyfed/0503/052003h1.htm.

53. See ibid.

54. U.S. Department of Defense, Office of the Inspector General, *Acquisition: Contracts Awarded for the Coalition Provisional Authority by the Defense Contracting Command-Washington,* Rep. No. D-2004-057 (2004), p 24, www.dodig.mil/audit/reports/fy04/04-057.pdf.

55. U.S. General Accounting Office, Comptroller General, *Sourcing and Acquisition,* Rep. No. GAO-03-771R (2003), p 1; see also Peterson, "Outsourcing Government." For a detailed discussion of the depletion of the acquisition workforce, see David A. Whiteford, "Negotiated Procurements: Squandering the Benefit of the Bargain," 32 *Public Contract Law Journal* 555–557 (2003).

56. See P.W. Singer, *Corporate Warriors: The Rise of the Privatized Military Industry* (Ithaca, NY: Cornell University Press, 2003), pp 123–124.

57. Ed Harriman, "Where Has All the Money Gone?," 27 *London Review of Books* 4–5 (2005)

58. SDPC, *Oversight Hearing,* 4.

59. See text accompanying note 36 on SDPC, *Oversight Hearing* and the statement by Alan Grayson at the hearing, at p 4.

60. See generally SDPC, *Oversight Hearing,* 10 (statement of Franklin Willis) Of course, the lack of oversight may have a more cynical explanation: it permits private contractors (who may have powerful connections within government) to reap profits without significant constraints.

61. The DOD has taken more and more control over reconstruction and emergency relief functions, normally the province of USAID. See Center for Public Integrity, "Contracts and Reports." The State Department, meanwhile, manages the contract with DynCorp to provide Iraqi police training. Ibid. And the State Department's Bureau of Population, Refugees, and Migration (PRM) manages refugee assistance funds.

62. Beelman, *Winning Contractors.*

63. Schooner, "Contractor Atrocities at Abu Ghraib," 564–570.

64. Ibid.

65. See, e.g., Harry P. Hatry, *Performance Measurement: Getting Results* (Washington, DC: Urban Institute Press, 1999), pp 3–10.

66. William D. Eggers, "Performance-Based Contracting: Designing State-of-the-Art Contract Administration and Monitoring Systems," *Reason Public Policy Institute: How-To Guide,* no. 17, (Los Angeles: Reason Public Policy Institute, 1997), p 5, reason.org/htg17.pdf.

67. See, e.g., Oklahoma Contract, §5.

68. Ibid., §§6.3–6.4.

69. See Freeman, "Private Role," 634–635 (describing contract between private corporation and state of Texas).

70. See Performance Standards Home, "Performance-Based Standards for Juvenile Correction and Detention Facilities," www.pbstandards.org; see also Geoffrey F. Segal and Adrian T. Moore, "Weighing the Watchmen: Evaluating the Costs and Benefits of Outsourcing Correctional Services," Reason Foundation Policy Study 290, http://www.reason.org/ps290.pdf, at 15–16 (2002).

71. "A Tale of Two Systems: Cost, Quality, and Accountability in Private Prisons," 115 *Harvard Law Review* 1889–1890 (2002).

72. 42 U.S.C. §604a(a)(1)(A) (2000).

73. See Pamela Winston et al., *Privatization of Welfare Services: A Review of the Literature* (2002), pp 3–6, aspe.hhs.gov/hsp/privatization02/report.pdf (discussing increase in private welfare providers).

74. See M. Bryna Sanger, *The Welfare Marketplace: Privatization and Welfare Reform* (Washington, DC: Brookings Institution Press, 2003), pp 28–48 (discussing issues raised by performance contracting for welfare services); Sheena McConnell et al., *Privatization in Practice: Case Studies of Contracting for TANF Case Management* (2003), pp 39–51, www.mathematica-mpr.com/PDFs/privatize.pdf (discussing use of performance measures in welfare contracts).

75. See Gillian Metzger, "Privatization as Delegation," 103 *Columbia Law Review* 1387–1388 (2003).

76. See, e.g., SDPC, *Oversight Hearing*, 3–4 (prepared statement of Franklin Willis).

77. For example, the CACI agreement was an ID/IQ contract. Compare Schooner, "Contractor Atrocities at Abu Ghraib," 569 (using the "Abu Ghraib experience" as an illustration of the dangers of ID/IQ contracts).

78. ID/IQ contracts are governed by Part 16.500–6 {2005} Code Fed. Reg. 48. For a discussion of ID/IQ contracts, see Karen DaPonte Thornton, "Fine-Tuning Acquisition Reform's Favorite Procurement Vehicle, the Indefinite Delivery Contract," 31 *Public Contract Law Journal* 383 (2002).

79. See Part 16.504 {2005} Code Fed. Reg. 48; Schooner, "Contractor Atrocities at Abu Ghraib," 565.

80. See Thornton, "Fine-Tuning," 387.

81. See, e.g., Schooner, "Contractor Atrocities at Abu Ghraib," 563.

82. Agreement between DOD and MPRI, Iraq Interpreters, No. GS-23F-9814H (April 28, 2003), www.publicintegrity.org/docs/wow/MPRI_Linguists.pdf.

83. Ibid.

84. Work Order No. 000071D004 issued under DOI-CACI, p 6.

85. See, e.g., Judith Tendler, "Turning Private Voluntary Organizations into Development Agencies: Questions for Evaluation" (127.49 AIG Program Evaluation Discussion Paper No. 12, 1982) (making recommendations regarding USAID's evaluation process for contracted projects).

86. See Agreement between USAID and Bechtel National, Inc., Iraq Infrastructure Reconstruction—Phase II, No. SPU-C-00-04-00001-00 (January 4, 2004), www.usaid.gov/iraq/contracts/iirii.html; Agreement between USAID and Bearing Point Inc., Economic Recovery, Reform, and Sustained Growth, No. RAN-C-00-03-00043-00 (July 25, 2003), www.usaid.gov/iraq/contracts/errsgi.html; Agreement between USAID and Skylink Air and Logistic Support (USA), Inc., Airport Administration, No. DFD-C-00-03-00026-00 (May 5, 2003), www.usaid.gov/iraq/contracts/aa.html; Agreement between USAID and Abt Associates, Inc., Public Health, No. RAN-C-00-03-0001-00 (April 30, 2003), www.usaid.gov/iraq/contracts/ph.html; Agreement between USAID and Bechtel, Inc., Capital Construction, No. EEE-C-00-03-00018-00 (April 17, 2003), www.usaid.gov/iraq/contracts/cc.html; Agreement between USAID and Creative Associates International, Inc., Primary and Secondary Education, No. EDG-C-00-03-00011-00 (April 11, 2003), www.usaid.gov/iraq/contracts/pse.html; Agreement between USAID and Research Triangle Institute, Local Governance, No. EDG-C-00-03-00010-00 (April 11, 2003), www.usaid.gov/iraq/contracts/lg.html.

87. See, e.g., Nestor Davidson, "Relational Contracts in the Privatization of Social Welfare: The Case of Housing," 24 *Yale Law and Policy Review* 264 (2006) (arguing for a "relational" approach to contracting that "shifts the locus of efficiency and accountability efforts from contractual specificity and enforcement to encouraging flexibility and fostering mutual responsibility for program goals"); Metzger, "Privatization as Delegation," 1388 ("[T]he operational flexibility of private providers can make them better able to improve staff performance and tailor their programs to meet the needs of particular participants of employers"); Martha Minow, "Public and Private Partnerships: Accounting for the New Religion," 116 *Harvard Law Review* 1262 (2003) ("Rigid standards could force private providers to behave like government and lose their potential for innovation, efficiency, and flexibility.").

88. See Eggers, "Performance-Based Contracting," 2.

89. See Sanger, *Welfare Marketplace*, 21–22, 42–43, 68–69, 104–106.

90. See generally Michael Power, *The Audit Society: Rituals of Verification* (New York: Oxford University Press, 1997).

91. See Smillie, "At Sea in a Sieve?" 10.

92. Ibid., 10–11.

93. See Kinney, "Private Accreditation," 52.

94. Although NCQA's accreditation program is voluntary, almost half the HMOs in the nation, covering three-quarters of all HMO enrollees, are currently involved in the NCQA accreditation process. Significantly, employers increasingly require or request NCQA accreditation of the plans with which they do business. See National Committee for Quality Assurance (NCQA): Overview, www.ncqa.org/Communications/Publications/overviewncqa.pdf (accessed 3/30/06).

95. Freeman, "Private Role," 618–619.
96. See, e.g., Oklahoma Contract; Freeman, "Private Role," 634 (describing model contract for private prison management drafted by the Texas Department of Criminal Justice that contains such a requirement).
97. See Freeman, "Private Role," 628–629. Freeman notes that, "throughout its history, the ACA has fostered professionalism in prison administration through the development of standards and promoted progressive reforms such as rehabilitation." Ibid.
98. See, e.g., Florida Contract, §5.21 (requiring prison to maintain accreditation); Oklahoma Contract, §5.2.
99. See Malcolm M. Feeley and Edward L. Rubin, *Judicial Policy Making and the Modern State: How the Courts Reformed America's Prisons* (New York: Cambridge University Press, 1998), pp 162–164.
100. Freeman, "Private Role," 629.
101. See Isabel V. Sawhill and Shannon L. Smith, "Vouchers for Elementary and Secondary Education," in C. Eugene Steuerle et al., eds., *Vouchers and the Provision of Public Services* (Washington, DC: Brookings Institution Press, 2000), p 263.
102. See "Accreditation: What Does It Mean?" *Parent Power!* December 2000, pp 2–3, www.edreform.com/_upload/00dec.pdf#ppArt75.
103. Stephen D. Sugarman and Emlei M. Kuboyama, "Approving Charter Schools: The Gate-Keeper Function," 53 *Administrative Law Review* 937 (2001).
104. As Freeman observes, in the prison context, "the ACA, rather than government agencies, may effectively establish correctional standards." Freeman, "Private Role," 629. Other private organizations—such as the American Medical Association, the National Sheriffs' Association, the American Public Health Association, and the National Fire Protection Association, all of which have published guidelines or standards governing "such things as medical care, sanitation, and safety in prisons"—play a similar role. Ibid. In the health care context, the Joint Commission on Healthcare and Accreditation also develops industry standards, through "a committee that includes representatives of professional and industry groups, as well as government representatives" from the Health Care Financing Administration. Ibid., 610–612.
105. Ibid., pp 612–613; see also Kinney, "Private Accreditation," 65.
106. Because ACA officials are generally chosen from the ranks of experienced corrections officials, for example, "personal and professional relationships between ACA overseers and prison management are not uncommon, creating a common sympathy and sense of purpose that tells against both more meaningful standards and more rigorous enforcement." Sharon Dolovich, "State Punishment and Private Prisons," 55 *Duke Law Journal* 492 (2005). Moreover, Dolovich argues that because the institutions pay for accreditation, thereby "providing income on which the ACA is dependent for its survival. a degree of capture is likely." Ibid.

107. Ibid., 490–491 (acknowledging benefits of ACA accreditation of prisons); Kinney, "Private Accreditation," 65 (acknowledging benefits of JCAHO accreditation of hospitals).

108. To be sure, the FAR does require the evaluation of all contracts in excess of $1,000,000, Part 42.1502 {2006} Code Fed. Reg. 48, and also requires contract officers to take into account the past performance of contractors in all competitively negotiated acquisitions expected to exceed $1,000,000. Part 15.304(c)(3) {2006} Code Fed. Reg. 48. Thus, in theory, an internal "blacklist" of rogue contractors could be created to guard against repeat abuses. But such an internal system hardly substitutes for independent accreditation.

109. See, e.g., "What is the Global Compact" (program, launched by United Nations Secretary-General Kofi Annan, to encourage corporations to agree voluntarily to respect nine principles, including the protection of human rights and the environment), www.unglobalcompact.org/abouttheGC/index.html (accessed 5/17/05); David Stout, "Oil and Mining Leaders Agree To Protect Rights in Remote Areas," New York Times, December 21, 2000, at A9 (describing agreement among oil and mining companies, the British and U.S. governments, and human rights organizations, providing that companies will voluntarily comply with human rights standards).

110. See the Sphere Project, Humanitarian Charter and Minimum Standards in Disaster Response, http://www.sphereproject.org/handbook/hdbkpdf/hdbk_hc.pdf (accessed 11/27/06).

111. See IPOA, "Code of Conduct."

112. Amnesty International has recently begun to take steps in this direction, by making military privatization a centerpiece of its annual report for 2006 and calling for reforms. See Amnesty International, 2006 Annual Report, www.amnestyusa.org/annualreport/2006/overview.html. However, to date neither Amnesty nor any other NGO has undertaken a comprehensive rating or accreditation program.

113. See work orders issued under DOI-CACI.

114. See Agreement between U.S. Department of State and Dyncorp, Iraq Law Enforcement, No. SLMAQM-03-C-0028 (April 18, 2003), www.publicintegrity.org/docs/wow/DynCorp.pdf.

115. See Barry Yeoman, "Need an Army? Just Pick Up the Phone," New York Times, April 2, 2004, at A19.

116. See the Sphere Project. Although Sphere itself is a project of the not-for-profit sector, see www.sphereproject.org (listing representatives of not-for-profits and governments as board members), nothing prevents contracting agencies from also requiring for-profit entities to follow Sphere guidelines in fulfilling contracts.

117. See Freeman, "Private Role," 634–635 (describing contract between private corporation and Texas Department of Criminal Justice).

118. See, e.g., NCQA, "What Does NCQA Review When It Accredits an HMO?", www.ncqa.org/Programs/Accreditation/mco/mcostdsoverview.htm (accessed 3/29/06).

119. See Center for Public Integrity, "Contracts and Reports."
120. Freeman, "Private Role," 608.
121. "A Tale of Two Systems," 1888; see also Alphonse Gerhardstein, "Private Prison Litigation: The 'Youngstown' Case and Theories of Liability," 36 *Criminal Law Bulletin* 198 (2000).
122. See CACI, "CACI in Iraq: Frequently Asked Questions," www.caci.com/iraq_faqs.shtml (accessed 5/21/05); CACI, "CACI Says the Fay Report Clearly Shifts Focus of Blame Away from Its Employee Named in a Previous Report," news release, August 26, 2004, www.caci.com/about/news/news2004/08_26_04_NR.html..
123. See CACI, "CACI in Iraq: Frequently Asked Questions."
124. Jody Freeman, for example, has suggested that, in order to protect public law values, "perhaps interested individuals, or representative groups should be entitled to participate in contract negotiation." Freeman, "Private Role," 668.
125. Alfred C. Aman, Jr., *The Democracy Deficit: Taming Globalization through Law Reform* (New York: New York University Press, 2004), p 155.
126. See ibid., 155–156 (critiquing a number of state privatization statutes for failing to provide adequate provisions for public participation in the design of contracts).
127. See Freeman, "Private Role," 624–625.
128. Mont. Code Ann. §2–8–302 (2005).
129. For a discussion of such provisions, see Aman, *Democracy Deficit,* 154–156.
130. See, e.g., Jonathan Turley, "The Military Pocket Republic," 97 *Northwestern University Law Review* 72 (2002) ("This layer of agencies creates obvious problems for theories of democracy that emphasize the ability of citizens to influence their government through participatory action or deliberative process."). But see Mark Seidenfeld, "A Civic Republican Justification for the Bureaucratic State," 105 *Harvard Law Review* 1542 (1992) (arguing that agencies, because they fall between the extremes of a "politically over-responsive Congress and the over-insulated courts," may be best situated to institute a civic republican model of policymaking).
131. See generally Tania Kaiser, "Participation or Consultation? Reflections on a 'Beneficiary Based' Evaluation of UNHCR's Programme for Sierra Leonean and Liberian Refugees in Guinea, June–July 2000," 17 *Journal of Refugee Studies* 186 (2004) (discussing ways to facilitate measuring the impact of aid programs).
132. See ibid.
133. See ibid.
134. See Laura A. Dickinson, "Privatization and Public Participation in Foreign Affairs," 34 Social Justice (2007).
135. See, e.g., Freeman, "Private Role," 1317.
136. For example, §313(2) of the Restatement (Second) of Contracts provides, "[A] promisor who contracts with a government or governmental agency

to do an act for or render a service to the public is not subject to contractual liability to a member of the public for consequential damages resulting from performance or failure to perform unless (a) the terms of the promise provide for such liability; or (b) the promisee is subject to liability to the member of the public for the damages and a direct action against the promisor is consistent with the terms of the contract and with the policy of the law authorizing the contract and prescribing remedies for its breach." *Restatement (Second) of Contracts* §313(2) (St. Paul, MN: American Law Institute Publishers, 1981). For further discussion of third-party beneficiary suits involving government contracts, see Melvin Aron Eisenberg, "Third-Party Beneficiaries," 92 *Columbia Law Review* 1406 (1992).

137. See Metzger, "Privatization as Delegation," 1494.

138. For examples of contracts with private operators that require grievance procedures, see Florida Contract §5.24; Oklahoma Contract, §5.15; Freeman, "Private Role," 142 (describing a similar prison privatization contract in Texas.

139. 42 U.S.C. §1395mm(c)(5)(A) (2000).

140. Such experiments might focus, at least initially, on those contracts deemed most vulnerable to serious abuses.

141. See Lori Udall, "The World Bank and Public Accountability: Has Anything Changed?" in Jonathan A. Fox and L. David Brown, eds., *The Struggle for Accountability: The World Bank, NGOs, and Grassroots Movements* (Cambridge, MA: MIT Press, 1998), pp 392–393.

142. 5 U.S.C. §2302 (1989). While it is true that such employees could bring a *qui tam* action for fraud, 31 U.S.C. §3730(b)(1), (c), (d), (h) (2000), such a suit would do nothing to protect the employee from being fired.

143. 31 U.S.C. §3730(h).

144. 31 U.S.C. §3730(c).

145. See, e.g., Jack M. Sabatino, "Privatization and Punitives: Should Government Contractors Share the Sovereign's Immunities from Exemplary Damages?" 58 *Ohio State Law Journal* 191 (1997) (expressing concern that litigation and administrative costs could "siphon away public resources that could have been devoted to, among other things, the effective implementation and oversight of the contractors' work").

146. See Metzger, "Privatization as Delegation," 1404–1405.

147. See, e.g., William E. Kovacic, "The Civil False Claims Act as a Deterrent to Participation in Government Procurement Markets," 6 *Supreme Court Economic Review* 205 (1998) (reporting contractors' concerns that the specter of *qui tam* suits is "a costly, substantial burden of doing business with the government").

148. See Stephen L. Schooner, "Fear of Oversight: The Fundamental Failure of Businesslike Government," 50 *American University Law Review* 668 (2001).

149. Indeed, as Bradley Karkkainen has pointed out, the Toxics Release Inventory (TRI), 42 U.S.C. §11023 (2000), which requires that industrial facilities

report the release and transfer of specific chemicals, has had a significant impact on pollution emissions. See Bradley C. Karkkainen, "Information as Environmental Regulation: TRI and Performance Benchmarking, Precursor to a New Paradigm?" 89 *Georgetown Law Journal* 257, 287–288 (2001). According to Karkkainen, the TRI, because it creates a performance metric, "both compels and enables facilities and firms to monitor their own environmental performance" and "encourages them to compare, rank, and track performance among production processes, facilities, operating units, and peer or competitor firms." Ibid., 261. In addition, Karkkainen argues that the TRI data "subjects the environmental performance of facilities and firms to an unprecedented degree of scrutiny by their peers, competitors, investors, employees, consumers, community residents, environmental organizations, activists, elected officials, regulators, and the public in general." Ibid., 261–262. As a result, this transparency scheme "unleashes, strengthens, and exploits multiple pressures, all tending to push in the direction of continuous improvement as facilities and firms endeavor to leapfrog over their peers to receive credit for larger improvements or superior performance." Ibid., 262. In addition, administrators—whether within companies or in government bureaucracies monitoring contract compliance—have a management incentive to improve transparency. Ibid., 295–305. Thus, although information by itself does not provide accountability, see ibid., 338–343 (noting that some small firms may be unconcerned about the mere release of information), it can enable other accountability mechanisms.

Contributors

ALFRED C. AMAN, JR.
Dean and Professor of Law, Suffolk University Law School

MATHEW BLUM
Associate Administrator of the Office of Federal Procurement Policy (OFPP),
Office of Management and Budget (OMB)

ALAN CHVOTKIN
Senior Vice President and Counsel, Professional Services Council

LAURA A. DICKINSON
Foundation Professor of Law, Arizona State University Sandra Day O'Connor
College of Law

SHARON DOLOVICH
Professor of Law, UCLA School of Law

JOHN D. DONAHUE
Raymond Vernon Lecturer in Public Policy, John F. Kennedy School of
Government, Harvard University

JODY FREEMAN
Professor of Law, Harvard Law School

STEVEN J. KELMAN
Albert J. Weatherhead III and Richard W. Weatherhead Professor of Public
Management, John F. Kennedy School of Government, Harvard University

NINA A. MENDELSON
Professor of Law, University of Michigan Law School

GILLIAN E. METZGER
Professor of Law, Columbia Law School

MARTHA MINOW
Jeremiah Smith, Jr. Professor of Law, Harvard Law School

WILLIAM J. NOVAK
Associate Professor of History, University of Chicago

MIRIAM SEIFTER
Harvard Law School, J.D., Environmental Law Fellow, 2005–2007

STAN SOLOWAY
President, Professional Services Council

PAUL R. VERKUIL
Professor of Law, Cardozo Law School, Yeshiva University

Index

The letter t following a number denotes a table.